Featured Papers in Finance and Society Wellbeing—in Honor of Professors Joe Gani and Chris Heyde

Featured Papers in Finance and Society Wellbeing—in Honor of Professors Joe Gani and Chris Heyde

Guest Editors

Shuangzhe Liu
Svetlozar (Zari) Rachev

MDPI

Basel • Beijing • Wuhan • Barcelona • Belgrade • Novi Sad • Cluj • Manchester

Guest Editors
Shuangzhe Liu
Faculty of Science and Technology
University of Canberra
Canberra
Australia

Svetlozar (Zari) Rachev
Department of Mathematics and Statistics
Texas Tech University
Lubbock
USA

Editorial Office
MDPI AG
Grosspeteranlage 5
4052 Basel, Switzerland

This is a reprint of the Special Issue, published open access by the journal *Journal of Risk and Financial Management* (ISSN 1911-8074), freely accessible at: https://www.mdpi.com/journal/jrfm/special_issues/R13LCHNHH0.

For citation purposes, cite each article independently as indicated on the article page online and as indicated below:

Lastname, Firstname, Firstname Lastname, and Firstname Lastname. Article Title. *Journal Name* **Year**, *Volume Number*, Page Range.

ISBN 978-3-7258-8165-9 (Hbk)
ISBN 978-3-7258-8166-6 (PDF)
https://doi.org/10.3390/books978-3-7258-8166-6

Contents

About the Editors

Shuangzhe Liu

Shuangzhe Liu currently works in the Faculty of Science and Technology, University of Canberra, Australia. His research interests include statistical science, econometrics, financial mathematics, and data science, with a focus on stochastic modeling and multivariate methods and their applications in finance and risk analysis. He has published widely in international journals and co-authored a book on time series analysis. He serves as Editor of *Statistical Papers* and holds editorial roles in several international statistical journals. His work aims to connect theoretical developments with practical applications in econometrics, finance, insurance, and related fields.

Svetlozar (Zari) Rachev

Svetlozar (Zari) Rachev is a Professor in the Department of Mathematics and Statistics at Texas Tech University. His research interests include probability theory, mathematical finance, quantitative risk management, econometrics, and asset pricing. He has authored and co-authored numerous books and research papers in financial mathematics, stochastic modeling, and risk analytics. He is also a co-founder of FinAnalytica and has contributed extensively to the development of advanced methods for portfolio optimization, heavy-tailed modeling, and financial risk management. He has supervised many doctoral students and collaborated internationally with scholars in finance, statistics, and applied probability.

Preface

This Reprint volume is dedicated to Professors Joseph Mark Gani and Christopher Charles Heyde, whose pioneering contributions have shaped applied probability, statistical science, stochastic processes, actuarial science, and financial risk analysis. Their work continues to influence research across finance, insurance, economics, and related quantitative fields.

The Reprint comprises a collection of selected research and review papers reflecting developments inspired by their scientific legacy. The contributions span stochastic modeling, statistical inference, financial econometrics, machine learning, actuarial science, risk management, ESG finance, cryptocurrency markets, fraud detection, epidemiological modeling, and computational methods.

A central theme is the integration of classical probabilistic and statistical theory with modern data-driven approaches, emphasizing rigorous modeling and empirical relevance. The volume also highlights key features of complex systems, including dependence, heavy tails, nonlinear dynamics, and model uncertainty, which are essential in financial and insurance applications.

This Reprint is intended for researchers, practitioners, and graduate students in statistics, econometrics, actuarial science, financial mathematics, applied probability, and risk management.

Shuangzhe Liu and Svetlozar (Zari) Rachev
Guest Editors

Journal of
Risk and Financial Management

MDPI

Editorial

Featured Papers in Finance and Society Wellbeing—In Honor of Professors Joe Gani and Chris Heyde

Shuangzhe Liu [1,*] and Svetlozar T. Rachev [2]

[1] Faculty of Science and Technology, University of Canberra, Bruce, ACT 2617, Australia
[2] Department of Mathematics and Statistics, Texas Tech University, Lubbock, TX 79409-1042, USA; zari.rachev@ttu.edu
* Correspondence: shuangzhe.liu@canberra.edu.au

This featured volume is dedicated to the memory of Professor Joe Gani (1924–2016) and Professor Chris Heyde (1939–2008), two outstanding scholars whose research, intellectual leadership, and mentorship had a lasting influence on applied probability, mathematical statistics, stochastic processes, actuarial science, and financial risk analysis.

The papers collected in this volume reflect both the breadth of contemporary research and the continuing relevance of their intellectual legacy. Many of the themes represented here trace directly to questions and ideas that Gani and Heyde helped bring to prominence through their research, collaboration, and encouragement of younger scholars. The contributions cover a broad range of topics, including stochastic modeling, statistical inference, financial econometrics, actuarial science, machine learning, risk management, macro-financial risk, ESG-related outcomes, retirement planning, cryptocurrency markets, fraud detection, epidemiological modeling, and Bayesian and computational methods. Together, these works illustrate the richness and breadth of modern applied probability and statistical science.

A recurring theme throughout the volume is the productive interaction between classical probabilistic modeling and modern data-driven methodology. This interaction between theory and application was central to the work of both Gani and Heyde. Machine learning, computational statistics, and high-dimensional data analysis are most powerful when embedded within coherent probabilistic and statistical frameworks. In this sense, the volume reflects Heyde's emphasis on inference under dependence, quasi-likelihood methodology, and robust statistical reasoning, as well as Gani's belief that probabilistic models should be directed toward meaningful practical problems.

Several contributions emphasize stochastic dependence, heavy-tailed behavior, structural uncertainty, and nonlinear dynamics. These features are essential for understanding financial returns, volatility, portfolio interactions, credit risk, option pricing, fraud detection, and systemic instability. The papers show the continuing need to balance mathematical tractability with empirical realism, predictive accuracy with interpretability, and computational flexibility with theoretical discipline.

Consistent with the perspectives of both Gani and Heyde, many contributions further emphasize that rigorous statistical and probabilistic thinking is most valuable when applied to important real-world problems. The volume therefore also highlights the societal importance of probabilistic and statistical reasoning. Contributions on pandemic dynamics, ESG performance, retirement sustainability, financial inclusion, and financial well-being demonstrate how rigorous modeling can support decision-making under uncertainty in complex and interconnected systems.

More broadly, this volume spotlights an important direction in contemporary research: the integration of probabilistic discipline, statistical rigor, and computational innovation. The principles associated with Gani and Heyde—clear assumptions, transparent inference, empirical grounding, and intellectual honesty—remain essential for modern research in finance, insurance, economics, actuarial science, and risk management. These qualities continue to inspire contemporary research and remain central to the development of sound statistical and financial methodology.

We hope that this volume will be useful to researchers, practitioners, and graduate students working in business statistics, econometrics, actuarial science, financial analytics, insurance, applied probability, and risk management.

In preparing this commemorative volume, we have benefited from the encouragement and support of many colleagues and friends. We express our sincere gratitude to Beth Heyde, Ross Maller, Eckhard Platen, and Eugene Seneta for their generous support and encouragement. We also thank Boris Buchmann, Roger Gay, Shigeyuki Hamori, Kazuhiko Kakamu, Yonghui Liu, Changyu Lu, Tiefeng Ma, Seng Huat Ong, Gilberto Paula, Milind Sathye, Kunio Shimizu, Dehui Wang, and Hailiang Yang for their valuable assistance. Above all, we thank the authors and reviewers whose generous contributions, time, and expertise made this commemorative volume possible.

Conflicts of Interest: The authors declare no conflict of interest.

 https://doi.org/10.3390/jrfm19050367

Journal of
Risk and Financial Management

MDPI

Article

The *t*-Distribution in Financial Mathematics and Multivariate Testing Contexts

Eugene Seneta [1,†] and Thomas Fung [2,*,†]

[1] School of Mathematics and Statistics, F07, The University of Sydney, Darlington, NSW 2006, Australia; eugene.seneta@sydney.edu.au
[2] School of Mathematical and Physical Sciences, Macquarie University, North Ryde, NSW 2109, Australia
* Correspondence: thomas.fung@mq.edu.au
† These authors contributed equally to this work.

Abstract: The Student's *t*-distribution provides a thematic connection between the historical and technical elements of this paper. The historical section offers a brief account of the early contributions of Chris Heyde and his collaborations with Madan and Seneta in the development of financial mathematics. The technical section focuses on hypothesis testing, motivated by the observation that, in a setting with pairwise exchangeable dependence for test statistics, the cutoff methods proposed by Sarkar and colleagues in 2016 can be viewed as a first iteration of the classical approach developed by Holm in 1979. These methods had already been refined earlier by Seneta and Chen in their work from 1997 and 2005, which laid the foundation for further improvements. Building on this, a new iteration of the Seneta-Chen method is presented, offering enhancements over the Sarkar approach. Numerical and graphical comparisons are provided, focusing on equal tails testing within the multivariate *t*-distribution framework. While the tabulated results clearly show improvements with the new procedure, the simulated family-wise error rates across varying correlations reveal only minor practical differences between the iterative methods. This suggests that, under suitable conditions, a single iteration suffices in practice. The paper concludes with personal reflections from the first author, sharing memories of Joe Gani and Chris Heyde, in keeping with the commemorative nature of this issue.

Keywords: Chris Heyde; two-tail hypothesis tests; Student's *t*-copula; iteration of cutoffs; familywise error rate (FWER); Joe Gani; personal recollections

1. Dedication

In Memory of Joe Gani and Chris Heyde.

2. Introduction

The *t*-distribution in its univariate and multivariate forms provides a thematic link to the historical and technical parts of this paper.

Most of the historical material is in Section 2.2, which is a brief account of the confluence and aftermath of the early work of Chris Heyde focused on the univariate *t*-distribution, and that of Dilip Madan and ES (the first author) focused on its dual, the Variance-Gamma (VG) distribution, both in the setting of financial mathematics.

Most of the technical part is in Sections 3 and 4. The general context is the step-down procedure of multivariate hypothesis testing when using equicorrelated pairwise dependent test statistics. In Fung and Seneta (2023), the cutoffs of Sarkar et al. (2016) were seen to be a first iteration improvement of Holm's classical cutoffs (Holm, 1979), under a convexity condition on the copula. The Sarkar et al. (2016) cutoffs (motivated by Seneta and Chen (2005)) improved on those of Seneta and Chen (1997)[1] which already improved on those of Holm (1979) by using pairwise dependence.

Section 3 summarizes this general theory, and notes that under the convexity condition on the copula, a first-iteration improvement of the cutoffs of Seneta and Chen (1997) improves those of Sarkar et al. (2016).

The first purpose of our technical part is to express the copula for a two-equal-tails testing procedure in a calculable form, and the familywise error rate (FWER) into a form calculable from repeated simulation of the sample values. The second purpose is to study numerically the degree of improvement of the improved cutoffs, and to compare the relative effectiveness of the two sets of cutoffs using the FWER, in the specific hypothesis testing setting of two equal-tail tests for multivariate equicorrelated t-distribution. This extends the small initial numerical study in Seneta and Chen (2005) and relates in structure to the examples in Sarkar et al. (2016)

2.1. The Multivariate t-Distribution

The multivariate skew equicorrelated t-distribution is a case of the multivariate skew Generalized Hyperbolic distribution, $GH(0, \mathbf{R_n}, \boldsymbol{\theta}, p, a, b)$ described by the mean-variance mixing expression

$$\mathbf{X} = \boldsymbol{\mu} + \boldsymbol{\theta} W + W^{\frac{1}{2}}\mathbf{Z} \tag{1}$$

where $\boldsymbol{\mu} = (\mu_1, \mu_2, \ldots, \mu_n)^\top, \boldsymbol{\theta} = (\theta_1, \theta_2, \ldots, \theta_n)^\top$,where $\mathbf{Z} \sim \mathbb{N}_\mathbf{n}(\mathbf{0}, \mathbf{R_n})$ is multivariate normal, with

$$\mathbf{R_n} = \mathbf{I_n}(1-\rho) + \rho\mathbf{1}\mathbf{1}^\top, \ -1/(n-1) < \rho < 1, \tag{2}$$

where $\mathbf{Z}$ and W are independently distributed. The random variable W has a (univariate) Generalized Inverse Gaussian (GIG) distribution, denoted by $GIG(p, a, b)$, that is, it has density

$$\begin{aligned} f_{GIG}(w) &= \frac{1}{2\overline{K}_p(a,b)} w^{p-1} \exp(-\frac{1}{2}(a^2 w^{-1} + b^2 w)), \quad w > 0; \\ &= 0, \quad \text{otherwise}; \end{aligned}$$

where

$$\overline{K}_p(a,b) = \begin{cases} (\frac{a}{b})^p K_p(ab), & p \in \mathbb{R}, \text{if } a, b > 0; \\ b^{-2p}\Gamma(p)2^{p-1}, & p, b > 0, \text{if } a = 0; \\ a^{2p}\Gamma(-p)2^{-p-1}, & a > 0 \text{ and } p < 0, \text{if } b = 0. \end{cases} \tag{3}$$

Here, $K_p(\omega)$, $\omega > 0$, is the modified Bessel function of the second kind (Erdélyi et al., 1954) with index $p \in \mathbb{R}$.

The case $a = 0$ encompasses the multivariate skew Variance-Gamma (VG) distribution.

The case $b = 0$, $p = -\nu/2$, $a = \sqrt{\nu}$, where ν is a positive integer, corresponds to the multivariate (n-variate) skewed equicorrelated t-distribution for $\mathbf{X}$ in (1) under (2). (ν is the "number of degrees of freedom" of the marginal t-distribution.)

This multivariate distribution is the central hypothesis testing example in Seneta and Chen (2005) and Sarkar et al. (2016) for testing with two tails under the null hypotheses $H_i : \mu_i = \theta = 0$, $i = 1, \ldots n$, and comparing the relative efficacy of the existing and new cutoffs numerically.

2.2. Historical Prelude

This paper as a whole is, however, part of a tribute issue to my (ES) friends Joe Gani and Chris Heyde, so it is necessary to first explain its descent from the setting of financial mathematics, and in particular the impetus and direction to that field of the work of Chris Heyde.

In mid-1979, I had moved to the University of Sydney from the teaching Department of Statistics at the Australian National University, Canberra, where my interest in financial mathematics developed through collaboration with Dilip Madan. Joe Gani asked me to co-edit a Festrschrift volume of papers in honor of Chris Heyde. The following is an extract from my own contribution, (Seneta, 2004), to that volume.

> My own interest up to the appearance of Madan and Seneta (1990) had been in the symmetric VG model. Dilip Madan had moved to the University of Maryland at College Park from the University of Sydney, and I was visiting the University of Virginia when we put the last touches to that paper in 1989. After some years of my own inactivity in this area, I became aware of Chris Heyde's penetration of yet another probabilistic field, that of financial modelling, and asked him to speak at the University of Sydney on 26 March 1999, on what was soon to be published as Heyde (1999). His opinion of the symmetric VG model was that, although it was heavier tailed than the normal, the tails were not heavy enough to account for what were occasionally relatively extreme values of X_t ; and of course the increments in the VG model had been assumed independent. Although the underlying stochastic process $\log(P_t/P_0), t \geq 0$, was closed under convolution and analytically convenient, a treatment such as he proposed could effectively reconstruct the $\{T_t\}$ process numerically from data. My occasional visits to Canberra allowed me to learn more about the FATGBM ideology, and to obtain advice from Chris on the statistical fitting of the symmetric VG model. The VG model had continued to be of interest. I had had several inquiries as to how to fit it to real data, and I needed to supervise the fourth-year Honours project[2] of Annelies Tjetjep in 2002. My focus was Dilip Madan's post-1990 successful extension and application of the VG models (see items in the references co-authored by Madan, especially Madan et al. (1998)), where fitting from data as well as modelling are integral issues. Madan et al. (1998), in the guise of its Research Report predecessor, was already described in a monograph (Epps, 2000). Dilip Madan, Wake Epps, and Eckhard Platen very kindly supplied me with current materials and information, as of course did Chris Heyde. The next section considers the procedure and effect of fitting the (general) VG by allowing for dependence of increments while retaining their stationarity. We do not address specifically the issue of adequacy of tail structure of the VG distribution. Important new work by Heyde and Kou (2004) suggests, in any case, that the heavy-tail (power-law) structure is not easily distinguishable in practice from the exponential-tail structure.

It is appropriate to note on this occasion that the papers authored by Hurst, Platen, and Rachev cited were written in Chris Heyde's Stochastic Analysis Group at the Australian National University, and are closely related to some of his own work, to which we now come.

To explain, let P_t be the price of a risky asset at some time $t \geq 0$, and assume that P_t follows subordinated geometric Brownian motion. Specifically, we have

$$P_t = P_0 e^{\mu t + \theta T_t + \sigma B(T_t)} \tag{4}$$

where μ, θ and $\sigma > 0$, are constants, and $\{B(t)\}$ is standard Brownian motion independent of $\{T_t\}$, which is a positive, nondecreasing random process with stationary, but not necessarily independent, increments and $T_0 = 0$. Denote the identically distributed increments over unit time by $\tau_t = T_t - T_{t-1}$; these form a discrete-time stationary process. The corresponding log increments of P_t, which can be interpreted as continuously compounded returns, are given by

$$X_t = \log P_t - \log P_{t-1} = \mu + \theta\tau_t + \sigma(B(T_t) - B(T_{t-1})) \tag{5}$$

Without loss of generality, take $E(\tau_t) = 1$, since any scaling can be absorbed into θ and σ as required (assuming that $E(\tau_t) < \infty$).

When t is a positive integer, as is appropriate when sampling at equally spaced points of time, the joint probability structure of the X_t is the same as for the model

$$X_t = \mu + \theta\tau_t + \sigma\tau_t^{\frac{1}{2}} W_t, \quad t = 1, 2, \ldots, \tag{6}$$

where the $W_t, t = 1, 2, \ldots$, are NID(0, 1) random variables, independent also of the process $\{\tau_t\}, t = 1, 2, \ldots$

The paradigm model for asset price movements, geometric Brownian motion, takes $\theta = 0, \tau_t = t$ in the above. The model is relatively simple, giving log returns as independent and identically distributed normal random variables. It has a number of shortcomings in the light of typical asset price data, which display the following characteristics as listed in Finlay and Seneta (2006) (see, for example, Heyde and Liu (2001) and the references therein): (i) a leptokurtic distribution (kurtosis greater than three)—higher peaks above the mean, and thicker tails, than a normal distribution; (ii) a heteroscedastic time series (time-dependent variance), unlike the geometric Brownian motion model; (iii) a long-range dependence structure in squared returns, violating the independence assumption; (iv) occasionally skewed distributions as opposed to the symmetry of a normal distribution; (v) little or no autocorrelation present in returns, at least past one or two lags. To deal with some of these issues, Heyde (1999) introduced a subordinator model (a model which gives asset prices as geometric Brownian motion driven by some nondecreasing stochastic 'activity time' or 'market time' process) based on fractal activity time: the fractal activity time geometric Brownian motion (FATGBM) model.

Heyde and Leonenko (2005)[3] expanded on this model to allow for t-distributed asset price increments, which incorporate self-similarity (a scaling property) and long-range dependence (LRD).

On the basis of preprints and reprints of this and related work, in Section 6, entitled 'Student' processes, of Seneta (2004), it was noted that the distribution of X_t in (6) when $\mu = 0 = \theta$, and the distribution of $\tau_t = T_t - T_{t-1}$ which is the reciprocal (inverse) gamma, is Praetz's-t distribution.

A multivariate version $\mathbf{X_t}$ of (5) is

$$\mathbf{X_t} = \mu + \tau_t\boldsymbol{\theta} + \mathbf{W}(\tau_t\mathbf{R_n}) \tag{7}$$

where $\mathbf{W}$ is the multivariate correlated Brownian motion (Wiener process) evaluated at positive integer time points t, univariate τ_t has an inverse gamma distribution, and $\mathbf{R_n} = \mathbf{I_n}(1-\rho) + \rho\mathbf{1}\mathbf{1}^\top$, $-1/(n-1) < \rho < 1$. The distribution of $\mathbf{X_t}$ is then a skewed equicorrelated multivariate t which at a given time point can be written as (1). All marginal distributions are the same as expressed in (5).

In conclusion to this historical account, after Seneta (2004), univariate theory was developed in a series of papers with Richard Finlay, the first of which was Finlay and Seneta (2006), and the multivariate theory, especially bivariate, with Thomas Fung, one of the first of which was Fung and Seneta (2011).

It is the skewed multivariate t-distribution with which we are concerned in the sequel, although in a context different from the preceding, namely multiple hypothesis testing. However, this different context and the multivariate financial mathematics context have in common the central role played by the Student's t-copula (see our Section 3.1).

3. Multivariate Hypothesis Testing Context

3.1. The Step-Down Procedure

We consider the multiple test problem when there are n hypotheses $H_1, H_2, \ldots, H_n$, and corresponding p-values $R_1, R_2, \ldots R_n$, assuming the test statistics $Y_1, Y_2, \ldots, Y_n$ are from a continuous distribution. Suppose that in such a multiple test procedure, the property

$$Pr(H_s, s \in I_m, \text{are accepted} | H_s, s \in I_m \text{ are true}) \geq 1 - \alpha \tag{8}$$

holds for a prespecified size of test α (familywise error: FWE) for every I_m, where I_m is any non-null subset of $\{1, 2, \ldots, n\}$, for every $m = 1, 2, \ldots, n$. Then, the FWE is said to be strongly controlled.

Let $R_{(1)}, R_{(2)}, \ldots, R_{(n)}$ be the ordered p-values, and $\Delta(i), 1 \leq i \leq n$ be a strictly increasing sequence of constants, with $0 < \Delta(i) < 1$, for each i. A step-down procedure begins by testing if $R_{(1)} < \Delta(1)$. If so, reject $H_{(1)}$ and go on to test if $R_{(2)} < \Delta(2)$. If not, accept all hypotheses. In general, if $R_{(i)} < \Delta(i), 1 \leq i \leq j-1$, then at step j, the remaining hypotheses are $H_{(j)}, H_{(j+1)}, \ldots, H_{(n)}$, and the inequality next to be checked is $R_{(j)} < \Delta(j)$. If it holds, reject $H_{(j)}$ and continue. Otherwise, accept $H_{(j)}, H_{(j+1)}, \ldots, H_{(n)}$. The process may continue until a decision is made on the basis of whether $R_{(n)} < \Delta(n)$. The step-down procedure of Holm (1979) uses the set of constants

$$\bar{\Delta}(i) = \frac{\alpha}{n - i + 1}, \; 1 \leq i \leq n, \tag{9}$$

and Holm proved that with these constants, the FWE is strongly controlled.

In the sequel, we shall have that $(Y_i, Y_j), i \neq j, i, j \in I_m$ are *exchangeable* (so that (R_i, R_j) are also) when $I_m, m \geq 2$ is the index set of assumed true hypotheses, and that their joint bivariate distribution is the same for each such I_m. The marginal distribution of each $R_i, i \in I_m, m \geq 1$ is $U(0,1)$. We shall need the notation

$$H(u) = Pr(R_1 \leq u, R_2 \leq u), u \in (0,1), \tag{10}$$

Under the above exchangeability setting, Seneta and Chen (1997), in their Sections 5 and 6, showed that then the critical cutoff constants

$$\tilde{\Delta}(i) = \frac{\alpha + (n_0 - 1)H(\frac{\alpha}{n_0})}{n_0}, \tag{11}$$

are monotonic increasing with i (that is, decreasing with increasing n_0), and the step-down procedure based on them strongly controls the FWE. Moreover, the step-down procedure with these constants provides tighter control on the FWE than Holm's since

$$\tilde{\Delta}(i) > \bar{\Delta}(i) = \frac{\alpha}{n_0}, 1 \leq i \leq n-1, \tilde{\Delta}(n) = \bar{\Delta}(n) = \alpha.$$

Note that $H(u), 0 < u < 1$, is a cdf. It also serves as the copula $C(u_1, u_2) = Pr(R_1 \leq u_1, R_2 \leq u_2), 0 < u_1, u_2 < 1$, of the bivariate joint distribution of the exchangeable pair (X_1, X_2), evaluated along the diagonal $u_1 = u_2 = u$. In one such application of the Student's t-copula, Sun et al. (2008) utilized a skewed Student's t-copula-based ARMA-GARCH model to capture tail dependence and asymmetric correlation, particularly relevant for financial markets, where extreme events and non-elliptical distributions are common.

Sarkar et al. (2016), motivated by Seneta and Chen (2005), made a substantial improvement. They showed, *under the condition that* $H(u)$ *in (10) is convex in* $u \in (0,1)$, that the monotonic increasing (with i) cutoffs

$$\hat{\Delta}(i) = \frac{\alpha^2/n_0}{G_{n_0}(\alpha/n_0)}, \tag{12}$$

where

$$G_{n_0}(u) = n_0 u - (n_0 - 1)H(u),\ 0 < u < 1, \tag{13}$$

provide tighter control on the FWE than (11) since they show

$$\hat{\Delta}(i) > \tilde{\Delta}(i),\ 1 \le i \le n-1, \tilde{\Delta}(n) = \bar{\Delta}(n) = \alpha.$$

Write

$$w_2(n_0) = \frac{\alpha w_1(n_0)}{G_{n_0}(w_1(n_0))}, \tag{14}$$

Clearly, $w_2(n_0)$ is (12) when $w_1(n_0)$ is (9);

Fung and Seneta (2023) showed, under the same convexity condition on $H(u)$, that $w_2(n_0)$ given by (14) when $w_1(n_0)$ is (11), provides tighter control on the FWE than (12). This is a consequence of their Theorem 1: since

$$w_1^*(n_0) = \frac{\alpha + (n_0 - 1)H(\frac{\alpha}{n_0})}{n_0} > \frac{\alpha}{n_0} = w_1(n_0)$$

it follows that

$$w_2^*(n_0) > \frac{\alpha^2/n_0}{G_{n_0}(\alpha/n_0)} = w_2(n_0)$$

3.2. *Two-Tail Tests*

Returning to (1) and (2), we take for $i = 1, 2, \ldots, n$ our ith null hypothesis to be $H_i : \mu_i = \theta_i = 0$, so that when all H_i are true,

$$\mathbf{X} = \sqrt{W}\mathbf{Z}, \tag{15}$$

and similarly for any subset of indices $\{1, 2, \ldots, n\}$.

For a two-sided equal-tails testing procedure, we take as our test statistics $Y_i = |X_i|$, $i = 1, 2 \ldots, n$. Their corresponding p-values $(R_i, R_j), i \neq j, i, j \in I_m$ are then also *exchangeable*, and their joint bivariate distribution is the same for each such I_m.

We shall work, for each of two specified values of n for numerical illustration, with three sets of cutoffs: those given by (11) which we call $w_1(n_0)$; those given by $\hat{\Delta}(i)$ in (12); and those given by (14) which we call $w_2(n_0)$. This involves the calculation of

$$H(u(n_0)) = Pr(R_1 \le u(n_0), R_2 \le u(n_0)),$$

at $u(n_0) = \frac{\alpha}{n_0}$ to produce (11) and $\hat{\Delta}(i)$ in (12), and $u(n_0) = w_1(n_0)$ to produce $w_2(n_0)$ for each value of $n_0 = n - i + 1$, $i = 1, 2, \ldots, n$.

We have indicated above that $w_1(n_0) < \hat{\Delta}(i) < w_2(n_0)$. Our intention is to compare numerically the relative efficacy of $\hat{\Delta}(i)$ and $w_2(n_0)$ as improvements on $w_1(n_0)$. For eventual use in the verification of convexity, and for numerical calculations in terms of test statistics, we first transform to a bivariate setting.

Since

$$Pr(R_1 \leq u(n_0), R_2 \leq u(n_0)) = Pr(Y_1 > x, Y_2 > x) \text{ where } x = F_X^{-1}(1 - \frac{u(n_0)}{2}), \quad (16)$$

we notice that the right-hand side of (16) may be written as

$$\begin{aligned} Pr(X_1 > x, X_2 > x) &+ Pr(X_1 > x, X_2 < -x) \\ &+ Pr(X_1 < -x, X_2 < -x) + Pr(X_1 < -x, X_2 > x) \end{aligned}$$

and then as

$$\begin{aligned} Pr(X_1 > x, X_2 > x) &+ Pr(X_1 > x, -X_2 > x) \\ &+ Pr(-X_1 > x, -X_2 > x) + Pr(-X_1 > x, X_2 > x). \end{aligned}$$

Putting $V_i = -X_i, i = 1,2$, since (V_1, V_2) has the same joint distribution as (X_1, X_2), and since (X_1, V_2) and (V_1, X_2) have the same joint distribution (namely, the joint distribution of (X_1, X_2) but with the sign of the correlation coefficient reversed), (16) is now

$$Pr(|X_1| > x, |X_2| > x) = 2Pr(X_1 > x, X_2 > x) + 2Pr(X_1 > x, V_2 > x) \quad (17)$$

Focus on the first summand on the right. Since

$$\begin{aligned} Pr(X_1 > x, X_2 > x) &= Pr(-X_1 < -x, -X_2 < x) = Pr(X_1 < -x, X_2 < -x) \\ &= Pr(X_{(2)} < -x) \end{aligned}$$

where $X_{(2)} = \max(X_1, X_2)$, and since $-x = -F_X^{-1}(1 - \frac{u(n_0)}{2}) = F_X^{-1}(\frac{u(n_0)}{2})$, it follows from (15) that

$$Pr(X_1 > x, X_2 > x) = Pr\Big(X_{(2)} \leq F_X^{-1}(u)\Big), \quad (18)$$

for $u = \frac{u(n_0)}{2}$.

To evaluate (17), the calculation of (18) needs to be repeated with ρ replaced by $-\rho$ to give $Pr(X_1 > x, V_2 > x)$.

It is important to note from the right-hand side of (17) that $Pr(|X_1| > x, |X_2| > x)$ is symmetric about 0 in the value of ρ.

For comparisons of the differential effects of various cutoffs, we use the familywise error rate (FWER) as a function of ρ as the means of comparison. This is in general defined as $Pr(\text{Reject at least one } H_i, i = 1,2,\ldots,n | H_i, i = 1,2,\ldots,n \text{ are all true})$. Thus, for the step-down procedure

$$\begin{aligned} \text{FWER} &= Pr(R_{(1)} < \Delta(1) | H_i, i = 1,2,\ldots,n \text{ are all true}) \\ &= Pr(R_{(1)} < w_j(n) | H_i, i = 1,2,\ldots,n \text{ are all true}) \\ &= Pr(\max_{i=1,2,\ldots,n} |X_i| > F_X^{-1}(1 - \frac{w_j(n)}{2}) | H_i, i = 1,2,\ldots,n \text{ are all true}) \quad (19) \end{aligned}$$

for fixed $j = 1,2$, in terms of sample values $X_i, i = 1,2,\ldots,n$. The expression (19) may be estimated from repeated simulation of the sample $X_i, i = 1,2,\ldots,n$, once $F_X^{-1}(1 - \frac{w_j(n)}{2})$ is numerically calculated. For our two sets of cutoffs, $u(n) = \frac{\alpha}{n}$ and $u(n) = w_1(n) = \frac{\alpha + (n-1)H(\frac{\alpha}{n})}{n}$, respectively.

Finally, the earlier numerical investigations of Seneta and Chen (2005), Sarkar et al. (2016), and Fung and Seneta (2023) have all been in the setting of $\rho > 0$.

4. Numerical Demonstration. Multivariate t-Distribution

For the specific multivariate t-distribution, Sarkar et al. (2016) proved that on account of the exchangeability, the copula $Pr(F_X(X_1) \leq u, F_X(X_2)) \leq u)$ is convex for $u \in (0,1)$, so from (17), $H(u)$ in (10) is convex as required.

In this section, we present some numerical results to illustrate the theoretical developments discussed earlier.

The work of Seneta and Chen (2005), in its Section 4, provides tabulated results (Table 4), with $\alpha = 0.05$ of (11) for $n_0 = 1, 2, \ldots, 8$ against $\rho = 0.0, 0.1, \ldots, 0.9, 0.95, 0.99$, and 1.00 for test statistic cutoffs from the multivariate normal for a two-tailed test for the zero mean; we extend that analysis. Specifically, we compute (11), (12) and (14) using (11) as $w_1(n_0)$ under two different multivariate t settings:

- Setting 1: multivariate t with $\nu = 64$ and $n = 16$.
- Setting 2: multivariate t with $\nu = 16$ and $n = 3$.

The results are presented in Tables 1–6. Specifically, we first compute (11), (12), and (14) when $w_1(n_0)$ is (11).

Table 1. Comparing the cutoffs $\tilde{\Delta}(i)$ under multivariate t with $n = 16$ and $\nu = 64$ for various ρ.

	ρ											
n_0	**0**	**0.1**	**0.2**	**0.3**	**0.4**	**0.5**	**0.6**	**0.7**	**0.8**	**0.9**	**0.95**	**0.99**
16	0.00314	0.00315	0.00317	0.00320	0.00326	0.00335	0.00348	0.00369	0.00400	0.00451	0.00493	0.00554
15	0.00335	0.00336	0.00338	0.00342	0.00348	0.00357	0.00372	0.00394	0.00427	0.00481	0.00525	0.00590
14	0.00359	0.00360	0.00362	0.00366	0.00373	0.00383	0.00399	0.00422	0.00458	0.00516	0.00563	0.00631
13	0.00387	0.00388	0.00390	0.00395	0.00402	0.00413	0.00430	0.00456	0.00494	0.00555	0.00605	0.00678
12	0.00419	0.00420	0.00423	0.00428	0.00436	0.00448	0.00467	0.00494	0.00535	0.00601	0.00655	0.00733
11	0.00458	0.00459	0.00462	0.00467	0.00476	0.00490	0.00510	0.00540	0.00584	0.00656	0.00714	0.00797
10	0.00504	0.00505	0.00508	0.00514	0.00524	0.00539	0.00562	0.00595	0.00643	0.00721	0.00783	0.00874
9	0.00560	0.00561	0.00565	0.00572	0.00583	0.00600	0.00625	0.00661	0.00715	0.00800	0.00868	0.00967
8	0.00630	0.00632	0.00636	0.00644	0.00657	0.00677	0.00705	0.00745	0.00804	0.00898	0.00973	0.01081
7	0.00721	0.00723	0.00728	0.00738	0.00752	0.00775	0.00807	0.00852	0.00919	0.01023	0.01107	0.01226
6	0.00842	0.00844	0.00850	0.00862	0.00879	0.00905	0.00942	0.00995	0.01070	0.01188	0.01282	0.01416
5	0.01012	0.01014	0.01022	0.01036	0.01057	0.01088	0.01132	0.01193	0.01280	0.01415	0.01521	0.01673
4	0.01266	0.01270	0.01280	0.01297	0.01324	0.01361	0.01414	0.01486	0.01589	0.01745	0.01868	0.02042
3	0.01691	0.01696	0.01709	0.01731	0.01765	0.01812	0.01876	0.01964	0.02086	0.02268	0.02411	0.02611
2	0.02539	0.02545	0.02562	0.02590	0.02632	0.02688	0.02764	0.02864	0.03001	0.03202	0.03356	0.03571
1	0.05000	0.05000	0.05000	0.05000	0.05000	0.05000	0.05000	0.05000	0.05000	0.05000	0.05000	0.05000

Table 2. Comparing the cutoffs $\hat{\Delta}(i)$ under multivariate t with $n = 16$ and $\nu = 64$ for various ρ.

	ρ											
n_0	**0**	**0.1**	**0.2**	**0.3**	**0.4**	**0.5**	**0.6**	**0.7**	**0.8**	**0.9**	**0.95**	**0.99**
16	0.00314	0.00315	0.00317	0.00320	0.00326	0.00336	0.00353	0.00381	0.00434	0.00561	0.00739	0.01373
15	0.00335	0.00336	0.00338	0.00342	0.00348	0.00359	0.00377	0.00407	0.00464	0.00599	0.00787	0.01448
14	0.00359	0.00360	0.00362	0.00366	0.00374	0.00385	0.00405	0.00437	0.00498	0.00642	0.00841	0.01532
13	0.00387	0.00388	0.00390	0.00395	0.00403	0.00416	0.00436	0.00472	0.00537	0.00691	0.00903	0.01625
12	0.00419	0.00420	0.00423	0.00428	0.00437	0.00451	0.00474	0.00512	0.00582	0.00748	0.00974	0.01729
11	0.00458	0.00459	0.00462	0.00467	0.00477	0.00493	0.00518	0.00559	0.00636	0.00815	0.01057	0.01847
10	0.00504	0.00505	0.00508	0.00515	0.00526	0.00543	0.00571	0.00617	0.00701	0.00895	0.01154	0.01982
9	0.00560	0.00561	0.00565	0.00573	0.00585	0.00604	0.00635	0.00686	0.00779	0.00991	0.01270	0.02135
8	0.00630	0.00632	0.00637	0.00645	0.00659	0.00681	0.00716	0.00774	0.00877	0.01110	0.01411	0.02313
7	0.00721	0.00723	0.00728	0.00738	0.00755	0.00780	0.00820	0.00885	0.01001	0.01259	0.01585	0.02521
6	0.00842	0.00844	0.00851	0.00863	0.00882	0.00912	0.00959	0.01033	0.01165	0.01451	0.01804	0.02767
5	0.01012	0.01014	0.01022	0.01037	0.01061	0.01097	0.01152	0.01239	0.01389	0.01709	0.02090	0.03060
4	0.01267	0.01270	0.01280	0.01299	0.01328	0.01372	0.01438	0.01541	0.01715	0.02071	0.02473	0.03414
3	0.01692	0.01696	0.01710	0.01734	0.01771	0.01826	0.01907	0.02028	0.02226	0.02609	0.03010	0.03846
2	0.02540	0.02546	0.02563	0.02593	0.02639	0.02704	0.02795	0.02926	0.03126	0.03475	0.03801	0.04375
1	0.05000	0.05000	0.05000	0.05000	0.05000	0.05000	0.05000	0.05000	0.05000	0.05000	0.05000	0.05000

Table 3. Comparing the cutoffs $w_2(n_0)$ when $w_1(n_0)$ is (11), under multivariate t with $n = 16$ and $\nu = 64$ for various ρ.

	ρ											
n_0	**0**	**0.1**	**0.2**	**0.3**	**0.4**	**0.5**	**0.6**	**0.7**	**0.8**	**0.9**	**0.95**	**0.99**
16	0.00314	0.00315	0.00317	0.00320	0.00326	0.00337	0.00354	0.00384	0.00440	0.00575	0.00762	0.01422
15	0.00335	0.00336	0.00338	0.00342	0.00349	0.00360	0.00378	0.00410	0.00470	0.00613	0.00811	0.01499
14	0.00359	0.00360	0.00362	0.00366	0.00374	0.00386	0.00406	0.00440	0.00504	0.00657	0.00867	0.01585
13	0.00387	0.00388	0.00390	0.00395	0.00403	0.00416	0.00438	0.00475	0.00544	0.00708	0.00931	0.01680
12	0.00419	0.00420	0.00423	0.00428	0.00437	0.00452	0.00476	0.00516	0.00590	0.00766	0.01004	0.01787
11	0.00458	0.00459	0.00462	0.00468	0.00478	0.00494	0.00520	0.00564	0.00645	0.00835	0.01089	0.01907
10	0.00504	0.00505	0.00508	0.00515	0.00526	0.00544	0.00573	0.00622	0.00711	0.00917	0.01189	0.02044
9	0.00560	0.00561	0.00565	0.00573	0.00585	0.00606	0.00638	0.00692	0.00790	0.01015	0.01308	0.02200
8	0.00631	0.00632	0.00637	0.00645	0.00660	0.00683	0.00719	0.00780	0.00889	0.01136	0.01452	0.02380
7	0.00721	0.00723	0.00728	0.00739	0.00756	0.00782	0.00824	0.00893	0.01015	0.01288	0.01629	0.02589
6	0.00842	0.00844	0.00851	0.00863	0.00883	0.00915	0.00963	0.01042	0.01181	0.01484	0.01853	0.02834
5	0.01012	0.01015	0.01023	0.01038	0.01062	0.01100	0.01157	0.01250	0.01409	0.01746	0.02141	0.03125
4	0.01267	0.01270	0.01281	0.01300	0.01330	0.01376	0.01446	0.01554	0.01738	0.02111	0.02527	0.03473
3	0.01692	0.01697	0.01711	0.01735	0.01774	0.01831	0.01916	0.02044	0.02252	0.02650	0.03061	0.03893
2	0.02541	0.02546	0.02564	0.02595	0.02642	0.02709	0.02804	0.02941	0.03148	0.03506	0.03835	0.04400
1	0.05000	0.05000	0.05000	0.05000	0.05000	0.05000	0.05000	0.05000	0.05000	0.05000	0.05000	0.05000

Table 4. Comparing the cutoffs $\tilde{\Delta}(i)$ under multivariate t with $n = 3$ and $\nu = 16$ for various ρ.

	ρ											
n_0	**0**	**0.1**	**0.2**	**0.3**	**0.4**	**0.5**	**0.6**	**0.7**	**0.8**	**0.9**	**0.95**	**0.99**
3	0.01718	0.01723	0.01738	0.01763	0.01800	0.01850	0.01916	0.02004	0.02124	0.02299	0.02434	0.02622
2	0.02572	0.02578	0.02595	0.02626	0.02669	0.02728	0.02805	0.02904	0.03038	0.03231	0.03378	0.03582
1	0.05000	0.05000	0.05000	0.05000	0.05000	0.05000	0.05000	0.05000	0.05000	0.05000	0.05000	0.05000

Table 5. Comparing the cutoffs $w_2(n_0)$ when $w_1(n_0)$ is (11), under multivariate t with $n = 3$ and $\nu = 16$ for various ρ.

	ρ											
n_0	**0**	**0.1**	**0.2**	**0.3**	**0.4**	**0.5**	**0.6**	**0.7**	**0.8**	**0.9**	**0.95**	**0.99**
3	0.01720	0.01725	0.01741	0.01769	0.01811	0.01872	0.01960	0.02090	0.02296	0.02686	0.03087	0.03904
2	0.02574	0.02580	0.02599	0.02632	0.02681	0.02751	0.02847	0.02982	0.03185	0.03533	0.03852	0.04406
1	0.05000	0.05000	0.05000	0.05000	0.05000	0.05000	0.05000	0.05000	0.05000	0.05000	0.05000	0.05000

Table 6. Comparing the cutoffs $w_2(n_0)$ when $w_1(n_0)$ is (11) under multivariate t with $n = 3$ and $\nu = 16$ for various ρ.

	ρ											
n_0	**0**	**0.1**	**0.2**	**0.3**	**0.4**	**0.5**	**0.6**	**0.7**	**0.8**	**0.9**	**0.95**	**0.99**
3	0.01720	0.01726	0.01742	0.01771	0.01815	0.01878	0.01970	0.02105	0.02320	0.02722	0.03130	0.03943
2	0.02575	0.02581	0.02601	0.02635	0.02686	0.02757	0.02856	0.02997	0.03205	0.03560	0.03881	0.04427
1	0.05000	0.05000	0.05000	0.05000	0.05000	0.05000	0.05000	0.05000	0.05000	0.05000	0.05000	0.05000

In Setting 1, $n = 16$ is as in Sarkar et al. (2016). To explain the other choices in a model framework, we go to Section 4 of Seneta and Chen (2005) for notation and discussion. Consider l treatments (the first of which is a control), and so l treatment groups, each of size J, and consider testing the simultaneous hypotheses $H_i : \mu_i - \mu_1 = 0$, $i = 2, \ldots, l$. Then, $n = l - 1$, and for the individual (equicorrelated) test statistics $\nu = lJ - l = l(J - 1)$. Then, $l = 16$, $J = 5$ implies $\nu = 64$, $n = 15$; while $l = 4$, $J = 5$ implies $\nu = 16$, $n = 3$. Thus, in Setting 2, the values of ν and n are precisely as in Section 5 of Seneta and Chen (2005), allowing some of the numerical results there to be cross-checked as well as for the graphic extension of those results.

Tables 1–6 demonstrate that (14) when $w_1(n_0)$ is (11) provides the tightest control on familywise error (FWE) among the three cutoffs.

Sarkar et al. (2016) presented a graphical comparison of the effect of their cutoff points (12) with those using (11) in the two-tailed setting with $n = 16$. Here, we extend this by graphically comparing the FWER resulting from each of four sets of cutoff constants: (9), (11), (12), and (14) when $w_1(n_0)$ is (11). The comparison is made with respect to error rates with increasing the values of ρ under our two multivariate t settings. The results can be found in Figures 1 and 2. All simulations were performed using the R software package (R Core Team, 2023), with one hundred thousand (100,000) independent replications in each case. The independent multivariate t samples were generated with the `mvtnorm` package version 1.3-3 of Genz et al. (2021). A generalized additive model (GAM) of Wood (2023) was used to smooth the resulting lines. Figures 1 and 2 parallel Figure 1a of Sarkar et al. (2016).

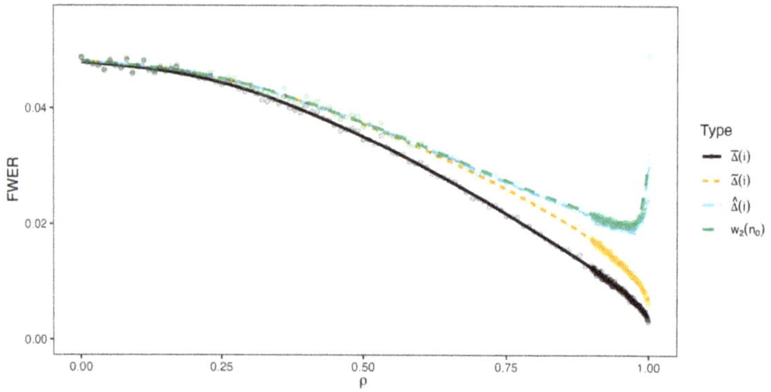

Figure 1. Comparing the familywise error rate with cutoff constants $\bar{\Delta}(i)$, $\tilde{\Delta}(i)$, $\hat{\Delta}(i)$, $w_2(n_0)$ when $w_1(n_0)$ is (11), the cutoff constants are given by (9), (11), (12) and (14), respectively, for various values of common correlation ρ at level $\alpha = 0.05$ for the multivariate and t_{64} with $n = 16$.

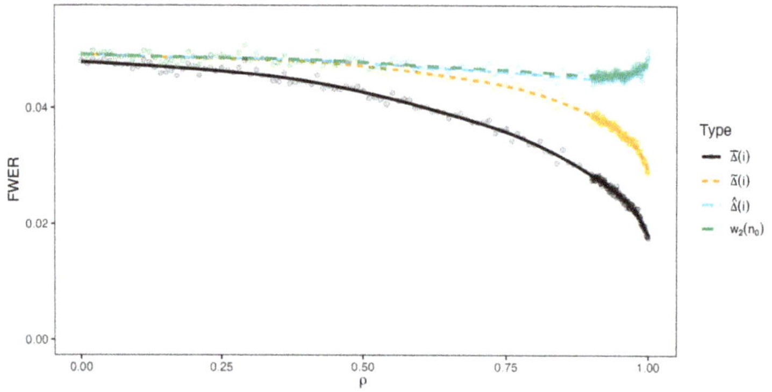

Figure 2. Comparing the familywise error rate with cutoff constants $\bar{\Delta}(i)$, $\tilde{\Delta}(i)$, $\hat{\Delta}(i)$, $w_2(n_0)$ when $w_1(n_0)$ is (11), and the cutoff constants are given by (9), (11), (12), and (14), respectively, for various values of common correlation ρ at level $\alpha = 0.05$ for the multivariate and t_{16} with $n = 3$.

From these two figures, we observe $\tilde{\Delta}(i)$, $\hat{\Delta}(i)$, and $w_2(n0)$ all provide significant improvement to the Holm values $\bar{\Delta}(i)$. There is some evidence from the two figures, for future investigation, that the FWER decreases as n increases, when the rest of the settings remain unchanged. Similarly, as ρ increases, the FWER generally decreases for most methods. However, at very high correlation values (such as $\rho \to 1$), $\hat{\Delta}(i)$ and $w_2(n_0)$ exhibit an upward spike towards α. This suggests that when the test statistics are perfectly correlated, only $\hat{\Delta}(i)$ and $w_2(n_0)$ appropriately adjust the FWER by collapsing the results.

However, the improvement in FWER due to $w_2(n_0)$ when $w_1(n_0)$ is (11) is so slight so as to be almost indistinguishable from $w_2(n_0)$ when $w_1(n_0)$ is (9). This is supported by the fact that even at $\rho = 0.99$ and $n_0 = 16$, $w_2(n_0)$ provides an approximately 3.5% improvement over $\hat{\Delta}(i)$.

In summary, our tabulated results demonstrate that (14), paired with (11) as $w_1(n_0)$, offers the most effective control of familywise error (FWE), particularly for higher values of ρ, under multivariate t-distributions. The graphical comparison suggests that a single iterative step from $w_1(n_0)$ to $w_2(n_0)$ is enough to stabilize the FWER irrespective of the choice of $w_1(n_0)$. The extent of improvement from $w_1(n_0)$ to $w_2(n_0)$ in the Sarkar et al. (2016) setting is remarkable.

Finally, recall that each of the two iterative steps is justified on account of the convex nature of the Student t-copula, a central result of Sarkar et al. (2016)

5. Some Personal Recollections (ES)

5.1. *Joe Gani and Chris Heyde, to September, 1974*

My first, indirect, contact with Joe Gani (1924–2016) occurred during my M.Sc. research year, 1964, at the University of Adelaide, when my supervisor John Darroch (1930–2024) made me aware of the work on applied probability centered in P.A.P. (Pat) Moran's department at the Australian National University (ANU), Canberra, and Joe Gani's intention there to found the *Journal of Applied Probability* (JAP) as a focus for publication in that subject area. John's intention was that our work on quasi-stationarity might eventually be published there as it was (Darroch & Seneta, 1965). In 1965, I began work on my PhD in Statistics enrolled in Moran's ANU Statistics Department in the Research School of Social Sciences, while working in E.J. (Ted) Hannan's ANU teaching Department in the School of General Studies (SGS). By then, all the illustrious and to-become-illustrious names associated with Moran's department had left it, including Joe Gani and Chris Heyde (1939–2008), who had been a PhD student there in 1962–1964. Chris's nominal supervisor had been J.E. (Jo) Moyal (1910–1998), then Reader in the Department, but Chris worked mainly on his own, following some suggestions made to him by Pat Moran.

Joe Gani and Ted Hannan (1921–1994) had been Moran's first PhD students at ANU, which had been established in 1946 by Act of Australian Federal Parliament as a centrepiece and focal point for Australian research and PhD training. Joe and Ted's deep friendship and mutual support, personal and academic continued until Ted's passing. Chris's relation with Joe was of a deeply loyal and filial nature.

In September 1964, Chris joined Joe Gani, first in the Department of Statistics at Michigan State University (MSU), East Lansing, where JAP was founded. When Joe Gani left MSU to take up the Chair of Probability and Statistics at the University of Sheffield, UK, at the end of 1965, Chris followed him there as a Lecturer. He was soon promoted to Special Lecturer in charge of the Statistical Laboratory at the University of Manchester in 1967, when the Manchester-Sheffield School of Probability and Statistics was formed.

Chris returned to Australia in September 1968 to take up a Readership in Ted Hannan's Department of Statistics, from which at the time I was absent on a one year's Study Leave in the UK. My paper (Seneta, 1968) on the sequence of constants $\{c_n\}$, (later called the "Seneta constants") giving convergence in distribution of $\{Z_n/c_n\}$ to a proper non-degenerate random variable W for the supercritical simple (at the time called the Galton–Watson) branching process, without any further conditions, had appeared in that year and Chris had noticed it. I received a letter in Cambridge from Chris that he had strengthened my result to almost sure convergence by noticing that $\{\exp(-Z_n/c_n)\}$ was a martingale with (obviously) bounded expectation. He published this in the same journal in 1970, and the result, in its variants and extensions became known as the Seneta–Heyde theorem or norming. Since that time, a principal theme of Chris's work became the theory and use of martingale methods in situations of statistical dependence.

The dominant theme of Chris's work prior to his return to Canberra in 1968 was the refinement of classical limit theory for sums of independent random variables, involving large and small deviations, rates of convergence and domains of attraction. His note of 1970 stimulated him to develop a theory for the supercritical process theory analogous to the classical rate of convergence theory. There was a continued focus on inference aspects of branching-type processes, which led to an inclination towards a framework of time-series type results, in which his martingale work was hugely influential. One of his favorite papers was a joint paper with Ted Hannan in this framework.

I had returned to Ted Hannan's department in the first half of 1969, and from that time our friendship and collaboration began.

At the time of Chris's return to Canberra in 1968, there was still a strong trend of research at ANU into population genetics, originating from Pat Moran's book on this topic, which had in fact partly motivated me to come to Canberra from Adelaide. Chris's interest in population genetics was invigorated by my note (Seneta, 1974), which extended, on its anniversary, Malécot's Markov chain formulation of the Fisher–Wright model to randomly fluctuating population size. The result uses the martingale convergence theorem, whose nature and use by Chris in his 1970 note had made me aware of its power and breadth of application. There followed a wealth of related and more general studies and papers by Chris, a few being collaborative. My fuller appreciation of Chris's work on branching processes and population genetics is the paper (Seneta, 2010).

Bienaymé

A second major common interest of mine with Chris was history. This evolved from our contact and collaboration on branching processes, and was initially stimulated by two historical papers published in 1966, one in this area by D. G. Kendall, on Galton and Watson's study of the criticality theorem for branching processes, the other by H.O. Lancaster on forerunners of the Pearson χ^2, which noted that the French statistician, I.J. Bienaymé, in a classic paper of 1853 had made considerable contributions to the theory. Lancaster had been Chris's M.Sc. supervisor at the University of Sydney (and, as it turned out, was to be my predecessor in the Chair of Mathematical Statistics there, to which I came in 1979). It was in the 1853 paper that Bienaymé had anticipated Chebyshev in the discovery of the inequality which should more appropriately be called the Bienaymé–Chebyshev Inequality.

My interest in whether Bienaymé had made other discoveries was aroused. Through Lancaster's bibliographic work, a list of Bienaymé's publications was available. Because of the title of one of Bienaymé's papers of 1845 on the duration of family names, I requested it on an interlibrary loan, and to my amazement, when it arrived, I found that it contained a completely correct (in contrast to Galton and Watson's) statement of the criticality theorem. I rushed down the passage from my office to Chris's to share the news, and we planned the future. The immediate result was the note (Heyde & Seneta, 1972), received February 1972. In time it led to the book, (Heyde & Seneta, 1977). And it became more correct to call the simple branching process the Bienaymé–Galton–Watson process.

5.2. September 1974–1993

From September 1974 to July 1981, Joe was back in Australia as Chief of the CSIRO Division of Mathematics and Statistics. The Division was now based in Canberra and located close to ANU.

Ted Hannan had retired as Professor and Head of the SGS Department in 1970, and C.R. (Chip) Heathcote (1931–2016), who like Chris, had been Reader in the Department, was eventually appointed in his place. Chris who had also applied for the position, joined Joe at the CSIRO in January 1975. Ross Maller (the first PhD student to be enrolled in the SGS Department) was one year into his PhD at the time. Chip asked me to take over as

Ross's supervisor for the remaining two or so years of Ross's candidature. My area of intersection with Ross's research was regularly varying functions, but Ross needed little supervision, and our relationship was good.

Chris took over as Acting Chief in 1981 when Joe Gani left the Division, until September 1983 when he was appointed Professor and Chairman of the Department of Statistics at the University of Melbourne. The 45th (100th anniversary) World Statistics Congress (WSC) of the International Statistical Institute took place in 1985 in Amsterdam, at which Chris and I had a happy reunion, although I was billeted at Valkenburg, and he, I think, in Maastricht. In particular I remember us at the van Gogh Museum in Amsterdam, commenting on van Gogh's *Sunflowers*, and his depiction of people.

In May 1986, Chris returned to the ANU, and was Professor and Head of the ANU Department of Statistics in the Institute of Advanced Studies from July 1986 to December 1988. Chris and I worked together again on history to motivate and jointly guest-edit for Australia's Bicentenary the Bicentennial History Issue of the Australian Journal of Statistics (Heyde & Seneta, 1988). That was Special Volume 30B of that year. Volume 30A was a Special Volume of "Papers in honour of J. Gani. C.C. Heyde (Editor)". to which both Chris and I also contributed.

From 1989 to 1992, Chris was the Foundation Dean of the ANU School of Mathematical Sciences (later the Mathematical Sciences Institute). Since 1993, while continuing at ANU, until his death in 2008, he had also been a Professor in the Department of Statistics at Columbia University, New York. He taught there for their Fall semester each year (September to December) till 2007, and was eventually the Director of that university's Center for Applied Probability.

5.3. Chris Heyde, 1993–2008

The First World Congress on Branching Processes was held in Varna, Bulgaria, on the Black Sea, in 1993 to celebrate the first 150 years of these processes. Chris presided over the opening session, and I was the first speaker (on history). I attended with Malcolm Quine, who had been my first PhD student. Chris later edited the Proceedings.

In 1995, the Christiaan-Huygens Committee on the History of Statistics of the International Statistical Institute (ISI) was reconstituted with Chris as Chair, and members of the committee became actively involved in what was to become the book *Statisticians of the Centuries*.

Chris was diagnosed with hairy-cell leukemia in about 1997. In one of his periods of rest during remission, at his and Beth's old home in Aranda, a Canberra suburb, when I called on him during one of my annual visits from Sydney, he told me about this task. This was the first time that I had learned of the hairy-cell leukemia. Our meeting was outside, on a sunny day. He looked fragile, was somewhat disheveled after rest, and said he did not feel up to the task, on which he had already been engaged for some time. He asked me to share the editorial task with him, and insisted on sharing equally the small initial funding grant from the ISI. And so *Centuries* came to be. Eventually we were joined by P. Crépel, S.E. Fienberg, and Joe Gani as Associate Editors. When the book was about to appear, he expressed to me great relief at having that millstone round his neck removed. The book appeared in 2001, when the world's attention was focused on 9/11 in the USA.

Soon after the diagnosis, at the award of a D.Sc. Honoris Causa from his Alma Mater, Sydney University, in 1998, I heard Chris give an inspiring speech to the new graduates, on the rewards of a life in science.

Especially memorable was the occasion of the 52nd WSC, 1999, in Helsinki, Finland, before which we made a side trip to St. Petersburg, Russia. In the company of our wives Beth and Ludmilla, and of our statistical colleagues Neville Weber and Mary Phipps, we enjoyed the warm hospitality of Yuri and Larissa Borovskikh, and experienced an adventure at border crossing out of Russia. On the train from St. Petersburg, before the border with Finland, Russian security decided to search Beth and Chris's baggage for items being taken out illegally. By the end of their search, they were disappointed that all they had found was a dried banana. Chris and Beth loved to repeat that story in later years.

A highlight of my memories of Chris in Australia was the celebration of his 65th birthday at ANU in 2004. In the speech he made that night following dinner at University House, he expressed gratitude for the extra years had been given him, and his happiness at being able to be present.

He had a special dedication to the Australian statistical tradition and activity. In 2005 the 55th WSC was held in Sydney. Chris was to give an invited lecture on the development of Statistics in our Australian state universities at the meeting He prepared this during one of the periodic flare-ups of his leukemia. As on some such occasions before and after, I was happy to play the role of Chris's back-up system. Joe Gani's was to be the opening historical talk, but early in the talk something went wrong. Joe, with obvious relief, discarded his notes and spoke impromptu, something at which he was very good.

Chris Heyde, Contact in Final Years

Chris made several visits from Columbia University, New York, to me at the University of Virginia (UVa.), Mr. Thomas Jefferson's university, in Charlottesville, where I spent a number of semesters teaching. My first visit to U.Va., with my wife, was 1988–89, for the full academic year. Then, I made fall semester visits within 1999–2001, and finally one in 2005.

In one of his talks at UVa., he described himself as a seeker after truth in the proper way to model random fluctuation of financial returns. That was characteristic of the man.

In late 2005, Leonard Scott my friend and colleague in the Mathematics Department, with experience in financial data and mathematics, organized a farewell conference. The following is from the poster:

> The Variance Gamma and Related Financial Models. A conference in honor of Eugene Seneta. University of Virginia, Charlottesville, Virginia. 22–23 October 2005. Speakers: Chris Heyde (Columbia University and ANU). Dilip Madan (University of Maryland), Eugene Seneta (University of Sydney)., +2 . Organizers: Patrick Dennis (U.Va.), Jeff Holt (U.Va.), Leonard Scott (U.Va.).

Chris, Dilip, and I also spoke impromptu at that evening's departmental dinner and party. The warmth and celebration were a joyful time, which lives in my memory. Among the things that Chris said was that I had successfully resisted a departmental farewell at ANU in 1979, and at Sydney University, but Leonard had, most remarkably, succeeded at UVa.

I had, in return, visited Chris in New York during his period at Columbia University. One Sunday, we walked by the foreshore of the Hudson to Grant's Tomb, and visited an almost deserted Wall Street, where I bought a wallet from a street vendor, a souvenir which I use to this day. In an email to me dated 20 January 2008, when the prognosis for his illness was already quite negative, Chris wrote the following:

> *Whatever happens, I certainly feel that I have had a fortunate life. I will be happy to have more, but if not, I have had a good innings and can go in peace.*

I last saw him at Canberra Hospital on the Friday before his death, in the company of Beth. They were hopeful, but prepared. His mind was clear, and we all spoke lightly of times together past, present and of possible futures.

Chris died in Canberra Thursday 6 March 2008, from the effects of metastatic melanoma.

Joe was too emotionally fragile to prepare a eulogy, and asked me to do it. He was in the front row of the congregation when I read it at the funeral ceremony on 13 March 2008.

I concluded the tribute with the words of St. Paul, which well describe Chris's life:

I have fought a good fight, I have finished the race, I have kept the faith.

5.4. ES Contact with Joe Gani

I had had almost no personal contact with Joe before I came to Sydney in mid-1979, and my news of Joe was largely through Ted Hannan and Chris. Prior to Sydney, there was some correspondence by mail relating to publications in his beloved creation, the *Journal of Applied Probability* (JAP), and then its companion journal *Advances in Applied Probability*, to be dedicated to longer articles. As the first article in 1969 he had kindly published a review paper originating from work around the creation of the norming constants for the supercritical branching process (Seneta, 1968).

He was a kind, generous, accommodating and efficient editor. At the time, the editorial policy was to use just one referee. I remember one occasion when an author had complained very strongly about a negative referee's report which indeed was very superficial. Joe then sent the paper to me, for a second opinion. I generally never liked refereeing since I felt that I should actually read a submission carefully, and Joe knew it. But indeed, the paper was a good piece of work. Sometimes people took advantage of the journal's one-referee policy and Joe's generosity. Joe could become very angry. One occasion was when a young author plagiarized a paper published earlier by another author in an obscure journal, and it was published in JAP before the plagiarism was discovered.

Concerning another occasion, to set the scene, in a late letter to me dated 16 March 2019, John Darroch (1930–2024) wrote "One of Joe's highly appreciated initiatives [during Joe's CSIRO period–ES] was to obtain funding to enable overseas statisticians to visit Australia for weeks or months in order to work jointly with their established research colleagues here in Australia". There were several Russian mathematical statisticians among such visitors. A problem was that such visitors, although provided with travel and accommodation, were not permitted to take any foreign currency out of the Soviet Union. On one occasion, I heard that Joe, taking pity on the penniless visitor, had given him USD 50 from his own pocket. This visitor had promptly spent all the money to buy himself a tennis racquet. It was one of several visitor occasions, even after the collapse of the Soviet Union in 1991, when Joe was very displeased at the exploitation, in ignorance of civilized norms, of his efforts.

5.4.1. 1983–2016, Varanasi, Mathematical Scientist, Doeblin, ANU

Even though from 1981 to 1994, Joe had been at the University of Kentucky, and the University of California at Santa Barbara, he and I got to know each other better from about this time.

There was to be an International Statistical Conference in India in 1983, and, characteristically, Joe was heavily involved in its organization. But something went wrong at the Indian end, and the locale and Indian organization were, fortunately, able to be moved to Varanasi at Banaras Hindu University, through the generosity and work of the local statisticians, under their Head, whose name I am not now sure of (Professor Singh?). I got one side of my clothes covered in mud from a fall outside the conference venue. Joe came to my rescue with particularly useful suggestions in view of my short supply of replacement trousers.

In the early 1980s, my work on history of probability and statistics in the 19th century had begun to focus strongly on the Russian Empire. I had submitted a long paper on this to *Archive for History of Exact Sciences*. After revision in response to review by a very eminent referee (van der Waerden), who identified himself, I did not hear for a very long time from the editor. In fact, as I learned later, the paper had been accepted, but an acceptance letter from the (at the time shaky) editorial system never arrived, so I had written to withdraw the paper, and turned to Joe who kindly agreed to publish it without further ado in his very personal creation *The Mathematical Scientist*. It appeared as Seneta (1984).

That particular issue of Joe's journal marked a high point in my hobby work on history since it also contained the first of my papers on Lewis Carroll, the author of the *Alice* books, as probabilist. Later, during his years resettled at ANU, Joe asked me, in line with his social organization activities, to give a seminar on Lewis Carroll there. The audience included a large number of ANU's mathematicians and mathematical statisticians. It was one of the most successful seminars, in terms of flow and audience reaction, of my professional career.

In his continuing promotion of personal contact and social interaction among probabilists and statisticians, and his intense interest in history and creativity of their subject area, Joe played a major part, with Harry Cohn, and Heinrich Hering (of Goettingen University), in a "By Invitation Only Conference":

> 50 Years After Doeblin: Developments in the Theory of Markov Chains, Markov Processes and Sums of Random Variables. Blaubeuren, Germany, 2–7 November 1991.

I had contributed in 1973 to the rediscovery of Doeblin's work on ergodicity coefficients, and study related to ergodicity coefficients was one of my main research areas.

This was a remarkably successful conference, the best organized in my professional experience, around the time of the collapse of the Soviet Union. It included K.L. Chung among the great names attending. The mornings were devoted to a small number of presentations. When one of the francophone speakers had difficulty with presentation in English, Joe stepped in to tell him to continue in French. After lunch, there was time for further social interaction, which at least once took the form of a companionable leisurely walk taking in scenery around a lake close to the conference/accommodation venue (Hotel "Terminus").

As Visiting Fellow at ANU from September 1989 to December 1999, and then continuously from 2001, Joe was primarily located within the Stochastic Analysis Group, in an office adjacent to Chris's, in the Moran Building. Joe was the social coordinator for the corridor. He formed a morning Coffee Club, an informal forum for exchange of views, and for Joe's Jewish jokes, for which he was famous.

During this period, he reestablished a caring personal contact with Jo Moyal, who after his retirement in 1977 as Professor at Macquarie University, had moved back to Canberra. Shortly before Moyal's passing in 1998, Joe organized an ANU Honorary D.Sc. for him. And after Moyal's passing, Joe put a great deal of effort and his own money for Macquarie University to award annually a Moyal Medal. It was appropriate that Joe was the first recipient in 2000.

On my annual visits to ANU, I would visit Chris first, and then Joe in his office, and then we would go to the Coffee Club.

In the early years of this century, the Australian Academy of Science had been arranging and conducting filmed interviews with its distinguished senior Fellows. The interview with Joe was scheduled for Friday, 28 March 2008, and, naturally, the interviewer was to be Chris. When Chris died on the 6th March, I was asked in his place. After my preparation, Joe and I met for an afternoon at his home on the 26 March for discussion. The long and successful interview took place as scheduled and is available as Seneta (2008). The following is the concluding part. The plain text is Joe speaking.

> I would say that although I've had a rather broken-up life, looking back I don't regret it. I consider myself to have been extremely lucky, not least in my marriage and in my children, but also professionally. I've had a lot of hurdles to overcome,

but fortunately I haven't been left with a nasty taste.
And you had two very important friends in your life, Ted Hannan and Chris Heyde.
Indeed. Ted was very much like a brother. We used to exchange views, we used to talk about everything – Ted was a person of very wide interests, extremely well read. I still have a copy of the poems of WB Yeats which he gave me on one occasion, and which he used to quote. I can never remember poetry, but he used to be very good at quotation from Yeats and other poets.
'An elderly man is like a stick with an esophagus'...
That's right! [laugh] Ted was a wonderful man. I am still very good friends with his widow, whom I visit regularly.
Chris was more like a son (there was a 15-year difference between us) and he was a very clever, very loyal colleague. Now it's our turn to support Beth Heyde, who has lost her very dear husband.
Ted and Chris were family. As, I might add, you are too.
Well, thank you for that, Joe. I think this interview will be a fitting tribute to your role.
And thank you very much. I really appreciate it.

After Chris's death in 2008, I continued the visits to Joe, and to walk with him to the Coffee Club. On our last meeting in this way, he asked me to stop, since he needed to rest on that walk.

He was first moved to Baptistcare Griffith (Griffith is a Canberra suburb) in July 2015, after a fall. I visited him there later that year. He was confined to bed at the time, fragile but mentally alert. On 4 April 2016, I heard from his daughter Sarah that he was back there after another fall. He died 12 April 2016.

5.4.2. Epilogue

A Memorial Service for Joe was held on 22 April 2016, in the Great Hall of University House, ANU. It was beautifully organized, with his four children speaking, led by Miriam Gani. I, Daryl Daley (1939–2023), and Bob Anderssen from the CSIRO, spoke as friends and former colleagues. The large gathering at this very significant venue for Joe's life included Chip Heathcote, even though incapacitated with a recently broken neck, in a wheelchair.

Joe, resolutely irreligious till the end, would have appreciated the coincidence of the date with the beginning of the Jewish Passover.

Another Memorial Session was held on 5 December 2016, at the Australian Statistical Conference, Hotel Realm in Canberra. The speakers were Eugene Seneta (overview of life and career), Sarah Gani (on her father, and family life), Frank de Hoog (presenting Ron Sandland's account of Joe's time at the CSIRO), Sue Wilson (1948–2020) (on Manchester-Sheffield), Gordon Smythe (on Santa Barbara), and Daryl Daley (Applied Probability and Joe's mathematical activity).

I treasure a happy photograph taken on 6 January, 1994, of Chris, Ted Hannan, Joe Gani, and myself at coffee at ANU's Calypso café, as shown in Figure 3.

It had been Chris who called me from Canberra to tell me that Ted had passed away the day after the photo was taken. At Ted's funeral at Canberra's St. Christopher's Cathedral, Joe read the eulogy from the pulpit. Chris, Daryl Daley, and I were in the congregation. Joe wrote Ted's official obituary for the Australian Academy of Science (Gani, 1994).

And Joe called me to tell me that Chris had passed away. Joe and I wrote Chris's obituary for the Academy (Seneta & Gani, 2009).

And I wrote Joe's official obituary (Seneta, 2019), after Joe passed away.

Joe was a visionary leader, of indomitable physical and mental energy. He helped a great many people, including me, in their academic careers, and was the moving influence of the golden years of applied probability.

Figure 3. From left: Chris Heyde, Ted Hannan, Joe Gani and Eugene Seneta (6 January 1994).

Author Contributions: The research part of this paper consist of Sections 2–4. Sections 2 and 3 were written by E.S., Section 4 by T.F. For these sections: conceptualization: E.S.; methodology: E.S. and T.F.; software: T.F.; validation: E.S. and T.F.; formal analysis: E.S. All authors have read and agreed to the published version of the manuscript.

Funding: This research received no external funding.

Institutional Review Board Statement: Not appicable.

Informed Consent Statement: Not applicable.

Data Availability Statement: All data was generated by analytical calculation, or by simulation, and is displayed. All the code used in the paper can be obtained by contacting the authors.

Acknowledgments: We thank the authors of `R` packages that we used to complete this work: `tidyverse` of Wickham and RStudio (2022), `ggplot2` of Wickham et al. (2024). ES is grateful to Shuangzhe Liu for his encouragement.

Conflicts of Interest: The authors declare no conflicts of interest.

Notes

1 The paper is available here: https://www.maths.usyd.edu.au/u/eseneta/SenetaChen(1997).pdf, accessed on 1 April 2025.
2 Eventually incorporated into Tjetjep and Seneta (2006).
3 Preprint version of this referred to as Heyde and Leonenko (2005) in Seneta (2004).

References

Darroch, J. N., & Seneta, E. (1965). On quasi-stationary distributions in absorbing discrete-time finite markov chains. *Journal of Applied Probability*, *2*(1), 88–100. [CrossRef]

Epps, T. W. (2000). *Pricing derivative securities*. G–reference, information and interdisciplinary subjects series. World Scientific.

Erdélyi, A., Magnus, W., Oberhettinger, F., & Tricomi, F. G. (1954). *Bateman manuscript project: Tables of integral transform* (Vol. 2.) McGraw-Hill.

Finlay, R., & Seneta, E. (2006). Stationary-increment student and variance-gamma processes. *Journal of Applied Probability, 43*(2), 441–453. [CrossRef]
Fung, T., & Seneta, E. (2011). Tail dependence and skew distributions. *Quantitative Finance, 11*(3), 327–333. [CrossRef]
Fung, T., & Seneta, E. (2023). On familywise error rate cutoffs under pairwise exchangeability. *Methodology and Computing in Applied Probability, 25*(2), 59. [CrossRef]
Gani, J. (1994). Obituary: Edward James Hannan. *Australian Journal of Statistics, 36*(1), 1–8. [CrossRef]
Genz, A., Bretz, F., Miwa, T., Mi, X., Leisch, F., Scheipl, F., Bornkamp, B., Maechler, M., & Hothorn, T. (2021). Mvtnorm: Multivariate normal and t distributions. R package version 1.1-3. Available online: https://cran.r-project.org/web/packages/mvtnorm/index.html (accessed on 1 April 2025).
Heyde, C. C. (1999). A risky asset model with strong dependence through fractal activity time. *Journal of Applied Probability, 36*(4), 1234–1239. [CrossRef]
Heyde, C. C., & Kou, S. G. (2004). On the controversy over tailweight of distributions. *Operations Research Letters, 32*(5), 399–408. [CrossRef]
Heyde, C. C., & Leonenko, N. N. (2005). Student processes. *Advances in Applied Probability, 37*(2), 342–365. [CrossRef]
Heyde, C. C., & Liu, S. (2001). Empirical realities for a minimal description risky asset model. The need for fractal features. *Journal of the Korean Mathematical Society, 38*, 1047–1059.
Heyde, C. C., & Seneta, E. (1972). Studies in the history of probability and statistics. XXXI. The simple branching process, a turning point test and a fundamental inequality: A historical note on I. J. Bienayme. *Biometrika, 59*(3), 680–683. [CrossRef]
Heyde, C. C., & Seneta, E. (1977). *I. J. Bienaymé: Statistical Theory Anticipated.* Springer, New York. [CrossRef]
Heyde, C. C., & Seneta, E. (Eds.). (1988). *The bicentennial history issue of the Australian journal of statistics* (Vol. 30B). John Wiley & Sons, Ltd.
Holm, S. (1979). A simple sequentially rejective multiple test procedure. *Scandinavian Journal of Statistics, 6*(2), 65–70.
Madan, D. B., Carr, P. P., & Chang, E. C. (1998). The variance gamma process and option pricing. *Review of Finance, 2*(1), 79–105. [CrossRef]
Madan, D. B., & Seneta, E. (1990). The variance gamma (V.G.) Model for share market returns. *The Journal of Business, 63*(4), 511–524. [CrossRef]
R Core Team. (2023). *R: A language and environment for statistical computing.* R Foundation for Statistical Computing.
Sarkar, S. K., Fu, Y., & Guo, W. (2016). Improving Holm's procedure using pairwise dependencies. *Biometrika, 103*(1), 237–243. [CrossRef]
Seneta, E. (1968). On recent theorems concerning the supercritical galton-watson process. *The Annals of Mathematical Statistics, 39*(6), 2098–2102. [CrossRef]
Seneta, E. (1974). A note on the balance between random sampling and population size (on the 30th anniversary of G. Malécot's paper). *Genetics, 77*(3), 607–610. [CrossRef]
Seneta, E. (1984). The central limit problem and linear least squares in pre-revoluationary Russia: The background. *Mathematical Scientist, 9*, 37–77.
Seneta, E. (2004). Fitting the variance-gamma model to financial data. *Journal of Applied Probability, 41*, 177–187. [CrossRef]
Seneta, E. (2008). Interview with Joe Gani. Interviews with Australian scientists. Australian Academy of Science. Available online: https://www.science.org.au/learning/general-audience/history/interviews-australian-scientists/professor-joe-gani-1924-2016 (accessed on 9 March 2024).
Seneta, E. (2010). Chris heyde on branching processes and population genetics. In R. Maller, I. Basawa, P. Hall, & E. Seneta (Eds.), *Selected works of C.C. Heyde* (pp. 12–15). Springer. [CrossRef]
Seneta, E. (2019). Joseph Mark Gani 1924–2016. *Historical Records of Australian Science, 30*(1), 32. [CrossRef]
Seneta, E., & Chen, J. T. (2005). Simple stepwise tests of hypotheses and multiple comparisons. *International Statistical Review/Revue Internationale de Statistique, 73*(1), 21–34. [CrossRef]
Seneta, E., & Chen, T. (1997). A sequentially rejective test procedure. *Theory of Stochastic Processes, 3*(19), 393–402.
Seneta, E., & Gani, J. (2009). Christopher Charles Heyde 1939–2008: [Obituary: Professor of statistics.]. *Historical Records of Australian Science, 20*(1), 67–90. [CrossRef]
Sun, W., Rachev, S., Stoyanov, S. V., & Fabozzi, F. J. (2008). Multivariate skewed student's t copula in the analysis of nonlinear and asymmetric dependence in the German equity market. *Studies in Nonlinear Dynamics & Econometrics, 12*(2). [CrossRef]
Tjetjep, A., & Seneta, E. (2006). Skewed normal variance-mean models for asset pricing and the method of moments. *International Statistical Review, 74*(1), 109–126. [CrossRef]
Wickham, H., Chang, W., Henry, L., Pedersen, T. L., Takahashi, K., Wilke, C., Woo, K., Yutani, H., Dunnington, D., van den Brand, T., Posit, & PBC. (2024). Ggplot2: Create elegant data visualisations using the grammar of graphics. Available online: https://cran.r-project.org/web/packages/ggplot2/index.html (accessed on 1 April 2025).

Wickham, H., & RStudio. (2022). Tidyverse: Easily Install and Load the 'Tidyverse'. Available online: https://cran.r-project.org/web/packages/tidyverse/index.html (accessed on 1 April 2025).
Wood, S. (2023). Mgcv: Mixed GAM computation vehicle with automatic smoothness estimation. Available online: https://cran.r-project.org/web/packages/mgcv/index.html (accessed on 1 April 2025).

Journal of
Risk and Financial Management

MDPI

Article

Bivariate Laplace Conditional Distributions for Modeling Non-Linearly Dependent Volatile Price Changes

Ashis SenGupta [1,2,*], Barry C. Arnold [3] and Moumita Roy [4]

1 Department of Population Health Sciences, Medical College of Georgia, Augusta University, Augusta, GA 30912, USA
2 Indian Statistical Institute, Kolkata 700108, India
3 Department of Statistics, University of California, Riverside, CA 92521, USA; barnold@ucr.edu
4 Department of Statistics, Midnapore College (Autonomous), Midnapore 721101, India; mouroy.roy@gmail.com
* Correspondence: amsseng@gmail.com

Abstract

In the spirit of the solution of for modeling price changes in high-volatility markets for univariate commodities, here we generalize an approach to the case of modeling price changes jointly for two related commodities. Often, conditional distributions are more easily understood in financial markets, where the fluctuations in one commodity can shed significant light on the behavior of a related commodity. With this observation, we enhance and characterize the entire family of bivariate joint densities for which both the conditional distributions are specified to be of the Laplace form. Such bivariate distributions will be referred to as bivariate Laplace conditional (BLC) distributions. We study the marginals of the BLC distributions and establish that they are not only sub-Gaussian but also super-Laplacian and, hence, super-Cauchy, i.e., they have heavier tails than Gaussian distributions but lighter tails than the usual Laplace and Cauchy distributions. Distance correlation is suggested as a measure of the association between the two marginal variables, as their product moment correlation is zero but they may be non-linearly dependent. A real-life data set is analyzed to illustrate the use of BCL distributions in practice. We believe that this is the first work using conditional specifications in bivariate financial data analysis.

Keywords: bivariate conditionally specified distributions; bivariate Laplace distribution; distance correlation; heavy tails; high volatility

1. Introduction

It is with deep respect and profound appreciation that we, the authors, dedicate this paper to the memory of the stalwart Professors Joe Gani and Chris Heyde. The first author fondly recalls the wonderful time he spent with Prof. Gani when he was a visiting faculty member at the University of California, Santa Barbara (UCSB), USA, and later also in Australia. It is a pleasure to share here two photos of Prof. Gani. One photo (Figure 1) is with his wife and Prof. S.T. (Zari) Rachev, one of the Editors of this volume, and the other (Figure 2), which reflects the kind and humorous nature of his otherwise serious personality, were taken while all three of them were at UCSB. Prof. Gani has always been an inspiring personality in research and a warm-hearted, cheerful friend.

Figure 1. Joe with Zari in Ashis's apartment at UCSB in early 1990s.

Figure 2. Joe in a humorous mood in Ashis's apartment at UCSB in early 1990s.

Rachev and SenGupta (1993) introduced Linnik, or geometric stable, families of distributions to model price change for a single commodity in high-volatility markets. In this paper, we generalize this approach to the case of modeling price changes jointly for two related (bivariate) commodities. Often, conditional distributions are more easily understood in financial markets where the fluctuations in one commodity can shed significant light on the behavior of a related commodity. In Section 2, we briefly introduce the usual Laplace distribution. In Section 3 we enhance and characterize the entire family of bivariate densities for which both the conditional distributions are specified as Laplace distributions, i.e., the family of bivariate conditionally specified Laplace or simply bivariate Laplace conditional (BLC) distributions. Section 4 generalizes the BLC distributions of Section 3 by introducing location parameters. We study in Section 5 the marginals of the BLC

 https://doi.org/10.3390/jrfm19050355

distribution and establish that these are not only sub-Gaussian but also super-Laplacian, i.e., they have lighter tails than the usual Laplace distribution and, hence, than the Gaussian distribution. So the BLC distribution is defined in terms of its tail behavior between the Gaussian and Cauchy distributions in the family of α-stable distributions, with $1 \leq \alpha \leq 2$, though it is neither a member of the α-stable nor of the Linnik family of distributions. The appealing property of the BLC distribution is that it can be represented in an elegant and analytical closed form in terms of its probability density function (p.d.f.). This property is not available for any distribution, save for merely three (Gaussian, Cauchy and Levy for $\alpha = 2$, 1 and 0.5 respectively) in the α-stable family, and one (Laplace for $\alpha = 2$) in the Linnik family. Section 6 presents further properties of the BLC and its marginal distributions. Section 7 recalls distance correlation as a useful measure of dependency when the two variables have zero linear correlation but are dependent, as is the case with the variables with the BLC distribution. The statistical inference procedures for the parameters are discussed in Section 8, and the CAN property of the maximum likelihood estimator is established. Section 9 illustrates our proposed model and the corresponding data analysis for a real-life data set on platinum and gold price changes. This example also serves to establish its superiority over the standard bivariate normal model. The closing remarks and conclusions are given in Section 10.

2. Univariate Laplace Models

The classical Laplace distribution is one with a density of the form

$$f(x;\lambda) = (\lambda/2)e^{-\lambda|x|}I(-\infty < x < \infty), \tag{1}$$

where λ is a positive intensity parameter.

In the quest for generalizations of the classical central limit theorem and of the family of heavy-tail distributions, Linnik (1963) presented a family of distributions which has been named after him as the family of Linnik distributions. This family essentially consists of symmetric distributions and is obtained through geometric compounding of the stable family of distributions, and hence, is often called the geometric stable family (see, e.g., Rachev & SenGupta, 1993). It has been shown by SenGupta and Roy (2023) that the Linnik family may be viewed as a complementary family to the stable family in terms of its tail behavior. The central role in this family is played by the Laplace distribution, as is done by the Gaussian (normal) distribution for the stable family. There have also been several generalizations of the Laplace distribution on non-Euclidean manifolds (see, e.g., Arnold & SenGupta, 2025).

A well-known property of a symmetric Laplace variable is that it can be represented as a sum or as a 1/2:1/2 mixture of a positive exponential variable and a negative exponential variable. Thus we can write the Laplace variable X in the following two forms in terms of two independent identically distributed exponential (λ) random variables, V_1 and V_2:

$$X = V_1 - V_2, \tag{2}$$

and

$$X = \begin{cases} V_1 & \text{with probability} \quad 1/2 \\ -V_2 & \text{with probability} \quad 1/2. \end{cases} \tag{3}$$

3. Distributions with Laplace Conditionals

We are interested in absolutely continuous bivariate distributions that have, for each $y \in \mathscr{R}$, a conditional density of X given $Y = y$ of the Laplace form, and for each $x \in \mathscr{R}$, a conditional density of Y given $X = x$ also of the Laplace form.

https://doi.org/10.3390/jrfm19050355

Thus there will exist two functions $\gamma(y), \delta(x)$ such that for $(x, y) \in \mathscr{R} \times \mathscr{R}$, we have

$$f_{X|Y}(x|y) = [\gamma(y)/2]e^{-\gamma(y)|x|}, \quad (4)$$
$$f_{Y|X}(y|x) = [\delta(x)/2]e^{-\delta(x)|y|}. \quad (5)$$

Denote the density of X as $f(x)$ and the density of Y as $g(y)$.

Now for any $(x, y) \in \mathscr{R} \times \mathscr{R}$ the joint density of (X, Y) can be written in two equivalent ways in terms of marginal and conditional densities. We thus will have

$$[\gamma(y)/2]e^{-\gamma(y)|x|}g(y) = [\delta(x)/2]e^{-\delta(x)|y|}f(x). \quad (6)$$

Define $\tau(y) = log[g(y)\gamma(y)/2]$ and $\psi(x) = log[f(x)\delta(x)]$, and we may rewrite this in the form

$$\tau(y) - \gamma(y)|x| = \psi_1(x) - \delta(x)|y| \quad (7)$$

Here τ, γ, ψ and δ are unknown functions. This is a simple functional equation of the Stephanos–Levi Civita–Suto form (see for example, Arnold et al. (1999, p. 13)). The solution is of the form

$$\begin{pmatrix} \tau(y) \\ \gamma(y) \end{pmatrix} = A \begin{pmatrix} 1 \\ -|y| \end{pmatrix} \quad (8)$$
$$\begin{pmatrix} \psi(x) \\ \delta(x) \end{pmatrix} = A^{-1} \begin{pmatrix} 1 \\ -|x| \end{pmatrix} \quad (9)$$

where

$$A = \begin{pmatrix} a_{00} & a_{01} \\ a_{10} & a_{11} \end{pmatrix}. \quad (10)$$

Upon substituting this solution into the expression for the density on $\mathscr{R} \times \mathscr{R}$ we obtain the following:

Theorem 1. *The family of all bivariate densities which possess Laplace conditionals (BLCs) is of the form*

$$\begin{aligned} f_{X,Y}(x, y) &= \exp[(1, -|x|)A(1, -|y|)'] \\ &= \exp[a_{00} - a_{01}|y| - a_{10}|x| + a_{11}|x||y|], \end{aligned} \quad (11)$$

where $-a_{11} < a_{01}.a_{10}, a_{01} > 0, a_{10} > 0$, *and* a_{00} *is chosen such that*

$$\int_{-\infty}^{\infty}\int_{-\infty}^{\infty} \exp[(1, -|x|)A(1, -|y|)']dx\, dy = 1.$$

A perhaps more useful version of this density which is amenable to statistical inference is as follows:

$$f_{X,Y}(x, y) = \kappa(\alpha, \beta, \gamma) \exp[-|x|/\alpha - |y|/\beta - (\gamma/\alpha.\beta)|x||y|]. \quad (12)$$

The parameters $\alpha, \beta > 0$, can be viewed as scale parameters, while γ is a dependency parameter, since X and Y are independent iff $\gamma = 0$.

Remark 1. *We note that a bivariate Laplace distribution is available from the characteristic function for the multivariate case as given by Anderson (1992).*

https://doi.org/10.3390/jrfm19050355

4. Introducing Location Parameters

There is no problem associated with a simple shift in location in the Laplace conditional density (11) to arrive at the density

$$\begin{aligned} f_{X,Y}(x,y) &= \exp\left[(1,-|x-\mu|)A(1,-|y-\nu|)'\right] \\ &= \exp\left[a_{00}-a_{01}|y-\nu|-a_{10}|x-\mu|+a_{11}|x-\mu||y-\nu|\right], \end{aligned} \tag{13}$$

where $a_{11} \leq 0, a_{01} > 0, a_{10} > 0$, and a_{00} is chosen such that

$$\int_{-\infty}^{\infty}\int_{-\infty}^{\infty} \exp\left[(1,-|x-\mu|)A(1,-|y-\nu|)'\right]dx\,dy = 1.$$

A more interesting problem will involve "conditional location shifts". To resolve this we will need to identify all bivariate densities on $\mathscr{R} \times \mathscr{R}$ such that the conditional densities will be of the form

$$f_{X|Y}(x|y) = [\gamma(y)/2]e^{-\gamma(y)|x-\mu(y)|}, \tag{14}$$

$$f_{Y|X}(y|x) = [\delta(x)/2]e^{-\delta(x)|y-\nu(x)|}. \tag{15}$$

where $\gamma(y)$ and $\delta(x)$ are positive real-valued functions and $\mu(y)$ and $\nu(x)$ are real-valued functions.

It appears that our old standby, the Stephanos–Levi Civita–Suto functional equation, will not help us here. This appears to be an intriguing open problem. Intuitively, unless the functions $\mu(y)$ and $\nu(x)$ are related (perhaps one is the inverse of the other), it is not obvious that these conditional densities will be compatible.

Henceforth, we will consider the bivariate Laplace conditional (BLC) distributions as members of the family of all possible bivariate distributions whose conditional distributions are Laplace. Thus, it is characterized by the following probability density function:

$$f(x,y) = K(\underline{m})\exp\{-(m_{01}|x|+m_{10}|y|+m_{11}|x||y|)\}, \quad -\infty < x,y < \infty \tag{16}$$

where $\underline{m} = (m_{01}, m_{10}, m_{11})$ and $K(\underline{m})$ is the normalizing constant.

Note that here we have slightly changed the notations for the parameters from those of (11) in the previous section. For $f(x,y)$ to exist, the necessary and sufficient condition is $m_{01} > 0, m_{10} > 0, -m_{11} < m_{01}.m_{10}$. Observe that when the first two conditions are satisfied, the third condition is trivially satisfied (as a sufficient condition) if $m_{11} \geq 0$.

5. Comparison of the Marginal Distributions with the Standard Laplace Distribution

The marginal distributions can be obtained from the bivariate distribution as given above in (16). The p.d.f of the marginal distribution of X is obtained as follows:

$$g(x) = C(\underline{m})\frac{\exp\{-m_{01}|x|\}}{m_{10}+m_{11}|x|}, \quad -\infty < x < \infty \tag{17}$$

where $C(\underline{m})$ is the normalizing constant of $g(x)$.

Taking $m_{01} = m_{11} = \eta$ (say) in (17) and using the transformation $t = \eta x$, the p.d.f. of t is obtained as

$$h(t) = D(m_{10})\frac{\exp\{-|t|\}}{m_{10}+|t|}, \quad -\infty < t < \infty,$$

where $D(m_{10})$ is the normalizing constant of $h(t)$. Thus, the scale parameter of the marginal distribution of x is $\frac{1}{\eta}$. Now letting $\eta = 1$ and taking different values of $m_{10} < 1$ (say, 0.2, 0.4, 0.6 and 0.8), we plot the graphs of $h(t)$ and superimpose them onto that of the standard Laplace density as shown in Figure 3. It is clear that the latter has heavier tails than the former.

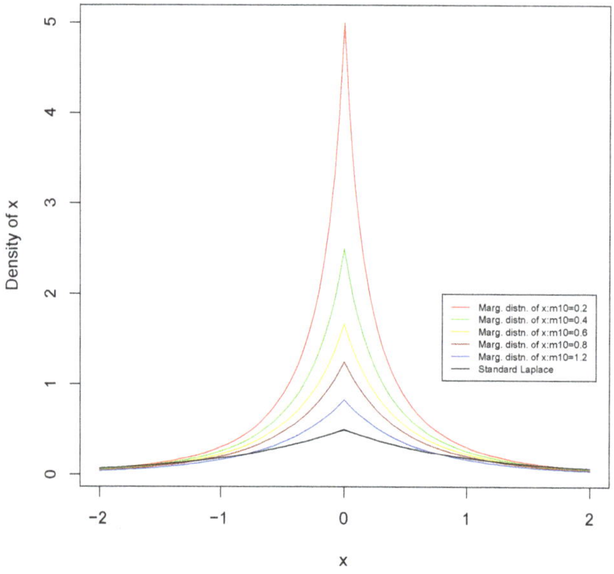

Figure 3. Overlay of standard Laplace over BLC marginal distributions.

The different upper (0.05, 0.1, 0.01, 0.001 and 0.00001) percentile points of the standard Laplace distribution are obtained using the VGAM 1.1-14 package in R for Laplace distribution. The computation for a BLC marginal is more involved. Taking the different values of $m_{10} < 1$, numerical integration of the p.d.f $h(t)$ is conducted using the cubature package in R. We set the lower limit to 0 and the upper limit to the corresponding percentile point of the standard Laplace distribution initially. This upper limit is then increased or decreased iteratively by such an amount as to obtain the required coverage probability. The percentile points of the marginals of the bivariate Laplace conditional distributions with different values of $m_{10} < 1$ and those of the standard Laplace distribution are presented in Table 1. Again, it is clear that the latter has heavier tails than the former.

Table 1. Comparison of percentile points of the marginal distribution and the standard Laplace distribution.

Upper Percentile	Standard Laplace	Marginal Distribution $l(t)$				
		$m_{10} = 0.2$	$m_{10} = 0.4$	$m_{10} = 0.6$	$m_{10} = 0.8$	$m_{10} = 1.2$
0.1	1.609438	0.1054379	0.2234379	0.3604379	0.5224379	0.9894379
0.05	2.302585	0.1215851	0.2640851	0.4337851	0.6465851	1.372585
0.01	3.912023	0.137023	0.300023	0.502023	0.769023	1.949023
0.001	6.214608	0.1403081	0.3084081	0.5146088	0.794608	2.178208
0.00001	10.81978	0.1406783	0.3087783	0.5198783	0.8027783	2.207878

 https://doi.org/10.3390/jrfm19050355

6. Further Properties of the BLC and Its Marginal Distributions

We now consider some useful and elegant properties of the BLC distribution.

- Observe that $E(XY) = E(X) = E(Y) = 0$, by virtue of symmetry. Thus the BLC distribution models the distribution of two uncorrelated, i.e., linearly independent, but possibly otherwise dependent random variables. Such a situation arises as with high-frequency data, where simple linear dependency within a small time frame may not be apparent, but dependency may exist in a more subtle manner.
- The BLC distribution does also include the case of independence, i.e., when $m_{11} = 0$.
- The BLC distribution is a member of the three-parameter regular exponential family (REF). This property is specially useful in developing optimal inference procedures for its parameters, as will be seen below.
- Explicit expressions for $K(\underline{m})$ and $\mathrm{Var}(X)$ can be obtained in terms of the classical exponential integral function but are inconsequential for this paper.
- The BLC distribution has Laplace marginals under independence, but not otherwise.

We now present some interesting and useful properties of the marginals of the BLC distribution.

It is well known that the family of α-stable distributions does not admit any distribution with an analytical, closed-form p.d.f. for $1 < \alpha < 2$, the two extreme values corresponding to the Cauchy and Gaussian distributions respectively. Similarly, the family of Linnik distributions also does not admit any distribution with an analytical, closed form p.d.f. for $1 < \alpha < 2$, the upper extreme value corresponding to the Laplace distribution. (Note that α, the index parameter, is not the same for the two families and its value thus does not quantitatively convey the same properties in the two families.)

- The previous section shows that the following tail ordering, in terms of their rate of decay, holds:

  $$\text{Gauss (normal)} \prec \text{BCL marginal} \prec \text{Laplace} \prec \text{Cauchy},$$

  where "$\prec$" represents "lighter tails than".
- In the family of α-stable distributions with $0 \leq \alpha \leq 2$, the sub-interval $1 \leq \alpha \leq 2$, has achieved widespread popularity and received special attention, especially for modeling heavy-tail distributions for financial data. Note that the two extremes of this support, $\alpha = 1$ and 2, correspond to the Gaussian and Cauchy distributions, respectively. However, there is no other distribution known to possess an analytical closed-form representation for it pdf in this interval, and this has led to difficulties in obtaining related optimal inference procedures. Thus, the search for such a distribution has been a challenging task. From the previous item, observe that a marginal of the BLC distribution in general (excluding the Laplace distribution in the case of independence) is defined in terms of its tail behavior between the Gaussian and Cauchy distributions. But, in general, it is neither a member of the α-stable family nor of the Linnik family of distributions. The appealing property of this distribution is that it can be represented in an elegant and analytical closed form in terms of its p.d.f., which is not available for any distribution in either of these two families within the tail ordering mentioned above.
- Marginals of the BLC distribution can capture very high kurtosis. This claim is supported by Figure 3.

https://doi.org/10.3390/jrfm19050355

7. Distance Correlation

The theoretical distance correlation (Szekely et al., 2007) is defined as the distance between the two random vectors $X\epsilon\Re^p$ and $Y\epsilon\Re^q$ with finite first-order moments, where p and q are positive integers. It is given by

$$R^2(X,Y) = \begin{cases} \frac{\nu^2(X,Y)}{\sqrt{\nu^2(X)}\sqrt{\nu^2(Y)}}, & \nu^2(X)\nu^2(Y) > 0 \\ 0, & \nu^2(X)\nu^2(Y) = 0 \end{cases}$$

where $\nu(X,Y)$ is the distance covariance given by

$$\nu^2(X,Y) = ||f_{X,Y}(t,s) - f_X(t)f_Y(s)||^2,$$

$\nu^2(X)$ is the square of the distance variance given by

$$\nu^2(X) = \nu^2(X,X) = ||f_{X,X}(t,s) - f_X(t)f_X(s)||^2,$$

$f_{X,Y}(t,s)$ is the joint characteristic function of X and Y, and $f_X(t)$ and $f_Y(s)$ are the marginal characteristic functions of X and Y respectively.

The empirical distance correlation $R_n(X,Y)$ based on a sample of n bivariate observations $(X_i,Y_i), i = 1,...,n$, is given by

$$R_n^2(X,Y) = \frac{V_n^2(X,Y)}{\sqrt{V_n^2(X)}\sqrt{V_n^2(Y)}},$$

where $V_n(X,Y)$ is the empirical distance covariance given by

$$V_n^2(X,Y) = \frac{1}{n^2}\sum_{k=1}^{n}\sum_{l=1}^{n} A_{kl}B_{kl},$$

$$A_{kl} = a_{kl} - \bar{a_{k.}} - \bar{a_{.l}} + \bar{a_{..}},$$

$$B_{kl} = b_{kl} - \bar{b_{k.}} - \bar{b_{.l}} + \bar{b_{..}},$$

$$a_{kl} = ||X_k - X_l||_p, b_{kl} = ||Y_k - Y_l||_q, k,l = 1,\ldots,n,$$

and the subscript "." denotes that the mean is computed for the index that it replaces. Also,

$$V_n^2(X) = \frac{1}{n^2}\sum_{k=1}^{n}\sum_{l=1}^{n} A_{kl}^2$$

8. Statistical Inference for the Parameters of the BLC Distribution

We consider now the method of obtaining the maximum likelihood estimator (MLE) of $\underline{m}$. The likelihood function of $\underline{m}$ based on a random sample of size n is given by

$$L(\underline{m}) = \prod_{i=1}^{n} K(\underline{m}) \exp\{-(m_{01}\sum_{i=1}^{n}|x_i| + m_{10}\sum_{i=1}^{n}|y_i| + m_{11}\sum_{i=1}^{n}|x_i||y_i|)\}$$

The likelihood equations can be written down easily save the part involving $K(\underline{m})$, which is represented in terms of a bivariate integral. An iterative method is thus needed to solve these equations, and one can use the 'optim' function in R.

For the iterative method, the initial values of the parameters m_{01} and m_{10} can be taken as the reciprocals of the standard deviations of $|X|$ and $|Y|$ respectively. For m_{11}, the initial value can be taken as the absolute value of the correlation between $|X|$ and $|Y|$ divided by the product of their two standard deviations.

 https://doi.org/10.3390/jrfm19050355

The efficiency of the MLEs can be measured through the computation of the standard errors of the estimators. The standard errors are obtained from the diagonal elements of the inverse of the Fisher information matrix based on n observations.

The Fisher information matrix, I, is given by

$$I(\underline{m}) = E\left[\left(\frac{\partial \ln f}{\partial \underline{m}}\right)\left(\frac{\partial \ln f}{\partial \underline{m}}\right)'\right] = E\begin{pmatrix} a^2 & ab & ac \\ ab & b^2 & bc \\ ac & bc & c^2 \end{pmatrix},$$

where

$$a = \frac{\partial \ln f}{\partial m_{01}} = K(\underline{m}) \int_{-\infty}^{\infty}\int_{-\infty}^{\infty} |x| \exp\{-m_{01}|x| - m_{10}|y| - m_{11}|x||y|\}\, dx\, dy - |x|$$
$$= E[|X|] - |X|,$$

$$b = \frac{\partial \ln f}{\partial m_{10}} = K(\underline{m}) \int_{-\infty}^{\infty}\int_{-\infty}^{\infty} |y| \exp\{-m_{01}|x| - m_{10}|y| - m_{11}|x||y|\}\, dx\, dy - |y|$$
$$= E[|Y|] - |Y|,$$

$$c = \frac{\partial \ln f}{\partial m_{10}} = K(\underline{m}) \int_{-\infty}^{\infty}\int_{-\infty}^{\infty} |x||y| \exp\{-m_{01}|x| - m_{10}|y| - m_{11}|x||y|\}\, dx\, dy - |x||y|$$
$$= E[|X||Y|] - |X||Y|.$$

Therefore, we get

$$E[a^2] = E\left[E^2|X|\right] + E\left[X^2\right] - 2E\left[|X|E|X|\right] = Var(|X|),$$
$$E[ab] = E\left[E|X|E|Y|\right] - E\left[|Y|E|X|\right] - E\left[|X|E|Y|\right] + E\left[|X||Y|\right] = Cov(|X|, |Y|),$$
$$E[ac] = E\left[E|X|E|X||Y|\right] - E\left[|X||Y|E|X|\right] - E\left[|X|E|X||Y|\right] + E\left[X^2|Y|\right] = Cov(|X|, |X||Y|),$$
$$E[b^2] = E\left[E^2|Y|\right] + E\left[Y^2\right] - 2E\left[|Y|E|Y|\right] = Var(|Y|),$$
$$E[bc] = E\left[E|Y|E|X||Y|\right] - E\left[|X||Y|E|Y|\right] - E\left[|Y|E|X||Y|\right] + E\left[Y^2|X|\right] = Cov(|Y|, |X||Y|),$$
$$E[c^2] = E\left[E^2|X||Y|\right] + E\left[X^2Y^2\right] - 2E\left[|X||Y|E|X||Y|\right] = Var(|X||Y|).$$

Remark 2. *The above results, though derived directly, also follow by appealing to the properties of the score functions of a multi-parameter REF.*

Since the BLC distribution is a member of the REF, the Cramer regularity conditions required to establish Theorem 2 are satisfied.

Theorem 2. *Let $\hat{\underline{m}}$ be the maximum likelihood estimator of $\underline{m}$. Then,*

$$\sqrt{n}(\hat{\underline{m}} - \underline{m}) \xrightarrow{L} \mathcal{N}_3(0, I^{-1}) \text{ as } n \to \infty.$$

The above result provides the consistency and asymptotic normality (CAN) properties of the MLE $\hat{\underline{m}}$ of $\underline{m}$. It can also be used to yield asymptotic confidence intervals and consistent tests for $\underline{m}$.

9. Real-Life Example

We now present a real-life data set to illustrate the application of our BLC model. Recall that this model does not apply to situations where the two variables have a non-zero product moment correlation.

 https://doi.org/10.3390/jrfm19050355

The daily price data on diamond and platinum were collected from the internet for the n paired observations for the months from May to July, 2025. Let the prices be denoted by x_{1t} and x_{2t} respectively.

We make the log-ratio transformation on x_{1t} and x_{2t} as follows.

$$y_{1t} = 100(\ln(x_{1t}) - \ln(x_{1,t-1})) \text{ and } y_{2t} = 100(\ln(x_{2t}) - \ln(x_{2,t-1})).$$

The obtained sample correlation between y_{1t} and y_{2t} is -0.01066954.

The obtained sample distance correlation between y_{1t} and y_{2t} is 0.1848587.

Observe that the linear correlation is very small and negligible. However, the distance correlation has a moderate value. This indicates that while linear dependency does not exist, non-linear dependency might. We thus advocate the use of our BCL model for this data set.

We follow the details given in Section 9 above for obtaining the MLE of $\underline{m}$. The initial estimates of the parameters m_{01}, m_{10} and m_{11} are 8.906111, 7.550306 and 49.7322 respectively. The following MLEs of the parameters are then obtained: $\hat{m_{01}} = 28.13994, \hat{m_{10}} = 7.83915$ and $\hat{m_{11}} = 30.19539$.

The empirical Fisher information matrix based on the n observations is obtained:

$$nI(\underline{m}) = \begin{pmatrix} 2.642579e-03 & -8.934507e-05 & 9.175539e-06 \\ -8.934507e-05 & 2.344128e-04 & 2.496011e-05 \\ 9.175539e-06 & 2.496011e-05 & 1.282111e-03 \end{pmatrix}$$

The corresponding inverse of the Fisher information matrix is obtained:

$$(nI(\underline{m}))^{-1} = \begin{pmatrix} 383.39849 & 146.72641 & -5.60029 \\ 146.72641 & 4330.99250 & -85.36571 \\ -5.60029 & -85.36571 & 781.66553 \end{pmatrix}$$

The standard errors of the estimators are obtained: $s.e.(m_{01}) = 19.58056$, $s.e.(m_{10}) = 65.81028$ and $s.e.(m_{11}) = 27.95828$. Given the small sample size, the estimators obtained can be considered to be reasonably efficient.

We have already noted that linear correlation is negligible, implying that there is no linear dependency between Y_1 and Y_2. The BLC model is a reasonable candidate here since it can capture possible non-linear dependency. Theorem 2 provides the necessary test (with large samples) by testing for $H_0 : m_{11} = 0$ against $H_1 : m_{11} \neq 0$. The critical region is given by:

$$\omega : |\hat{\underline{m}}| > [s.e.(m_{11})]\tau_{\alpha/2},$$

where τ_α is the upper α-percentile point of the standard normal distribution. Taking $\alpha = 0.30$, $\tau_{0.15}$ is 1.02. Hence, for this example (for a somewhat moderate level of significance), independence between Y_1 and Y_2 is rejected in favor non-linear dependency.

To demonstrate its usefulness in real-life applications, the performance of the proposed BLC distribution is compared with the bivariate normal distribution for the above data set. We do this through the use of the formal goodness-of-fit metrics viz. the Akaike information criterion (AIC) and Bayesian information criterion (BIC). The Akaike information criterion (AIC) is given by

$$AIC = -2\ln L_{max} + 2 \times k$$

The Bayesian information criterion (BIC) is given by

$$BIC = -2\ln L_{max} + k \times \ln(n)$$

 https://doi.org/10.3390/jrfm19050355

where n is the number of observations and k is the number of estimated parameters. In the case of the BLC distribution, $k = 3$, while for the bivariate normal distribution, $k = 5$.

The smaller the AIC or BIC value of a distribution, the better the fit of the distribution to the given data.

We now compare the performance of our BLC distribution and the bivariate normal distribution models for this data set. The AIC and BIC values for the data are displayed in Table 2.

Table 2. AIC and BIC values for bivariate normal and BLC distributions.

Distribution	BIC	AIC
Bivariate normal	−891.4517	−905.3892
Bivariate Laplace conditionals	−85,109.22	−85,119.69

It is clear from the above table that the bivariate Laplace conditional distribution gives a better fit to the given data than the bivariate normal distribution.

10. Remarks and Conclusions

This paper was prompted by several facts: 1. There is no distribution with a closed-form p.d.f. in the α-stable family in the important region $1 < \alpha < 2$, i.e., there are no tails in between the normal and Cauchy distributions. 2. Bivariate distributions with marginals as stated in item 1 are not readily available. 3. High-frequency data on a bivariate random variable may exhibit zero linear correlation, but strong dependency can exist. 4. In practice, it is often easier and more meaningful to specify the conditionals of a bivariate distribution. The bivariate Laplace conditional distribution proposed here provides a solution to items 1–3 based on its construction, which is enhanced by item 4. Further, asymptotic optimal inference procedures for the parameters of this model have been readily derived. We believe that this is the first work using conditional specifications in bivariate financial data analysis. It is hoped that the elegant representation of the bivariate p.d.f. for the BLC family of distributions, coupled with its attractive and useful properties for real-life applications, will motivate further research in this new direction.

Author Contributions: Conceptualization, A.S.; methodology, A.S.; writing—original draft preparation, A.S., B.C.A. and M.R.; writing—review and editing, A.S., B.C.A. and M.R.; numerical computations—M.R. All authors have read and agreed to the published version of the manuscript.

Funding: This research received no external funding.

Institutional Review Board Statement: Not applicable.

Informed Consent Statement: Not applicable.

Data Availability Statement: Data used in the Example was collected from the Internet and are available from the first author on request.

Acknowledgments: The authors would like to thank the two Referees and the Associate Editor for their careful reading of the manuscript and for their comments, which have improved the presentation of the current version.

Conflicts of Interest: The authors declare no conflicts of interest.

References

Anderson, D. N. (1992). A multivariate Linnik distribution. *Statistics and Probability Letters, 14*, 333–336. [CrossRef]

Arnold, B. C., Castillo, E., & Sarabia, J.M. (1999). *Conditional specification of statistical models*. Springer.

https://doi.org/10.3390/jrfm19050355

Arnold, B. C., & SenGupta, A. (2025). Wrapping generalized Laplace and generalized discrete Laplace distributions. *Axioms*, *14*(7), 529. [CrossRef]
Linnik, J. V. (1963). Linear forms and statistical criteria I, II. In *Selected transactions in mathematical statistics and probability* (Vol. 3, pp. 1–90). American Mathematical Society.
Rachev, S. T., & SenGupta, A. (1993). Laplace—Weibull mixtures for modelling price changes. *Management Science*, *39*, 1029–1038. [CrossRef]
SenGupta, A., & Roy, M. (2023). A characteristic function based circular distribution family and its goodness of fit: The flexible wrapped Linnik family. *Journal of Applied Statistics*, *51*(12), 2364–2381. [CrossRef] [PubMed]
Szekely, G. J., Rizzo, M. L., & Bakirov, N. K. (2007). Measuring and testing dependence by correlation of distances. *Annals of Statistics*, *35*(6), 2769–2794. [CrossRef]

 https://doi.org/10.3390/jrfm19050355

Journal of
Risk and Financial Management

MDPI

Review

Recent Progress on Financial Risk Detection in the Context of Transaction Fraud Based on Machine Learning Algorithms

Teli Chen [1,*], Ruili Sun [2], Tiefeng Ma [3] and Sergey Sergeev [1]

[1] Faculty of Science and Technology, University of Canberra, Canberra 2617, Australia
[2] College of Mathematics and Information Science, Zhengzhou University of Light Industry, Zhengzhou 450001, China
[3] School of Statistics, Southwestern University of Finance and Economics, Chengdu 611130, China
* Correspondence: teli.chen@canberra.edu.au

Abstract

Transaction Fraud, a type of financial operational risk, remains a major threat to financial sectors and continuously imposes devastating financial impacts. This study comprehensively reviews 41 cutting-edge publications on financial transaction fraud detection using Machine Learning from January 2018 to October 2025. We establish a taxonomy to categorize the selected work into four themes: Traditional Machine Learning, Deep Learning, Ensemble Method, and Hybrid Method. Each theme is evaluated in-depth, from strengths to weaknesses. Ensemble exhibits better performance over other methods with a recall of 92.7%, a precision of 96% and an F1-score of 92.66% on average, while Traditional ML ranks last in terms of average F1-score. Preprocessing strategies, like data balancing, can enhance performance, while feature engineering requires careful evaluation before implementation. Significantly, we assess financial implications, suggesting it is essential to integrate financial metric design, feature explanation, time series patterns, and data privacy considerations into financial fraud detection—a focus that aligns with risk management frameworks and regulations. By revealing current research gaps and suggesting future directions, our study provides practical guidance for researchers and practitioners to advance financial fraud detection strategies within a highly intricate financial ecosystem.

Keywords: card transaction fraud/scam detection; machine learning; deep learning; financial risk; financial fraud

1. Introduction

Background: Technology advancements have facilitated people's lives over the past decades, leading to the prevalence of cashless, electronic, and online payments in the financial sector. However, these advancements in financial sectors have been accompanied by a rise in various forms of fraud and scams, such as identity theft, account takeover, card skimming, phishing, money laundering, and cyberattacks (Vashistha & Tiwari, 2024). Most fraudulent activities result in financial losses, causing substantial harm to financial institutions, individuals, and organizations. These losses also escalate operational risk, a key category defined by the Basel Framework, a comprehensive set of measures to strengthen the regulation, supervision, and risk management of the global banking sector (Basel Committee on Banking Supervision, 2024). Consumers in the United States lost more than USD 10 billion to fraud, marking a 14% increase from 2022, according to statistics of the Federal Trade Commission of the USA (Federal Trade Commission, 2024). In 2023,

AUD 2.7 billion was stolen by scammers from Australian consumers (The Treasury, 2024). Although these financially external frauds emerged over a decade, they consistently pose a huge threat to the world's economy and society's well-being as people are more dependent on the digital world during the COVID and post-COVID era. Inadequate regulatory oversight concerning this risk could even result in severe breakdown for banks and financial institutions. Capital requirements, such as those based on Risk-Weighted Assets (RWA) within the Basel Framework, manage risk by ensuring banks maintain sufficient capital buffers. Complementing this, effective fraud detection strategies are imperative to tackle operational risk directly, minimizing financial losses and protecting customers from harm.

Motivation and Purpose: Machine Learning (ML), along with its subset Deep Learning (DL), is widely leveraged by researchers and practitioners to build fraud detection systems because of its effectiveness in prediction and forecasting by identifying intricate patterns and learning historical behaviors from large volumes of data (Dal Pozzolo et al., 2014). However, interpretability of "Black Box Model", data imbalance, data inaccessibility, and misclassification are common challenges in financial fraud detection by ML (Abdul Salam et al., 2024; Ahmed et al., 2025; Baisholan et al., 2025b; Tayebi & El Kafhali, 2025). This study aims to survey recent ML methods applied to financial transaction fraud detection—which work by forecasting the probability of fraud to mitigate financial risk—and to evaluate their progress and weaknesses. Although several similar reviews (Baisholan et al., 2025a; Chen et al., 2025; Hafez et al., 2025; Moradi et al., 2025) were released recently, making substantial progress in this field, they still suffer from certain limitations. These include a lack of focus on transaction fraud detection specifically, insufficient discussion of preprocessing strategies, and a failure to address financial implications or link them systematically to financial risk, etc. Our work will distinguish itself from existing reviews by addressing these research gaps (Table 1).

Table 1. Comparison with recent reviews in 2025.

Citation	Coverage											
	Card Transaction Fraud Focus	Various Datasets Description	Comprehensive Preprocessing Analysis			Pros and Cons	Financial implications					Current Issue and Future Scope
			Data Balancing	Feature Engineering	Hyperparameter Tunning		Financial Metrics	Financial Risk and Direct Impact	IML	Time Series	Data Privacy with Regulation Compliance	
This work	✓	✓	✓	✓	✓	✓	✓	✓	✓	✓	✓	✓
(Moradi et al., 2025)	✓									✓		✓
(Hafez et al., 2025)	✓	✓	✓		✓	✓			✓			✓
(Chen et al., 2025)			✓	✓			✓		✓		✓	✓
(Baisholan et al., 2025a)	✓	✓							✓			✓

Specifically, we are going to provide a critical analysis of ML techniques for transaction fraud detection, structured thematically to address advances, challenges, and opportunities. This analysis encompasses their classification methods, preprocessing strategies, highlights, results, and limitations. Additionally, we will conduct a deeper evaluation of preprocessing strategies. Moreover, we intend to emphasize the financial implications and significance of these methods from the perspective of the financial sector. This will involve aspects such as financial metric design, feature explainability, time-series considerations, and financial data privacy. By linking our analysis to risk management and regulatory compliance, we aim to bridge a critical research gap: few studies have systematically addressed the financial

https://doi.org/10.3390/jrfm19010014

impact when applying ML to detect transaction fraud, despite it being a problem rooted in the financial sector itself. The overall goal is to provide a comprehensive review of recent ML methods in handling transaction fraud detection and to offer insights into future directions for both researchers and practitioners in this field.

Scope: This research primarily focuses on peer-reviewed journal articles and conference papers from the past seven years (January 2018–October 2025) that employ ML algorithms to detect card transaction fraud, a specific form of external fraud in operational risk under the Basel Framework. Since financial transaction data is usually structured, the datasets used among selected studies are tabular. They include features such as transaction time, amount, receiving account, type of transaction, age group, monthly salary, etc. The target is a binary feature (typically labeled 0 or 1) that indicates whether a transaction is fraudulent, defining the classification task.

This study contributes to the literature in the following key ways:

- We assess recent ML progress in transaction fraud detection for financial risk, using a structured taxonomy that covers advances and limitations to provide a comprehensive domain overview.
- Simultaneously, we specifically evaluate preprocessing methods, including data balancing, feature engineering, and hyperparameter optimization techniques, which are critical for enhancing ML performance in classification tasks, emphasizing a potential future focus.
- Comparisons across studies by aggregation are conducted to critically analyze our reviews, presenting key findings.
- Additionally, we address the financial implications and significance of these methods, linking them to risk management.
- Finally, the review concludes with a comprehensive discussion of the limitations and future scope of current studies, highlighting directions for further work by researchers and practitioners in this domain.

The rest of the study is arranged in the following way: Section 2 briefly explains the review methodology employed to conduct this research. In Section 3, we review and analyze these approaches in-depth based on four subthemes: Traditional ML, DL, Ensemble method, and Hybrid method. Key topics such as dataset descriptions, preprocessing strategies, and cross-validation are considered. Discussions on performance comparisons across our reviews are carried out. Section 4 discusses the financial implications, closely connected to risk management. Section 5 focuses on gaps and limitations in this domain and provides future directions. In Section 6, we conclude this study.

2. Review Methodology

In this study, we perform an exhaustive and rigorous evaluation of the most recent publications on financial risk detection in the context of card transaction fraud using state-of-the-art ML. To ensure the quality of our evaluations, we referred to some of the Preferred Reporting Items for Systematic Reviews and Meta-Analyses (PRISMA) (Page et al., 2021) and Kitchenham Systematic Review Process guidelines (Kitchenham & Charters, 2007). Detailed steps are described in the following.

Initially, a comprehensive search was conducted using a combination of keywords: ("credit card fraud detection" OR "transaction fraud detection" OR "financial fraud detection") and ("machine learning" OR "deep learning"). These search queries were applied to databases including Google Scholar, Springer Nature Link, ScienceDirect, Scopus, and IEEE Xplore to search publications published from January 2018 to October 2025. Then publications between the first five and ten pages of the search results in the above databases were screened. In addition, we conducted another search in terms of the above keywords

https://doi.org/10.3390/jrfm19010014

on Google Scholar from January 2024 to October 2025 and browsed publications of the first ten pages to ensure our reviews keep up with the times. Only studies written in English and published in peer-reviewed journals or conferences were considered.

After screening 200 publications with their abstracts, experimental results, and summaries, we selected 41 publications for further in-depth reviews. Our selection criteria include relevance (whether the method is a Machine Learning based algorithm and applied to financial transaction/credit card fraud datasets), citation times according to Google Scholar, journal quality, etc. Specifically, studies that did not employ ML/DL techniques or that were not focused on transaction fraud detection with tabular data were excluded. In addition to satisfying the relevance, publications must also meet the following: (citation times > 50) OR (journal indexed in SCI with IF > 1.5) OR (journal indexed in ESCI with IF > 1.5). First, a minimum of 50 citations, a benchmark for influential work, ensured the credibility and impact of selected work. Second, to mitigate the recency bias in citation counts, we included papers from journals with an Impact Factor (IF) > 1.5, a threshold that captures quality emerging research while maintaining a baseline of editorial rigor. We also conducted snowballing through Research Rabbit to scan the reference lists of selected publications to find other related studies, but no additional publications were selected according to our selection criteria and their publishing years. To ensure the quality of included papers, the following components were assessed and satisfied by all selected works:

- Data & Reproducibility: Datasets are clearly described, and a source link is provided if publicly accessible.
- Experimental Rigor: The methodology and experimental steps are explicitly stated.
- Model Credibility: The proposed model is compared with baselines or prior work.
- Analysis: The results are discussed and analyzed.

With organized reviewing, we gathered information from the 41 selected publications, including their years, journals published, citation times (Google Scholar), methods used/developed, data balancing techniques, feature engineering techniques, datasets used, highlights, results, limitations/challenges, and financial significance, extracting and categorizing all the information into an Excel form. ML used to be categorized into two groups: Supervised Learning and Unsupervised Learning. But in financial fraud detection, no matter what preprocessing strategies (Supervised, Unsupervised, Statistical, or others) are employed, the last step is usually classification, which is a type of Supervised Learning. Thus, it is meaningless to classify in the traditional way since all these fraud detection techniques can be categorized as Supervised Learning (Chhabra et al., 2023). Alternatively, we established a taxonomy in terms of the specific ML strategies employed and divided them into four subgroups: Traditional ML, DL, Ensemble, and Hybrid. The fundamental distinction among them lies in their core mechanisms: from human-driven feature engineering (Traditional ML) to automatic feature learning (DL), to collective prediction (Ensemble), and finally to integrative system design (Hybrid). Each subgroup was reviewed in depth, and its strengths and limitations were thoroughly described to enlighten future studies.

A full review process diagram can be seen in Figure 1. The workflow of identification, screening, and inclusion ties closely to the framework of PRISMA and Kitchenham to ensure the trustworthiness of our research. Furthermore, an analysis part following the inclusion is presented in the workflow, providing readers with a clear understanding of the overall evaluation process. Through the proposed methodology, a comprehensive study is performed to present various ML techniques employed in financial risk prevention, with a particular focus on transaction fraud detection.

 https://doi.org/10.3390/jrfm19010014

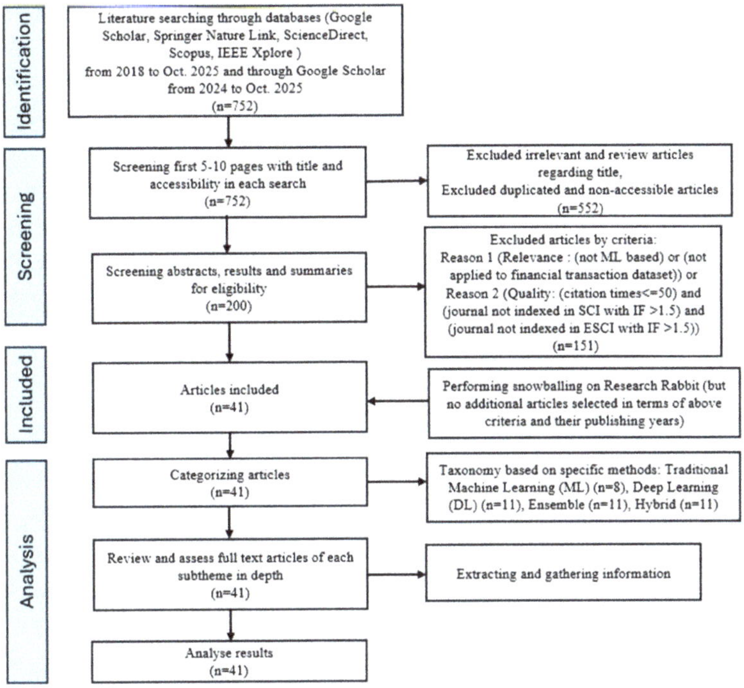

Figure 1. Review workflow.

3. Analysis of Approaches

ML has been widely adopted in the financial domain to solve practical problems, like financial fraud and transaction fraud, particularly where this research focuses. Overall, the number of papers has increased over time. In Figure 2, the four methods used are almost evenly distributed, with DL, Ensemble, and Hybrid slightly higher than Traditional ML in our reviewed papers. It suggests that DL, Ensemble, and Hybrid methods attract more attention than Traditional ML in transaction fraud detection.

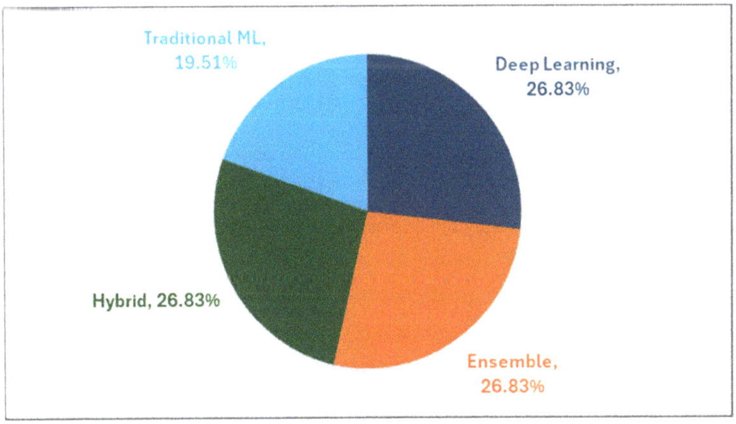

Figure 2. Distribution of methods by category.

https://doi.org/10.3390/jrfm19010014

3.1. Traditional Machine Learning (ML)

Traditional ML refers to algorithms such as Logistic Regression (LR), Naïve Bayes (NB), K-Nearest Neighbors (KNN), Decision Tree (DT), etc., which are generally less complex, more interpretable, and perform well with smaller datasets. LR provides a linear, probabilistic foundation by modeling outcomes with a logistic curve, while NB relies on probability and the assumption of feature independence to perform quick probabilistic classification. In contrast, KNN is an instance-based, non-parametric method that classifies data points based on the majority vote of their k closest neighbors in the feature space. DT uses a hierarchical, rule-based structure to split data recursively, creating an interpretable model for classifications or predictions. In this subsection, we incorporate publications if they include any of the traditional ML methods mentioned above. Thus, the traditional ML subgroup comprises publications that may include both traditional ML and other types of methods.

Three traditional ML algorithms, including LR, NB, and KNN with Random Under Sampling (RUS), were employed by Itoo et al. (2021) to detect card transaction fraud. In this study, LR outperformed NB and KNN with a maximum accuracy of 95%. This result indicates that LR shows optimal performance when processing fewer data samples, reduced by RUS. Another study (Tanouz et al., 2021) compared Random Forest (RF), DT, LR, and NB with RUS resampling. RF, composed of multiple decision trees that output a mean prediction, achieved the best result with a recall of 91.11% due to its inherent ability to reduce overfitting. Although these 2 studies demonstrate excellent performance of Traditional ML models on transaction fraud detection, the reduced training data resulting from RUS may negatively impact the model's stability and generalizability.

Both studies (Ileberi et al., 2022; Mienye & Sun, 2023b) introduced Genetic Algorithm (GA) with Traditional ML models on the same dataset. IG-GAW (Mienye & Sun, 2023b), which uses Extreme Learning Machine (ELM) as its classification method and achieves a sensitivity of 99.7%, outperforms GA-RF (Ileberi et al., 2022), which uses RF with a sensitivity of 72.56%. Due to its simpler learning process and robust generalizability, the ELM—a feedforward neural network that uses randomly fixed hidden weights and analytically solves output weights—demonstrates superior capability over RF in this case.

Afriyie et al. (2023) revealed the weakness of RF in their study, showing that it achieved low performance in terms of F1-score and precision, with only 17% and 9%. This performance would inconvenience customers, subsequently raising operational costs and risks for financial institutions if deploying the model to a real-time system. All reviewed publications associated with Traditional ML are comprehensively summarized in Table 2.

Table 2. Selected work on Transaction Fraud Detection by Traditional ML.

Citation	Specific Method	Resample Tech	Feature Engineering	Dataset	Highlight	Result	Limitation/Challenge
(Itoo et al., 2021)	LR, NB, KNN	RUS		European credit card dataset		LR achieved an accuracy of 95.9%, NB achieved 91% while KNN achieved 75%	Fewer data points are trained, which may result in poor generalizability
(Tanouz et al., 2021)	RF, DT, LR, NB	RUS	Removing highly correlated features	European credit card dataset		RF with 96.77% accuracy, 100% precision, 91.11% recall, 95.35% F1-scores, and 95.55% ROC-AUC score	Model generalizability, robustness

https://doi.org/10.3390/jrfm19010014

Table 2. *Cont.*

Citation	Specific Method	Resample Tech	Feature Engineering	Dataset	Highlight	Result	Limitation/Challenge
(Dang et al., 2021)	RF, KNN, DT, LR, AdaBoost, XGBoost, DNN	SMOTE, Adaptive Synthetic Sampling (ADASYN)		European credit card dataset		High performance when resampling methods are applied to both the train and test datasets. DRL is ineffective when detecting fraud.	Model generalization, data availability, and low performance when the test data is not balanced
(Ileberi et al., 2022)	DT, RF, LR, ANN, NB with GA	SMOTE	GA with fitness function RF and an accuracy measure to reduce feature dimension	European credit card dataset, Synthetic Credit Card Fraud Dataset		GA-RF with an accuracy of 99.98%, GA-DT with an accuracy of 99.92%	Recall and F1-score still need improvements, due to their importance in the context
(Mienye & Sun, 2023b)	IG-GAW (ELM with information gain and GA)		Combination of IG and GA with ELM and a fitness measure of geometric means to select features	European credit card dataset		Sensitivity: 0.997; Specificity: 0.994 (stratified 10-fold cross-validation)	Other state-of-the-art ML models can be combined with the proposed feature selection method to compare performance
(Afriyie et al., 2023)	RF, DT, LR			Sparkov Dataset	Exploratory data analysis is conducted with feature interpretation	RF achieved an AUC value of 98.9% and an accuracy value of 96.0%	Bad performance on F1-score and precision, with only 17% and 9% respectively
(Abdul Salam et al., 2024)	RF, KNN, DT, NB, CNN	RUS, ROS, SMOTE, ADASYN		European credit card dataset	Data privacy concerns are addressed by proposing a federated learning framework	RF with an accuracy of 99.99% under cross-validation	More advanced algorithms are expected under the federal learning framework
(Ileberi & Sun, 2024)	DT, RF, XGBoost, LightGBM, and LR	ADASYN	Recursive Feature Elimination Cross Validation (RFECV) for feature elimination	European credit card dataset		XGBoost and RF with ADASYN and RFECV achieved the best Matthew's Correlation Coefficient (MCC) of 0.9994 and 0.9991, respectively	Model generalization on other datasets

3.2. Deep Learning (DL)

DL is a subset of ML but is more complex and usually adopts multilayer neural network architectures to learn the intricate patterns from vast amounts of data. A detailed review is listed in Table 3 at the end of this subsection.

Table 3. Selected work on Transaction Fraud Detection by DL.

Citation	Specific Method	Resample Tech	Feature Engineering	Dataset	Highlight	Result	Limitation/Challenge
(Kim et al., 2019)	Challenger (Deep Feed-Forward Network) and Champion		Hand-engineered by highly experienced domain experts	Real-world data from a South Korean bank		The Challenger outperforms the Champion, with +3.8% of recall and +5.5% of cost reduction rate	Model interpretability of features' contributions to the results
(Najadat et al., 2020)	BiLSTM-MaxPooling-BiGRU-MaxPooling	ROS, RUS, SMOTE	Categorical features are embedded by spatial dropout and a dropout layer	IEEE-CIS Fraud Detection Dataset		AUC of 91.37% with ROS	Model interpretability. The time series feature (date) is removed before modelling, and it's better to consider the temporal pattern in the future, as LSTM has the potential to capture the pattern and may promote performance

 https://doi.org/10.3390/jrfm19010014

Table 3. *Cont.*

Citation	Specific Method	Resample Tech	Feature Engineering	Dataset	Highlight	Result	Limitation/Challenge
(Nguyen et al., 2020)	LSTM	RUS, NM (Near Miss), SMOTE		European credit card dataset, Small Card Data, Tall Card Data		F1-Score of 84.85% on the European dataset	Model interpretability and poor performance with SCD and TCD datasets
(Zhang et al., 2021)	DBN, CNN, RNN with HOBA		HOBA to extract feature variables	A real-world dataset from a Chinese bank	A novel feature engineering method, HOBA	DBN with HOBA outperforms others with an accuracy of 98.25%, a recall of 51.96% and an accuracy of 96.51%, a recall of 75% under the tolerance of 3% FPR (10-fold cross-validation)	Intensive computing resources, low recall without data resampling
(Alarfaj et al., 2022)	CNN with 20 layers	Removing non-fraudulent transactions		European credit card dataset		Accuracy, F1-score, precision and AUC are 99.9%,85.71%,93%, and 98%, respectively	Model interpretability, Data availability
(Yu et al., 2024)	Transformer	Random sampling (not specifically mentioned)	T-SNE, PCA, SVD	European credit card dataset		The transformer model with a multi-head attention mechanism achieved a recall of 0.998, an F1-score of 0.998 (cross-validation)	Model interpretability
(Cherif et al., 2024)	Encoder–decoder-based GNNs		GNN for graph (node) representation and encoder–decoder for feature representation	Sparkov dataset		Precision of 0.82, recall of 0.92, F1-score of 0.86, AUC-ROC of 0.92	Model interpretability, relatively low performance for the graph method
(Harish et al., 2024)	GNNS with RGCN		GNN for graph (node) representation and RGCN for feature representation	IBM TabFormer Dataset, Sparkov dataset		F1-score of 0.78 and recall rate of 0.66 for the IBM dataset, and F1-score of 0.61 and recall rate of 0.46 for the Sparkov dataset	Model interpretability, poor performance
(Khaled Alarfaj & Shahzadi, 2025)	GNNs, Autoencoders (AE)	Min-Max Scaling	GNN for graph (node) representation	Real-world datasets from two Pakistani banks		Autoencoder achieves accuracy, precision, recall, F1-score of 79.01%, 79.98%, 80.68%, 79.78% while GNN achieves accuracy, precision, recall, F1-score of 78.01%, 80.98%, 79.68%, 80.78%	Model interpretability, relatively low performance for the graph method

 https://doi.org/10.3390/jrfm19010014

Table 3. *Cont.*

Citation	Specific Method	Resample Tech	Feature Engineering	Dataset	Highlight	Result	Limitation/Challenge
(Wu et al., 2025)	CCNN	SMOTE	The features are sequentially placed in a 6 × 6 matrix to fit the deep learning method	European credit card dataset		Accuracy of 0.9998, precision of 0.9996, recall of 1.00, and an F1-score of 0.9998 (10-fold cross-validation)	Model interpretability, data availability
(Dong et al., 2025)	Enhanced AE			The Bank Account Fraud (BAF) dataset, The BankSim Dataset		Accuracy of 0.8194, precision of 0.9969, recall of 0.8200, specificity of 0.7664, and F1-score of 0.8999 on BAF, while precision of 0.9996, recall of 0.9520, F1-score of 0.9752, and specificity of 0.9700 on BankSim	Model interpretability

Convolutional Neural Network (CNN) with 20 layers achieved an accuracy of 99.9%, an F1-score of 85.71%, a precision of 93% and an AUC of 98% (Alarfaj et al., 2022) while Continuous-Coupled Neural Network (CCNN) with Synthetic Minority Over-sampling Technique (SMOTE) achieved an accuracy of 99.98%, a precision of 99.96%, a recall of 100%, and an F1-score of 99.98% (Wu et al., 2025). CNN was designed to automatically extract spatial features from image data via convolutional layers with learnable filters, while CCNN improved the representation of intricate spatiotemporal patterns by continuous neuron activation and dynamic coupling. These strong results demonstrate their efficacy in processing financial transaction data. Yu et al. (2024) adopted the Transformer model, a deep learning architecture originally developed for natural language processing tasks on financial transaction datasets. The transformer model with a multi-head attention mechanism successfully captured the intricate correlations between attributes of financial transaction datasets and obtained a recall of 99.8% and an F1-score of 99.8% under cross-validation. These state-of-the-art DL algorithms, particularly CCNN and Transformer, demonstrated impressive performance due to their inherently robust architectures. However, the substantial computational resources required for training and classifying, along with challenges in interpretability, hinder these methods from becoming the most effective solution for mitigating financial risks associated with transaction fraud in real-world systems.

Graph Neural Networks (GNNs) captured researchers' interests in transaction fraud detection (Cherif et al., 2024; Harish et al., 2024; Khaled Alarfaj & Shahzadi, 2025). In the financial fraud context, unlike other techniques that only consider single transactions, GNNs usually transform tabular datasets into graphs with customer nodes and merchant nodes and link nodes to uncover the intricate relations and behavior patterns between customer (transaction initiator), merchant (transaction receiver), and transactions before classification. GNNs with lambda architecture—which processes large-scale data through a combined batch and real-time structure—achieved an F1-score of 80.78% and a recall of 79.68% (Khaled Alarfaj & Shahzadi, 2025). In contrast, GNNs with Relational Graph Convolutional Network (RGCN), used to learn node representations, achieved a lower F1-score of 61% and a recall of 46% (Harish et al., 2024). Cherif et al. (2024) proposed an encoder–decoder-based GNN model to detect transaction fraud. The encoder–decoder architecture was applied to represent the nodes, and the proposed model yielded better results than the previous two studies, achieving a recall of 92%, an F1-score of 86%, and an AUC of 92%. Overall, GNNs demonstrate lower performance relative to other

https://doi.org/10.3390/jrfm19010014

DL algorithms. The effectiveness of GNNs in transaction fraud detection needs further investigation, as poor performance may lead to increased operational risk.

3.3. Ensemble Method

Ensemble methods are learning algorithms that construct two or more classifiers (also called weak learners) and then classify new data points by averaging, stacking, or taking a (weighted) vote of their predictions (Dietterich, 2000). They balance bias and variance of weak learners and usually yield a more robust result, improving overall performance compared to any single constituent model. Ensemble could be a powerful tool to combat financial risk in the context of transaction fraud.

The voting ensemble, which outputs classification results by aggregating (hard or soft) votes from multiple weak learners, has drawn attention in transaction fraud detection. All the work (Ahmed et al., 2025; Chhabra et al., 2023; Khalid et al., 2024) achieved promising accuracy (exceeding 99.9%) on the same dataset by employing a voting ensemble composed of different base classifiers. Another study (Talukder et al., 2024) proposed a voting-based multistage ensemble ML classifier (EIBMC), leveraging the diversity of the fundamental ML models and combining the finest aspects of multiple multistage ensemble models into a more robust and trustworthy detection technique. EIBMC achieved an accuracy score of 99.94% and an AUC score of 100% under stratified 5-fold cross-validation. However, EIBMC used accuracy—a metric known to be biased in imbalanced datasets—to assign weights to its ensemble classifiers. For future work, metrics like recall could be adopted to improve model robustness.

A cost-sensitive and ensemble deep forest (CE-gcForest) method, inspired by Zhou and Feng (2019), was employed to detect transaction fraud (Zhao et al., 2023). The ensemble-gcForest model enhances diversity and improves performance by selecting the best-performing base-classifiers in each round based on their Type II error rate. This process results in a more robust and efficient ensemble. The model achieved the best performance compared to other baseline ML models, with AUC 98.01% and 98.25% respectively, on real-world datasets.

Mienye and Sun (2023a) implemented a stacking ensemble approach involving deep learning base-classifiers, Long Short-Term Memory (LSTM), Gated Recurrent Unit (GRU), and a meta-classifier, Multilayer Perception (MLP), to address the problem of dynamic patterns in card transactions. In a stacking ensemble, the base classifiers are trained on the original features, and the meta-classifier is trained on the results of the base classifiers to produce the final output. The proposed model obtained promising results with a recall value of 100%, a precision value of 99.7% and an AUC value of 100% under a 10-fold cross-validation technique.

The examples discussed above highlight the outstanding proficiency of Ensemble in detecting transaction fraud. Leveraging the strengths and diversities of multiple base learners, Ensemble successfully enhances models' performance, making them particularly effective in handling complex and unbalanced datasets commonly found in financial transactions. A comprehensive summary regarding the reviewed Ensemble methods can be found in Table 4 below.

https://doi.org/10.3390/jrfm19010014

Table 4. Selected work on Transaction Fraud Detection by Ensemble Method.

Citation	Specific Method	Resample Tech	Feature Engineering	Dataset	Highlight	Result	Limitation/Challenge
(Sailusha et al., 2020)	RF, Adaboost			European credit card dataset		RF and AdaBoost had the same accuracy, but RF performed better according to precision, recall, and F1-score	Low performance without any data resampling or feature engineering
(Ileberi et al., 2021)	DT-AdaBoost, RF-AdaBoost, ET-AdaBoost, XGB-AdaBoost, LR-AdaBoost	SMOTE		European credit card dataset		Both ET-AdaBoost and XGB-AdaBoost achieved an accuracy of 99.98% and an MCC of 0.99	Data availability, model interpretability
(Alfaiz & Fati, 2022)	AllKNN-CatBoost	AllKNN and the other 18 resampling methods		European credit card dataset	Comprehensive comparison study of a combination of 19 different resampling methods and ML algorithms to address the unbalanced issue	AllKNN-CatBoost achieved AUC value of 97.94%, Recall value of 95.91%, and F1-score value of 87.40%	Model generalizability, interpretability
(Hajek et al., 2023)	XGBoost, XGBOD	RUS	Outlier detection algorithms are used to generate new features	Paysim, Banksim	A novel measure of cost savings (CS) metric is proposed to evaluate the financial impact	XGBoost- RUS with best CS total 4,866.9. XGBOD with best AUC 99.68% (5-fold cross-validation)	Cost savings (CS) do not apply to test data
(Chhabra et al., 2023)	Voting ensemble with base classifiers KNN, RF, LR	RUS, ROS		European credit card dataset		Accuracy of 100% and 99% for training and testing, when applying ROS and assigning the highest weight to RF	Model generalizability, synthetic dataset
(Zhao et al., 2023)	CE-gcForest			European credit card dataset, a real-world dataset from a Chinese bank	Higher costs are assigned to the fraud class by the cost-sensitive gcForest to address the data imbalance problem	AUC of 98.01% and 98.25% respectively, on the two datasets	
(Mienye & Sun, 2023a)	Stacking with base learners of LSTM, GRU, and a meta-learner of MLP	SMOTE-ENN		European credit card dataset	LSTM and GRU consider the sequential patterns	Sensitivity: 1; specificity: 99.7%; AUC: 100% (10-fold cross-validation)	Model interpretability
(Khalid et al., 2024)	Voting ensemble with base classifiers SVM, LR, KNN, RF, Bagging	RUS, SMOTE		European credit card dataset		The proposed model with SMOTE achieved an accuracy of 99.96%, but performed poorly with RUS.	Model generalizability, synthetic dataset
(Talukder et al., 2024)	EIBMC	IHT+EMC		European credit card dataset		AUC score of 100%	Model generalizability; the voting weights were defined by accuracy, which may introduce biases
(Ahmed et al., 2025)	Voting ensembles with base classifiers RF, KNN, AdaBoost	SMOTE-ENN		European credit card dataset		Accuracy, recall, and an F1-score of 99.9%, 100%, and 99.9%	Model generalizability, synthetic dataset
(Baisholan et al., 2025b)	FraudX AI			European credit card dataset	SHAP was conducted to interpret the contributions of features to the result.	Recall value of 95% and AUC-PR of 97%	Model generalization on other datasets and the SHAP method could be tried on datasets with specific feature names

https://doi.org/10.3390/jrfm19010014

3.4. Hybrid Method

Unlike Ensemble methods, which combine the predictions of multiple base learners, Hybrid methods integrate two or more ML algorithms sequentially or in parallel to exploit their individual strengths. They are used for tasks such as parameter optimization, feature engineering, data balancing, and classification. This architecture allows a more robust, accurate, and reliable model to be developed.

Du et al. (2024) employed an Autoencoder (AE) for feature learning and Extreme Gradient Boosting (XGBoost) for classification, achieving a recall of 89.29%. Here, the AE compresses input data to extract features, while XGBoost serves as the predictive ensemble model. Another hybrid deep learning architecture, the Zeiler and Fergus Network integrated with Dwarf Mongoose–Shuffled Shepherd Political Optimization (DMSSPO_ZFNet), was proposed (Ganji & Chaparala, 2024). In this model, feature fusion is performed using Wave Hedge distance and a Deep Neuro-Fuzzy Network (DNFN), hyperparameters are optimized via DMSSPO, and classification is handled by ZFNet. It achieved an accuracy of 96.1%, a sensitivity of 96.1%, and a specificity of 95.1%.

Meta-heuristic algorithms inspired by animal behaviors have recently gained popularity for optimizing hyperparameters in transaction fraud detection. Jovanovic et al. (2022) introduced Group Search Fireflies algorithms (GSFA) coupled with XGBoost to detect transaction fraud. The GSFA utilizes a fitness function based on firefly brightness and attraction. It also employs a disputation operator, which searches for solutions within a selected subgroup of the population to optimize the hyperparameters of ML algorithms. XGBoost-GSFA achieved a recall of 99.97%, an F1-score of 99.97%, and an AUC of 100%. Reddy et al. (2025) introduced XGBoost with Elephant Herd Optimization (EHO) to tune hyperparameters. EHO finds an optimal hyperparameter set by mimicking elephant herding behavior, guided by specific evaluation metrics. The result showed XGBoost with EHO had an accuracy of 98% and an AUC of 99.7% under 20-fold cross-validation.

These statistics indicate that the capability of Hybrid techniques on transaction fraud detection is exceptional. Meta-heuristic algorithms, in particular, which are more flexible and more efficient at finding near-optimal solutions and less prone to becoming stuck in local optima, show a superior ability to enhance ML models' performance through hyperparameter optimization. Nevertheless, most Hybrid methods incorporate deep neural network structures, resulting in the same issues as DL, like interpretability and requiring intensive computing resources. Table 5 presents the review summary of the Hybrid method.

Table 5. Selected work on transaction fraud detection by a hybrid method.

Citation	Specific Method	Resample Tech	Feature Engineering	Dataset	Highlight	Result	Limitation/Challenge
(Zheng et al., 2018)	GAN with Denoising AE and GMMs	GAN with decoders and GMMs		Real-world data from two commercial banks in China	The generator, along with GMMs, makes the resample more robust and credible	The system successfully detects 321 of 367 true fraudulent cases (87%) and reduces customer losses of nearly 10 million RMB over 12 weeks, and the misclassification rate is about 0.68%	
(Malik et al., 2022)	AdaBoost + LightGBM	SMOTE-ENN	SVM-RFE	IEEE-CIS Fraud Detection Dataset		AUC-ROC value of 0.82, recall value of 0.64, precision of 0.97, F1-score of 0.77	Relatively low performance

 https://doi.org/10.3390/jrfm19010014

Table 5. *Cont.*

Citation	Specific Method	Resample Tech	Feature Engineering	Dataset	Highlight	Result	Limitation/Challenge
(Jovanovic et al., 2022)	SVM, ELM, and XGBoost with GSFA	SMOTE		European credit card dataset	Nature-inspired meta-heuristic algorithms adopted to optimize hyperparameters	XGBoost-GSFA without SMOTE achieves the best performance with a recall of 0.9997, an F1-score of 0.9997, AUC-ROC of 1	Model generalization, intensive computing resources
(Alharbi et al., 2022)	Novel text2IMG with CNN and Coarse-KNN		Transactional data to image by text2ING	European credit card dataset		An accuracy of 99.87% under 5 and 10-fold cross-validation	Low Recall. Is tabular data to image necessary? Model interpretability
(Cheah et al., 2023)	FNN + CNN with GANified-SMOTE	GANified-SMOTE,		European credit card dataset		F1-score of 0.89	Model interpretability and generalizability
(Zioviris et al., 2024)	LSTM with AE and VAE	SMOTE, K-MEANS SMOTE, Borderline SMOTE, ADASYN	Dimensionality reduction by AE and VAE	BankSim	The proposed model considers the temporal pattern of the dataset since LSTM is good at dealing with time series data	AUC of 99.61% by K-Means SMOTE—AE—LSTM	Model interpretability and generalizability
(Du et al., 2024)	AE-XGB-SMOTE-CGAN	SMOTE-CGAN	AE for feature extraction and presentation	European credit card dataset		Recall of 0.8929	Model interpretability and generalizability
(Ganji & Chaparala, 2024)	DMSSPO_ZFNet		Wave Hedge distance and DNFN for feature fusion	European credit card dataset		Accuracy, sensitivity, and specificity at 0.961, 0.961, and 0.951	Model interpretability and generalizability
(Tayebi & El Kafhali, 2025)	GB_ALSTM with ASVM	AVSM (AE with Support Vector Machine)		European credit card dataset	AVSM ensures the robustness of the generation. LSTM captures the temporal pattern of the feature.	99.99% accuracy, 98% precision, 99.99% recall, and 97.77% F-measure	Interpretability, generalization to other datasets
(Zeng et al., 2025)	NNEnsLeG (Neural Network Based Ensemble Learning with Generation)	GAN		European credit card dataset		AUC-ROC of 0.9862	Model generalization, intensive computing resources
(Reddy et al., 2025)	XGBoost, CatBoost, and LightGBM with EHO, MSA, and SMA	BorderLine SMOTE		Paysim	Nature-inspired meta-heuristic algorithms adopted to optimize hyperparameters	XGBoost with EHO had an accuracy of 98% and an AUC-ROC of 0.997 (20-fold cross-validation)	Model generalization, intensive computing resources

3.5. Analysis

3.5.1. Datasets Description

Datasets for detecting transaction fraud are usually collected in two ways: online open sources or private data from banks or financial institutions. Most researchers adopt online open-source data to build their ML models on card transaction fraud detection, since private data from banks is inaccessible in most cases due to the private nature, while in some reviewed studies, researchers cooperate with banks and financial institutions so that they can access real-world data to build detection systems.

Online open-source data:

The European credit card dataset is a highly adopted dataset to train ML models in transaction fraud. There are two versions, which were made in 2013 and 2023, respectively. The first version contains 284,807 transactions, where 492 out of 284,807 (0.172%) transactions are fraudulent, made by European cardholders in September 2013 (ULB Machine Learning Group, 2018). The second version contains 550,000 credit card transactions, which

https://doi.org/10.3390/jrfm19010014

are evenly distributed and made by European cardholders in 2023 (Elgiriyewithana, 2023). Most features in these datasets are transformed by Principal Component Analysis (PCA) and anonymized due to privacy concerns.

The Sparkov dataset is used by several studies. It was simulated using the Sparkov Data Generation tool, covering credit cards of 1000 customers doing transactions with a pool of 800 merchants from the duration 1 January 2019 to 31 December 2020 (Shenoy, 2022). This dataset is highly unbalanced.

The BankSim dataset is a synthetic dataset of bank payments based on a Spanish bank. It contains 594,643 records in total and is highly unbalanced, with normal payments of 587,443 and fraudulent transactions of 7200 (Lopez-Rojas, 2017a).

The PaySim dataset is another synthetic dataset generated from a private dataset containing mobile money transactions in an African country to solve the lack of publicly available datasets in financial fraud (Lopez-Rojas, 2017b). This dataset is very huge, containing more than 6 million instances, and is highly unbalanced.

Private data:

Private data from banks or financial institutions often contains real-world transactions. ML models developed with real-world data are usually more efficient and accurate because real data preserves all the authentic information of transactions. However, private data is hard to access due to the private nature of financial security.

Table 6 provides a summary of the datasets used in the reviewed papers. As shown, the European credit card dataset is most welcomed, and the adoption times are substantially greater than other datasets. This is because the European credit card dataset is easily accessible and the attributes have already been processed by PCA, providing researchers with clean and standardized data to develop their models (Chen et al., 2025).

Table 6. Datasets used by the reviewed work.

Datasets Name	Times Used
European credit card dataset	28
Sparkov dataset	3
BankSim dataset	3
PaySim dataset	2
IEEE-CIS Fraud Detection dataset	2
The Bank Account Fraud (BAF) dataset	1
IBM TabFormer dataset	1
Small Card Data	1
Tall Card Data	1
Real-world data from financial institutions	5 out of 41 studies

Although synthetic datasets offer valuable utility, they might introduce significant risks in transaction fraud detection (Tayebi & El Kafhali, 2025). Firstly, synthetic data may fail to capture the complex and non-linear interactions and subtle behavioral cues presented in real-world transactions. Moreover, it often lacks the rare and evolving attack patterns that define emerging fraud. Consequently, models that perform well in training or testing might fail when deployed on different, more complex real-world datasets. Access to rich, up-to-date real transaction data, therefore, remains essential. Real data provides the ground truth needed to validate models, capture live threat intelligence, and ensure that detection systems adapt to novel fraud schemes in real time, thereby maintaining both robustness and regulatory credibility.

https://doi.org/10.3390/jrfm19010014

3.5.2. Preprocessing

Preprocessing plays a crucial part in ML-based applications before training and classification, especially in financial fraud detection, which typically involves datasets with unbalanced classes and redundant features. Regardless of the ML algorithms implemented, most of the reviewed papers adopted at least one of the three preprocessing methods: data balancing, feature engineering, or hyperparameter tuning/optimization to enhance the performance of their ML models. This subsection provides an analysis of these methods applied by selected publications.

Data Balancing

Data resampling is the most popular choice for researchers to address issues of highly unbalanced datasets in transaction fraud detection. It can create a more balanced data distribution, consequently leading to better model performance. Traditional resampling techniques include undersampling, oversampling, and a combination of undersampling and oversampling, which usually generate synthetic data instances of the minority class or reduce the instances of the majority class by statistical methods (Alfaiz & Fati, 2022). RUS, Random Over Sampling (ROS), and SMOTE are widely adopted traditional resampling methods. RUS reduces the majority class by randomly removing instances, while ROS randomly duplicates existing minority class instances. SMOTE can generate new synthetic examples of the minority class by interpolating between existing minority instances. Dang et al. (2021) compared the model performance with and without SMOTE, concluding that ML models achieve high performance when resampling methods are applied to both of training and testing datasets, but poor results are obtained by applying resampling methods only to the training dataset. However, oversampling can introduce noise and result in overfitting, while undersampling may result in the loss of information (Cherif et al., 2024). ML methods are alternatives for data resampling, and their generations are usually more robust and credible. Zheng et al. (2018) constructed a Hybrid method, Generative Adversarial Network (GAN) with Gaussian Mixture Models (GMMs) to generate transaction samples. In this architecture, generator networks integrated with GMMs create and validate synthetic fraud samples, resulting in a more robust generation process. The result in a real-world system showed strong financial significance. Similarly, Tayebi and El Kafhali (2025) leveraged an Autoencoder (AE) coupled with a Support Vector Machine (SVM) in their Hybrid model for data creation and verification. SVM is a traditional supervised ML method that finds the optimal separating hyperplane by maximizing the margin between classes for linear classification and efficiently handles non-linear problems using the kernel trick. In this combined approach, newly generated fraud data points from AE were added to the dataset only if they were correctly classified by the SVM model. This approach yielded promising results, with 99.99% accuracy, 98% precision, 99.99% recall, and a 97.77% F1-score. The validation process in these two examples demonstrated robust data generation.

Assigning class weights that are inversely related to the class frequencies is another alternative to solve the class imbalance (Alharbi et al., 2022; Baisholan et al., 2025b; Cherif et al., 2024; Zhao et al., 2023). This strategy is preferred because it maintains a realistic distribution to prevent overfitting and avoids biased results caused by artificially generated samples of the minority class (Cherif et al., 2024). Zhao et al. (2023) employed cost-sensitive gcForest to address the data imbalance issue by assigning higher classification costs to fraud cases, while Baisholan et al. (2025b) tuned the threshold and adjusted minority class weight. In these examples, a higher penalty was assigned to the model for misclassifying fraud samples. This cost-sensitive approach increases the model's sensitivity to fraud during training, leading to better performance on imbalanced classification tasks.

https://doi.org/10.3390/jrfm19010014

Feature Engineering

Feature engineering is another hot topic in detecting financial fraud by ML algorithms because it enhances models' performance by removing redundant information and extracting useful information. This is achieved by cleaning and restructuring the data through steps such as selecting the optimal set of features and creating new features through aggregation, decomposition, or interaction of existing variables. The goal is to highlight the underlying patterns and relationships within the data, making it easier for the model to learn effectively, rather than simply feeding it raw or unstructured information. Zhang et al. (2021) proposed a feature engineering method, Homogeneity-Oriented Behaviour Analysis (HOBA), inspired and developed from a marketing technique called recency-frequency-monetary (RFM) (Van Vlasselaer et al., 2015), to extract feature variables by aggregation. RFM analyzes and aggregates variables related to three key customer behaviors: recency (how recently they purchased), frequency (how often they purchase), and monetary value (how much they spend). HOBA is an enhanced version of RFM that formalizes this approach in the financial fraud detection context through a structured aggregation strategy, extracting features based on four components: the aggregation characteristic, aggregation period, transaction behavior measure, and aggregation statistic. This strategy helps the model capture fraudulent transaction patterns. GA, a type of Evolutionary-inspired Algorithm (EA), was introduced to find the optimized feature subsets by computing model fitness (Ileberi et al., 2022; Mienye & Sun, 2023b). GNNs were applied to represent the graph nodes (Cherif et al., 2024; Harish et al., 2024; Khaled Alarfaj & Shahzadi, 2025), while an Autoencoder (AE) was implemented for feature extraction and representation (Du et al., 2024; Zioviris et al., 2024). All the work mentioned improved their models' performance by integrating feature engineering. However, Nguyen et al. (2020) failed to achieve optimal results without implementing feature engineering, as the features in the datasets had little correlation.

Hyperparameter Tuning/Optimization

Hyperparameter tuning and optimization are the processes of finding the optimal set of hyperparameters to achieve the best possible model performance and play an important role in ML algorithms. Several researchers (Ganji & Chaparala, 2024; Jovanovic et al., 2022; Reddy et al., 2025) applied Hybrid methods, incorporating hyperparameter tuning to enhance performance in transaction fraud detection. (see Section 3.4) Since huge computing resources are required, the feasibility of implementing it in a real-world system could be tested in the future.

3.5.3. Cross-Validation

Cross-validation is a fundamental statistical technique in ML used to evaluate the stability and reliability of predictive models and prevent overfitting (Wu et al., 2025). As mentioned before, a few studies employed cross-validation techniques to ensure the robustness of their models. The most common implementation is k-fold cross-validation. In this approach, the dataset is first randomly partitioned into k equal, non-overlapping subsets (folds). The model is then trained and evaluated k times; in each iteration, one subset is held out as the test set while the remaining k-1 subsets are used for training. This process ensures every data point is used for testing exactly once. Finally, the k performance scores are averaged to produce a robust and generalized estimate of model performance (Zheng et al., 2018). Stratified k-fold cross-validation is a crucial variant. This method ensures each fold (subset) maintains the same proportion of class labels as the original dataset, making it essential for imbalanced classification tasks (Alfaiz & Fati, 2022). Figure 3 gives an example of 5-fold cross-validation.

https://doi.org/10.3390/jrfm19010014

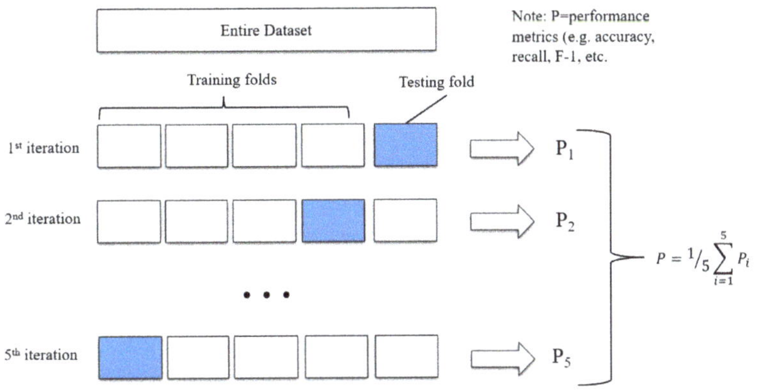

Figure 3. 5-fold cross-validation workflow.

3.6. Discussion

We selected several traditional metrics, involving accuracy, recall, precision, AUC, F1-score, and ROC-AUC, that are prevalent to measure the performance of ML models for comparison across studies. The results are presented in Table 7. As shown, many studies report high accuracy. However, this can be misleading due to severe class imbalance in fraud datasets, as a classifier that always predicts "not fraud" will achieve high accuracy while failing to detect fraud. Several studies show low performance on metrics like recall, precision, and F1-score. This variation in performance is influenced by factors such as the datasets used, preprocessing methods, and the ML models employed.

Table 7. Comparison of reviewed work among widely adopted metrics.

Citation	Accuracy	Recall (Sensitivity)	Precision	AUC	F1-Score	ROC-AUC
(Zheng et al., 2018)		88.33%	4.51%			
(Kim et al., 2019)		91.5%				
(Sailusha et al., 2020)	100%	77%	95%	94.29%	85%	
(Najadat et al., 2020)		94.59%	91.14%	91.37%	92.81%	
(Itoo et al., 2021)	95.9%	83.9%	99.1%	91.8%	90.9%	
(Nguyen et al., 2020)					84.85%	
(Tanouz et al., 2021)	96.77%	91.11%	100%		95.35%	95.55%
(Ileberi et al., 2021)	99.98%	99.96%	99.93%			
(Dang et al., 2021)	99.99%	100%	99.98%	100%	99.99%	
(Zhang et al., 2021)	96.51%	75%				
(Alarfaj et al., 2022)	99.9%		93%	98%	85.71%	
(Alfaiz & Fati, 2022)	99.96%	95.91%	80.28%	97.94%	87.4%	
(Malik et al., 2022)		64%	97%		77%	82%
(Ileberi et al., 2022)	99.98%	72.56%	95.34%		82.41%	
(Jovanovic et al., 2022)	99.97%	99.97%	99.97%		99.97%	100%
(Alharbi et al., 2022)	99.87%	51.22%			57.8%	
(Hajek et al., 2023)	99.94%	77.93%	99.42%	99.58%	87.37%	
(Chhabra et al., 2023)	99.99%					

https://doi.org/10.3390/jrfm19010014

Table 7. *Cont.*

Citation	Accuracy	Recall (Sensitivity)	Precision	AUC	F1-Score	ROC-AUC
(Zhao et al., 2023)		82.11%	88.45%	98.01%	85.14%	
(Afriyie et al., 2023)	96%	93%	9%	98.9%	17%	
(Mienye & Sun, 2023a)		100%		100%		
(Mienye & Sun, 2023b)		99.7%		99%		
(Cheah et al., 2023)		85%	94%		89%	
(Ziovíris et al., 2024)		99.89%	98.94%	99.61%	99.14%	
(Abdul Salam et al., 2024)	99.99%	100%	99.98%		99.99%	
(Khalid et al., 2024)	99.96%	99.96%	99.96%		99.96%	100%
(Ileberi & Sun, 2024)	99.98%	99.99%	99.92%		99.95%	
(Yu et al., 2024)		99.8%	99.8%		99.8%	99%
(Du et al., 2024)	99.87%	89.29%				
(Talukder et al., 2024)	99.84%	99.14%	99.91%	100%	99.52%	
(Ganji & Chaparala, 2024)	96.1%	96.1%				
(Cherif et al., 2024)	97%	92%	82%		86%	92%
(Harish et al., 2024)		66%	94%		78%	
(Khaled Alarfaj & Shahzadi, 2025)	79.01%	80.68%	79.98%		79.78%	
(Tayebi & El Kafhali, 2025)	99.99%	99.99%	98%		97.77%	
(Zeng et al., 2025)						98.62%
(Reddy et al., 2025)	98%	97.2%	97.8%		98%	99.7%
(Ahmed et al., 2025)	99.9%	100%	99.9%		99.9%	100%
(Baisholan et al., 2025b)	99%	95%	100%		97%	
(Wu et al., 2025)	99.98%	100%	99.96%		99.98%	
(Dong et al., 2025)	95.23%	95.2%	99.96%		97.52%	96%

To better understand the performance among various groups, box plots (Figures 4–6) with average values are drawn to compare recall, precision, and F1-scoreacross different taxonomies, with and without data balancing and feature engineering (Note: due to insufficient sample sizes within individual datasets, comparisons were conducted across multiple datasets). We chose these three metrics for comparison because more than half of the reviewed work adopted them. Accuracy is excluded since it is unreliable for highly unbalanced binary classification tasks. Figure 4 presents the results of the comparison across subgroups. As shown, Ensemble outperforms the other three methods according to the average recall, precision, and F1-score. Traditional ML has two outliers while Hybrid has one. F1-score, a comprehensive metric combining precision and recall, provides a balanced view of an ML model's performance. The graph indicates that Ensemble obtains the highest average F1-score with 92.66%, DL ranks second with 89.38%, Hybrid is slightly lower with 88.38% while Traditional ML has the lowest value with 83.66%. DL, Ensemble, and Hybrid outperform Traditional ML according to F1-score due to their superior powers and more robust architectures to identify intricate patterns. This is consistent with the observation that more studies employ DL, Ensemble, and Hybrid methods for transaction fraud detection compared to Traditional ML approaches.

In terms of Figure 5, studies that applied data balance techniques demonstrate higher performance overall compared to studies without data balancing, although there are several outliers. The average recall, precision, and F1-scores of studies using data balance techniques are 91.02%, 93%, and 91.57%, respectively, markedly greater than those of studies without data balancing, which are 86.69%, 74%, and 69.38%. This is aligned with the previous observation that data balance techniques are widely adopted by researchers to enhance the performance of transaction fraud detection systems.

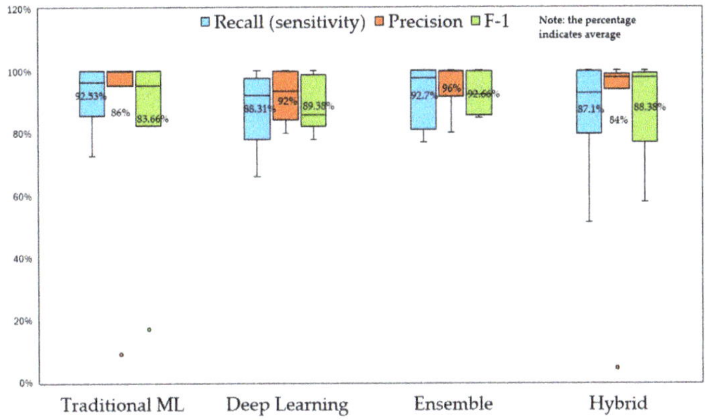

Figure 4. Comparison of metrics across subgroups.

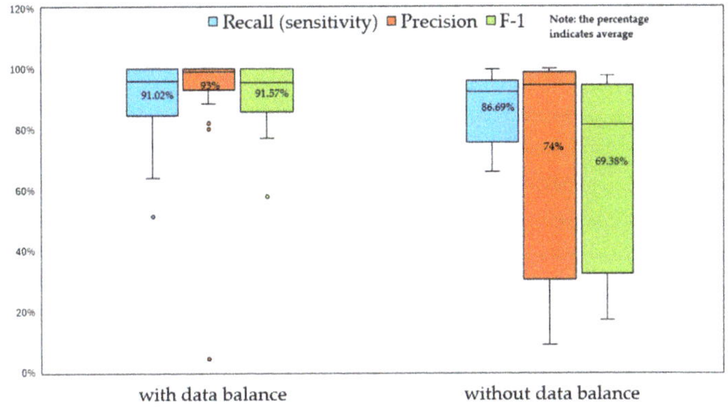

Figure 5. Comparison of metrics across data balance techniques.

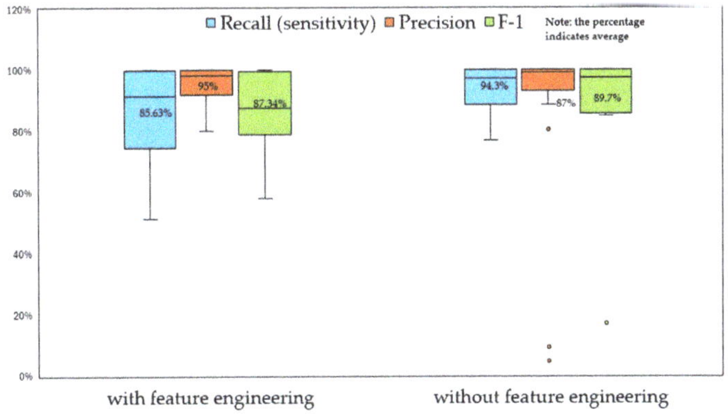

Figure 6. Comparison of metrics across feature engineering techniques.

In Figure 6, studies with feature engineering have a higher average precision over studies without feature engineering, which also display some outliers according to precision

https://doi.org/10.3390/jrfm19010014

and F1-score. However, studies without feature engineering show a higher performance in terms of recall and F1-score, contradicting the assumption that feature engineering can improve models' performance by removing unrelated information and extracting valuable information. One of the reasons might be that inappropriate adoption of feature engineering techniques could lead to poor performance. For example, Alharbi et al. (2022) implemented a text2IMG conversion technique, which converted the transactional data with 30 features into 5 × 6-dimensional images for modelling, but the output yielded only 51.22% recall and 57.8% F1-score. The necessity of converting tabular data into images is questionable. Another study (Malik et al., 2022) employed SVM- recursive feature elimination (RFE) for feature dimension reduction. The process iteratively selects features to identify the optimal subset. However, this approach may eliminate valuable information, resulting in a recall of 64% and an F1-score of 77%. Low recalls would allow more fraudulent transactions to be approved, causing tremendous financial losses and escalating the operational risk. The results of these 2 studies significantly bias the overall average performance of studies with feature engineering. Moreover, several studies (Khaled Alarfaj & Shahzadi, 2025; Kim et al., 2019; Zhang et al., 2021) with feature engineering applied their models to real-world datasets from banks. Their recalls are 80.68%, 91.5%, and 75%, respectively. As we know, real-world data that has better quality is usually more complex than synthetic datasets in transaction fraud. ML models often have lower performance on real-world data than on synthetic data. This could also negatively affect the box plots and overall averages.

Finally, after comprehensive analysis and exhaustive examination, a general workflow (Figure 7) of applying ML to mitigate financial risk in the context of transaction fraud detection is developed. One single study may not contain all the depicted steps, but this depiction provides a general picture and helps readers understand the overall process, and key procedures may be incorporated in this domain. The last three steps are considerable, as preprocessing techniques are essential to enhance the model's performance, and the classification is the final step to predict the possibility of fraud.

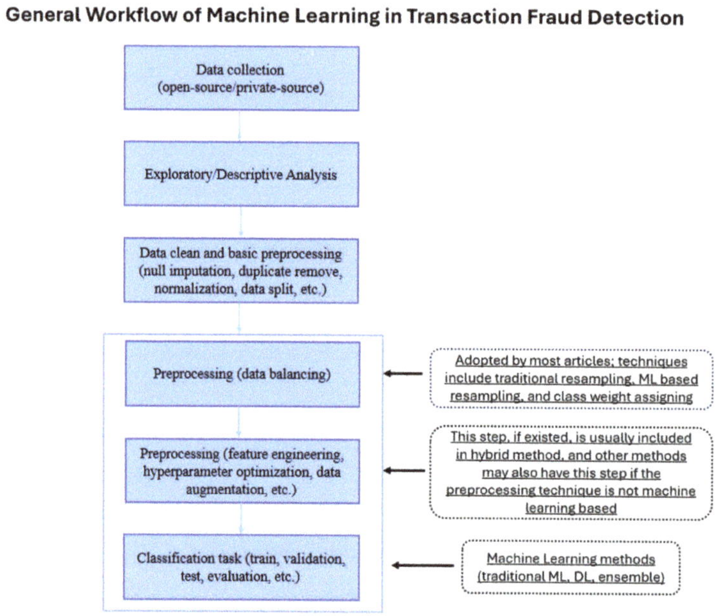

Figure 7. General workflow.

https://doi.org/10.3390/jrfm19010014

4. Financial Implication

In the research field, addressing financial implications is critical and helpful to investigate the insights into financial risk in transaction fraud, as the goal is to protect stakeholders in the financial domains. Generally, advanced automated fraud detection systems, like ML-based methods that improve their detection performance through training, are more efficient for financial institutions and their customers to fight against external fraud than manual and traditional fraud detection systems. These approaches provide alternatives to deal with operational risk under the Basel Framework. Implementing ML also complied with regulations, such as the Scam Detection Framework, recently activated in Australia, designating financial institutions like banks as one of the initial sectors to introduce robust systems to combat fraud and scams, managing the risks that might cause financial losses (The Treasury, 2024). However, most reviewed studies focus on developing ML models, which mainly rely on traditional ML evaluation metrics, like accuracy, ignoring the specific significance in financial domains. This section highlights a selection of reviewed publications that emphasize financial significance, addressing key aspects such as financial metric design, feature interpretation, time series considerations, and financial data privacy.

4.1. Financial Metric Design and Direct Impact

The primary role of card transaction fraud detection is to reduce financial losses and preserve the reputation of financial institutions. Two studies adopted or designed financial metrics to evaluate ML models' performance in this context. The Cost Reduction Rate (CRR) was introduced to quantify the cost savings achieved by the new model compared to the old one in a financial transaction fraud detection system (Kim et al., 2019). The metric is calculated by first aggregating the total cost for each model, which comprises financial losses from falsely approved fraudulent transactions and operational costs of incorrectly rejected legitimate transactions. The difference between the total cost of the old and new models is then divided by the old model's total cost. The result, expressed as a percentage, represents the relative cost reduction achieved by the new model. Similarly, Cost Savings (CS) measure, inspired by profit-based systems in loan default prediction, measures the net financial benefit an ML algorithm provides on a fraud dataset (Hajek et al., 2023). Its value is derived from the difference between the savings generated by correctly identified fraudulent transactions and the total costs incurred due to misclassifications (both false positives and false negatives). This metric provides a direct and absolute basis for comparing algorithms, where a higher CS score signifies greater overall cost-effectiveness. In real-world applications, high performance on traditional metrics such as accuracy and recall does not guarantee that a model will effectively mitigate financial risk. For instance, a high accuracy rate indicates that most samples are classified correctly. However, if the misclassified samples consist of approved fraudulent transactions, substantial financial losses can still occur, thereby escalating risk. Similarly, a model with high recall successfully identifies many fraudulent transactions but may misclassify numerous legitimate ones, leading to high operational costs from manual reviews, which also increases risk. In contrast, CRR and CS directly quantify financial costs, offering a more meaningful approach to assessing the true financial impact of ML models in fraud detection and providing significant value for practical risk management (The Treasury, 2024). Another study (Zheng et al., 2018) showed direct financial impact in a real-world implementation by ML in transaction fraud detection. The system successfully detected 321 of 367 true fraudulent cases (87%) and reduced customer losses of nearly 10 million RMB for two commercial banks in China over 12 weeks. The statistics demonstrate how ML effectively mitigates external fraud in operational risk by detecting anomalies and reducing financial losses. Consequently, advanced ML for fraud detection could even

https://doi.org/10.3390/jrfm19010014

affect banks' strategies of capital requirements against financial risk, like RWA, allowing them to allocate more assets to other investments and subsequently resulting in economic growth. Zhang et al. (2021) highlighted the importance of setting a tolerance for the False Positive Rate (FPR) to balance the capture of fraudulent transactions against the misclassification of legitimate ones. Financial institutions typically prioritize a lower FPR to protect customer relationships and reputations. This strategy, however, often leads to a higher False Negative Rate (FNR), indirectly exposing customers to greater financial losses from undetected fraud. This preference can be understood through a risk-adjusted return framework. From the institution's perspective, models are tuned to accept a certain level of risk (financial losses from false negatives) in exchange for a greater "return": lower operational costs and preserved customer trust. Consequently, while this calibration may maximize the institution's operational efficiency and profitability, it does so by effectively transferring a portion of the financial risk to the customer.

4.2. Feature Explanation

Interpreting the models and explaining the contributions of features to the results are always hard tasks for ML methods, especially for DL, as they are defined as "Black Box Models", but it is important for financial institutions to understand attributes of people who are prone to be deceived and set up effective protection measures, as mentioned in Scam Detection Framework (The Treasury, 2024). Afriyie et al. (2023) analyzed the characteristics of fraudulent transactions on the Sparkov dataset. Their analysis reveals that fraudulent transactions tend to involve higher amounts than legitimate ones and disproportionately target older adults. Furthermore, fraudulent transactions occur most frequently on Sundays, a day of higher consumer activity, and during nighttime hours when monitoring may be less vigilant. These insights can help financial institutions strengthen their protective measures and mitigate this risk. Baisholan et al. (2025b) employed the Interpretable Machine Learning (IML) method, Shapley additive explanations (SHAP), to explain features' contributions to the results. Although the features' names in the dataset are anonymous, this is a good attempt to refine their models by understanding the attributes' contributions.

Interpretable Machine Learning (IML) Overview

SHAP, Local Interpretable Model-agnostic Explanations (LIME), and Partial Dependence Plot (PDP) are widely adopted IML methods for explaining feature influence in tabular datasets (Wang et al., 2025).

SHAP, a method inspired by cooperative game theory, explains ML model outputs by attributing importance to each input feature. The framework treats each feature as a contributor and calculates its average marginal contribution across all possible feature combinations for a given prediction. The results are typically presented as a ranked list of feature importance, allowing users to easily identify the most influential factors (Wang et al., 2025). A key limitation is its potential to be misleading when features are highly correlated, as SHAP may distribute importance unevenly among them. Additionally, the method can be computationally expensive for large datasets, as the exact calculation grows exponentially with the number of features.

LIME explains individual predictions by ranking the contribution of each feature to that specific outcome. It does so by constructing a simple, interpretable local surrogate model, such as a linear regression, which explains how the complex "Black Box Model" behaves around one specific instance (Wang et al., 2025). While LIME is computationally efficient, it is designed only for local interpretation and does not provide a global view of feature importance.

https://doi.org/10.3390/jrfm19010014

In contrast to methods that explain individual predictions, PDP provides a global perspective by visualizing the average marginal effect of a feature across the entire dataset. It calculates how the model's prediction changes on average when one specific feature is varied while all other features are held at their typical observed values. The result is a curve that shows the overall trend between the feature and the predicted outcome, along with an indication of the uncertainty around that average effect (Wang et al., 2025). However, this approach can produce misleading results when features are highly correlated, as it may extrapolate to unrealistic combinations of feature values.

All these methods are valuable for transaction fraud detection and financial risk prevention. However, selecting the appropriate method requires careful consideration of the specific task (whether to explain local or global influence), the application context, dataset characteristics, and the inherent strengths and limitations of each technique. A summary can be found in Figure 8.

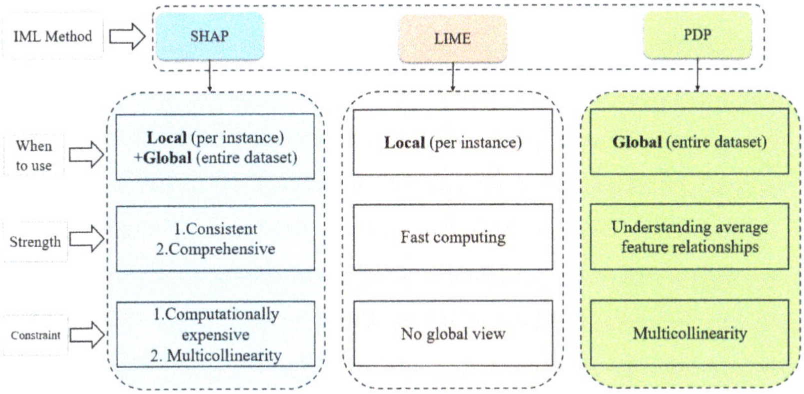

Figure 8. Interpretable Machine Learning (IML) methods overview.

4.3. Time Series Consideration

Applications in financial contexts usually involve time series data. Most of the studies in transaction fraud detection by ML remove the "time" attribute before training, as they think this attribute is redundant and not contributory, ignoring concept drift, the common phenomenon that statistical properties always change over time in time series data. Neglecting "time" can harm a model's performance by limiting its generalizability to new or real-world data. A few (Mienye & Sun, 2023a; Tayebi & El Kafhali, 2025; Zioviris et al., 2024) consider the importance of temporal and sequential patterns during training. These studies involve Recurrent Neural Network (RNN), including LSTM and GRU, which are well-suited for sequential data like time series, and this inherent suitability enables them to generate more robust results. RNN introduces the basic concept of memory for sequences. This approach can learn temporal dependencies among instances. LSTM and GRU are enhanced versions that overcome the vanishing gradient problem and capture long-term dependencies through their gated architectures. This allows them to capture relationships between instances that are widely separated in time. These approaches offer examples of how concept drift is considered and handled, and could inspire other financial time series-related problems, like stock market prediction, loan default, and insurance fraud etc.

https://doi.org/10.3390/jrfm19010014

4.4. Financial Data Privacy

The data privacy concerns cause underperformance in transaction fraud detection for financial institutions. Without sufficient data to be trained and learned, ML-based detection systems would be more likely to yield poor results and fail to correctly classify transactions. The Federated Learning (FL) framework was proposed to address financial data privacy issues (Abdul Salam et al., 2024). It enables multiple financial institutions to cooperatively train ML models using their dispersed data without sharing the raw data itself, thereby bypassing privacy concerns. This framework helps mitigate the risk of financial data leakage while ensuring compliance with stringent data protection laws, such as the EU's General Data Protection Regulation (GDPR), a comprehensive data privacy and security standard (Sgantzos et al., 2025; Yang et al., 2019). Table 8 summarizes the financial significance addressed by relevant papers.

Table 8. Publications that addressed Financial Significance.

Citation	Method Category	Metho Used	Financial Significance
(Zheng et al., 2018)	Hybrid	GAN with Denoising AE and GMMs	This experiment was conducted in a real-world scenario and successfully reduced huge losses (10 million RMB)
(Kim et al., 2019)	DL	Challenger (Deep Feed-Forward Network) and Champion	Cost reduction rate (CRR) was adopted to estimate the financial impact of different models
(Zhang et al., 2021)	DL	DBN, CNN, RNN with HOBA	Tolerance of FPR is usually low for financial institutions to preserve reputations (but a lower FPR causes more fraud transactions to be approved), transferring a portion of the financial risk to the customer
(Hajek et al., 2023)	Ensemble	XGBoost, XGBOD	The Cost Savings (CS) metric was proposed and effectively identified how many losses were reduced by the proposed model
(Afriyie et al., 2023)	Traditional ML	RF, DT, LR	The characteristics of individuals who are easily deceived were analyzed. And this helps financial institutions efficiently set up protection measures.
(Mienye & Sun, 2023a)	Ensemble	Stacking with base learners of LSTM, GRU, and a meta-learner of MLP	Sequential and temporal patterns were considered, inspiring other financial contexts
(Cioviris et al., 2024)	Hybrid	LSTM with AE and VAE	Sequential and temporal patterns were considered, inspiring other financial contexts
(Abdul Salam et al., 2024)	Traditional ML	RF, KNN, DT, NB, CNN	FL framework allows different financial institutions to cooperate regardless of data privacy concerns, aligning with regulation compliance, like GDPR
(Tayebi & El Kafhali, 2025)	Hybrid	GB_ALSTM	Sequential and temporal patterns were considered, inspiring other financial contexts
(Baisholan et al., 2025b)	Ensemble	FraudX AI	The IML method is important in this context as it helps financial institutions understand the characteristics of fraudulent transactions

https://doi.org/10.3390/jrfm19010014

5. Limitations/Challenges and Future Scopes

To wrap up, this section extracts limitations and challenges from previous analysis and develops research gaps and future scopes in managing risks associated with detecting financial transaction fraud.

5.1. Limitations/Challenges

An appropriate performance metric might be the most urgent concern in detecting financial fraud by ML for financial institutions. Some studies focus on improving accuracy, a metric that always has a misleadingly high value in unbalanced data classification tasks. Although a higher accuracy marginally reduces losses, it is an indirect and weaker measure than metrics like the F1-score or financial indicators (e.g., CRR, CS), which correlate more directly with actual risk and cost outcomes. Furthermore, since this is fundamentally a financial risk problem, few studies adopted financially significant metrics that assess the cost of fraud under the risk. This is inconsistent with the risk management framework to mitigate financial losses.

Interpretability is another important limitation confronted by all types of ML methods, which are often called "Black Box Models". This is especially true for DL, Ensemble, and Hybrid methods, which employ more complicated architectures that are difficult to understand. Under the Scam Prevention Framework, identifying individuals who could be impacted by scams is required (The Treasury, 2024). So, it is important for financial institutions to set up prevention measures by understanding the intricate relationship between features and their contributions to the results. However, only one publication in the review used IML techniques, representing a significant gap in the literature.

Data privacy/availability is one of the biggest obstacles faced by financial fraud detection. Open-source datasets are insufficient and might exclude important information as they are usually synthetic and generated, while private-source or real-world datasets are inaccessible to most researchers, except for those who cooperate with financial institutions or industries. In addition, financial institutions are less likely to collaborate to build a more robust detection system due to data privacy regulations, like GDPR. For example, A bank in country A cannot simply share its customers' transaction records with a partner bank in country B, even if the goal is to protect those same customers from cross-border fraud. Without sufficient and accurate data, ML algorithms are hindered from leveraging their full potential to learn the historical behaviors from vast amounts of data, thus leading to poor performance.

Model replicability and concept drift are challenges for financial fraud detection. Most studies only involve one dataset, and while a model obtains promising results on a specific dataset does not guarantee it performs well on other datasets. Moreover, many studies ignore concept drift, which happens a lot in time series data, and exclude the time attribute while training. This will probably cause negative effects on the models' performance.

Data resampling is one of the techniques to address data imbalance problems, faced by all studies and methods in the field of financial fraud detection, as fraudulent transactions are usually much fewer than legitimate transactions. Although data resampling techniques help improve models' performances, they, especially the traditional ways like undersampling and oversampling, also increase the risk of introducing bias, potential loss of valuable information, and the creation of noisy or inaccurate synthetic samples that can lead to overfitting.

Intensive computing resources required are a disadvantage for DL and Hybrid, which usually involve more complex structures, requiring more training and processing time. However, real-time detection systems always allow little response time to approve or reject a transaction. For instance, when a customer makes an online purchase, the fraud detection

 https://doi.org/10.3390/jrfm19010014

system must analyze the transaction, check historical patterns, and decide whether to block or approve it—often within a few hundred milliseconds. During that brief window, high latency causes system inefficiency and leads to customer complaints.

5.2. Future Scopes

Involving financial metrics and addressing more of the financial impact are pressing issues anticipated in future studies to mitigate this financial risk. Instead of relying on traditional ML model evaluation metrics like accuracy, future research can prioritize CS (Hajek et al., 2023) or CRR (Kim et al., 2019) to estimate the model's performance financially, aligning with operational risk management. Moreover, the trade-off between FPR and True Positive Rate (TPR) is encouraged to be considered (Zhang et al., 2021).

Incorporating IML strategies to explain models, features, and results in future studies of financial fraud detection is imperative. IML methods, including SHAP, feature permutations, feature occlusion, PDP, and LIME (Allen et al., 2024), are good ways to address the interpretability of "Black Box Model" and understand the models' decisions. Moreover, it helps detect unfair bias. For example, auditors can use IML techniques to check whether a model's decisions are overly influenced by sensitive attributes like age or location.

Integrating novel technologies like GNNs, metaheuristics, time series forecasting models, blockchain, and FL to emphasize different sides of financial fraud detection could be considered. GNNs and metaheuristic algorithms could be used for feature representation and hyperparameter optimization to enhance performance, while time series forecasting models could be included to solve concept drift. Blockchain, known for its distributed ledger and secured blocks, together with FL, can enhance the performance of ML in real-time financial transaction fraud detection without sharing sensitive information between financial institutions. This combination could effectively mitigate the data privacy constraints that prevent banks from sharing sensitive information with each other. Moreover, FL framework allows organizations across sectors like financial institutions and telecommunication companies, etc. working together to integrate multimodal data, such as financial transaction data (tabular), customers' portraits (image), message contents (text), phone call contents (audio), etc., developing more robust and resilient detection system, and complying with regulations, like GDPR simultaneously.

Assigning class weights or implementing ML algorithms for combating data imbalance lacks investigation. Assigning class weights (Alharbi et al., 2022; Baisholan et al., 2025b; Cherif et al., 2024; Zhao et al., 2023) can maintain a realistic distribution in the dataset while ML algorithms (Tayebi & El Kafhali, 2025; Zheng et al., 2018) make the generated data points more reliable.

Various advanced feature engineering and hyperparameter tuning strategies are expected to enhance model performance. More preprocessing strategies could be focused on in future studies of financial fraud detection. For example, our findings suggest that methods like the statistical HOBA framework and complex neural networks, such as Autoencoder (AE), demonstrate superior power for model improvement. Future work could leverage such approaches, including statistical feature selection that aggregates fraud-related components and advanced neural networks for effective feature representation.

6. Conclusions

This research exhaustively analyzes 41 recent papers on ML for detecting transaction fraud—a key financial operational risk. It provides a comprehensive review of their advantages and disadvantages. Traditional ML methods like Logistic Regression (LR) and Random Forest (RF) demonstrate strong classification performance on small, randomly undersampled transaction fraud datasets. However, they may show instability

 https://doi.org/10.3390/jrfm19010014

when classifying new data points. DL approaches, particularly Transformer models and Continuous-Coupled Neural Networks (CCNNs)—which were originally designed for unstructured data—have shown superior power on transactional tabular data. However, DL suffers from difficulties such as poor interpretability and intensive computational demands. Ensemble and Hybrid methods, which strategically combine multiple ML techniques, tend to deliver more robust performance in fraud detection. Nonetheless, they face limitations, such as issues with generalizability, interpretability, or high resource consumption, depending on the specific base algorithms used. A comparison across the taxonomy indicates that Ensemble methods demonstrate superior average performance over the other three categories. Data balancing generally improves model performance, while inappropriate feature engineering can negatively impact results. Employing financial metrics, applying feature explanation techniques, considering temporal patterns, and addressing financial data privacy are all crucial for assessing financial significance in external fraud prevention. These elements are also key to aligning with risk management frameworks, such as the Basel operational risk standards (Basel Committee on Banking Supervision, 2024), and regulations like GDPR and Scam Prevention Framework (The Treasury, 2024).

Future work in this domain could employ more preprocessing alternatives, focus on metrics such as the False Positive Rate (FPR), True Positive Rate (TPR), and other financial metrics like Cost Reduction Rate (CRR), Cost Savings (CS), to evaluate model performance and financial impact, and implement Interpretable ML (IML) strategies to explain the results. Advanced technologies like Federated Learning (FL), which allows collaborations across multiple organizations, could be considered to mitigate data privacy concerns. The use of the Hybrid Method, which integrates multiple ML techniques for tasks such as data balancing, feature engineering, hyperparameter optimization, and classification to enhance model performance, and the Ensemble Method, which leverages the diversity of the various ML models to yield a more robust result, might be a trend for future-generation financial fraud detection systems.

Author Contributions: Conceptualization, T.C. and T.M.; methodology, T.C. and R.S.; formal analysis, T.C., R.S., T.M. and S.S.; writing—original draft preparation, T.C.; writing—review and editing, T.C., R.S., T.M. and S.S. All authors have read and agreed to the published version of the manuscript.

Funding: This research received no external funding.

Institutional Review Board Statement: Not applicable.

Informed Consent Statement: Not applicable.

Data Availability Statement: No new data were created or analyzed in this study.

Acknowledgments: We would like to thank the editors and reviewers for their constructive comments and insightful advice, which helped us to significantly improve the presentation of this manuscript.

Conflicts of Interest: The authors declare no conflicts of interest.

References

Abdul Salam, M., Fouad, K. M., Elbably, D. L., & Elsayed, S. M. (2024). Federated learning model for credit card fraud detection with data balancing techniques. *Neural Computing and Applications*, *36*(11), 6231–6256. [CrossRef]

Afriyie, J. K., Tawiah, K., Pels, W. A., Addai-Henne, S., Dwamena, H. A., Owiredu, E. O., Ayeh, S. A., & Eshun, J. (2023). A supervised machine learning algorithm for detecting and predicting fraud in credit card transactions. *Decision Analytics Journal*, *6*, 100163. [CrossRef]

Ahmed, K. H., Axelsson, S., Li, Y., & Sagheer, A. M. (2025). A credit card fraud detection approach based on ensemble machine learning classifier with hybrid data sampling. *Machine Learning with Applications*, *20*, 100675. [CrossRef]

https://doi.org/10.3390/jrfm19010014

Alarfaj, F. K., Malik, I., Khan, H. U., Almusallam, N., Ramzan, M., & Ahmed, M. (2022). Credit card fraud detection using state-of-the-art machine learning and deep learning algorithms. *IEEE Access*, *10*, 39700–39715. [CrossRef]

Alfaiz, N. S., & Fati, S. M. (2022). Enhanced credit card fraud detection model using machine learning. *Electronics*, *11*(4), 662. [CrossRef]

Alharbi, A., Alshammari, M., Okon, O. D., Alabrah, A., Rauf, H. T., Alyami, H., & Meraj, T. (2022). A novel text2IMG mechanism of credit card fraud detection: A deep learning approach. *Electronics*, *11*(5), 756. [CrossRef]

Allen, G. I., Gan, L., & Zheng, L. (2024). Interpretable machine learning for discovery: Statistical challenges and opportunities. *Annual Review of Statistics and Its Application*, *11*(1), 97–121. [CrossRef]

Baisholan, N., Dietz, J. E., Gnatyuk, S., Turdalyuly, M., Matson, E. T., & Baisholanova, K. (2025a). A Systematic review of machine learning in credit card fraud detection under original class imbalance. *Computers*, *14*(10), 437. [CrossRef]

Baisholan, N., Dietz, J. E., Gnatyuk, S., Turdalyuly, M., Matson, E. T., & Baisholanova, K. (2025b). FraudX AI: An interpretable machine learning framework for credit card fraud detection on imbalanced datasets. *Computers*, *14*(4), 120. [CrossRef]

Basel Committee on Banking Supervision. (2024). *Basel framework*. Bank for International Settlements. Available online: https://www.bis.org/basel_framework/index.htm?m=97 (accessed on 3 December 2025).

Cheah, P. C. Y., Yang, Y., & Lee, B. G. (2023). Enhancing financial fraud detection through addressing class imbalance using hybrid SMOTE-GAN techniques. *International Journal of Financial Studies*, *11*(3), 110. [CrossRef]

Chen, Y., Zhao, C., Xu, Y., Nie, C., & Zhang, Y. (2025). Deep learning in financial fraud detection: Innovations, challenges, and applications. *Data Science and Management*, S2666764925000372. [CrossRef]

Cherif, A., Ammar, H., Kalkatawi, M., Alshehri, S., & Imine, A. (2024). Encoder–decoder graph neural network for credit card fraud detection. *Journal of King Saud University—Computer and Information Sciences*, *36*(3), 102003. [CrossRef]

Chhabra, R., Goswami, S., & Ranjan, R. K. (2023). A voting ensemble machine learning based credit card fraud detection using highly imbalance data. *Multimedia Tools and Applications*, *83*(18), 54729–54753. [CrossRef]

Dal Pozzolo, A., Caelen, O., Le Borgne, Y.-A., Waterschoot, S., & Bontempi, G. (2014). Learned lessons in credit card fraud detection from a practitioner perspective. *Expert Systems with Applications*, *41*(10), 4915–4928. [CrossRef]

Dang, T. K., Tran, T. C., Tuan, L. M., & Tiep, M. V. (2021). Machine learning based on resampling approaches and deep reinforcement learning for credit card fraud detection systems. *Applied Sciences*, *11*(21), 10004. [CrossRef]

Dietterich, T. G. (2000). Ensemble methods in machine learning. In G. Goos, J. Hartmanis, & J. Van Leeuwen (Eds.), *Multiple classifier systems* (Vol. 1857, pp. 1–15). Springer. [CrossRef]

Dong, H., Liu, S., & Tran, D. (2025). Enhanced autoencoder model for robust anomaly detection in financial fraud with imbalanced data. In M. Mahmud, M. Doborjeh, K. Wong, A. C. S. Leung, Z. Doborjeh, & M. Tanveer (Eds.), *Neural information processing* (Vol. 2293, pp. 184–198). Springer Nature. [CrossRef]

Du, H., Lv, L., Wang, H., & Guo, A. (2024). A novel method for detecting credit card fraud problems. *PLoS ONE*, *19*(3), e0294537. [CrossRef] [PubMed]

Elgiriyewithana, N. (2023). *Credit card fraud detection dataset 2023* [Dataset]. Kaggle. Available online: https://www.kaggle.com/datasets/nelgiriyewithana/credit-card-fraud-detection-dataset-2023 (accessed on 18 September 2025).

Federal Trade Commission. (2024). *As nationwide fraud losses top $10 billion in 2023, FTC steps up efforts to protect the public*. Available online: https://www.ftc.gov/news-events/news/press-releases/2024/02/nationwide-fraud-losses-top-10-billion-2023-ftc-steps-efforts-protect-public (accessed on 23 August 2025).

Ganji, V. R., & Chaparala, A. (2024). Wave Hedges distance-based feature fusion and hybrid optimization-enabled deep learning for cyber credit card fraud detection. *Knowledge and Information Systems*, *66*(11), 7005–7030. [CrossRef]

Hafez, I. Y., Hafez, A. Y., Saleh, A., Abd El-Mageed, A. A., & Abohany, A. A. (2025). A systematic review of AI-enhanced techniques in credit card fraud detection. *Journal of Big Data*, *12*(1), 6. [CrossRef]

Hajek, P., Abedin, M. Z., & Sivarajah, U. (2023). Fraud detection in mobile payment systems using an XGBoost-based framework. *Information Systems Frontiers*, *25*(5), 1985–2003. [CrossRef]

Harish, S., Lakhanpal, C., & Jafari, A. H. (2024). Leveraging graph-based learning for credit card fraud detection: A comparative study of classical, deep learning and graph-based approaches. *Neural Computing and Applications*, *36*(34), 21873–21883. [CrossRef]

Ileberi, E., & Sun, Y. (2024). Advancing model performance with ADASYN and recurrent feature elimination and cross-validation in machine learning-assisted credit card fraud detection: A comparative analysis. *IEEE Access*, *12*, 133315–133327. [CrossRef]

Ileberi, E., Sun, Y., & Wang, Z. (2021). Performance evaluation of machine learning methods for credit card fraud detection using SMOTE and AdaBoost. *IEEE Access*, *9*, 165286–165294. [CrossRef]

Ileberi, E., Sun, Y., & Wang, Z. (2022). A machine learning based credit card fraud detection using the GA algorithm for feature selection. *Journal of Big Data*, *9*(1), 24. [CrossRef]

Itoo, F., Meenakshi, & Singh, S. (2021). Comparison and analysis of logistic regression, Naïve Bayes and KNN machine learning algorithms for credit card fraud detection. *International Journal of Information Technology*, *13*(4), 1503–1511. [CrossRef]

Jovanovic, D., Antonijevic, M., Stankovic, M., Zivkovic, M., Tanaskovic, M., & Bacanin, N. (2022). Tuning machine learning models using a group search firefly algorithm for credit card fraud detection. *Mathematics*, *10*(13), 2272. [CrossRef]

 https://doi.org/10.3390/jrfm19010014

Khaled Alarfaj, F., & Shahzadı, S. (2025). Enhancing fraud detection in banking with deep learning: Graph neural networks and autoencoders for real-time credit card fraud prevention. *IEEE Access, 13*, 20633–20646. [CrossRef]

Khalid, A. R., Owoh, N., Uthmani, O., Ashawa, M., Osamor, J., & Adejoh, J. (2024). Enhancing credit card fraud detection: An ensemble machine learning approach. *Big Data and Cognitive Computing, 8*(1), 6. [CrossRef]

Kim, E., Lee, J., Shin, H., Yang, H., Cho, S., Nam, S., Song, Y., Yoon, J., & Kim, J. (2019). Champion-challenger analysis for credit card fraud detection: Hybrid ensemble and deep learning. *Expert Systems with Applications, 128*, 214–224. [CrossRef]

Kitchenham, B., & Charters, S. (2007). *Guidelines for performing systematic literature reviews in software engineering* (Version 2.3, EBSE Technical Report No. EBSE-2007-01). Keele University and University of Durham. Available online: https://www.researchgate.net/publication/302924724_Guidelines_for_performing_Systematic_Literature_Reviews_in_Software_Engineering (accessed on 11 August 2025).

Lopez-Rojas, E. (2017a). *Synthetic data from a financial payment system* [Dataset]. Kaggle. Available online: https://www.kaggle.com/datasets/ealaxi/banksim1 (accessed on 18 September 2025).

Lopez-Rojas, E. (2017b). *Synthetic financial datasets for fraud detection* [Dataset]. Kaggle. Available online: https://www.kaggle.com/datasets/ealaxi/paysim1 (accessed on 18 September 2025).

Malik, E. F., Khaw, K. W., Belaton, B., Wong, W. P., & Chew, X. (2022). Credit card fraud detection using a new hybrid machine learning architecture. *Mathematics, 10*(9), 1480. [CrossRef]

Mienye, I. D., & Sun, Y. (2023a). A deep learning ensemble with data resampling for credit card fraud detection. *IEEE Access, 11*, 30628–30638. [CrossRef]

Mienye, I. D., & Sun, Y. (2023b). A machine learning method with hybrid feature selection for improved credit card fraud detection. *Applied Sciences, 13*(12), 7254. [CrossRef]

Moradi, F., Tarif Hokmabadi, M., & Homaei, M. (2025). A systematic review of machine learning in credit card fraud detection. *Preprints*. [CrossRef]

Najadat, H., Altiti, O., Aqouleh, A. A., & Younes, M. (2020, April 7–9). *Credit card fraud detection based on machine and deep learning*. 2020 11th International Conference on Information and Communication Systems (ICICS) (pp. 204–208), Irbid, Jordan. [CrossRef]

Nguyen, T. T., Tahir, H., Abdelrazek, M., & Babar, A. (2020). Deep learning methods for credit card fraud detection. *arXiv*. [CrossRef]

Page, M. J., McKenzie, J. E., Bossuyt, P. M., Boutron, I., Hoffmann, T. C., Mulrow, C. D., Shamseer, L., Tetzlaff, J. M., Akl, E. A., Brennan, S. E., Chou, R., Glanville, J., Grimshaw, J. M., Hróbjartsson, A., Lalu, M. M., Li, T., Loder, E. W., Mayo-Wilson, E., McDonald, S., ... Moher, D. (2021). The PRISMA 2020 statement: An updated guideline for reporting systematic reviews. *BMJ, 372*, n71. [CrossRef]

Reddy, S. S., Amrutha, K., Mnssvkr Gupta, V., Vssr Murthy, K., & Rao, V. V. R. M. (2025). Optimizing hyperparameters for credit card fraud detection with nature-inspired metaheuristic algorithms in machine learning. *Journal of The Institution of Engineers (India): Series B, 106*, 2005–2030. [CrossRef]

Sailusha, R., Gnaneswar, V., Ramesh, R., & Rao, G. R. (2020, May 13–15). *Credit card fraud detection using machine learning*. 2020 4th International Conference on Intelligent Computing and Control Systems (ICICCS), Madurai, India.

Sgantzos, K., Tzavaras, P., Al Hemairy, M., & Porras, E. R. (2025). Triple-entry accounting and other secure methods to preserve user privacy and mitigate financial risks in AI-empowered lifelong education. *Journal of Risk and Financial Management, 18*(4), 176. [CrossRef]

Shenoy, K. (2022). *Credit card transactions fraud detection dataset* [Dataset]. Kaggle. Available online: https://www.kaggle.com/datasets/kartik2112/fraud-detection (accessed on 18 September 2025).

Talukder, M. A., Khalid, M., & Uddin, M. A. (2024). An integrated multistage ensemble machine learning model for fraudulent transaction detection. *Journal of Big Data, 11*(1), 168. [CrossRef]

Tanouz, D., Subramanian, R. R., Eswar, D., Reddy, G. V. P., Kumar, A. R., & Praneeth, C. V. N. M. (2021, May 6–8). *Credit card fraud detection using machine learning*. 2021 5th International Conference on Intelligent Computing and Control Systems (ICICCS) (pp. 967–972), Madurai, India. [CrossRef]

Tayebi, M., & El Kafhali, S. (2025). Combining autoencoders and deep learning for effective fraud detection in credit card transactions. *Operations Research Forum, 6*(1), 8. [CrossRef]

The Treasury. (2024). *Scams prevention framework—Summary of reforms*. Available online: https://treasury.gov.au/sites/default/files/2024-09/c2024-573813-summary.pdf (accessed on 16 October 2025)

ULB Machine Learning Group. (2018). *Credit card fraud detection* [Dataset]. Kaggle. Available online: https://www.kaggle.com/datasets/mlg-ulb/creditcardfraud (accessed on 18 September 2025).

Van Vlasselaer, V., Bravo, C., Caelen, O., Eliassi-Rad, T., Akoglu, L., Snoeck, M., & Baesens, B. (2015). APATE: A novel approach for automated credit card transaction fraud detection using network-based extensions. *Decision Support Systems, 75*, 38–48. [CrossRef]

Vashistha, A., & Tiwari, A. K. (2024). Building resilience in banking against fraud with hyper ensemble machine learning and anomaly detection strategies. *SN Computer Science, 5*(5), 556. [CrossRef]

Wang, Z., Chen, X., Wu, Y., Jiang, L., Lin, S., & Qiu, G. (2025). A robust and interpretable ensemble machine learning model for predicting healthcare insurance fraud. *Scientific Reports, 15*(1), 218. [CrossRef]

 https://doi.org/10.3390/jrfm19010014

Wu, Y., Wang, L., Li, H., & Liu, J. (2025). A deep learning method of credit card fraud detection based on continuous-coupled neural networks. *Mathematics*, *13*(5), 819. [CrossRef]
Yang, Q., Liu, Y., Chen, T., & Tong, Y. (2019). Federated machine learning: Concept and applications. *ACM Transactions on Intelligent Systems and Technology*, *10*(2), 1–19. [CrossRef]
Yu, C., Xu, Y., Cao, J., Zhang, Y., Jin, Y., & Zhu, M. (2024, August 12–14). *Credit card fraud detection using advanced transformer model*. 2024 IEEE International Conference on Metaverse Computing, Networking, and Applications (MetaCom) (pp. 343–350), Hong Kong, China. [CrossRef]
Zeng, Q., Lin, L., Jiang, R., Huang, W., & Lin, D. (2025). NNEnsLeG: A novel approach for e-commerce payment fraud detection using ensemble learning and neural networks. *Information Processing & Management*, *62*(1), 103916. [CrossRef]
Zhang, X., Han, Y., Xu, W., & Wang, Q. (2021). HOBA: A novel feature engineering methodology for credit card fraud detection with a deep learning architecture. *Information Sciences*, *557*, 302–316. [CrossRef]
Zhao, F., Li, G., Lyu, Y., Ma, H., & Zhu, X. (2023). A cost-sensitive ensemble deep forest approach for extremely imbalanced credit fraud detection. *Quantitative Finance*, *23*(10), 1397–1409. [CrossRef]
Zheng, Y.-J., Zhou, X.-H., Sheng, W.-G., Xue, Y., & Chen, S.-Y. (2018). Generative adversarial network based telecom fraud detection at the receiving bank. *Neural Networks*, *102*, 78–86. [CrossRef]
Zhou, Z.-H., & Feng, J. (2019). Deep forest. *National Science Review*, *6*(1), 74–86. [CrossRef]
Ziovis, G., Kolomvatsos, K., & Stamoulis, G. (2024). An intelligent sequential fraud detection model based on deep learning. *The Journal of Supercomputing*, *80*(10), 14824–14847. [CrossRef]

 https://doi.org/10.3390/jrfm19010014

Journal of
Risk and Financial Management

MDPI

Article

Accuracy Comparison Between Feedforward Neural Network, Support Vector Machine and Boosting Ensembles for Financial Risk Evaluation

Dat Tran and Allan W. Tham *

Faculty of Science and Technology, University of Canberra, Canberra 2617, Australia; dat.tran@canberra.edu.au
* Correspondence: allan.tham@canberra.edu.au

Abstract: Loan defaults have become an increasing concern for lending institutions, presenting significant challenges to profitability and operational stability. However, with the advent of advanced data processing capabilities, greater data availability, and the development of sophisticated machine learning techniques—particularly neural networks—new opportunities have emerged for classifying and predicting loan defaults beyond traditional manual methods. This, in turn, can reduce risk and enhance overall financial performance. In recent years, institutions have increasingly employed these advanced techniques to mitigate the risk of non-performing loans (NPLs) by improving loan approval efficiency. This study aims to address a gap in the literature by examining the predictive performance of different neural network architectures on financial loan datasets. Specifically, it compares the effectiveness of Feedforward Neural Networks (FNNs), Long Short-Term Memory (LSTM) networks, and one-dimensional Convolutional Neural Networks (1D-CNNs) in forecasting loan defaults. Despite the growing body of research in this area, comparative studies focusing on the application of various neural network techniques to loan default prediction remain relatively scarce.

Keywords: financial data analysis; machine learning algorithms; loan default assessment; classification; neural network

1. Introduction

Many factors can directly or indirectly influence the rate of loan defaults. Croux et al. (2020) emphasized the importance of various contractual loan features, borrower characteristics, and macroeconomic variables—such as loan maturity, ownership status, loan purpose, and occupational background—in determining the likelihood of default. They advocated for greater transparency, enhanced risk assessment practices, and the use of alternative data sources to improve the prediction of default rates. Researchers such as Lai (2020) and Wang and Perkins (2019) have highlighted the transformative potential of machine learning in credit analysis, arguing that the combination of advanced algorithms and vast datasets enables lending institutions to build more robust and accurate models for identifying potential defaulters. Wang and Perkins (2019) highlighted additional factors, such as borrowers' local economic conditions (e.g., unemployment rates), which can significantly influence the realized outcome of a loan.

While much research has focused on the importance of accurate credit risk prediction to improve the financial performance of lending institutions, another crucial area of inquiry is the advancement of predictive algorithms. Historically, researchers have relied on parametric approaches such as regression, logistic regression, and linear discriminant analysis for financial modelling (Beaver, 1966; Altman, 1968; Black & Scholes, 1973). Among these, Logit Regression (LR) and Multivariate Discriminant Analysis (MDA) were the most commonly used statistical models. However, these models depend heavily on assumptions that are often violated due to the complex and non-linear nature of financial data. Acknowledging these limitations, researchers across disciplines, including in financial risk, have increasingly turned to more flexible, data-driven approaches.

The 1990s marked a pivotal shift away from traditional parametric methods. During this period, advanced techniques such as Feedforward Neural Networks (also known as Multi-Layer Perceptrons or MLPs) began to be rigorously compared to conventional models. Due to their simplicity and promising early results, MLPs gained traction, leading to further advancements in neural network architectures. Today, variants such as MLPs, Recurrent Neural Networks (RNNs), and Convolutional Neural Networks (CNNs) have become mainstream, particularly in applications that require modelling non-linear relationships between variables. In fields, such as life sciences, finance, transportation, and energy, the demand for predictive modelling, such as housing price forecasts, has shifted away from traditional methods toward machine learning techniques, especially neural networks.

In the existing literature, comparisons between traditional models (both parametric and non-parametric) and single neural network architectures are common. However, comprehensive studies comparing multiple neural network architectures applied to loan default prediction remain limited.

This research contributes to the literature in the following key ways:

- Comparative Evaluation of Model Performance:
- We assess the influence of data characteristics (e.g., sparse vs. dense, temporal vs. non-temporal) on the performance of various algorithms, including Support Vector Machines (SVMs), Gradient Boosting, XGBoost, LightGBM, and several neural network models. The neural network architectures examined include Feedforward Neural Networks (FNNs/MLP), Long Short-Term Memory (LSTM), and 1D Convolutional Neural Networks (1D-CNNs).
- Assessment of Architecture Suitability:
- We explore the suitability of each neural network architecture based on data characteristics, aiming to generalize their effectiveness in different contexts. For example, we compare the performance of 1D-CNNs and FNNs on smaller datasets containing categorical features, evaluating their capacity to learn from varying data structures.
- Analysis of Data Preprocessing Techniques:
- We investigate the effects of data scaling using various pipelines and hyperparameter optimization. Additionally, we assess the impact of the Synthetic Minority Oversampling Technique (SMOTE) when applied to imbalanced datasets.

This study is arranged in the following way:

- Section 2: Literature Review
  This section reviews foundational studies from the 1960s to early 2000s, focusing on traditional methods such as regression, logistic regression, and discriminant analysis. It also highlights early applications of MLPs and other machine learning models, including SVM, k-Nearest Neighbours (KNNs), Gradient Boosting, XGBoost, and LightGBM.
- Section 3: Methodology
  We outline the methodology used to compare the seven algorithms in predicting loan defaults, using two publicly available datasets (German Credit and Taiwan Credit) from the University of California at Irvine (UCI). This section introduces the analytics

lifecycle methodology, selection of packages, preprocessing techniques (scaling, encoding, dimensionality reduction), imbalance handling strategies (e.g., SMOTE), and model tuning processes. To ensure rigor, this study prioritizes reproducibility and methodological validity.

- Section 4: Results and Evaluation
  This section presents performance metrics, such as accuracy, AUC-ROC, precision, recall, and F1 score. Results are discussed across three permutations:
  - With/without SMOTE, using default hyperparameters and the full feature set.
  - With/without SMOTE, using optimized hyperparameters and the full feature set.
  - With/without SMOTE, using optimized hyperparameters and a reduced feature set (top predictors).

2. Related Work

Prior to the widespread adoption of Neural Networks in loan default prediction, most studies employed traditional parametric methods. One of the earliest efforts in this domain was Altman's (1968) seminal "Z-Score" model, which pioneered multivariate financial distress prediction. Beaver (1966) introduced a univariate approach, and both Altman and Beaver extended this to multivariate modelling in 1968. Drawing from these foundations, subsequent studies—such as those by Blum (1974), Deakin (1972), and Edmister (1972)—used discriminant analysis to test the predictive power of financial ratios in assessing small business failures.

However, discriminant analysis has notable limitations, particularly its reliance on restrictive assumptions: (1) independent variables must follow a normal distribution, and (2) the variance–covariance matrices of the two groups must be equal. Recognizing these shortcomings, Karels and Prakash (1987), Martin (1977), and Ohlson (1980) questioned the efficacy of discriminant analysis for datasets that deviate from these assumptions, especially financial data, which are often non-linear and non-normal. As a response, studies such as Martin (1977) and Ohlson (1980) proposed logistic regression (LR) as a more flexible alternative. While LR addressed some of the challenges of Multivariate Discriminant Analysis (MDA), it was still constrained by the requirement of monotonic relationships between variables. Thus, despite the popularity of LDA/MDA, their application remained limited by statistical assumptions like Gaussian normality, linearity, and homoscedasticity.

Although Altman's foundational work in LDA and MDA laid the groundwork for corporate failure prediction, their adoption in practice remained limited. Seeking less restrictive alternatives, Altman et al. (1994) conducted one of the first comparative studies between LDA and Neural Networks. Around the same time, empirical studies by Lacher et al. (1995), Sharda and Wilson (1996), and Tam and Kiang (1990) demonstrated that Neural Networks outperformed LDA and MDA. For instance, Fletcher and Goss (1993) reported that Neural Networks achieved an accuracy of 91.7%, compared to 85.4% for LDA. Salchenberger et al. (1992) and Zhang et al. (1999) also highlighted the superior performance of Multi-Layer Perceptrons (MLPs), showing that MLPs reached 88.2% accuracy versus 78.6% for LDA. Tam and Kiang (1990), using a backpropagation algorithm, showed that MLPs outperformed MDA, LDA, and K-Nearest Neighbours (KNN).

However, not all studies universally favoured Neural Networks. For example, Jo et al. (1997) compared Neural Networks, MDA, and Case-Based Reasoning (CBR), finding that Neural Networks achieved 83.79% accuracy, marginally higher than MDA (82.22%) and CBR (81.52%). Other researchers, including Boritz et al. (1995) and Altman et al. (1994), also reported mixed results. The latter examined 1000 Italian industrial firms but did not find consistent evidence supporting the superiority of Neural Networks.

Several other researchers, including White (1989), Cheng and Titterington (1994), Sarle (1994), and Ripley (1994), explored the theoretical connections between Neural Networks and traditional methods. They recognized links between perceptrons and regression, discriminant analysis, and cluster analysis. Ripley (1994), in particular, acknowledged the potential of Neural Networks for classification tasks, while also highlighting challenges such as parameter estimation and classifier evaluation. Researchers, like Bell et al. (1990), Hart (1992), Yoon et al. (1993), Curram and Mingers (1994), and Wilson and Sharda (1994), further contributed by comparing the classification performance of Neural Networks with traditional statistical models, paving the way for broader adoption.

In more recent years, an increasing number of studies have applied Neural Networks to loan default prediction. Zhao et al. (2008), for example, compared Support Vector Machines (SVMs), Naïve Bayes, and Random Forest (RF) to 1D Convolutional Neural Networks (1D-CNNs) using performance metrics such as accuracy (ACC) and the area under the ROC curve (AUC). Their study on personal loan data demonstrated that 1D-CNN could autonomously learn and extract relevant features without predefined mathematical relationships, outperforming traditional models due to its feature learning capabilities.

Liu and Feng (2024) further extended this research by comparing 1D-CNN with six baseline models (SVM, KNN, LR, RF, AdaBoost, and XGBoost), incorporating a detailed data preprocessing pipeline. This included standardization, SMOTE for class imbalance, Recursive Feature Elimination (RFE), Information Value (IV), and Principal Component Analysis (PCA). Their model achieved 99.57% accuracy and an AUC of 0.9998, surpassing XGBoost (98.02% accuracy, 0.9980 AUC).

Ciampi and Gordini (2013) applied Neural Networks to a dataset of 7000 Italian small enterprises and found that Neural Networks outperformed both MDA and LR in evaluating credit risk. Notably, performance improved when models were segmented by firm size, geographic region, and business sector. Neural Networks were particularly effective at detecting weak signals indicative of credit deterioration—signals that traditional models often missed due to their reliance on parametric assumptions.

Dutta et al. (2021) proposed a hybrid CNN-Gated Recurrent Unit (GRU) model and compared it with MLP, KNN, and Decision Trees (DTs). To mitigate overfitting, they employed dropout layers and the Adam optimizer. Their hybrid model achieved 89.59% accuracy, outperforming all baseline models.

Serengil et al. (2021) evaluated the performance of various models—SVM, LightGBM, XGBoost, RF, bagging classifiers, and LSTM—on a private Turkish banking dataset. Using metrics, such as precision, recall, F1 score, Imbalanced Accuracy Metric (IAM), and specificity, they found LightGBM to be the best performer. LSTM followed closely due to its strength in capturing temporal dependencies.

Li et al. (2018) combined LSTM and SVM to predict defaults using both dynamic (user browsing behaviour) and static (demographics, billing) information. Their hybrid model achieved 99% accuracy, outperforming standalone models, such as Naïve Bayes (79%), KNN, and Deep Neural Networks (DNNs), all of which reached 90%.

Gao et al. (2021) proposed a novel approach by feeding LSTM outputs into XGBoost. This method reduced the need for manual feature engineering, achieving AUC and accuracy scores of 0.954 and 0.937, respectively, compared to 0.895 and 0.873 for XGBoost alone.

Jiang (2022) compared six models, including Ordered Logit (OL), Neural Networks, SVM, Bagged Decision Trees (BDTs), RF, and Gradient-Boosted Machines (GBMs), to demonstrate the suitability of machine learning for empirical credit rating tasks. Similarly, Dong et al. (2024) conducted a comparative analysis of popular machine learning algorithms applied to financial datasets, although their study notably excluded Neural Network models.

3. Case Study—Advanced Machine Learning for Financial Risk Mitigation

3.1. Methodology—Computational Approach

This research adopts a quantitative approach with an experimental design. While numerous deep learning frameworks exist—such as Microsoft Cognitive Toolkit (CNTK), Theano (developed by the University of Montreal), and Google's TensorFlow and Keras—each differs in terms of implementation, execution, and performance. For the purposes of this study, TensorFlow and Keras are selected due to their maturity, active development, and widespread adoption within the deep learning community. By leveraging these leading frameworks, this study ensures the validity and repeatability of controlled experiments, encompassing all major stages: data preparation, model training, and performance evaluation.

TensorFlow, developed by the Google Brain team, employs a flexible dataflow-based programming model. As noted by Abadi et al. (2016), this approach offers several advantages, including modularity and an extensive library of pre-built operations, which facilitate rapid prototyping and scalable deployment. One of its most compelling strengths is its ability to execute computational graphs across a wide range of hardware platforms—from mobile devices to large-scale GPU clusters—without requiring significant modifications to the code. This scalability is particularly beneficial given the high computational demands of Deep Neural Networks. TensorFlow enables efficient parallelism and distributed processing, making it suitable for large-scale model training.

Keras, also developed under the Google umbrella, serves as a high-level Neural Network API that simplifies deep learning development while preserving the robustness of the TensorFlow backend. According to Al-Bdour et al. (2019), Keras's modular and extensible design allows for fast experimentation and prototyping, making it an ideal choice for researchers and practitioners alike. Its user-friendly interface supports rapid model building and testing, reducing the overhead typically associated with deep learning pipeline development.

The research methodology will adhere to the analytics lifecycle framework.

Step 1	**Step 2**	**Step 3**	**Step 4**	**Step 5**
Research Objectives	Data Understanding	Data Pre-Processing	Model Building & Analysis	Model Validation & Conclusion
Target Research questions	Identify data availability	Data Cleansing	Model methodology	Model evaluation & Analysis
Appropriateness of algorithms	Determine initial data requirements	Determine initial data requirements	Feature selection	Model risk interpretation
Appropriateness of data sets	Explore data characteristics	Imbalance treatment	Model construction	Model insights and limitations
		Data leakage detection	Model Scoring	Summary & recommendations
		Encoding & transformation	Model Assessment	
		Dimensional reduction	Model Comparison	

Rigorous data preparation is a critical component of this study. Prior to model development, several preprocessing steps will be implemented, including the treatment of class imbalance, mitigation of data leakage, normalization, and encoding. As noted by Zhao et al. (2008) in their work within the sensor field, the primary challenge of data preparation lies in identifying and extracting the most relevant information for a given analytical task. They also emphasize the importance of data transformation techniques, such as scaling, which help tailor the data for optimal performance with specific learning systems. Thus, understanding the unique requirements of Neural Networks enables a more targeted and effective data preparation process.

Beyond improving model accuracy, data preprocessing plays a vital role in ensuring the fairness and robustness of machine learning models. Tae et al. (2019) and Whang et al. (2023) both argue that data quality, rather than algorithm design, is often the root cause of bias and unreliability in predictive models. Whang et al. (2023) further advocate that data preparation should receive equal, if not greater, attention to algorithm development. Echoing this perspective, Roh et al. (2019) introduced a paradigm shift that refocuses efforts on data quality through the use of intelligent metrics and transformative operations. In line with their recommendations, this study adopts a data-centric approach aimed at maximizing data integrity before training, testing, and scoring the Neural Network models.

To address the issue of imbalanced datasets—common in loan default prediction—the Synthetic Minority Oversampling Technique (SMOTE) will be employed. Since its introduction in 2002, SMOTE has become the de facto standard for handling class imbalance. It works by interpolating new minority class examples between existing ones, thus improving the classifier's generalization ability. As highlighted by García et al. (2016), SMOTE is among the most influential data preprocessing algorithms in machine learning due to its effectiveness and ease of implementation.

Given that Neural Networks are sensitive to high-dimensional input data, dimensionality reduction will be applied to enhance computational efficiency and minimize overfitting. This is particularly relevant when working with small datasets, where a large number of input features can lead to data sparsity. To address this, this study uses Principal Component Analysis (PCA), which identifies uncorrelated components (principal components) that capture the most variance in the data. Hasan and Abdulazeez (2021) demonstrated that PCA enhances model interpretability while preserving essential information, making it a valuable tool in pre-modelling stages.

The following Neural Network architectures will be evaluated in this study:

- Feedforward Neural Networks (FNNs)
  FNNs represent the most basic form of neural networks, in which data flow unidirectionally, from input nodes through one or more hidden layers to output nodes. These networks do not contain cycles or feedback connections, making them computationally efficient and easy to implement. In an FNN, the input layer accepts features from the dataset, the hidden layers perform intermediate computations using activation functions, and the output layer generates final predictions. Despite their simplicity, FNNs may underperform in tasks where feedback or sequential dependencies are crucial.
- Recurrent Neural Networks (RNNs) and Long Short-Term Memory (LSTM)
  For sequential data, such as time series, this study employs RNNs with an LSTM architecture. LSTM networks are specifically designed to capture long-term dependencies while mitigating the vanishing gradient problem. The many-to-one configuration—where multiple input time steps yield a single output—is used here, appropriate for time-ordered loan data. Since the dataset contains multiple sequences (e.g., multiple customers), a three-dimensional input structure is adopted, unlike the two-dimensional input typically used for non-temporal data. Each data point is modeled as a single time step, and the output reflects the probability of loan default.
- Convolutional Neural Networks (CNNs)

Although CNNs are traditionally used in image and video processing, recent studies have shown their effectiveness in time-series tasks due to their ability to extract local patterns using convolutional filters. CNNs can identify trends, seasonality, and anomalies in sequential data, making them a promising tool for loan default prediction. As noted by Wibawa et al. (2022), CNNs can outperform RNNs in some scenarios due to their parallel execution capabilities and ability to model both local and global dependencies by stacking multiple convolutional layers. In multivariate time-series analysis, each variable (channel) can be treated as a separate input layer, thereby enabling more structured pattern recognition. This study will incorporate 1D-CNNs to explore their performance in modeling temporal dependencies in loan default data.

3.2. Data Collection

This study utilizes two credit card client datasets obtained from the UCI Machine Learning Repository. The first dataset, known as the Taiwan Credit Card Default dataset, was provided by Yeh and Lien (2009) and Yeh (2016). It contains data from a major bank in Taiwan for the year 2005. The dataset comprises 30,000 observations, of which 6636 instances (22.12%) represent clients who defaulted on their payments (indicated by the target variable ID_x24 = 1), while the remaining 23,364 instances (77.88%) correspond to non-default cases.

Importantly, the dataset is free of duplicate and missing values, making it well suited for supervised learning applications. However, the class distribution is significantly imbalanced, with a skewed ratio of healthy to default cases (approximately 78:22), which may affect model performance if not properly addressed. The target variable used for classification is ID_x24, while the predictor variables span features X1 to X23, as summarized in Table 1.

Table 1. Dataset 1: Taiwan credit card client dataset features and types.

Total Missing Values	Taiwan Credit Data Set Features		
	Feature ID/Name	**Description**	**Numeric/Nominal/Ordinal**
0	x1 (limit_bal)	Amount of the given credit (NT dollar): includes both the individual consumer credit and his/her family (supplementary) credit	Numeric
0	x2 (sex)	Gender (1 = male, 2 = female).	Numeric
0	x3 (education)	Education (1 = graduate school, 2 = university, 3 = high school, 4 = others)	Numeric
0	x4 (marriage)	Marital status (1 = married, 2 = single, 3 = others)	Numeric
0	x5 (age)	Age (year)	Numeric
0	x6–x11 (pay_1 to pay_6)	History of past payment. We tracked the past monthly payment records (from April to September 2005) as follows: X6 = the repayment status in September 2005, X7 = the repayment status in August 2005, X11 = the repayment status in April 2005. The measurement scale for the repayment status is: −1 = pay duly, 1 = payment delay for one month, 2 = payment delay for two months, 8 = payment delay for eight months, 9 = payment delay for nine months and above.	Numeric
0	x12–x17 (bill_amt1 to bill_amt6)	Amount of bill statement (NT dollar). X12 = amount of bill statement in September 2005, X13 = amount of bill statement in August 2005, X17 = amount of bill statement in April 2005	Numeric
0	x18–x23 (pay_amt1 to pay_amt6)	Amount of previous payment (NT dollar). X18 = amount paid in September 2005, X19 = amount paid in August 2005, X23 = amount paid in April 2005	Numeric
0	x24 (default_payment_next_ month)	Default or not (default = 1, health = 0)	Numeric

The first dataset consists exclusively of numerical features and serves as a control group within the analytics pipeline due to its larger sample size. It plays a key role in validating the end-to-end pipeline—including data transformation, class imbalance handling, feature reduction/selection, and model fitting. Given its similar class imbalance ratio to the second dataset, the first dataset also serves a secondary purpose: assessing the predictive performance and generalization capability of Neural Network models in a large-scale data setting.

The second dataset, known as the German Credit Card Client dataset, was obtained from the UCI Machine Learning Repository (Hofmann, 1994). It contains 1,000 observations, with a target variable indicating credit risk in a binary format. The class distribution is imbalanced, with 70% classified as "no default" and 30% as "default." Like the first dataset, it contains no missing or duplicate values, making it suitable for modelling. Table 2 provides an overview of the dataset's features, including descriptions and data types.

Table 2. Dataset 2: German Credit Card Client dataset features and types.

Total Missing Values	German Credit Data Set Features		
	Feature	**Description**	**Numeric/Nominal/Ordinal**
0	checking_balance	Status of existing checking account	Ordinal
0	months_loan_duration	Duration in months	Numeric
0	credit_history	Credit history	Ordinal
0	purpose	Purpose of loan	Nominal
0	amount	Credit amount	Numeric
0	savings_balance	Saving accounts/bonds	Ordinal
0	employment_duration	Present employment since	Ordinal
0	percent_of_income	Install rate (% of disposable income)	Numeric
0	years_at_residence	Present residence since	Numeric
0	age	Age in years	Numeric
0	other_credit	Other installment plans	Nominal
0	housing	Housing Situation	Nominal
0	existing_loans_count	Number of existing credits	Numeric
0	job	Job skill level	Ordinal
0	dependents	Number of dependents	Numeric
0	phone	Holding Telephone or not	Nominal
0	default	Default or not	Nominal

Since this dataset contains both numerical and categorical features, the data preprocessing pipeline includes one-hot encoding for categorical variables. Additionally, the target variable, originally labelled as "yes" and "no", requires label encoding to convert it into a binary numerical format suitable for classification tasks. Both the encoding of categorical features and the transformation of the target variable are performed prior to model training and classifier fitting, ensuring that the dataset is fully prepared for subsequent machine learning procedures.

3.3. Visual Data Exploration

Before initiating the data preprocessing stage, a critical component of the methodology involves validating the soundness of the dataset to ensure reliable model training and fitting. In particular, visual exploration of the German Credit dataset plays an essential role in uncovering its underlying structure and characteristics. This includes examining feature correlations, data distributions (linear or non-linear), the presence of multicollinearity, and detecting any anomalies or outliers that may distort the analysis or degrade model performance.

Such exploratory data analysis (EDA) is especially important when applying complex classifiers, like Support Vector Machines (SVMs), Gradient Boosting, XGBoost, LightGBM, and various Neural Network architectures. A robust understanding of the data's intrinsic patterns and relationships enhances the effectiveness and interpretability of these models. Table 3 presents the correlation matrix for the dataset's numerical features, highlighting potential multicollinearity and interdependencies among predictors.

Table 3. Correlation between numerical features—German Credit dataset.

	Correction Matrix						
	F1	**F2**	**F3**	**F4**	**F5**	**F6**	**F7**
F1	1.0000	0.6250	0.0747	0.0341	−0.0361	−0.0113	−0.0238
F2	0.6250	1.0000	−0.2713	0.0289	0.0327	0.0208	0.0171
F3	0.0747	−0.2713	1.0000	0.0493	0.0583	0.0217	−0.0712
F4	0.0341	0.0289	0.0493	1.0000	0.2664	0.0896	0.0426
F5	−0.0361	0.0327	0.0583	0.2664	1.0000	0.1493	0.1182
F6	−0.0113	0.0208	0.0217	0.0896	0.1493	1.0000	0.1097
F7	−0.0238	0.0171	−0.0712	0.0426	0.1182	0.1097	1.0000

Note: Dataset Feature Labels: F1—months_loan_duration, F2—amount, F3—percent_of_income, F4—years_at_residence, F5—age, F6—existing_loans_count, F7—dependents.

As shown in Table 3, the German Credit dataset exhibits low correlation among most features. The highest observed correlation is 0.6250, found between "months loan duration" and "amount", suggesting a moderately positive linear relationship. In contrast, other features such as "age" and "percent of income" show minimal correlation, with values of –0.0361 and 0.0747, respectively. These low coefficients indicate an absence of linear relationships between most feature pairs.

This observation is further supported by the scatterplots in Figure 1, which reveal a lack of visible patterns or trends among the majority of feature combinations. While the "months loan duration" and "amount" pair displays a clear upward trend, neither "age" nor "percent of income" demonstrates a discernible relationship with "months loan duration." This suggests that, apart from the primary correlated pair, the dataset is largely composed of independent or weakly related features, which may influence model selection and feature engineering strategies.

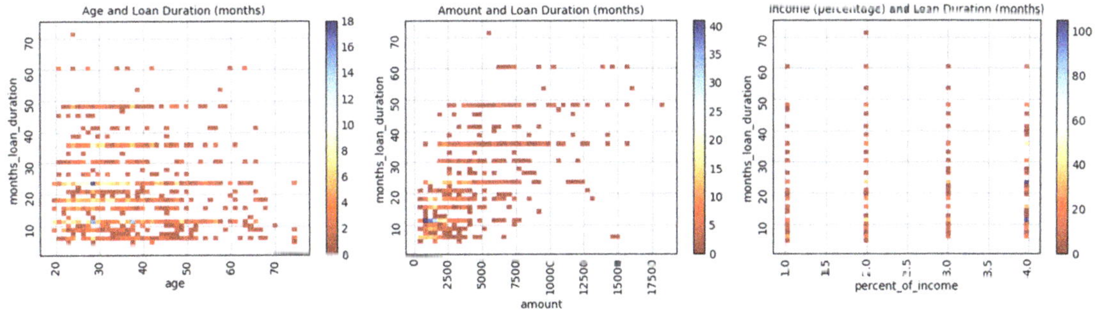

Figure 1. Scatterplots for selected numeric features.

A deeper analysis of multicollinearity within the German Credit dataset (as shown in Table 4) reveals that the Variance Inflation Factor (VIF) values for all predictors fall well within acceptable thresholds, indicating that multicollinearity is not a concern and does not pose a risk to model reliability.

Table 4. VIF—German Credit dataset.

Feature	VIF
months_loan_duration	7.3588
amount	4.5758
percent_of_income	7.9587
years_at_residence	7.7354
age	10.9257
existing_loans_count	6.6793
dependents	8.7906

The distribution of data can be considered partially normal or normal (right skewed) for only three predictors, as seen in Figure 2. The remaining numerical predictors are dichotomous in nature.

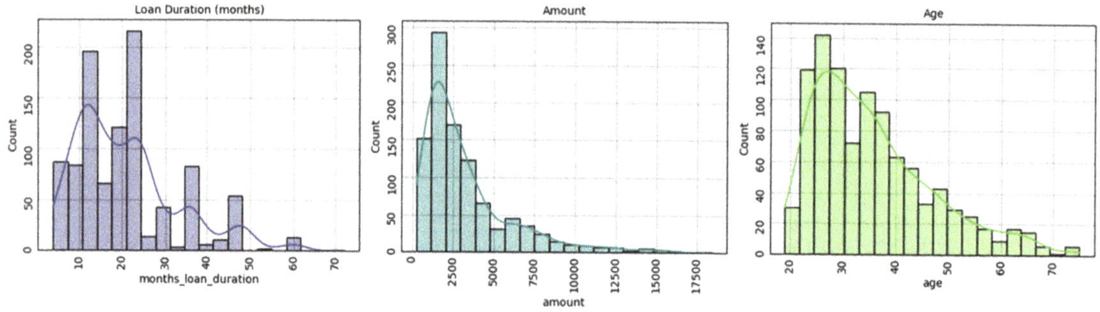

Figure 2. Data distributions—German Credit dataset.

Although boosting algorithms are generally more robust to outliers, models such as Support Vector Machines (SVMs) and Feedforward Neural Networks (FNNs) are more sensitive to extreme values. Therefore, it is imperative to minimize the impact of outliers to maintain model stability and ensure reliable performance. In this study, preliminary diagnostic tests confirm that the German Credit dataset contains no missing values or significant outliers, thereby reducing the need for additional corrective measures during preprocessing.

3.4. Data Preprocessing

In the data preprocessing phase, the primary objective is to prepare the datasets in a way that enables models to leverage the underlying data structure effectively. This involves initial checks for outliers and missing values. Since both the German and Taiwan datasets are free from missing values, imputation techniques were excluded from the preprocessing pipelines.

To streamline and modularize data transformation, Scikit-learn's ColumnTransformer is employed as the core functionality within the pipelines. The transformation process begins with scaling, including both standardization and normalization. This step is critical, particularly for models such as Support Vector Machines (SVMs) and Feedforward Neural Networks (FNNs), which are highly sensitive to feature scaling. In contrast, tree-based boosting algorithms—such as Gradient Boosting, XGBoost, and LightGBM—are generally more robust to unevenly scaled features. However, Gradient Boosting is more susceptible to the effects of unscaled features than XGBoost and LightGBM, which possess built-in mechanisms to mitigate scaling issues.

For instance, in Gradient Boosting, features with larger scales may dominate gradient updates, potentially skewing the model by overemphasizing these variables while neglecting more predictive but smaller-scale features. Furthermore, such large-scale features often produce greater reductions in the loss function, making them preferred candidates for tree splits. This imbalance can disrupt the regularization mechanism and slow down convergence.

Additionally, encoding categorical variables is an essential preprocessing step, particularly for the German Credit dataset, which includes a mix of numerical and categorical data. While LightGBM can automatically handle categorical features internally, all other models require explicit one-hot encoding to ensure categorical variables are properly utilized. The transformation process is followed by imbalanced data treatment using the SMOTE algorithm, as recommended by Alam et al. (2020), to address class distribution issues and enhance classification performance.

Subsequently, the pipeline performs dimensionality reduction—either using system defaults or a predefined number of features—to reduce model complexity and computational cost. In total, seven distinct permutations are constructed, each with its own corresponding pipeline. These pipelines maintain a consistent train–test split of 70:30, using stratified sampling to preserve the class distribution in both sets.

Each pipeline is designed to handle both numerical and categorical features, applying scaling and encoding as necessary. Only pipelines configured for dimensionality reduction include this additional step. Finally, all pipelines encompass the full machine learning workflow, including training, scoring, and performance evaluation, forming a complete end-to-end analytics process.

3.5. Model Construction and Evaluation

A total of seven algorithms are employed in the training and model-fitting stages of the analytics pipeline. These classifiers—Support Vector Machine (SVM), Gradient Boosting, XGBoost, LightGBM, Feedforward Neural Network (FNN), Long Short-Term Memory (LSTM), and 1D Convolutional Neural Network (1D-CNN)—are selected based on their unique characteristics and suitability for the given classification problem.

- Support Vector Machine (SVM)
  SVM is a distance-based algorithm known for its effectiveness in handling classification problems and its inherent robustness to overfitting, particularly in high-dimensional spaces. SVM can operate with different kernel functions: the linear kernel, which assumes a parametric linear relationship between input features and the target, and the Radial Basis Function (RBF) kernel, which captures non-linear boundaries. The decision boundary is formed by identifying a hyperplane that maximizes the margin between classes. However, SVM is sensitive to outliers with both linear and RBF kernels, as extreme values can shift the decision boundary. The two most critical hyperparameters for tuning SVM performance are the regularization parameter (C) and the kernel parameter (γ). Of these, C plays a key role in balancing model complexity and generalization. A low value of C allows for a wider margin but may increase classification errors, while a high value of C seeks to classify all training examples correctly, potentially leading to overfitting.
- Boosting-Based Algorithms
  Three tree-based boosting methods are incorporated: traditional Gradient Boosting, as well as its modern, optimized counterparts, XGBoost and LightGBM.
  - Gradient Boosting serves as a baseline model, building weak learners sequentially to minimize the overall loss.

- XGBoost improves upon traditional Gradient Boosting by offering regularization, parallelization, and handling of missing values, which enhances speed and accuracy.
- LightGBM further optimizes performance through leaf-wise tree growth, and it natively supports categorical features, one-hot encoding, and efficient training on large, sparse datasets.

Unlike models such as SVM and FNN, boosting methods do not require features to be scaled or normally distributed. They are also relatively robust to outliers. Key hyperparameters to tune for these models include learning rate, number of estimators (trees), and maximum tree depth, which collectively influence training speed and prediction accuracy.

- Feedforward Neural Network (FNN)

  FNN is a parametric model composed of layers of interconnected nodes, where the primary learnable parameters are weights and biases. Training involves the forward pass, where inputs are transformed through hidden layers using activation functions (typically ReLU), and the output layer produces classification probabilities. The loss function (e.g., Cross-Entropy for classification) quantifies prediction error, which is minimized through backpropagation and optimization algorithms like Stochastic Gradient Descent (SGD) or Adam.

  FNNs are most effective when trained on large datasets, as their predictive performance can deteriorate in low-data environments. Tuning FNN performance involves optimizing several hyperparameters:

  - Number of hidden layers and neurons per layer;
  - Learning rate;
  - Choice of optimizer (e.g., SGD vs. Adam);
  - Regularization techniques (e.g., dropout, L2);
  - Batch size and number of epochs.

  For instance, an excessively high learning rate may cause the model to overshoot the optimal weights, while a very low rate may result in slow convergence or getting stuck in local minima. The Adam optimizer often improves convergence speed and performance by dynamically adjusting the learning rate for each parameter.

The Feedforward Neural Network (FNN) used in this study is implemented using the tf.keras.Sequential API from TensorFlow, with the following architectural and training specifications:

- Input Layer: Configured to match the number of input features in the dataset.
- Hidden Layers: A single dense (fully connected) layer with 64 units, followed by:
  - Batch Normalization to stabilize and accelerate training.
  - ReLU activation function to introduce non-linearity.
  - Dropout (rate = 0.5) to prevent overfitting, combined with L2 regularization ($\lambda = 0.001$) to penalize large weights.
- Output Layer: A dense layer with a sigmoid activation function, suitable for binary classification tasks.
- Optimizer: Stochastic Gradient Descent (SGD) with a learning rate of 0.001 and momentum of 0.9, promoting smoother convergence and mitigating oscillations.
- Loss Function: Binary Cross-Entropy, commonly used in binary classification to quantify the difference between predicted and actual labels.
- Evaluation Metric: Accuracy, which measures the proportion of correct predictions during training and evaluation.
- Training Configuration: The model is trained for 50 epochs using a batch size of 16.

- Validation Strategy: A 20% validation split is applied to the training data to monitor generalization performance and detect overfitting during training.

Table 5 summarizes the key characteristics of the various classifiers implemented in this study.

Table 5. High-level characteristics of classifiers.

Classifier	Type	Dependence (H/L) and Tolerance (H/L) for Various Characteristics								
		Features/Capabilities								
		F1	F2	F3	F4	F5	F6	F7	F8	F9
support vector (svm)	P–DB	Y	N	Y	N	H	Y	N	H	M
gradient boosting (gbm)	NP–TB	N	N	N	N	H	N	N	M	M
xgboost (xgb)	NP–TB	N	N	N	Y	L	N	Y	M	M
lightgbm (lgm)	NP–TB	N	Y	N	Y	L	N	Y	M	M
feedforward (ff)	P–NB	N	N	Y	N	H	Y	N	H	H

Note: L—low, H—high, M—Medium. P—parametric, NP—non-parametric. DB—distance-based, TB—tree-based, NB—neural-base. F1—linearity assumption, F2—automatic categorical encoding, F3—scaling required, F4—automatic missing data handling, F5—outliers' sensitivity, F6—affected by multicollinearity, F7—automatic regularization, F8—affected by imbalanced class, F9—affected by small data size.

In this study, the primary evaluation metric is the Area Under the Receiver Operating Characteristic Curve (AUC-ROC). AUC-ROC is widely used to evaluate classification models as it reflects the model's ability to rank predictions by analyzing the trade-off between the True-Positive Rate (Recall) and the False-Positive Rate (1: specificity). Unlike accuracy, AUC does not directly measure misclassification errors; instead, it assesses how well the model discriminates between classes across various threshold settings.

However, while AUC is a popular metric, it is not without limitations. As discussed by Lobo et al. (2008), AUC can be insensitive to class imbalance, potentially yielding high values even when a model performs poorly on the minority class. This can be misleading in highly imbalanced datasets, where AUC may fail to reflect the model's actual precision or recall. Furthermore, AUC does not account for the cost of different types of errors and may be inappropriate for scenarios where specific decision thresholds or business rules are important. AUC is especially less informative when comparing models that prioritize precision over recall, or vice versa.

To complement AUC, this study includes additional performance metrics to offer a more comprehensive evaluation of model effectiveness. As noted by Han et al. (2022), relying solely on error rate—a common practice in earlier works such as Jain et al. (2000) and Nelson et al. (2003)—can be misleading, especially in the context of imbalanced datasets. This is particularly relevant to the Taiwan Credit Card dataset, which is skewed, with 77.88% of observations labelled as "non-risky" and only 22.12% as "risky."

To address this, the following four metrics are also employed (see Table 6) to provide a multi-dimensional assessment of model performance:

- Accuracy: Measures the proportion of total correct predictions relative to all predictions.
- Precision: Assesses the proportion of true-positive predictions among all instances predicted as positive.
- Recall (Sensitivity): Measures the proportion of actual positive cases that are correctly identified by the model.
- F1 Score: Represents the harmonic mean of precision and recall, offering a balanced measure that is particularly valuable for imbalanced classification tasks.
- Together, these metrics ensure a robust evaluation framework that goes beyond AUC alone, accounting for the complexities of imbalanced data and diverse classification objectives.

Table 6. Performance measurements.

Evaluation Metrics	Formula
Accuracy Score	$\frac{TP + TN}{TP + FN + TN + FP}$
Precision Score	$\frac{TP}{TP + FP}$
Recall Score (Sensitivity)	$\frac{TP}{TP + FN}$
F1 Score	$\frac{2 * (Precision * Recall)}{(Precision + Recall)}$

Note: N—sample size, TP—true positive, FN—false negative, TN—true negative, FP—false positive.

Table 6 depicts the performance metrics used throughout the model comparisons. All the scores used in this study are based on prediction results.

4. Results

The experimental results are presented in both tabular and graphical formats, supplemented by variable importance visualizations. These results compare the performance of two distinct datasets—the German Credit and Taiwan Credit Card datasets—across three variations of analytics pipelines. Due to the stochastic nature of several classifiers (particularly Neural Networks), slight variations in results were observed across different runs.

Included in the analysis are feature importance rankings generated from various algorithms, providing insight into the most influential predictors. The ROC-AUC curves illustrate model discrimination performance, where the grey dotted line represents the baseline of random guessing.

This study employs three pipeline variations, each designed to evaluate classifier performance under different preprocessing and optimization scenarios. These include the following:

- Permutation-1: With or without SMOTE; uses default hyperparameters and evaluates performance based on the full feature set.
- Permutation-2: With or without SMOTE; uses optimized hyperparameters with the full feature set.
- Permutation-3: With or without SMOTE; uses optimized hyperparameters with a reduced feature set, consisting of top-performing predictors.

Each pipeline includes the following preprocessing steps: data scaling, categorical encoding, and SMOTE treatment for class imbalance.

The results of these permutations are summarized as follows:

- Table 7 and Figure 3: Permutation-1 applied to the German Credit dataset, using default hyperparameters and all features.
- Table 8, Figures 4 and 6: Permutation-2 applied to the German Credit dataset, using optimized hyperparameters and all features.
- Table 9, Figures 5 and 7: Permutation-3 applied to the German Credit dataset, using optimized hyperparameters and reduced features.
- Table 10, Figures 14 and 15: Permutation-2 applied to the Taiwan Credit dataset, using optimized hyperparameters and all features.
- Figures 8 and 9: Comparative results of Permutations 2 and 3 for the German Credit dataset, highlighting the impact of full versus reduced feature sets.
- Figures 10 and 11: Permutation-1 for Feedforward Neural Networks on the German Credit dataset, distinguishing models by the presence or absence of SMOTE treatment.

- Figures 12 and 13: Permutation-1 with optimized hyperparameters for Feedforward models, again differentiated by SMOTE application.
- Figures 16 and 17: Application of Permutation-1 using LSTM and 1D CNN architectures on the German Credit dataset, using the full feature set.

Table 7. German Credit Card dataset—Permutation-1.

	Default Hyperparameters									
	Full Features (without SMOTE)					Full Features (with SMOTE)				
	M1	M2	M3	M4	M5	M1	M2	M3	M4	M5
svc	0.7367	0.6279	0.3000	0.4060	0.7678	0.7233	0.5333	0.6222	0.5744	0.7685
gbm	0.7233	0.5479	0.4444	0.4908	0.7534	0.7267	0.5444	0.5444	0.5444	0.7553
xgb	0.7133	0.5286	0.4111	0.4625	0.7370	0.7167	0.5316	0.4667	0.4970	0.7357
lgb	0.7433	0.5867	0.4889	0.5333	0.7711	0.7000	0.5000	0.4222	0.4578	0.7452
ff	0.7267	0.5488	0.5000	0.5233	0.7719	0.7400	0.5625	0.6000	0.5806	0.7839

Note: M1—accuracy score, M2—precision score, M3—recall score, M4—F1 score, M5—AUC.

Table 8. German Credit Card dataset—Permutation-2.

	Best Hyperparameters									
	Full Features (without SMOTE)					Full Features (with SMOTE)				
	M1	M2	M3	M4	M5	M1	M2	M3	M4	M5
svc	0.8567	0.8730	0.6111	0.7190	0.9179	0.8633	0.7333	0.8556	0.7897	0.9138
gbm	0.8967	0.9041	0.7333	0.8098	0.9553	0.8600	0.7791	0.7444	0.7614	0.9331
xgb	0.9767	0.9882	0.9333	0.9600	0.9970	0.9933	1.0000	0.9778	0.9888	0.9999
lgb	0.9867	1.0000	0.9556	0.9773	0.9993	0.9800	0.9773	0.9556	0.9663	0.9956
ff	0.7300	0.5882	0.3333	0.4255	0.6167	0.7033	0.5053	0.5333	0.5189	0.6548

Note: M1—accuracy score, M2—precision score, M3—recall score, M4—F1 score, M5—AUC.

Table 9. German Credit Card dataset—Permutation-3.

	Best Hyperparameters									
	Reduced Features (without SMOTE)					Reduced Features (with SMOTE)				
	M1	M2	M3	M4	M5	M1	M2	M3	M4	M5
svc	0.7000	0.0000	0.0000	0.0000	0.5614	0.6000	0.4138	0.8000	0.5455	0.7094
gbm	0.9700	1.0000	0.9000	0.9474	0.9985	1.0000	1.0000	1.0000	1.0000	1.0000
xgb	0.9150	0.9574	0.7500	0.8411	0.9898	0.9900	0.9833	0.9833	0.9833	0.9998
lgb	0.9700	1.0000	0.9000	0.9474	0.9994	0.9400	0.8750	0.9333	0.9032	0.9874
ff	0.7300	0.5882	0.3333	0.4255	0.6167	0.7100	0.5146	0.5889	0.5492	0.6754

Note: M1—accuracy score, M2—precision score, M3—recall score, M4—F1 score, M5—AUC.

Table 10. Taiwan Credit Card dataset—Permutation-1.

	Default Hyperparameters									
	Full Features (without SMOTE)					Full Features (with SMOTE)				
	M1	M2	M3	M4	M5	M1	M2	M3	M4	M5
svc	0.8175	0.6929	0.3142	0.4324	0.7078	0.7802	0.5029	0.5606	0.5302	0.7568
gbm	0.8206	0.6780	0.3599	0.4703	0.7825	0.7978	0.5478	0.4922	0.5185	0.7684
xgb	0.8136	0.6374	0.3650	0.4642	0.7622	0.8017	0.5704	0.4198	0.4836	0.7497
lgb	0.8208	0.6760	0.3650	0.4740	0.7794	0.8105	0.6036	0.4173	0.4935	0.7714
ff	0.8192	0.7050	0.3147	0.4352	0.7660	0.8131	0.6068	0.4414	0.5111	0.7571

Note: M1—accuracy score, M2—precision score, M3—recall score, M4—F1 score, M5—AUC.

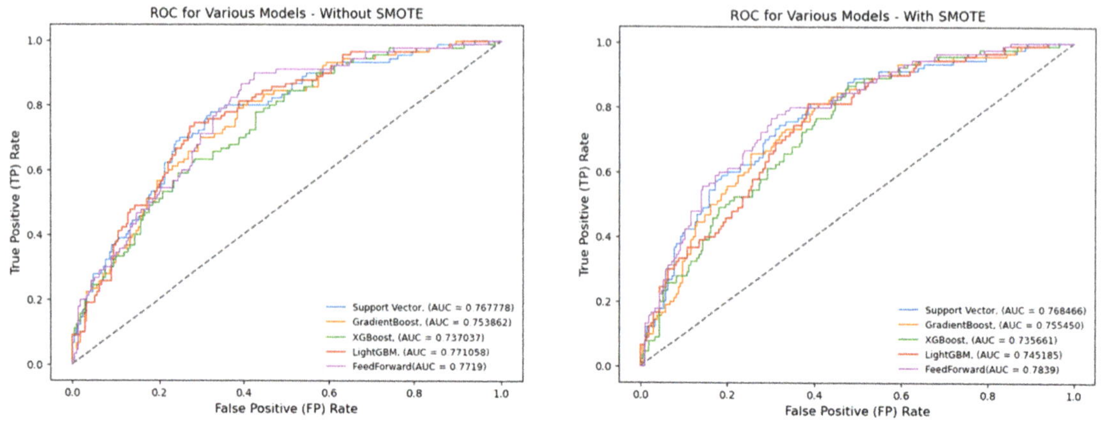

Figure 3. ROC for default hyperparameters (full features)—German Credit dataset (Permutation-1).

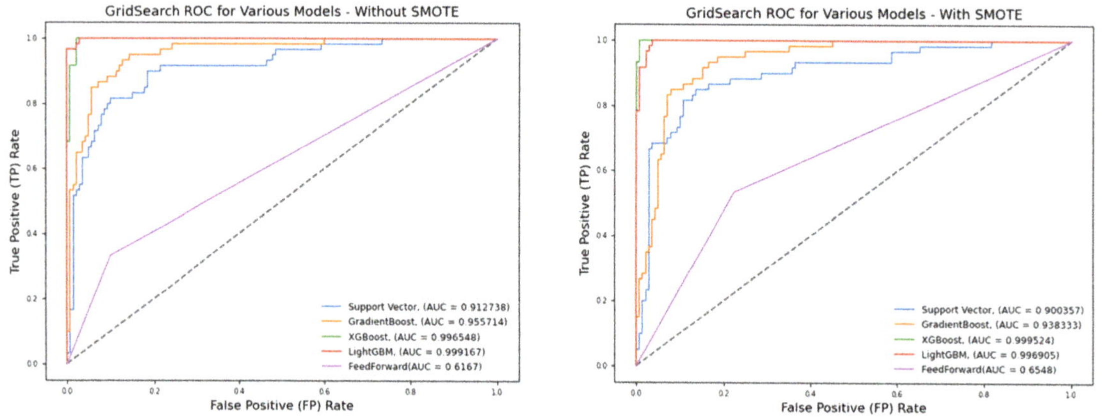

Figure 4. ROC for best hyperparameters (full features)—German Credit dataset (Permutation-2).

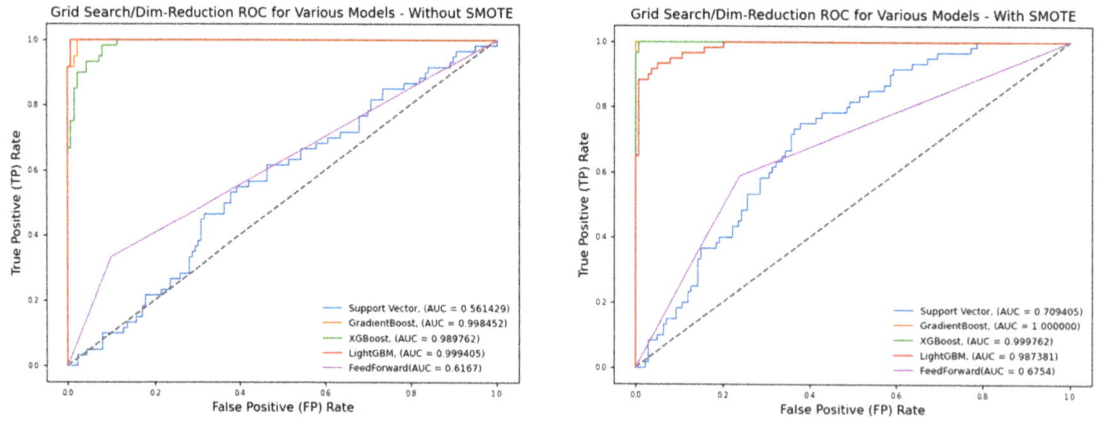

Figure 5. ROC for best hyperparameters (reduced features)—German Credit dataset (Permutation-3).

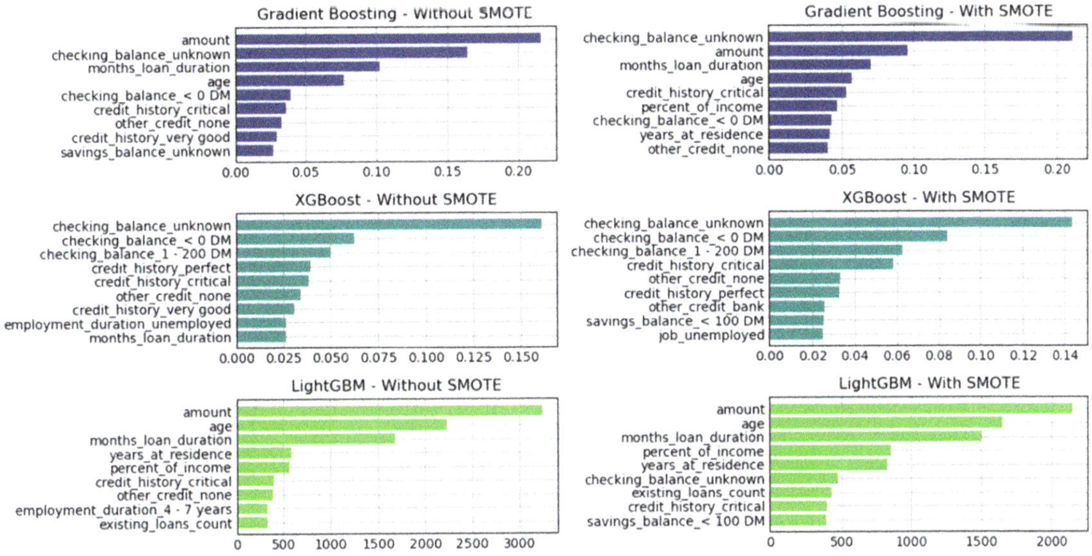

Figure 6. Variable of importance for best hyperparameters (full features)—German Credit dataset (Permutation-2).

This structured approach allows for the systematic comparison of model performance under varying preprocessing conditions, classifier configurations, and dataset characteristics.

The optimal hyperparameters for each classifier, identified through grid search with and without SMOTE, are summarized as follows:

- Support Vector Machine (SVM):
  {'C': 1, 'gamma': 0.1, 'kernel': 'poly'}
- Gradient Boosting:
  {'learning_rate': 0.1, 'max_depth': 5, 'n_estimators': 100}
- XGBoost:
  {'colsample_bytree': 0.6, 'learning_rate': 0.05, 'max_depth': 7, 'n_estimators': 100, 'subsample': 1.0}
- LightGBM:
  {'learning_rate': 0.01, 'max_depth': 10, 'n_estimators': 500, 'num_leaves': 31}
- Feedforward Neural Network (FNN):
  {'dropout_rate': 0.2, 'learning_rate': 0.001, 'momentum': 0.9}

Each of the three pipeline permutations is accompanied by graphical depictions of performance metrics across all classifiers. Additionally, Permutations-2 and -3 include feature importance analyses, identifying the most significant predictors for Decision Tree-based models such as Gradient Boosting, XGBoost, and LightGBM. The remaining classifiers, including SVM and FNN, produced comparable performance, though without native feature importance mechanisms.

As shown in Figures 7 and 8, the three tree-based algorithms consistently highlight the same key predictive features across all permutations—whether using default hyperparameters, grid-searched hyperparameters, or reduced feature sets. Specifically, the features "amount", "checking_balance", "credit_history", and "saving_balance" repeatedly emerge as the top contributors to model performance.

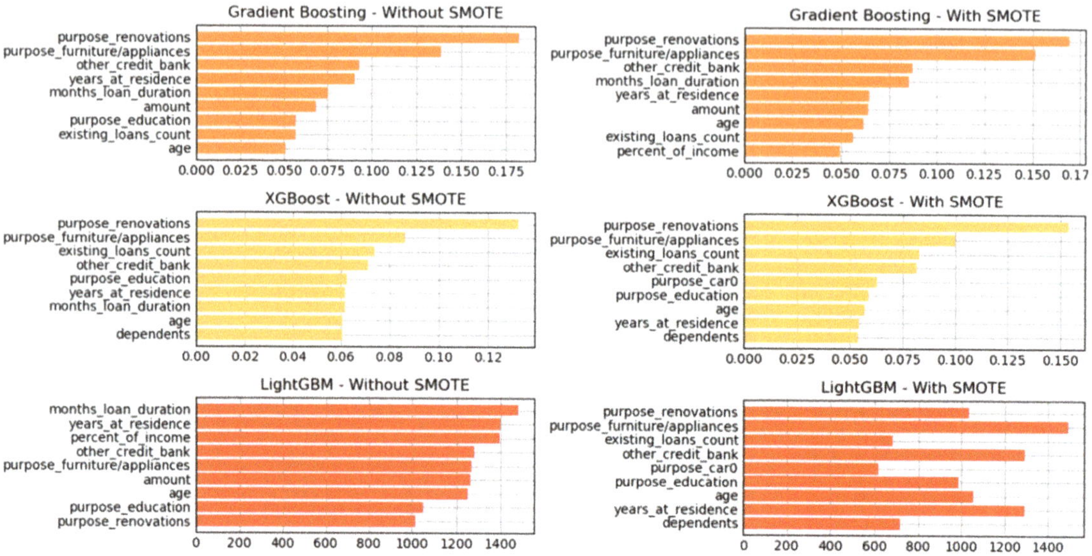

Figure 7. Variable of importance for best hyperparameters (reduced features)—German Credit dataset (Permutation-3).

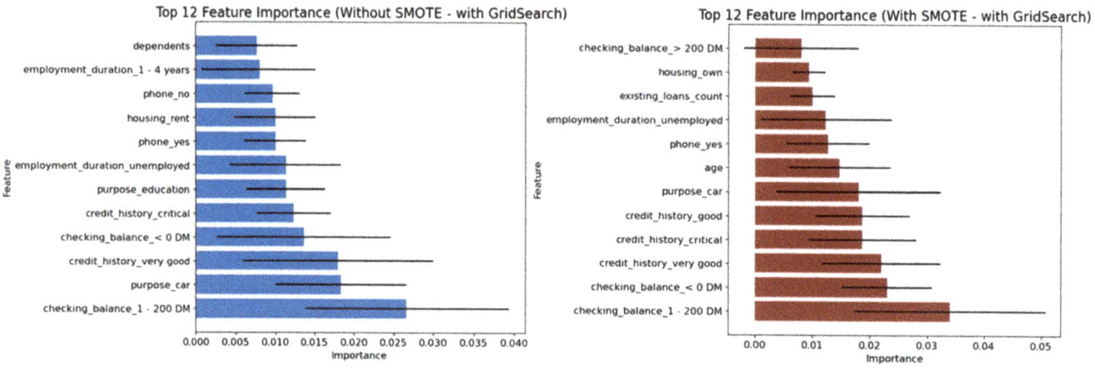

Figure 8. Variable of importance for best hyperparameters (full features)—German Credit dataset (Permutation-2) with Feedforward Neural Network.

Similarly, Figures 9 and 10 illustrate the Feedforward Neural Network's variable importance, derived from permutation runs using both default and optimized hyperparameters. These results also reinforce the central role of "checking_balance" and "credit_history" as the two most influential features, mirroring the findings from the tree-based classifiers.

Figure 11, which presents the results of Permutation-1 without SMOTE, displays the Cross-Entropy loss curve for the feedforward model using the full feature set and default hyperparameters. The loss pattern suggests potential overfitting and a lack of convergence, indicating that the model may have struggled to generalize to unseen data. This behaviour is likely attributed to the class imbalance, which can hinder the model's ability to learn meaningful patterns, especially in underrepresented classes.

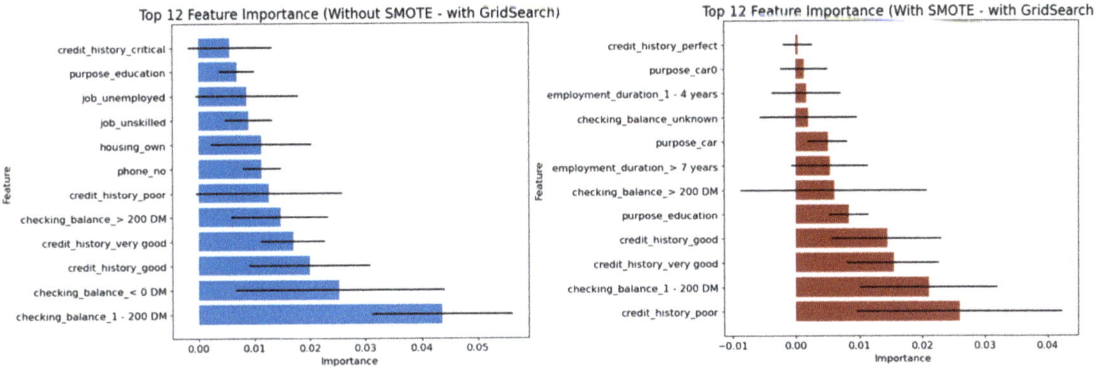

Figure 9. Variable of importance for best hyperparameters (reduced features)—German Credit dataset (Permutation-3) with Feedforward Neural Network.

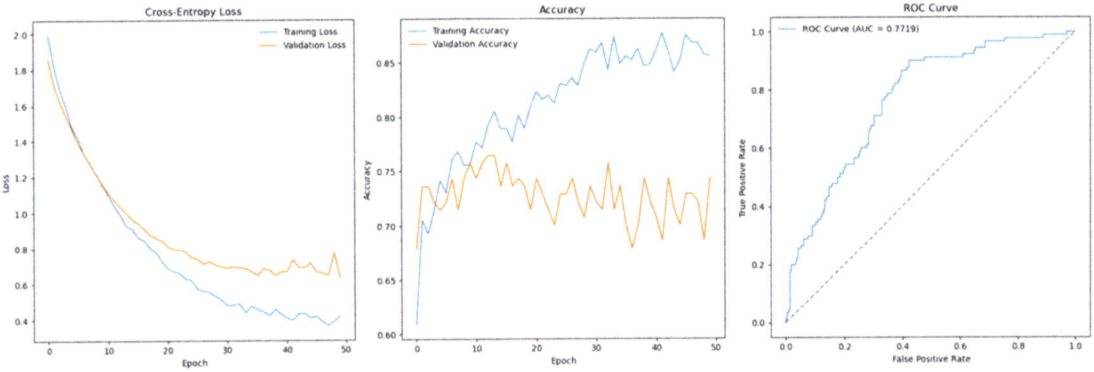

Figure 10. Cross-Entropy (full features without SMOTE)—German Credit dataset (Permutation-1) with Feedforward Neural Network.

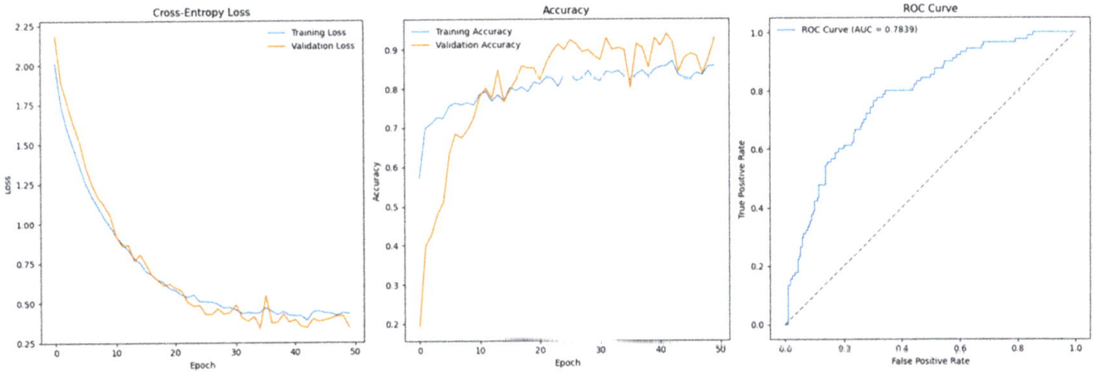

Figure 11. Cross-Entropy (full features with SMOTE)—German Credit dataset (Permutation-1) with Feedforward Neural Network.

In contrast, Figure 12 shows the same feedforward model under Permutation-1 with SMOTE applied during preprocessing. The model demonstrates convergence and a stable decrease in Cross-Entropy loss, reflecting improved generalization and reduced overfitting. This highlights the effectiveness of SMOTE in addressing class imbalance, thereby enhancing the model's learning stability and predictive performance.

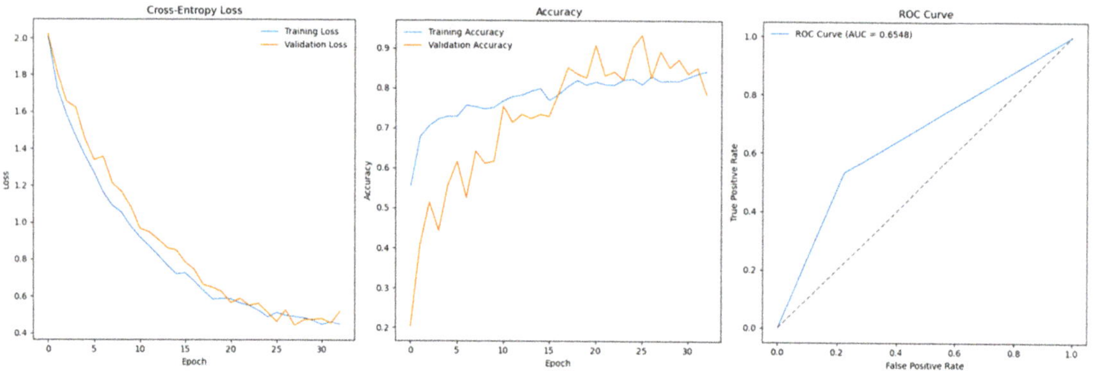

Figure 12. Cross-Entropy (GridSearch full features without SMOTE)—German Credit dataset (Permutation-2) with Feedforward Neural Network.

Figure 13, corresponding to Permutation-2 without SMOTE, illustrates the Cross-Entropy loss curve for the Feedforward Neural Network using the full feature set and grid-searched hyperparameters. The loss curve shows clear signs of convergence, and the accuracy plot indicates that validation accuracy closely tracks training accuracy throughout the training process. This alignment suggests that the model is generalizing well to unseen data, and the risk of overfitting is significantly reduced.

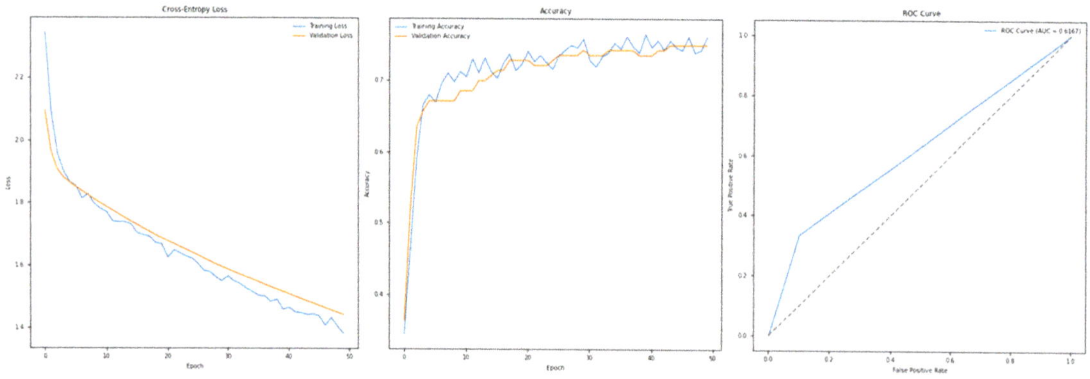

Figure 13. Cross-Entropy (GridSearch full features with SMOTE)—German Credit dataset (Permutation-2) with Feedforward Neural Network.

Similarly, Figure 14, which represents the same model configuration but with SMOTE applied, also demonstrates convergence and stable learning behaviour. The inclusion of SMOTE further enhances the model's ability to generalize by addressing class imbalance. As with Figure 13, the model trained with SMOTE achieves strong generalization performance and avoids overfitting, reinforcing the importance of both hyperparameter optimization and class imbalance treatment in Neural Network training.

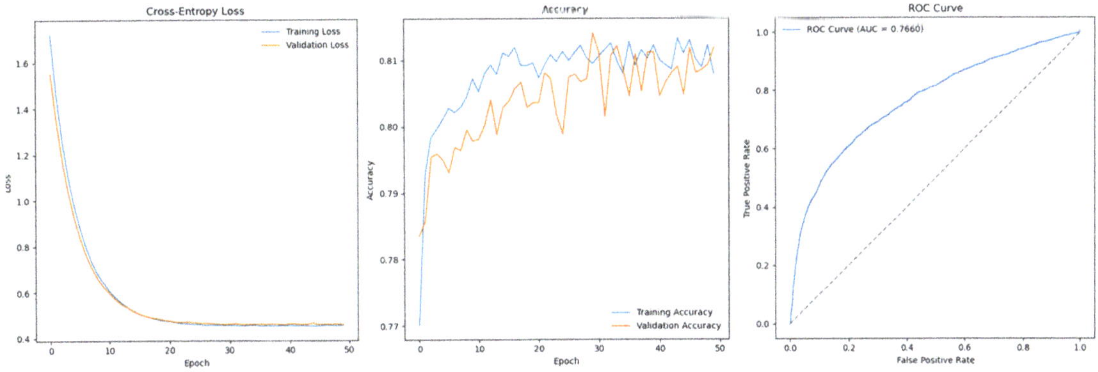

Figure 14. Cross-Entropy (default hyperparameters, full features without SMOTE)—Taiwan Credit dataset (Permutation-1) with Feedforward Neural Network.

Finally, this study incorporates a control dataset from a Taiwanese credit card client, comprising 30,000 observations, which is significantly larger than the German Credit dataset. To maintain consistency and ensure comparability, the same Permutation-1 analytics pipeline, including all data transformation steps, is applied to this control dataset prior to model training. The Feedforward Neural Network architecture and configuration used here mirror those applied to the German dataset.

Table 10 presents the performance results. As expected, the larger dataset size enhances the predictive performance of the feedforward model, demonstrating improved accuracy and generalization. However, this improvement comes at the cost of increased training time, which is notably higher for the larger dataset.

Regarding classifier performance, Support Vector Machine, Gradient Boosting, XGBoost, and LightGBM all exhibit strong training and generalization capabilities using default hyperparameters, as reflected in Table 10. For the Feedforward Neural Network, Figure 15 shows a smooth convergence of the model trained with default hyperparameters, indicating good generalization.

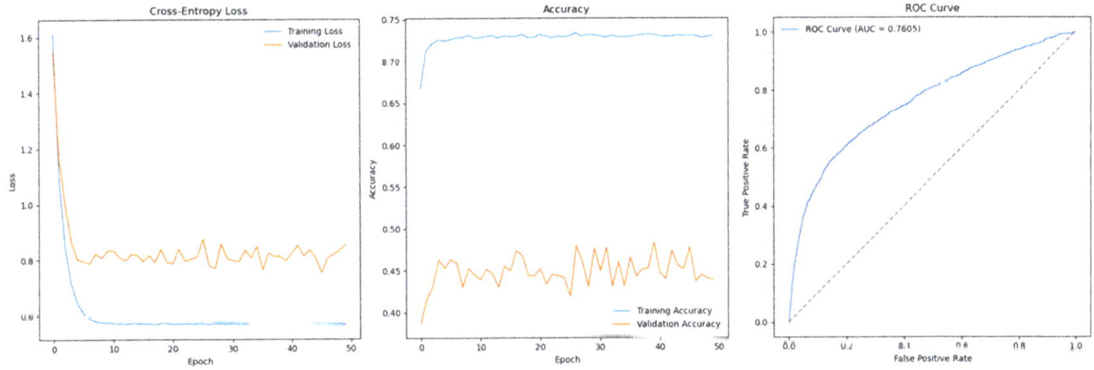

Figure 15. Cross-Entropy (default hyperparameters, full features with SMOTE)—Taiwan Credit dataset (Permutation-1) with Feedforward Neural Network.

Interestingly, when SMOTE is applied to address class imbalance, the feedforward model exhibits non-convergent behaviour, as shown in Figure 16. Contrary to expectations, the model trained with SMOTE generalizes poorly, highlighting a counterintuitive result. This suggests that while SMOTE is generally beneficial in imbalanced scenarios, its effectiveness may vary depending on dataset characteristics, model architecture, and hyperparameter configurations.

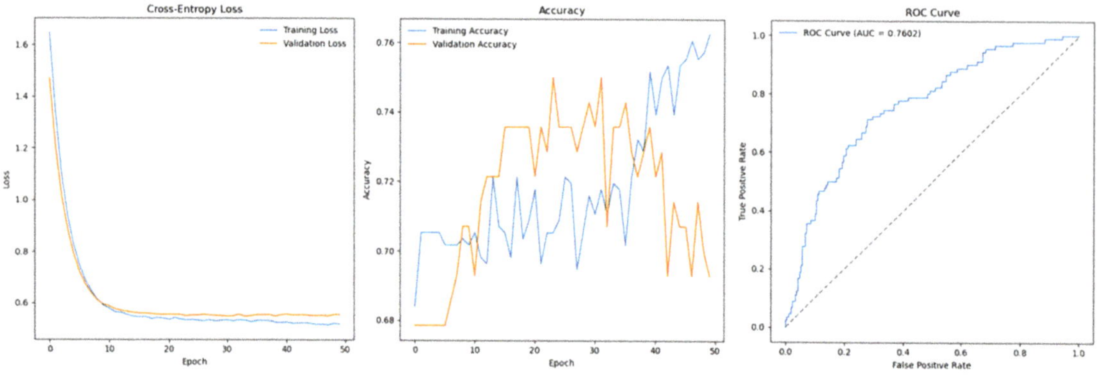

Figure 16. Cross-Entropy (default hyperparameters, full features with SMOTE)—German Credit dataset (Permutation-1) with LSTM.

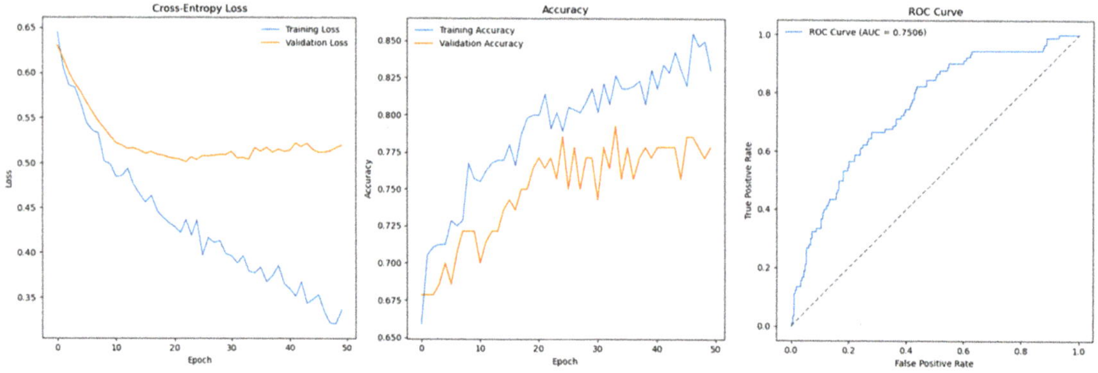

Figure 17. Cross-Entropy (default hyperparameters, full features with SMOTE)—German Credit dataset (Permutation-1) with 1D-CNN.

The final two configurations tested in this study are based on Long Short-Term Memory (LSTM) networks and 1D Convolutional Neural Networks (1D-CNNs). Given that both the German Credit and Taiwan Credit datasets are tabular in nature, only the German dataset is used for illustration purposes in this context.

- LSTM Configuration
  The LSTM model is designed to handle sequential input data and includes the following components:
  - Data Transformation: The dataset is reshaped to ensure that the number of features is divisible by the number of time steps, allowing for the proper formation of 3D input tensors required by LSTM models.
  - LSTM Layer: The first layer consists of 64 units (neurons) with return_sequences = True, which outputs a sequence of hidden states across all time steps, maintaining the 3D tensor structure. L2 regularization is applied with a value of 0.01 to penalize large weights and reduce the risk of overfitting.
  - Dropout Layer: A dropout rate of 0.3 is used to randomly deactivate 30% of the neurons during training, further mitigating overfitting.

    - Output Layer: A sigmoid activation function is used to produce a binary classification output, indicating the likelihood of default.
- 1D-CNN Configuration
  The 1D Convolutional Neural Network is structured to process tabular data treated as 1D sequences and consists of the following layers:
    - First Convolutional Layer: Contains 64 filters with a kernel size of 3, using ReLU activation. This layer extracts 64 local features (feature maps) from the input.
    - Max Pooling Layer: Uses a pool size of 2 to reduce the length of each feature map by half, thereby lowering dimensionality and retaining dominant features. This also helps reduce overfitting.
    - Dropout Layer: A dropout rate of 0.3 is applied following the pooling layer to randomly deactivate 30% of the neurons during training.
    - Second Convolutional Layer: Comprises 32 filters to extract deeper, more abstract patterns from the previously pooled feature maps.
    - Global Average Pooling: This layer reduces each feature map to a single scalar value by averaging its values, reducing the output to a fixed-size vector and minimizing overfitting risk.
    - Second Dropout Layer: An additional dropout rate of 0.2 is applied to further regularize the model by deactivating 20% of the neurons before final classification.

A comparative analysis of model performance between Table 7 (Permutation-1) and Table 8 (Permutation-2) clearly demonstrates that, with or without SMOTE treatment, pipelines consistently perform better when grid-searched hyperparameters are applied. For instance, under default hyperparameter settings, classifiers, such as Support Vector Machine, Gradient Boosting, XGBoost, and LightGBM, achieve accuracy scores ranging from 0.7133 to 0.7367 without SMOTE. With SMOTE treatment, these values decrease slightly to between 0.7000 and 0.7267. In terms of AUC, models without SMOTE range from 0.7370 to 0.7719, whereas SMOTE-treated models show marginal improvements, with AUCs between 0.7357 and 0.7685.

Interestingly, while the Feedforward Neural Network (FNN) performs comparably to other models under Permutation-1, Table 8 highlights a more significant performance gap when grid-searched hyperparameters are used. Under Permutation-2, the AUC scores for all models (excluding FNN) improve markedly, ranging from 0.8567 to 0.9867 without SMOTE and from 0.7033 to 0.9933 with SMOTE. A similar trend is observed in reduced feature scenarios, where AUC ranges from 0.9179 to 0.9993 (without SMOTE) and 0.9138 to 0.9999 (with SMOTE).

However, this performance improvement does not extend to the FNN, where SMOTE application results in deteriorating performance, with AUC dropping from 0.7300 to 0.6548. This outcome is counterintuitive, as all other algorithms either maintain or improve performance when SMOTE is applied.

Across all three permutations, it is evident that SMOTE fails to enhance FNN performance. Neither hyperparameter tuning nor dimensionality reduction improves its ability to generalize on imbalanced data. In Permutation-3, although Support Vector Machine shows some degradation in performance under reduced features, Gradient Boosting, XGBoost, and LightGBM maintain their robustness and strong predictive capacity.

Similar findings are reflected in the control dataset (Taiwan Credit), which has a larger number of observations. Table 10 shows that under Permutation-1 with default hyperparameters, all classifiers, including FNN, achieve comparable performance. Accuracy for models without SMOTE ranges from 0.8136 to 0.8208, while SMOTE-treated models range from 0.7802 to 0.8131. AUC values range from 0.7078 to 0.7825 (without SMOTE) and 0.7497 to 0.7714 (with SMOTE). Of note, the Support Vector Machine performs slightly worse with SMOTE, suggesting that not all algorithms benefit uniformly from synthetic oversampling.

The feedforward network, however, demonstrates a distinct behaviour. As seen in Figure 15, the model converges well under default hyperparameters without SMOTE—training and validation loss curves are closely aligned by epoch 10, indicating good generalization. In contrast, Figure 16 shows failure to converge when SMOTE is applied, with Cross-Entropy loss increasing and poor generalization emerging.

The model configuration for FNN includes the following:

- Input layer matching the number of features;
- Dense hidden layer with 64 neurons (initialized using He Uniform);
- ReLU activation, Batch Normalization, and dropout (rate = 0.5);
- Sigmoid activation in the output layer;
- L2 regularization ($\lambda = 0.01$);
- Training with SGD optimizer, momentum = 0.9, learning rate = 0.001, and 5-fold stratified cross-validation to preserve class balance.

Despite testing multiple hyperparameter combinations, FNN continues to exhibit overfitting when trained on SMOTE-augmented data. The issue arises because SMOTE-generated synthetic samples may not adequately represent the true distribution of the minority class, leading the model to overfit on synthetic patterns rather than learning generalizable features. With the minority class comprising only 20% of the dataset, SMOTE overcompensates, inflating the minority class and exacerbating the overfitting problem.

In the case of the LSTM model, applying this architecture to non-temporal tabular data introduces several limitations. LSTM networks are specifically designed to capture temporal dependencies, which are absent in tabular datasets like the German Credit data. Reshaping features into sequences to mimic time steps leads the LSTM to artificially learn dependencies between unrelated features, resulting in poor generalization or unnecessary model complexity. In such scenarios, non-sequential models like SVM, tree-based algorithms, or FNNs are more suitable.

Similarly, the 1D-CNN model assumes that neighbouring features exhibit meaningful sequential patterns—a condition often met in domains like signal or image processing but not in standard tabular data. Without natural feature ordering or sequential relationships, convolutional filters in 1D-CNNs fail to extract meaningful patterns, potentially learning artificial correlations that reduce performance. As a result, 1D-CNNs perform suboptimally when applied to tabular data lacking temporal or structured spatial characteristics.

5. Discussion

The following points summarize the main observations and provide possible explanations for the performance of the models evaluated in this study:

- Support Vector Machine (SVM) demonstrates consistent performance across most experimental configurations. However, a slight drop in accuracy is observed when SMOTE is applied to the larger Taiwan dataset. This may be attributed to the linear interpolation mechanism of SMOTE, which can generate synthetic minority class samples that overlap with the majority class, especially in high-dimensional spaces. As a distance-based model, SVM is sensitive to boundary distortions, and non-representative synthetic samples may compromise the decision margin, leading to degraded performance.
- The three tree-based ensemble algorithms—Gradient Boosting, XGBoost, and LightGBM—deliver the most consistent and superior performance overall. All experimental results confirm their robustness in binary classification tasks for tabular

data. These algorithms outperform both SVM and Feedforward Neural Networks across several dimensions:
  - Imbalance Handling: Even when the minority class is underrepresented, tree-based ensembles perform well, with or without SMOTE.
  - Improved Accuracy: As ensemble methods, they reduce bias and variance by aggregating multiple base learners.
  - Generalization Capability: Overfitting is less evident in these models, as validation on unseen data consistently yields high accuracy.
  - Model Stability: Tree-based ensembles are resilient to outliers and noise, as they "average out" the effects of less reliable base models, leading to more stable predictions.
- The Feedforward Neural Network (FNN) underperforms in comparison to both SVM and the tree-based methods. Notably, FNN fails to converge when trained on SMOTE-treated datasets. The network tends to overfit synthetic samples, which are interpolated between real minority class instances. As demonstrated in Permutations-1 and -2, FNNs are particularly prone to overfitting on these artificially generated patterns. Moreover, once overfitting occurs, hyperparameter tuning becomes more difficult, further limiting performance improvements.
- LSTM and 1D-CNN architectures prove to be unsuitable for the datasets used in this study. Both the German Credit dataset and the Taiwan Credit dataset are tabular in nature and lack an inherent temporal structure. While attempts were made to reshape the data into time step sequences (e.g., simulating transactions over time), these transformations fail to introduce meaningful sequential patterns. As a result, both the LSTM and 1D-CNN models exhibit unstable generalization performance, particularly when evaluated on unseen data (as shown in Figure 17). These architectures are more appropriate for domains where sequential or spatial dependencies naturally exist.
- Finally, this study reinforces the importance of careful treatment of class imbalance during preprocessing. While SMOTE is a widely adopted oversampling technique, it does not universally improve performance. In this study, algorithms such as SVM, FNN, LSTM, and 1D-CNN show reduced generalization when trained on SMOTE-augmented data. This outcome underscores the need for the algorithm-specific evaluation of oversampling strategies and highlights the superior robustness of tree-based ensemble methods under class imbalance conditions.

6. Further Studies

While SMOTE was the primary oversampling technique explored in this study for addressing class imbalance, alternative resampling methods merit further investigation. As suggested by Alam et al. (2020), methods, such as Random Oversampling, ADASYN, k-means SMOTE, Borderline-SMOTE, and SMOTE-Tomek, offer distinct mechanisms for generating synthetic samples and may lead to more robust generalization. The poor performance observed with SMOTE in conjunction with Feedforward Neural Networks highlights the need for more nuanced oversampling strategies that avoid overfitting on synthetic data.

An alternative method introduced by Chen et al. (2018), the Synthetic Neighbourhood Generation (SNG) approach, shows promise by creating synthetic samples near the decision boundary of the minority class. Unlike traditional interpolation methods, SNG emphasizes generating higher-quality synthetic examples that enhance classifier learning without inducing bias or redundancy. Incorporating SNG or similar techniques in future studies may lead to better performance, particularly for classifiers like Neural Networks, which are sensitive to noisy or unrepresentative input patterns.

Beyond oversampling, further research should explore non-standardized preprocessing pipelines, as proposed by Zelaya (2019), which involve selectively including or excluding specific transformation steps (e.g., handling outliers, dealing with missing data, or applying normalization). This concept of pipeline volatility encourages adaptive strategies that tailor the preprocessing flow to the model and data characteristics, which could yield more consistent and interpretable results.

Given the superior performance of tree-based boosting algorithms (Gradient Boosting, XGBoost, and LightGBM), future research should investigate how these models perform under additional pipeline permutations, such as the following:

- Introducing clear outliers to evaluate robustness.
- Applying dimensionality reduction techniques such as Principal Component Analysis (PCA) and Recursive Feature Elimination (RFE).
- Utilizing built-in parameters like scale_pos_weight (available in XGBoost and LightGBM) to handle class imbalance more effectively.

Furthermore, in high-dimensional settings, enhancements such as adaptive feature selection and the use of custom loss functions that penalize noisy or redundant features may improve learning efficiency. For example, Grønlund et al. (2020) argue that the success of Gradient Boosting cannot be fully explained by margin size alone and propose considering base learner prediction strength as a more accurate explanatory factor. Combining boosting methods with other models—such as k-Nearest Neighbours (k-NN), Support Vector Machines (SVMs), or clustering-based approaches—may also offer gains through hybrid ensemble frameworks.

The results of this study indicate that the Feedforward Neural Network (FNN), while powerful in theory, underperformed compared to tree-based methods and SVMs, particularly when trained on SMOTE-treated data. Further investigation is warranted into the architectural design and optimization strategies of FNNs.

Key areas for future exploration include the following:

- Network depth and width: The number of layers (depth) and neurons per layer (width) can significantly impact model performance. Finding the optimal architecture for a given dataset requires both technical rigor and intuitive design.
- Regularization strategies: Methods such as dropout, L2 regularization, and Early Stopping play a vital role in reducing overfitting. A more exhaustive tuning of these techniques could improve generalization.
- Optimization techniques: This study primarily relied on SGD with momentum; however, further exploration of adaptive optimizers such as Adam and RMSprop, as well as learning rate schedules, may improve convergence and final performance.
- Advanced training techniques: Techniques like Batch Normalization (to stabilize and speed up training) and Gradient Clipping (to address vanishing/exploding gradients) were not fully explored and could further enhance model robustness.

Given the complexity of tuning deep learning models, future studies would benefit from systematic hyperparameter search strategies, such as Bayesian optimization or AutoML frameworks, to more efficiently explore the configuration space.

7. Conclusions

This study offers a comprehensive exploration of various classifiers, analyzing their unique characteristics and performance across different data preprocessing techniques, including data cleansing, feature and label encoding, feature importance analysis, dimensionality reduction, class imbalance handling, and cross-validation. It highlights how model performance is closely tied to the permutations of preprocessing steps, the complexity of the model, the size and structure of the dataset, and the presence of underlying patterns within the data.

Notably, the findings confirm the superiority of tree-based ensemble methods, specifically Gradient Boosting, XGBoost, and LightGBM, which consistently outperform other classifiers across all experimental configurations. In contrast, Support Vector Machines and Feedforward Neural Networks exhibit inconsistent performance, particularly when trained on data treated with SMOTE. These results underscore the fact that not all classifiers benefit equally from oversampling techniques and that model choice must be tailored to both data characteristics and preprocessing strategies.

Another key insight is the importance of hyperparameter tuning. This study clearly shows that reliance on default settings often leads to suboptimal outcomes, whereas grid search optimization significantly enhances model performance. While hyperparameter tuning is effective for SVM and tree-based models, it proves less feasible for Feedforward Neural Networks, primarily due to their tendency to overfit on synthetic samples and their sensitivity to class imbalance. This highlights the importance of computational resources and tuning strategies in the successful deployment of machine learning models in real-world applications such as credit risk assessment.

Furthermore, this study underscores that factors, such as data distribution, multicollinearity, class imbalance, and feature relevance, all play a significant role in shaping model performance, with different classifiers responding differently to these factors. This further reinforces the idea that model selection must be informed by a deep understanding of the dataset.

A final and critical conclusion concerns the importance of aligning model architecture with data structure. Attempts to impose artificial sequential structures in LSTM and 1D-CNN models—on tabular datasets lacking temporal dependencies—proved ineffective. These models failed to generalize, confirming that deep learning architectures must be applied where their assumptions (e.g., temporal or spatial continuity) are valid. As such, model selection must be grounded in domain knowledge and a careful assessment of the data's intrinsic properties.

In summary, this study concludes that for tabular, imbalanced, and non-sequential credit data, models such as Support Vector Machines and especially tree-based boosting algorithms provide superior stability, scalability, and accuracy. Moving forward, practitioners and researchers must ensure they thoroughly understand the data and apply preprocessing and model selection techniques that align with both the statistical and structural nature of the dataset, to build models that are not only high-performing but also interpretable and robust.

Author Contributions: Conceptualization, A.W.T. and D.T.; methodology, A.W.T. and D.T.; software, A.W.T. and D.T.; validation, A.W.T. and D.T.; formal analysis, A.W.T. and D.T. All authors have read and agreed to the published version of the manuscript.

Funding: This research received no external funding.

Informed Consent Statement: Informed consent was obtained from all subjects involved in the study.

Data Availability Statement: Data are contained within the article.

Acknowledgments: Sincere thanks to Ong Seng Huat, UCSI, Malaysia, and Dat Tran, University of Canberra, for their constructive comments.

Conflicts of Interest: The authors declare no conflicts of interest.

References

Abadi, M., Agarwal, A., Barham, P., Brevdo, E., Chen, Z., Citro, C., Corrado, G. S., Davis, A., Dean, J., & Devin, M. (2016). Tensorflow: Large-scale machine learning on heterogeneous distributed systems. *arXiv*, arXiv:1603.04467.

Alam, T. M., Shaukat, K., Hameed, I. A., Luo, S., Sarwar, M. U., Shabbir, S., Li, J., & Khushi, M. (2020). An investigation of credit card default prediction in the imbalanced datasets. *IEEE Access*, *8*, 201173–201198.

Al-Bdour, G., Al-Qurran, R., Al-Ayyoub, M., & Shatnawi, A. (2019). A detailed comparative study of open source deep learning frameworks. *arXiv*, arXiv:1903.00102.

Altman, E. I. (1968). Financial ratios, discriminant analysis and the prediction of corporate bankruptcy. *The Journal of Finance*, *23*(4), 589–609. [CrossRef]

Altman, E. I., Marco, G., & Varetto, F. (1994). Corporate distress diagnosis: Comparisons using linear discriminant analysis and neural networks (the Italian experience). *Journal of Banking & Finance*, *18*(3), 505–529. [CrossRef]

Beaver, W. H. (1966). Financial ratios as predictors of failure. *Journal of Accounting Research*, *4*, 71–111. [CrossRef]

Bell, T. B., Ribar, G. S., & Verichio, J. (1990). *Neural nets versus logistic regression: A comparison of each model's ability to predict commercial bank failures*. Available online: https://egrove.olemiss.edu/cgi/viewcontent.cgi?article=1081&context=dl_proceedings (accessed on 25 October 2024).

Black, F., & Scholes, M. (1973). The pricing of options and corporate liabilities. *Journal of Political Economy*, *81*(3), 637–654. [CrossRef]

Blum, M. (1974). Failing company discriminant analysis. *Journal of Accounting Research*, *12*, 1–25. [CrossRef]

Boritz, J. E., Kennedy, D. B., & Albuquerque, A. d. M. e. (1995). Predicting corporate failure using a neural network approach. *Intelligent Systems in Accounting, Finance and Management*, *4*(2), 95–111. [CrossRef]

Chen, Z., Lin, T., Xia, X., Xu, H., & Ding, S. (2018). A synthetic neighborhood generation based ensemble learning for the imbalanced data classification. *Applied Intelligence*, *48*, 2441–2457. [CrossRef]

Cheng, B., & Titterington, D. M. (1994). Neural networks: A review from a statistical perspective. *Statistical Science*, *9*, 2–30.

Ciampi, F., & Gordini, N. (2013). Small enterprise default prediction modeling through artificial neural networks: An empirical analysis of i talian small enterprises. *Journal of Small Business Management*, *51*(1), 23–45. [CrossRef]

Croux, C., Jagtiani, J., Korivi, T., & Vulanovic, M. (2020). Important factors determining Fintech loan default: Evidence from a lendingclub consumer platform. *Journal of Economic Behavior & Organization*, *173*, 270–296. [CrossRef]

Curram, S. P., & Mingers, J. (1994). Neural networks, decision tree induction and discriminant analysis: An empirical comparison. *Journal of the Operational Research Society*, *45*(4), 440–450. [CrossRef]

Deakin, E. B. (1972). A discriminant analysis of predictors of business failure. *Journal of Accounting Research*, *10*, 167–179. [CrossRef]

Dong, H., Liu, R., & Tham, A. W. (2024). Accuracy comparison between five machine learning algorithms for financial risk evaluation. *Journal of Risk and Financial Management*, *17*(2), 50. [CrossRef]

Dutta, S., Bose, P., Goyal, V., Bandyopadhyay, P., & Kumar, S. (2021). Applying convolutional-GRU for term deposit likelihood prediction. *International Journal of Engineering and Management Research*, *11*, 265–272. [CrossRef]

Edmister, R. O. (1972). An empirical test of financial ratio analysis for small business failure prediction. *Journal of Financial and Quantitative Analysis*, *7*(2), 1477–1493. [CrossRef]

Fletcher, D., & Goss, E. (1993). Forecasting with neural networks: An application using bankruptcy data. *Information & Management*, *24*(3), 159–167.

Gao, J., Sun, W., & Sui, X. (2021). Research on default prediction for credit card users based on XGBoost-LSTM model. *Discrete Dynamics in Nature and Society*, *2021*(1), 5080472. [CrossRef]

García, S., Luengo, J., & Herrera, F. (2016). Tutorial on practical tips of the most influential data preprocessing algorithms in data mining. *Knowledge-Based Systems*, *98*, 1–29. [CrossRef]

Grønlund, A., Kamma, L., & Green Larsen, K. (2020). Margins are insufficient for explaining gradient boosting. *Advances in Neural Information Processing Systems*, *33*, 1902–1912.

Han, J., Pei, J., & Tong, H. (2022). *Data mining: Concepts and techniques*. Morgan Kaufmann.

Hart, A. (1992). Using neural networks for classification tasks–some experiments on datasets and practical advice. *Journal of the Operational Research Society*, *43*(3), 215–226.

Hasan, B. M. S., & Abdulazeez, A. M. (2021). A review of principal component analysis algorithm for dimensionality reduction. *Journal of Soft Computing and Data Mining*, *2*(1), 20–30.

Hofmann, H. (1994). *Statlog (german credit data)*. UCI Machine Learning Repository.

Jain, A. K., Duin, R. P. W., & Mao, J. (2000). Statistical pattern recognition: A review. *IEEE Transactions on Pattern Analysis and Machine Intelligence*, *22*, 4–37.

Jiang, Y. (2022). A primer on machine learning methods for credit rating modeling. In B. W. Sloboda (Ed.), *Econometrics—Recent advances and applications*. IntechOpen. [CrossRef]

Jo, H., Han, I., & Lee, H. (1997). Bankruptcy prediction using case-based reasoning, neural networks, and discriminant analysis. *Expert Systems with Applications*, *13*(2), 97–108. [CrossRef]
Karels, G. V., & Prakash, A. J. (1987). Multivariate normality and forecasting of business bankruptcy. *Journal of Business Finance & Accounting*, *14*(4), 573–593.
Lacher, R. C., Coats, P. K., Sharma, S. C., & Fant, L. F. (1995). A neural network for classifying the financial health of a firm. *European Journal of Operational Research*, *85*(1), 53–65. [CrossRef]
Lai, L. (2020, August 21–23). *Loan default prediction with machine learning techniques*. 2020 International Conference on Computer Communication and Network Security (CCNS), Xi'an, China.
Li, X., Long, X., Sun, G., Yang, G., & Li, H. (2018, October 8–12). *Overdue prediction of bank loans based on LSTM-SVM*. 2018 IEEE SmartWorld, Ubiquitous Intelligence & Computing, Advanced & Trusted Computing, Scalable Computing & Communications, Cloud & Big Data Computing, Internet of People and Smart City Innovation (SmartWorld/SCALCOM/UIC/ATC/CBDCom/IOP/SCI), Guangzhou, China.
Liu, Y., & Feng, H. (2024). Hybrid 1DCNN-attention with enhanced data preprocessing for loan approval prediction. *Journal of Computer and Communications*, *12*(8), 224–241. [CrossRef]
Lobo, J. M., Jiménez-Valverde, A., & Real, R. (2008). AUC: A misleading measure of the performance of predictive distribution models. *Global Ecology and Biogeography*, *17*, 145–151. [CrossRef]
Martin, D. (1977). Early warning of bank failure: A logit regression approach. *Journal of Banking & Finance*, *1*(3), 249–276.
Nelson, B. J., Runger, G. C., & Si, J. (2003). An error rate comparison of classification methods with continuous explanatory variables. *IIE Transactions*, *35*, 557–566. [CrossRef]
Ohlson, J. A. (1980). Financial ratios and the probabilistic prediction of bankruptcy. *Journal of Accounting Research*, *18*, 109–131. [CrossRef]
Ripley, B. D. (1994). Neural networks and related methods for classification. *Journal of the Royal Statistical Society: Series B (Methodological)*, *56*(3), 409–437. [CrossRef]
Roh, Y., Heo, G., & Whang, S. E. (2019). A survey on data collection for machine learning: A big data-ai integration perspective. *IEEE Transactions on Knowledge and Data Engineering*, *33*(4), 1328–1347. [CrossRef]
Salchenberger, L. M., Cinar, E. M., & Lash, N. A. (1992). Neural networks: A new tool for predicting thrift failures. *Decision Sciences*, *23*(4), 899–916. [CrossRef]
Sarle, W. S. (1994, April 10–13). *Neural networks and statistical models*. 19th Annual SAS Users Group International Conference, Dallas, TX, USA.
Serengil, S. I., Imece, S., Tosun, U. G., Buyukbas, E. B., & Koroglu, B. (2021, September 15–17). *A comparative study of machine learning approaches for non performing loan prediction*. 2021 6th International Conference on Computer Science and Engineering (UBMK), Ankara, Turkey.
Sharda, R., & Wilson, R. (1996). Neural network experiments in business-failure forecasting: Predictive performance measurement issues. *International Journal of Computational Intelligence and Organizations*, *1*(2), 107–117.
Tae, K. H., Roh, Y., Oh, Y. H., Kim, H., & Whang, S. E. (2019, June 30). *Data cleaning for accurate, fair, and robust models: A big data-AI integration approach*. 3rd International Workshop on Data Management for End-to-End Machine Learning, Amsterdam, The Netherlands.
Tam, K. Y., & Kiang, M. (1990). Predicting bank failures: A neural network approach. *Applied Artificial Intelligence an International Journal*, *4*(4), 265–282. [CrossRef]
Wang, J. C., & Perkins, C. B. (2019). *How magic a bullet is machine learning for credit analysis? An exploration with FinTech lending data*. Federal Reserve Bank of Boston.
Wibawa, A. P., Utama, A. B. P., Elmunsyah, H., Pujianto, U., Dwiyanto, F. A., & Hernandez, L. (2022). Time-series analysis with smoothed convolutional neural network. *Journal of Big Data*, *9*(1), 44. [CrossRef]
Wilson, R. L., & Sharda, R. (1994). Bankruptcy prediction using neural networks. *Decision Support Systems*, *11*(5), 545–557. [CrossRef]
Whang, S. E., Roh, Y., Song, H., & Lee, J.-G. (2023). Data collection and quality challenges in deep learning: A data-centric ai perspective. *The VLDB Journal*, *32*(4), 791–813. [CrossRef]
White, H. (1989). Learning in artificial neural networks: A statistical perspective. *Neural Computation*, *1*(4), 425–464. [CrossRef]
Yeh, I. C. (2016). Default of credit card clients. *UCI Machine Learning Repository*, *10*, C55S3H. [CrossRef]
Yeh, I. C., & Lien, C. H. (2009). The comparisons of data mining techniques for the predictive accuracy of probability of default of credit card clients. *Expert Systems with Applications*, *36*, 2473–2480. [CrossRef]
Yoon, Y., Swales, G., Jr., & Margavio, T. M. (1993). A comparison of discriminant analysis versus artificial neural networks. *Journal of the Operational Research Society*, *44*(1), 51–60. [CrossRef]
Zelaya, C. V. G. (2019, April 8–11). *Towards explaining the effects of data preprocessing on machine learning*. 2019 IEEE 35th International Conference on Data Engineering (ICDE), Macao, China.

Zhang, G., Hu, M. Y., Patuwo, B. E., & Indro, D. C. (1999). Artificial neural networks in bankruptcy prediction: General framework and cross-validation analysis. *European Journal of Operational Research*, *116*(1), 16–32. [CrossRef]

Zhao, W., Bhushan, A., Santamaria, A. D., Simon, M. G., & Davis, C. E. (2008). Machine learning: A crucial tool for sensor design. *Algorithms*, *1*(2), 130–152. [CrossRef]

Journal of
Risk and Financial Management

MDPI

Article

Stochastic Modelling of the COVID-19 Epidemic

Eckhard Platen [1,2,3]

[1] School of Mathematical and Physical Sciences and Finance Discipline Group, University of Technology Sydney, P.O. Box 123, Broadway, NSW 2007, Australia; eckhard.platen@uts.edu.au
[2] Department of Actuarial Science, University of Cape Town, Cape Town 7701, South Africa
[3] College of Business and Economics, Australian National University, Canberra, ACT 2600, Australia

Abstract: The need to manage the risks related to the COVID-19 epidemic in health, economics, finance, and insurance became obvious after its outbreak. As a basis for the respective quantitative methods, this paper models, in a novel manner, the dynamics of an epidemic via a four-dimensional stochastic differential equation. Crucial time-dependent input parameters include the reproduction number, the average number of externally and newly infected cases, and the average number of new vaccinations. The proposed model is driven by a single Brownian motion process. When fitted to COVID-19 data, it generates the observed features. It captures widely observed fluctuations in the number of newly infected cases. The fundamental probabilistic properties of the dynamics of an epidemic can be deduced from the proposed model. These can form the basis for successfully managing an epidemic and the related economic and financial risks. As a general tool for quantitative studies, a simulation algorithm is provided. A case study illustrates the model and discusses strategies for reopening an economy during an epidemic.

Keywords: stochastic epidemic model; stochastic differential equations; squared Bessel process; COVID-19 epidemic; simulation

MSC: 91G60; 60H10; 92D30

1. Introduction

This paper is written in memory of Joe Gani and Chris Heyde with whom the author shared a close friendship and worked for several years at the Institute of Advanced Studies at the Australian National University. Both worked in the areas of probability theory and stochastic processes with a strong interest in modelling epidemics.

The COVID-19 pandemic has demonstrated that there exist risks that have not been accounted for. There is an urgent need to quantitatively assess the risks related to an epidemic or pandemic with similar rigour as is common, e.g., for derivatives in quantitative finance. Given the way that viruses are known to mutate and move from animals to humans, it is not a question of whether a pandemic will occur, but rather when it will occur again. Epidemics can emerge at any time and require appropriate long-term risk management. To provide a basis for the accurate quantitative risk management of an epidemic, one requires an accurate understanding of its stochastic dynamics. This paper aims to improve that understanding. The stochastic model it proposes should be suitable for risk management in areas such as health economics, finance, and insurance. The fundamental probabilistic properties of the model are deduced, and a simulation algorithm is provided.

A particular challenge in modelling epidemics emerges when the proportion of newly infected cases in the population is relatively small, which is typically the case when an

https://doi.org/10.3390/jrfm18020097

epidemic is managed in its early stages. The challenge for the health authorities in such a situation is to keep a delicate balance between the emerging number of newly infected cases and the imposed degree of social distancing and travel restrictions, aiming to reopen the economy as soon as possible. The understanding of the stochastic nature of the widely observed fluctuations in the number of newly infected cases is critical for the decision making of health authorities in a pandemic like COVID-19, which had relatively high infection rates.

Important questions that typically arise include the following: How much can a health authority relax social distancing to keep the number of newly infected cases below a critical level? How important are severe travel restrictions? How many externally and newly infected cases are, on average, permitted to keep the number of newly infected cases still below a critical threshold? How long does it take to reopen the economy? How many susceptibles must be vaccinated per day to reopen an economy at a target date?

The proposed model is different from the models that were typically employed by most health authorities during the COVID-19 pandemic. The model is based on the fact that a pandemic evolves like a branching process, see (Feller, 1971), and it provides, in a unified and transparent manner, a quantitative model for answering these and other questions, which is demonstrated in a case study. The paper was written in April 2020, during the beginning of the pandemic, aiming to answer some of the above-mentioned questions. To underline the predictive abilities of the proposed model, most of the paper, along with its illustrations and case study, is based on (Platen, 2020).

The model captures the stochastic dynamics of an epidemic at all stages of its evolution. It adequately models an epidemic when the number of newly infected cases is small and fluctuates considerably. The key to understanding the stochastic nature of an epidemic is the insight into the evolution of the number of newly infected individuals, as closely follows a generalized, time-transformed squared Bessel process; see, e.g., (Feller, 1971; Revuz & Yor, 1999).

The proposed model characterizes the dynamics of an epidemic via a four-dimensional system of stochastic differential equations (SDEs) with time and state-dependent drift and diffusion coefficient functions. An introduction to the theory of SDEs and the methods for their numerical solution can be found in (Kloeden & Platen, 1999). SDE solutions can be discretised with different time step sizes without changing parameters. A discrete-time approximation for the solution of the system of SDEs describing the model is provided in the paper. This algorithm represents a flexible tool that can be widely applied for quantitative risk management related to epidemics by using simulation methods.

The literature on epidemic modelling is rich. The variants of the SIR (Susceptible-Infectious-Recovered) model are widely used and rather popular, using deterministic ordinary differential equations; see (Katriel, 2010) and the references therein. Other models employ Markov chains; see, e.g., (Chang et al., 2020) and the references therein. Markov chain models for state variables of an epidemic can become extremely complex when many geographical and network details are incorporated. The complexity of Markov chain models, particularly the characterization of transition probabilities, makes it difficult to obtain, on an aggregate level, a deeper understanding of the modelled stochastic dynamics. As shown in this paper, a reasonably accurate model needs to only consider about four evolving state variables, not requiring much detail about the transition probabilities as in Markov chain models.

There exists some literature on the modelling of epidemics with SDEs, including some SDE models with time delay, where one may refer to (Chunyan & Jiang, 2014) and references therein.

An advantage of the SDE models is that these aggregate unimportant minor details that average out in the continuous time evolution of state variables, e.g., the number of newly infected individuals. What remains are the core properties of the dynamics, characterized locally in time and space via drift and diffusion coefficient functions. In the case of the proposed branching process model, its SDE can be transformed into a standardized form that has been well studied in the literature, see, e.g., (Feller, 1971), which reveals its fundamental probabilistic properties. These properties can produce rather accurate quantitative statements and values of interest, which would not be possible without a deeper understanding of the underlying nature of the stochastic dynamics. Beyond that, SDE models are not only parsimonious, buy they also grant us access to the powerful tools of stochastic analysis, which have been the key to deriving accurate quantitative methods in many areas, e.g., in quantitative finance.

The paper is organized as follows: Section 2 describes a time-discrete model that can be used as a simulation algorithm. Section 3 provides the continuous time version of the model. The fundamental properties of the proposed model are discussed in Section 4. Section 5 fits the model to Australian COVID-19 data and provides a case study for the early stage of the pandemic.

2. Discrete-Time Model

This section presents a discrete-time model for the evolution of key state variables that characterize the dynamics of an epidemic. The discrete-time model is designed in a way that permits the simulation of scenarios for studying the dynamic properties of an epidemic. The algorithm can also be employed to calculate values of interest via Monte Carlo simulation.

One time unit is set to one day because most reported data during the outbreak of the COVID-19 epidemic have been provided daily. Let us introduce the equidistant time points t_i, $i = 0, 1, 2, \dots$, where $t_{i+1} - t_i = 1$ such that $t_i = i$ is counting the days from the initial time point $t_0 = 0$. We consider a population of an *initial size* $n_0 > 0$ at the initial time $t_0 = 0$ that experiences an epidemic outbreak, like the COVID-19 epidemic, with time-dependent *reproduction number* R_i at time $i \geq 0$. This number can be interpreted as the expected number of infections directly generated by one infected person during the entire time the person is infectious, if all individuals in the population are susceptible to infection. For the COVID-19 epidemic, various sources estimated $R_i \approx 2.25$ when no social distancing measures were implemented; see e.g., (Dorigatti et al., 2020; Roser & Ritchie, 2020). Strong social distancing, with only essential services working and with most parts of the population staying at home, achieves a potential reproduction number of about $R_i \approx 0.5$. For simplicity, we assume that a person can only become infected once, and when recovered, the infected becomes immune. The parameter $\sigma \geq 1$ characterizes the *average number of days during which a person infects* other people. Various studies show that for COVID-19, one finds a likely value of about $\sigma \approx 4.5$, see e.g., (Dorigatti et al., 2020), which we assume throughout the paper. The *infection variance* $\nu \geq 0$ is proportional to the variance of the number of individuals that an infected individual infects when there are only susceptible individual and the reproduction number equals 1.0. The case study at the end of this paper finds that $\nu = 6$ generates the magnitude of fluctuations that one typically observes, and we assume this number to be the case throughout the paper. When the entire population is susceptible, the average number of persons at time i who would become *externally infected* per day is denoted by $\epsilon_i \geq 0$.

Our main state variable Y_i denotes the number of persons that become *newly infected* at the i-th day. The second state variable X_i counts the number of *new deaths* at the i-th day. Our third state variable, denoted by Z_i, captures the number of *non-susceptible individuals* at time i. The latter includes individuals who had the disease and recovered, and those who became immune through vaccination. Finally, the changing size n_i of the population represents our fourth state variable.

Let the number of newly infected individuals start at time $t_0 = 0$ with $0 \leq Y_0 \leq n_0 - Z_0$, satisfying, at time $i+1, i = 0, 1, 2, \ldots$, the relation

$$Y_{i+1} = Y_i + \left(\frac{Y_i}{\sigma}(R_i(1 - Z_i/n_i) - 1) + \epsilon_i(1 - Z_i/n_i)\right) + \sqrt{\frac{\nu Y_i}{\sigma} R_i(1 - Z_i/n_i)} U_i, \tag{1}$$

if the right-hand side of (1) is non-negative and less than $n_i - Z_i$. We set $Y_{i+1} = 0$, if the right-hand side of (1) is negative, and we set $Y_{i+1} = n_i - Z_i$ if the right-hand side of (1) is greater than $n_i - Z_i$. Here, $U_i, i = 0, 1, 2, \ldots$, are independent standard Gaussian-distributed random variables.

The second summand (in large round brackets) on the right hand side of (1) models the trend of the number of newly infected individuals. As long as no external infections occur in the population ($\epsilon_i = 0$), the number of newly infected cases is, on average, increasing (decreasing) with *return rate*

$$g_i = \frac{1}{\sigma}(R_i(1 - Z_i/n_i) - 1) \tag{2}$$

where $R_i(1 - Z_i/n_i)$ is greater (smaller) than 1.0. Social distancing reduces the reproduction number R_i, and thus, the return rate. An increased number of non-susceptibles Z_i also decreases the return rate. There is an additional increase in the average number of newly infected individuals if there are susceptibles and external infections, that is, when $1 - Z_i/n_i > 0$ and $\epsilon_i > 0$. Travel restrictions between populations reduce ϵ_i. When the proportion of susceptibles $1 - Z_i/n_i$ has decreased so that $R_i(1 - Z_i/n_i) < 1$, then, the average number of newly infected individuals fluctuates around the *reference level*

$$\bar{Y}_i = \frac{\sigma \epsilon_i (1 - Z_i/n_i)}{1 - R_i(1 - Z_i/n_i)}. \tag{3}$$

This level is proportional to the average number of new externally infected individuals and increases when the reproduction number increases. This means, relaxing travel restrictions and/or reducing social distancing raises the average number of newly infected individuals.

So far, the average dynamics models a typical deterministic SIR-type dyamics. However, when the number of infected individuals is small, as it is when an epidemic is initially managed to avoid overloading the health system, one observes substantial fluctuations in the trajectory of the number of newly infected individuals. These fluctuations are not due to reporting errors. They represent an important stochastic property of the dynamics of an epidemic. The proposed model captures the fluctuations of the number of newly infected individuals Y_i through the third summand on the right-hand side of Equation (1), where the *variance* of the increment of the number of newly infected individuals is made *proportional to the number of newly infected individuals*.

To understand the reasoning behind this assumed property, assume that all infected individuals each infect an independent, identically distributed random number of individuals during a given day. Then, due to the assumed independence, the variance of the increment of the total number of newly infected individuals equals the sum of the variances of the newly infected individuals caused by everyone that was infected at the beginning of the day. Thus, the variance of the increment of the total number of newly infected individuals turns out to be proportional to the number of individuals that were infected at the beginning of the day. This fundamental fact underpins the dynamics of branching processes, see (Feller, 1971), and determines the feedback in the fluctuations of the number of newly infected individuals because of the nature of the spread of infections.

The variance of the number of newly infected individuals in (1) turns out to be proportional to the contact intensity, which is the product of the infection variance ν, the reproduction number R_i, the proportion of susceptibles $1 - Z_i/n_i$, and the inverse of the average number of days, σ, during which an infected person infects others. This means that one can observe larger fluctuations in the number of newly infected individuals when the reproduction number is higher or when the proportion of non-susceptibles is lower, and vice versa.

For simplicity, we do not consider cases where individuals move between populations and do not account for deaths that are not caused by an epidemic infection. We also do not consider the possibility that non-susceptibles can become susceptible again. However, such features could be easily included in the model. It is important to consider the possibility that a vaccine becomes available, which permits us to model the immunization of susceptibles. We denote by ξ_i the number of *newly vaccinated* susceptibles per day at time i with $\xi_0 = 0$.

Unfortunately, an epidemic such as that of COVID-19 causes a relatively high proportion of deaths among the infected. To model the number of deaths we introduce the *mortality rate* $\lambda_i \geq 0$, which captures the proportion of persons that pass away at time i because of an epidemic infection. We make the mortality rate time-dependent because this rate may change over time in a population, e.g., when more vulnerable persons become strongly isolated from most of the population or when better or fewer treatments become available. In the case of COVID-19, the vulnerable are the elderly and those with prior health conditions. In some developed countries with a good health system, a mortality rate of about $\lambda \approx 0.01$ has been observed; see (Dorigatti et al., 2020). However, this may vary considerably and is most likely higher in many populations.

Let $\psi > 0$ denote the average *lag time* (in days) between infection and death. A realistic number for this average time seems to be about $\psi \approx 17$; see (Dorigatti et al., 2020). For simplicity, we assume that when there were no infections in the population before time $t_0 = 0$, the number of *daily new deaths* X_i in the population at time $i = \psi, \psi + 1, \psi + 2, \ldots$ takes the form

$$X_i = \lambda_i Y_{i-\psi}, \tag{4}$$

where we set $Y_{-1} = Y_{-2} = \ldots = Y_{-\psi} = 0$. When non-susceptible individuals pass away at time i, caused by an epidemic infection, this reduces the total size n_i of the population to

$$n_{i+1} = n_i - X_i \tag{5}$$

as long as the right-hand side of (5) is non-negative, where we set it to zero otherwise. With these notations, the number Z_{i+1} of *non-susceptibles* at time $i + 1$ equals

$$Z_{i+1} = Z_i + Y_{i+1} + \xi_i - X_i, \tag{6}$$

as long as the right-hand side of (6) remains non-negative and not greater than n_{i+1}. We set $Z_{i+1} = n_{i+1}$ in case the right-hand side of (6) becomes larger than n_{i+1}, and we set $Z_{i+1} = 0$ when it becomes negative. We start with an initial value of $Y_0 \leq Z_0 \leq n_0$. Note that Equation (6) is different in the literature that uses SIR-type models; see e.g., (Chunyan & Jiang, 2014). This difference turns out to be crucial for a realistic model of the stochastic dynamics of an epidemic. The four state variables Y_i, X_i, Z_i, and n_i evolve jointly over time, in accordance with Equations (1), (4), (6), and (5).

Often-reported quantities that can be easily derived from the model include the total number of deaths until time i,

$$V_i = \sum_{k=0}^{i} X_k, \tag{7}$$

and the total number of individuals that become infected until time i,

$$M_i = \sum_{k=0}^{i} Y_k. \tag{8}$$

The total number of recovered individuals is the difference between the total number of those who became infected and the total number of deaths.

It is straightforward to simulate scenarios of the above-modelled dynamics. These scenarios can help to compare the impact of alternative variants of strategies in the management of an epidemic. Furthermore, the above algorithm can be used to evaluate values of interest via Monte Carlo simulation; see e.g., (Kloeden & Platen, 1999). To gain a deeper understanding of the stochastic dynamics under the model, it is beneficial to study the probabilistic properties of the continuous time limit of the above dynamics, which emerge when letting the time step size to tend to zero. The weak convergence of the respective stochastic processes can be secured by theorems given, e.g., in Chapter 14 of (Kloeden & Platen, 1999). This weak convergence still holds if the Gaussian random variables in Equation (1) are substituted by other independent random variables with the same first and second moment and a finite third moment. This indicates the important invariance of stochastic differential equation models towards details of specific randomness at a discrete-time level.

3. Continuous Time Model

This section presents the continuous time model that follows by weak convergence from the above-described discrete-time model when letting the time step size converge to zero. The continuous time model results in the four-dimensional form of the stochastic differential equation (SDE). We keep the notations and interpretations of the previous section for the parameters of the continuous time model. From a mathematical perspective, it is advantageous to normalize, in continuous time, the number of newly infected individuals for large populations and the number of non-susceptibles by the actual size of the population because the respective normalized quantities become uniformly bounded. Our normalized main state variable $y_t \approx Y_t/n_t$ becomes the proportion of the population that is *newly infected* at time t. Our second normalized state variable, denoted by $z_t \approx Z_t/n_t$, captures the proportion of the population that is *not susceptible* at time $t \geq 0$.

Under the proposed model, the proportion y_t of the newly infected individuals in the population satisfies the SDE

$$dy_t = \left(\frac{y_t}{\sigma}(R_t(1-z_t)-1) + \frac{\epsilon_t}{n_t}(1-z_t)\right)dt + \sqrt{\frac{\nu y_t R_t}{\sigma n_t}}(1-z_t)dW_t, \tag{9}$$

for $t \geq 0$ with $y_0 \geq 0$. Here, $W = \{W_t, t \geq 0\}$ is the standard Brownian motion that models the randomness in the dynamics of the epidemic in t-time. This uncertainty is driving the fluctuations of the number of newly infected individuals in the population. Note that when the size of the population is large and the number of infected individuals is so large that it makes sense to study the proportion of newly infected individuals in the population, then, the diffusion coefficient in (9) can be neglected and there is almost no randomness in the trajectory of the proportion of newly infected individuals. However, in the case of an initially managed epidemic, the number of newly infected individuals is small. This number can fluctuate considerably in this case, as typically observed. Such fluctuations, when observed in COVID-19 data, were sometimes misinterpreted as observation errors. The proposed model explains the strong fluctuations observed. This understanding is important for proper decision making during the initial management of an epidemic, e.g., when aiming at reopening an economy after a lockdown.

According to (4), the expected proportion of new deaths $E(x_t) = E(\frac{X_t}{n_t})$ (per day) at time t satisfies the differential equation with time delay

$$dE(x_t) = \lambda_t dE(y_{t-\psi}), \tag{10}$$

where $E(X)$ denotes the expected value of a random variable X. Note that with a constant mortality rate $\lambda_t = \lambda > 0$, the SDE for $E(x_t)$ follows (9), approximately in the form

$$dE(x_t) \approx \left(\frac{E(x_t)}{\sigma}(R_{t-\psi}(1 - E(z_{t-\psi})) - 1) + \lambda E(\frac{\epsilon_{t-\psi}}{n_{t-\psi}})(1 - E(z_{t-\psi})) \right) dt. \tag{11}$$

This reveals the fact that the expected proportion of new deaths has, with time delay ψ, the same return rate as the proportion of newly infected individuals. More precisely, one can estimate the (by the time ψ) delayed return rate of newly infected individuals from the return rate of the number of new deaths. This return rate may give more accurate estimates for the reproduction number than the reliance on the reported number of newly infected individuals, which is often missing a large number of cases.

The differential equation for the proportion $z_t = Z_t/n_t$ of non-susceptibles in the population starting with $y_0 \leq z_0 \leq 1$ is given as

$$dz_t = (y_t + \frac{\xi_t}{n_t} - x_t)dt \tag{12}$$

for $t \geq 0$, as long as z_t stays in the interval $[0, 1]$. The proportion of non-susceptibles z_t is pulled back to the boundaries of this interval when the right hand side of (12) pushes z_t beyond these boundaries, which is analogous to the boundary behaviour modelled in (6). Finally, we obtain from (5) a differential equation for n_t in the form

$$dn_t = -x_t n_t dt \tag{13}$$

for $t \geq 0$ with $n_0 > 0$ and $x_t = \frac{X_t}{n_t}$.

The fluctuations of the proportion of newly infected individuals y_t is modelled in the SDE (9) via the diffusion coefficient. We emphasize the crucial property of the model which follows that the variance of the increments of the proportion of the infected individuals in the population is proportional to the proportion of the infected individuals in the population. This crucial property of the proposed model for the stochastic evolution of the number of newly infected individuals reflects the fundamental fact that we model the continuous time limit of a branching process; see (Feller, 1971). Recall that we explained in Section 2 why the variance of the increments of the number of newly infected individuals evolves proportionally to this number. Explanations for the form of the drift and the diffusion coefficient functions of the four-dimensional system of SDEs (9), (10), (12), and (13) remain analogous to those given in Section 2 for the respective equations.

The four state variables of the above model are, at time t, the proportion of the newly infected individuals in the population y_t , the proportion of new deaths x_t, the proportion of non-susceptible individuals in the population z_t , and the size of the population n_t. These quantities evolve jointly together according to the above four-dimensional system of SDEs. The existence and uniqueness of a strong solution for this system of SDEs can be secured by a combination of respective theorems in (Ikeda & Watanabe, 1989). What makes the respective proof work is the fact that the key state variables are bounded. A

Yamada condition for the diffusion coefficient of (9) is satisfied, and the delayed proportion of deaths can be captured as an additional component in a respective five-dimensional Markovian SDE, which satisfies an existence and uniqueness theorem of the type given in (Ikeda & Watanabe, 1989).

4. Fundamental Properties and Strategies

The dynamics of y_t in (9) can be identified as that of a generalized, time-transformed squared Bessel process; see, e.g., (Revuz & Yor, 1999). To deduce the fundamental probabilistic properties from its dynamics, we introduce the *intrinsic time* τ_t with derivative

$$\frac{d\tau_t}{dt} = \frac{\nu R_t}{4\sigma n_t}(1 - z_t) \tag{14}$$

for $t \geq 0$ with $\tau_0 = 0$. The intrinsic time runs faster when the reproduction number is higher and the proportion of non-susceptibles is smaller. When the proportion of non-susceptibles reaches the value 1.0, then, the intrinsic time stops. This time evolves *slower for larger populations*, which reveals the fundamental probabilistic property of epidemics that determines the schedule of its typical evolution. Furthermore, we obtain the crucial *dimension* δ_t of the underlying generalized squared Bessel process using the formula

$$\delta_t = \frac{4\sigma\epsilon_t}{\nu R_t}. \tag{15}$$

Finally, we introduce the *intrinsic growth rate* η_t in the form

$$\eta_t = \frac{4n_t}{\nu}(1 - \frac{1}{R_t(1 - z_t)}). \tag{16}$$

These notations allow us to rewrite the SDE (9) in the standardized form

$$dy_t = (\delta_t + \eta_t y_t)d\tau_t + 2\sqrt{y_t}d\tilde{W}_{\tau_t}. \tag{17}$$

Here, $\tilde{W}$ denotes a standard Brownian motion that evolves in the intrinsic time τ_t. It aggregates, in intrinsic time, the randomness driving the dynamics of an epidemic.

Due to the standardized form of the SDE (17), we can deduce the probabilistic properties of the dynamics of the proportion of the number of newly infected individuals from well-established properties of time-transformed squared Bessel processes; see, e.g., (Revuz & Yor, 1999).

4.1. Eradicating the Disease

When the dimension δ_t is less than two, y_t becomes *absorbed* at zero, with a strictly positive probability at some random future time. This is a fundamental property which tells us that, due to (15), the ratio $\frac{\epsilon_t}{R_t}$ has to be less than $\frac{1}{2\sigma}$ to potentially *eradicate the disease.* This insight specifies the average number of new externally infected individuals ϵ_t that one can allow and still potentially eradicate the disease at some future time.

As mentioned earlier, a realistic parameter choice is $\sigma \approx 4.5$, which we keep in all our calculations and which yields the inequality $\epsilon_t < 0.11R_t$. Without social distancing, that is, with $R_t \approx 2.25$, this choice is on average equivalent to less than one externally infected person every four days. Anything more would not keep the epidemic on a path where its infections can potentially become eradicated.

Most importantly, the number of new externally infected individuals allowed for eradicating infections becomes smaller when social distancing is in place. Say, for social distancing equivalent to a reproduction number of $R_t \approx 0.5$, one can only allow on average one externally infected individual every nine days to achieve still eradication.

Unfortunately, these are extremely small numbers. They show that, for the management of an epidemic, it is imperative to keep the number of externally infected individuals as close to zero as possible. If one does not respect this major requirement and allows too many new external infections to occur, then, one faces, according to the model, the scenario during which the epidemic continues until almost no susceptibles exist anymore.

When there are no new external infections, that is, $\epsilon_t = 0$, we obtain, by Formula (15), the dimension $\delta_t = 0$. In this case, the disease can be potentially eradicated; see (Revuz & Yor, 1999). To make this specific, let $\rho = \{\inf t | Y_t = 0\}$ denote the first time t when the number of newly infected individuals Y_t hits zero, where the number of newly infected individuals at time $t = 0$ is set to $Y_0 = Y > 0$. It is then possible to calculate, for the proposed model, the conditional probability $P(\rho \leq t | Y_0 = Y)$. According to (2), we have the return rate g_t (with respect to t-time) given by the formula

$$g_t = \frac{1}{\sigma}(R_t(1 - z_t) - 1). \tag{18}$$

When assuming, for simplicity, the return rate $g_t = g$ to be constant, then it follows from Corollary (1.4) in Chapter XI of (Revuz & Yor, 1999) that

$$P(\rho \leq t | Y_0 = Y) = \exp\left\{ -\frac{2Y}{\nu(1 + \frac{1}{\sigma g})(1 - \exp(-gt))} \right\}. \tag{19}$$

This formula captures the probability to potentially eradicate the disease until time t. Recall that we are assuming in (19) a constant return rate g and no external new infections. For a reproduction number R_t less than 1.0 and almost no non-susceptibles, the return rate g is negative and one can, over time and with probability one, *eradicate the disease*. For a reproduction number greater than 1.0, one has a positive return rate g, and the Formula (19) shows that it takes an extremely long time to eradicate the disease. The probability for such a scenario is approximately given by (19) as

$$P(\rho = \infty | Y_0 = Y) \approx 1 - \exp\left(-\frac{2Y}{\nu(1 + \frac{1}{R-1})} \right). \tag{20}$$

Already, for a reproduction number of $R_t = R = 1.1$ and $Y_0 = 20$, the probability is greater than 50% that one does not eradicate the disease at any finite time. This makes clear that one has a good chance of eradicating the disease over time, only in the case where one reduces the number of newly infected individuals down to zero and maintains the reproduction number significantly below 1.0. Lifting social distancing restrictions too early under this strategy would considerably delay eradication and may even jeopardize the prospects of eradicating the disease when the return rate becomes slightly positive. We will illustrate later, in a case study, how the degree of social distancing impacts the time it takes to eradicate the disease.

When the dimension δ_t is greater than two, then, y_t will never reach zero with probability one, even with a negative return rate. In this case, the disease will continue to circulate in the population, supported from time to time by new external infections, until there are no susceptibles left in the population. This means that almost the entire population must contract the disease if no vaccine is introduced. According to the mortality rate, many individuals will pass away in this scenario.

In summary, a realistic strategy for managing an epidemic is to keep the dimension of the above generalized squared Bessel process y at zero through strong travel restrictions. If, additionally, one implements strong social distancing measures, then, this makes the growth rate of the newly infected individuals negative and significantly reduces the average time until eradication, as will be illustrated in the next section. When eradication is achieved, one can relax social distancing but must maintain the number of new external infections at zero. Therefore, one must vigorously chase every infection and isolate potentially infected individuals. Otherwise, a new outbreak almost certainly emerges from the new externally infected individuals if the reproduction number is not clearly below 1.0. It needs to be emphasized that the populations that eradicate the disease must remain isolated until a vaccine is introduced or until all other populations have also eradicated the disease.

4.2. Flattening the Curve

When the return rate g_t is positive and there are no externally infected individuals, then, the number of infected individuals rises, on average, exponentially due to (16) and (14). The observed return rate may be used to estimate the reproductive number from a smoothed version of a visibly exponentially growing trajectory of the number of newly infected individuals. Note, however, that Y_t fluctuates considerably, and the reported number of newly infected individuals may significantly underestimate the true number. On the other hand, when an outbreak is experienced, it is not important to estimate the reproductive number that is driving the observed growing curve of newly infected individuals. What is important is to stop this growth.

Of strategic importance in managing an outbreak of an epidemic is the 'flattening of the curve' of newly infected individuals, which is typically achieved by two measures as follows:

First, by imposing strong travel restrictions so that these reduce ϵ_t to such a low level that the term $\frac{\epsilon_t}{n_t}(1 - z_t)$ in the drift of the SDE (9) can be neglected.

Second, by implementing social distancing that reduces the product of the reproductive number R_t and the proportion of the susceptibles $1 - z_t$ to a level clearly below 1.0, typically 0.9, so that the return rate (18) becomes sufficiently negative.

At the start of an epidemic, the proportion of non-susceptibles, z_t, can be approximately assumed to be zero. When the epidemic is managed reasonably well with a small number of deaths, this proportion can be neglected for a long time. Thus, at the beginning of an epidemic, with no social distancing measures in place, the return rate would be about $g_t \approx 0.28$, which yields the typically observed fast exponential growth of the COVID-19 epidemic when not managed via social distancing.

This exponential growth should alarm health officials. By implementing very strong social distancing measures, one can achieve a reproduction number R_t of about 0.5, which yields a return rate of about $g_t \approx -0.11$. With such strong social distancing implemented, one can expect, after a few days, the curve of the number of newly infected individuals to flatten and then decline on average, in accordance with this negative return rate. The curve of newly infected individuals will, by its stochastic nature, continue to fluctuate visibly when the number of newly infected individuals is in the typical range in which epidemics are managed. It is difficult to make decisions based on the strongly fluctuating numbers of newly infected individuals when one has no quantitative understanding of the random nature of the underlying dynamics. The proposed model provides an understanding of these fluctuations and a probabilistic description of the future evolution of the epidemic.

To provide some information about the expected number of newly infected individuals, we denote by $\mu_t = E(Y_t)$ the expected value of the number of newly infected individuals. Note that $Y_t = y_t n_t$ fluctuates and evolves rather independently from the proportion of non-susceptibles z_t, which is not fluctuating and is growing extremely slowly. By (9), it approximately follows that

$$d\mu_t \approx \Big(\frac{\mu_t}{\sigma}(R_t(1 - E(z_t)) - 1) + \epsilon_t(1 - E(z_t))\Big)dt \tag{21}$$

for $t \geq 0$ with $\mu_0 = Y_0$. Similarly, we can calculate (by applying the Ito formula) the variance of the number of newly infected individuals, which approximately satisfies, for constant return rate $g_t = g < 0$ and constant dimension $\delta_t = \delta \geq 0$, the formula

$$E((Y_t - \mu_t)^2) \approx Y_0 \nu (1 + \frac{1}{\sigma g})(\exp(2gt) - \exp(gt)) + \frac{\delta \nu^2}{8}(1 + \frac{1}{\sigma g})^2 (1 - \exp(gt))^2 \quad (22)$$

for $t \geq 0$. It turns out that both equations can provide predictions for the number of newly infected individuals Y_t, which can be confirmed and visualized via scenario simulation; see Figures 6 and 7. We note from (22) that the variance of the number of newly infected individuals is, after a short time, approximately proportional to the number of newly infected individuals. This is consistent with what was mentioned earlier about the discrete-time version of the model. On the other hand, after a long time, the variance becomes proportional to the dimension. This means that the case of no new externally infected individuals finally leads to zero variance after absorption. For strictly positive dimension $\delta > 0$, where new externally infected individuals arrive, the number of newly infected individuals enters an equilibrium and obtains a stationary variance proportional to the dimension.

4.3. Newly Infected Individuals in Local Equilibrium

When the return rate in (18) becomes negative through social distancing and/or an increased proportion of non-susceptibles, that is, $R_t(1 - z_t) < 1$, then, a local (in time) *equilibrium* emerges for the number of infected individuals Y_t. As already mentioned in (3), this number fluctuates by (18) around the *reference level*

$$\bar{Y}_t = \frac{\epsilon_t (1 - z_t)}{-g_t}, \quad (23)$$

which is proportional to the average number of new externally infected individuals ϵ_t and does not depend on the size of the population n_t. This reference level is lower when ϵ_t is lower due to stronger travel restrictions or when the (negative) return rate is lower, which means that the reproduction number R_t is reduced through further social distancing. This is also lower when the proportion of non-susceptibles is higher. Note, when the return rate approaches zero from below, then, the reference level of the local equilibrium tends to infinity, indicating that the number of newly infected individuals will, on average, grow towards the respective reference level.

The fluctuations around the above reference level approximately occur by (22) with a variance as

$$E((Y_t - \mu_t)^2) \approx \frac{\sigma \epsilon_t \nu}{2R_t} \left(1 + \frac{1}{R_t(1 - E(z_t)) - 1}\right)^2, \quad (24)$$

which is not depending on n_t. This variance increases proportionally to ϵ_t, σ, ν, and the proportion of susceptibles $1 - z_t$. When the proportion of non-susceptibles reaches 1.0, then one has no longer any fluctuations. Note that when $R_t(1 - z_t)$ approaches 1.0 from below in (24), then, major fluctuations in the number of newly infected individuals are expected. This also means that when one relaxes social distancing and comes too close to 1.0 for the value of the product $R_t(1 - z_t)$, one may observe, as a *warning sign*, significant fluctuations in the number of newly infected individuals.

In a local equilibrium, the number of currently infected individuals Y_t can be kept with some probability below a critical level C_t. This critical level may be chosen, for instance, as the number of newly infected individuals related to the number of cases with severe disease that the health system could still handle. To calculate the above-mentioned probability, one can exploit another fundamental probabilistic property of the model, which is the shape of the stationary density for the number of newly infected individuals. This density is a gamma density with mean (23) and variance (24). The respective gamma density is given by the formula

$$p_t(Y) = \frac{Y^{\alpha-1}}{\beta^\alpha \Gamma(\alpha)} \exp(-\frac{Y}{\beta}), \tag{25}$$

with $\alpha = \frac{\delta}{2}$ and

$$\beta = 0.5\nu(\frac{1}{R_t(1-z_t)} - 1)^{-1}, \tag{26}$$

where

$$\Gamma(\alpha) = \int_0^\infty s^{\alpha-1} e^{-s} ds \tag{27}$$

is the gamma function for $\alpha > 0$.

In a local equilibrium, the probability $P(Y_t < C_t)$ used to keep, at time t, the number of newly infected individuals Y_t below a critical level C_t is about

$$P(Y_t < C_t) \approx \int_0^{C_t} p_t(y) dy. \tag{28}$$

This probability may be useful in assessing the social distancing measures to be implemented to control the risk of overloading the health system through random upward excursions in the number of newly infected individuals. By relying on the above gamma distribution, it is easy to calculate the targeted probability $P(Y_t < C_t)$ and the respective critical level C_t, and vice versa. For a given proportion of non-susceptibles z_t and a given number of the average externally infected individuals per day ϵ_t, one can identify, via the above relation, the permissible level for the reproduction number R_t. This then translates to the required level of social distancing that must be imposed to keep the fluctuating number of newly infected individuals below the critical threshold C_t.

4.4. Herd Immunization

Let us interpret the so-called 'herd immunity' as the case of a sufficiently high proportion of non-susceptibles that allows authorities to remove social distancing and travel restrictions while staying in a local equilibrium. This means that the value of the product $R_t(1-z_t)$ has to be clearly below 1.0. With a reproductive number $R_t \approx 2.25$ for the case where no social distancing is implemented, one needs a proportion of about 60% of non-susceptibles to remove all social distancing measures and still secure a local equilibrium. Note that this theoretical proportion is a *critical borderline*, which may have to be higher for some populations with higher reproductive numbers. Even if a population has such a high level of non-susceptibles, one must (according to Formula (23)) be very cautious about relaxing travel restrictions, because relaxing these increases ϵ_t. As pointed out, the average number of newly infected individuals is proportional to the number ϵ_t of new externally infected individuals per day. By Formula (24) the variance of the number of infected individuals is also proportional to ϵ_t. As described above, one can calculate the probability $P(Y_t < C_t)$ of staying with Y_t below a critical level C_t and enforce travel restrictions and social distancing measures that keep this probability within a target level.

When managing an epidemic by keeping the number of infected individuals in a local equilibrium, with a large probability $P(Y_t < C_t)$ that avoids overloading the health system, it takes a long time to reach the critical borderline of 60% of non-susceptibles through immunization by infection and recovery. This also means that one must let a proportion of more than 60% of the population contract the disease. For a population of about 25 million and a mortality rate of 1%, a toll of about 150,000 deaths would be the consequence of that strategy, which would be tragic. Even if the health system could handle about $C_t = 100,000$ newly infected individuals per day because many infected individuals may show only mild symptoms, about 1000 infected individuals would pass away each day. Then, it would still take about five months to reach the proportion of non-susceptibles necessary to remove social distancing measures. This would be a horror scenario with a high death toll. Since social distancing would still have to be sufficiently strict to be effective, major parts of the economy would suffer dramatically over a long period of time, and large parts of the population would be unable to work with severe consequences. One can see the risks for the vulnerable, employees, the economy, and the financial market when embarking on the strategy of 'herd immunity'. 'Herd immunization' is in stark contrast to the strategy of aiming to eradicate the disease.

Under 'herd immunization' with some social distancing, if one opens the economy too early, the number of newly infected individuals would grow exponentially for some time, and the epidemic would quickly force its way through the entire population. This would create potentially catastrophic consequences for the overwhelmed health system until the critical borderline level of non-susceptibles is reached. After that, the epidemic would slow down. It would finally stop the spread of new infections because there would be almost no susceptibles left. Many infected individuals would pass away without a chance of receiving reasonable medical care because the health system would not have enough capacity. Consequently, the mortality rate for infected individuals would be much higher than otherwise due to the lack of medical care. This scenario should be avoided if possible.

4.5. Delaying Flattening the Curve

As mentioned earlier, to avoid a high death toll and to ensure the economy is reinvigorated, the leadership of a population must act 'hard and fast', from the very beginning of the epidemic. It must impose, as soon as possible, strict travel restrictions and social distancing measures, aiming to lower the number of infections and the fast eradication of the disease. This strategy is realistic and can achieve, within reasonable time, the eradication of the disease. However, it requires the living conditions, leadership, and discipline of the population to keep the reproduction number clearly below 1.0, for a sufficiently long time, while avoiding new external infections. If one cannot avoid a few new external infections, the above strategy does not lead to the eradication of the disease but keeps the number of newly infected individuals extremely low in a local equilibrium, which allows the health authority to track and isolate emerging clusters.

If a health authority does not act 'fast and hard' and delays its response with soft social distancing measures, then, it allows the number of newly infected individuals to exponentially grow for some time, and the population faces many avoidable deaths. When imposing, with delay, strong social distancing measures, through the exponential decline of the number of newly infected individuals, the health authority can potentially still manage the disease to some extent. This takes longer, and the death toll would still be substantially higher due to the higher total number of infected individuals.

Also, to the 'delayed flattening the curve' response, the rule still applies that if social distancing measures are relaxed too early then an additional avoidable death toll arises in a 'second wave' of deaths caused by the once more exponentially growing number of newly infected individuals. To stop this second wave, one would have to impose stronger social distancing measures once more. The population may not be able to go through strict social distancing again, and one may have to give up controlling the epidemic. From this perspective, it is extremely important to have a clear strategy and implement it strictly from the beginning without compromise.

4.6. No Possibility for Sufficient Social Distancing

For populations that are living under conditions that do not allow for strong social distancing at a level where the reproduction number is low enough for a sufficiently long time, the arrival of an epidemic like COVID-19 can be catastrophic. When the epidemic begins, it may not look serious because social distancing and travel bans are often implemented, which reduce the return rate of the number of newly infected individuals but may not sustainably 'flatten the curve'. In many countries, a large part of the population needs to continue to work and socialise when performing economic activities needed to survive. For such a population, it is very difficult to successfully manage an epidemic because it does not allow for the main weapon used to fight the epidemic, social distancing, capable of sufficiently bringing the reproduction number down. A sufficient level of social distancing, when implemented, slows down the speed of the epidemic. This may give infected individuals with severe disease access to medical care, which may reduce the mortality rate.

One possibility for a population to fight an epidemic is to isolate, almost totally, the vulnerable part of the population and let the epidemic take its course with some social distancing measures in place to avoid too many deaths, while at the same time allowing for better medical care. There is in this case not much need for travel restrictions from the perspective of this population. The number of non-susceptibles will exponentially rise through the large number of individuals infected and recovered. The epidemic continues until the proportion of non-susceptibles is so high that there is only a small chance that a vulnerable individual becomes infected. In the case of COVID-19, the mortality rate may be lower than 1% for an on average young population. In many developing countries, different generations often live together. The above-mentioned 'herd immunization' strategy could become very painful if the vulnerable could not be sufficiently protected.

It is unfortunate that the populations that cannot implement social distancing on a sufficient level and for a sufficiently long time do not have many options in the absence of a vaccine.

4.7. Reopening with Vaccination

Let us finally discuss the possibility that a vaccine would become available, thus providing immunization. We denoted by ξ_t the number of vaccinations per day at time t. The SDE (12) captures the evolution of the proportion of non-susceptibles. At the beginning of the epidemic, one has almost no non-susceptibles. When managing the epidemic with a low number of new deaths, there is, for a long time, only a rather small proportion of non-susceptibles in the population. The number of vaccinations per day determines when the critical borderline of about 60% of non-susceptibles is reached, where another major outbreak is unlikely because the number of newly infected individuals evolves in a local equilibrium, even without social distancing. One could at this point slowly start to remove some of the travel restrictions because one would be in a local equilibrium. However, new externally infected individuals would increase the number of newly infected individuals and, therefore, the number of new externally infected individuals should remain rather small compared to the vaccinated individuals per day.

Assume again a population of 25 million. To reach the critical borderline of a level of non-susceptibles of 60% in about one month, one needs to immunize approximately 500,000 susceptibles per day. As the proportion of non-susceptibles increases during the vaccination campaign, the reproduction number can be increased accordingly, ensuring that the number of newly infected individuals remains in equilibrium and on a low level. This means, during the vaccination campaign, one can gradually relax social distancing. When aiming for a value below 1.0 of the product $L_t = R_t(1 - z_t)$ of the reproduction number and proportion of susceptibles, during the vaccination campaign, one can gradually relax social distancing because of the possible higher reproduction number given by the formula

$$R_t = \frac{L_t}{1 - z_t}. \tag{29}$$

In summary, the most recommendable strategy in fighting the epidemic with a minimal number of deaths is to aim for the eradication of the disease and open the economy only in populations that have eradicated the disease. It may take a long time to develop a vaccine that would allow for the economy to be reopened.

The likely mistakes that the leadership of a population could make in managing an epidemic like COVID-19 seem to be as follows:

(i) Not acting 'hard and fast' enough due to delays in implementing social distancing and travel restrictions, prioritising keeping the economy open as long as possible.

(ii) Relaxing social distancing too early when 'flattening the curve' because one wants to reopen the economy as soon as possible.

(iii) Underestimating the number of externally infected individuals that may emerge in the population because one needs to let some travellers and external workers in.

(iv) Not sufficiently protecting vulnerable individuals because it seems expensive or is too restrictive.

(v) Letting the epidemic evolve towards 'herd immunization' because the death toll is underestimated and the economic toll of social distancing appears to be too high.

4.8. Aggregation of Epidemics in a Pandemic

After closing the borders, it was observed, during the COVID-19 pandemic, that epidemics evolve independently in different countries. One may ask the following question: What is the nature of the resulting dynamics for the entire pandemic? Our understanding of important insights will be discussed below, supporting that *the stochastic dynamics of a pandemic are of the same nature as those of each of its epidemics*

Let, for the k-th population, Y_t^k denote the number of newly infected individuals, z_t^k the proportion of non-susceptibles, n_t^k its size, R_t^k its reproduction number, and W_t^k its independent driving Brownian motion at time $t \geq 0$, $k = 1, 2, \ldots, d$, with $d > 1$. For simplicity, assume that the proportion of new externally infected individuals per day in each population can be neglected because most travel between populations is severely restricted in a pandemic. For the total number $\hat{Y}_t$, at time $t \geq 0$, of newly infected individuals in the independently evolving epidemics d, we obtain, from SDE (9), the SDE

$$d\hat{Y}_t = \sum_{k=1}^{d} \left(\left(\frac{Y_t^k}{\sigma}(R_t^k(1 - z_t^k) - 1) \right) dt + \sqrt{\frac{\nu Y_t^k}{\sigma} R_t^k (1 - z_t^k)} dW_t^k \right), \tag{30}$$

with

$$\hat{Y}_t = \sum_{k=1}^{d} Y_t^k. \tag{31}$$

Thus, with an average reproduction number

$$\hat{R}_t = \sum_{k=1}^{d} \frac{Y_t^k}{\hat{Y}_t} R_t^k \tag{32}$$

and an average proportion of non-susceptibles

$$\hat{z}_t = \sum_{k=1}^{d} \frac{Y_t^k R_t^k}{\hat{Y}_t \hat{R}_t} z_t^k \tag{33}$$

we obtain, for the number of newly infected individuals $\hat{Y}_t$, the SDE

$$d\hat{Y}_t = \frac{\hat{Y}_t}{\sigma}(\hat{R}_t(1-\hat{z}_t)-1)dt + \sqrt{\frac{\nu\hat{Y}_t}{\sigma}\hat{R}_t(1-\hat{z}_t)}d\hat{W}_t \tag{34}$$

for $t \geq 0$. Here, $\hat{W}$ denotes standard Brownian motion in t-time. One notes that this type of dynamics is the same as the one obtained for a single population. Thus, it turns out that one can aggregate the numbers of infected individuals of different independently evolving epidemics and remain within the *same model class*. This is a fundamental fact concerning the aggregation of epidemics. The dynamics of the newly infected individuals of an entire pandemic are, therefore, once more, similar to those of a generalized, time-transformed squared Bessel process. This squared Bessel process is of dimension zero if there are no new externally infected individuals. Thus, one can eradicate the pandemic, unless the number of new externally infected individuals excessively increases, through, e.g., transmission from animals or due to non-susceptibles becoming susceptible once more. It follows from (14) that the *intrinsic time for the pandemic runs slower* for a large population.

A strategy to manage the pandemic worldwide is to let each population eradicate its epidemic before it opens itself up to other populations that have done the same. Self-sustained island populations have an advantage because they can better isolate themselves than populations that are close to other populations and possess many natural ties. It can be predicted that small islands will be the first to eradicate the epidemic. Large populations will take more time to eradicate the disease. One may consider subdividing a population of a large country into smaller parts (e.g., states) to first eradicate the disease in each part before opening the scope of the strategy.

Gained immunity may become lost after time, which is a fact that health authorities may have to face in the future for the COVID-19 pandemic. One could capture this feature in an obvious extension of the model, which leads to an SDE with an additional time delay.

5. A Case Study

5.1. Fitting the Model

It is desirable to fit the proposed model to some observed data. There exist various sources capturing the evolution of the COVID-19 epidemic in different countries. We rely on the website of (Roser & Ritchie, 2020) for the Australian data employed and for checking whether the evolution of the observed data makes sense under the proposed model.

The reported number of newly infected individuals at the beginning of an epidemic is rather unreliable and often significantly underestimates the number of newly infected individuals. A more informative number is the number of new deaths. Therefore, we display in Figure 1 (in blue) the number of new deaths reported in Australia, where we set t_0 to zero for 25 January 2020, the day when the first case of a COVID-19 infection was reported in Australia. By using the Equations (10) and (21) and the average time delay between infection and death of $\psi = 17$ days, as well as, a mortality rate of $\lambda = 0.01$, we calculate the expected number of deaths under the model, as shown in Figure 1 (in red), with the parameters chosen as explained below. Note that the number of new deaths appears, in reality, to be a smoothed number, which makes it a less fluctuating number than the number of newly infected individuals and potentially more suitable for estimating the reproductive number. When a large proportion of the population can be regularly tested, with good accuracy, for infections, then, the number of newly infected individuals provides a reasonable basis for estimating the reproductive number. However, as we will see later in a scenario simulation, due to the randomness in the number of newly infected individuals, it still remains difficult to estimate the reproductive number.

A key parameter is the average number ϵ_t of new externally infected individuals per day. Since Australia had detected several externally infected individuals during a period of several months and still had externally infected individuals coming in after the 'curve became flattened', we assume, for simplicity, the parameter ϵ_t is constant, with one external infection every ten days, until $t = 102$. This seems to be an extremely small number. However, it is sufficient to generate the number of infected individuals initially detected in Australia. Moreover, the model shows that any number much higher than $\epsilon_t = 0.1$ seems unable of producing a reasonable fit to the observed data. This means it was extremely important to close the Australian borders soon after the outbreak to avoid large numbers of external infections. After $t = 102$, we set ϵ_t to zero and assume no new external infections are possible under the given travel restrictions, which opens the possibility of eradicating the disease.

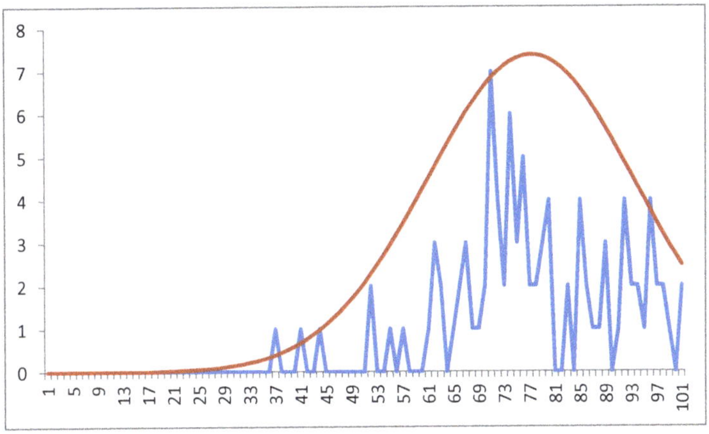

Figure 1. Number of new deaths in Australia (blue) and the expected number under the model (red).

Australia aimed, from the beginning of the pandemic, to avoid the high death toll associated with the 'herd immunization' strategy and to manage the epidemic with a low number of infections. Fortunately, Australia has a developed health system with significant capacity. It can afford to isolate the vulnerable and has an economy that can hopefully sustain a longer partial lockdown. Thus, when managing the epidemic in Australia under these circumstances, it all boils down to the timing of travel restrictions, the imposed degree of social distancing, and the strategy implemented to eradicate the disease with the help of vaccinations that will hopefully become available.

After controlling new external infections through travel restrictions, Australia needed to rapidly bring the exponential growth of newly infected individuals under control. The model clearly shows that in order to achieve this, Australia had to reduce the reproduction number R_t to a level below 1.0. Recall that sufficiently reducing the reproduction number is the primary weapon used to successfully manage an epidemic. This governs the exponential decrease of the average number of newly infected individuals.

The number of newly infected individuals influences, through the mortality rate λ, the number of new deaths X_t, which we display in Figure 1. Under the model, the expected number of new deaths $E(X_t)$ is, by (10), proportional to the mortality rate $\lambda_t = 0.01$ and proportional to ψ, the delayed expected number of newly infected individuals, $E(Y_{t-\psi})$. This allows us to deduce, from the expected number of new deaths, the expected number of newly infected individuals

$$E(Y_t) \approx E(X_{t+\psi})/\lambda_t. \tag{35}$$

Let us continue to use an average timespan of $\sigma = 4.5$ days, during which an infected individual infects others, and choose $\nu = 6$, which generates the typically observed magnitude of fluctuations in the number of newly infected individuals. The data fitted to the number of observed daily new deaths and the history of the implemented social distancing measures for Australia suggest an approximately linear decline in the reproduction number R_t, starting from a relatively high level of about 2.0 at $t = 0$, which is slightly below the 2.25 level, in which case, no social distancing measures would be in place. From that time onward, with every day, social distancing was increasingly implemented. In our modelling, it reached 0.5 at the end of April 2020, which approximately corresponds to $t = 102$. The simplified, linear decrease in the reproduction number during the first period of about 100 days seems to be a reasonable reflection of the impact of social distancing on the reproduction number in Australia for February, March, and April of 2020. It is interesting to note that even a minor increase or decrease in the average level of this linearly declining reproduction number would have substantially changed the expected number of new deaths predicted under the model, which is also shown in Figure 1. In this way, we use the reported number of new deaths to fit the (time-dependent) reproduction number for the observation period of the first 102 days.

The model allows us to calculate, via the differential Equation (21), the expected number of newly infected individuals μ_t. The trajectory of μ_t and the reported number of newly infected individuals in Australia are shown in Figure 2.

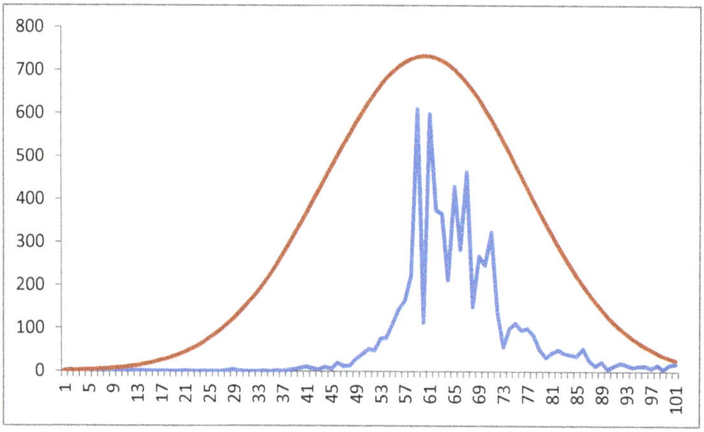

Figure 2. Number of newly infected individuals (blue) and the expected number (red).

Notably, the number of reported newly infected individuals (in blue) and the corresponding theoretical expected number (in red) evolve in an approximately similar shape from the right-hand peak in the figure. However, the reported number of newly infected individuals evolves on a lower level. Before its peak, the reported number of newly infected individuals appears to even be significantly smaller than what the model expects. This is most likely the case because many newly infected individuals have only mild or no symptoms and were not reported. Around the time of the peak in Figure 2, public awareness of COVID-19 was becoming stronger every day, so reporting became more accurate but may still not fully reflect the true number of newly infected individuals. Better testing also became available, which, over time, provided more accurate numbers for the newly infected individuals. Testing is extremely helpful when aiming to eradicate the disease.

5.2. Eradication

Let us now position ourselves at the end of the observed data, towards the end of April 2020, that is, around $t = 102$. By using its properties, the model allows one to probabilistically describe the future evolution of the epidemic using the assumed parameter set. Due to the small number of 18 newly infected individuals at $t = 102$, the numbers of new deaths and newly infected individuals can be expected to fluctuate strongly in the forthcoming period. As explained earlier, this is a property of the underlying stochastic dynamics. After fitting the model, one can use the theoretical predictions of the stochastic evolution of the epidemic to draw probabilistically conclusions.

An ideal strategy would be to aim directly at eradicating the disease. As an island nation, Australia has a good chance of achieving this. Of course, one has to then deal with the fact that the population remains susceptible, which must be changed via vaccination as soon as possible. Many economic activities can be allowed, which is crucial for sustainably mastering the epidemic from an economic point of view. As mentioned earlier, in larger populations, the epidemic evolves intrinsically slower. Therefore, it is recommended to keep the populations of the states of Australia separated from each other and to aim for the eradication of the disease in each state.

Let us give some examples for the time it may take to eradicate the disease, which follow from Formula (19) when assuming that no new externally infected individuals and almost no non-susceptibles exist. When having a reproduction number of $R_t = 0.9$ and 18 newly infected individuals, then the disease would be eradicated in about 90 days, with a probability of 90%. On the other hand, if the reproduction number was lower, at about $R_t = 0.5$, then, the disease would be eliminated in about 36 days, with a 90% probability. These are reasonable times; however, they also show how the early relaxation of social distancing would considerably delay the eradication of the disease. Fortunately, Australia acted relatively 'fast and hard' and brought itself into a position of having to deal with only a few new infections that could be tracked and isolated.

If the number of newly infected individuals would have risen to 100, then, eradicating the disease with a probability of 90% and a reproduction number of $R_t = 0.9$ would take about 170 days. This shows that it is extremely important to act early to keep the number of newly infected individuals from becoming too high. Not only would the death toll be high, but the the health system would also become overwhelmed. The time needed to eventually bring the epidemic under control would become too long to be sustainable for the economy.

The number of days one needs to eradicate the disease with a 90% probability depends on the number of newly infected individuals for a given reproduction number. To provide a visual representation of this fact, we display, in Figure 3, the respective curves for $R_t = 0.5, 0.6, 0.7, 0.8, 0.88, 0.92$, and 0.96. The vertical axis shows the number of newly infected individuals and the horizontal axis shows the number of days needed until eradication. It is important to note that, in this figure, stronger social distancing dramatically reduces the time needed to eradicate the disease.

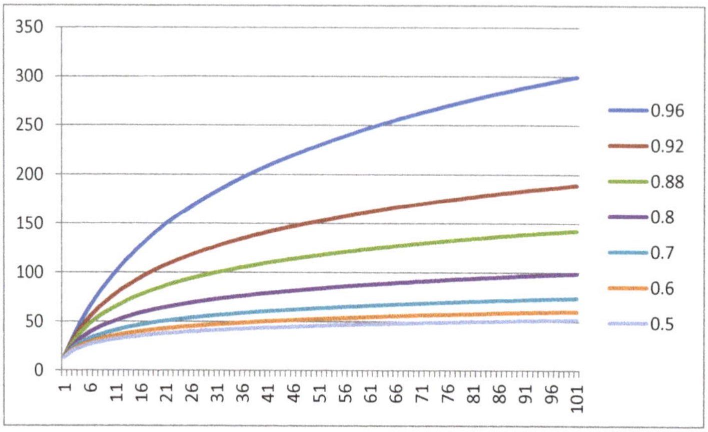

Figure 3. Number of days needed to eradicate the disease depending on the number of newly infected individuals for a given reproduction number.

5.3. Easing Restrictions

If the eradication of the disease in Australia is not achievable because a few new externally infected individuals arrive from time to time, then, it is clear from our discussion in the previous section, that to secure a local equilibrium, the product $R_t(1 - z_t)$ of the reproduction number and the proportion of susceptibles has to remain below 1.0, for example, about $R_t = 0.9$. This number can be confirmed as a suitable number through scenario simulation for the given set of parameters; see, e.g., Figure 6. The easing of social distancing around $t = 102$ should be slowly and carefully executed to make sure that one does not reach a reproduction number too close to 1.0, or even above 1.0. As we have pointed out, a warning sign would be the strongly fluctuating number of newly infected individuals. This should raise an alarm and should lead to stronger social distancing to avoid a major increase in the number of newly infected individuals.

As discussed in the previous section, what would be a severe mistake is the easing of travel restrictions to countries that still have infections circulating. According to Equation (23), the average number of newly infected individuals increases proportionally to the average number of new externally infected individuals per day. This means that, while keeping social distancing on a level where one remains in a local equilibrium, the number of newly infected individuals can become rather large when lifting travel restrictions.

In a local equilibrium, it is important to know how large the number of newly infected individuals may become when it occasionally exhibits an upward excursion. The gamma distribution, as a stationary distribution for the equilibrium dynamic, is given in (28) and allows one to characterize the probability for the number of newly infected individuals below a given threshold $C_t = C$. Let us assume $R_t = R = 0.9$ and $\epsilon_t = \epsilon = 0.1$, for an equilibrium regime where the respective gamma distribution is as shown in Figure 4. We note that the probability for less than 14 newly infected individuals is about 90%, and for less than 55, it is about 99%.

Note, the average number of newly infected individuals per day Y_t is, by (23), around $\bar{Y}_t \approx 4.5$, and its deviation is, by (24), about $\sqrt{(E((Y_t - \mu_t)^2)} \approx 11$. Recall that $\bar{Y}_t$ is the average, which the number of newly infected individuals approaches asymptotically, when we have, on average, one new externally infected individual every ten days. In the case where there are no new externally infected individuals, the number of newly infected individuals would drop to zero, and the disease in Australia would be eradicated relatively early.

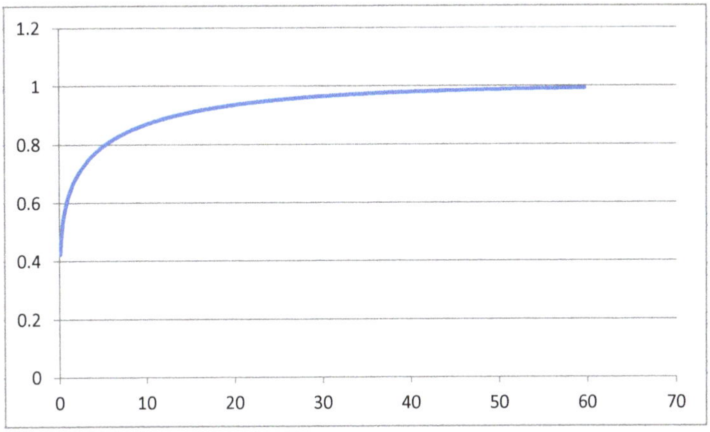

Figure 4. Stationary distribution for newly infected individuals.

In the case where one lifts travel restrictions and several new external infections occur on average, then, eradication is not possible, and one would face a significant number of newly infected individuals, even if one would keep the reproduction number clearly below 1.0. By using (28), we calculate, as shown in Figure 5 for a given average number of new externally infected individuals per day (vertical axis) and the implemented social distancing equivalent to a reproduction number $R = 0.5, 0.6, 0.7, 0.8, 0.88, 0.92$, and 0.96, the probability of the number of newly infected individuals rising above the given critical level $C = 1500$.

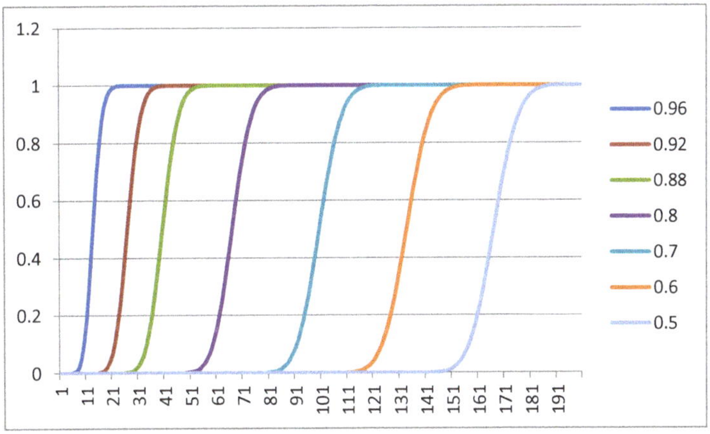

Figure 5. Probability to exceed 1500 newly infected individuals, depending on the average number of new externally infected individuals for a given reproduction number.

An equilibrium regime, such as the one described above, is likely to become for several months the new normal until a vaccine becomes available, unless the Australian population succeeds, through strong social distancing and the tracking of new cases, to eradicate the disease. The eradication scenario seems to be preferable but requires strong social distancing, significant testing, and the tracking of new cases. Once the disease would be eradicated, many social and economic activities could go back to 'normal'. The vulnerable must remain very cautious until a vaccine is introduced.

5.4. Vaccination Strategy

Assume that a vaccine could be rolled out to immunize larger parts of the population. Then, it depends on how fast the immunization could be achieved. Until that time, we assume that the proportion of non-susceptibles would be almost negligible. As indicated in the previous section, when vaccinating fast, one can take advantage of the increasing proportion of non-susceptibles. For example, when aiming, during the vaccination campaign, for a product of reproduction number and a proportion of non-susceptibles close to 0.9, one can increasingly relax social distancing equivalent to a level of

$$R_t = \frac{0.9}{1 - z_t} \tag{36}$$

for the assumed reproduction number. For instance, when vaccinating with a daily number of immunizations of about $\xi = 100,000$, it takes about 156 days until the level of 2.25, for the reproduction number, is reached. This means that no more social distancing is required after that time. The vaccination campaign would take about 5 months; however, it could end much earlier if the number of vaccinations per day would be much higher. Still, only about 60% of the population would be non-susceptible at that time, and it would then take several extra months to vaccinate most of the population. Of course, if vulnerables become vaccinated first, then one would have fewer potential deaths.

5.5. Scenario Simulation

To round up the case study for the Australian COVID-19 epidemic, we use scenario simulation to generate some likely paths for solutions of the SDE (9) by using the algorithm described in Equation (1), together with the related equations. Figure 6 shows the expected value (in blue) and three paths for the simulated number of newly infected individuals when, after the arrival of one newly infected individual at time $t = 0$, the reproduction number is linearly decreasing via social distancing, from 2.0 down to 0.5, during the first 102 days. After $t = 102$, we set R_t to a level of 0.9, where the number of new externally infected individuals is kept at 0.1 to yield a local equilibrium.

We see in Figure 6 some similarity between the three paths. However, during the first 100 days, the number of newly infected individuals varies by magnitudes because of the randomness of the dynamics. Small random differences in the way the number of newly infected individuals evolves at the beginning have a major effect on the magnitude at the peak later. Thus, even if a population implements social distancing similarly to Australia, the number of newly infected individuals at the peak can vary considerably. Therefore, it should be no surprise that some countries did not report large numbers of newly infected individuals during the first 100 days after their first reported infection and the implementation of social distancing. The figure also shows that it is extremely difficult to accurately estimate the reproduction number from the observed number of newly infected individuals or the number of new deaths.

We simulate in Figure 6 the equilibrium paths after $t = 102$, which appear to stay, as theoretically predicted in Figure 4, with a probability of 90% , below 14 and, with a 99% probability, below 55.

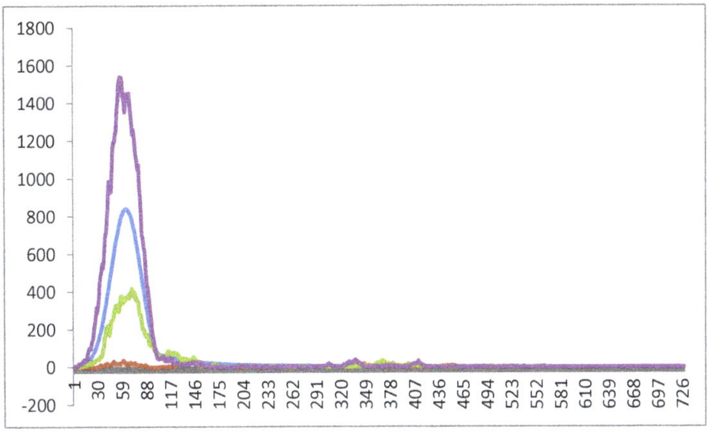

Figure 6. Simulated scenarios for newly infected individuals and the expected number (blue) for $R_t = 0.9$ after $t = 102$.

Let us assume, before time $t = 102$, a parameter setting like the one just discussed. However, we assume, after $t = 102$, that social distancing is only implemented in a way that yields a reproductive number of 1.05, which is slightly above 1.0. This may easily happen when social distancing is relaxed too much. In Figure 7, we show the path of the expected value (in blue) and three likely paths for the number of newly infected individuals. For the first 102 days, these paths show a similar random behaviour to those in Figure 6. However, for the remaining time, we see, among the three simulated paths, one with a significant upward excursion (in green) of the number of newly infected individuals. Like the expected number (in blue), this excursion starts to decrease at around $t = 370$ because the proportion of susceptibles at that time has increased to a level where the product of the number of susceptibles and the reproductive number became less than 1.0, causing the visible decline. This indicates that, already, rather small deviations from 1.0 for the product of the reproductive number and the number of susceptibles can lead to significant random upward excursions.

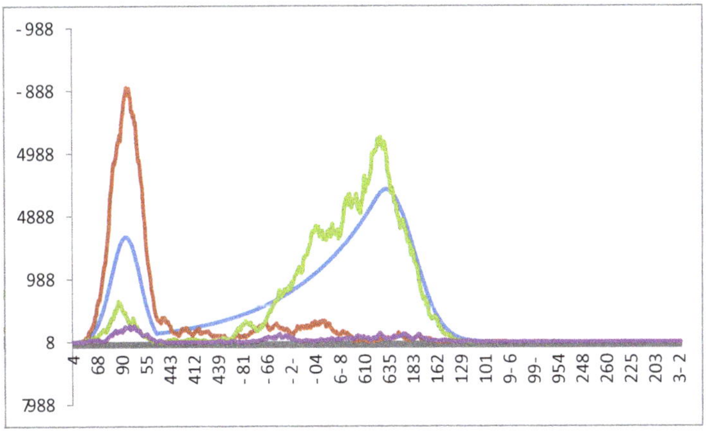

Figure 7. Simulated paths of newly infected individuals and the expected path (blue) with $R_t = 1.05$ after $t = 102$.

The above examples show that scenario simulation can provide, under the model, some valuable insights into the potential evolution of the epidemic. They also demonstrate that it is extremely difficult to accurately estimate the reproductive number when the number of newly infected individuals is not very large.

6. Conclusions

The proposed model provides a tool for quantitatively managing an epidemic and related risks. The provided algorithm for scenario simulation is widely applicable. Furthermore, the revealed fundamental probabilistic properties of the dynamics under the model give important insights into the stochastic evolution of an epidemic. They allow for the calculation of quantities that are crucial for strategies aiming to manage an epidemic. The model explains the dynamics of small numbers of newly infected individuals, which fluctuate strongly in reality. It is explained that, under major travel restrictions and with strong social distancing, one can bring the number of newly infected individuals to an extremely low level and even eradicate the disease within a reasonable time. The probabilistic properties that this paper derives go beyond the known results for popular SIR-type models. They capture different possible regimes of the stochastic dynamics of an epidemic. The proposed model provides a deeper understanding of epidemics. Its properties can support the management of an epidemic and the related risks in finance and insurance.

Funding: This research received no external funding.

Institutional Review Board Statement: Not applicable.

Informed Consent Statement: Not applicable.

Data Availability Statement: Data is contained within the article.

Conflicts of Interest: The author declares no conflicts of interest.

References

Chang, S. L., Harding, N., Zachreson, C., Cliff, O. M., & Prokopenko, M. (2020). Modelling transmission and control of the COVID-19 pandemic in Australia. *Nature Communications, 11*, 5710. [CrossRef]

Chunyan, J., & Jiang, D. (2014). Threshold behaviour of a stochastic SIR model. *Applied Mathematical Modelling, 38*(21–22), 5067–5079.

Dorigatti, I., Okell, L., & Cori, A. (2020). *Severity of 2019-novel coronavirus (nCoV)*. Available online: http://hdl.handle.net/10044/1/77154 (accessed on 28 April 2020).

Feller, W. (1971). *An introduction to probability theory and its applications* (2nd ed., Vol. 2). Wiley.

Ikeda, N., & Watanabe, S. (1989). *Stochastic differential equations and diffusion processes* (2nd ed.). North-Holland. (Original work Published 1981).

Katriel, G. (2010). Epidemics with partial immunity to reinfection. *Mathematical Bioscience, 228*, 153–159. [CrossRef] [PubMed]

Kloeden, P. E., & Platen, E. (1999). *Numerical solution of stochastic differential equations* (3rd ed., Vol. 23). Springer. (Original work Published 1992).

Platen, E. (2020). *Stochastic modelling of the COVID-19 epidemic Stochastic modelling of the COVID-19 epidemic*. Available online: https://www.uts.edu.au/sites/default/files/article/downloads/rp409.pdf (accessed on 30 December 2024).

Revuz, D., & Yor, M. (1999). *Continuous martingales and brownian motion* (3rd ed.). Springer.

Roser, M., & Ritchie, H. (2020). *Coronavirus disease (COVID-19)—The data*. Available online: https://ourworldindata.org/coronavirus (accessed on 28 April 2020).

Journal of
Risk and Financial Management

MDPI

Article

Diagnostic for Volatility and Local Influence Analysis for the Vasicek Model

Manuel Galea [1,*], Alonso Molina [1] and Isabelle S. Beaudry [2]

1 Departamento de Estadística, Pontificia Universidad Católica de Chile, Santiago 7820436, Chile; aomolina@uc.cl
2 Department of Mathematics and Statistics, Mount Holyoke College, South Hadley, MA 01075, USA; ibeaudry@mtholyoke.edu
* Correspondence: manuel.galea@uc.cl; Tel.: +56-9-5504-5973

Abstract: The Ornstein–Uhlenbeck process is widely used in modeling biological systems and, in financial engineering, is commonly employed to describe the dynamics of interest rates, currency exchange rates, and asset price volatilities. As in any stochastic model, influential observations, such as outliers, can significantly influence the accuracy of statistical analysis and the conclusions we draw from it. Identifying atypical data is, therefore, an essential step in any statistical analysis. In this work, we explore a set of methods called local influence, which helps us understand how small changes in the data or model can affect an analysis. We focus on deriving local influence methods for models that predict interest or currency exchange rates, specifically the stochastic model called the Vasicek model. We develop and implement local influence diagnostic techniques based on likelihood displacement, assessing the impact of the perturbation of the variance and the response. We also introduce a novel and simple way to test whether the model's variability stays constant over time based on the Gradient test. The purpose of these methods is to identify potential risks of reaching incorrect conclusions from the model, such as the inaccurate prediction of future interest rates. Finally, we illustrate the methodology using the monthly exchange rate between the US dollar and the Swiss franc over a period exceeding 20 years and assess the performance through a simulation study.

Keywords: influence diagnostics; Ornstein–Uhlenbeck processes; likelihood inference; stochastic interest rate models; gradient test

1. Introduction

Understanding and predicting interest rate movements plays a significant role in investment decisions and financial risk management. The main objective of this paper is to diagnose certain assumption violations in classical stochastic interest rate models. In particular, we derive closed-form expressions of the local influence methodology for the one-factor models, a popular class of interest rate models mainly used in pricing interest rate derivatives. These models are represented by the following stochastic differential equation (Black & Scholes, 1973; Hassler, 2016; Rémillard, 2013):

$$dr(t) = m(t, r(t))dt + v(t, r(t))dW(t), \tag{1}$$

where m is the drift function, v is the volatility function, $r(t)$ denotes the interest rate at time $t \geq 0$, and W denotes a Brownian motion or Wiener process. Various models for the interest rates $\{r(t); t \geq 0\}$ have been proposed in the literature. Overviews may be found in the books by Brigo and Mercurio (2006), Filipović (2009), McDonald (2013), and Rémillard (2013), and in the papers by Merton (1973), Vasicek (1977), and Cox et al. (1985), among others. Equation (2) presents a common class of drift and volatility functions (Chan et al., 1992; Nowman, 1997):

$$m(t, r(t)) = \alpha(\beta - r(t)) \quad v(t, r(t)) = \sigma r^{\tau}(t), \tag{2}$$

where α is the mean reversion parameter and β is the long-term mean rate of the process, σ is the volatility of the short-term rate and τ is the proportional volatility exponent (the symbols appearing in the interest rate models are summarized in Appendix A). A class of well-known interest rate processes is obtained by imposing restrictions on the parameters of the stochastic model (2). For more details on this family of models, see, for example, Chan et al. (1992) and Nowman (1997, 1998).

Remark 1. *The drift function in Equation (2) may also be written as* $m(t, r(t)) = a + br(t)$ *(Chan et al., 1992). However, this paper follows the parametrization presented in Rémillard (2013) and Mazzoni (2018). The advantage of Equation (2) is that the parameters have straightforward economic interpretations.*

Estimating the parameters in the process (2) has been vastly discussed in the literature. Lo (1986), Duan (1994), Valdivieso et al. (2009), Rémillard (2013) and Fergusson and Platen (2015), among others, present maximum likelihood estimation in processes of the Ornstein–Uhlenbeck type. Chan et al. (1992) estimate the parameters of several continuous-time models for short-term rates using the generalized method of moments. In this work, we derive the maximum likelihood (ML) estimators for the Vasicek model, which corresponds to the special case when $\tau = 0$. Subsequently, we develop the local influence methods for stochastic models defined in (2). To our knowledge, the local influence methodology has not been applied to this type of stochastic models.

As mentioned in Galea and Giménez (2019), influence analysis is a group of techniques designed to evaluate the sensitivity of some statistics to perturbations in the data or model assumptions. Detecting atypical (outliers) and influential observations is an essential step in any financial model's econometric analysis. Also, this is important to evaluate the sensitivity (robustness) of the results obtained using the available data set, since atypical interest rates can distort predictions and statistics of interest, leading to, in some cases, wrong decisions. In this direction, van der Hart et al. (2003) showed that outliers are one of the important factors in the selection of stocks in emerging markets. In addition, decisions based on distorted inferences may be incorrect or suboptimal. Several approaches exist to assess the influence of data and model perturbations on parameter estimates. Overviews may be found in the books by Cook and Weisberg (1982) and Chatterjee and Hadi (1988) and the papers by Cook (1986), Escobar and Meeker (1992) and Zhu et al. (2007). Case deletion is a popular way to assess the impact of individual cases on the estimation process. This approach, referred to as global influence analysis, consists of quantifying the effect of a given observation by completely removing it. However, this approach is impractical for data collected at regular time intervals, as eliminating certain observations would disrupt the consistency of those intervals.

Local influence is an alternative approach based on differential geometry rather than complete deletion. This method employs a differential comparison of parameter estimates before and after a given perturbation to the data or model assumptions. Recently, Galea and Giménez (2019) applied the local influence approach to the capital asset pricing model under the multivariate normal distribution for modeling asset returns. However, the application of this methodology to the Vasicek model has not been considered in the literature. The main contribution of this paper is to apply the local influence methodology under various perturbation schemes to identify influential outliers among the observations or assumption violations of the Vasicek model. We consider a parametrization of the model that substantially simplifies the development of the influence measures.

We apply the methodology to the monthly exchange rates of the US dollar and the Swiss franc from January 2001 to November 2024. This application is particularly relevant, as both currencies are regarded as "safe-haven" assets. Understanding the relationship between these two currencies is of significant interest to financial market stakeholders, including investors seeking stability during periods of economic uncertainty. Moreover, the Swiss National Bank implemented a notable shift in its monetary policies during the analyzed period, which likely influenced the volatility of the Swiss franc. By utilizing the methods developed in this paper, we aim to uncover meaningful patterns in the volatility of this exchange rate over time. We also assess the performance of the proposed methodology through a simulation study.

The paper is structured as follows. In Section 2, we describe the Vasicek model for the modeling of interest rates. In Section 3, we present the ML estimators for the classical Ornstein–Uhlenbeck process used in the Vasicek model. In that section, we also propose a statistic to test the hypothesis of constant volatility based on the Gradient test. The local influence methodology and explicit calculations of the influence measures are then derived in Section 4. Section 5 presents a simulation study and an application based on the monthly exchange rate between the US dollar and the Swiss franc after 31 December 2000. Finally, we discuss some concluding remarks in Section 6.

2. The Vasicek Model

Interest rate modeling finds most of its applications in investment and financial decisions, portfolio management, and insurance. The Vasicek model (Vasicek, 1977) is a stochastic model describing the evolution of interest rates and is based on an arithmetic Brownian motion with mean reversion. The Vasicek model was developed assuming an efficient market economy, that is, based on the assumptions that (1) complete information is available to all the economic agents acting in the markets, and (2) privileged information providing any advantage does not exist. Furthermore, the Vasicek model assumes that interest rates have a regressive behavior towards a fixed value representing the long-term value of the interest rate. This model is known as the mean regression model and is based on the Wiener and Ornstein–Uhlenbeck processes, which we define below. The Wiener process, also referred to as a Brownian motion, is a continuous-time stochastic process with independent increments. In finance, the Wiener process is used to describe changes in stock prices or interest rates.

Definition 1. *A stochastic process* $W = \{W(t); t \geq 0\}$ *is a standard Wiener process or standard Brownian motion if (i)* $W(0) = 0$*, (ii)* W *has independent increments, that is,* $W(t_2) - W(t_1), W(t_3) - W(t_2), \ldots, W(t_n) - W(t_{n-1})$ *are independent random variables for* $t_1 \leq t_2 \leq \ldots \leq t_n$*, (iii) for each time interval* (t_i, t_{i-1})*,* $W(t_i) - W(t_{i-1}) \sim N(0, t_i - t_{i-1})$*, and (iv) the realizations of* W *are continuous; that is,* $t \to W(t)$ *is a continuous function of* $t \geq 0$.

Also, we know that the Wiener process is a Gaussian process, and its covariance function is given by $\mathrm{Cov}\{W(s), W(t)\} = \min(s, t)$, for $s, t \geq 0$.

Definition 2. *Let $\{r(t); t \geq 0\}$ be a stochastic process. The process defined by $dr(t) = \alpha(\beta - r(t))dt + \sigma dW(t)$ is called an Ornstein–Uhlenbeck process, where W is Brownian motion and $\sigma > 0$. The solution of this equation is:*

$$r(t) = \beta + e^{-\alpha t}(r_0 - \beta) + \sigma \int_0^t e^{-\alpha(t-u)} dW(u), \ \ t \geq 0, \tag{3}$$

with known $r(t_0) = r_0$, and where α, β, and σ are parameters of the process. The Ornstein–Uhlenbeck process is a Gaussian and Markovian process. For properties of stochastic integrals of the form $\int_0^t f(u)dW(u)$, see Appendix B.

Definition 3. *If the interest rate follows an Ornstein–Uhlenbeck mean-reverting process, defined by (3), where α is the mean speed of reversion, β is the mean interest rate level, σ is the instantaneous volatility, and W is a standard Brownian motion, then the resulting process is referred to as the Vasicek model.*

From the properties of the integral of a deterministic function relative to a Brownian motion, see Appendix B, it follows that the interest rate $r(t)$, conditional on $\mathcal{F}_s$, the information set at time s, for $s \leq t$, is normally distributed with mean and variance functions given by:

$$\begin{aligned} \mathrm{E}\{r(t)|\mathcal{F}_s\} &= r(s)\mathrm{e}^{-\alpha(t-s)} + \beta\{1 - \mathrm{e}^{-\alpha(t-s)}\}, \\ \mathrm{Var}\{r(t)|\mathcal{F}_s\} &= \frac{\sigma^2}{2\alpha}\{1 - \mathrm{e}^{-2\alpha(t-s)}\}, \end{aligned} \tag{4}$$

respectively. Hence $P(r(t) < 0) > 0$, which is inappropriate when $r(t)$ represents the rate of interest at time t. However, this probability is typically negligible. On the other hand, the long-term distribution of the Ornstein–Uhlenbeck process is stationary and is Gaussian with mean β and variance $\sigma^2/2\alpha$, which we denote as $r_\infty \sim N(\beta, \sigma^2/2\alpha)$. So, in the long-term equilibrium, the probability of negative values of r_∞ is given by:

$$P(r_\infty < 0) = \Phi\Big(- \beta\sqrt{2\alpha/\sigma^2}\Big), \tag{5}$$

where $\Phi(x)$ denotes the cumulative distribution function of a standard normal distribution.

Note that if observations are collected at regular intervals of length $h > 0$, we can write:

$$r(t+h) = \beta + \mathrm{e}^{-\alpha h}(r(t) - \beta) + \sigma \int_t^{t+h} \mathrm{e}^{-\alpha(t+h-u)} dW(u). \tag{6}$$

Remark 2. *To simulate n observations from a Vasicek model, we can use the following equation:*

$$r(k+h) = \beta + e^{-\alpha h}(r(k) - \beta) + \sigma\sqrt{\frac{1 - exp\{-2\alpha h\}}{2\alpha}} Z_k, \tag{7}$$

where, $Z_k, k = 0, 1, ..., n$ are random variables independent and identically distributed $N(0,1)$.

Remark 3. *Another important application of the Ornstein–Uhlenbeck process, and in particular of the Vasicek model, is the modeling of exchange rates. The exchange rate is a very important macroeconomic variable that plays a crucial role in international trade. See, for example, Mostafa and Mohammed (2016), Sikora et al. (2019) and Serafin et al. (2020).*

Let $\theta = (\alpha, \beta, \sigma^2)^T$. To simplify the statistical analysis of the Vasicek model given in Definition 3, we consider the following parametrization (Brigo & Mercurio, 2006; Rémillard,

2013). Let $\gamma = (\gamma_0, \gamma_1, \gamma_2)^T$, where $\gamma_0 = \beta(1-\gamma_1)$, $\gamma_1 = \exp\{-\alpha h\}$, and $\gamma_2 = \sigma^2(1-\gamma_1^2)/2\alpha$. We also assume n observations of $r(t)$ at times $\{t_1, t_2, ..., t_n\}$, where $0 < t_1 < t_2 < ... < t_n$. Let $r = (r_1, ..., r_n)^T$, where $r_i = r(t_i)$ for $i = 1, ..., n$ and $r(t_0) = r_0$ is known. Usually, interest rates are observed at equally spaced time points $\{h, 2h, ..., nh\}$ over a given time interval $[0, T]$, where $T = nh$. Therefore, we may rewrite Equation (7) with the above parametrization, such that:

$$r_i = \gamma_0 + \gamma_1 r_{i-1} + \epsilon_i, \tag{8}$$

where $\epsilon_i \sim N(0, \gamma_2)$, for $i = 1, ..., n$.

Let $p(r|\gamma, r_0)$ denote the density function of r given r_0. As described in Lo (1986), the density p may be written as the product of conditional densities:

$$p(r|\gamma, r_0) = p_1(r_1|\gamma, r_0)p_2(r_2|\gamma, r_1, r_0)....p_n(r_n|\gamma, r_{n-1}, ..., r_0). \tag{9}$$

However, because the interest rate $r(t)$ follows a Markovian process, Equation (9) reduces to:

$$p(r|\gamma, r_0) = p_1(r_1|\gamma, r_0)p_2(r_2|\gamma, r_1)....p_n(r_n|\gamma, r_{n-1}),$$

and since the increments of the Wiener process are normally distributed, we have that:

$$p(r_i|\gamma, r_{i-1}) = \frac{1}{\sqrt{2\pi\gamma_2}}\exp\Big\{-\frac{(r_i - \gamma_1 r_{i-1} - \gamma_0)^2}{2\gamma_2}\Big\},$$

which corresponds to the probability density function of a normal distribution with mean $\gamma_1 r_{i-1} + \gamma_0$ and variance γ_2, for $i = 1, ..., n$. Finally, the joint density function of the sample $r = (r_1, ..., r_n)^T$ takes the following form:

$$p(r|\gamma, r_0) = \prod_{i=1}^{n} \frac{1}{\sqrt{2\pi\gamma_2}}\exp\Big\{-\frac{(r_i - \gamma_1 r_{i-1} - \gamma_0)^2}{2\gamma_2}\Big\}, \tag{10}$$

that is, $r|r_0 \sim N_n(X\gamma^*, \gamma_2 I_n)$, with $X^T = \begin{pmatrix} 1 & . & . & . & 1 \\ r_0 & . & . & . & r_{n-1} \end{pmatrix}$ and $\gamma^* = (\gamma_0, \gamma_1)^T$, a simple linear regression model.

3. Likelihood Inference

In this section, we briefly discuss the likelihood inference for the model parameters and their associated standard errors, as well as hypothesis testing for constant volatility.

3.1. Maximum Likelihood Estimation

Maximum likelihood estimation in processes of theOrnstein–Uhlenbeck type has been discussed in the literature, for instance, see Lo (1986), Duan (1994), Brigo and Mercurio (2006), Valdivieso et al. (2009), Rémillard (2013) and Fergusson and Platen (2015). Chan et al. (1992) estimate the parameters of several continuous-time models for the short-term interest rates using the Generalized Method of Moments. In this section, we present some results for the ML estimation following Rémillard (2013) and Fergusson and Platen (2015), using the parametrization of the Vasicek model discussed in the previous section.

From Equation (10), it follows that the log-likelihood function for γ takes the following form:

$$\mathcal{L}(\gamma) = \sum_{i=1}^{n} \mathcal{L}_i(\gamma), \tag{11}$$

where $\mathcal{L}_i(\gamma) = -\frac{1}{2}\ln 2\pi - \frac{1}{2}\ln\gamma_2 - \frac{1}{2\gamma_2}(r_i - \gamma_1 r_{i-1} - \gamma_0)^2$, for $i = 1, ..., n$. The score functions for γ then follow, which are given by:

$$\begin{aligned}\frac{\partial\mathcal{L}(\gamma)}{\partial\gamma_0} &= \frac{1}{\gamma_2}\sum_{i=1}^{n}(r_i - \gamma_1 r_{i-1} - \gamma_0),\\ \frac{\partial\mathcal{L}(\gamma)}{\partial\gamma_1} &= \frac{1}{\gamma_2}\sum_{i=1}^{n}(r_i - \gamma_1 r_{i-1} - \gamma_0)r_{i-1},\\ \frac{\partial\mathcal{L}(\gamma)}{\partial\gamma_2} &= \sum_{i=1}^{n}\Big\{-\frac{1}{2\gamma_2} + \frac{1}{2\gamma_2^2}(r_i - \gamma_1 r_{i-1} - \gamma_0)^2\Big\}.\end{aligned} \tag{12}$$

From Equation (12), we obtain the following ML estimators for γ_0, γ_1 and γ_2:

$$\begin{aligned}\hat\gamma_0 &= \frac{1}{n}\sum_{i=1}^{n}(r_i - \hat\gamma_1 r_{i-1}),\\ \hat\gamma_1 &= \frac{n\sum_{i=1}^{n} r_i r_{i-1} - \sum_{i=1}^{n} r_i \sum_{i=1}^{n} r_{i-1}}{n\sum_{i=1}^{n} r_{i-1}^2 - \{\sum_{i=1}^{n} r_{i-1}\}^2},\\ \hat\gamma_2 &= \frac{1}{n}\sum_{i=1}^{n}(r_i - \hat\gamma_1 r_{i-1} - \hat\gamma_0)^2.\end{aligned} \tag{13}$$

As described in Appendix C, we may also derive an estimator of the covariance matrix for $\hat\gamma$, which leads to the following result:

$$D(\hat\gamma) = \begin{pmatrix} \hat\gamma_2(X^TX)^{-1} & 0 \\ 0 & 2\hat\gamma_2^2/n \end{pmatrix}.$$

Due to the invariance property of the ML estimators, we also obtain the ML estimators for α, β and σ^2:

$$\begin{aligned}\hat\alpha &= -\frac{1}{h}\ln\hat\gamma_1,\\ \hat\beta &= \hat\gamma_0/(1-\hat\gamma_1),\\ \hat\sigma^2 &= -2\hat\gamma_2\ln\hat\gamma_1/h(1-\hat\gamma_1^2),\end{aligned} \tag{14}$$

and an estimator of the covariance matrix of $\hat\theta = (\hat\alpha, \hat\beta, \hat\sigma^2)^T$ is given by $D(\hat\theta) = L_\theta^{-1}(\hat\theta)$, as shown in Appendix C.

3.2. Diagnostic for Constant Volatility

An important feature of the class of stochastic models defined in Equation (2) is the evolution of the volatility, $v(t, r(t)) = \sigma r^\tau(t)$. The dynamics of volatility can be modeled using the parameter τ. For example, if $\tau = 0$, the volatility is constant and Equation (2) corresponds to the Vasicek model (Vasicek, 1977), while $\tau = 1/2$ corresponds to the CIR model (Cox et al., 1985). In the latter case, the volatility is not constant. In this section, we propose a statistic for testing the hypothesis of constant volatility. The hypothesis that $\tau = 1/2$ may be tested similarly.

To test the null hypothesis $H_0 : \tau = 0$, we use the Gradient test (Lemonte, 2016; Terrell, 2002), defined as:

$$Ga = \mathcal{U}^T(\tilde\gamma)(\hat\gamma - \tilde\gamma), \tag{15}$$

where $\hat\gamma$ and $\tilde\gamma$ are the ML estimators of $\gamma = (\gamma_0, \gamma_1, \gamma_2, \tau)^T$ based on the full and reduced ($\tau = 0$) models, respectively, and $\mathcal{U}(\gamma)$ is the score function for a sample of the process shown in Equation (2). Under the null hypothesis, Ga asymptotically follows a χ^2-distribution with $p = 1$ degree of freedom.

Following Nowman (1997), the discrete model we use for estimation is given by:

$$r_i = \gamma_0 + \gamma_1 r_{i-1} + \epsilon_i, \tag{16}$$

where $\epsilon_i \sim N(0, \gamma_2 r_{i-1}^{2\tau})$, for $i = 1, ..., n$, $\gamma_0 = \beta(1 - \exp(-\alpha))$, $\gamma_1 = \exp(-\alpha)$ and $\gamma_2 = \frac{\sigma^2}{2\alpha}(1 - \exp(-2\alpha))$.

Remark 4. *Using the approximation that* $\exp(-2\alpha) \approx 1 - 2\alpha$*, we have that* $\gamma_2 \approx \sigma^2$*, and, in this case, the models proposed by Chan et al. (1992) and Nowman (1997, 1998) coincide.*

From Equation (16), it follows that the log-likelihood function for γ under the full model takes the form:

$$\mathcal{L}(\gamma) = \sum_{i=1}^{n} \mathcal{L}_i(\gamma), \tag{17}$$

where $\mathcal{L}_i(\gamma) = -\frac{1}{2}\ln 2\pi - \frac{1}{2}\ln \gamma_2 - \tau \ln r_{i-1} - \frac{1}{2\gamma_2 r_{i-1}^{2\tau}}(r_i - \gamma_1 r_{i-1} - \gamma_0)^2$, for $i = 1, ..., n$. The associated score functions for γ are given by:

$$\begin{aligned}
\frac{\partial \mathcal{L}(\gamma)}{\partial \gamma_0} &= \sum_{i=1}^{n} \Big(\frac{1}{\gamma_2 r_{i-1}^{2\tau}}\Big)(r_i - \gamma_1 r_{i-1} - \gamma_0), \\
\frac{\partial \mathcal{L}(\gamma)}{\partial \gamma_1} &= \sum_{i=1}^{n} \Big(\frac{1}{\gamma_2 r_{i-1}^{2\tau}}\Big)(r_i - \gamma_1 r_{i-1} - \gamma_0) r_{i-1}, \\
\frac{\partial \mathcal{L}(\gamma)}{\partial \gamma_2} &= \sum_{i=1}^{n} \Big\{-\frac{1}{2\gamma_2} + \frac{1}{2\gamma_2^2 r_{i-1}^{2\tau}}(r_i - \gamma_1 r_{i-1} - \gamma_0)^2\Big\}, \\
\frac{\partial \mathcal{L}(\gamma)}{\partial \tau} &= \sum_{i=1}^{n} \Big\{-\ln r_{i-1} + \frac{\ln r_{i-1}}{\gamma_2 r_{i-1}^{2\tau}}(r_i - \gamma_1 r_{i-1} - \gamma_0)^2\Big\}.
\end{aligned} \tag{18}$$

Let $c_i = c_i(\tau) = 1/r_{i-1}^{2\tau}$, for $i = 1, ..., n$. If we set $\mathcal{U}(\gamma) = 0_4$, then it follows that:

$$\begin{aligned}
\hat{\gamma}_0 &= \sum_{i=1}^{n} c_i(r_i - \hat{\gamma}_1 r_{i-1}) / \sum_{i=1}^{n} c_i, \\
\hat{\gamma}_1 &= \frac{\sum_{i=1}^{n} c_i r_i r_{i-1} - (\sum_{i=1}^{n} c_i r_i)(\sum_{i=1}^{n} c_i r_{i-1}) / \sum_{i=1}^{n} c_i}{\sum_{i=1}^{n} c_i r_{i-1}^2 - (\sum_{i=1}^{n} c_i r_{i-1})^2 / \sum_{i=1}^{n} c_i}, \\
\hat{\gamma}_2 &= \frac{1}{n}\sum_{i=1}^{n} c_i(r_i - \hat{\gamma}_1 r_{i-1} - \hat{\gamma}_0)^2,
\end{aligned} \tag{19}$$

$$g(\tau) = 0, \tag{20}$$

where $g(\tau) = \hat{\gamma}_2 \sum_{i=1}^{n} \ln r_{i-1} - \sum_{i=1}^{n} \ln r_{i-1}\big[c_i(r_i - \hat{\gamma}_1 r_{i-1} - \hat{\gamma}_0)^2\big]$. The parameter vector $\gamma = (\gamma_0, \gamma_1, \gamma_2, \tau)^T$ may be estimated through the following iterative process:

Step 0: Set an initial value for $\hat{\gamma}^{(0)}$ and $k = 0$.

Step 1: Calculate the weights $c_i(\hat{\tau}^{(k)})$, for $i = 1, ..., n$.

Step 2: Using Equation (19), calculate the estimates $\hat{\gamma_0}^{(k+1)}$, $\hat{\gamma_1}^{(k+1)}$, and $\hat{\gamma_2}^{(k+1)}$.

Step 3: Solve Equation (20) to obtain $\hat{\tau}^{(k+1)}$. The Newton-type algorithm provides a recursive expression for $\hat{\tau}^{(k+1)}$ given by:

$$\hat{\tau}^{(k+1)} = \hat{\tau}^{(k)} - g(\hat{\tau}^{(k)})/g'(\hat{\tau}^{(k)}),$$

where $g'(\hat{\tau}^{(k)}) = 2\sum_{i=1}^{n} c_i(\hat{\tau}^{(k)})(\ln r_{i-1})^2(r_i - \hat{\gamma}_1^{(k+1)} r_{i-1} - \hat{\gamma}_0^{(k+1)})^2$, for $k = 0, 1, ...$

the variance given by $\omega_i^{-1}\gamma_2$, for $i = 1, \ldots, n$, the density function of the perturbed model is given by:

$$p(r|\gamma,\omega,r_0) = \prod_{i=1}^{n} \frac{1}{\sqrt{2\pi\gamma_2\omega_i^{-1}}} \exp\Big\{ -\frac{(r_i - \gamma_1 r_{i-1} - \gamma_0)^2}{2\gamma_2\omega_i^{-1}} \Big\}, \tag{22}$$

and the corresponding perturbed log-likelihood function is given by:

$$\mathcal{L}(\gamma|\omega) = \sum_{i=1}^{n} \mathcal{L}_i(\gamma|\omega_i),$$

where $\mathcal{L}_i(\gamma|\omega_i) = -\frac{1}{2}\ln 2\pi - \frac{1}{2}\ln\gamma_2 + \frac{1}{2}\ln\omega_i - \frac{\omega_i}{2\gamma_2}\{r_i - \gamma_1 r_{i-1} - \gamma_0\}^2$, for $i = 1, ..., n$.

In this case, the elements $g_{ij}(\omega) = (1/2\omega_i^2)\delta_{ij}$ for $i, j = 1, ..., n$, where δ_{ij} is the Kronecker delta, see Appendix E for more details. Therefore, the metric matrix $G(\omega_0) = (1/2)I_n$, with $\omega_0 = (1, ..., 1)^T$. Thus, the perturbation scheme of the variance is appropriate and allows us to assess the effect of the heteroskedasticity on the ML estimators. The Δ matrix for this perturbation scheme takes the form of $\Delta = (\Delta_1, ..., \Delta_n)$ where $\Delta_i = (1/\hat{\gamma}_2)(e_i, e_i r_{i-1}, e_i^2/2\hat{\gamma}_2)^T$, where $e_i = r_i - \hat{\gamma}_1 r_{i-1} - \hat{\gamma}_0$, for $i = 1, ..., n$.

4.2.2. Perturbation of the Interest Rate

In this section, we discuss the perturbation of the response. Specifically, we consider an additive perturbation scheme $r_{i\omega} = r_i + \omega_i$, $i = 1, ..., n$. In this case, $\omega = (\omega_1, ..., \omega_n)^T$ and $\omega_0 = 0_n$, where 0_n represents an $n \times 1$ vector of zeros. After some algebraic manipulations, we obtain that the metric matrix is $G(\omega) = (1/\gamma_2)I_n$. Thus, the additive perturbation of the response is appropriate too. With this perturbation scheme, we can assess the effect of outliers on the ML estimators. The Δ matrix is given by $\Delta^T = (1/\hat{\gamma}_2)(X, e/\hat{\gamma}_2)$, where $e = (e_1, ..., e_n)^T$ is the vector of residuals (Schwarzmann, 1991). In this case, the influence matrix $F = \Delta^T L_\gamma^{-1}(\gamma)\Delta = (1/\hat{\gamma}_2)\{H + 2hh^T\}$, where the hat matrix $H = X(X^TX)^{-1}X^T$ and the normalized residual vector $h = e/\|e\|$, with $Hh = 0_n$. The direction of the maximum curvature is proportional to the residual vector, $d_{max} = h$. For more details, see Schwarzmann (1991). Finally, since $\mathrm{tr}(F) = 4/\hat{\gamma}_2$ and $f_{ii} = (h_{ii} + 2h_i^2)/\hat{\gamma}_2$, we have $B_i = (h_{ii} + 2h_i^2)/4$, for $i = 1, ..., n$. Note that $f_{ii} = 4B_i/\hat{\gamma}_2$ and therefore, both diagnostic measures highlight the same potentially influential observations, if any.

5. Applications and Simulation Study

5.1. Historical USD to CHF Exchange Rate

This section describes the results we obtained when applying the methods discussed in this paper to the monthly exchange rate between the US dollar (USD) and the Swiss franc (CHF). The data cover the period from January 2001 to November 2024 and therefore include 287 monthly observations. Table 1 presents a descriptive summary of the series. We see that in the period considered, the exchange rate fluctuates between a minimum of 0.779 and a maximum of 1.784, with an average of 1.080. We also observe that the exchange rate is right-skewed (skewness = 1.448) and the observed kurtosis (4.479) is greater than what would be expected under the normal distribution.

Table 1. Summary statistics for monthly USD to CHF exchange rate over the period from January 2001 to November 2024.

n	Min	Median	Mean	Max	SD	Skewness	Kurtosis
287	0.779	0.989	1.080	1.784	0.214	1.448	4.479

Figure 1a shows the fluctuation in the exchange rates in the covered period and the fitted Vasicek model in red. In addition to the overall downward trend in the exchange rate over that period, we note the close fit of the model to the data. Figure 1b displays the exchange rates in the current period against the value in the previous one, (r_{i-1}, r_i), $i = 1, ..., n$. From this figure, we observe a linear relationship between the exchange rates of consecutive months. Consequently, both plots suggest that the Vasicek model appears to be reasonable for modeling these exchange rates.

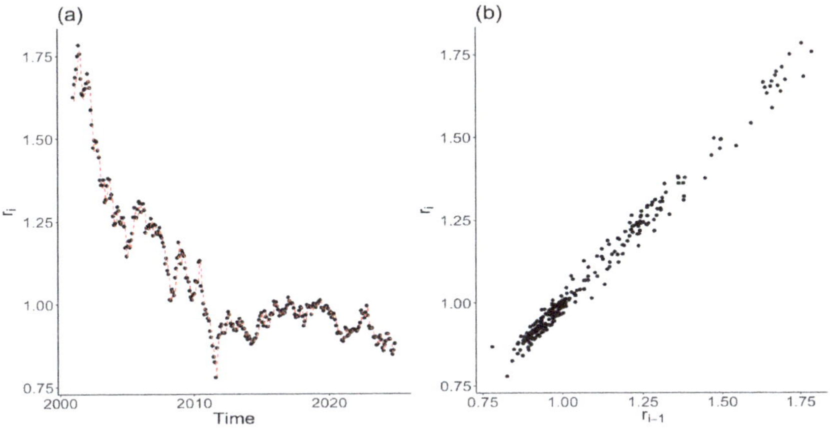

Figure 1. (**a**) Monthly exchange rate between the US dollar and the Swiss franc from January 2001 to November 2024 and the fitted Vasicek model in red. and (**b**) Dispersion plot of the exchange rates of the current period (r_i) against those of the previous one (r_{i-1}).

The maximum likelihood (ML) estimates and their standard errors are shown in Table 2, and the resulting estimated Vasicek model is as follows:

$$\hat{r}_i = 0.92120 + \mathrm{e}^{-0.1983}(r_{i-1} - 0.92120), \quad \text{for } i = 1, ..., n. \tag{23}$$

Using the Wald test, we determined that the coefficients α and β and the volatility σ^2 are all statistically significant at a significance level of 0.05. Furthermore, from Equation (5), the estimated probability (in the long-term equilibrium) of a negative exchange rate is $\hat{P}(r_\infty < 0) = 2.19 \times 10^{-12}$. These results do not provide us with evidence against the adequacy of the Vasicek model.

Table 2. ML estimates of the Vasicek model and their respective standard errors.

Parameter	ML Estimate	Standard Error
α	0.19833	(0.08095)
β	0.92120	(0.10793)
σ^2	0.00702	(0.00059)

Panel (a) of Figure 2 shows a Q–Q plot of the studentized residuals $r_1^*, \ldots, r_n^*$ and panel (b), a plot of the studentized residuals against the fitted values of the USD to CHF exchange rate. Figure 2a shows a moderate departure from the normality assumption. Figure 2b does not display any distinctive patterns indicating violations of the model assumptions. Again, both plots indicate that the model assumptions are reasonably met.

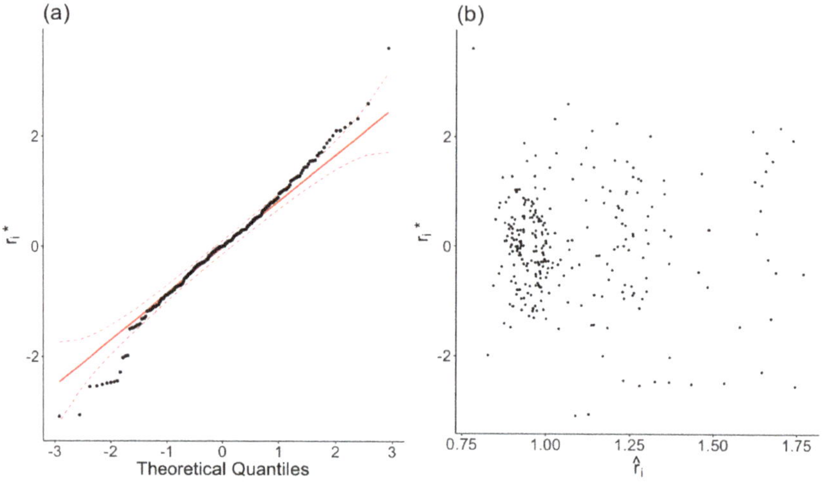

Figure 2. (**a**) Q–Q plots of the studentized residuals and (**b**) of the studentized residuals against the fitted values of the USD to CHF exchange rate.

Figure 3 displays diagnostic plots for the constant volatility assumption. Figure 3a presents the index plot of the B_i statistics of the local influence method for the perturbation of the variance scheme. The dashed line represents the threshold of $\bar{B} + 2\text{sd}(B)$, signaling that the observation is potentially influential. As we may observe, several observations fall above the threshold, but the observations 2011–09 and 2001–08 are the most significant influential observations for this perturbation scheme. Figure 3b shows the Cook–Weisberg plots (Cook & Weisberg, 1983) to assess the constant volatility assumption in regression models. Interestingly, this plot also identifies observation 2011–09 as the most potentially influential under the constant volatility assumption. It is interesting to note that this influential observation happened shortly after the National Swiss Bank adopted a minimum exchange rate at CHF 1.20 per euro in an attempt to limit the overvaluation of the Swiss franc (Swiss National Bank, 2011) and that both methods detect its influence. Also, none of the influential observations occurred after 2012. This may indicate that the monetary policy reduced the volatility between the two currencies and that using the Vasicek model for the entire period from 2001 to 2024 is inappropriate. Finally, both graphs suggest that $\tau \neq 0$.

The Gradient statistics test that $H_0 : \tau = 0$ is $Ga = 23.687$ with a p−value of 1.13×10^{-6} so we reject the hypothesis that $H_0 : \tau = 0$ at a 5% significance level. Finally, we also calculated the Box Pierce portmanteau statistic (Nowman, 1997) to assess the dynamic specification of the model. We obtained an S statistic equal to 18.944, corresponding to a p-value of 0.0899. Thus, we have moderate evidence against the null hypothesis of white noise. To some extent, both tests indicate that the variance is not constant across the full duration of the data. Since the perturbation of the variance also suggests that using the Vasicek model may not be appropriate over the entire period, we broke the data into two segments: before 2012 and after 2011, and repeated the Gradient and Box Pierce Portmanteau tests. After splitting the data, both tests failed to reject the null hypothesis of constant variance within each segment, contradicting the initial conclusion of the tests. This outcome could be attributed to the reduced statistical power from using fewer observations to fit the model, or it may indicate that separately modeling the two time periods is more appropriate.

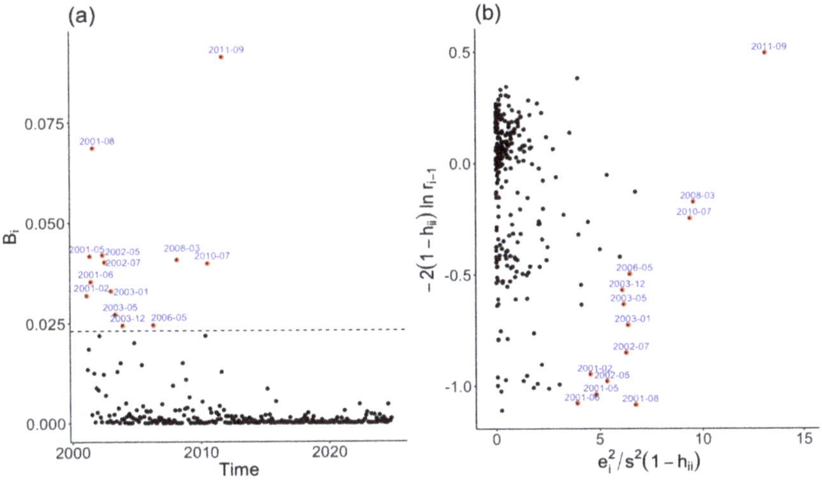

Figure 3. (**a**) Index plot of the B_i statistics of the local influence method for the perturbation of the variance scheme. (**b**) Cook–Weisberg plot. The detected influential observations are shown in red, and their dates of occurrence are indicated next to them in both plots.

Finally, Figure 4 displays the diagnostic plot for the additive perturbation of the exchange rates. Figure 4a presents the index plot of the B_i statistics of the local influence method for that perturbation scheme. The dashed line represents the threshold of $\bar{B} + 2\text{sd}(B)$, indicating that the observation is potentially influential. Again, the most influential observations correspond to 2011–09 and 2001–08. This result suggests that the Swiss National Bank monetary policy adopted in September 2011 might have significantly impacted that year's exchange rate. Figure 4b shows the monthly exchange rate between the US dollar and the Swiss franc from January 2001 to November 2024 and the fitted Vasicek model in red. The blue points represent the detected influential observations. We again note that none of the influential observations occur after 2011. The Vasicek model may be more appropriate for the USD-CHF exchange rates after the introduction of the monetary policy.

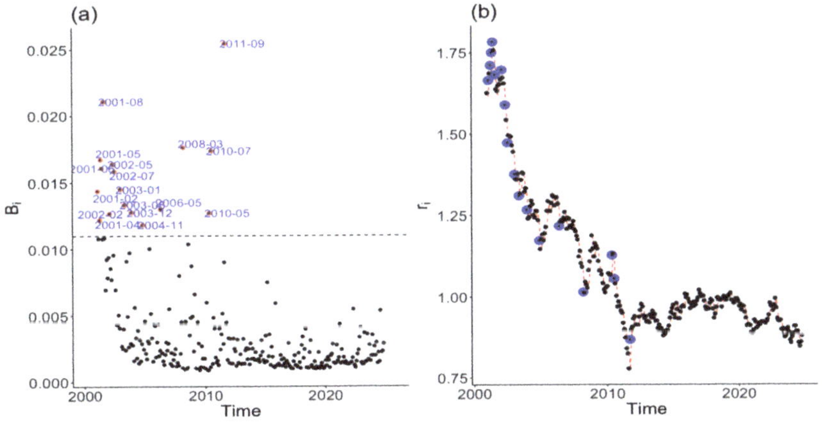

Figure 4. (**a**) Index plot of the B_i statistics for the perturbation of the exchange rate. The detected influential observations are shown in red, and their dates of occurrence are indicated next to them. (**b**) Monthly exchange rate between the US dollar and the Swiss franc from January 2001 to November 2024 and the fitted Vasicek model in red. The blue points represent the detected influential observations.

5.2. Simulation Study

To evaluate the Gradient test's performance in finite samples, we conducted a simulation study to assess the empirical level and the power of the test at a nominal significance level of 5% when testing the hypothesis H_0 that $\tau = 0$. We simulated 5000 series of returns from the stochastic model (2), with $\alpha = 0.10, \beta = 0.20, \sigma^2 = 0.001, \tau = 0, \tau = 1/2, h = 1/12$ and $r_0 = 0.50$.

Table 3 summarizes some of the results of the simulations. Rejection rates from the Gradient test are close to 5%, independently of the sample size. As expected, when $\tau \neq 0$, the rejection rates tend to 1.00 as the sample size increases. These results suggest that the Gradient test detects with a high probability non-constant interest rate when it is indeed non-constant, as long as the sample size is sufficiently large. Therefore, investors may reconsider their exposure to a financial product if the Gradient test identifies non-constant variability, particularly if maintaining stability in variability is among their investment objectives. However, while doing so, they must recall that, by design, the Gradient test has a probability, 5% in this case, of incorrectly detecting a non-constant variance when the variance is, in fact, constant, irrespective of the sample size.

Table 3. Rejection rates of the Gradient test for the hypothesis of constant volatility at a 5% significance level.

n	$\tau = 0$ (Vasicek Model)	$\tau = 0.5$ (CIR Model)
50	0.0554	0.0692
120	0.0488	0.2170
200	0.0480	0.5210
300	0.0514	0.8074
1000	0.0542	0.9988

Figure 5 shows the empirical histograms of the Gradient test values for the simulated data under different scenarios, where we see clear evidence of the agreement between the empirical and theoretical distributions under the null hypothesis.

In response to reviewers' feedback, we conducted additional simulations using two alternative models to assess their impact on the Gradient test's ability to detect heteroskedasticity. We chose the parameters of the alternative models to ensure that the long-term expected value of the interest rate and their volatility were similar to those of the Vasicek and CIR models. The results showed that the proposed Gradient test has higher power for the alternative models than the CIR model for the selected sample sizes. This can be attributed to the fact that, while the average volatility is comparable across models, the alternative models exhibit greater variability in volatility across samples. It thus suggests that the data are noisier, making it easier for the Gradient test to detect the non-constant variance. In addition, these simulations revealed that the Gradient test performs better for the four models we considered when the initial interest rate, r_0, is higher than the long-term equilibrium rate.

We further investigated the proposed influence measures' empirical performance, based on one simulated data set, with two added outliers; the observation 100, r_{100} was changed to $1.10r_{100}$ and r_{200} was changed to $1.15r_{200}$. Figure 6 presents the index plots of B_i and the Cook–Weisberg plot for this simulated data set. We see that both influence measures can effectively detect the two perturbed observations.

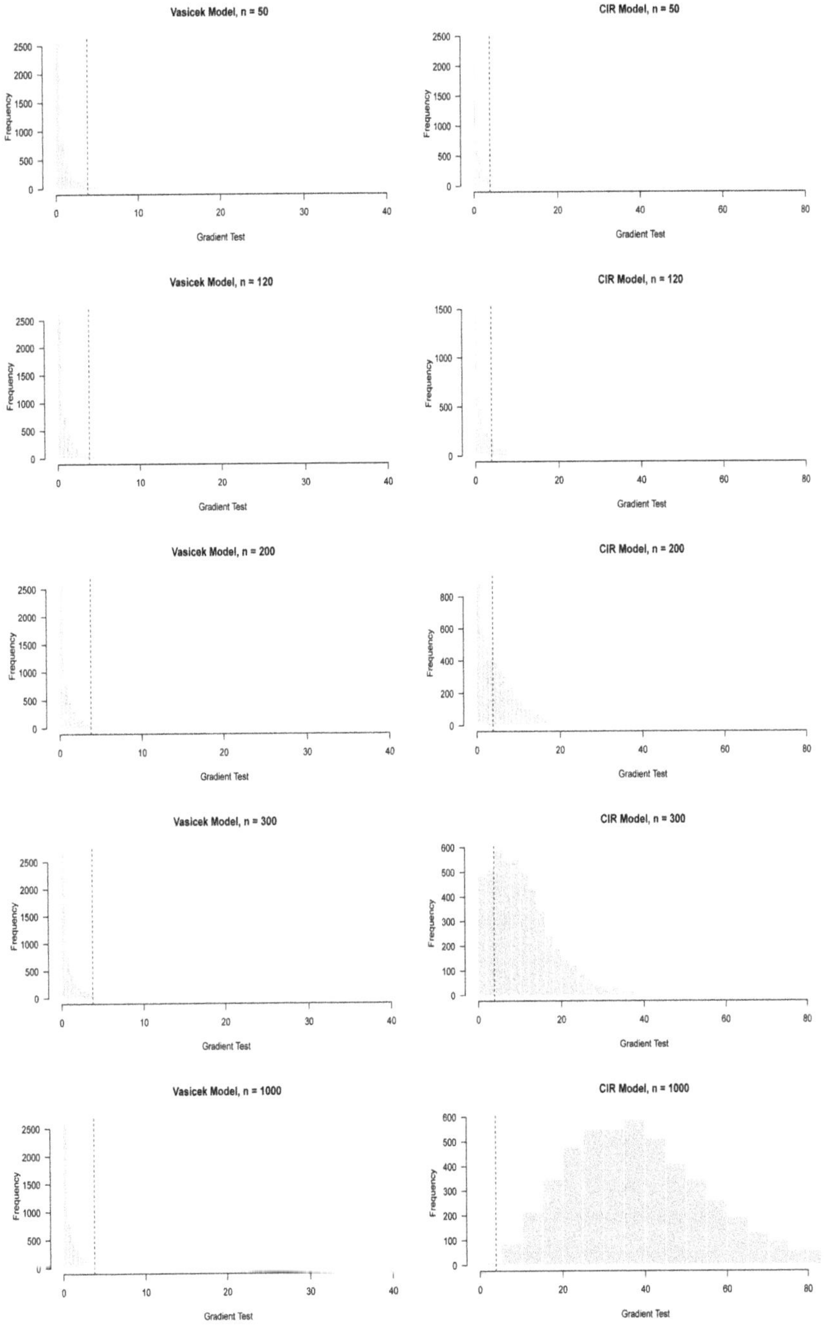

Figure 5. Empirical histograms of the Gradient test for the simulated data.

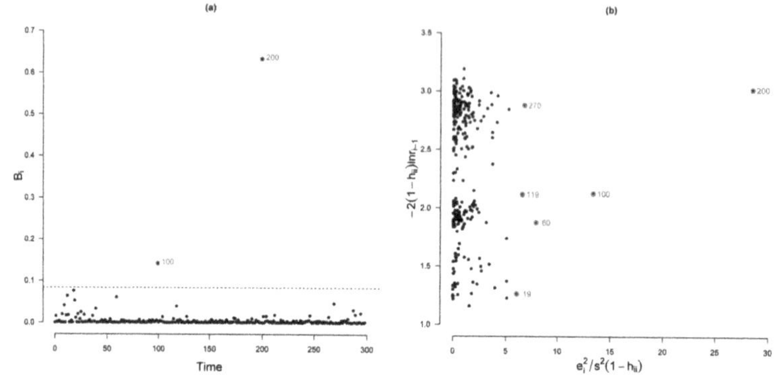

Figure 6. (**a**) Index plots of B_i. (**b**) Cook–Weisberg plot for a simulated data set.

6. Conclusions

Understanding interest rates' fluctuations play an essential role in investment decisions and financial markets' risk management. One approach to understanding the behavior of interest rates is through stochastic modelling. However, inferences for stochastic models may be sensitive to the presence of atypical rates. Since outliers may significantly distort estimators and statistical tests, potentially leading to incorrect or suboptimal decision making, assessing the results' sensitivity to such observations is an essential step to stochastic model inference. The local influence methodology is an approach to identify outliers that may significantly affect the value of statistics of interest in a given model. This work's main contribution is to apply the local influence methodology in stochastic interest rate models. In particular, the proposed local influence measures we present in this work aim at detecting atypical rates for the Vasicek model.

After describing the parametrization of the Vasicek model, we discussed the likelihood inference for the model parameters. We also presented methods for the diagnostic of constant volatility, which, in some instances, we adapted for the Vasicek model. Then, we explained how the local influence approach could also be applied to this stochastic model. To do so, we derived closed-form expressions for the delta matrices under the perturbation of the variance. Subsequently, we illustrated the methods in an application using the monthly exchange rate between the US dollar and the Swiss franc from January 2001 to November 2024. We found similarities in the detection of influential observations among the methodologies.

We also developed the local influence diagnostic for the perturbation in the interest rates and the associated delta matrices. We evaluated the performance of the method through a simulation study in which we artificially added outliers. Empirical results show that the proposed influence measures are able to detect outliers' rates.

This paper's proposed diagnostic measures may be extended to other stochastic models (Brigo & Mercurio, 2006; Chan et al., 1992; Nowman, 1997; Rémillard, 2013). For example, they may be applied to (i) more complex Ornstein–Uhlenbeck Process, (ii) the Black-Scholes Model, (iii) Stochastic Volatility Models, and (iv) stochastic models for selecting investment portfolios. However, the normality assumption is key for these types of stochastic models, and we know that this assumption is not reasonable in many cases. Therefore, another interesting area of research is the development of statistical methodology using alternative distributions, such as elliptical and/or elliptical skew distributions (Cambanis et al., 1981; Galea et al., 2008; Kelker, 1970) which offer a more flexible framework for modeling interest and exchange rates.

Author Contributions: All authors have contributed substantially to the work reported. In particular, the authors have contributed in the following ways: Conceptualization: M.G.; methodology: M.G., and I.S.B.; software: A.M., and I.S.B.; validation: M.G., and I.S.B.; formal analysis, M.G., A.M., and I.S.B.; investigation, A.M., and I.S.B.; resources, not applicable; data curation, A.M., and I.S.B.; writing—original draft preparation, M.G., and I.S.B.; writing—review and editing, M.G., and I.S.B.; visualization, A.M., and I.S.B.; supervision, M.G.; project administration, M.G.; funding acquisition: not applicable. All authors have read and agreed to the published version of the manuscript.

Funding: This research received no external funding.

Institutional Review Board Statement: Not applicable.

Informed Consent Statement: Not applicable.

Data Availability Statement: In this paper, we used the monthly exchange rates between the US dollar and the Swiss franc published on the website https://www.bcentral.cl/inicio accessed on 30 November 2024.

Conflicts of Interest: The authors declare no conflicts of interest.

Appendix A. Interest Rate Model Symbols and Their Interpretation

Table A1. Interpretation of the symbols appearing in the interest rate models.

Symbol	Interpretation
r_i	Response variable (e.g., interest) at time i
α	Mean speed of the interest rate reversion
β	Mean interest rate level
σ	Volatility of the short-term rate
τ	Proportional volatility exponent
γ_0	Intercept of the relation between r_i and r_{i-1}
γ_1	Slope of the relation between r_i and r_{i-1}
γ_2	Variance of the error term of the relation between r_i and r_{i-1}

Appendix B. The Stochastic Integral

If f is a deterministic square integrable function, and $W(t)$ is a Wiener process, then the stochastic integral

$$M(t) = \int_0^t f(u)dW(u),$$

has a normal distribution with mean 0 and variance $\int_0^t f^2(u)du$. For instance, if $f(u) = \sigma\exp\{-\alpha(t-u)\}$, then $\int_0^t f^2(u)du = \int_0^t \sigma^2\exp\{-2\alpha(t-u)\}du = \frac{\sigma^2}{2\alpha}\{1-\exp(-2\alpha t)\}$, for $t > 0$. Also, the covariance function of $\{M(t), t \geq 0\}$ is given by:

$$\text{Cov}\{M(t), M(s)\} = \text{Cov}\Big\{\int_0^t f_1(u)dW(u), \int_0^s f_2(u)dW(u)\Big\} = \int_0^{t\wedge s} f_1(u)f_2(u)du,$$

where $t \wedge s = \min\{t, s\}$.

Appendix C. The Observed Information Matrix

The second derivatives of the log-likelihood function are given by:

$$\begin{aligned}
\frac{\partial^2 \mathcal{L}(\gamma)}{\partial \gamma_0^2} &= -\frac{n}{\gamma_2}, \\
\frac{\partial^2 \mathcal{L}(\gamma)}{\partial \gamma_0 \partial \gamma_1} &= -\frac{1}{\gamma_2}\sum_{i=1}^{n} r_{i-1}, \\
\frac{\partial^2 \mathcal{L}(\gamma)}{\partial \gamma_0 \partial \gamma_2} &= -\frac{1}{\gamma_2^2}\sum_{i=1}^{n} (r_i - \gamma_1 r_{i-1} - \gamma_0), \\
\frac{\partial^2 \mathcal{L}(\gamma)}{\partial \gamma_1^2} &= -\frac{1}{\gamma_2}\sum_{i=1}^{n} r_{i-1}^2, \\
\frac{\partial^2 \mathcal{L}(\gamma)}{\partial \gamma_1 \partial \gamma_2} &= -\frac{1}{\gamma_2^2}\sum_{i=1}^{n} (r_i - \gamma_1 r_{i-1} - \gamma_0) r_{i-1}, \\
\frac{\partial^2 \mathcal{L}(\gamma)}{\partial \gamma_2^2} &= \sum_{i=1}^{n} \left\{ \frac{1}{2\gamma_2^2} - \frac{1}{\gamma_2^3}(r_i - \gamma_1 r_{i-1} - \gamma_0)^2 \right\}.
\end{aligned}$$

This leads to the following observed information matrix for γ:

$$L_\gamma(\gamma) = \frac{1}{\gamma_2}\begin{pmatrix} X^T X & 0 \\ 0 & n/2\gamma_2 \end{pmatrix},$$

and the following estimator of the covariance matrix of $\hat{\gamma}$:

$$D(\hat{\gamma}) = \begin{pmatrix} \hat{\gamma}_2 (X^T X)^{-1} & 0 \\ 0 & 2\hat{\gamma}_2^2/n \end{pmatrix}.$$

The Fisher information depends on the parametrization of the statistical model. If $\gamma = a(\theta)$ is a continuously differentiable function of θ, then $L_\theta(\theta) = J^T L_\gamma(\theta) J$, where the (i,j)th element of the 3×3 Jacobian matrix J is defined by $J_{ij} = \partial a_i(\theta)/\partial \theta_j$, for $i, j = 1, 2, 3$. In our case:

$$J = \begin{pmatrix} h\beta\gamma_1 & 1-\gamma_1 & 0 \\ -h\gamma_1 & 0 & 0 \\ \sigma^2(2\alpha h\gamma_1^2 + \gamma_1^2 - 1)/2\alpha^2 & 0 & (1-\gamma_1^2)/2\alpha \end{pmatrix},$$

with $\gamma_1 = \exp\{-\alpha h\}$.

Appendix D. Invariant of C_d and B_d

The conformal normal curvature has two important properties. For details and applications see Poon and Poon (1999) and Zhu and Lee (2005).

(i) The normal curvatures C_d and B_d do not depend on the parametrization. Then, C_d and B_d are invariant with respect to any parametrization $\gamma = a(\theta)$ where a is a differentiable function of θ. (ii) The conformal normal curvature B_d in any direction unit d at ω_0 is invariant with respect to the conformal parametrization $\omega^* = \omega^*(\omega)$.

Appendix E. Determination of $g_{ij}(\omega)$ for the Variance Perturbation Scheme

As described in Section 4.1, $g_{ij}(\omega)$ is defined as:

$$g_{ij}(\omega) = E_\omega\Big[\frac{\partial}{\partial\omega_i}\mathcal{L}(\gamma|\omega)\frac{\partial}{\partial\omega_j}\mathcal{L}(\gamma|\omega)\Big], \quad \text{for } i,j = 1,\ldots,n.$$

For the perturbation of the variance, we have that:

$$\begin{aligned}
g_{ii}(\omega) &= E_\omega\Big[\Big(\frac{\partial}{\partial\omega_i}\mathcal{L}(\gamma|\omega)\Big)^2\Big] \\
&= E_\omega\Big[\Big(\frac{1}{2\omega_i} - \frac{(r_i - \gamma_1 r_{i-1} - \gamma_0)^2}{2\gamma_2}\Big)^2\Big] \\
&= E_\omega\Big[\frac{1}{4\omega_i^2} - \frac{1}{2\omega_i^2}\Big(\frac{r_i - \gamma_1 r_{i-1} - \gamma_0}{(\gamma_2\omega_i^{-1})^{0.5}}\Big)^2 + \frac{1}{4\omega_i^2}\Big(\frac{r_i - \gamma_1 r_{i-1} - \gamma_0}{(\gamma_2\omega_i^{-1})^{0.5}}\Big)^4\Big] \\
&= \frac{1}{4\omega_i^2}E_\omega\Big[1 - 2Z_i^2 + Z_i^4\Big] \qquad \text{(where } Z_i \sim N(0,1))\\
&= \frac{1}{2\omega_i^2},
\end{aligned}$$

for $i = 1,2,\ldots,n$. Also, for $i \neq j \in \{1,2,\ldots,n\}$, we have that:

$$\begin{aligned}
g_{ij}(\omega) &= E_\omega\Big[\frac{\partial}{\partial\omega_i}\mathcal{L}(\gamma|\omega)\frac{\partial}{\partial\omega_j}\mathcal{L}(\gamma|\omega)\Big] \\
&= E_\omega\Big[\Big(\frac{1}{2\omega_i} - \frac{(r_i - \gamma_1 r_{i-1} - \gamma_0)^2}{2\gamma_2}\Big)\Big(\frac{1}{2\omega_j} - \frac{(r_j - \gamma_1 r_{j-1} - \gamma_0)^2}{2\gamma_2}\Big)\Big] \\
&= \frac{1}{4\omega_i\omega_j}E_\omega\Big[1 - \Big(\frac{r_i - \gamma_1 r_{i-1} - \gamma_0}{(\gamma_2\omega_i^{-1})^{0.5}}\Big)^2 - \Big(\frac{r_j - \gamma_1 r_{j-1} - \gamma_0}{(\gamma_2\omega_j^{-1})^{0.5}}\Big)^2 \\
&\quad + \Big(\frac{(r_i - \gamma_1 r_{i-1} - \gamma_0)(r_j - \gamma_1 r_{j-1} - \gamma_0)}{(\gamma_2\omega_i^{-1}\gamma_2\omega_j^{-1})^{0.5}}\Big)^2\Big] \\
&= \frac{1}{4\omega_i\omega_j}E_\omega\Big[1 - Z_i^2 - Z_j^2 + Z_i^2 Z_j^2\Big] \qquad \text{(where } Z_i \text{ and } Z_j \text{ are i.i.d. } N(0,1))\\
&= 0.
\end{aligned}$$

Therefore, we have that: $g_{ij}(\omega) = (1/2\omega_i^2)\delta_{ij}$ for $i,j = 1,\ldots,n$, where δ_{ij} is the Kronecker delta.

References

Black, F., & Scholes, M. (1973). The pricing of options and corporate liabilities. *Journal of Political Economy, 81*, 637–659. [CrossRef]

Brigo, D., & Mercurio, F. (2006). *Interest rate models—Theory and practice, with smile, inflation and credit* (2nd ed.). Springer.

Cambanis, S., Huang, S., & Simons, G. (1981). On the theory of elliptical contoured distributions. *Journal of Multivariate Analysis, 11*, 368–385. [CrossRef]

Chan, K. C., Karolyi, G. A., Longstaff, F. A., & Sanders, A. B. (1992). An empirical comparison of alternative models of the short-term interest rate. *Journal of Finance, 47*, 1209–1227.

Chatterjee, S., & Hadi, A. S. (1988). *Sensitivity analysis in linear regression*. John Wiley.

Cook, R. D. (1986). Assessment of local influence. *Journal of the Royal Statistical Society, B, 48*, 133–169. [CrossRef]

Cook, R. D., & Weisberg, S. (1982). *Residuals and influence in regression*. Chapman and Hall.

Cook, R. D., & Weisberg, S. (1983). Diagnostics for heteroscedasticity in regression. *Biometrika, 70*(1), 1–10. [CrossRef]

Cox, D. R., & Reid, N. (1987). Parameter orthogonality and approximate conditional inference. *Journal of the Royal Statistical Society, B, 49*, 1–39. [CrossRef]

Cox, J. C., Ingersoll, J. E., & Ross, S. A. (1985). A theory of the term structure of interest rates. *Econometrica, 53*, 385–407. [CrossRef]

Duan, J. C. (1994). Maximum likelihood estimation using price data of the derivative contract. *Mathematical Finance*, *4*, 155–167. [CrossRef]

Escobar, E., & Meeker, W. (1992). Assessing influence in regression analysis with censored data. *Biometrics*, *48*, 507–528. [CrossRef] [PubMed]

Fergusson, K., & Platen, E. (2015). Application of maximum likelihood estimation to stochastic short rate models. *Annals of Financial Economics*, *10*, 1–26. [CrossRef]

Filipović, D. (2009). *Term-structure models. A graduate course*. Springer.

Galea, M., Díaz-García, J. A., & Vilca, F. (2008). Influence diagnostics in the capital asset pricing model under elliptical distributions. *Journal of Applied Statistics*, *35*(2), 179–192. [CrossRef]

Galea, M., & Giménez, P. (2019). Local influence diagnostics for the test of mean-variance efficiency and systematic risks in the capital asset pricing model. *Statistical Papers*, *60*, 293–312. [CrossRef]

Hassler, U. (2016). *Stochastic processes and calculus: An elementary introduction with applications*. Springer International Publishing.

Kelker, D. (1970). Distribution theory of spherical distributions and location-scale parameter generalization. *Sankhya*, *32*, 419–430.

Lemonte, A. (2016). *The Gradient test: Another likelihood-based test*. Academic Press.

Lo, A. (1986). Statistical tests of contingent-claims asset-pricing models: A new methodology. *Journal of Financial Economics*, *17*, 143–173. [CrossRef]

Mazzoni, T. (2018). *A first course in quantitative finance*. Cambridge University Press.

McDonald, R. L. (2013). *Derivatives markets* (3rd ed.). Pearson.

Merton, R. C. (1973). Theory of rational option pricing. *Bell Journal of Economics and Management Science*, *4*, 141–183. [CrossRef]

Mostafa, H., & Mohammed, H. (2016). Modeling of Exchange Rate Risk. *American Journal of Mathematics and Statistics*, *6*, 233–237.

Nowman, K. B. (1997). Gaussian estimation of single-factor continuous time models of the term structure of interest rates. *Journal of Finance*, *52*, 1695–1706.

Nowman, K. B. (1998). Continuous time short rate interest rate models. *Applied Financial Economics*, *8*, 401–407. [CrossRef]

Poon W., & Poon Y. S. (1999). Conformal normal curvature and assessment of local influence. *Journal of the Royal Statistical Society, B*, *61*, 51–61. [CrossRef]

Rémillard, B. (2013). *Statistical methods for financial engineering*. CRC Press.

Schwarzmann, B. (1991). A connection between local-influence analysis and residual diagnostics. *Technometrics*, *33*, 103–104. [CrossRef]

Serafin, T., Michalak, A., Bielak, L., & Wylomanska, A. (2020). Averaged-calibration-length prediction for currency exchange rates by a time-dependent vasicek model. *Theoretical Economics Letters*, *10*, 579–599. [CrossRef]

Sikora, G., Michalak, A., Bielak, L., Mista, P., & Wylomanska, A. (2019). Stochastic modeling of currency exchange rates with novel validation techniques. *Physica A*, *523*, 1202–1215. [CrossRef]

Swiss National Bank. (2011, September 6). *Swiss National Bank sets minimum exchange rate at CHF 1.20 per euro*. Available online: https://www.snb.ch/en/publications/communication/press-releases/2011/pre_20110906 (accessed on 19 December 2024).

Terrell, G. (2002). The gradient statistic. *Computing Science and Statistics*, *34*, 206–215.

Valdivieso, L., Schoutens, W., & Tuerlinckx, F. (2009). Maximum likelihood estimation in processes of Ornstein-Uhlenbeck type. *Statistical Inference for Stochastic Processes*, *12*, 1–19. [CrossRef]

van der Hart, J., Slagter, E., & van Dijk, D. (2003). Stock selection strategies in emerging markets. *Journal of Empirical Finance*, *10*, 105–132 [CrossRef]

Vasicek, O. A. (1977). An equilibrium characterization of the term structure. *Journal of Financial Economics*, *5*, 177–188. [CrossRef]

Zhu, H. T., Ibrahim, J. G., Lee, S., & Zhang, H. (2007). Perturbation selection and influence measures in local influence analysis. *The Annals of Statistics*, *35*, 2565–2588. [CrossRef]

Zhu, H. T., & Lee, S. Y. (2001). Local influence for incomplete-data models. *Journal of the Royal Statistical Society, B*, *63*, 111–126. [CrossRef]

Journal of
Risk and Financial Management

MDPI

Article

On the Use of the Harmonic Mean Estimator for Selecting the Hypothetical Income Distribution from Grouped Data

Kazuhiko Kakamu

School of Data Science, Nagoya City University, Nagoya 467-8601, Japan; kakamu@ds.nagoya-cu.ac.jp;
Tel.: +81-52-872-5720

Abstract: It is known that the harmonic mean estimator is a consistent estimator of the marginal likelihood and is easy to implement, but it has severe biases and does not change as much as the prior distribution changes. In this study, we investigate the use of the harmonic mean estimator to select the hypothetical income distribution from grouped data through Monte Carlo simulations and apply it to real data in Japan. From the results, we confirm that there are significant biases, but it can be reliably used to select an appropriate model only when the sample size is large enough under appropriate prior settings.

Keywords: harmonic mean estimator; hypothetical income distribution; Metropolis–Hastings algorithm; marginal likelihood; Markov chain Monte Carlo (MCMC) method

1. Introduction

Non-negative statistical distributions and their applications are studied and used in areas such as finance (Higbee & McDonald, 2024), among others. One such example is the work of Professor Chris Heyde; see, for example, Heyde (1964, 1986). Among them, income distribution is widely considered to be one of the most important research areas involving non-negative-valued random variables, and such distributions are relevant to societal outcomes in general. In estimating an income distribution, the choice of the initial hypothetical income distribution is a crucial consideration. However, we face a trade-off between fitting a precise hypothetical income distribution and the interpretability of the parameters. Therefore, in empirical studies, we often start with distributions such as the lognormal (LN) distribution, the Dagum (DA) distribution introduced by Dagum (1977), the Singh–Maddala (SM) distribution proposed by Singh and Maddala (1976), and others. These distributions are preferred for better interpretability of the parameters. In addition, the estimation of the more flexible generalized beta distribution of the second kind (hereinafter referred to as GB2 distribution), introduced by McDonald (1984), is also examined within a Bayesian framework by Kakamu and Nishino (2019).

Several Bayesian model selection criteria exist for choosing the most appropriate hypothetical income distribution from a set of candidate distributions (see, for example, Ando (2010) for Bayesian model selection). Among these criteria, the marginal likelihood is a common choice for selecting the hypothetical income distribution, and various estimators have been proposed for its accurate estimation. Accurate estimation of the marginal likelihood is critical when dealing with Bayesian model averaging (BMA) or Bayes factor estimation. Inaccurate estimates can lead to inappropriate inference. Therefore, the precision of marginal likelihood estimators is extensively studied in the literature, with works such as Friel and Wyse (2012); Kass and Raftery (1995) providing valuable insights. On the other hand, the harmonic mean estimator introduced by Newton and Raftery (1994) is a consistent estimator of the marginal likelihood and is easy to implement. However, it has been criticized for its significant biases and limited responsiveness to changes in prior information. Consequently, its use in BMA or Bayes factor estimation is controversial. However, if the sole objective is to select an appropriate hypothetical income distribution, it remains unclear whether the harmonic mean estimator can effectively serve this purpose.

This study explores the application of the harmonic mean estimator in selecting a hypothetical income distribution from grouped data using Monte Carlo simulations. We also apply this estimator to real data from a Japanese case study. Our results confirm the presence of significant biases in the harmonic mean estimator. Nevertheless, it can prove valuable in selecting an appropriate model, but its effectiveness is significantly more pronounced when the sample size is sufficiently large under appropriate prior settings.

The remainder of this paper is organized as follows. In Section 2, we explain the method for selecting the hypothetical income distribution using marginal likelihoods from grouped data. In Section 3 we implement the Monte Carlo simulations. Section 4 examines the real data in Japan. Finally, brief conclusions are given in Section 5.

2. Selecting the Hypothetical Income Distribution

Income data are published as grouped data in many countries. In grouped data, suppose that the income units are grouped into K income classes, viz., $(x_{[0]}, x_{[1]})$, $(x_{[1]}, x_{[2]})$, $\ldots$, $(x_{[K-1]}, x_{[K]})$, with $x_{[0]} = 0$ and $x_{[K]} \leq \infty$: Let n be the total number of units and n_k be the number of units in the interval $x_{[k-1]}$ and $x_{[k]}$ for $k = 1, 2, \ldots, K$ and therefore $n = \sum_{k=1}^{K} n_k$. There are two types of grouped data (see Eckernkemper & Gribisch, 2021) and we assume the type of quantile form in this study (see Nishino & Kakamu, 2011). From the grouped data, we assume the hypothetical distribution and estimate its parameters.

Let $\boldsymbol{\theta}$ be a $d \times 1$ vector of parameters for the assumed hypothetical income distribution. Let $f(x|\boldsymbol{\theta})$ and $F(x|\boldsymbol{\theta})$ be the probability density function (PDF) and cumulative distribution function (CDF) of the hypothetical income distribution, respectively. Given the grouped data, $\mathbf{x}_{[K]} = (x_{[1]}, x_{[2]}, \ldots, x_{[K-1]})'$ and $\mathbf{n} = (n_1, n_2, \ldots, n_K)'$, the likelihood function based on the selected order statistics by Nishino and Kakamu (2011) is given as follows:

$$L(\mathbf{x}_{[K]}|\boldsymbol{\theta}, \mathbf{n}) = n! \frac{F(x_{[1]}|\boldsymbol{\theta})^{n_1 - 1}}{(n_1 - 1)!} f(x_{[1]}|\boldsymbol{\theta}) \times \left\{ \prod_{k=2}^{K-1} \frac{\left(F(x_{[k]}|\boldsymbol{\theta}) - F(x_{[k-1]}|\boldsymbol{\theta})\right)^{n_k - 1}}{(n_k - 1)!} f(x_{[k]}|\boldsymbol{\theta}) \right\} \frac{\left(1 - F(x_{[K-1]}|\boldsymbol{\theta})\right)^{n_K}}{n_K!}. \quad (1)$$

To proceed with the Bayesian analysis, we need to assume the prior distribution as $\pi(\boldsymbol{\theta})$. Given the likelihood function (1) and prior distribution $\pi(\boldsymbol{\theta})$, the posterior distribution is expressed as

$$\pi(\boldsymbol{\theta}|\mathbf{x}_{[K]}, \mathbf{n}) = \frac{\pi(\boldsymbol{\theta}) L(\mathbf{x}_{[K]}|\boldsymbol{\theta}, \mathbf{n})}{m(\mathbf{x}_{[K]}|\mathbf{n})} \propto \pi(\boldsymbol{\theta}) L(\mathbf{x}_{[K]}|\boldsymbol{\theta}, \mathbf{n}),$$

where $m(\mathbf{x}_{[K]}|\mathbf{n})$ is called the marginal likelihood and used as a criterion to select the hypothetical income distribution. Using the posterior distribution, posterior inference via the Markov chain Monte Carlo (MCMC) method is implemented. This procedure is explained in Appendix A. In this study, the LN, DA, and SM distributions, which are denoted by $\mathcal{LN}(\mu, \sigma^2)$, $\mathcal{DA}(a, b, p)$, and $\mathcal{SM}(a, b, q)$, respectively, are assumed as hypothetical income distributions.[1]

In this study, we focus on the estimation of the marginal likelihood, which is estimated from the MCMC draws $\{\boldsymbol{\theta}^{(r)}\}_{r=1}^{R}$. As is shown by Gelfand and Dey (1994), for any proper PDF $g(\boldsymbol{\theta})$,

$$\begin{aligned}\frac{1}{m(\mathbf{x}_{[K]}|\mathbf{n})} &= \frac{1}{m(\mathbf{x}_{[K]}|\mathbf{n})}\int_{\Theta} g(\boldsymbol{\theta})d\boldsymbol{\theta} \\ &= \int_{\Theta} \frac{g(\boldsymbol{\theta})}{\pi(\boldsymbol{\theta})L(\mathbf{x}_{[K]}|\boldsymbol{\theta},\mathbf{n})}\frac{\pi(\boldsymbol{\theta})L(\mathbf{x}_{[K]}|\boldsymbol{\theta},\mathbf{n})}{m(\mathbf{x}_{[K]}|\mathbf{n})}d\boldsymbol{\theta} \\ &= \int_{\Theta} \frac{g(\boldsymbol{\theta})}{\pi(\boldsymbol{\theta})L(\mathbf{x}_{[K]}|\boldsymbol{\theta},\mathbf{n})}\pi(\boldsymbol{\theta}|\mathbf{x}_{[K]},\mathbf{n})d\boldsymbol{\theta}\end{aligned}$$

for any hypothetical income distribution. Therefore, using the MCMC draws, we can obtain the estimator of the marginal likelihood as follows:

$$\hat{m}_{\mathrm{GD}}(\mathbf{x}_{[K]}|\mathbf{n}) = \left[\frac{1}{R}\sum_{r=1}^{R}\frac{g(\boldsymbol{\theta}^{(r)})}{\pi(\boldsymbol{\theta}^{(r)})L(\mathbf{x}_{[K]}|\boldsymbol{\theta}^{(r)},\mathbf{n})}\right]^{-1}. \quad (2)$$

In Equation (2), the choice of $g(\boldsymbol{\theta})$ is important and we need to specify it. Two major approaches are the harmonic mean estimator by Newton and Raftery (1994) and modified harmonic mean estimator by Geweke (1999). If we set $g(\boldsymbol{\theta}) = \pi(\boldsymbol{\theta})$, then it becomes the harmonic mean estimator by Newton and Raftery (1994) as follows:

$$\hat{m}_{\mathrm{NR}}(\mathbf{x}_{[K]}|\mathbf{n}) = \left[\frac{1}{R}\sum_{r=1}^{R}\frac{1}{L(\mathbf{x}_{[K]}|\boldsymbol{\theta}^{(r)},\mathbf{n})}\right]^{-1}. \quad (3)$$

It is a consistent estimator of the marginal likelihood and easy to implement. However, it is also known that its variance can go to infinity, since it contains the inverse of the likelihood function, and that the harmonic mean estimator will not change much as the prior changes, even though the marginal likelihood is very sensitive to changes in the prior distribution.

To overcome the severe downside to this estimator, Geweke (1999) proposed the modified harmonic mean estimator. It is calculated as follows:

$$\hat{m}_{\mathrm{G}}(\mathbf{x}_{[K]}|\mathbf{n}) = \left[\frac{1}{R}\sum_{r=1}^{R}\frac{h(\boldsymbol{\theta}^{(r)})}{\pi(\boldsymbol{\theta}^{(r)})L(\mathbf{x}_{[K]}|\boldsymbol{\theta}^{(r)},\mathbf{n})}\right]^{-1}, \quad (4)$$

where $h(\boldsymbol{\theta}^{(r)})$ is a truncated normal distribution as follows:

$$h(\boldsymbol{\theta}^{(r)}) = P^{-1}(2\pi)^{-d/2}|\hat{\boldsymbol{\Sigma}}|^{-1/2}\exp\left\{-\frac{(\boldsymbol{\theta}^{(r)}-\hat{\boldsymbol{\theta}})'\hat{\boldsymbol{\Sigma}}^{-1}(\boldsymbol{\theta}^{(r)}-\hat{\boldsymbol{\theta}})}{2}\right\}$$

where $\hat{\boldsymbol{\theta}}$ and $\hat{\boldsymbol{\Sigma}}$ are the sample mean and covariance matrix from $\{\boldsymbol{\theta}^{(r)}\}_{r=1}^{R}$ and P is the normalizing constant, which satisfies $(\boldsymbol{\theta}^{(r)}-\hat{\boldsymbol{\theta}})'\hat{\boldsymbol{\Sigma}}^{-1}(\boldsymbol{\theta}^{(r)}-\hat{\boldsymbol{\theta}}) \leq \chi^2_{\alpha}(d)$ and $\chi^2_{\alpha}(d)$ is the α quantile of the χ^2 distribution with degrees of freedom d. This approach is popular and is used in the analyses of income distribution, for example, by Griffiths et al. (2005) for the purpose of the BMA.

Another approach is proposed by Chib (1995) and Chib and Jeliazkov (2001) for the Gibbs sampler and Metropolis–Hastings (MH) algorithm, respectively. Their idea is based on the basic marginal likelihood identity as follows:

$$m(\mathbf{x}_{[K]}|\mathbf{n}) = \frac{\pi(\boldsymbol{\theta})L(\mathbf{x}_{[K]}|\boldsymbol{\theta},\mathbf{n})}{\pi(\boldsymbol{\theta}|\mathbf{x}_{[K]},\mathbf{n})}.$$

At any point $\bar{\boldsymbol{\theta}}$, which is, for example, the posterior mean, in the case of the MH algorithm, Chib and Jeliazkov (2001) showed that $\pi(\bar{\boldsymbol{\theta}}|\mathbf{x}_{[K]}, \mathbf{n})$ can be estimated as follows:

$$\hat{\pi}(\bar{\boldsymbol{\theta}}|\mathbf{x}_{[K]}, \mathbf{n}) = \frac{R^{-1}\sum_{r=1}^{R} \alpha(\boldsymbol{\theta}^{(r)}, \bar{\boldsymbol{\theta}}) q(\boldsymbol{\theta}^{(r)}, \bar{\boldsymbol{\theta}})}{R^{-1}\sum_{r=1}^{R} \alpha(\bar{\boldsymbol{\theta}}, \boldsymbol{\theta}^{(r)})},$$

where $q(\boldsymbol{\theta}^{(r)}, \bar{\boldsymbol{\theta}})$ is the PDF of the proposal distribution.

Using the quantity, the marginal likelihood can be calculated as follows:

$$\hat{m}_{\mathrm{CJ}}(\mathbf{x}_{[K]}|\mathbf{n}) = \frac{\pi(\bar{\boldsymbol{\theta}}) L(\mathbf{x}_{[K]}|\bar{\boldsymbol{\theta}}, \mathbf{n})}{\hat{\pi}(\bar{\boldsymbol{\theta}}|\mathbf{x}_{[K]}, \mathbf{n})}. \tag{5}$$

From the number of citations which these articles have gained, it is clear that their approach is popular among practitioners.

As a final note to this section, we briefly discuss the properties of marginal likelihood estimators. All estimators are consistent but biased. The difference lies in the size of the biases and the computational procedures. From the point of view of biases, the harmonic mean estimator is highly sensitive to the values of the likelihood in low-probability regions, a few extreme samples can dominate the estimate, and outliers in the parameter space can significantly affect the estimation result, making the method less robust. The modified harmonic mean estimator is proposed to overcome the problem of the harmonic mean estimator, but it is known that the estimators have biases when estimating high-dimensional parameter models such as latent variable models (see Chan & Grant, 2015). Finally, for the estimator of Chib and Jeliazkov (2001), difficulties can arise when this method is applied to mixture models, hidden Markov models, and other models that give rise to label switching and parameter non-identifiability, and the bias in these estimates is reported in Chan and Eisenstat (2015). From a computational point of view, the harmonic mean estimator is the easiest method to implement. On the other hand, the method by Chib and Jeliazkov (2001) increases in computational complexity as the dimension of parameters increases. Moreover, implementation is more involved, especially for computing numerical standard errors of marginal likelihood estimates. For a more comprehensive review of marginal likelihood estimation, see Chan and Eisenstat (2015); Friel and Wyse (2012); Han and Carlin (2001).

Using these three estimators of the marginal likelihood, we examine the selection of the hypothetical income distribution through Monte Carlo simulations and apply it to real data in Japan. All the results reported here were generated using Ox 9.10 (macOS_64/Parallel) (see Doornik, 2013).

3. Simulation Studies

We now explain the setup for the Monte Carlo simulations. First, we set the number of observations as n = 1000, 10,000, and 100,000 to evaluate the effect of the number of observations. In addition, we assume the number of groups as decile ($K = 10$).[2] Given n and $K = 10$, we consider two scenarios in which the true data generating processes (DGPs) follow the LN distribution and GB2 distribution[3], denoted by $\mathcal{GB}2(a, b, p, q)$, and L samples of $x_{[k]}$ for $k = 1, 2, \ldots, K-1$ are generated. That is, we perform L simulation runs for these two distributions; in this section, L = 1000.

The simulation procedure is as follows:

(i) Given the true DGP, we generate random numbers x_is, $i = 1, 2, \ldots, n$ from the distribution.

(ii) We sort the random numbers in ascending order and pick up $x_{[k]} = x_{n_k}$, where $n_k = n \times \dfrac{k}{K}$ for $k = 1, 2, \ldots, K-1$.

(iii) Given $\mathbf{x}_{[K]} = (x_{[1]}, x_{[2]}, \ldots, x_{[K-1]})'$ and the hyper-parameters $(\mu_0, \tau_0^2, \nu_0, \lambda_0)$, we obtain the estimates and marginal likelihoods assuming the LN, DA, and SM distributions. In the MCMC procedure, we run a random walk MH (RWMH) algorithm, with 4000 iterations excluding the first 2000 iterations. For the modified harmonic mean estimator, $\alpha = 0.5, 0.75$ and 0.9 are considered.

(iv) We repeat (i)–(iii) L times, where $L = 1000$, as mentioned above.

(v) From L marginal likelihoods, we count the distribution with the largest marginal likelihood.

In the first scenario, we assume the true DGP as the LN distribution with $\mu = 1$ and $\sigma^2 = 0.5$ and examine the prior sensitivity. Therefore, we assume $(\mu_0, \tau_0^2, \nu_0, \lambda_0) = (0, 100, 2, 1)$, $(0, 1, 2, 1)$, $(0, 1000, 2, 1)$, $(0, 100, 0.01, 0.01)$, $(0, 100, 20, 10)$ for the LN distribution and the same hyper-parameters (ν_0, λ_0) with the LN distribution for the SM and DA distributions.[4]

In the second scenario, the purpose of the analysis is to analyze whether the true distribution can be properly selected and what selection is made when the true distribution is not included in the candidate distributions. Therefore, we assume the GB2 distribution with $(a, b, p, q) = (2, 1, 1.5, 1)$, $(2, 1, 3, 1)$, $(2, 1, 1, 1.5)$, $(2, 1, 1, 3)$, $(2, 1, 2.5, 1.5)$, $(2, 1, 1.5, 2.5)$, where the first two cases assume that the true distributions are the DA distributions, the second two cases assume the true distributions are the SM distributions, and last two cases assume that the true distributions are not included in the candidate distributions. It should be mentioned that, as shown by Kakamu (2016), the SM distributions are selected if $p < q$ and $p > 1$, while the DA distributions are selected if $p > q$ and $q > 1$, in terms of AIC.[5] As the hyper-parameters, we set $(\mu_0, \tau_0^2, \nu_0, \lambda_0) = (0, 100, 2, 1)$ for all cases.

Table 1 displays the results of our Monte Carlo simulations, assuming the LN distribution. The results reveal that when the sample size n is sufficiently large, for example, n =100,000, the LN distribution is consistently selected correctly across all estimators, regardless of the hyper-parameter choices. However, as the sample size n decreases, the choice of hyper-parameters begins to influence the selection of the hypothetical income distribution, particularly when using Equations (4) and (5). In cases where the prior for μ becomes diffuse, i.e., when τ_0^2 is large, the DA or SM distributions are preferred over the LN distribution, even if the true DGP is the LN distribution. Moreover, when ν_0 and λ_0 are large, the DA distribution is favored. It seems to be affected by the prior information when the sample size is not large enough, because it is well-known that biases of Equations (4) and (5) are relatively smaller than Equation (3). It is also consistent with the previous literature because the harmonic mean estimator will not change much as the prior changes. Therefore, it is worth noting that the use of the harmonic mean estimator should be criticized when the sample size is not large enough and/or when we assume some tight prior distribution.

To investigate why the true distribution is not selected in small samples and under certain prior settings, we examined the empirical distributions of the log of marginal likelihoods and the posterior means from the LN, DA, and SM distributions. Table 2 presents the means and standard deviations of the log of marginal likelihoods obtained from Monte Carlo simulations. The results reveal the following: First, the distribution with the highest mean marginal likelihood was consistently selected. Second, the means reported by Geweke (1999) and Chib and Jeliazkov (2001) are similar, whereas those of Newton and Raftery (1994) differ from Geweke (1999) and Chib and Jeliazkov (2001) across all cases. Third, when n = 1000, the marginal likelihood estimates appear relatively stable for Newton and Raftery (1994). However, these estimates change when τ_0^2 is altered or when ν_0 and λ_0 are adjusted. In particular, the changes in the marginal likelihood estimates for LN, when ν_0 and λ_0 are varied, indicate greater sensitivity to the choice of hyper-parameters compared to changes in τ_0^2. Needless to say, the marginal likelihood estimates are even more sensitive to the choice of hyper-parameters in Geweke (1999) and Chib and Jeliazkov (2001). Based on these observations, we proceed to examine the posterior estimates derived from the three distributions.

Table 1. Monte Carlo results of the log of marginal likelihoods for the LN distribution.

	$\mu_0 = 0, \tau_0^2 = 100, \nu_0 = 2, \lambda_0 = 1$								
	n = 1000			n = 10,000			n = 100,000		
	LN	DA	SM	LN	DA	SM	LN	DA	SM
Newton and Raftery (1994)	726	136	138	990	3	7	1000	0	0
Geweke (1999) ($\alpha = 0.5$)	280	379	341	986	9	5	1000	0	0
Geweke (1999) ($\alpha = 0.75$)	289	373	338	986	9	5	1000	0	0
Geweke (1999) ($\alpha = 0.9$)	289	371	340	986	9	5	1000	0	0
Chib and Jeliazkov (2001)	322	362	316	988	7	5	1000	0	0
	$\mu_0 = 0, \tau_0^2 = 1, \nu_0 = 2, \lambda_0 = 1$								
	n = 1000			n = 10,000			n = 100,000		
	LN	DA	SM	LN	DA	SM	LN	DA	SM
Newton and Raftery (1994)	733	128	139	990	3	7	1000	0	0
Geweke (1999) ($\alpha = 0.5$)	699	158	143	992	4	4	1000	0	0
Geweke (1999) ($\alpha = 0.75$)	704	157	139	992	4	4	1000	0	0
Geweke (1999) ($\alpha = 0.9$)	700	159	141	992	4	4	1000	0	0
Chib and Jeliazkov (2001)	708	152	140	993	3	4	1000	0	0
	$\mu_0 = 0, \tau_0^2 = 10{,}000, \nu_0 = 2, \lambda_0 = 1$								
	n = 1000			n = 10,000			n = 100,000		
	LN	DA	SM	LN	DA	SM	LN	DA	SM
Newton and Raftery (1994)	742	128	130	988	4	8	1000	0	0
Geweke (1999) ($\alpha = 0.5$)	10	508	482	971	19	10	1000	0	0
Geweke (1999) ($\alpha = 0.75$)	15	508	477	971	19	10	1000	0	0
Geweke (1999) ($\alpha = 0.9$)	14	513	473	971	19	10	1000	0	0
Chib and Jeliazkov (2001)	29	507	464	972	18	10	1000	0	0
	$\mu_0 = 0, \tau_0^2 = 100, \nu_0 = 0.01, \lambda_0 = 0.01$								
	n = 1000			n = 10,000			n = 100,000		
	LN	DA	SM	LN	DA	SM	LN	DA	SM
Newton and Raftery (1994)	740	145	115	988	6	6	1000	0	0
Geweke (1999) ($\alpha = 0.5$)	999	0	1	1000	0	0	1000	0	0
Geweke (1999) ($\alpha = 0.75$)	999	0	1	1000	0	0	1000	0	0
Geweke (1999) ($\alpha = 0.9$)	999	0	1	1000	0	0	1000	0	0
Chib and Jeliazkov (2001)	998	0	2	999	1	0	1000	0	0
	$\mu_0 = 0, \tau_0^2 = 100, \nu_0 = 20, \lambda_0 = 10$								
	n = 1000			n = 10,000			n = 100,000		
	LN	DA	SM	LN	DA	SM	LN	DA	SM
Newton and Raftery (1994)	750	88	162	989	4	7	1000	0	0
Geweke (1999) ($\alpha = 0.5$)	348	568	84	991	5	4	1000	0	0
Geweke (1999) ($\alpha = 0.75$)	344	575	81	991	5	4	1000	0	0
Geweke (1999) ($\alpha = 0.9$)	351	569	80	991	5	4	1000	0	0
Chib and Jeliazkov (2001)	390	538	72	991	5	4	1000	0	0

Table 2. Summary statistics of the log of marginal likelihoods for the LN distribution.

				$\mu_0 = 0$, $\tau_0^2 = 100$, $\nu_0 = 2$, $\lambda_0 = 1$					
	n = 1000			n = 10,000			n = 100,000		
	LN	DA	SM	LN	DA	SM	LN	DA	SM
Newton and Raftery (1994)	11.771	10.242	10.224	22.071	8.905	8.924	32.519	−92.521	−92.283
	(2.037)	(2.314)	(2.299)	(2.066)	(5.411)	(5.393)	(1.977)	(15.708)	(15.742)
Geweke (1999) ($\alpha = 0.5$)	3.894	4.581	4.516	11.882	0.029	0.011	20.015	−104.840	−104.681
	(1.893)	(2.219)	(2.161)	(1.946)	(5.350)	(5.304)	(1.826)	(15.629)	(15.754)
Geweke (1999) ($\alpha = 0.75$)	3.889	4.564	4.504	11.879	0.022	0.002	20.014	−104.849	−104.689
	(1.892)	(2.219)	(2.158)	(1.945)	(5.353)	(5.304)	(1.823)	(15.630)	(15.752)
Geweke (1999) ($\alpha = 0.9$)	3.886	4.555	4.497	11.877	0.016	−0.007	20.012	−104.856	−104.697
	(1.893)	(2.219)	(2.158)	(1.945)	(5.352)	(5.303)	(1.823)	(15.630)	(15.753)
Chib and Jeliazkov (2001)	4.103	4.571	4.449	12.084	−0.043	−0.066	20.215	−104.904	−104.756
	(1.926)	(2.277)	(2.213)	(1.992)	(5.357)	(5.306)	(1.865)	(15.652)	(15.739)
				$\mu_0 = 0$, $\tau_0^2 = 1$, $\nu_0 = 2$, $\lambda_0 = 1$					
	n = 1000			n = 10,000			n = 100,000		
	LN	DA	SM	LN	DA	SM	LN	DA	SM
Newton and Raftery (1994)	11.800	10.242	10.224	22.069	8.905	8.924	32.560	−92.521	−92.283
	(1.989)	(2.314)	(2.299)	(2.035)	(5.411)	(5.393)	(1.962)	(15.708)	(15.742)
Geweke (1999) ($\alpha = 0.5$)	5.698	4.581	4.516	13.692	0.029	0.011	21.823	−104.840	−104.681
	(1.897)	(2.219)	(2.161)	(1.950)	(5.350)	(5.304)	(1.823)	(15.629)	(15.754)
Geweke (1999) ($\alpha = 0.75$)	5.698	4.564	4.504	13.687	0.022	0.002	21.822	−104.849	−104.689
	(1.896)	(2.219)	(2.158)	(1.949)	(5.353)	(5.304)	(1.823)	(15.630)	(15.752)
Geweke (1999) ($\alpha = 0.9$)	5.694	4.555	4.497	13.685	0.016	−0.007	21.819	−104.856	−104.697
	(1.896)	(2.219)	(2.158)	(1.949)	(5.352)	(5.303)	(1.822)	(15.630)	(15.753)
Chib and Jeliazkov (2001)	5.911	4.571	4.449	13.911	−0.043	−0.066	22.039	−104.904	−104.756
	(1.936)	(2.277)	(2.213)	(2.025)	(5.357)	(5.306)	(1.858)	(15.652)	(15.739)
				$\mu_0 = 0$, $\tau_0^2 = 10{,}000$, $\nu_0 = 2$, $\lambda_0 = 1$					
	n = 1000			n = 10,000			n = 100,000		
	LN	DA	SM	LN	DA	SM	LN	DA	SM
Newton and Raftery (1994)	11.797	10.242	10.224	22.099	8.905	8.924	32.567	−92.521	−92.283
	(2.023)	(2.314)	(2.299)	(2.051)	(5.411)	(5.393)	(1.945)	(15.708)	(15.742)
Geweke (1999) ($\alpha = 0.5$)	1.594	4.581	4.516	9.585	0.029	0.011	17.720	−104.840	−104.681
	(1.895)	(2.219)	(2.161)	(1.945)	(5.350)	(5.304)	(1.824)	(15.629)	(15.754)
Geweke (1999) ($\alpha = 0.75$)	1.591	4.564	4.504	9.581	0.022	0.002	17.716	−104.849	−104.689
	(1.894)	(2.219)	(2.158)	(1.945)	(5.353)	(5.304)	(1.823)	(15.630)	(15.752)
Geweke (1999) ($\alpha = 0.9$)	1.590	4.555	4.497	9.579	0.016	−0.007	17.713	−104.856	−104.697
	(1.893)	(2.219)	(2.158)	(1.945)	(5.352)	(5.303)	(1.823)	(15.630)	(15.753)
Chib and Jeliazkov (2001)	1.804	4.571	4.449	9.783	−0.043	−0.066	17.937	−104.904	−104.756
	(1.935)	(2.277)	(2.213)	(1.977)	(5.357)	(5.306)	(1.864)	(15.652)	(15.739)
				$\mu_0 = 0$, $\tau_0^2 = 100$, $\nu_0 = 0.01$, $\lambda_0 = 0.01$					
	n = 1000			n = 10,000			n = 100,000		
	LN	DA	SM	LN	DA	SM	LN	DA	SM
Newton and Raftery (1994)	11.778	10.211	10.114	22.097	8.942	8.961	32.531	−92.485	−92.298
	(2.026)	(2.364)	(2.320)	(2.063)	(5.392)	(5.377)	(1.869)	(15.638)	(15.769)
Geweke (1999) ($\alpha = 0.5$)	−0.149	−7.093	−7.048	7.838	−11.643	−11.626	15.976	−116.513	−116.319
	(1.894)	(2.191)	(2.161)	(1.945)	(5.351)	(5.307)	(1.823)	(15.636)	(15.750)
Geweke (1999) ($\alpha = 0.75$)	−0.149	−7.113	−7.059	7.835	−11.653	−11.634	15.970	−116.522	−116.327
	(1.891)	(2.189)	(2.162)	(1.945)	(5.351)	(5.306)	(1.822)	(15.637)	(15.750)
Geweke (1999) ($\alpha = 0.9$)	−0.153	−7.118	−7.066	7.834	−11.660	−11.641	15.967	−116.529	−116.336
	(1.891)	(2.194)	(2.163)	(1.946)	(5.350)	(5.308)	(1.822)	(15.636)	(15.752)
Chib and Jeliazkov (2001)	0.056	−7.131	−7.095	8.054	−11.736	−11.692	16.180	−116.597	−116.387
	(1.954)	(2.213)	(2.215)	(1.989)	(5.378)	(5.338)	(1.860)	(15.681)	(15.759)

Table 2. *Cont.*

	$\mu_0 = 0, \tau_0^2 = 100, \nu_0 = 20, \lambda_0 = 10$								
	n = 1000			n = 10,000			n = 100,000		
	LN	DA	SM	LN	DA	SM	LN	DA	SM
Newton and Raftery (1994)	11.864	9.169	10.227	22.096	7.963	8.893	32.558	−92.636	−92.303
	(1.969)	(2.566)	(2.324)	(2.062)	(5.534)	(5.359)	(1.894)	(15.653)	(15.745)
Geweke (1999) ($\alpha = 0.5$)	5.037	5.689	3.389	13.068	−0.238	−0.923	21.206	−105.418	−105.596
	(1.898)	(2.762)	(2.266)	(1.947)	(5.414)	(5.297)	(1.819)	(15.620)	(15.750)
Geweke (1999) ($\alpha = 0.75$)	5.033	5.675	3.379	13.064	−0.248	−0.931	21.204	−105.426	−105.604
	(1.897)	(2.758)	(2.266)	(1.947)	(5.415)	(5.296)	(1.822)	(15.618)	(15.751)
Geweke (1999) ($\alpha = 0.9$)	5.028	5.668	3.368	13.060	−0.255	−0.936	21.200	−105.433	−105.612
	(1.896)	(2.758)	(2.264)	(1.947)	(5.415)	(5.294)	(1.822)	(15.617)	(15.750)
Chib and Jeliazkov (2001)	5.252	5.785	3.293	13.266	−0.317	−0.991	21.423	−105.528	−105.689
	(1.929)	(2.762)	(2.321)	(1.964)	(5.408)	(5.317)	(1.873)	(15.637)	(15.755)

Tables 3–5 present summaries of the empirical distributions of the posterior means derived from the LN, DA, and SM distributions. The means and standard deviations of the posterior means from the LN distribution (see Table 3) exhibit minimal variation, whereas those from the DA and SM distributions (see Tables 4 and 5) show noticeable changes, particularly when the sample size is small (n = 1000). Additionally, it is noteworthy that the influence of the prior settings persists even when the sample size increases to n = 100,000 (e.g., for $\nu_0 = 20$ and $\lambda_0 = 10$). This indicates that the choice of hyper-parameters affects the posterior estimates of the hypothetical income distribution, leading to variations in the marginal likelihood estimates, particularly for Chib and Jeliazkov (2001); Geweke (1999).

Table 3. Summary statistics of the LN distribution.

Hyper-Parameters	n = 1000		n = 10,000		n = 100,000	
	μ	σ^2	μ	σ^2	μ	σ^2
$\mu_0 = 0, \tau_0^2 = 100,$	1.000	0.504	1.000	0.501	1.000	0.500
$\nu_0 = 2, \lambda_0 = 1$	(0.023)	(0.027)	(0.007)	(0.009)	(0.002)	(0.003)
$\mu_0 = 0, \tau_0^2 = 1,$	0.999	0.504	1.000	0.501	1.000	0.500
$\nu_0 = 2, \lambda_0 = 1$	(0.023)	(0.027)	(0.007)	(0.009)	(0.002)	(0.003)
$\mu_0 = 0, \tau_0^2 = 10{,}000,$	1.000	0.504	1.000	0.501	1.000	0.500
$\nu_0 = 2, \lambda_0 = 1$	(0.023)	(0.027)	(0.007)	(0.009)	(0.002)	(0.003)
$\mu_0 = 0, \tau_0^2 = 100,$	1.000	0.504	1.000	0.501	1.000	0.500
$\nu_0 = 0.01, \lambda_0 = 0.01$	(0.023)	(0.027)	(0.007)	(0.009)	(0.002)	(0.003)
$\mu_0 = 0, \tau_0^2 = 100,$	1.000	0.503	1.000	0.501	1.000	0.500
$\nu_0 = 20, \lambda_0 = 10$	(0.023)	(0.025)	(0.007)	(0.009)	(0.002)	(0.003)

Note: The means and standard deviations (in parentheses) of the empirical distribution of the posterior means from the LN distribution are displayed when the true DGPs are from the LN distribution.

To sum up, when the sample size is sufficiently large, the posterior estimates of the LN, DA, and SA do not change and the weight of the prior distribution seems to be sufficiently small (see Tables 3–5). Therefore, the marginal likelihood estimates of Newton and Raftery (1994), Geweke (1999), and Chib (1995) do not change, even when the hyper-parameters have changed (see Table 2). On the other hand, the posterior estimates of the DA and SM distributions are different when the hyper-parameters have changed (see Tables 4 and 5), but the posterior estimates of the LN distribution, especially the ones of σ^2, have small biases; however, the biases do not change so much, even when the hyper-parameters have changed (see Table 3). Moreover, the marginal likelihood estimates of Geweke (1999) and Chib (1995) require prior distribution to estimate them. We think these facts lead to small changes in the marginal likelihoods of Geweke (1999) and Chib (1995) and the wrong choice of hypothetical income distribution depending on the hyper-parameter settings (see Table 2). These results suggest that selecting appropriate hyper-parameters is crucial, especially when the sample size is small. However, with a sufficiently large sample size and appropriate prior settings, valid model selection can still be achieved.

Table 4. Summary statistics of the DA distribution.

Hyper-Parameters	n = 1000			n = 10,000			n = 100,000		
	a	b	p	a	b	p	a	b	p
$\nu_0 = 2, \lambda_0 = 1$	2.316 (0.148)	2.538 (0.309)	1.169 (0.233)	2.343 (0.047)	2.640 (0.100)	1.052 (0.060)	2.348 (0.015)	2.653 (0.032)	1.040 (0.018)
$\nu_0 = 0.01, \lambda_0 = 0.01$	2.350 (0.159)	2.610 (0.329)	1.124 (0.247)	2.347 (0.047)	2.648 (0.101)	1.047 (0.060)	2.348 (0.015)	2.654 (0.032)	1.040 (0.018)
$\nu_0 = 20, \lambda_0 = 10$	2.149 (0.084)	2.160 (0.179)	1.451 (0.173)	2.310 (0.044)	2.566 (0.096)	1.099 (0.061)	2.344 (0.015)	2.645 (0.032)	1.045 (0.019)

Note: The means and standard deviations (in parentheses) of the empirical distribution of the posterior means from the DA distribution are displayed when the true DGPs are from the LN distribution.

Table 5. Summary statistics of the SM distribution.

Hyper-Parameters	n = 1000			n = 10,000			n = 100,000		
	a	b	p	a	b	p	a	b	p
$\nu_0 = 2, \lambda_0 = 1$	2.342 (0.144)	2.928 (0.364)	1.128 (0.212)	2.345 (0.048)	2.804 (0.107)	1.050 (0.060)	2.347 (0.015)	2.790 (0.033)	1.042 (0.018)
$\nu_0 = 0.01, \lambda_0 = 0.01$	2.352 (0.158)	2.927 (0.429)	1.127 (0.256)	2.347 (0.048)	2.800 (0.108)	1.048 (0.060)	2.347 (0.015)	2.790 (0.033)	1.041 (0.018)
$\nu_0 = 20, \lambda_0 = 10$	2.280 (0.085)	2.993 (0.201)	1.173 (0.114)	2.332 (0.045)	2.830 (0.102)	1.066 (0.057)	2.345 (0.015)	2.793 (0.033)	1.043 (0.018)

Note: The means and standard deviations (in parentheses) of the empirical distribution of the posterior means from the SM distribution are displayed when the true DGPs are from the LN distribution.

Table 6 presents the results of our Monte Carlo simulations under the assumption of the GB2 distribution. Similar to the findings under the LN distribution, when the sample size n is sufficiently large, for instance, n = 100,000, the true distribution is consistently favored, aligning with Kakamu (2016), even when the true distributions are not included among the candidate distributions. However, as the sample size n decreases, the performance of Equation (3) declines compared to Equations (4) and (5).[6] Consequently, when the sample size n is not sufficiently large, caution is warranted when using Equation (3).

Table 6. Monte Carlo results of the log of marginal likelihoods for the GB2 distribution.

	$\mathcal{GB}2(2,1,1.5,1) = \mathcal{DA}(2,1,1.5)$								
	n = 1000			n = 10,000			n = 100,000		
	LN	DA	SM	LN	DA	SM	LN	DA	SM
Newton and Raftery (1994)	119	631	250	0	765	235	0	996	4
Geweke (1999) ($\alpha = 0.5$)	15	917	68	0	944	56	0	998	2
Geweke (1999) ($\alpha = 0.75$)	14	923	63	0	939	61	0	998	2
Geweke (1999) ($\alpha = 0.9$)	13	926	61	0	938	62	0	998	2
Chib and Jeliazkov (2001)	25	853	122	0	926	74	0	998	2

Table 6. *Cont.*

	$\mathcal{GB}2(2,1,3,1) = \mathcal{DA}(2,1,3)$								
	n = 1000			n = 10,000			n = 100,000		
	LN	DA	SM	LN	DA	SM	LN	DA	SM
Newton and Raftery (1994)	3	818	179	0	964	36	0	1000	0
Geweke (1999) ($\alpha = 0.5$)	0	885	115	0	993	7	0	1000	0
Geweke (1999) ($\alpha = 0.75$)	0	884	116	0	993	7	0	1000	0
Geweke (1999) ($\alpha = 0.9$)	0	887	113	0	993	7	0	1000	0
Chib and Jeliazkov (2001)	0	894	106	0	994	6	0	1000	0
	$\mathcal{GB}2(2,1,1,1.5) = \mathcal{SM}(2,1,1.5)$								
	n = 1000			n = 10,000			n = 100,000		
	LN	DA	SM	LN	DA	SM	LN	DA	SM
Newton and Raftery (1994)	123	377	500	0	229	771	0	6	994
Geweke (1999) ($\alpha = 0.5$)	17	20	963	0	64	936	0	4	996
Geweke (1999) ($\alpha = 0.75$)	17	22	961	0	65	935	0	4	996
Geweke (1999) ($\alpha = 0.9$)	16	26	958	0	64	936	0	4	996
Chib and Jeliazkov (2001)	25	57	918	0	78	922	0	3	997
	$\mathcal{GB}2(2,1,1,3) = \mathcal{SM}(2,1,3)$								
	n = 1000			n = 10,000			n = 100,000		
	LN	DA	SM	LN	DA	SM	LN	DA	SM
Newton and Raftery (1994)	7	227	766	0	35	965	0	0	1000
Geweke (1999) ($\alpha = 0.5$)	0	27	973	0	5	995	0	0	1000
Geweke (1999) ($\alpha = 0.75$)	0	25	975	0	5	995	0	0	1000
Geweke (1999) ($\alpha = 0.9$)	0	25	975	0	5	995	0	0	1000
Chib and Jeliazkov (2001)	0	24	976	0	7	993	0	0	1000
	$\mathcal{GB}2(2,1,2.5,1.5)$								
	n = 1000			n = 10,000			n = 100,000		
	LN	DA	SM	LN	DA	SM	LN	DA	SM
Newton and Raftery (1994)	192	643	165	2	968	30	0	1000	0
Geweke (1999) ($\alpha = 0.5$)	5	961	34	0	999	1	0	1000	0
Geweke (1999) ($\alpha = 0.75$)	5	956	39	0	999	1	0	1000	0
Geweke (1999) ($\alpha = 0.9$)	5	951	44	0	999	1	0	1000	0
Chib and Jeliazkov (2001)	11	909	80	1	997	3	0	1000	0
	$\mathcal{GB}2(2,1,1.5,2.5)$								
	n = 1000			n = 10,000			n = 100,000		
	LN	DA	SM	LN	DA	SM	LN	DA	SM
Newton and Raftery (1994)	199	246	555	1	25	974	0	0	1000
Geweke (1999) ($\alpha = 0.5$)	6	15	979	0	2	998	0	0	1000
Geweke (1999) ($\alpha = 0.75$)	5	16	979	0	2	998	0	0	1000
Geweke (1999) ($\alpha = 0.9$)	7	17	976	0	2	998	0	0	1000
Chib and Jeliazkov (2001)	10	46	944	0	1	999	0	0	1000

In summary, when employing the marginal likelihood for selecting the hypothetical income distribution, Equations (4) and (5) are typically preferred. However, it is essential to exercise caution in choosing the hyper-parameters when using these equations. On the other hand, if the sample size n is sufficiently large, Equation (3) can also be used effectively without the need to be overly concerned about hyper-parameter selection.

4. Empirical Example

Using the Japanese household survey, Family Income and Expenditure Survey in 2020, which was compiled by the Statistics Bureau of the Ministry of Internal Affairs and

Communications, we will consider the choice of the hypothetical income distributions. There are data on two types of households: two-or-more-person households and workers' households (unit: million yen). The sample size for each dataset is n = 10,000 and the dataset in decile form is utilized; therefore, n_k = 1000 for $k = 1, 2, \ldots, K = 10$.[7] Finally, we set the hyper-parameters to $\mu_0 = 0$, $\tau_0^2 = 100$, $\nu_0 = 2$ and $\lambda_0 = 1$ and run the RWMH algorithm using 22,000 iterations while discarding the first 2000 iterations.

Table 7 shows the results for the log of the marginal likelihoods for both two-or-more person households and workers' households. From the table, although we can confirm that there are severe biases in the values of the log of the marginal likelihood using (3), we can see that the LN distribution was chosen as the most suitable hypothetical income distribution in both datasets, as was using (4) and (5). In this sense, if the model selection is only performed using the marginal likelihoods, then using (3) is not considered to be a major problem.

Table 7. Empirical results of the log of marginal likelihoods.

	Two-or-More Person Household			Workers' Household		
	LN	DA	SM	LN	DA	SM
Newton and Raftery (1994)	**−9.997**	−54.578	−61.286	**9.078**	−6.012	0.770
Geweke (1999) ($\alpha = 0.5$)	**−22.427**	−64.823	−70.826	**−5.310**	−19.474	−11.330
Geweke (1999) ($\alpha = 0.75$)	**−22.391**	−64.795	−70.879	**−5.339**	−19.491	−11.351
Geweke (1999) ($\alpha = 0.9$)	**−22.394**	−64.841	−70.900	**−5.323**	−19.490	−11.374
Chib and Jeliazkov (2001)	**−22.140**	−64.109	−71.014	**−4.670**	−19.948	−10.987

Since the LN distributions are selected from three hypothetical income distributions for both datasets, the posterior estimates from the LN distribution are shown in Table 8 with the trace plots shown in Figure 1. The trace plots confirm that the convergence of the MCMC chains is fast with respect to mixing. Therefore, we can conclude that the algorithm described in Appendix A works well for the LN distribution with the datasets. Focusing on the posterior estimates, we see that the standard deviations are very small, with narrow 95% credible intervals. This suggests that the fits of the LN distribution are very good and is the reason why the LN distributions are chosen as the hypothetical income distribution for the datasets.

Table 8. Posterior estimates of the LN distribution.

	Two-or-More Person Household				Workers' Household			
	Mean	SD	95%CI		Mean	SD	95%CI	
μ	1.688	0.006	1.677	1.699	1.906	0.004	1.898	1.915
σ^2	0.313	0.005	0.303	0.323	0.200	0.003	0.194	0.207

Note: The posterior means (Mean), standard deviations (SD), and 95% credible intervals (95%CI) are displayed.

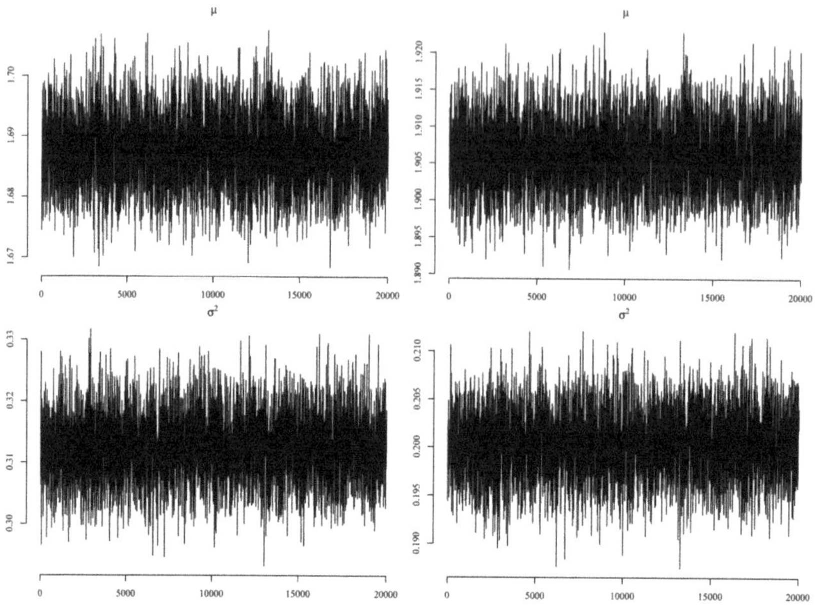

Figure 1. The trace plots for two-or-more person (**left**) and workers' (**right**) households.

5. Conclusions

This study investigated the performance of the marginal likelihood in selecting the hypothetical income distribution from grouped data, with a specific focus on the harmonic mean estimator, using Monte Carlo simulations. The results confirmed that the harmonic mean estimator can effectively choose the appropriate hypothetical income distribution when the sample size is sufficiently large under appropriate prior settings, despite the presence of severe biases observed in the empirical example. Consequently, the harmonic mean estimator, due to its pronounced bias, may cause problems when used to compute BMA or Bayes factors, but it remains a valuable tool for selecting the appropriate model, provided the sample size is sufficient under the appropriate prior settings.

As the remaining issue, it is reasonable to examine other marginal likelihood estimators, such as those by Chan and Eisenstat (2015) and Chan (2023). It is our future remark, but our findings represent an interesting first step.

Funding: This research was partially supported by JSPS KAKENHI (grant numbers: JP20H00080 and JP20K01590).

Institutional Review Board Statement: Not applicable.

Informed Consent Statement: Not applicable.

Data Availability Statement: The data is available from the author upon request.

Acknowledgments: We would like to thank the editor and reviewers for their useful comments, which substantially improve the study. We would also like to thank Conan Liu for English language editing.

Conflicts of Interest: The author declares no conflict of interest.

Appendix A

In this appendix, we introduce a MCMC method using a RWMH algorithm to estimate the parameters of the distributions, which is used by Chotikapanich and Griffiths (2000) and Kakamu (2016). To obtain the posterior estimates for the LN, DA, and SM distributions, we implement the following RWMH algorithm in the general setting.

1. Set $r = 1$ and initial value $\boldsymbol{\theta}^{(0)}$.
2. Generate a candidate value $\boldsymbol{\theta}^{new}$ from $\mathcal{N}(\boldsymbol{\theta}^{(r-1)}, c^2\boldsymbol{\Sigma})$, where c is a tuning parameter and $\boldsymbol{\Sigma}$ is the maximum likelihood covariance estimate.[8]
3. Compute

$$\alpha(\boldsymbol{\theta}^{(r-1)}, \boldsymbol{\theta}^{new}) = \min\left\{1, \frac{\pi(\boldsymbol{\theta}^{new}|\mathbf{x}_{[K]}, \mathbf{n})}{\pi(\boldsymbol{\theta}^{(r-1)}|\mathbf{x}_{[K]}, \mathbf{n})}\right\},$$

and if any of the elements of $\boldsymbol{\theta}^{new}$ fall outside the feasible parameter region, then $\alpha(\boldsymbol{\theta}^{(r-1)}, \boldsymbol{\theta}^{new}) = 0$.
4. Generate a value u from $\mathcal{U}(0,1)$, where $\mathcal{U}(a,b)$ is a uniform distribution on the interval (a,b).
5. If $u \le \alpha(\boldsymbol{\theta}^{(r-1)}, \boldsymbol{\theta}^{new})$, set $\boldsymbol{\theta}^{(r)} = \boldsymbol{\theta}^{new}$, otherwise $\boldsymbol{\theta}^{(r)} = \boldsymbol{\theta}^{(r-1)}$.
6. Return to step 2, with r set to $r + 1$.

Appendix B

In this appendix, we report the Monte Carlo experiments for the information criteria. To examine the performance of the information criteria, we examined the Akaike information criterion (AIC), Bayesian information criterion (BIC), and deviance information criterion (DIC), as in Doğan (2023), through Monte Carlo simulation. The simulation settings are the same as those in Section 3. Tables A1 and A2 show the results of our Monte Carlo simulation, which counts the distribution with the smallest information criteria, for the cases where the true DGPs are the LN and GB2 distributions, respectively. From the tables, we can confirm that the performance of the information criteria is almost the same as that of Newton and Raftery (1994) in general. The differences appear when n = 1000. Especially, in the case of the LN distribution, as is different from the marginal likelihoods, the LN distributions are preferred to other distributions without being affected by the prior distributions. Moreover, the performance of AIC and BIC seems to be poorer than that of DIC in both cases. It suggests that the penalty term of DIC works well, while the number of parameters does not work well to select an appropriate hypothetical income distribution. Therefore, we can conclude that DIC becomes a candidate for selecting a hypothetical income distribution when the sample size is small.

Table A1. Monte Carlo results of the information criteria for the LN distribution.

	$\mu_0 = 0, \tau_0^2 = 100, \nu_0 = 2, \lambda_0 = 1$								
	n = 1000			n = 10,000			n = 100,000		
	LN	DA	SM	LN	DA	SM	LN	DA	SM
AIC	699	66	235	987	8	5	1000	0	0
BIC	699	66	235	987	8	5	1000	0	0
DIC	776	156	71	991	3	5	1000	0	0
	$\mu_0 = 0, \tau_0^2 = 1, \nu_0 = 2, \lambda_0 = 1$								
	n = 1000			n = 10,000			n = 100,000		
	LN	DA	SM	LN	DA	SM	LN	DA	SM
AIC	696	67	237	987	8	5	1000	0	0
BIC	696	67	237	987	8	5	1000	0	0
DIC	781	149	70	990	4	6	1000	0	0

Table A1. *Cont.*

	$\mu_0 = 0, \tau_0^2$ = 10,000, $\nu_0 = 2, \lambda_0 = 1$								
	n = 1000			n = 10,000			n = 100,000		
	LN	DA	SM	LN	DA	SM	LN	DA	SM
AIC	697	67	236	987	8	5	1000	0	0
BIC	697	67	236	987	8	5	1000	0	0
DIC	783	150	67	991	3	6	1000	0	0
	$\mu_0 = 0, \tau_0^2 = 100, \nu_0 = 0.01, \lambda_0 = 0.01$								
	n = 1000			n = 10,000			n = 100,000		
	LN	DA	SM	LN	DA	SM	LN	DA	SM
AIC	698	73	229	986	9	5	1000	0	0
BIC	698	73	229	986	9	5	1000	0	0
DIC	787	150	63	991	3	6	1000	0	0
	$\mu_0 = 0, \tau_0^2 = 100, \nu_0 = 20, \lambda_0 = 10$								
	n = 1000			n = 10,000			n = 100,000		
	LN	DA	SM	LN	DA	SM	LN	DA	SM
AIC	725	75	200	989	4	7	1000	0	0
BIC	725	75	200	989	4	7	1000	0	0
DIC	781	80	139	992	3	5	1000	0	0

Table A2. Monte Carlo results of the information criteria for the GB2 distribution.

	$\mathcal{GB}2(2,1,1.5,1) = \mathcal{DA}(2,1,1.5)$								
	n = 1000			n = 10,000			n = 100,000		
	LN	DA	SM	LN	DA	SM	LN	DA	SM
AIC	113	305	582	0	801	199	0	997	3
BIC	113	305	582	0	801	199	0	997	3
DIC	108	787	105	0	806	194	0	997	3
	$\mathcal{GB}2(2,1,3,1) = \mathcal{DA}(2,1,3)$								
	n = 1000			n = 10,000			n = 100,000		
	LN	DA	SM	LN	DA	SM	LN	DA	SM
AIC	2	479	519	0	953	47	0	1000	0
BIC	2	481	517	0	953	47	0	1000	0
DIC	1	929	70	0	977	23	0	1000	0
	$\mathcal{GB}2(2,1,1,1.5) = \mathcal{SM}(2,1,1.5)$								
	n = 1000			n = 10,000			n = 100,000		
	LN	DA	SM	LN	DA	SM	LN	DA	SM
AIC	80	438	482	0	192	808	0	1	999
BIC	80	438	482	0	192	808	0	1	999
DIC	128	390	482	0	196	804	0	1	999
	$\mathcal{GB}2(2,1,1,3) = \mathcal{SM}(2,1,3)$								
	n = 1000			n = 10,000			n = 100,000		
	LN	DA	SM	LN	DA	SM	LN	DA	SM
AIC	5	302	693	0	32	968	0	0	1000
BIC	5	302	693	0	32	968	0	0	1000
DIC	8	192	800	0	32	968	0	0	1000
	$\mathcal{GB}2(2,1,2.5,1.5)$								
	n = 1000			n = 10,000			n = 100,000		
	LN	DA	SM	LN	DA	SM	LN	DA	SM

Table A2. *Cont.*

AIC	180	432	388	1	992	7	0	1000	0
BIC	180	432	388	1	992	7	0	1000	0
DIC	186	747	67	1	992	7	0	1000	0
				$\mathcal{GB}2(2,1,1.5,2.5)$					
	n = 1000			n = 10,000			n = 100,000		
	LN	**DA**	**SM**	**LN**	**DA**	**SM**	**LN**	**DA**	**SM**
AIC	153	249	598	0	10	990	0	0	1000
BIC	153	249	598	0	10	990	0	0	1000
DIC	213	217	570	1	9	990	0	0	1000

Notes

1 For prior distributions, we assume $\mu \sim \mathcal{N}(\mu_0, \tau_0^2)$, $1/\sigma^2 \sim \mathcal{G}(\nu_0, \lambda_0)$ for the LN distribution, $a \sim \mathcal{G}(\nu_0, \lambda_0)$, $b \sim \mathcal{G}(\nu_0, \lambda_0)$, $p \sim \mathcal{G}(\nu_0, \lambda_0)$ for the DA distribution, and $a \sim \mathcal{G}(\nu_0, \lambda_0)$, $b \sim \mathcal{G}(\nu_0, \lambda_0)$, $q \sim \mathcal{G}(\nu_0, \lambda_0)$ for the SM distribution, respectively, where $\mathcal{N}(\mu_0, \tau_0^2)$ is a normal distribution and $\mathcal{G}(\nu_0, \lambda_0)$ is a gamma distribution.

2 It should be mentioned that the number of income classes K also plays an important role in the performance of the estimator. As it has already been discussed in Kakamu and Nishino (2019) that the estimates become worse when K is small, we focus on the effects of n and prior hyper-parameters in this study.

3 The probability density function of the GB2 distribution is expressed by

$$f(x|\boldsymbol{\theta}) = \frac{ax^{ap-1}}{b^{ap}B(p,q)\left[1+\left(\frac{x}{b}\right)^{a}\right]^{p+q}},$$

where $\boldsymbol{\theta} = (a,b,p,q)'$ and $B(p,q)$ is a beta function.

4 From the nature of the gamma distribution, as ν_0 increases, the expectation and variance increase, while as λ_0 increases, the expectation is larger and variance is smaller. As is well known, as τ_0^2 increases, the variance becomes large in the case of a normal distribution, i.e., the prior distribution becomes diffuse.

5 It is not our concern, but it is interesting to examine the performance of the information criteria for selecting the hypothetical income distribution (see Doğan (2023) for the case of spatial models). These results are reported in Appendix B.

6 It is worthwhile to mention that if $p \to 1$ for the DA distribution or $q \to 1$ for the SM distribution, the performance of the model selection becomes worse. It is also consistent with the results from Kakamu (2016).

7 For more details, see http://www.stat.go.jp/english/ (accessed on 31 January 2025).

8 It is sometimes difficult to find the mode of the parameters by the maximum likelihood method. Therefore, we implement the simulated annealing of Goffe et al. (1994). In addition, if the Cholesky decomposition of $\boldsymbol{\Sigma}$ fails, the modified Cholesky of Nocedal and Wright (2000) is used. The appropriate choice of step sizes used in the random walk chain is determined by the procedure in Holloway et al. (2002) during the burn-in period.

References

Ando, T. (2010). *Bayesian model selection and statistical modeling*. Statistics: A Series of Textbooks and Monographs. Taylor & Francis.

Chan, J. C. C. (2023). Comparing stochastic volatility specifications for large Bayesian VARs. *Journal of Econometrics*, *235*(2), 1419–1446. [CrossRef]

Chan, J. C. C., & Eisenstat, E. (2015). Marginal likelihood estimation with the cross-entropy method. *Econometric Reviews*, *34*(3), 256–285. [CrossRef]

Chan, J. C. C. & Grant, A. L. (2015). Pitfalls of estimating the marginal likelihood using modified harmonic mean. *Economics Letters*, *131*, 29–33. [CrossRef]

Chib, S. (1995). Marginal likelihood from the Gibbs output. *Journal of the American Statistical Association*, *90*(432), 1313–1321. [CrossRef]

Chib, S., & Jeliazkov, I. (2001). Marginal likelihood from the Metropolis–Hastings output. *Journal of the American Statistical Association*, *96*(453), 270–281. [CrossRef]

Chotikapanich, D., & Griffiths, W. E. (2000). Posterior distributions for the Gini coefficient using grouped data. *Australian & New Zealand Journal of Statistics*, *42*(4), 383–392.

Dagum, C. (1977). A new model of personal income distribution: Specification and estimation. *Economie Appliquée*, *30*, 413–437. [CrossRef]

Doğan, O. (2023). Modified harmonic mean method for spatial autoregressive models. *Economics Letters*, *223*, 110978. [CrossRef]
Doornik, J. A. (2013). *Ox^{TM} 7: An object-oriented matrix programming language*. Timberlake Consultants Press.
Eckernkemper, T., & Gribisch, B. (2021). Classical and Bayesian inference for income distributions using grouped data. *Oxford Bulletin of Economics and Statistics*, *83*(1), 32–65. [CrossRef]
Friel, N., & Wyse, J. (2012). Estimating the evidence—A review. *Statistica Neerlandica*, *66*(3), 288–308. [CrossRef]
Gelfand, A. E., & Dey, D. K. (1994). Bayesian model choice: Asymptotics and exact calculations. *Journal of the Royal Statistical Society. Series B (Methodological)* *56*(3), 501–514. [CrossRef]
Geweke, J. (1999). Using simulation methods for Bayesian econometric models: Inference, development, and communication. *Econometric Reviews*, *18*(1), 1–73. [CrossRef]
Goffe, W. L., Ferrier, G. D., & Rogers, J. (1994). Global optimization of statistical functions with simulated annealing. *Journal of Econometrics*, *60*(1–2), 65–99. [CrossRef]
Griffiths, W. E., Chotikapanich, D., & Rao, D. S. P. (2005). Averaging income distributions. *Bulletin of Economic Research*, *57*(4), 347–367. [CrossRef]
Han, C., & Carlin, B. P. (2001). Markov chain Monte Carlo methods for computing Bayes factor: A comparative review. *Journal of the Statistical Association*, *96*(455), 1122–1132. [CrossRef]
Heyde, C. C. (1964). On a property of the lognormal distribution. *Journal of the Royal Statistical Society. Series B (Methodological)*, *25*(2), 392–393. [CrossRef]
Heyde, C. C. (1986). Random sum distributions. In N. L. Johnson, & S. Kotz (Eds.), *Encyclopedia of statistical sciences* (Vol. 7, pp. 565–567). Wiley.
Higbee, J. D., & McDonald, J. B. (2024). A comparison of the GB2 and skewed generalized log-*t* distributions with an application in finance. *Journal of Econometrics*, *240*(2), 105064. [CrossRef]
Holloway, G., Shankar, B., & Rahmanb, S. (2002). Bayesian spatial probit estimation: A primer and an application to HYV rice adoption. *Agricultural Economics*, *27*(3), 383–402. [CrossRef]
Kakamu, K. (2016). Simulation studies comparing Dagum and Singh-Maddala income distributions. *Computational Economics*, *48*, 593–605. [CrossRef]
Kakamu, K., & Nishino, H. (2019). Bayesian estimation of beta-type distribution parameters based on grouped data. *Computational Economics*, *54*, 625–645. [CrossRef]
Kass, R.E., & Raftery, A.E. (1995). Bayes factors. *Journal of the American Statistical Association*, *90*(430), 773–795. [CrossRef]
McDonald, J. B. (1984). Some generalized functions for the size distribution of income. *Econometrica*, *52*(3), 647–665. [CrossRef]
Newton, M. A., & Raftery, A. E. (1994). Approximate bayesian inference with the weighted likelihood bootstrap. *Journal of the Royal Statistical Society. Series B (Methodological)*, *56*(1), 3–48. [CrossRef]
Nishino, H., & Kakamu, K. (2011). Grouped data estimation and testing of Gini coefficients using lognormal distributions. *Sankhyā: The Indian Journal of Statistics, Series B*, *73*(2), 193–210. [CrossRef]
Nocedal, J., & Wright, S. (2000). *Numerical optimization* (2nd ed.). Springer.
Singh, S. K., & Maddala, G. S. 1976. A function for size distribution of incomes. *Econometrica*, *44*(5), 963–970. [CrossRef]

Journal of
Risk and Financial Management

MDPI

Article

ESG Ratings and Financial Performance in the Global Hospitality Industry

Kefan Lu [1], Cagri Berk Onuk [1], Yifei Xia [1] and Jianing Zhang [1,2,3,*]

[1] College of Business and Public Management, Wenzhou-Kean University, Wenzhou 325060, China; 1129485@wku.edu.cn (K.L.); conuk@kean.edu (C.B.O.); yxia@wku.edu.cn (Y.X.)
[2] Quantitative Finance Research Institute, Wenzhou-Kean University, Wenzhou 325060, China
[3] Center for Big Data and Decision-Making Technologies, Wenzhou-Kean University, Wenzhou 325060, China
* Correspondence: jzhang@kean.edu

Abstract: Existing research critically examines the influence of environmental, social, and governance (ESG) ratings on corporate financial performance (CFP), with outcomes varying considerably. This study employs a dataset of publicly traded firms across 16 countries within the hospitality sector from 2005 to 2022 to examine the ESG-CFP relationship. Fixed effects regression results demonstrate a positive linkage between ESG ratings and CFP, utilizing both comprehensive ESG ratings and discrete pillar ratings. These findings remain robust across various performance measures including return on assets, return on equity, and Tobin's Q. Heteroscedasticity and endogeneity concerns are mitigated through generalized least squares and two-stage least squares methods, respectively. Moreover, the positive impact of ESG on CFP exhibits greater potency in the United States relative to other countries and was more pronounced during the COVID-19 era. These findings offer valuable insights for business executives, investors, and policymakers in supporting ESG initiatives, guiding investment decisions, and formulating effective policy directives.

Keywords: ESG rating; corporate financial performance; hospitality sector

JEL Classification: G32; G15; L25; L83; M14

1. Introduction

The United Nations-endorsed Principles for Responsible Investment pioneered the concept of environmental, social, and governance (ESG) to underscore the significance of sustainable investment.[1] In recent years, many scholars and investors have shown interest in the correlation between a firm's ESG and corporate financial performance (CFP). Concurrently, numerous governments have established regulations for corporate sustainability initiatives and mandate firms to enhance the transparency of ESG reporting (Taherdangkoo et al., 2017). Thus, companies are motivated to incorporate sustainable development strategies for an enduring advantage. However, ESG undertakings, such as procuring eco-friendly infrastructure, fostering an environment-friendly reputation, and implementing green programs, necessitate persistent financial backing, escalating the risk of financial constraints that negatively affect the company's financial performance (Branco & Rodrigues, 2006). In this study, we investigate the relationship between ESG and CFP within the global hospitality sector to augment our comprehension of the economic repercussions of ESG.

We investigate the ESG effect utilizing a sample of companies in the hospitality sector for three key reasons. First, the hospitality sector is pivotal in stimulating local economic growth and enhancing employment prospects.[2] Second, despite its considerable economic benefits, the hospitality sector has taken few initiatives to contribute significantly toward global sustainable development goals (Wu & Pearce, 2013). Third, the growth of the hospitality sector is inherently linked to social sustainability (Moscardo & Murphy, 2014). For instance, sub-sectors within hospitality are susceptible to accidental events and negative publicity, such as the gaming and entertainment industries, potentially engendering an adverse societal impact that impairs corporate reputation and long-term performance. Consequently, social responsibility is vital, yet it receives insufficient attention within the hospitality sector. In this study, we scrutinize the relationship between ESG and CFP to enhance our comprehension of a firm's sustainable development and underscore the role of ESG in societal advancement and economic growth.

Myriad studies probe the association between ESG and CFP, yet they yield diverse outcomes, encompassing positive, negative, non-linear, U-shaped, and seemingly negligible correlations (Brammer et al., 2006; Ersoy et al., 2022; Fatemi et al., 2015; Crisóstomo et al., 2011). Additionally, firms' ESG initiatives vary with industry characteristics (S. Lee et al., 2013; Casado-Díaz et al., 2014; Ionescu et al., 2019). Thus, insights from ESG research in other industries might not directly apply to the hospitality sector. Considering the vast array of businesses subsumed within hospitality, it is essential to examine ESG influences in this industry, mitigating the effect of sectoral discrepancies and promoting the comprehension of ESG functions in this specific industry (McIntosh et al., 1995). Additionally, environmental, social, and governance activities constitute three independent pillars of ESG efforts. Utilizing a single composite ESG rating might not fully capture a firm's pursuits toward sustainable development (Alareeni & Hamdan, 2020). Limited studies address ESG implications using individual ESG pillars in the hospitality industry. In this study, we examine the relationship between ESG and CFP using the composite ESG rating and the three ESG pillars to enhance our understanding of the ESG effect. Moreover, we perform an extensive examination to ascertain if the impact of ESG on CFP in the hospitality industry diverges across countries and between pre- and post-COVID periods (Eccles et al., 2014; Keceli & Cankaya, 2020; Siueia et al., 2019; Nicola et al., 2020; Sigala, 2020).

Using a sample comprising publicly traded hospitality firms across 16 countries, we employ fixed effects ordinary least squares (OLS) regression methodologies to scrutinize the correlation between ESG and CFP. Our findings reveal that the composite ESG rating exerts a substantial positive influence on CFP, mirroring the impact of the individual ESG pillars. Interestingly, the correlation between ESG and CFP intensifies in the United States relative to other nations and is amplified during the COVID-19 pandemic. Within the scope of this research, we gauge corporate performance from a tripartite perspective, using market performance, as denoted by Tobin's Q, and accounting performance, as signified by return on asset (ROA) and return on equity (ROE). The main results persist when applying generalized least squares (GLS) and two-stage least squares (2SLS) regression methodologies.

The study contributes to the literature in several different ways. Firstly, this research enriches the ESG scholarship by presenting empirical insights regarding the relation between ESG activities and CFP within the global hospitality sector, where ESG is integral to enduring corporate growth yet is often neglected (S. Lee et al., 2013). Our analysis bears implications for hospitality industry leaders making ESG investment determinations. Secondly, most investigations evaluate ESG effects utilizing the composite ESG score, overlooking the distinct influence of ESG pillar components (Abdi et al., 2022; Taherdangkoo et al., 2017). We secure individual ratings for each ESG pillar and independently examine their relationships with CFP. Thirdly, we accentuate the nation-specific disparities in the correlation between ESG and CFP, emphasizing that regional factors may have significant implications when examining ESG influences. Fourthly, we elucidate the moderating role of the COVID-19 pandemic in the ESG-CFP relationship, emphasizing the significance of global health crises.

The arrangement of this study is as follows: Section 2 discusses pertinent theories that support the ESG-CFP relationship. Section 3 encompasses a literature review and the formulation of research hypotheses. Section 4 offers a detailed description of the sample, the variables, and the research methodology. Empirical findings are presented and analyzed in Section 5. Finally, Section 6 concludes the study.

2. Theoretical Framework

2.1. Signaling Theory

ESG activities are frequently viewed as signals through which firms convey information about their values, qualities, and efforts to consumers, investors, and other related parties. Signaling theory effectively explains behavior when two parties (individuals or organizations) possess unequal access to information. The sender must decide whether and how to communicate the information, while the receiver must determine how to interpret the signal. At its core, signaling theory aims to mitigate information asymmetry between the parties (Connelly et al., 2011).

In recent decades, corporate brands have heavily invested in sustainability to enhance their reputations, responding to increasing expectations for such practices (Torelli et al., 2012). In the digital age, brand value creation appears to have shifted toward information sharing and signaling among firms, consumers, and independent entities such as online reviewers and social media influencers (M. T. Lee et al., 2022). As a result, the content and manner of firms' signals in this interconnected environment significantly influence brand valuation.

The 2015 Nielsen Global Corporate Sustainability Report highlights that nearly 66% of consumers worldwide are willing to pay a premium for products from sustainable brands.[3] Moreover, over 80% of millennials expect their favorite companies to make public commitments to good corporate citizenship. Similarly, Cowan and Guzman (2020) find that positive sustainability signals from corporate brands correlate with higher sales growth—both domestically and internationally—and greater brand equity. Conversely, Sen and Bhattacharya (2001) show that consumers may undervalue sustainability efforts, suggesting that such initiatives can increase costs without yielding the anticipated benefits. While most evidence supports the view that ESG initiatives signal positively to consumers and investors, there are instances where misalignment between consumer values and ESG efforts may result in unintended negative perceptions.

2.2. Legitimacy Theory

Suchman (1995) defines legitimacy as "a generalized perception or assumption that the actions of an entity are desirable, proper, or appropriate within some socially constructed system of norms, values, beliefs, and definitions". A business organization must justify its existence through legitimate economic and social actions that contribute to both the society in which it operates and the broader environment (Burlea & Popa, 2013).

In the Spanish context, Reverte (2009) identified that the key variables explaining firms' corporate social responsibility (CSR) ratings are media exposure, firm size, and industry, particularly those in environmentally sensitive sectors. These variables are linked to public or social visibility, suggesting that legitimacy theory is the most pertinent framework for understanding CSR disclosure practices of publicly listed Spanish firms. Similarly, in Bangladesh, Khan et al. (2013) demonstrate that firms with higher foreign ownership tend to report more CSR disclosures as a legitimacy strategy to address the concerns of ethical foreign investors.

In summary, legitimacy theory asserts that firms undertake CSR or ESG activities to preserve their social license to operate and validate their existence within the framework of societal norms and values. Such actions can enhance their public image, improve investor perception, and mitigate potential regulatory or societal risks. By aligning their practices with societal expectations, legitimacy theory forecasts a positive ESG-CFP relationship, provided the firm successfully demonstrates its legitimacy through effective ESG initiatives.

2.3. Stakeholder Theory

The concept of CSR—the idea that businesses must assume responsibility to society and a broader range of stakeholders beyond shareholders—gained wider acceptance in the 1960s (H. Wang et al., 2016). In response, economist Milton Friedman introduced the Friedman doctrine in 1970, arguing that a company holds no social responsibility to society, with its sole obligation being to its shareholders (Friedman, 2007). However, CSR gained further prominence in the 1980s following the rise in stakeholder theory, introduced by Edward Freeman in 1984, where he defined a stakeholder as "any group or individual who can affect or is affected by the achievement of the firm's objectives" (Freeman, 2010). According to this theory, firms must consider not only their owners and customers, but also employees, the local community, the environment, consumer advocates, special interest groups, and other relevant parties.

H. Wang et al. (2016) show that companies that actively engage with stakeholders tend to display superior social performance and higher CSR standards, contributing to long-term sustainable growth. However, a limitation arises as companies face resource constraints, leading to potential conflicts of interest among stakeholder groups competing for financial resources and managerial attention. The challenge for many corporations is determining how managers should prioritize the needs of diverse stakeholders (H. Wang et al., 2016).

3. Literature Review and Hypothesis Development

3.1. ESG Practices in the Hospitality Industry

Simultaneously fostering the local economy, expanding the hospitality sector might impose adverse environmental implications. Take hotels as an example; typically situated near heritage locations, they draw in large volumes of tourists, thus escalating the environmental detriment triggered by human interaction (Kirk, 1998; Legrand, 2021). Even though stakeholders across diverse sectors emphasize sustainability and voice the necessity for global attainment, the practical application of sustainability approaches, in reality, continues to be daunting (Higgins-Desbiolles, 2010). Research delving into ESG protocols within the hospitality industry primarily targets developed nations or conducts assessments with a minimal sample of fewer than 20 firms, culminating in an informational deficit regarding the ESG impact in the hospitality sector (Carlsen et al., 2001; Kasim, 2007; Holcomb et al., 2007; Scanlon, 2007; Bohdanowicz & Zientara, 2008).

Nonetheless, sustainability is a crucial factor in facilitating the advancement of the hospitality industry. Firstly, due to the resource-intensive nature of the hospitality sector (Gil et al., 2001), it is imperative to establish sustainable management systems for coping with the constraints of worldwide resource paucity (J. Lu & Nepal, 2009). Sustainability crises undermine the prospects of hospitality firms and their clientele, as climate change renders numerous global destinations less appealing. In more severe cases, rising sea levels threaten to inundate hospitality industry properties (Legrand & Matthew-Bolofinde, 2022). Secondly, consumers' burgeoning focus on sustainability is reflected in their willingness to financially support corporate initiatives to bolster energy efficiency and environmental conservation (Laroche et al., 2001; Rivera, 2002). The hospitality industry relies heavily on both natural resources and human capital. Consequently, integrating ESG practices is essential not only for implementing effective food waste management systems and preserving clean water but also for ensuring the fair treatment of employees and fostering community engagement (Back, 2024). As such, exploring the implementation of sustainability strategies within the hospitality industry will contribute to the expanding body of the literature on the ESG effect.

3.2. ESG Ratings and Firm Performance

Assessing ESG impact proves challenging.[4] Existing inquiries into the ESG-CFP interconnection yield inconclusive outcomes. According to the conventional neoclassical perspective, the investment expenditure required for corporations to undertake ESG initiatives supersedes the returns accruing to the corporation (Palmer et al., 1995). Moreover, firms committed to ESG norms persistently generate non-positive returns to shareholders (Lyon et al., 2013). L. Wang et al. (2024) demonstrate that ESG ratings have a significant and negative impact on the stock performance of publicly listed Chinese firms. Baklaci et al. (2024) demonstrate that ESG exchange-traded funds underperform conventional exchange-traded funds in many aspects. Conversely, recent research illustrates that the ramifications of ESG adoption vary among corporations across distinct industries (Elzahar et al., 2015; Moon, 2007). ESG adherence in some sectors exhibits a neutral effect, suggesting corporations equilibrate the cost of ESG against the financial return they generate (Lahouel et al., 2019).

Contrarily, stakeholder theory substantiates a positive association between ESG activities and CFP (Ionescu et al., 2019). The returns from ESG investments can surpass the associated costs, resulting in a favorable ESG influence on CFP (Aouadi & Marsat, 2018). This can be attributed to various factors. Firstly, a superior ESG rating corresponds to reduced financial risk, positively impacting investors' propensity to invest in the enterprise (Benlemlih & Girerd-Potin, 2017; Jo & Na, 2012). Nguyen et al. (2022) find that among financial performance metrics such as ROA, ROE, and Tobin's Q, the latter is most positively influenced by ESG activities, highlighting investors' growing interest in firms actively engaging in ESG initiatives. Secondly, corporations' ESG endeavors enhance employees' job satisfaction, improving their operational and financial performance (Edmans, 2011). Thirdly, the economic advantage of ESG activities becomes more conspicuous when a company embraces a long-term investment approach as opposed to a short-term strategy (Statman & Glushkov, 2009), since the ESG effort is more prone to bolster corporate competitiveness, curtail business risks, and augment financial profitability over a more extended period (Moravcikova et al., 2015). Fourthly, firms may be subject to higher debt and equity financing costs if they lack social responsibility, escalating the likelihood of financial constraints (El Ghoul et al., 2011; Goss & Roberts, 2011). Fifthly, ESG activities can augment the firm's societal reputation and elevate customer loyalty, fostering customer repurchase behavior (Pérez & del Bosque, 2015) and reducing price sensitivity by narrowing the perceived quality gap between firms (Boehe & Cruz, 2010).

Pursuing a different trajectory, the implications of each ESG pillar on CFP remain ambiguous. The first ESG pillar is the environment. Consumers demonstrate sensitivity to environmental disclosure information (Jacobs et al., 2010). Specific research indicates that a corporation's disclosure of environmental initiatives has a positive bearing on CFP, implying that the adoption of eco-friendly policies can foster corporate growth (Emeka-Nwokeji & Osisioma, 2019; Murray et al., 2006; Saleh et al., 2011). Nevertheless, some academics argue that the environmental impact across diverse organizations is not universally applicable (Elsayed & Paton, 2005). Initiatives like becoming a climate leader may not resonate with market interest and might trigger negative financial consequences for the company (Fisher-Vanden & Thorburn, 2011). Moreover, firms might commit to environmental projects to fulfill obligatory governmental stipulations at the expense of shareholders, engendering negative financial implications (Reid & Toffel, 2009). Besides the potential positive and negative effects, a neutral correlation between environmental actions and CFP could be attributed to the firms experiencing audit threats, compelling them to make environmental disclosures (Nakao et al., 2007; Lyon & Maxwell, 2011).

The second ESG pillar pertains to the social dimension. Escalated expenditure on social initiatives aids in preserving and cultivating stakeholder relationships, diminishes the company's operational costs, and enhances CFP (Fombrun et al., 2000). Moreover, nurturing strong stakeholder relationships may confer intangible value on a corporation (Hillman & Keim, 2001). Liu et al. (2024) find that employee stock ownership plans positively influence corporate ESG ratings in a sample of 4464 publicly listed Chinese firms. Nevertheless, some studies also negatively correlate social initiatives and CFP (Emeka-Nwokeji & Osisioma, 2019). Given the diverse industries in which companies operate, a negative linkage might exist between social initiatives and CFP (Brammer et al., 2006; Fisher-Vanden & Thorburn, 2011). Other research implies that social endeavors and CFP could be neutrally connected (Patten, 1991).

The third ESG pillar refers to corporate governance. Numerous studies exhibit a positive correlation between corporate governance and CFP (Brown & Caylor, 2006; Emeka-Nwokeji & Osisioma, 2019; Xie et al., 2019). Superior governance can preempt financial crises (Nollet et al., 2016). Furthermore, an elevated governance pillar score signifies reduced information asymmetry, thereby ensuring optimal benefits for the stakeholders (Patten, 1991). Shaikh (2022) also finds that among the three ESG pillars, governance exerts the strongest positive impact on financial performance.

Despite the heterogeneous outcomes of ESG effects in the previous literature, we postulate that corporations in the hospitality sector are more inclined to exhibit a positive ESG-CFP relationship due to the significant emphasis on sustainable development within this industry. Indeed, Bianco et al. (2023) demonstrate that ESG certifications can enable a hotel to achieve higher occupancy rates and increased revenue per available room, particularly when it is the first in its local area to obtain such a certification. Moreover, ESG dimensions are three independent aspects jointly capturing the company's performance of sustainability (Galbreath, 2013). Evaluating ESG performance using individual dimension ratings can furnish supplementary information beyond what is provided by employing a singular composite ESG rating as a measure (Ionescu et al., 2019; McWilliams et al., 1999). Consequently, it is imperative to scrutinize the ESG effects utilizing both composite and disaggregated dimension ratings. Based on the discussions above, we derive the following hypothesis:

Hypothesis 1. *ESG ratings are positively related to CFP in the hospitality industry.*

3.3. *Role of Regional Factors in the ESG-CFP Relationship*

Existing research suggests that merely scrutinizing the effect of ESG on CFP is insufficient; additional variables are in play and geographic factors warrant further exploration (S. Lee et al., 2013). First, historical evidence suggests that in the US, ESG disclosures are positively correlated with improved CFP (Eccles et al., 2014). In contrast, the performance of companies from other countries does not uniformly inspire optimism. Notably, for Europe and Latin America, there is no discernible correlation between ESG disclosure and CFP (Keceli & Cankaya, 2020). Conversely, sub-Saharan country samples illustrate a positive association between ESG disclosure and CFP (Siueia et al., 2019). In Australia, however, the relationship between ESG disclosure and CFP emerges only in the context of high performance (Gholami et al., 2022). Similarly, in China, the positive relationship between ESG and financial performance is observed specifically among Growth Enterprise Market companies, smaller firms with growth potential that do not meet the full listing requirements of the main board of the Hong Kong exchange (Zheng et al., 2022).

Second, the United States ranks among the highest globally in individualism and also scores significantly high on masculinity, according to Hofstede's cultural dimensions.[5] Shin et al. (2023) find that cultures characterized by high individualism or masculinity amplify the relationship between ESG and financial performance. The rationale is that in highly individualistic societies, ESG practices are less ingrained and thus must provide stronger financial incentives. Similarly, in societies with higher masculinity, ESG efforts are financially incentivized, whereas more feminine societies may view ESG as a firm's social obligation, offering fewer financial rewards for such practices.

Third, compared to other nations, US firms focus more on regional diversification and strategize regional operations to cater to local market requirements, thereby capturing further market opportunities and augmenting profits (J. W. Lu & Beamish, 2004; Koh et al., 2009). Achieving regional diversification necessitates a company to acknowledge the variegated needs of stakeholders across political, economic, and cultural spheres, among others (Abrahamson & Fombrun, 1994). Furthermore, firms employing regional diversification strategies must accommodate an expanded spectrum of societal demands and diverse pressures (Sharfman et al., 2004). Moreover, research indicates that a firm's ESG activities are intimately tied to stakeholder needs, and regional diversification bolsters firms in fulfilling their ESG obligations (Brammer et al., 2006). Hence, this study incorporates regional disparities to delve deeper into the influence of varying national contexts on ESG disclosure and CFP. Based on the discussions above, we derive the following hypothesis:

Hypothesis 2. *The positive ESG effect on CFP is more pronounced in the United States compared to other countries.*

3.4. Impact of COVID-19 on the ESG-CFP Relationship

The COVID-19 pandemic has precipitated a significant upheaval in the global hospitality industry (Bai, 2020). Policy reactions to COVID-19 have constrained global hospitality operations by curtailing social activities and travel plans (Sigala, 2020). Past research confirms the substantial effects of non-financial events on equity markets; for instance, Taiwanese hotel industry stocks experienced a notable downturn in the month following the SARS outbreak (M. H. Chen et al., 2005). More recently, many scholars have delineated and explicated the devastating impact of COVID-19 on global economics and finance (Rehman et al., 2021; Arbulú et al., 2021). The deleterious effect of the pandemic on equity markets surpasses the damage wrought by economic crises (Baker et al., 2020). Liu et al. (2023) ascertain that equities in the hospitality sector undergo significant volatility following the dissemination of COVID-19 announcements. C. D. Chen et al. (2022) demonstrate that during the COVID-19 pandemic, hotel corporation stocks with higher ESG ratings acted as more defensive assets, offering investors a safe haven amid market turbulence. Consequently, in analyzing the ESG-CFP relationship, the pandemic's influence cannot be overlooked. These preceding discussions provide the foundation for the following hypothesis:

Hypothesis 3. *The positive influence of ESG on CFP is more discernible during the COVID-19 pandemic than in prior periods.*

4. Data and Methodology

4.1. Data

Data on the ESG of the hospitality industry were collected from the Bloomberg Terminal. Using the Bloomberg ESG Classification System (BECS), we selected all 89 international hospitality companies within the "Leisure Facilities & Services" category, encompassing "Hotels", "Recreational Facilities", and "Restaurants". We also acquired datasets regarding ROA, ROE, and Tobin's Q as dependent variables, alongside ESG and individual pillar scores as primary explanatory variables. Control variables encompass firm size, firm age, leverage, capital expenditure, the market-to-book ratio, dividend payout ratio, board size, the proportion of independent directors, CEO age, CEO tenure, and the dual role of the CEO and chairman. Any missing datasets, such as the dividend payout ratio, were manually supplemented by sourcing the information from the respective company's website or annual report. The annual GDP growth data, sourced from the World Bank, represent the annual percentage change in GDP at market prices, adjusted to constant 2015 US dollars.[6] The dataset represents all publicly listed hospitality firms globally for which Bloomberg provides comprehensive ESG and financial data. The sample begins in 2005 because this is the earliest year for which Bloomberg provides ESG data for the hospitality sector. However, it is important to note that ESG disclosures vary significantly across countries, and many firms—particularly in emerging markets—only began reporting ESG metrics in recent years.

Our sample spans 2005 to 2022, a period marked by substantial advancements in ESG reporting and evolving trends in the hospitality sector. In 2015, the Task Force on Climate-Related Financial Disclosures was established to develop recommendations for corporate disclosures, enabling investors and lenders to better assess climate-related risks.[7] These guidelines achieved widespread global adoption. During this period, many countries also introduced mandatory ESG disclosure requirements for publicly listed firms.[8] In the hospitality sector, technological innovations and sustainability concerns drove significant transformations. The most notable disruption was Airbnb's 2008 entry, introducing home-sharing and short-term rentals, which exerted pressure on the revenues and profits of traditional hotel companies.[9] Simultaneously, hospitality providers intensified sustainability efforts, including energy-efficient designs, renewable energy adoption, water conservation, and waste reduction initiatives.[10]

We also executed winsorization on all variables at the 1st and 99th percentiles. The final sample incorporates 1110 firm-year observations spanning 2005 to 2022, indicative of 86 distinct firms. Table 1 delineates the sample composition across 16 countries, with the United States constituting the most extensive sample and accounting for 48.83% of total observations. The geographic distribution of the sample reflects the structure of the global hospitality industry, the concentration of publicly listed firms in specific regions such as the United States, and the fact that not all hospitality firms are publicly listed, particularly in emerging countries. Countries with fewer publicly listed firms, such as Korea and Mexico, naturally appear underrepresented. Although some countries are over- or underrepresented, we address potential geographic biases by employing country-level fixed effects in the regression models, which account for unobserved heterogeneity across countries.

Table 1. Sample composition.

Country	Observations	%
Australia	33	2.97
Canada	24	2.16
China	54	4.86
United Kingdom	156	14.05
France	41	3.69
Germany	29	2.61
Hong Kong	51	4.59
India	30	2.70
Italy	18	1.62
Japan	42	3.78
Korea	8	0.72
Mexico	13	1.17
Philippines	11	0.99
Spain	32	2.88
Thailand	26	2.34
United States	542	48.83
Total	1110	100.00

Note: This table presents the compositional distributions of the entire sample, encompassing publicly listed global hospitality firms from 2005 to 2022.

4.2. Variables

Our dependent variable is CFP, which is represented by ROA, ROE, and Tobin's Q. Dao and Ta's (2020) meta-analysis on firm performance divides proxies for such performance into two principal categories, namely accounting-based measures such as ROA and ROE and a market-based ratio such as Tobin's Q. Of the 245 studies, those deploying accounting indicators (ROA, ROE) comprise roughly 73.1% in contrast to 26.9% incorporating the market ratio (Tobin's Q). An extensive body of the literature, encompassing Aouadi and Marsat (2018) and S. Lee et al.'s (2013) work, posits that Tobin's Q also signals CFP. In alignment with the extant literature, we define Tobin's Q as the ratio of a firm's total market value to its book value of assets (Chung & Pruitt, 1994).

Our primary explanatory variables are the ESG score and individual ESG pillar scores. Bloomberg ESG ratings have been recognized as reliable sources for academic research (Abdi et al., 2022; Egorova et al., 2022). Leveraging public ESG data, Bloomberg assesses companies' composite ESG scores on a scale from zero to a hundred. The environmental rating quantifies the impact of corporate operations on the environment, covering factors such as greenhouse gas and carbon dioxide emissions, energy and water consumption, pollutant levels, and additional ecological concerns. The social rating mirrors business–community interactions with elements like the proportion of female staff, community investment, accident rates, supplier management, output per employee, and research and development outlays. The governance rating includes various factors, such as board composition, the ratio of female directors, director autonomy, the average director age, board meeting frequency, and the engagement levels of independent and non-independent directors. A composite score, which amalgamates factors from all three ESG dimensions, measures overall ESG performance.

We incorporate temporally sensitive firm characteristics pertinent to the ESG-CFP relationship into our control variables (Li et al., 2018; D'Amato & Falivena, 2020; Abdi et al., 2022; Shakil, 2022). The regression model integrates firm-level control variables, encompassing firm size (*FirmSize*), firm age (*FirmAge*), the leverage ratio (*Lev*), capital expenditure (*Capex*), the market-to-book ratio (*MTB*), and dividend payout ratio (*DivPay*). It also subsumes board-level control variables such as board size (*BoardSize*) and the proportion of independent directors (*IndeptDir*). The regression schema incorporates executive-level control variables, comprising the CEO's age (*CEOAge*), the CEO's tenure (*CEOTenure*), and the dual role of the CEO and chairman (*Duality*). Following D'Amato and Falivena (2020), we utilize the firm's age as a control variable. Numerous studies utilize the leverage and dividend payout ratios as control variables (Shakil, 2022; Li et al., 2018). A lower leverage ratio indicates reduced insolvency risk and lesser financial stress to pursue social responsibilities. The dividend payout ratio provides insights into the company's worth (Gordon, 1959). Investors can infer a company's expansion aspirations based on its dividend payout ratio. The GDP growth rate (*GDPGrow*) is also included as a control variable, as it accounts for country-level economic variations that may impact financial performance. Additionally, we consider country and year fixed effects (FEs) to regulate for time-constant attributes inherent in each nation and a specific annum. All variables are defined in Table 2.

Table 2. Variable definitions.

Variable	Definition
ROA	Return on assets. The firm's net income divided by its total assets.
ROE	Return on equity. The firm's net income divided by its shareholders' equity.
TobinQ	Tobin's Q. The firm's total market value divided by its book value of assets.
ESG	The firm's aggregate rating score encompassing environmental, social, and governance aspects.
E	The firm's rating score pertaining to the environmental pillar.
S	The firm's rating score pertaining to the social pillar.
G	The firm's rating score pertaining to the governance pillar.
FirmSize	Firm size. The natural logarithm of the firm's total assets.
FirmAge	Firm age. The years elapsed since the firm's inception.
Lev	Leverage ratio. The firm's total liabilities divided by its total assets.
Capex	Capital expenditure. The outlays made by the firm on the acquisition, upkeep, or augmentation of assets relative to its aggregate assets.
MTB	Market-to-book ratio. The firm's total market value of equity divided by its book value of equity.
DivPay	Dividend payout ratio. The firm's dividend payments divided by its net income.
BoardSize	Board size. The number of directors comprising the firm's board of directors.
IndeptDir	Percentage of independent directors. The proportion of independent directors in service on the firm's board of directors.
CEOAge	CEO's age in years.
CEOTenure	CEO's tenure. The duration for which an individual assumes the role of the company's CEO.
Duality	The circumstance in which an individual concurrently assumes the roles of CEO and board chairman within the firm.
GDPGrow	Annual percentage change in GDP at market prices, adjusted for constant 2015 US dollars.

4.3. Methodology

We employ the following fixed effects OLS regression model to investigate whether ESG ratings are positively related to companies' financial performance:

$$\begin{aligned} Perf_{it} = \; & \beta_0 + \beta_1 ESG_{it} + \beta_2 FirmSize_{it} + \beta_3 FirmAge_{it} + \beta_4 Lev_{it} + \beta_5 Capex_{it} + \beta_6 MTB_{it} \\ & + \beta_7 DivPay_{it} + \beta_8 BoardSize_{it} + \beta_9 IndeptDir_{it} + \beta_{10} CEOAge_{it} + \beta_{11} CEOTenure_{it} \\ & + \beta_{12} Duality_{it} + \beta_{13} GDPGrow_{it} + \text{Country FE} + \text{Year FE} + \varepsilon_{it} \end{aligned} \tag{1}$$

where $Perf_{it}$ is the CFP of firm i in year t, proxied by ROA, ROE, and Tobin's Q. ESG_{it} is the composite ESG rating of firm i in year t. All other control variables are defined in Table 2.

We also use three ESG pillar ratings to measure their impact on CFP as follows:

$$\begin{aligned} Perf_{it} = \; & \beta_0 + \beta_1 ESGPillar_{it} + \beta_2 FirmSize_{it} + \beta_3 FirmAge_{it} + \beta_4 Lev_{it} + \beta_5 Capex_{it} + \beta_6 MTB_{it} \\ & + \beta_7 DivPay_{it} + \beta_8 BoardSize_{it} + \beta_9 IndeptDir_{it} + \beta_{10} CEOAge_{it} + \beta_{11} CEOTenure_{it} \\ & + \beta_{12} Duality_{it} + \beta_{13} GDPGrow_{it} + \text{Country FE} + \text{Year FE} + \varepsilon_{it} \end{aligned} \tag{2}$$

where *ESGPillar* represents the firm's environmental (*E*), social (*S*), and governance (*G*) pillar ratings, respectively.

4.4. Descriptive Statistics

Table 3 portrays the summary statistics for all variables within the regression schemas. The ROA's mean stands at 5.36%, indicating that corporations in the sector demonstrate potent profitability and exhibit a high capability to transmute their assets into earnings. Tobin's Q presents a mean of 2.66, ranging from 0.59 to 22.95. Among the triadic dimension ratings of ESG, the governance rating exhibits the peak average value, intimating that hospitality sector corporations invest more effort into corporate governance than environmental and societal endeavors. The logarithm of firm size spans from 1.64 to 5.10, signifying considerable variation in size among hospitality industry corporations. The average leverage ratio is 44.82%, implying a middling debt proportion in the hospitality sector. The mean board size approximates ten directors, and the proportion of independent directors roughly equates to 62.24%. The average CEO's age is 55.71 years. Approximately 23% of the corporations host a CEO who simultaneously functions as the board's chairman.

Table 3. Descriptive statistics.

Variable	Obs.	Mean	Std. Dev.	Min	P25	Median	P75	Max
ROA	1110	5.36	9.12	−97.00	1.53	4.62	9.27	50.00
ROE	1110	29.04	82.85	−204.42	5.34	14.80	29.30	654.00
TobinQ	1110	2.66	2.34	0.59	1.39	1.84	3.08	22.95
ESG	1110	36.39	10.33	6.86	29.80	34.51	43.40	73.20
E	1110	1.53	2.00	0.00	0.00	0.73	2.24	8.38
S	1110	1.92	1.50	0.00	1.25	1.40	2.17	8.47
G	1110	6.19	1.36	2.15	5.36	6.50	7.31	8.41
FirmSize	1110	3.39	0.55	1.64	3.06	3.42	3.78	5.10
FirmAge	1110	44.61	40.97	1.00	24.00	36.00	54.00	299.00
Lev	1110	44.82	43.88	0.00	22.27	37.18	55.28	389.20
Capex	1110	−0.06	0.06	−0.36	−0.08	−0.05	−0.03	−0.00
MTB	1110	17.89	65.47	0.11	1.99	3.70	7.45	552.00
DivPay	1110	63.10	266.03	0.00	0.00	34.50	60.50	8055.42
BoardSize	1110	9.59	2.58	2.00	8.00	9.00	11.00	20.00
IndeptDir	1110	62.24	22.24	0.00	44.40	66.70	81.80	100.00
CEOAge	1110	55.71	7.47	34.00	50.00	55.00	60.00	86.00
CEOTenure	1110	9.04	8.86	0.00	2.17	6.42	12.80	44.30
Duality	1110	0.23	0.42	0.00	0.00	0.00	0.00	1.00
GDPGrow	1110	2.16	3.09	−10.94	1.56	2.46	2.95	14.23

Note: This table delineates summary statistics for all variables. Table 2 furnishes the definitions of the variables.

We present the correlation matrix in Table 4 before performing the regression analyses. Though ESG does not demonstrate direct correlations with corporate performance, the individual ESG pillars reveal substantial negative or positive correlations. As anticipated, ROA, ROE, and Tobin's Q are positively correlated. ESG and the three pillars are also positively intertwined. Most control variables significantly correlate with ROA, except firm age, the dividend payout ratio, the CEO's age, and duality.

To ensure the robustness of our regression models, we performed a variance inflation factor (VIF) analysis to identify potential multicollinearity among the independent variables. The VIF results for all four baseline regressions are presented in Table 5. According to Hair et al. (2013), a VIF value exceeding 10 indicates high multicollinearity, which could distort estimation results. In all models, the VIF values for the variables remain well below the threshold of 10, indicating no significant multicollinearity concerns.

Table 4. Pearson correlation analysis.

		(1)	(2)	(3)	(4)	(5)	(6)	(7)	(8)	(9)	(10)	(11)	(12)	(13)	(14)	(15)	(16)	(17)	(18)	(19)
(1)	*ROA*	1																		
(2)	*ROE*	0.43 ***	1																	
(3)	*TobinQ*	0.50 ***	0.19 ***	1																
(4)	*ESG*	−0.02	0.04	−0.03	1															
(5)	*E*	−0.05 *	−0.04	−0.10 ***	0.54 ***	1														
(6)	*S*	−0.06 *	0.03	−0.11 ***	0.61 ***	0.70 ***	1													
(7)	*G*	0.20 ***	0.26 ***	0.05	0.31 ***	−0.16 ***	0.00	1												
(8)	*FirmSize*	−0.17 ***	−0.16 ***	−0.33 ***	0.48 ***	0.32 ***	0.36 ***	0.05	1											
(9)	*FirmAge*	0.02	0.05 *	−0.11 ***	0.24 ***	0.12 ***	0.09 ***	0.18 ***	0.21 ***	1										
(10)	*Lev*	0.22 ***	0.17 ***	0.43 ***	0.22 ***	0.04	0.06 **	0.22 ***	0.02	0.26 ***	1									
(11)	*Capex*	−0.17 ***	0.01	−0.21 ***	0.25 ***	0.12 ***	0.27 ***	0.09 ***	0.36 ***	−0.04	0.14 ***	1								
(12)	*MTB*	0.12 ***	0.68 ***	0.11 ***	0.05 *	−0.03	0.00	0.19 ***	−0.14 ***	0.04	0.17 ***	0.06 **	1							
(13)	*DivPay*	−0.03	−0.01	0.04	0.04	−0.02	−0.03	0.07 **	0.01	0.01	0.04	0.02	0.01	1						
(14)	*BoardSize*	−0.10 ***	−0.00	−0.15 ***	0.26 ***	0.26 ***	0.14 ***	−0.04	0.42 ***	0.17 ***	0.02	−0.11 ***	−0.02	0.02	1					
(15)	*IndeptDir*	0.17 ***	0.18 ***	0.14 ***	0.22 ***	−0.11 ***	0.00	0.66 ***	0.01	0.01	0.26 ***	0.04	0.14 ***	0.06 **	−0.06 *	1				
(16)	*CEOAge*	−0.04	0.01	−0.13 ***	0.14 ***	0.17 ***	0.14 ***	0.02	0.15 ***	0.09 ***	−0.07 **	0.12 ***	0.03	0.02	0.05 *	−0.03	1			
(17)	*CEOTenure*	0.14 ***	−0.04	0.12 ***	0.04	0.20 ***	0.15 ***	−0.21 ***	−0.05	−0.04	0.01	−0.04	−0.11 ***	0.04	−0.02	−0.13 ***	0.13 ***	1		
(18)	*Duality*	0.05	−0.05 *	0.06 *	−0.10 ***	0.08 ***	0.01	−0.12 ***	−0.02	−0.10 ***	−0.10 ***	−0.11 ***	−0.03	0.05	−0.12 ***	0.02	0.23 ***	0.22 ***	1	
(19)	*GDPGrow*	0.16 ***	0.04	0.12 ***	−0.15 ***	−0.10 ***	−0.14 ***	−0.11 ***	−0.16 ***	−0.08 ***	−0.05	−0.07 **	0.00	−0.02	−0.08 ***	−0.03	−0.09 ***	0.05 *	−0.02	1

Note: This table exhibits the Pearson correlations among the variables. Table 2 furnishes the definitions of the variables. ***, **, and * represent the 1%, 5%, and 10% levels of significance, respectively.

Table 5. Multicollinearity tests.

Variable	VIF Values			
	(1)	(2)	(3)	(4)
ESG	1.54			
E		1.24		
S			1.24	
G				2.03
FirmSize	1.93	1.76	1.80	1.70
FirmAge	1.21	1.20	1.19	1.24
Lev	1.26	1.25	1.24	1.24
Capex	1.42	1.41	1.44	1.41
MTB	1.11	1.10	1.10	1.11
DivPay	1.01	1.01	1.01	1.01
BoardSize	1.41	1.43	1.40	1.40
IndeptDir	1.18	1.14	1.12	1.94
CEOAge	1.15	1.15	1.14	1.14
CEOTenure	1.13	1.15	1.15	1.13
Duality	1.20	1.19	1.18	1.21
GDPGrow	1.04	1.04	1.05	1.05

Note: this table reports the VIF values to assess multicollinearity among the independent variables used in the regression models.

5. Results and Discussion

5.1. ESG Effects on Financial Performance

Building on Equations (1) and (2), we utilize fixed effects OLS regression models to assess the impact of composite ESG ratings and individual ESG pillars on CFP. Table 6 exhibits the findings. The regression results indicate that the firm's ESG undertakings, gauged by an integrated ESG rating and trio ESG pillar ratings, are markedly positively linked to CFP, supporting Hypothesis 1. We find that the coefficient for ESG is 0.21 and statistically significant at the 1% level. The results suggest a positive ESG-CFP relationship in the hospitality sector, aligning with the discoveries in preceding studies (Alareeni & Hamdan, 2020). It appears that stakeholders recompense corporations for ESG activities within the hospitality sector.

Table 6. Baseline regressions of ROA on aggregate ESG ratings and individual ESG pillar ratings.

Variable	Dependent Variable = *ROA*			
	(1)	(2)	(3)	(4)
ESG	0.21 ***			
	(6.49)			
E		0.54 ***		
		(3.90)		
S			0.68 ***	
			(3.49)	
G				1.24 ***
				(3.30)
FirmSize	−1.95 *	−1.14	−1.17	−0.60
	(−1.82)	(−1.13)	(−1.19)	(−0.59)
FirmAge	−0.02 **	−0.02 **	−0.02 **	−0.02 **
	(−2.50)	(−2.15)	(−2.19)	(−2.34)
Lev	0.06 ***	0.06 ***	0.06 ***	0.06 ***
	(9.62)	(9.36)	(9.42)	(9.28)
Capex	−20.53 ***	−22.39 ***	−23.65 ***	−21.88 ***
	(−2.63)	(−2.87)	(−2.98)	(−2.78)
MTB	0.01 ***	0.01 ***	0.01 ***	0.01 ***
	(4.05)	(4.14)	(4.06)	(3.56)

Table 6. *Cont.*

Variable	Dependent Variable = *ROA*			
	(1)	(2)	(3)	(4)
DivPay	−0.00 ***	−0.00 ***	−0.00 ***	−0.00 ***
	(−3.12)	(−2.64)	(−2.67)	(−2.75)
BoardSize	−0.23 **	−0.15	−0.10	−0.16
	(−2.09)	(−1.32)	(−0.88)	(−1.49)
IndeptDir	0.08 ***	0.10 ***	0.10 ***	0.07 ***
	(4.83)	(5.93)	(6.23)	(3.67)
CEOAge	−0.01	−0.01	−0.01	−0.01
	(−0.18)	(−0.17)	(−0.16)	(−0.35)
CEOTenure	0.17 ***	0.18 ***	0.18 ***	0.19 ***
	(5.58)	(5.78)	(6.01)	(6.52)
Duality	−1.02 *	−1.18 *	−1.04 *	−0.84
	(−1.66)	(−1.93)	(−1.68)	(−1.37)
GDPGrow	0.03	−0.06	−0.02	0.00
	(0.20)	(−0.42)	(−0.17)	(0.01)
Constant	5.95	6.49	4.86	−1.40
	(1.39)	(1.58)	(1.17)	(−0.32)
Country FE	Yes	Yes	Yes	Yes
Year FE	Yes	Yes	Yes	Yes
Observations	1110	1110	1110	1110
R^2	0.35	0.34	0.34	0.34

Note: This table presents the baseline regression outcomes of ROA on the firm's ESG composite and individual pillar rating scores, respectively. Table 2 provides the descriptions of the variables. The robust *t*-values are reported within parentheses below the corresponding coefficient. ***, **, and * represent the 1%, 5%, and 10% levels of significance, respectively.

Following Equation (2), the coefficients are notably positive when the triadic ESG pillar ratings assess the ESG activities. The affirmative influence of the environmental pillar on CFP implies that corporate actions to safeguard the environment and higher degrees of environmental disclosure amplify the firm's positive image from the stakeholders' perspectives. Customers may favor "green hotels" and demonstrate an increased propensity to finance environmental initiatives (Jacobs et al., 2010; Nor et al., 2016). Moreover, heightened participation in social activities enhances the firm's operational and financial efficiency, positively impacting firm value (Ersoy et al., 2022; Xie et al., 2019). The results indicate that social activities significantly affect CFP, signifying that superior firm performance offsets the company's expenses toward employees, customers, and communities and that investment in social activities can yield enduring benefits. Finally, the result aligns with the research probing the correlation between corporate governance disclosure and CFP (Rouf, 2011). Optimal corporate governance disclosure can aid companies in operating effectively, curtail information asymmetry, and mitigate corporate financial risk, thereby augmenting corporate value.

Regarding the control variables, the positive influence of leverage on CFP is significant, implying that greater financial leverage of a corporation enhances the CFP of publicly traded firms in the hospitality sector, in alignment with the overall perspective that leverage can serve as a crucial instrument for achieving long-term performance (Alareeni & Hamdan, 2020; Popli et al., 2017). Additionally, a firm's age negatively impacts CFP, suggesting that younger firms tend to exhibit better CFP. The dividend payout ratio exerts a negative effect on CFP. As anticipated, more independent directors bolster CFP, and extended CEO tenure benefits CFP.

5.2. Alternative Performance Measures

Furthermore, we reassess the ESG-CFP relationship by substituting the dependent variable with ROE and Tobin's Q. The regression results presented in Table 7 align with the results yielded when employing ROA. Specifically, the coefficients for ESG stand at 1.26 and 0.05, respectively, and are significant at the 1% level. The coefficients for each ESG pillar rating are likewise significant, except for the coefficient on governance with respect to Tobin's Q. In unison, the regression results suggest that enhanced efforts committed to both composite and individual pillar ESG ratings can augment CFP, providing additional backing to Hypothesis 1.

Table 7. Alternative performance measures of ROE and Tobin's Q.

Variable	Dependent Variable = *ROE*				Dependent Variable = *TobinQ*			
	(1)	(2)	(3)	(4)	(5)	(6)	(7)	(8)
ESG	1.26 ***				0.05 ***			
	(5.50)				(6.79)			
E		2.04 **				0.09 ***		
		(2.18)				(3.24)		
S			6.74 ***				0.20 ***	
			(5.16)				(5.56)	
G				13.18 ***				−0.05
				(4.17)				(−0.74)
FirmSize	−24.55 ***	−18.60 ***	−21.49 ***	−15.67 **	−1.14 ***	−0.93 ***	−0.99 ***	−0.86 ***
	(−3.70)	(−2.94)	(−3.30)	(−2.58)	(−5.64)	(−4.74)	(−4.92)	(−4.35)
FirmAge	0.01	0.02	0.01	0.00	−0.01 ***	−0.01 ***	−0.01 ***	−0.01 ***
	(0.16)	(0.61)	(0.36)	(0.09)	(−7.13)	(−6.51)	(−6.63)	(−6.48)
Lev	0.12 ***	0.12 ***	0.13 ***	0.12 ***	0.03 ***	0.03 ***	0.03 ***	0.03 ***
	(3.47)	(3.37)	(3.74)	(3.54)	(10.78)	(10.68)	(10.87)	(10.73)
Capex	69.44 *	58.16	45.17	63.10 *	−7.33 ***	−7.75 ***	−8.12 ***	−7.75 ***
	(1.90)	(1.60)	(1.26)	(1.71)	(−4.02)	(−4.24)	(−4.46)	(−4.26)
MTB	0.83 ***	0.83 ***	0.83 ***	0.82 ***	0.00	0.00	0.00	0.00
	(8.82)	(8.79)	(8.85)	(8.80)	(0.67)	(0.74)	(0.59)	(0.92)
DivPay	−0.01 ***	−0.01 **	−0.01 **	−0.01 **	0.00	0.00	0.00	0.00
	(−2.62)	(−2.19)	(−2.09)	(−2.32)	(0.97)	(1.19)	(1.23)	(1.10)
BoardSize	1.29 *	1.89 **	2.16 ***	1.51 **	−0.03	−0.00	0.01	0.00
	(1.73)	(2.48)	(2.85)	(2.15)	(−0.96)	(−0.18)	(0.20)	(0.16)
IndeptDir	0.28 **	0.40 ***	0.42 ***	0.07	0.01 *	0.01 ***	0.01 ***	0.01 ***
	(2.07)	(3.00)	(3.21)	(0.52)	(1.90)	(3.13)	(3.44)	(3.22)
CEOAge	0.11	0.13	0.08	0.01	−0.02 ***	−0.02 ***	−0.02 ***	−0.02 ***
	(0.40)	(0.45)	(0.31)	(0.02)	(−3.13)	(−3.02)	(−3.11)	(−2.75)
CEOTenure	0.46 **	0.55 ***	0.51 ***	0.66 ***	0.03 ***	0.04 ***	0.03 ***	0.04 ***
	(2.41)	(2.90)	(2.70)	(3.52)	(4.12)	(4.39)	(4.41)	(4.66)
Duality	−16.79 ***	−17.44 ***	−16.91 ***	−14.80 ***	0.11	0.08	0.11	0.10
	(−3.84)	(−4.01)	(−3.87)	(−3.34)	(0.51)	(0.37)	(0.49)	(0.45)
GDPGrow	−0.18	−0.66	−0.49	−0.21	−0.01	−0.03	−0.02	−0.02
	(−0.15)	(−0.56)	(−0.42)	(−0.19)	(−0.23)	(−0.86)	(−0.64)	(−0.72)
Constant	33.20	31.04	29.31	−36.94 *	5.53 ***	5.51 ***	5.33 ***	5.35 ***
	(1.51)	(1.41)	(1.38)	(−1.67)	(5.38)	(5.48)	(5.20)	(5.06)
Country FE	Yes	Yes	Yes	Yes	Yes	Yes	Yes	Yes
Year FE	Yes	Yes	Yes	Yes	Yes	Yes	Yes	Yes
Observations	1110	1110	1110	1110	1110	1110	1110	1110
R^2	0.54	0.53	0.54	0.54	0.46	0.45	0.45	0.44

Note: This table shows the regression results of ROE and Tobin's Q on the firm's ESG composite and individual pillar rating scores, respectively. Table 2 provides the descriptions of the variables. The robust t-values are reported within parentheses below the corresponding coefficient. ***, **, and * represent the 1%, 5%, and 10% levels of significance, respectively.

5.3. GLS and 2SLS Regressions

To mitigate the impact of heteroscedasticity in OLS regression and procure an unbiased estimate (Reed & Ye, 2011), we implement fixed effects GLS regressions and delineate the results in Table 8. The coefficient on ESG and the triadic pillars persist in being significantly positive, in alignment with the baseline results.

Table 8. Heteroscedasticity assessment employing GLS regressions.

Variable	Dependent Variable = *ROA*			
	(1)	(2)	(3)	(4)
ESG	0.21 ***			
	(5.71)			
E		0.54 ***		
		(3.63)		
S			0.68 ***	
			(3.38)	
G				1.24 ***
				(3.77)
FirmSize	−1.95 ***	−1.14 **	−1.17 **	−0.60
	(−3.27)	(−1.99)	(−2.03)	(−1.06)
FirmAge	−0.02 ***	−0.02 ***	−0.02 ***	−0.02 ***
	(−3.05)	(−2.63)	(−2.70)	(−2.84)
Lev	0.06 ***	0.06 ***	0.06 ***	0.06 ***
	(10.54)	(10.42)	(10.59)	(10.47)
Capex	−20.53 ***	−22.39 ***	−23.65 ***	−21.88 ***
	(−3.95)	(−4.29)	(−4.51)	(−4.19)
MTB	0.01 ***	0.01 ***	0.01 ***	0.01 ***
	(4.09)	(4.11)	(4.03)	(3.65)
DivPay	−0.00 **	−0.00 **	−0.00 **	−0.00 **
	(−2.40)	(−2.16)	(−2.16)	(−2.44)
BoardSize	−0.23 **	−0.15	−0.10	−0.16
	(−2.04)	(−1.32)	(−0.87)	(−1.40)
IndeptDir	0.08 ***	0.10 ***	0.10 ***	0.07 ***
	(4.06)	(5.00)	(5.34)	(3.30)
CEOAge	−0.01	−0.01	−0.01	−0.01
	(−0.21)	(−0.20)	(−0.19)	(−0.39)
CEOTenure	0.17 ***	0.18 ***	0.18 ***	0.19 ***
	(5.43)	(5.73)	(5.91)	(6.41)
Duality	−1.02	−1.18 *	−1.04	−0.84
	(−1.58)	(−1.81)	(−1.59)	(−1.29)
GDPGrow	0.03	−0.06	−0.02	0.00
	(0.19)	(−0.41)	(−0.16)	(0.01)
Constant	5.95	6.49	4.86	−1.40
	(1.44)	(1.54)	(1.17)	(−0.32)
Country FE	Yes	Yes	Yes	Yes
Year FE	Yes	Yes	Yes	Yes
Observations	1110	1110	1110	1110

Note: This table displays the outcomes of heteroscedasticity assessments using GLS regressions. Table 2 provides the descriptions of the variables. The robust *t*-values are reported within parentheses below the corresponding coefficient. ***, **, and * represent the 1%, 5%, and 10% levels of significance, respectively.

Subsequently, we employ 2SLS regressions to assuage our regression models' apprehension regarding the endogeneity issue. In line with preceding studies (Attig et al., 2016; Wintoki et al., 2012), we utilize the lagged ESG ratings as the instrumental variable. The second-stage results of the 2SLS regressions are presented in Table 9. The *F*-value surpasses ten, implying that the instrumental variable is suitable and efficient. The coefficients for the composite and pillar ESG ratings predicted from the first stage remain significantly positive. Once again, the regression results correspond with the primary findings.

Table 9. Endogeneity assessment employing 2SLS regressions.

Variable	Dependent Variable = *ROA*			
	(1)	(2)	(3)	(4)
Predicted ESG	0.23 ***			
	(5.56)			
Predicted E		0.46 ***		
		(2.97)		
Predicted S			0.62 ***	
			(2.92)	
Predicted G				1.73 ***
				(4.88)
FirmSize	−2.89 ***	−1.87 ***	−1.93 ***	−1.31 **
	(−4.90)	(−3.37)	(−3.43)	(−2.42)
FirmAge	−0.02 ***	−0.02 ***	−0.02 ***	−0.02 ***
	(−3.61)	(−3.12)	(−3.20)	(−3.48)
Lev	0.06 ***	0.06 ***	0.06 ***	0.06 ***
	(11.44)	(11.26)	(11.40)	(11.42)
Capex	−16.01 ***	−18.28 ***	−19.42 ***	−17.08 ***
	(−3.12)	(−3.52)	(−3.72)	(−3.31)
MTB	0.01 ***	0.01 ***	0.01 ***	0.01 ***
	(4.00)	(4.06)	(3.98)	(3.39)
DivPay	−0.00 ***	−0.00 **	−0.00 **	−0.00 ***
	(−2.75)	(−2.44)	(−2.45)	(−2.80)
BoardSize	−0.16	−0.05	−0.01	−0.08
	(−1.47)	(−0.47)	(−0.06)	(−0.75)
IndeptDir	0.08 ***	0.10 ***	0.11 ***	0.06 ***
	(4.08)	(5.10)	(5.51)	(2.83)
CEOAge	0.01	0.01	0.01	0.00
	(0.36)	(0.41)	(0.40)	(0.00)
CEOTenure	0.16 ***	0.17 ***	0.18 ***	0.20 ***
	(5.52)	(5.95)	(6.13)	(6.77)
Duality	−1.07 *	−1.23 **	−1.11 *	−0.78
	(−1.74)	(−1.97)	(−1.78)	(−1.26)
GDPGrow	0.00	−0.08	−0.05	−0.01
	(0.01)	(−0.56)	(−0.34)	(−0.09)
Constant	−3.94	−1.00	−2.48	−10.35 ***
	(−1.26)	(−0.31)	(−0.78)	(−2.96)
Country FE	Yes	Yes	Yes	Yes
Year FE	Yes	Yes	Yes	Yes
Observations	1024	1024	1024	1024
R^2	0.40	0.39	0.39	0.40

Note: The table reports the second-stage results of the 2SLS regression of ROA on the firm's predicted ESG composite and individual pillar ratings, using the lagged ESG ratings as the instrumental variable. Table 2 provides the descriptions of the variables. The robust *t*-values are reported within parentheses below the corresponding coefficient. ***, **, and * represent the 1%, 5%, and 10% levels of significance, respectively.

5.4. Subsamples of US and Non-US Firms

In response to the heterogeneity within country-specific contexts (Keceli & Cankaya, 2020; Siueia et al., 2019; Gholami et al., 2022), we partition the sample into two subgroups, US and non-US enterprises, given that the United States represents the single largest category, accounting for approximately half of the entire sample. Table 10 reveals that the ESG coefficient is both more significant and larger in magnitude for US firms compared to non-US firms, supporting Hypothesis 2. These findings align with observations that ESG disclosures are positively correlated with superior CFP in US businesses (Eccles et al., 2014). Intriguingly, the governance and social coefficients are markedly positive for US firms, whereas the environmental and social coefficients are significantly positive for non-US firms. It infers that US firms prioritize corporate governance and social issues, which are critical components of firm performance. In contrast, non-US firms place greater emphasis on environmental and societal concerns.

Table 10. Subsamples of US firms and firms from other countries.

Variable	Dependent Variable = *ROA*							
	US Firms				Firms from Other Countries			
	(1)	(2)	(3)	(4)	(5)	(6)	(7)	(8)
ESG	0.25 ***				0.11 **			
	(6.00)				(2.29)			
E		0.30				0.70 ***		
		(1.46)				(3.20)		
S			0.49 **				0.86 **	
			(2.07)				(2.43)	
G				1.84 ***				−0.19
				(4.39)				(−0.23)
FirmSize	−0.65	0.72	0.76	1.18	−2.83	−2.31	−2.71	−2.30
	(−0.69)	(0.76)	(0.82)	(1.40)	(−1.25)	(−1.02)	(−1.25)	(−1.03)
FirmAge	−0.02	−0.01	−0.01	−0.02	−0.00	−0.00	−0.00	0.00
	(−1.12)	(−0.36)	(−0.72)	(−1.26)	(−0.37)	(−0.24)	(−0.00)	(0.06)
Lev	0.08 ***	0.08 ***	0.08 ***	0.08 ***	−0.01	−0.02	−0.01	−0.02
	(14.43)	(13.38)	(13.65)	(13.44)	(−0.42)	(−0.60)	(−0.47)	(−0.54)
Capex	−28.91 ***	−30.39 ***	−32.38 ***	−24.56 ***	−15.69	−16.63	−16.32	−16.57
	(−3.50)	(−3.51)	(−3.66)	(−2.98)	(−1.31)	(−1.40)	(−1.38)	(−1.46)
MTB	0.02 ***	0.02 ***	0.01 ***	0.01 ***	0.02 **	0.02 **	0.02 **	0.02 **
	(3.65)	(3.60)	(3.56)	(2.68)	(2.34)	(2.15)	(2.42)	(2.45)
DivPay	−0.00 ***	−0.00 ***	−0.00 ***	−0.00 ***	−0.01	−0.01 *	−0.01 *	−0.01
	(−3.89)	(−3.42)	(−3.42)	(−3.27)	(−1.52)	(−1.83)	(−1.68)	(−1.46)
BoardSize	−0.12	−0.06	−0.02	−0.14	−0.26	−0.29 *	−0.20	−0.16
	(−0.80)	(−0.39)	(−0.15)	(−0.96)	(−1.63)	(−1.68)	(−1.24)	(−1.14)
IndeptDir	0.05 **	0.10 ***	0.10 ***	0.03	0.09 ***	0.07 **	0.09 ***	0.09 ***
	(2.33)	(4.33)	(4.30)	(1.26)	(2.98)	(2.52)	(2.97)	(2.95)
CEOAge	−0.05	−0.06	−0.07	−0.09	−0.01	−0.02	−0.01	0.00
	(−0.90)	(−1.17)	(−1.22)	(−1.63)	(−0.13)	(−0.38)	(−0.11)	(0.07)
CEOTenure	0.26 ***	0.29 ***	0.29 ***	0.31 ***	0.04	0.01	0.03	0.04
	(6.09)	(6.33)	(6.40)	(7.11)	(1.05)	(0.38)	(1.00)	(1.20)
Duality	−0.15	−0.34	−0.23	−0.33	−1.14	−1.90	−1.73	−1.23
	(−0.21)	(−0.46)	(−0.31)	(−0.47)	(−0.84)	(−1.39)	(−1.24)	(−0.96)
GDPGrow	7.86 ***	5.17 ***	5.16 ***	3.71 ***	−0.13	−0.16	−0.13	−0.16
	(4.00)	(3.47)	(3.53)	(2.68)	(−0.71)	(−0.93)	(−0.75)	(−0.90)
Constant	−31.47 ***	−23.57 ***	−24.39 ***	−25.41 ***	11.81 *	14.67 ***	12.09 **	12.65 **
	(−4.99)	(−4.22)	(−4.45)	(−4.65)	(1.94)	(2.64)	(2.05)	(2.18)
Country FE	Yes	Yes	Yes	Yes	Yes	Yes	Yes	Yes
Year FE	Yes	Yes	Yes	Yes	Yes	Yes	Yes	Yes
Observations	542	542	542	542	568	568	568	568
R^2	0.47	0.44	0.44	0.46	0.32	0.32	0.32	0.31

Note: This table shows the regression results of ROA on the firm's ESG composite and individual pillar rating scores for US and non-US firm subsamples. Table 2 provides the descriptions of the variables. The robust *t*-values are reported within parentheses below the corresponding coefficient. ***, **, and * represent the 1%, 5%, and 10% levels of significance, respectively.

5.5. Subperiods of Pre- and During COVID-19

According to the World Health Organization, the hospitality sector, constituting a significant portion of the tourism industry, experienced considerable repercussions from the COVID-19 pandemic.[11] The recurring lockdown measures during the pandemic severely impacted the hotel industry, resulting in substantial financial distress for numerous firms.[12] The pandemic might have escalated corporations' financial risk and stock volatility to an unprecedented level (Shakil, 2022).

Following prior research, we reapply the regression analysis to a subsample characterized by abbreviated sample durations (Abdi et al., 2022; Moneva et al., 2020). Our sample is bifurcated into two subsections, 2005–2019 for the pre-COVID-19 phase and 2020–2022 for the COVID-19 phase. The baseline regression is executed by applying ROA on ESG and its three pillars. The outcomes are exhibited in Table 11. The coefficients on the composite ESG rating are positive and statistically significant, aligning with the findings in our principal regressions. However, it is observable that the coefficient's magnitude is more profound during COVID-19 than before, supporting Hypothesis 3. Additionally, the coefficients on environmental and governance pillars, while not significant pre-COVID-19, gain significance during the pandemic. This subperiod analysis suggests that our finding, namely the positive influence of hospitality industry firms' ESG rating on CFP, gains salience amidst COVID-19. This aligns with the notion that stakeholders' attention to ESG issues heightens during a global health crisis.

Table 11. Analysis of pre- and during COVID-19 subperiods.

	Dependent Variable = *ROA*							
Variable	**Pre-COVID-19**				**During COVID-19**			
	(1)	**(2)**	**(3)**	**(4)**	**(5)**	**(6)**	**(7)**	**(8)**
ESG	0.14 ***				0.33 ***			
	(3.88)				(4.75)			
E		0.27				0.83 ***		
		(1.62)				(2.91)		
S			0.56 **				0.69 **	
			(2.21)				(2.18)	
G				0.77				2.67 ***
				(1.48)				(4.21)
FirmSize	−1.71	−1.12	−1.23	−0.90	−2.51 *	−0.78	−0.64	0.78
	(−1.19)	(−0.82)	(−0.93)	(−0.66)	(−1.73)	(−0.61)	(−0.47)	(0.68)
FirmAge	−0.01	−0.01	−0.01	−0.01	−0.04 **	−0.04 **	−0.04 **	−0.04 **
	(−1.63)	(−1.42)	(−1.44)	(−1.54)	(−2.42)	(−2.02)	(−2.14)	(−2.22)
Lev	0.07 ***	0.07 ***	0.07 ***	0.07 ***	0.06 ***	0.06 ***	0.06 ***	0.06 ***
	(9.28)	(9.23)	(9.21)	(9.08)	(3.51)	(3.21)	(3.34)	(3.47)
Capex	−22.24 **	−23.42 **	−24.42 **	−22.96 **	−2.40	−5.19	−4.34	5.04
	(−2.36)	(−2.50)	(−2.57)	(−2.39)	(−0.15)	(−0.31)	(−0.25)	(0.31)
MTB	0.01 **	0.01 **	0.01 **	0.01	0.02 ***	0.02 ***	0.02 ***	0.02 ***
	(1.98)	(2.03)	(1.98)	(1.64)	(3.74)	(3.92)	(3.93)	(3.45)
DivPay	−0.00 ***	−0.00 ***	−0.00 ***	−0.00 ***	−0.00	−0.00	−0.00	−0.00
	(−3.29)	(−2.96)	(−2.94)	(−2.98)	(−0.64)	(−0.61)	(−0.43)	(−0.85)
BoardSize	−0.16	−0.11	−0.07	−0.12	−0.28	0.04	0.07	0.04
	(−1.18)	(−0.76)	(−0.53)	(−0.97)	(−1.13)	(0.16)	(0.30)	(0.18)
IndeptDir	0.07 ***	0.08 ***	0.08 ***	0.07 ***	0.08	0.14 **	0.15 **	0.05
	(4.07)	(4.96)	(5.00)	(3.10)	(1.45)	(2.22)	(2.41)	(0.82)
CEOAge	0.09 *	0.09 *	0.09 *	0.09 **	−0.22 ***	−0.22 ***	−0.24 ***	−0.28 ***
	(1.91)	(1.87)	(1.88)	(2.00)	(−2.99)	(−2.87)	(−3.06)	(−3.75)
CEOTenure	0.18 ***	0.19 ***	0.19 ***	0.19 ***	0.08	0.09	0.12	0.18 **
	(5.54)	(5.71)	(5.84)	(5.98)	(1.08)	(1.22)	(1.61)	(2.36)
Duality	−0.53	−0.62	−0.49	−0.41	−0.64	−0.26	−0.58	1.05
	(−0.79)	(−0.92)	(−0.74)	(−0.62)	(−0.38)	(−0.15)	(−0.32)	(0.60)
GDPGrow	0.11	0.02	0.04	0.04	−0.15	−0.17	−0.14	−0.15
	(0.50)	(0.09)	(0.20)	(0.21)	(−0.63)	(−0.77)	(−0.61)	(−0.67)
Constant	1.91	2.31	1.56	−2.43	−3.77	−4.73	−6.22	−16.78 **
	(0.38)	(0.48)	(0.32)	(−0.51)	(−0.52)	(−0.65)	(−0.86)	(−2.31)
Country FE	Yes	Yes	Yes	Yes	Yes	Yes	Yes	Yes
Year FE	Yes	Yes	Yes	Yes	Yes	Yes	Yes	Yes
Observations	852	852	852	852	258	258	258	258
R^2	0.26	0.25	0.26	0.26	0.46	0.43	0.42	0.45

Note: This table shows the regression results of ROA on the firm's ESG composite and individual pillar rating scores for the pre-COVID-19 period (2005–2019) and during the COVID-19 era (2020–2022). Table 2 provides the descriptions of the variables. The robust *t*-values are reported within parentheses below the corresponding coefficient. ***, **, and * represent the 1%, 5%, and 10% levels of significance, respectively.

6. Conclusions

Using a sample of 86 publicly traded companies across 16 nations from 2005 to 2022, we explore the association between ESG ratings and CFP within the hospitality sector, where ESG stands as a pivotal investment catalyzing an organization's growth potential and long-term evolution. Many studies probe the connection between ESG and financial performance, yielding a blend of empirical outcomes. This research manifests a positive ESG impact on corporate value in the global hospitality sector, applicable to composite ESG ratings and individual ESG pillar ratings. A suite of additional tests is conducted to ascertain the robustness of our findings. The foundational results persist for three alternative measures of firm performance (ROA, ROE, and Tobin's Q). Additionally, concerns regarding heteroscedasticity and endogeneity are addressed using GLS and 2SLS regressions, respectively. These findings confirm Hypothesis 1, demonstrating that ESG ratings are positively associated with CFP in the hospitality industry. Furthermore, our findings demonstrate significant geographic heterogeneity. The positive ESG-CFP relationship is notably stronger for US firms compared to non-US entities, lending support to Hypothesis 2. In US firms, governance assumes a predominant role, whereas the environmental pillar is commanding in non-US companies. We also observe that the ESG-CFP linkage is stronger during the COVID-19 era than in the pre-pandemic period, especially for the environmental and governance pillars, supporting Hypothesis 3, which posits that the pandemic amplified ESG's impact on CFP. These findings underscore the pivotal role of ESG in driving sustainable corporate value, particularly amid heightened uncertainty.

This study enhances the body of knowledge on ESG by scrutinizing the impact of ESG activities on CFP within the global hospitality sector. By utilizing cross-national ESG information and disaggregated pillar ratings on ESG, our conclusions proffer additional proof and enrich the comprehension of ESG implications. The cross-country variation and temporal analysis in the ESG-CFP relationship propose that ESG impact might diverge across geographical regions and temporal spans. Furthermore, our results hold practical value for executives and policymakers, supporting informed decision-making on ESG investments. The following subsections detail the study's implications across four key areas, which are theoretical implications to the ESG literature, practical insights for corporate managers, policy recommendations to enhance ESG practices, and a discussion of the study's limitations alongside future research opportunities.

6.1. Theoretical Implications

One of the most intriguing questions in ESG research is whether companies can perform well financially by doing good socially. If a strong business case exists for positive social action, all stakeholders—employees, customers, shareholders, the environment, and society at large—stand to benefit. Margolis et al. (2009) explored this question through a meta-analysis of 167 studies conducted over 35 years. Their findings indicate that while a positive relationship between CSR and CFP exists, it is not particularly strong. Notably, only 2% of the studies reviewed found that sustainability activities directly impose costs on shareholders. In the hospitality sector, Bianco et al. (2023) demonstrate that within the United States, sustainability certifications can improve key performance indicators such as occupancy rates. Extending this analysis to an international context, our study shows that hospitality firms with higher ESG commitments enhance their financial performance, as measured by ROA, ROE, and Tobin's Q.

The findings of this study provide critical theoretical insights into signaling theory, legitimacy theory, and stakeholder theory concerning ESG ratings and CFP. From a signaling theory perspective, ESG ratings serve as credible signals that reduce information asymmetry by conveying a firm's commitment to sustainability and resilience to investors and stakeholders. In the context of legitimacy theory, the results demonstrate how ESG initiatives help align corporate actions with societal norms and expectations, thereby enhancing legitimacy and contributing to improved financial performance. Finally, through the lens of stakeholder theory, the observed positive ESG-CFP relationship underscores the importance of addressing diverse stakeholder interests, including environmental stewardship, employee well-being, and governance practices. Together, these contributions enrich the theoretical understanding of ESG as a multidimensional construct that simultaneously reflects corporate responsibility and bolsters firm value through enhanced stakeholder engagement and societal alignment.

6.2. Implications for Corporate Managers

A McKinsey global survey reveals that 76% of executives believe CSR initiatives positively impact long-term shareholder value, while 55% agree that sustainability strengthens their company's reputation.[13] Our findings align with these perspectives, particularly regarding shareholder value. Emphasizing ESG initiatives that resonate with stakeholder expectations enhances both financial performance and corporate valuation. Additionally, our results suggest that US firms should prioritize robust governance mechanisms, whereas non-US firms may achieve greater benefits by focusing on environmental issues. These findings highlight the importance of tailoring ESG strategies to regional and industry-specific contexts, ensuring that initiatives align with the expectations and demands of various stakeholders to maximize their impact.

Managers in the hospitality sector should view ESG initiatives not merely as compliance or ethical obligations but as strategic assets that can drive financial performance and enhance corporate valuation. The amplified ESG-CFP relationship observed during the COVID-19 pandemic underscores the critical role of resilience-focused ESG strategies in navigating periods of crisis. Integrating such strategies into core business operations can help firms adapt to dynamic challenges while fostering long-term sustainability. By aligning ESG efforts with stakeholder interests and addressing region-specific priorities, corporate managers can not only mitigate risks and enhance resilience but also capitalize on opportunities for growth, innovation, and strengthened stakeholder trust. These efforts ultimately contribute to building a sustainable competitive advantage and securing enduring value for their organizations.

6.3. Implications for Policymakers

Our findings advocate for policy frameworks that incentivize ESG adoption, particularly in sectors like hospitality, where sustainable practices can significantly and positively influence economic and social outcomes. Policymakers should prioritize making ESG adoption an industry norm through government action, as it has the potential to drive both economic performance and societal benefits. The study's insights on the heightened relevance of ESG during the COVID-19 era emphasize the necessity for policies that encourage resilience-focused ESG strategies. Beyond enhancing firm performance, ESG activities contribute to greater resilience in turbulent times (Xu et al., 2023), supporting stable and sustainable economic growth.

In this context, policymakers should establish regulatory frameworks that promote ESG transparency and standardize reporting metrics to reduce information asymmetry and enable more informed decision-making by investors and stakeholders. Given the observed geographic variation in the ESG-CFP relationship, region-specific policies that address unique ESG priorities are crucial for maximizing the impact of ESG initiatives. Furthermore, fostering collaboration between governments, industry leaders, and local communities can ensure ESG practices align with broader societal objectives while supporting economic resilience and long-term growth. By integrating these elements, policymakers can create a sustainable foundation for the hospitality sector and other industries alike.

6.4. Limitations and Future Research Directions

While this study provides significant insights into the ESG-CFP relationship, it is not without limitations. The analysis focuses exclusively on publicly traded hospitality firms due to the limited availability of ESG data from Bloomberg. This narrow scope may limit the generalizability of the findings to private enterprises, which might demonstrate unique ESG practices and financial outcomes. Additionally, reliance on Bloomberg ESG ratings may not fully capture the intricate nuances of sustainability practices across different organizations. The study's focus on the hospitality sector, while valuable, inherently reflects the unique sustainability and reputational demands of the industry, which may not apply uniformly across other sectors with differing environmental and social priorities.

Regional disparities observed in the ESG-CFP relationship further underscore the potential influence of cultural and institutional factors, which were not explicitly controlled in this study. These disparities suggest that the ESG-CFP dynamic may vary based on national contexts, regulatory environments, and cultural norms. Such contextual factors highlight the need for further research to disentangle the role of these influences on the effectiveness of ESG strategies. Addressing these limitations through expanded datasets and more granular analyses could provide a more comprehensive understanding of the ESG-CFP nexus across diverse industries and regions. Methodologically, while robust regression techniques such as 2SLS were employed to address endogeneity, potential limitations remain. The validity of 2SLS depends heavily on the choice of instrumental variables, and alternative instrumental variables or methods, such as the generalized method of moments or quasi-experimental designs, could further strengthen the analysis.

Future research should explore the ESG-CFP relationship across various sectors and conduct cross-country comparisons to examine how cultural, regulatory, and institutional dynamics shape this linkage in different contexts. Additionally, longitudinal studies investigating the enduring impact of ESG initiatives on firm performance, particularly in the post-pandemic era, could offer critical insights into the long-term benefits of sustainability practices. These directions would not only enrich academic discourse but also provide actionable guidance for businesses and policymakers seeking to align ESG strategies with both financial performance and societal expectations.

Author Contributions: Conceptualization, K.L.; methodology, K.L. and J.Z.; software, K.L. and J.Z; validation, K.L., C.B.O., Y.X. and J.Z.; formal analysis, K.L., C.B.O., Y.X. and J.Z.; investigation, K.L., C.B.O., Y.X. and J.Z.; resources, K.L. and J.Z.; data curation, K.L. and J.Z.; writing—original draft preparation, K.L.; writing—review and editing, K.L., C.B.O., Y.X. and J.Z.; visualization, K.L. and J.Z.; supervision, C.B.O., Y.X. and J.Z.; project administration, J.Z.; funding acquisition, J.Z. All authors have read and agreed to the published version of the manuscript.

Funding: This research was funded by the General Program of the Zhejiang Provincial Department of Education (Y202353438), the Wenzhou-Kean University International Collaborative Research Program (ICRP2023002), and the Wenzhou-Kean University Student Partnering with Faculty Research Program (WKUSPF202411).

Institutional Review Board Statement: Not applicable.

Informed Consent Statement: Not applicable.

Data Availability Statement: The original data presented in the study are openly available in the commercially subscribed Bloomberg Terminals at [https://www.bloomberg.com/professional/products/bloomberg-terminal/, accessed on 29 December 2024].

Conflicts of Interest: The authors declare no conflicts of interest.

Notes

1 "Integrate the Principles for Responsible Investment", United Nations Global Compact. Available online: https://www.unglobalcompact.org/take-action/action/responsible-investment (accessed on 7 June 2023).

2 "Economic Impact Reports", World Travel & Tourism Council. Available online: https://wttc.org/research/economic-impact (accessed on 7 June 2023).

3 "Insights", Nielsen. Available online: https://www.nielsen.com/insights/type/report/ (accessed on 27 December 2024).

4 "ESG Impact Is Hard to Measure—But It's Not Impossible", Jennifer Howard-Grenville. Available online: https://hbr.org/2021/01/esg-impact-is-hard-to-measure-but-its-not-impossible (accessed on 7 June 2023).

5 "Country Comparison Graphs", Geert Hofstede. Available online: https://geerthofstede.com/country-comparison-graphs/ (accessed on 26 December 2024).

6 "GDP growth (annual %)", World Bank Group. Available online: https://data.worldbank.org/indicator/NY.GDP.MKTP.KD.ZG (accessed on 29 December 2024).

7 "About", Task Force on Climate-Related Financial Disclosures. Available online: https://www.fsb-tcfd.org/about/ (accessed on 29 December 2024).

8 "Countries affected by mandatory ESG reporting", Worldfavor. Available online: https://blog.worldfavor.com/countries-affected-by-mandatory-esg-reporting-here-is-the-list (accessed on 29 December 2024).

9 "How Airbnb has affected the hotel industry", US Bureau of Labor Statistics. Available online: https://www.bls.gov/opub/mlr/2018/beyond-bls/how-airbnb-has-affected-the-hotel-industry.htm (accessed on 29 December 2024).

10 "The Growth of Sustainability in Hotels: An Industry in Transformation", ROIBACK. Available online: https://en.roiback.com/rb-academy/the-growth-of-sustainability-in-hotels (accessed on 29 December 2024).

11 "Achieved: WHO timeline—COVID-19", World Health Organization. Available online: https://www.who.int/news/item/27-04-2020-who-timeline---covid-19 (accessed on 7 June 2023).

12 "The leisure and hospitality industry: Short-term growth, long-term challenges", United States Congress Joint Economic Committee. Available online: https://www.jec.senate.gov/public/index.cfm/republicans/analysis?ID=71F83A28-1113-4C90-B33F-EF8EB78FF0EB (accessed on 7 June 2023).

13 "How companies manage sustainability", McKinsey. Available online: https://www.mckinsey.com/capabilities/sustainability/our-insights/how-companies-manage-sustainability-mckinsey-global-survey-results (accessed on 28 December 2024).

References

Abdi, Y., Li, X., & Càmara-Turull, X. (2022). Exploring the impact of sustainability (ESG) disclosure on firm value and financial performance (FP) in airline industry: The moderating role of size and age. *Environment, Development and Sustainability*, *24*(4), 5052–5079. [CrossRef]

Abrahamson, E., & Fombrun, C. J. (1994). Macrocultures: Determinants and consequences. *Academy of Management Review*, *19*(4), 728–755. [CrossRef]

Alareeni, B. A., & Hamdan, A. (2020). ESG impact on performance of US S&P 500-listed firms. *Corporate Governance*, *20*(7), 1409–1428.

Aouadi, A., & Marsat, S. (2018). Do ESG controversies matter for firm value? Evidence from international data. *Journal of Business Ethics*, *151*, 1027–1047. [CrossRef]

Arbulú, I., Razumova, M., Rey-Maquieira, J., & Sastre, F. (2021). Measuring risks and vulnerability of tourism to the COVID-19 crisis in the context of extreme uncertainty: The case of the Balearic Islands. *Tourism Management Perspectives*, *39*, 100857. [CrossRef] [PubMed]

Attig, N., Boubakri, N., El Ghoul, S., & Guedhami, O. (2016). Firm internationalization and corporate social responsibility. *Journal of Business Ethics*, *134*, 171–197. [CrossRef]

Back, K. J. (2024). ESG for the hospitality and tourism research: Essential demanded research area for all. *Tourism Management*, *105*, 104954. [CrossRef]

Bai, H. M. (2020). The socio-economic implications of the coronavirus pandemic (COVID-19): A review. *ComFin Research*, *8*(4), 8–17.

Baker, S. R., Bloom, N., Davis, S. J., Kost, K., Sammon, M., & Viratyosin, T. (2020). The unprecedented stock market reaction to COVID-19. *Review of Asset Pricing Studies*, *10*(4), 742–758. [CrossRef]

Baklaci, H. F., Cheng, I. W., & Zhang, J. (2024). Performance attributes of environmental, social, and governance exchange-traded funds. *Asia-Pacific Financial Markets*, *31*(2), 307–334. [CrossRef]

Benlemlih, M., & Girerd-Potin, I. (2017). Corporate social responsibility and firm financial risk reduction: On the moderating role of the legal environment. *Journal of Business Finance & Accounting*, *44*(7–8), 1137–1166.

Bianco, S., Bernard, S., & Singal, M. (2023). The impact of sustainability certifications on performance and competitive action in hotels. *International Journal of Hospitality Management*, *108*, 103379. [CrossRef]
Boehe, D. M., & Cruz, L. B. (2010). Corporate social responsibility, product differentiation strategy and export performance. *Journal of Business Ethics*, *91*, 325–346. [CrossRef]
Bohdanowicz, P., & Zientara, P. (2008). Corporate social responsibility in hospitality: Issues and implications. A case study of Scandic. *Scandinavian Journal of Hospitality and Tourism*, *8*(4), 271–293. [CrossRef]
Brammer, S., Brooks, C., & Pavelin, S. (2006). Corporate social performance and stock returns: UK evidence from disaggregate measures. *Financial Management*, *35*(3), 97–116. [CrossRef]
Branco, M. C., & Rodrigues, L. L. (2006). Corporate social responsibility and resource-based perspectives. *Journal of Business Ethics*, *69*, 111–132. [CrossRef]
Brown, L. D., & Caylor, M. L. (2006). Corporate governance and firm valuation. *Journal of Accounting and Public Policy*, *25*(4), 409–434. [CrossRef]
Burlea, A. S., & Popa, I. (2013). Legitimacy theory. *Encyclopedia of Corporate Social Responsibility*, *21*, 1579–1584.
Carlsen, J., Getz, D., & Ali-Knight, J. (2001). The environmental attitudes and practices of family businesses in the rural tourism and hospitality sectors. *Journal of Sustainable Tourism*, *9*(4), 281–297. [CrossRef]
Casado-Díaz, A. B., Nicolau, J. L., Ruiz-Moreno, F., & Sellers, R. (2014). Industry-specific effect of CSR initiatives: Hotels and airlines. *Kybernetes*, *43*(3/4), 547–564. [CrossRef]
Chen, C. D., Su, C. H. J., & Chen, M. H. (2022). Are ESG-committed hotels financially resilient to the COVID-19 pandemic? An autoregressive jump intensity trend model. *Tourism Management*, *93*, 104581. [CrossRef] [PubMed]
Chen, M. H., Kim, W. G., & Kim, H. J. (2005). The impact of macroeconomic and non-macroeconomic forces on hotel stock returns. *International Journal of Hospitality Management*, *24*(2), 243–258. [CrossRef] [PubMed]
Chung, K. H., & Pruitt, S. W. (1994). A simple approximation of Tobin's Q. *Financial Management*, *23*(3), 70–74. [CrossRef]
Connelly, B. L., Certo, S. T., Ireland, R. D., & Reutzel, C. R. (2011). Signaling theory: A review and assessment. *Journal of Management*, *37*(1), 39–67. [CrossRef]
Cowan, K., & Guzman, F. (2020). How CSR reputation, sustainability signals, and country-of-origin sustainability reputation contribute to corporate brand performance: An exploratory study. *Journal of Business Research*, *117*, 683–693. [CrossRef]
Crisóstomo, V. L., de Souza Freire, F., & De Vasconcellos, F. C. (2011). Corporate social responsibility, firm value and financial performance in Brazil. *Social Responsibility Journal*, *7*(2), 295–309. [CrossRef]
D'Amato, A., & Falivena, C. (2020). Corporate social responsibility and firm value: Do firm size and age matter? Empirical evidence from European listed companies. *Corporate Social Responsibility and Environmental Management*, *27*(2), 909–924. [CrossRef]
Dao, B. T. T., & Ta, T. D. N. (2020). A meta-analysis: Capital structure and firm performance. *Journal of Economics and Development*, *22*(1), 111–129. [CrossRef]
Eccles, R. G., Ioannou, I., & Serafeim, G. (2014). The impact of corporate sustainability on organizational processes and performance. *Management Science*, *60*(11), 2835–2857. [CrossRef]
Edmans, A. (2011). Does the stock market fully value intangibles? Employee satisfaction and equity prices. *Journal of Financial Economics*, *101*(3), 621–640. [CrossRef]
Egorova, A. A., Grishunin, S. V., & Karminsky, A. M. (2022). The impact of ESG factors on the performance of information technology companies. *Procedia Computer Science*, *199*, 339–345. [CrossRef]
El Ghoul, S., Guedhami, O., Kwok, C. C., & Mishra, D. R. (2011). Does corporate social responsibility affect the cost of capital? *Journal of Banking & Finance*, *35*(9), 2388–2406.
Elsayed, K., & Paton, D. (2005). The impact of environmental performance on firm performance: Static and dynamic panel data evidence. *Structural Change and Economic Dynamics*, *16*(3), 395–412. [CrossRef]
Elzahar, H., Hussainey, K., Mazzi, F., & Tsalavoutas, I. (2015). Economic consequences of key performance indicators' disclosure quality. *International Review of Financial Analysis*, *39*, 96–112. [CrossRef]
Emeka-Nwokeji, N., & Osisioma, B. C. (2019). Sustainability disclosures and market value of firms in emerging economy: Evidence from Nigeria. *European Journal of Accounting, Auditing and Finance Research*, *7*(3), 1–19.
Ersoy, E., Swiecka, B., Grima, S., Özen, E., & Romanova, I. (2022). The impact of ESG scores on bank market value? Evidence from the US banking industry. *Sustainability*, *14*(15), 9527. [CrossRef]
Fatemi, A., Fooladi, I., & Tehranian, H. (2015). Valuation effects of corporate social responsibility. *Journal of Banking & Finance*, *59*, 182–192.
Fisher-Vanden, K., & Thorburn, K. S. (2011). Voluntary corporate environmental initiatives and shareholder wealth. *Journal of Environmental Economics and Management*, *62*(3), 430–445. [CrossRef]
Fombrun, C. J., Gardberg, N. A., & Barnett, M. L. (2000). Opportunity platforms and safety nets: Corporate citizenship and reputational risk. *Business and Society Review*, *105*(1), 85–106. [CrossRef]
Freeman, R. E. (2010). *Strategic management: A stakeholder approach*. Cambridge University Press.

Friedman, M. (2007). The social responsibility of business is to increase its profits. In W. C. Zimmerli, M. Holzinger, & K. Richter (Eds.), *Corporate ethics and corporate governance* (pp. 173–178). Springer.
Galbreath, J. (2013). ESG in focus: The Australian evidence. *Journal of Business Ethics, 118*, 529–541. [CrossRef]
Gholami, A., Sands, J., & Rahman, H. U. (2022). Environmental, social and governance disclosure and value generation: Is the financial industry different? *Sustainability, 14*(5), 2647. [CrossRef]
Gil, M. A., Jiménez, J. B., & Lorente, J. C. (2001). An analysis of environmental management, organizational context and performance of Spanish hotels. *Omega, 29*(6), 457–471.
Gordon, M. J. (1959). Dividends, earnings, and stock prices. *Review of Economics and Statistics, 41*(2), 99–105. [CrossRef]
Goss, A., & Roberts, G. S. (2011). The impact of corporate social responsibility on the cost of bank loans. *Journal of Banking & Finance, 35*(7), 1794–1810.
Hair, J. F., Black, W. C., Babin, B. J., & Anderson, R. E. (2013). *Multivariate data analysis*. Pearson Higher Education.
Higgins-Desbiolles, F. (2010). The elusiveness of sustainability in tourism: The culture-ideology of consumerism and its implications. *Tourism and Hospitality Research, 10*(2), 116–129. [CrossRef]
Hillman, A. J., & Keim, G. D. (2001). Shareholder value, stakeholder management, and social issues: What's the bottom line? *Strategic Management Journal, 22*(2), 125–139. [CrossRef]
Holcomb, J. L., Upchurch, R. S., & Okumus, F. (2007). Corporate social responsibility: What are top hotel companies reporting? *International Journal of Contemporary Hospitality Management, 19*(6), 461–475. [CrossRef]
Ionescu, G. H., Firoiu, D., Pirvu, R., & Vilag, R. D. (2019). The impact of ESG factors on market value of companies from travel and tourism industry. *Technological and Economic Development of Economy, 25*(5), 820–849. [CrossRef]
Jacobs, B. W., Singhal, V. R., & Subramanian, R. (2010). An empirical investigation of environmental performance and the market value of the firm. *Journal of Operations Management, 28*(5), 430–441. [CrossRef]
Jo, H., & Na, H. (2012). Does CSR reduce firm risk? Evidence from controversial industry sectors. *Journal of Business Ethics, 110*, 441–456. [CrossRef]
Kasim, A. (2007). Towards a wider adoption of environmental responsibility in the hotel sector. *International Journal of Hospitality & Tourism Administration, 8*(2), 25–49.
Keceli, B., & Cankaya, S. (2020). The effects of ESG and financial data on stock value: The Nordic and Latin European sample. *Turkish Joirnal of Entrepreneurship, 4*(7), 31–49.
Khan, A., Muttakin, M. B., & Siddiqui, J. (2013). Corporate governance and corporate social responsibility disclosures: Evidence from an emerging economy. *Journal of Business Ethics, 114*, 207–223. [CrossRef]
Kirk, D. (1998). Attitudes to environmental management held by a group of hotel managers in Edinburgh. *International Journal of Hospitality Management, 17*(1), 33–47. [CrossRef]
Koh, Y., Lee, S., & Boo, S. (2009). Does franchising help restaurant firm value? *International Journal of Hospitality Management, 28*(2), 289–296. [CrossRef]
Lahouel, B. B., Gaies, B., Zaied, Y. B., & Jahmane, A. (2019). Accounting for endogeneity and the dynamics of corporate social–corporate financial performance relationship. *Journal of Cleaner Production, 230*, 352–364. [CrossRef]
Laroche, M., Bergeron, J., & Barbaro-Forleo, G. (2001). Targeting consumers who are willing to pay more for environmentally friendly products. *Journal of Consumer Marketing, 18*(6), 503–520. [CrossRef]
Lee, M. T., Raschke, R. L., & Krishen, A. S. (2022). Signaling green! firm ESG signals in an interconnected environment that promote brand valuation. *Journal of Business Research, 138*, 1–11. [CrossRef]
Lee, S., Seo, K., & Sharma, A. (2013). Corporate social responsibility and firm performance in the airline industry: The moderating role of oil prices. *Tourism Management, 38*, 20–30. [CrossRef]
Legrand, W. (2021). Luxury tourism in remote destinations: An inquiry into sustainability. In J. S. Chen (Ed.), *Advances in hospitality and leisure* (pp. 65–81). Emerald Publishing Limited.
Legrand, W., & Matthew-Bolofinde, A. (2022). ESG, SDGs, and hospitality: Challenges and opportunities in activating sustainability. In C. N. Berrones-Flemmig, F. Contreras, & U. Dornberger (Eds.), *Business in the 21st century: A sustainable approach* (pp. 25–39). Emerald Publishing Limited.
Li, Y., Gong, M., Zhang, X. Y., & Koh, L. (2018). The impact of environmental, social, and governance disclosure on firm value: The role of CEO power. *British Accounting Review, 50*(1), 60–75. [CrossRef]
Liu, Y., Cheng, X., Liao, S. S., & Yang, F. (2023). The impact of COVID-19 on the tourism and hospitality Industry: Evidence from international stock markets. *North American Journal of Economics and Finance, 64*, 101875. [CrossRef]
Liu, Y., McDowell, S., Xue, C., & Zhang, J. (2024). Environmental, social, and governance performance: The role of Chinese employee stock ownership plans. *Environmental Economics, 25*(2), 1–12. [CrossRef]
Lu, J., & Nepal, S. K. (2009). Sustainable tourism research: An analysis of papers published in the Journal of Sustainable Tourism. *Journal of Sustainable Tourism, 17*(1), 5–16. [CrossRef]

Lu, J. W., & Beamish, P. W. (2004). International diversification and firm performance: The S-curve hypothesis. *Academy of Management Journal, 47*(4), 598–609. [CrossRef]

Lyon, T. P., & Maxwell, J. W. (2011). Greenwash: Corporate environmental disclosure under threat of audit. *Journal of Economics & Management Strategy, 20*(1), 3–41.

Lyon, T. P., Lu, Y., Shi, X., & Yin, Q. (2013). How do investors respond to green company awards in China? *Ecological Economics, 94*, 1–8. [CrossRef]

Margolis, J. D., Elfenbein, H. A., & Walsh, J. P. (2009). *Does it pay to be good... and does it matter? A meta-analysis of the relationship between corporate social and financial performance*. SSRN Working Paper. Available online: https://ssrn.com/abstract=1866371 (accessed on 29 December 2024).

McIntosh, R. W., Goeldner, C. R., & Ritchie, J. B. (1995). *Tourism: Principles, practices, philosophies*. John Wiley and Sons.

McWilliams, A., Siegel, D., & Teoh, S. H. (1999). Issues in the use of the event study methodology: A critical analysis of corporate social responsibility studies. *Organizational Research Methods, 2*(4), 340–365. [CrossRef]

Moneva, J. M., Bonilla-Priego, M. J., & Ortas, E. (2020). Corporate social responsibility and organisational performance in the tourism sector. *Journal of Sustainable Tourism, 28*(6), 853–872. [CrossRef]

Moon, J. (2007). The contribution of corporate social responsibility to sustainable development. *Sustainable Development, 15*(5), 296–306. [CrossRef]

Moravcikova, K., Stefanikova, L'., & Rypakova, M. (2015). CSR reporting as an important tool of CSR communication. *Procedia Economics and Finance, 26*, 332–338. [CrossRef]

Moscardo, G., & Murphy, L. (2014). There is no such thing as sustainable tourism: Re-conceptualizing tourism as a tool for sustainability. *Sustainability, 6*(5), 2538–2561. [CrossRef]

Murray, A., Sinclair, D., Power, D., & Gray, R. (2006). Do financial markets care about social and environmental disclosure? Further evidence and exploration from the UK. *Accounting, Auditing & Accountability Journal, 19*(2), 228–255.

Nakao, Y., Amano, A., Matsumura, K., Genba, K., & Nakano, M. (2007). Relationship between environmental performance and financial performance: An empirical analysis of Japanese corporations. *Business Strategy and the Environment, 16*(2), 106–118. [CrossRef]

Nguyen, D. T., Hoang, T. G., & Tran, H. G. (2022). Help or hurt? The impact of ESG on firm performance in S&P 500 non-financial firms. *Australasian Accounting, Business and Finance Journal, 16*(2), 91–102.

Nicola, M., Alsafi, Z., Sohrabi, C., Kerwan, A., Al-Jabir, A., Iosifidis, C., Agha, M., & Agha, R. (2020). The socio-economic implications of the coronavirus pandemic (COVID-19): A review. *International Journal of Surgery, 78*, 185–193. [CrossRef]

Nollet, J., Filis, G., & Mitrokostas, E. (2016). Corporate social responsibility and financial performance: A non-linear and disaggregated approach. *Economic Modelling, 52*, 400–407. [CrossRef]

Nor, N. M., Bahari, N. A. S., Adnan, N. A., Kamal, S. M. Q. A. S., & Ali, I. M. (2016). The effects of environmental disclosure on financial performance in Malaysia. *Procedia Economics and Finance, 35*, 117–126. [CrossRef]

Palmer, K., Oates, W. E., & Portney, P. R. (1995). Tightening environmental standards: The benefit-cost or the no-cost paradigm? *Journal of Economic Perspectives, 9*(4), 119–132. [CrossRef]

Patten, D. M. (1991). Exposure, legitimacy, and social disclosure. *Journal of Accounting and Public Policy, 10*(4), 297–308. [CrossRef]

Pérez, A., & del Bosque, I. R. (2015). Corporate social responsibility and customer loyalty: Exploring the role of identification, satisfaction and type of company. *Journal of Services Marketing, 29*(1), 15–25. [CrossRef]

Popli, M., Ladkani, R. M., & Gaur, A. S. (2017). Business group affiliation and post-acquisition performance: An extended resource-based view. *Journal of Business Research, 81*, 21–30. [CrossRef]

Reed, W. R., & Ye, H. (2011). Which panel data estimator should I use? *Applied Economics, 43*(8), 985–1000. [CrossRef]

Rehman, M. U., Kang, S. H., Ahmad, N., & Vo, X. V. (2021). The impact of COVID-19 on the G7 stock markets: A time-frequency analysis. *North American Journal of Economics and Finance, 58*, 101526. [CrossRef]

Reid, E. M., & Toffel, M. W. (2009). Responding to public and private politics: Corporate disclosure of climate change strategies. *Strategic Management Journal, 30*(11), 1157–1178. [CrossRef]

Reverte, C. (2009). Determinants of corporate social responsibility disclosure ratings by Spanish listed firms. *Journal of Business Ethics, 88*, 351–366. [CrossRef]

Rivera, J. (2002). Assessing a voluntary environmental initiative in the developing world: The Costa Rican Certification for Sustainable Tourism. *Policy Sciences, 35*(4), 333–360. [CrossRef]

Rouf, A. (2011). The financial performance (profitability) and corporate governance disclosure in the annual reports of listed companies of Bangladesh. *Journal of Economics and Business Research, 17*(2), 103–117.

Saleh, M., Zulkifli, N., & Muhamad, R. (2011). Looking for evidence of the relationship between corporate social responsibility and corporate financial performance in an emerging market. *Asia-Pacific Journal of Business Administration, 3*(2), 165–190. [CrossRef]

Scanlon, N. L. (2007). An analysis and assessment of environmental operating practices in hotel and resort properties. *International Journal of Hospitality Management, 26*(3), 711–723. [CrossRef]

Sen, S., & Bhattacharya, C. B. (2001). Does doing good always lead to doing better? Consumer reactions to corporate social responsibility. *Journal of Marketing Research, 38*(2), 225–243. [CrossRef]
Shaikh, I. (2022). Environmental, social, and governance (ESG) practice and firm performance: An international evidence. *Journal of Business Economics and Management, 23*(1), 218–237. [CrossRef]
Shakil, M. H. (2022). Environmental, social and governance performance and stock price volatility: A moderating role of firm size. *Journal of Public Affairs, 22*(3), e2574. [CrossRef]
Sharfman, M. P., Shaft, T. M., & Tihanyi, L. (2004). A model of the global and institutional antecedents of high-level corporate environmental performance. *Business & Society, 43*(1), 6–36.
Shin, J., Moon, J. J., & Kang, J. (2023). Where does ESG pay? The role of national culture in moderating the relationship between ESG performance and financial performance. *International Business Review, 32*(3), 102071. [CrossRef]
Sigala, M. (2020). Tourism and COVID-19: Impacts and implications for advancing and resetting industry and research. *Journal of Business Research, 117*, 312–321. [CrossRef] [PubMed]
Siueia, T. T., Wang, J., & Deladem, T. G. (2019). Corporate social responsibility and financial performance: A comparative study in the sub-Saharan Africa banking sector. *Journal of Cleaner Production, 226*, 658–668. [CrossRef]
Statman, M., & Glushkov, D. (2009). The wages of social responsibility. *Financial Analysts Journal, 65*(4), 33–46. [CrossRef]
Suchman, M. C. (1995). Managing legitimacy: Strategic and institutional approaches. *Academy of Management Review, 20*(3), 571–610. [CrossRef]
Taherdangkoo, M., Ghasemi, K., & Beikpour, M. (2017). The role of sustainability environment in export marketing strategy and performance: A literature review. *Environment, Development and Sustainability, 19*(5), 1601–1629. [CrossRef]
Torelli, C. J., Monga, A. B., & Kaikati, A. M. (2012). Doing poorly by doing good: Corporate social responsibility and brand concepts. *Journal of Consumer Research, 38*(5), 948–963. [CrossRef]
Wang, H., Tong, L., Takeuchi, R., & George, G. (2016). Corporate social responsibility: An overview and new research directions. *Academy of Management Journal, 59*(2), 534–544. [CrossRef]
Wang, L., Weng, Z., Xue, C., & Zhang, J. (2024). ESG ratings and stock performance in the internet industry. *Investment Management and Financial Innovations, 21*(1), 38–50. [CrossRef]
Wintoki, M. B., Linck, J. S., & Netter, J. M. (2012). Endogeneity and the dynamics of internal corporate governance. *Journal of Financial Economics, 105*(3), 581–606. [CrossRef]
Wu, M. Y., & Pearce, P. L. (2013). Tourists to Lhasa, Tibet: How local youth classify, understand and respond to different types of travelers. *Asia Pacific Journal of Tourism Research, 18*(6), 549–572. [CrossRef]
Xie, J., Nozawa, W., Yagi, M., Fujii, H., & Managi, S. (2019). Do environmental, social, and governance activities improve corporate financial performance? *Business Strategy and the Environment, 28*(2), 286–300. [CrossRef]
Xu, N., Chen, J., Zhou, F., Dong, Q., & He, Z. (2023). Corporate ESG and resilience of stock prices in the context of the COVID-19 pandemic in China. *Pacific-Basin Finance Journal, 79*, 102040. [CrossRef]
Zheng, J., Khurram, M. U., & Chen, L. (2022). Can green innovation affect ESG ratings and financial performance? Evidence from Chinese GEM listed companies. *Sustainability, 14*(14), 8677. [CrossRef]

Journal of
Risk and Financial Management

Article

The Modelling of Auto Insurance Claim-Frequency Counts by the Inverse Trinomial Distribution

Seng Huat Ong [1,2,*], Shin Zhu Sim [3] and Shuangzhe Liu [4]

1 Institute of Actuarial Science and Data Analytics, UCSI University, Kuala Lumpur 56000, Malaysia
2 Institute of Mathematical Sciences, University of Malaya, Kuala Lumpur 50603, Malaysia
3 School of Mathematical Sciences, University of Nottingham Malaysia, Semenyih 43500, Malaysia; sim.shinzhu@nottingham.edu.my
4 Faculty of Science and Technology, University of Canberra, Canberra 2600, Australia; shuangzhe.liu@canberra.edu.au
* Correspondence: ongsh@ucsiuniversity.edu.my

Abstract: In the transportation services industry, the proper assessment of insurance claim count distribution is an important step to determine insurance premiums based on policyholders' risk profiles. Risk factors are identified through regression analysis. In this paper, the inverse trinomial distribution is proposed as a count data model for insurance claims characterised by having long tails and a high index of dispersion. Two regression models are developed to identify associated risk factors. Other popular models, such as the negative binomial and COM-Poisson, are fitted and compared to information criteria. The risk profiles of policyholders are determined based on the selected model. To illustrate the application of the inverse trinomial regression models, the ausprivautolong dataset of automobile claims in Australia has been fitted with identification of risk factors.

Keywords: insurance premiums; negative binomial; COM-Poisson; long tail; over dispersion; transportation services

1. Introduction

A basic objective of insurance companies is to determine the appropriate insurance premium for the insured to cover a particular risk. Based upon the risk characteristics of the insured, a standard procedure to calculate the premium is to multiply the conditional expectation of the claim frequency by the expected cost of the claims (David, 2015). Evaluation of the risks to calculate an insurance premium uses regression by generalized linear models (GLM). Poisson regression is a popular model for claim counts in non-life insurance contexts but suffers from the restrictive equality of mean and variance. In practice, the data often exhibit over-dispersion, where the variance is greater than the mean. To account for over-dispersion, many alternative models have been proposed. One such family of models is the mixed Poisson distribution with negative binomial (NB) distribution as a popular choice for modelling claim frequency counts in auto insurance (Denuit et al., 2007). The NB distribution, as a mixed Poisson distribution, is formulated by allowing the Poisson mean to vary as a gamma random variable. In accident-proneness studies, as initially proposed by Greenwood and Yule (1920), the number of accidents is assumed to be Poisson distributed, but there is individual heterogeneity which is modelled by the Poisson mean varying as a gamma distribution. The NB regression model has been particularly effective in analysing motor vehicle crash data, as demonstrated in the work of Lord et al. (2005), Lord (2006) and Li et al. (2008). The unique distributional characteristics of insurance data, such as a very long tail and high kurtosis, present challenges for traditional negative binomial (NB) regression models. To better accommodate these data characteristics and improve model fit, alternatives to NB regression have been developed. For instance, Dean et al. (1989) examined the Poisson-inverse Gaussian regression model. The Poisson-inverse Gaussian distribution has a longer tail than the NB distribution. Willmot (1987) proposed this distribution as an alternative to the NB distribution.

In this paper, the inverse trinomial (IT) regression model is proposed to analyse claim-frequency count data with very long tails and high over-dispersion. The ausprivautolong dataset of automobile claims in Australia over one and two periods are characterised by their long tails and index of dispersion greater than three. Shimizu and Yanagimoto (1991) introduced IT distribution as a one-dimensional random walk distribution on a nonnegative line with an absorbing barrier at the origin, where the particle performing the random walk is allowed to remain at a position with positive probability. Aoyama et al. (2008) generalised this random walk model. NB distribution is a special case of IT distribution. As a comparison of the overdispersion, NB and Poisson-inverse Gaussian distributions have quadratic variance functions of the mean (Morris, 1982), while IT distribution has a cubic variance (Letac & Mora, 1990) function of the mean. This property adds flexibility to IT distribution when modelling over-dispersion. Phang et al. (2013) examined statistical inference in IT distribution based on minimum distance estimation with probability-generating function (Sim & Ong, 2010). Phang et al. (2013) showed that the IT distribution as a viable alternative to NB and Poisson-inverse Gaussian distributions for the empirical modelling of data. Recently, Ong et al. (2024) derived and discussed some probabilistic properties of IT distribution. Regression analysis has proven useful in various contexts, for instance, in the analysis of bus travel times in effective journey planning (Cheok et al., 2024). Due to these aforementioned advantages, it is of interest to consider the application of IT distribution to auto insurance.

This paper is arranged as follows: In Section 2, we introduce IT distribution and the formulation of the regression models. In Section 3, we describe the auto insurance claim-frequency count in Australia, the ausprivautolong dataset, and present the results of the analysis with IT distribution and identify the risk factors. Finally, in Section 4, our study shows the IT model consistently outperforms traditional NB and flexible COM-Poisson (Conway & Maxwell, 1962; Sellers et al., 2012) models, as indicated by their lower Akaike information criterion (AIC) and Bayesian information criterion (BIC) scores. This highlights the IT model's effectiveness for long-tailed and highly over-dispersed datasets.

2. The Inverse Trinomial Distribution and Regression Models

In this section, some basic properties of IT distribution are stated, followed by a presentation of two IT regression models.

2.1. Basic Properties

In the random walk model for the IT distribution, we let the probability of a $-1, 0$, or $+1$ step be given by p, q and r, respectively. IT distribution has the probability mass function (pmf) (Shimizu & Yanagimoto, 1991) given by

$$Pr(X=x)=\frac{\lambda p^{\lambda}q^{x}}{x+\lambda}\sum_{t=0}^{\lfloor x/2\rfloor}\binom{x+\lambda}{t,t+\lambda,x-2t}\left(\frac{pr}{q^{2}}\right)^{t}, x=0,1,2,\cdots, \quad (1)$$

where $\lambda>0, p\geq r, p+q+r=1\ (p,q,r\geq 0)$, $\lfloor x\rfloor$ represents the greatest integer less than or equal to x and

$$\binom{x+\lambda}{t,t+\lambda,x-2t}=\frac{(x+\lambda)!}{t!(t+\lambda)!(x-2t)!}.$$

In terms of the Gauss hypergeometric function, the pmf is given by

$$Pr(X = x) = p^{\lambda}(q + 2\sqrt{pr})^{x}\frac{(\lambda)_x}{x!}{}_2F_1\left[-x, \lambda + 1/2; 2\lambda + 1; \frac{4\sqrt{pr}}{(q + 2\sqrt{pr})}\right], \quad (2)$$

where $(\lambda)_x$ is the Pochhammer function and ${}_2F_1$ denotes the Gauss hypergeometric function.

The probability-generating function (pgf) has the following simple form (Shimizu et al., 1997):

$$G(u) = \left(\frac{2p}{(1 - qu) + \sqrt{(1 - qu)^2 - 4pru^2}}\right)^{\lambda},$$

where $\lambda > 0, p + q + r = 1, 0 < \frac{4pr}{(1-q)^2} < 1$. When $r = 0$, the NB pgf is obtained. The mean and variance of the IT distribution, respectively, with $p > r$, are as follows:

$$E[X] = \mu = \lambda\{[1 - (p - r)]/(p - r)\},$$

$$Var[X] = \sigma^2 = \lambda\{1 - (p - r) + 2r/(p - r)\}/(p - r)^2.$$

Let $a = p - r$. The index of dispersion (ID) is as follows:

$$ID = \frac{Var[X]}{E[X]} = \frac{a(1 - a) + 2r}{(1 - a)a^2} = \phi. \quad (3)$$

Note that the ID is a function of a and is independent of the parameter λ.

2.2. The Inverse Trinomial Regression Models

To apply IT distribution in regression analysis, it is assumed that the response Y_i is influenced by a set of explanatory variables or covariates. This is achieved by expressing the parameters as functions of these explanatory variables. To include the covariates, we consider a GLM with log link function. The log link for a parameter, μ, is given by

$$\log(\mu) = \boldsymbol{x}_i^T\boldsymbol{\beta},$$

where $\boldsymbol{x}_i$ is a vector of the explanatory variables and $\boldsymbol{\beta}$ is the vector of regression parameters, $i = 1, \ldots, n$.

The simple form of the IT mean facilitates the development of the regression models. With the equations

$$\mu = \lambda\left(\frac{1 - a}{a}\right) = \lambda\theta, a = p - r, \theta = \frac{1 - a}{a},$$

we consider the log link function for the mean as the following:

$$\mu = \lambda\theta = exp\left(\boldsymbol{x}_i^T\boldsymbol{\beta}\right). \quad (4)$$

Since $\mu = \lambda\theta$, the covariates $\boldsymbol{x}_i^T$ may be linked either through λ or θ. This avoids the need to reparametrize the model in terms of the mean, μ. The regression models may be formulated as follows:

$$\text{(a) } \lambda = \theta^{-1}exp\left(\boldsymbol{x}_i^T\boldsymbol{\beta}\right)$$

The parameter λ is regarded as a function of θ and the covariates x_i^T. This is designated IT Regression I.

$$\text{(b) } \theta = \frac{1-a}{a} = \lambda^{-1} exp\left(x_i^T \beta\right)$$

The parameter θ is regarded as a function of λ and the covariates x_i^T. That is, θ, as a function of a, is allowed to vary. Since ID is a function of a, this may be called the varying dispersion index regression model. This is designated IT Regression II.

For IT Regression I, regression model (a), substitute $\lambda = \theta^{-1} exp(x_i^T \beta)$ in the IT pmf. while for IT Regression II, model (b), we make the following substitution:

$$p = \frac{1}{1 + \lambda^{-1} exp(x_i^T \beta)} + r.$$

2.3. The Random Intercept Regression Model for Clustered Data

The regression model in the previous section may be extended to model clustered data by including a random intercept. Let y_{ij} be the count for cluster $i = 1, 2, \ldots, m$, where m is the number of clusters, and individual $j = 1, 2, \ldots, m_i$, where m_i is the number of individuals in the i-th cluster. This regression model, corresponding to IT Regression Model I, is defined as follows:

$$y_{ij} | \gamma_i \sim IT(\lambda_{ij}, \theta)$$

$$\log(\lambda_{ij}) = x_{ij}^T \beta + \gamma_i$$

$$\gamma_i \sim f(\gamma_i; \delta),$$

where $f(\gamma_i; \delta)$ is the probability density function of the random intercept γ_i, with the vector of parameters δ. The conditional pmf of individual j in cluster i is given by

$$P(Y_{ij} = y_{ij} | x_{ij}, \gamma_i) = \frac{\lambda_{ij} p^{\lambda_{ij}} q^{y_{ij}}}{y_{ij} + \lambda_{ij}} \sum_{t=0}^{\lfloor x/2 \rfloor} \binom{y_{ij} + \lambda_{ij}}{t, t + \lambda_{ij}, y_{ij} - 2t} \left(\frac{pr}{q^2}\right)^t. \quad (5)$$

2.4. Parameter Estimation

If $Y_1, Y_2, \ldots, Y_N$ is a random sample, the log-likelihood function can be written as follows:

$$lnL(\lambda, p, r) = \sum_i lnP(Y_i = y_i; \lambda, p, r), \quad (6)$$

where $\lambda > 0, p \geq r, p + q + r = 1$ $(p, q, r \geq 0)$. The links to the explanatory variables are given by Equation (4), either through λ or θ. Due to the complicated log-likelihood function, we consider the direct numerical optimisation of Equation (6). Examples of global optimization algorithms are the simulated annealing (SA) algorithm (Metropolis et al., 1953) and basin-hopping (Wales & Doye, 1997). Challenges to the use of these algorithms are in the choice of starting points and appropriate tuning parameters, the time used to search for the whole space and ensuring, with great confidence, the global optimum has been determined. Simulated annealing is a stochastic search algorithm, based on the physics of annealing in metallurgy, that finds the global optimum of a complex function. Basin-hopping is a global optimization technique motivated by problems in physical chemistry; it iterates between the random perturbation of coordinates to jump basins and local optimization to optimize each basin in order to get the best optimum.

In the random intercept regression model, the marginal likelihood for the i-th cluster is given by

$$L_i(\boldsymbol{\beta},\ p, r, \delta) = \int \prod_{j=1}^{m_i} P(Y_{ij} = y_{ij} | \boldsymbol{x}_{ij}, \gamma_i) f(\gamma_i; \delta) d\gamma_i, \tag{7}$$

where $P(Y_{ij} = y_{ij} | \boldsymbol{x}_{ij}, \gamma_i)$ is given by Equation (5). The distribution of γ_i is usually taken to be the normal (Gaussian) distribution $N(\mu,\ \sigma^2)$. In this case, we call this the regression model the IT-Gaussian random intercept regression model. The marginal likelihood for the i-th cluster is given by Equation (7) with

$$f(\gamma_i; \delta) = \frac{1}{\sigma\sqrt{2\pi}} e^{-\frac{(\gamma_i - \mu)^2}{2\sigma^2}} \tag{8}$$

where $\delta = (\mu, \sigma^2)$. The log-likelihood function is

$$ln\ L(\boldsymbol{\beta},\ p, r, \delta) = \sum_{i=1}^{m} lnL_i(\boldsymbol{\beta},\ p, r, \delta).$$

3. Application to the Modelling of Auto Insurance Claim-Frequency Counts

3.1. Auto Insurance Claim-Frequency Count Dataset

We analysed the ausprivautolong dataset from the dataset ausprivauto of automobile claim in Australia, included in the R package 'CASdatasets' (https://cas.uqam.ca/pub/web/CASdatasets-manual.pdf (accessed on 3 November 2024)). The ausprivautolong is a simulated dataset containing counts of claims from 40,000 policies over three periods (years). The simulation is based on a true non-life portfolio. Each policy is regarded as a cluster, hence there are 3 × 40,000 = 120,000 records. The variables are as follows:

IDpol is the policy identification number.
DrivAge is the age of the policyholder.
VehValue is the vehicle value in thousands of AUD.
Period is tthe period number.
ClaimNb is tthe number of claims.
ClaimOcc indicates occurrence of a claim.

The risk factors are DrivAge (driver's age) and VehValue (vehicle value). In this study, the datasets are analysed separately by period, specifically focusing on Period 1 and Period 2. The claim-frequency count for both Period 1 and 2 has a very long tail and a high index of dispersion; see Tables 1 and 2.

Both datasets are analysed with the IT regression models. Due to the complexity of the clustered regression model, we have considered the non-clustered case. For comparison the data are fitted with the NB and COM-Poisson regression models. The NB pmf is given by

$$Pr(k) = \binom{\frac{1}{\varphi} + k - 1}{k} \left(\frac{1}{1+\varphi\theta}\right)^{\frac{1}{\varphi}} \left(\frac{\varphi\theta}{1+\varphi\theta}\right)^{k},$$

where $\varphi, \theta > 0$. The COM-Poisson distribution, has pmf given by

$$P(X = x) = \frac{\lambda^x}{(x!)^v Z(\lambda, v)},$$

where $Z(\lambda, v) = \sum_{j=0}^{\infty} \frac{\lambda^j}{(j!)^v}$ for $\lambda > 0$ and $v \geq 0$. The COM-Poisson distribution is under-dispersed when $\nu > 1$ and over-dispersed for $\nu < 1$. If $\nu = 1$, the Poisson distribution is obtained.

Table 1. Fitting of automobile claim dataset in Australia, Period 1 (without covariates).

	Observed Frequency	Expected Frequency		
		NB	COM-Poisson	IT
0	34,764	34,817.81	32,847.04	34,814.06
1	3704	3293.50	5952.58	3391.38
2	875	1078.85	1006.49	1008.93
3	301	437.18	163.42	401.10
4	129	194.13	25.78	183.67
5	87	90.73	4.69 ^	91.36
6	39	43.81		47.97
7	22	21.64		26.16
8	17	10.87		14.67
9	17	5.53		8.41
10	9	2.84		4.91
11	8	1.47		2.90
12	7	1.63 ^		1.74
13	6			1.05
14+	15			1.69 ^
χ^2		652.17	120,55.59	256.35
$\hat{\theta}$		0.24		
$\hat{\varphi}$		5.74		
$\hat{\upsilon}$			0.01	
$\hat{\lambda}$			0.18	0.25
$\hat{p}$				0.57
$\hat{r}$				0.04
Log-likelihood		−21,073.78	−22,571.02	−20,990.19
AIC		42,151.56	45,146.05	41,986.34
BIC		42,152.69	45,145.63	41,988.50

^ Indicates the expected frequency is grouped. The index of dispersion = 3.11.

Table 2. Fitting of automobile claim dataset in Australia, Period 2 (without covariates).

	Observed Frequency	Expected Frequency		
		NB	COM-Poisson	IT
0	34,346	34,408.04	32,263.66	34,401.50
1	3901	3468.01	6249.50	3583.95
2	1005	1178.66	1202.17	1102.91
3	343	494.52	230.32	451.40
4	155	227.18	44.00	212.54
5	75	109.80	8.39	108.66
6	56	54.82	1.97 ^	58.62
7	33	27.99		32.85
8	19	14.53		18.94
9	11	7.64		11.15
10	15	4.06		6.68
11	6	2.17		4.06
12	7	1.17		2.50
13	3	1.40 ^		1.55
14+	25			2.68 ^
χ^2		733.41	17,113.73	295.70
$\hat{\theta}$		0.22		
$\hat{\varphi}$		5.93		
$\hat{\upsilon}$			0.01	
$\hat{\lambda}$			0.19	0.25
$\hat{p}$				0.55
$\hat{r}$				0.04
Log-likelihood		−22,530.84	−2,4361.47	−22,434.82
AIC		45,065.68	48,726.95	44,875.64
BIC		4,5066.96	48,726.84	44,877.77

^ Indicates the expected frequency is grouped. The index of dispersion = 3.40.

3.2. Fit to the Auto Claim Count Data

To assess goodness-of-fit and for model selection, the IT distribution was compared to the NB and COM-Poisson models by means of chi-square goodness-of-fit statistics, log-likelihood, AIC and BIC. The fitting process was conducted using Python, employing basin-hopping as the global optimisation algorithm and sequential least squares programming (SLSQP) as the local optimiser. Basin-hopping was tuned using the parameters niter = 50, T = 0.5 and step size = 0.2. The results from the local SLSQP optimization were used as the starting point for the basin-hopping algorithm. SLSQP was specifically chosen for its suitability in handling constrained optimization problems, where both parameter bounds and custom constraints are enforced. In this case, the constraints for the model are $p + q + r = 1$ and $p > r$. The Python modules used include scipy.optimize, from which the functions "basinhopping" and "minimize" were imported for global and local optimization, respectively.

To estimate the standard errors of the parameters, we approximated the Hessian matrix of the log-likelihood function using numerical gradients. This is achieved by calculating the gradient of the log-likelihood function with small changes in the parameter values. We used the numdifftools package, available in Python, to compute the Hessian matrix numerically. The standard errors were then calculated by taking the square roots of the diagonal elements of the inverse of the Hessian matrix. The Python sample codes are given in Appendix A. Due to possible numerical issues in the Hessian matrix calculation, some alternatives, such as bootstrapping and jackknife, could provide better estimates for the asymptotic covariance matrices. See, for instance, Shao and Tu (1995). In clustered data, not accounting for clustering will result in very biased standard error estimates. For a discussion of some methods of clustered regression, see Skinner and de Toledo Vieira (2007).

Tables 1 and 2 display the fit without covariates. Based on chi-square statistics, the IT distribution fits better than the NB and COM-Poisson distributions. The distribution of claims, irrespective of claim amounts, may be applied to build bonus–malus systems for auto insurance (Lemaire, 1976, 1985). It was observed that the count data contained many zeroes. The zero-inflated version of the NB, COM-Poisson (Sim et al., 2018) and IT distributions were also fitted, without much improvement, based on chi-square statistics.

The regression fits are shown in Tables 3 and 4. Statistically significant covariates at a level of 5 percent are indicated with an asterisk. It is shown the IT regression models provide a better fit than the NB and COM-Poisson regressions. It appears young drivers and vehicles of low value (VehValue 50–75 kAUD) are prone to claims.

Table 3. Fitting of automobile claim dataset in Australia, Period 1 (with covariates).

Parameters/Coefficients	Estimate and Its Standard Error			
	NB Regression	**COM-Poisson Regression**	**IT Regression I**	**IT Regression II**
Intercept	−1.36 (0.05) *	−1.58 (0.03) *	−1.42 (0.06) *	−1.33 (0.08) *
DrivAgeyoung people	−0.11 (0.06)	−0.08 (0.04)	−0.02 (0.06)	−0.11 (0.09)
DrivAgeworking people	−0.20 (0.06) *	−0.16 (0.04) *	−0.09 (0.06)	−0.19 (0.09) *
DrivAgeolder work people	−0.22 (0.02) *	−0.18 (0.04) *	−0.11 (0.06) *	−0.22 (0.09) *
DrivAgeold people	−0.39 (0.07) *	−0.32 (0.04) *	−0.20 (0.07) *	−0.40 (0.10) *
DrivAgeoldest people	−0.40 (0.08) *	−0.33 (0.05) *	−0.22 (0.08)	−0.41 (0.11) *
VehValue50–75 kAUD	0.15 (0.04) *	0.12 (0.03) *	0.08 (0.04)	0.15 (0.06) *
VehValue 75–100 kAUD	0.18 (0.12)	0.14 (0.07)	0.06 (0.12)	0.18 (0.17)
VehValue 100–125 kAUD	−0.90 (0.55)	−0.79 (0.43)	−0.62 (0.58)	−0.90 (0.67)
VehValue >125 kAUD	−0.02 (0.67)	−0.003 (0.41)	−0.77 (1.00)	−0.04 (0.93)
$\hat{\varphi}$	5.85 (0.15) *	-	-	-
$\hat{\upsilon}$	-	0.01 (0.03)	-	-
$\hat{\lambda}$	-	-	-	0.07 (0.002) *
$\hat{p}$	-	-	0.25 (0.01) *	-
$\hat{r}$	-	-	0.01 (0.003) *	0.01 (0.005) *
Log-likelihood	−21,036.95	−22,660.24	−16,050.81	−16,043.59
AIC	42,095.89	45,342.49	32,125.62	32,111.18
BIC	42,190.45	45,437.05	32,228.78	32,214.34

The bracketed figures indicate the standard errors of the parameter estimates, while an asterisk (*) denotes statistically significant estimates at a 5% level.

In Table 3, the total computational time reported for IT Regression I is 3170.27 s, which includes both basin-hopping and local SLSQP optimization processes. We performed 50 basin-hopping iterations (niter = 50) and assumed approximately 100 function evaluations per SLSQP iteration. Given the total computation time of 3170 s, the average time per function evaluation is estimated as 3170/50/100 = 0.634 s per evaluation. The mathematical order of computational complexity is given by O(Complexity of SLSQP × Temperature steps × Total number of iterations).

Table 4. Fitting of automobile claim dataset in Australia, Period 2 (with covariates).

Parameters/Coefficients	Estimate and Its Standard Error			
	NB Regression	COM-Poisson Regression	IT Regression I	IT Regression II
Intercept	−1.22 (0.05) *	−1.48 (0.03) *	−1.23 (0.05) *	−1.18 (0.08) *
DrivAge young people	−0.19 (0.06) *	−0.15 (0.03) *	−0.15 (0.06) *	−0.21 (0.09) *
DrivAge working people	−0.23 (0.06) *	−0.18 (0.03) *	−0.17 (0.06) *	−0.23 (0.09) *
DrivAge older work people	−0.26 (0.06) *	−0.21 (0.03) *	−0.19 (0.06) *	−0.27 (0.09) *
DrivAge old people	−0.44 (0.07) *	−0.35 (0.04) *	−0.35 (0.07) *	−0.45 (0.09) *
DrivAge oldest people	−0.32 (0.07) *	−0.25 (0.04) *	−0.25 (0.07) *	−0.33 (0.10) *
VehValue 50–75 kAUD	0.19 (0.04) *	0.15 (0.02) *	0.11 (0.04) *	0.20 (0.06) *
VehValue 75–100 kAUD	0.14 (0.12)	0.11 (0.07)	0.03 (0.12)	0.14 (0.17)
VehValue 100–125 kAUD	−0.59 (0.47)	−0.45 (0.33)	−0.36 (0.50)	−0.61 (0.61)
VehValue >125 kAUD	−0.62 (0.76)	−0.51 (0.55)	−0.83 (1.00)	−0.62 (0.98)
$\hat{\varphi}$	5.67 (0.14) *	- -	-	-
$\hat{\upsilon}$	-	0.01 (0.03)	-	-
$\hat{\lambda}$	-	-	-	0.07 (0.002) *
$\hat{p}$	-	-	0.23 (0.01) *	-
$\hat{r}$	-	-	0.01 (0.003) *	0.01 (0.005) *
Log-likelihood	−22,492.96	−24,289.21	−16,803.29	−16,803.16
AIC	45,007.92	48,600.42	33,630.58	33,630.31
BIC	45,104.62	48,697.13	33,736.08	33,735.81

The bracketed figures indicate the standard errors of the parameter estimates, while an asterisk (*) denotes statistically significant estimates at a 5% level.

4. Conclusions

The proper assessment of insurance claim count distribution is an important step to determine insurance premiums based on policyholders' risk profiles. Most of the analyses of insurance claim count distributions in the literature involve short-tailed count frequency distributions. In this paper, the inverse trinomial distribution was used to model insurance claim counts characterised by long tails and high over-dispersion. Two regression models were developed for the identification of associated risk factors and were demonstrated to significantly outperform the NB and COM-Poisson regression models. The results indicate the COM-Poisson model fails to fit the data, both with and without covariates, as evidenced by it having the highest chi-square, AIC, and BIC values. This highlights the reliability and flexibility of the IT model to handle count data with long tails and significant over-dispersion. The IT model would be useful in the construction of an improved bonus–malus system for auto insurance. Upon analysis of the ausprivautolong dataset of automobile claims in Australia, driving age was identified as a significant factor; as the claim frequency decreased, driver age increased. Additionally, lower-value vehicles were shown to be more prone to claims.

The IT model's adaptability suggests it could be applied to other fields with highly over-dispersed count data such as healthcare, social sciences and public safety. For example, it could help analyse medical claim frequencies or accident counts, where the data often have long tails and high variability, improving risk assessment and policy planning.

Author Contributions: Conceptualization, S.H.O.; Methodology, S.H.O., S.Z.S. and S.L.; Validation, S.H.O. and S.L.; Formal analysis, S.H.O., S.Z.S. and S.L.; Investigation, S.H.O., S.Z.S. and S.L.; Resources, S.Z.S.; Data curation, S.H.O. and S.Z.S.; Writing—original draft, S.H.O., S.Z.S. and S.L.; Writing—review & editing, S.H.O., S.Z.S. and S.L.; Supervision, S.H.O.; Project administration, S.H.O. All authors have read and agreed to the published version of the manuscript.

Funding: This research received no external funding.

Institutional Review Board Statement: Not applicable.

Informed Consent Statement: Not applicable.

Data Availability Statement: The data utilized in this study are publicly available from the R package CASdatasets.

Acknowledgments: The authors wish to thank the reviewers for their insightful comments, which have greatly improved this paper.

Conflicts of Interest: The authors declare no conflict of interest.

Appendix A

The following is a sample of the code used for log-likelihood, optimization and Hessian approximation:

```
# Import the necessary libraries.
import numpy as np
import numdifftools as nd
from scipy.optimize import minimize, basinhopping

# Log-likelihood function.
def log_likelihood(params, X, y, N):
""

Calculate the total log-likelihood function of the IT Regression I model.

Parameters:
-params: parameters [beta, p, r]
-X: design matrix (numpy array of shape (N, P-2))
-y: observed data (numpy array of length N)
-N: size of the dataset (number of observations)

Returns:
-float: The negative log-likelihood value to be minimized.
""

P = X.shape [1] + 2 # Number of parameters, including p and r.
beta = params[:P-2] # Beta parameters.
p = params[P-2] # p parameter.
r = params[P-1] # r parameter.
q = 1.0 − p − r # q parameter (based on p and r).

large_negative = −1e10 # Penalty value for invalid cases.

LL = np.zeros(N)
for k in range(N):
linear_predictor = np.dot(X[k, :], beta)
```

```
Lam = (p − r) * np.exp(linear_predictor)/(1.0 − (p − r))

# Check if Lam, p and q are positive.
if Lam <= 0 or p <= 0 or q <= 0:
LL[k] = large_negative
continue

if y[k] == 0:
LL[k] = Lam * np.log(p)

elif y[k] == 1:
LL[k] = Lam * np.log(p) + np.log(Lam) + np.log(q)

else:
LL[k] = custom_log_likelihood_for_y_greater_than_1(y[k], Lam, p, r, q)

return-np.sum(LL)

def constraint_sum(params):
p = params[P-2]
r = params[P-1]
return 1.0 − (p + r)

def constraint_diff(params):
p = params[P-2]
r = params[P-1]
return p − r

constraints = [
{'type': 'ineq', 'fun': constraint_sum},
{'type': 'ineq', 'fun': constraint_diff},
]

# Initial guess for SLSQP optimization.
P = 12 # Total number of parameters (e.g., 12 for 10 beta parameters, p and r)
initial_guess = np.concatenate((np.full(P-2, 0.5), [0.5, 0.1])) # Initial guess for beta,
p and r.

# Example bounds for beta, p, and r.
bounds = [(−5, 5) for _ in range(P-2)] + [(0.01, 0.999), (0.01, 0.499)] # Adjust bounds if
necessary.

# Run SLSQP locally to obtain initial parameter estimates.
slsqp_result = minimize(
log_likelihood,
initial_guess,
args = (X, y, N),
method = 'SLSQP',
bounds = bounds,
constraints = constraints,
options = {'disp': True}
)

# Extract the estimated parameters from SLSQP.
initial_basin_hopping = slsqp_result.x

# Define local minimizer for basin-hopping (SLSQP).
minimizer_kwargs = {
'method': 'SLSQP',
```

```
'args': (X, y, N),
'bounds': bounds,
'constraints': constraints
}

# Perform basin-hopping using the initial SLSQP result.
result = basinhopping(
log_likelihood,
x0 = initial_basin_hopping,
minimizer_kwargs = minimizer_kwargs,
niter = 50,
T = 0.5,
stepsize = 0.2,
disp = True
)

def hessian_approximation(params):
""""
Approximate the Hessian matrix using numdifftools.

Parameters:
-params: parameters [beta, p, r]

Returns:
-hessian: Hessian matrix.
""""
try:
# Use numdifftools to compute the Hessian matrix.
hessian_func = nd.Hessian(lambda p: log_likelihood(p, X, y, N))
hessian = hessian_func(params)

# Regularization to ensure stability (optional, based on context).
regularization = 1e−6
hessian += regularization * np.eye(len(params))

# Validate Hessian.
if np.any(np.isnan(hessian)) or np.any(np.isinf(hessian)):
raise ValueError("Hessian contains NaN or infinity values.")
if np.any(np.diag(hessian) <= 0):
print("Warning: Hessian has non-positive diagonal elements.")

except Exception as e:
print(f"Error in Hessian computation: {e}")
return np.full((len(params), len(params)), np.nan)

return hessian
```

References

Aoyama, K., Shimizu, K., & Ong, S. H. (2008). A first-passage time random walk distribution with five transition probabilities: A generalization of the shifted inverse trinomial. *Annals of the Institute of Statistical Mathematics*, *60*, 1–20. [CrossRef]

Cheok, C. C. T., Khoo, W. C., & Khoo, H. L. (2024). Bus travel time variability modelling using Burr type XII regression: A case study of Klang Valley. *KSCE Journal of Civil Engineering*, *28*, 3998–4009. [CrossRef]

Conway, R. W., & Maxwell, W. L. (1962). A queueing model with state dependent service rates. *Journal of Industrial Engineering*, *12*, 132–136.

David, M. (2015). Auto insurance premium calculation using generalized linear models. *Procedia Economics and Finance*, *20*, 147–156. [CrossRef]

Dean, C., Lawless, J. F., & Willmot, G. E. (1989). A mixed Poisson–Inverse-Gaussian regression model. *Canadian Journal of Statistics, 17*, 171–181. [CrossRef]
Denuit, M., Maréchal, X., Pitrebois, S., & Walhin, J. F. (2007). *Modeling of claim counts. Risk classification, credibility and bonus-malus systems*. Wiley.
Greenwood, M., & Yule, G. U. (1920). An Inquiry into the nature of frequency distributions of multiple happenings, with particular reference to the occurrence of multiple attacks of disease or repeated accidents. *Journal of the Royal Statistical Society A, 83*, 255–279. [CrossRef]
Lemaire, J. (1976). Driver Versus Company. *Scandinavian Actuarial Journal, 1976*, 209–219. [CrossRef]
Lemaire, J. (1985). *Automobile insurance: Actuarial models*. Kluwer-Nijhoff.
Letac, G., & Mora, M. (1990). Natural real exponential families with cubic variance functions. *Annals of Statistics, 18*, 1–37. [CrossRef]
Li, X., Lord, D., Zhang, Y., & Xie, Y. (2008). Predicting motor vehicle crashes using Support Vector Machine models. *Accident Analysis and Prevention, 40*(2008), 1611–1618. [CrossRef]
Lord, D. (2006). Modeling motor vehicle crashes using Poisson-gamma models: Examining the effects of low sample mean values and small sample size on the estimation of the fixed dispersion parameter. *Accident Analysis & Prevention, 38*(4), 751–766.
Lord, D., Washington, S. P., & Ivan, J. N. (2005). Poisson, Poisson-Gamma and zero inflated regression models of motor vehicle crashes: Balancing statistical fit and theory. *Accident Analysis & Prevention, 37*(1), 35–46.
Metropolis, N., Rosenbluth, A. W., Rosenbluth, M. N., Teller, A. H., & Teller, E. (1953). Equation of state calculations by fast computing machines. *Journal of Chemical Physics, 21*, 1087–1092. [CrossRef]
Morris, C. (1982). Natural exponential families with quadratic variance functions. *Annals of Statistics, 10*(1), 65–80. [CrossRef]
Ong, S. H., Liew, K. W., Shimizu, K., & Loh, Y. F. (2024). *Mixed Poisson formulation of inverse trinomial distribution and other properties*, [Submitted].
Phang, Y. N., Sim, S. Z., & Ong, S. H. (2013). Statistical analysis for the inverse trinomial distribution. *Communications in Statistics—Simulation and Computation, 42*, 2073–2085. [CrossRef]
Sellers, K. F., Borle, S., & Shmueli, G. (2012). The COM-Poisson model for count data: A survey of methods and applications. *Applied Stochastic Models in Business and Industry, 28*, 104–116. [CrossRef]
Shao, J., & Tu, D. (1995). *The jackknife and bootstrap*. Springer.
Shimizu, K., & Yanagimoto, T. (1991). The inverse trinomial distribution. *Japanese Journal of Applied Statistics, 20*(2), 89–96. (In Japanese) [CrossRef]
Shimizu, K., Nishii, N., & Minami, M. (1997). Multivariate inverse trinomial distribution as a Lagrangian probability model. *Communications in Statistics—Theory and Methods, 26*(7), 1585–1598. [CrossRef]
Sim, S. Z., & Ong, S. H. (2010). Parameter estimation for discrete distributions by generalized Hellinger-type divergence based on probability generating function. *Communications in Statistics—Simulation and Computation, 39*, 305–314. [CrossRef]
Sim, S. Z., Gupta, R. C., & Ong, S. H. (2018). Zero-inflated Conway-Maxwell Poisson distribution to analyze discrete data. *International Journal of Biostatistics, 14*(1), 20160070. [CrossRef]
Skinner, C. J., & de Toledo Vieira, M. (2007). Variance estimation in the analysis of clustered longitudinal survey data. *Survey Methodology, 33*(1), 3–12.
Wales, D. J., & Doye, J. P. (1997). Global Optimization by Basin-Hopping and the Lowest Energy Structures of Lennard-Jones Clusters Containing up to 110 Atoms. *The Journal of Physical Chemistry A, 101*(28), 5111–5116. [CrossRef]
Willmot, G. E. (1987). The Poisson-Inverse Gaussian distribution as an alternative to the Negative Binomial. *Scandinavian Actuarial Journal, 1987*, 113–127. [CrossRef]

Journal of
Risk and Financial Management

MDPI

Article

The Relationship Between Sociodemographic Attributes and Financial Well-Being of Low-Income Urban Families Amid the COVID-19 Pandemic: A Case Study of Malaysia

Abdullah Sallehhuddin Abdullah Salim [1], Norzarina Md Yatim [2,*] and Al Mansor Abu Said [3]

1 Faculty of Accountancy and Management, Universiti Tunku Abdul Rahman, Kajang 43000, Selangor, Malaysia; sallehhuddin@utar.edu.my
2 Faculty of Management, Multimedia University, Cyberjaya 63100, Selangor, Malaysia
3 Faculty of Business, Multimedia University, Bukit Beruang 75450, Melaka, Malaysia; almansor.abu.said@mmu.edu.my
* Correspondence: norzarina.yatim@mmu.edu.my

Abstract: The COVID-19 pandemic and the Movement Control Order (MCO) have had a negative impact on the financial well-being of low-income families in urban areas. This study involved respondents living in the public housing project (PPR) residential areas in Kuala Lumpur—the capital of Malaysia. The key finding is that the financial well-being of low-income urban families was negatively impacted due to the COVID-19 pandemic and the MCO implementation. Furthermore, the impact on the financial well-being of low-income urban families is significantly different in terms of types of families, type and sector of employment, type of home ownership, household monthly income, and education level. Reforms to the financial assistance system and the community empowerment of low-income urban families are necessary to increase the community's preparedness and resilience in the face of new shocks in the future.

Keywords: financial well-being; low-income families; urban poverty; COVID-19 pandemic; sociodemographic

1. Introduction

The context of well-being in the current study focuses on family well-being. The National Population and Family Development Board (NPFDB 2017, p. 2) cited family well-being from McKeown et al. (2003) as "associated with family happiness, which includes both physical and psychological well-being, the quality of the relationship between the parents and the quality of the interactions between the parents and the children". Additionally, Newland (2015) suggested that the family well-being dimension is inclusive of family resilience, self-ability, mental health, and physical health. Additionally, Frey et al. (1989) and Armstrong et al. (2005) proposed the inclusion of the family organizational structure, interpersonal relationships, psychological status of parents, and self-efficacy of parents in the family well-being domain.

For a more in-depth trajectory, the current study zoomed into the impact of the COVID-19 pandemic on low-income or B40 urban families' financial well-being. Researchers like Joo et al. (2008) and Sabri and Falahati (2012) described financial well-being as "a state of being financially healthy, happy, and free from worry which is typically based on a subjective appraisal of one's financial situation". In a more recent research study, Mahdzan et al. (2020, p. 289) defined financial well-being as "the feeling of self-fulfilment over one's present financial standing, being assured of meeting regular living expenses and emergency costs, possessing financial freedom to conduct activities as one pleases and feeling confident about one's future retirement". However, the COVID-19 pandemic has led to unprecedented economic shut down or scaling back in Malaysia in a nationwide effort to stop the transmission of the evil coronavirus. Of concern, one segment of the population that appears more vulnerable to the downward economic effects of the pandemic is the urban poor—those with the lowest earnings, the fewest financial resources, and the most lacking digital devices, coupled with living in high-density areas and overcrowded flats—which increase the risk of infections (Megat Muzafar and Kunasekaran 2020). The pandemic-driven Movement Control Order (MCO) created more pressure on the already distressed low-income urban families, particularly those living in the Projek Perumahan Rakyat (PPR) residential area.

According to Jabatan Perumahan Negara's (JPN) 2017 report, there are 73,622 PPR units nationwide, with 32,762 units or 44.5% in the Federal Territory of Kuala Lumpur. The PPR initiative is a government program for the resettlement of urban pioneers for those who are qualified as well as who meet the housing requirements for low-income groups. These urban pioneers migrate from rural and semi-urban areas around the country to the capital city seeking opportunities to alleviate their socioeconomic status (Awang Besar 2018; Awang Besar et al. 2018). There are two categories of PPR occupants, namely owned or rented. The eligibility conditions to apply and have a PPR are as follows: (i) the applicant and spouse are Malaysian citizens; (ii) aged 18 years and above; (iii) gross household income of RM 3000 per month; and (iv) the applicant and spouse do not own a home.

Past shocks or crises have disproportionately hurt the working poor in urban areas, and it seems that the COVID-19 outbreak is not an exception. The government has ordered the people to stay at home and discouraged them from going out except to perform necessary tasks and errands. Meanwhile, companies are now adopting 'work from home' policies to reduce unnecessary travelling. However, these protective measures might have overlooked one thing: the poor urban workers whose work either requires physical presence and cannot be performed remotely or provides a much-needed income where not working means not having enough money to put food on the table. Contrary to white-collar workers, working from home is not an option for some of the households in the PPRs, as their work requires them to be physically present, e.g., lorry drivers, restaurant workers, and grocery store clerks. The nature of these jobs requires them to interact with others almost daily which increases their risk of contracting the disease, and subsequently spreading it. Furthermore, to make things worse, UNICEF and UNFPA's (2020) report informed us that not all PPR residents have reliable access to the internet and rely on public internet centers like PIK, which are usually built within the PPR complex. However, not all PPR housing areas have the PIK. Therefore, they are less able to perform tasks remotely such as working from home or even participating in online learning.

However, there is a particular gap in the evidence on the impact of COVID-19 on low-income Malaysian urban families' financial well-being. Additionally, little is yet known about whether the launched relief packages, e.g., (1) PRIHATIN (Prihatin Rakyat Economic Stimulus Package, (2) PRIHATIN TAMBAHAN (Langkah Tambahan Bagi Pakej Rangsangan Ekonomi Prihatin Rakyat), (3) PENJANA (Pelan Jana Semula Ekonomi Negara), (4) KITA PRIHATIN (Prihatin Supplementary Initiative Package, (5) PERMAI (Pakej Bantuan Perlindungan Ekonomi dan Rakyat Malaysia), (6) PEMERKASA (Program Strategik Memperkasa Rakyat dan Ekonomi), (7) PEMERKASA TAMBAHAN (Program Strategik Memperkasa Rakyat dan Ekonomi Tambahan), and (8) PEMULIH (Pakej Perlindungan Rakyat dan Pemulihan Ekonomi), were offering sufficient assistance to low-income urban families across sociodemographic attributes; hence, ensuring vigorous financial well-being during the economic and health crises. In Malaysia, the Malaysian Family Well-Being Index (MFWBI) has been used as a measurement of family well-being; however, the last assessment was carried out in 2019, before the pandemic hit. Hence, this study highlights how the COVID-19-compelled MCO could impact low-income urban families' well-being and the challenges that they may face during these trying times financially. The possibility of MCO extension and future shock would cause these B40 urban families to be worse off if prompt actions are not taken. Nevertheless, this study offers more inclusive and comprehensive measures, as the government, authorities, and policymakers would benefit from soliciting the input of the head of the family of PPR residents with diverse sociodemographic backgrounds. Therefore, this study intends to achieve the following objectives: (1) to examine the impact of the COVID-19 pandemic and the MCO on the financial well-being of low-income urban families, and (2) to assess the impact of the COVID-19 pandemic and the MCO on the financial well-being across selected sociodemographic attributes of low-income urban families.

2. Materials and Methods

2.1. Impact of COVID-19 Pandemic and Movement Restriction Order on Families' Financial Well-Being

A study by Jusoh et al. (2020) highlighted that during the COVID-19 pandemic, household spending was influenced by income shocks, and not by financial wealth shocks. Furthermore, Jusoh et al. (2020) underlined that Malaysia's unemployment rate rose to 5 percent in April 2020 at the beginning of the COVID-19 pandemic. Therefore, it was concluded that the low-income group was facing the highest risk of unemployment, and their job opportunities would be severely curtailed by the constriction of the job market, and with their comparatively lower incomes, many would struggle to feed their families.

A study by Abdul Rahim et al. (2021) examined the impact of sociodemographic attributes, such as job sector, type of job, income, education, housing type and number of dependents, toward the financial well-being of single mothers in the state of Negeri Sembilan during the COVID-19 pandemic. The findings indicated that respondents who were working in the private sector, earning a monthly income of less than RM 1000, and renting a house had the financial well-being of the family significantly impacted by COVID-19.

In another study, Magli et al. (2021) evaluated the factors affecting the financial well-being of low-income households in the state of Selangor during the COVID-19 pandemic. The findings indicated that financial stress has a positive impact on financial vulnerability, while an internal locus of control and financial literacy have a negative influence on financial vulnerability. Additionally, financial behavior was found to have full mediation only toward the influence of the internal locus of control on financial vulnerability. Hence, the study concluded that improving self-control among low-income households is essential to avoid financial vulnerability, in particular during a crisis situation.

Meanwhile, Lee et al. (2021) assessed the financial vulnerability among civil servants in Peninsular Malaysia surrounding the wake of the COVID-19 pandemic. The analysis found that financial attitude and self-efficacy, except financial literacy, positively correlated with financial vulnerability. Financial management practices were the most significant predictor, as indicated by multivariate analysis. Moreover, mediation analysis found that financial management practices significantly mediated the relationships between variables and financial vulnerability.

In addition, Sabri et al. (2021) evaluated the relationships between financial literacy, financial behavior, and gender with financial vulnerability among households in Malaysia during the COVID-19 pandemic period. A total of 578 respondents engaged through a multi-stage random sampling approach. The results revealed that financial literacy positively influenced financial behavior. In addition, financial behavior negatively influenced financial vulnerability. Besides, financial behavior mediates the relationship between financial literacy and financial vulnerability. Moreover, gender moderates the relationship between financial behavior and financial vulnerability.

From the international perspective, a study by Barrafrem et al. (2020) examined the impact of the COVID-19 pandemic on the household financial well-being in Sweden and England. The study revealed that in general, families are optimistic that the household economy is better than the country and the global economy. Furthermore, the pessimistic overview about families' financial well-being is driven by financially ignorant behavior. In the United States, the administration of Biden–Harris launched two major pillars, namely the American Jobs Plan dan the American Families Plan with an allocation of USD 2 trillion, which will be spent for the range of eight years (Apostolopoulos et al. 2022). The first plan focused on building and rebuilding the aging infrastructure, and the second plan emphasized education, healthcare, and childcare. Both plans are expected to improve the economic output of the United States by USD 6.07 trillion in the next ten years (Apostolopoulos et al. 2022). For the low-income households who lost their jobs during the pandemic, the American Jobs Plan offered employment in sectors like construction, clean energy and caregiving, and provided skills training programs and apprenticeships for high-demand jobs, as well as allocated funding to build and retrofit affordable housing. In addition, the American Families Plan improved the disposable income of low-income households by offering direct cash relief, reduced living expenses by subsidized childcare, healthcare, and community college education fees, and supported economic mobility through paid family and medical leave. Additionally, the Japanese government announced the Special Cash Payments Program with the amount of USD 909 or 100,000 yen per person to every registered person in Japan, including foreigners (Gogineni and Martin 2022). This program helped families cover essential expenses such as food, utilities, and rent, reducing financial stress, including helping low-income households. In addition, the Japanese government also introduced Special Allocation for Revitalization to cope with COVID-19 for local governments in the forms of grants and direct money payments (Gogineni and Martin 2022).

In the neighboring country of the Philippines, Eadie and Yacub (2024) mentioned the roles of the Republic Act (RA) 11469 (Bayanihan to Heal as One Act) and the RA 11494 (Bayanihan to Recover as One Act) in supporting the Filipino people, especially the low-income households, in cushioning the impact of the pandemic. There were 5 features of the RA 11469 consisting of the Social Amelioration Program (SAP) with provisions of 5000 to 8000 pesos, depending on the regional minimum wages, to low-income households for two months, food and non-cash assistance, a moratorium on loan payment, utilities support, and expanded medical and health access. Furthermore, RA 11494 focused on additional cash assistance, wages subsidies, loan and rent relief, supports for farmers and fishermen, and free COVID-19 testing and healthcare. These two acts provided short-term relief, reduction in financial stress, support for livelihoods, and enhanced accessibility to healthcare and education for low-income households in the country.

In another bordering country, the Republic of Indonesia, the immediate social security net programs to protect low-income households from the severe impact of the pandemic consisted of having additional recipients of the Family Hope Program or Program Keluarga Harapan (PKH), staple food cards (Kartu Sembako Program), pre-employment cards (Kartu Pra-Kerja Program), electricity subsidies, additional market and logistical operations, credit payment relief for informal workers, and the Village Fund BLT (direct cash assistance) (Roziqin et al. 2021). For low-income households, such programs offered short-term relief, improved food security, and provided employment support; thus, enabling these groups in meeting daily needs during the income disruption period.

Thailand, to the north of Malaysia, announced an initial USD 61 billion or 2.2 trillion Thai Baht relief package, with special attention provided to financial assistance for low-income households (Marome and Shaw 2021). This group received USD 150 or 5000 Thai Baht per family on a monthly basis for the duration of three months. The package also covered 62% of wages for 90 days for workers who were forced to stay at home due to mandated movement restriction, in order to compensate for the income loss. Additionally, the packages covered subsidized utility bills, and introduced a tax reduction, exemption, and delays (financial moratorium).

2.2. Types and Sectors of Employment

An observation by Megat Muzafar and Kunasekaran (2020) highlighted the concern of the Malaysian Institute of Economic Research (MIER) that the continuation or prolonging of the MCO shall result in some 2.4 million people losing their jobs, where 67% of the layoffs will be unskilled workers. Additionally, 3.8% of the heads of the PPR households are temporary or part-time workers, making them further dispensable considering the current economic uncertainty. Furthermore, approximately 20% of households in PPR are self-employed and/or earn income through their small businesses (Megat Muzafar and Kunasekaran 2020). However, the outbreak led to these businesses having to either scale back or close shops, cutting these households off from one of their main sources of income. Additionally, Megat Muzafar and Kunasekaran (2020) discovered that a considerable proportion of PPR households work in informal employment such as petty traders, tailors, and freelancers. Therefore, these employees lack the social security that formal workers enjoy such as paid leave, EPF, and SOSCO coverage (Sazali and Gen 2019). Consequently, this also means they are not sufficiently covered by social protection measures introduced by the government such as allowing RM500 monthly EPF withdrawals.

The International Labour Organisation (ILO) Report by Lim (2020) highlighted B40 households as one of the vulnerable communities in the surge of the pandemic in Malaysia. The ILO's 2020 report elaborated that the majority of approximately 2.8 million B40 households are low-skilled workers in the informal job sector who are more likely to lose their income, causing financial hardship. The Malaysian Institute of Economic Review (MIER) 2020 estimated that around two-thirds of job losses will fall on low-skilled workers.

The predicament of low-income urban families' financial well-being due to the pandemic is further elaborated on by the survey of the Department of Statistics Malaysia (DOSM) in 2020. The survey showed half of those self-employed reported being out of work, while up to one-third said their income dropped by more than 90%. The results exposed alarming concerns that vulnerable households were experiencing income shocks. Moreover, the survey disclosed that half of them only had enough savings to last two weeks, while only 28% said they had enough to last two months. In addition, the survey indicated that the average expenditure on household consumption during the MCO decreased by 48%.

Additionally, Jusoh et al. (2020) highlighted that during the COVID-19 pandemic, household spending was influenced by income shocks, especially among the self-employed group. Additionally, Abdul Rahim et al. (2021) evidenced that private-sector employees were in worse positions in terms of financial well-being, compared to other types and sectors of jobs, during the COVID-19 pandemic. The preceding arguments have led to the formulation of the hypothesis as follows:

H_1. *The significant difference in the types and sectors of employment impacted the financial well-being of low-income urban families during the COVID-19 pandemic.*

2.3. Monthly Household Income

A study by Abdul Rahim et al. (2021) showed that families with a monthly income of less than 1000 in Negeri Sembilan, Malaysia were suffering more during the COVID-19 pandemic. Therefore, lower household income leads to a lack of affordability to purchase important items including sufficient internet data or the right devices to support online learning for children (Zainol et al. 2021). In a related analysis, Abdul Hamid and Khalidi (2020) expressed concern about the potential impact of the COVID-19 pandemic toward unequal learning. As the pandemic hit the family economy, many households, particularly those who became unemployed, experienced financial constraints, and the priority was to ensure the purchase of food rather than to obtain other items like online learning devices. Despite multiple relief packages and assistance schemes by the government, many low-income urban families struggled to cover recurring expenses, i.e., rent, utilities, and food. This context highlights the potential variations in financial well-being among families with differing levels of income during the pandemic, underscoring the need to analyze the direct relationship between monthly income and financial stability. According to Megat Muzafar and Kunasekaran (2020), the pandemic intensified income inequality, disproportionately affecting those already at an economic disadvantage, as the lower-income families, especially in urban areas, tend to be more vulnerable to economic shocks.

In contrast, higher-income groups may have had more financial buffers (e.g., savings or access to credit) to withstand temporary income disruptions. This disparity suggests that income level may be a critical factor influencing financial well-being under pandemic-related economic stress. Furthermore, low-income urban families often work in sectors that were severely impacted by the pandemic, such as hospitality, retail, and informal services. These sectors faced high unemployment rates or reduced working hours, resulting in a direct income reduction for many households. The loss or reduction in monthly income may have created financial instability, making it harder for families to meet basic needs and maintain financial security. The preceding arguments have led to the formulation of the hypothesis as follows:

H_2. *The significant difference in monthly household income impacted the financial well-being of low-income urban families during the COVID-19 pandemic.*

2.4. Type of Accommodation Ownership

In addition, living in overcrowded conditions like PPRs, having to practice social distancing, coupled with illiteracy and often not being able to work from home, put the residents at a greater risk (Lim 2020). Additionally, Abdul Rahim et al. (2021) found that a family that occupies a rented house is suffering more during the pandemic as they are more vulnerable to losing their house due to their inability to pay monthly rent. Furthermore, families that own their accommodations have a greater tendency to experience faster and better-quality internet connection, compared to families that rent accommodations (Gong 2020; Kamaruzuki 2020). Those without their own property experience physical access challenges to computers, the internet, and devices. The preceding arguments have led to the formulation of the hypothesis as follows:

H_3. *The significant difference in the types of accommodation ownership impacted the financial well-being of low-income urban families during the COVID-19 pandemic.*

2.5. Highest Education Qualification

Additionally, Megat Muzafar and Kunasekaran (2020) found that 59% of the heads of households in PPRs attained education up to the secondary level, while around 7% of them have never attended school. Having a lower education level means that their options for work are limited to low-skilled types of work such as jobs in the retail industry (KRI 2018). In addition, Barrafrem et al. (2020) found that families with higher education qualifications are more optimistic toward the households' economic well-being during the COVID-19 pandemic, while families with lower education qualifications are more pessimistic toward the households' economic well-being during the health crisis due to financially ignorant behavior. Furthermore, Magli et al. (2021) contended that the level of education influences financial literacy and locus control of the head of the family. Individuals with a higher education qualification are stronger in terms of financial competencies; hence, they enjoy better control of the family's financial well-being compared to individuals with a lower academic qualification. Moreover, Lee et al. (2021) and Sabri et al. (2021) showed that an individual with a better education achievement is superior to those with lower qualifications in terms of financial management skills. As a result, the individual has a better financial attitude and financial literacy. The preceding arguments have led to the formulation of the hypothesis as follows:

H_4. *The significant difference in education qualification has impacted the financial well-being of low-income urban families during the COVID-19 pandemic.*

2.6. Types of Families

A study by Chong and Khong (2018) of Bank Negara Malaysia (BNM) estimated that a single adult living in Klang Valley needs to earn at least RM 2700 a month to have a dignified life, while a nuclear family consisting of a married couple with two children require around RM 6500. In addition, Abdul Hamid et al. (2019) argued that the number of family members living together influences the level of comfortable living and exhibits consumption patterns that are "aspirational". The data from JPN (2017) showed that 65.8% of the head of the households in PPRs nationwide earn below RM 2000, whilst the average monthly income of households in PPRs hovers around RM 2000 in more urbanized states—RM 2039.40 for Selangor and RM 1994.40 in Kuala Lumpur—while on average, the monthly income of the head of the households of PPR residents nationwide earn RM 1786.80. In other words, these households were probably already struggling to make ends meet and the repercussions from the outbreak will create a huge dent in their finances. Additionally, Abdul Rahim et al. (2021) found that a family with a single mother as the head of the family is suffering more during the pandemic. Moreover, Chan and Chong (2022) argued that a family led by a single parent does not enjoy strong and quality support from spouses or partners, making them more economically vulnerable. The preceding arguments have led to the formulation of the hypothesis as follows:

H_5. *There is a significant difference in types of families on the financial well-being of low-income urban families during the COVID-19 pandemic.*

2.7. Research Design

The research design of this study was cross-sectional and quantitative. The literature review revealed that empirical studies in family well-being were dominated by the positivism paradigm, and the majority of the studies deployed the quantitative method. The most common quantitative method adopted was survey research. Therefore, this study decided to adopt positivist cross-sectional quantitative research design. It is consistent with previous investigations by AKPK (2018), Abdullah et al. (2019), Mahdzan et al. (2020), Barrafrem et al. (2020), Jusoh et al. (2020), NPFDB (2020a), Magli et al. (2021), Mohamed et al. (2021), Abdul Wahab et al. (2021), and Abdul Rahim et al. (2021) in the context of the financial well-being and low-income urban family literature. The cross-sectional design was preferred considering the logistics, convenience, and cost, the operationalization of the research, and the ability to generalize results (Neuman 2007). Furthermore, the cross-sectional design was appropriate to meet the objectives of the study, which were to ascertain the impact of the COVID-19 pandemic and the movement restriction rules on financial well-being during the crisis point in time.

2.8. Population and Sample

The population designated for this study consisted of families living in PPRs in the Federal Territory of Kuala Lumpur, since they represented nearly 45 percent of family units in urban areas across the country. Moreover, based on the requirements to own or to rent PPR units, there was a higher possibility to obtain low-income urban families as respondents. The implementation of PPR residents as respondents is consistent with previous studies by Abdul Wahab et al. (2021), UNICEF and UNFPA (2020), and Megat Muzafar and Kunasekaran (2020) in assessing the impact of the pandemic on the low-income urban groups' financial well-being. This study decided to adopt a stratified random sampling technique. From its name, the technique involves a process of stratification or segregation, followed by a random selection of respondents from each stratum (Sekaran 2000). In addition, the stratified random sampling technique "guarantees representativeness of different strata within a sample" (Neuman 2007, p. 153).

Based on the JPN's 2017 report, the population of families in PPR residential areas in the Federal Territory of Kuala Lumpur is 32,762. According to Krejcie and Morgan (1970), the recommended sample size for 32,762 subjects in the population is 380. Subsequently, the study determined the percentage of families residing in individual PPR residential areas in the Federal Territory of Kuala Lumpur. The study found that the largest family unit was 2844 in PPR Kg Muhibah which represents 8.7% of the total population of 32,762; while the smallest family unit was 316 in PPR Seri Anggerik or 1.1% of the entire population. Proportionately, using the required total sample size of 380, the required sample size of 8.7% for PPR Kg Muhibah was 34, and the expected sample size of 1.1% for PPR Seri Anggerik was 5. A similar procedure was deployed to determine the expected sample size for other PPR residential areas in the study. The following Table 1 indicates the sample size of the study and the name of the PPR residential area in Kuala Lumpur involved in the study.

Table 1. Sample size of the study.

No.	Registered Name	Commercial Name	Population of Family, *N*	Percentage, %	Sample Size Required, *S*
		State: Federal Territory of Kuala Lumpur			
1	PPR Bukit Jalil I	PPR Pinggiran Bukit Jalil	1896	5.8%	22
2	PPR Bukit Jalil II	PPR Pinggiran Bukit Jalil	1896	5.8%	22
3	PPR Kg Muhibah	PPR Kg Muhibah	2844	8.7%	34
4	PPR Lembah Pantai, Kerinchi	PPR Kerinchi	1896	5.8%	22
5	PPR KL Linear City II, Fasa 1	PPR Pantai Ria	1264	3.9%	15
6	PPR KL Linear City II, Fasa 2	PPR Seri Cempaka	632	1.9%	7
7	PPR Kg Limau Pantai Dalam	PPR Kg Limau	632	1.9%	7
8	PPR Salak Selatan	PPR Salak Selatan	632	1.9%	7
9	PPR KL Linear City I	PPR Seri Anggerik	316	1.1%	5
10	PPR Seri Malaysia	PPR Seri Malaysia	632	1.9%	7
11	PPR Jln Lapangan Terbang Lama F1	PPR Seri Alam	660	2.0%	8
12	PPR Jln Lapangan Terbang Lama F2	PPR Seri Alam	920	2.8%	10
13	PPR Pudu Hulu	PPR Pudu Ulu	948	2.9%	11
14	PPR Kg Malaysia Permai	PPR Raya Permai	1264	3.9%	14
15	PPR Jalan Cochrane	PPR Perkasa	1620	4.9%	19
16	PPR Pekan Kepong	PPR Pekan Kepong	948	2.9%	11
17	PPR Taman Wahyu II	PPR Wahyu	948	2.9%	11
18	PPR Taman Wahyu I	PPR Beringin	1896	5.8%	22
19	PPR Kg Batu Muda	PPR Batu Muda	2132	6.5%	25
20	PPR Pekan Batu	PPR Pekan Batu	632	1.9%	7
21	PPR Kg Baru Air Panas Tambahan	PPR Kg Baru Air Panas	2528	7.7%	30
22	PPR Sg Bunus Air Jernis	PPR Seri Semarak	632	1.9%	7
23	PPR Sg Bunus Air Jernis	PPR Sg Bonus	1580	4.8%	18
24	PPR Ampang Hiliran	PPR Hiliran Ampang	948	2.9%	11
25	PPR Sungai Besi	PPR Desa Petaling	632	1.9%	7
26	PPR Intan Baiduri	PPR Intan Baiduri	1834	5.6%	21
	Total		32,762	100%	380

2.9. Development of Questionnaire

The final survey form has two parts: part A (sociodemographic attributes), and part B (financial well-being with 10 indicators). The final survey form will use a 5-point Likert scale. The 5-point Likert scale for this final survey form consists of the following responses: 1 = strongly disagree, 2 = disagree, 3 = somewhat agree, 4 = agree, and 5 = strongly agree. The financial well-being items are adapted from previous related studies such as Abdul Wahab et al. (2021), Sabri et al. (2021), Jusoh et al. (2020), Mahdzan et al. (2020), Lim (2020),

Megat Muzafar and Kunasekaran (2020), and NPFDB (2015, 2017, 2020b). Initially, there were 12 items developed based on those studies.

In order to ensure the instrument's validity and reliability, the items were examined by two experts. The first expert was a registered financial planner and had extensive experience in the financial industry such as insurance, takaful, retirement funds, and trust funds for almost 20 years. The second expert was a professor and dean at one of the top institutes of higher learning in Malaysia with extensive experience in the field of consumer financial management and who had carried out numerous research projects and publications in the area. Furthermore, the instrument was also scrutinized by the funding agency's Research Grants Technical Committee, where the majority of them are well-experienced in formulating the instrument to measure the national Family Well-Being Index. Finally, the instrument was also pilot tested involving the low-income urban head of the families in the list of the microcredit participants of the Amanah Ikhtiar Malaysia (AIM) Kuala Lumpur branch. The pilot study provided Cronbach's alpha score of more than the threshold of 0.70, as suggested by Nunally and Bernstein (1994). Based on the expert review, the technical committee feedback, and the results of the pilot study, the final survey consisted of 10 items on measuring financial well-being, as well as the sociodemographic information.

2.10. Data Collection Procedure

The data collection procedure was adapted from the study of Mohamed et al. (2021). First, the research team engaged the chairman of each PPR residents' association to seek logistical support. The chairman's assistance was sought to publicize and disseminate information about the research, as well as to openly invite the heads of families or representatives in respective PPRs to participate in completing the survey. Any heads of families or representatives who were willing to voluntarily participate in the study were required to register with the chairman of the PPR residents' association. The registration remained open until the number was met of the expected sample size for each PPR residential area. Later, the appointment was set for a meeting with respondents who had registered with the chairman and volunteered to participate at the respective office of the PPR residents' association. During the meeting, a short briefing about the study's background and the survey structure was given by the research team. After the short briefing, each respondent would answer the survey questionnaire through a Google Form using their own gadgets like handphones. Furthermore, the research team also prepared a laptop with internet access if respondents were without appropriate gadgets.

2.11. Data Analysis Technique

For the final data analysis, this study used SPSS 28. The analysis techniques carried out were frequency analysis, descriptive analysis, and sociodemographic impact analysis. Frequency analysis aims to identify the respondents' background such as monthly household income, type and sector of employment, highest education level achieved, types of families and types of accommodation ownership. The next analysis was descriptive. In this analysis, the minimum, maximum, mean, and standard deviation values for each indicator of financial well-being were obtained. Next, the mean or average for the financial well-being domain was derived. Since the final survey form used a five-point Likert scale, the interpretation of the mean domain score refers to the guidance provided by Pallant (2005) and Masruki and Mohd Hanefah (2021), when a mean score of 1.00 to 2.33 is a low level, a mean score of 2.34 to 3.66 is a moderate level, and a mean score of 3.67 to 5.00 is a high level. Next was the sociodemographic impact analysis, conducted by adopting one-way ANOVA analysis. This intended to ascertain the existence of a significantly different impact on the financial well-being of the sociodemographics of the respondents.

This study employed ANOVA for examining the effect of sociodemographic information on the financial well-being of lower income urban families as it offered a robust analysis by comparing the means of multiple groups, which was particularly useful when examining the categorical data of sociodemographics such as types and sectors of employment, household income, types of families, level of education, and types of accommodation, and their effects on a continuous outcome, i.e., financial well-being. ANOVA was also appropriate as compared to other similar analysis techniques such as the Kruskal–Wallis test which is more suitable for non-normality data, or the chi-squared test since the dependent variable in the study, i.e., financial well-being was continuous rather than categorical. Furthermore, compared to multiple linear regression, ANOVA is less complex, simpler, and more interpretable given the categorical sociodemographic data as the predictor.

3. Results

3.1. Respondents' Profiles

Table 2 shows the profiles of respondents. About 146 respondents or 35 percent work in the private sector, followed by 55 respondents or 13.2 percent are self-employed, 45 respondents or 10.8 percent are civil servants, 34 respondents or 8.2 percent run businesses, 26 respondents or 6.2 percent are freelancers, 15 respondents or 3.6 percent of workers are in the gig economy sector, while 96 respondents or 23 percent are unemployed. Furthermore, 267 respondents or 64 percent are in group B1 with a monthly household income of less than RM 2500. There are 82 respondents or 19.7 percent in group B2 with a monthly household income between RM 2501 and RM 3169, followed by group B3 with a monthly household income between RM 3170 and RM 3969 for a total of 34 people or 8.2 percent, and group B4 with a monthly household income between RM 3970 and RM 4849 for a total of 25 people or 6 percent. There are 9 respondents or 2.1 percent who belong to the M40 group with a monthly household income exceeding RM 4850. Additionally, 308 respondents or 73.9 percent rent residential units in PPRs, followed by 59 respondents or 14.1 percent with self ownership, and 15 respondents or 3.6 percent with joint ownership. There are 12 respondents or 2.9 percent with a boarding status, as well as 16 respondents or 3.8 percent still borrowing. Additionally, 260 respondents or 62.3 percent have passed the Malaysian Certificate of Education (SPM). There are 55 respondents or 13.2 percent who graduated up to Form 3 or equivalent. There are also 50 respondents or 12 percent who have passed the Sijil Tinggi Pelajaran Malaysia (STPM) or equivalent, while 23 respondents or 5.5 percent have at least a first degree. There is also a small number of respondents who attend religious schools like tahfiz and pondok, and technical and vocational training. Next are 307 respondents or 73.6 percent with nuclear family status (a family consisting of a father, mother, and children only), followed by 62 respondents or 14.9 percent with the status of a single-parent family (a family that has one of either the mother or the father and a child; this may be due to divorce or even death), and 22 respondents or 5.3 percent with the status of an extended family (a family consisting of several generations; for example, grandfathers, relatives, and cousins also living together).

One notable highlight from Table 2 is 64% or 267 respondents earn less than RM 2500 monthly in terms of household income. Financial resilience or the capacity to withstand financial shocks is particularly low among those earning below RM 2500. With limited disposable income, saving is challenging, resulting in a lack of emergency funds or other financial buffers. Additionally, lower-income households are often less likely to have access to insurance or other protective measures, increasing their vulnerability to crises, whether personal (e.g., illness) or economic (e.g., job loss). This lack of a financial safety net contributes to the lower financial well-being observed among respondents with incomes below this threshold. Additionally, households earning below RM 2500 may face heightened economic pressures and stress, which can impact their ability to save, invest, or plan financially. This inequality ultimately limits social mobility and creates cyclical poverty, as lower-income families have fewer means to improve their financial situation over time. Income inequality further compounds financial challenges for low-income households, who may already feel disadvantaged relative to higher-income groups. The gap between these groups not only reflects disparities in access to resources but also influences financial behaviors and stress levels.

Table 2. Respondents' profiles (indicator of selected sociodemographic attributes, N = 417).

Demographic Attributes	*N*	(%)	Demographic Attributes	*N*	(%)
Types and sectors of employment			*Monthly household income*		
Self employment	55	13.2	B1: Less than RM 2500	267	64.0
Running own business	34	8.2	B2: 2501–3169	82	19.7
Freelancing	26	6.2	B3: 3170–3969	34	8.2
Gig economy, i.e., p-hailing and e-hailing	15	3.6	B4: 3970–4849	35	6.0
Private sector	146	35.0	M1: 4850–5879	6	1.4
Public sector	45	10.8	M2: 5880–7099	2	0.5
Not working	96	23.0	M3: 7100–8699	1	0.2
			Types of families		
			Mixed	10	2.4
			Dyad	8	1.9
Highest education qualification			Single Parent	62	14.9
Other	5	1.2	Co-habitation	8	1.9
Informal education	2	0.5	Extended	22	5.3
First degree	22	5.3	Nuclear	307	73.6
Postgraduate–Master's	1	0.2	*Types of Accommodation Ownership*		
Religious school (incl. tahfiz and pondok)	5	1.2	Sharing	6	1.4
Primary school	10	2.4	Boarding	12	2.9
LCE/SRP/PMR/PT3	55	13.2	Renting	308	73.9
STPM/Diploma/Matriculation/A-Level	50	12.0	Leasing	1	0.2
SPM	260	62.3	Joint ownership	15	3.6
Technical and Vocational	7	1.7	Self ownership	59	14.1
			Borrowing/financing	16	3.8

3.2. Descriptive Analysis

Table 3 shows a descriptive analysis of 10 indicators of financial well-being. The four indicators with the lowest mean scores are items 3,4,5, and 6, respectively, with mean scores of 1.8825, 1.9257, 1.9424, and 2.0791; hence, reflecting the respondents' difficulty in amassing savings, obtaining insurance or takaful protection, meeting unexpected expenses, and providing emergency funds during a health crisis. The pandemic placed substantial pressure on household finances, especially for low-income urban families who are more vulnerable to income shocks. Reduced work hours, job losses, and heightened uncertainty affected their financial resilience. For many, any existing savings were likely depleted during the crisis, making it even harder to create or maintain emergency funds, prepare for unexpected expenses, or secure insurance. Health crises in particular, increase both immediate healthcare costs and the need for a financial safety net, which many respondents lack. Additionally, for families facing economic hardship, immediate needs like food, rent, and utilities take precedence over long-term financial planning, such as savings or insurance. The psychological toll of financial instability often leads to "survival mode" decision making, where day-to-day expenses overshadow the motivation or ability to prepare for future risks. This prioritization can explain the difficulty in meeting expenses for unforeseen events or health crises.

Only items 7 and 8 received somewhat agreeable responses, with a mean score of 3.0480 and 3.2590, respectively. This feedback gives the impression that the COVID-19 pandemic and the MCO have changed the spending patterns of urban B40 families by causing them to sacrifice the basic expenses for food and medicine to buy health-related items following the implementation of related regulations to curb transmissions such as hand sanitizer, face masks, and temperature scanners. The overall response to the ten indicators of financial well-being has contributed to a mean score of the financial well-being domain of 2.3115, thus reflecting the low level of financial well-being experienced by urban B40 families coping with the challenging periods of the COVID-19 pandemic and the MCO. The mean score indicated that on average, respondents experienced financial difficulty during the crisis. Many low-income families have limited disposable income due to high living expenses, especially in urban areas where costs for housing, transportation, and basic necessities are higher. This restricts their ability to save and accumulate funds for unexpected or emergency needs. With their budgets already stretched, even small financial setbacks can greatly impact their ability to manage daily expenses, let alone save or invest in insurance.

Table 3. Descriptive results of financial well-being indicators and domain ($N = 417$).

No.	Indicator	Min	Max	Mean	Std. Deviation
1	Throughout the COVID-19 pandemic and MCO, I can pay back debts and loans with consistency.	1.00	5.00	2.1631	1.15287
2	Throughout the COVID-19 pandemic and MCO, I can pay rent, utility bills, fees, and other charges.	1.00	5.00	2.3501	1.14447
3	Throughout the COVID-19 pandemic and MCO, I can still afford to make savings.	1.00	5.00	1.8825	1.08889
4	Throughout the COVID-19 pandemic and MCO, I can still afford to provide an emergency fund.	1.00	5.00	2.0791	1.18320
5	Throughout the COVID-19 pandemic and MCO, I can still afford to meet unexpected expenditures.	1.00	5.00	1.9424	1.07710
6	During the COVID-19 pandemic and MCO, I can still afford to provide insurance/takaful coverage.	1.00	5.00	1.9257	1.14007
7	Throughout the COVID-19 pandemic and MCO, the major expenditure of my family is on health items compared to other expenses.	1.00	5.00	3.0480	1.30738
8	Throughout the COVID-19 pandemic and MCO, I had to reduce basic expenses such as food.	1.00	5.00	3.2590	1.28605
9	In general, throughout the COVID-19 outbreak and MCO, my financial well-being has been good.	1.00	5.00	2.2206	1.14952
10	In general, throughout the COVID-19 outbreak and MCO, my family's financial well-being has been good.	1.00	5.00	2.2446	1.15718
	Financial well-being domain mean score	1.00	5.00	2.3115	0.79385

3.3. Sociodemographic Analysis

Table 4 shows the results of the ANOVA analysis related to the difference in the impact of the types and sectors of employment on the aspects of financial well-being related to dealing with the COVID-19 pandemic and the MCO. This analysis reflects that there is a significant difference from the perspective of the type and sector of employment on financial well-being with $p = 0.000$. For the effect of size, the eta squared is $\eta^2 = 0.06$ (medium to large effect). This result suggests that financial well-being varied significantly among respondents based on the type and sector of their employment during the COVID-19 pandemic and the Movement Control Order (MCO) period in Malaysia. It also indicates that the types and sectors of employment explained the financial well-being of respondents during the crisis by 6%. This suggests that employment characteristics had a notable impact on financial stability, with different employment sectors and job types contributing substantially to the financial resilience of individuals during the crisis. In practical terms, the 6% variance explained by employment type and sector highlights that certain types of jobs and sectors may have faced unique challenges or financial pressures during the pandemic. For instance, respondents employed in sectors heavily affected by COVID-19 restrictions—such as tourism, retail, or hospitality—may have experienced greater financial strain than those in more stable sectors like healthcare or government services. Similarly, those in informal or temporary employment might have been more financially vulnerable compared to those with secure, permanent positions. These findings underscore the importance of employment type and sector as key factors in financial well-being during crisis periods. They suggest that targeted economic support for workers in affected sectors and flexible, income-stabilizing policies could be essential for enhancing financial resilience, especially in times of economic disruption.

Table 4. ANOVA results for types and sectors of employment.

		Sum of Squares	df	Mean Square	F	Sig.
Financial Well-Being	Between Groups	15.020	6	2.503	4.153	0.000
	Within Groups	247.145	410	0.603		
	Total	262.165	416			

The following Table 5 shows the results of the ANOVA analysis related to the difference in the impact of household monthly income on the aspects of financial well-being related to dealing with the COVID-19 pandemic and the MCO. This analysis reflects that there is a significant difference from the perspective of household monthly income on financial well-being with $p = 0.003$. For the effect of size, the eta squared is $\eta^2 = 0.03$ (small to medium effect). This suggests that there are meaningful differences in financial well-being among respondents with different household income levels during the COVID-19 pandemic and the Movement Control Order (MCO) in Malaysia. It also indicates that the monthly household income explained the financial well-being of respondents during the crisis by 3%. While this may seem modest, it nonetheless highlights that household income plays a meaningful role in financial resilience and stability, even if other factors are likely also influencing financial well-being during the crisis. In practical terms, the 3% variance explained by household income suggests that respondents from different income groups experienced varying degrees of financial impact due to the pandemic and lockdowns. Lower-income households, for instance, may have had more difficulty managing their finances, meeting unexpected expenses, or maintaining savings compared to higher-income groups. These findings underscore the role of household income as an important factor influencing financial well-being in crisis contexts and highlight the need for income-sensitive support policies that can alleviate financial stress for vulnerable income groups during economic disruptions.

Table 5. ANOVA results for monthly household income.

		Sum of Squares	df	Mean Square	F	Sig.
Financial Well-Being	Between Groups	7.419	2	3.710	6.029	0.003
	Within Groups	254.746	414	0.615		
	Total	262.165	416			

Additionally, Table 6 shows the results of the ANOVA analysis related to the difference in the type of home ownership on the aspects of financial well-being related to dealing with the COVID-19 pandemic and the MCO. This analysis reflects that there is a significant difference from the perspective of the type of accommodation ownership of financial well-being with $p = 0.023$. For the effect of size, the eta squared is $\eta^2 = 0.03$ (small to medium effect). This result suggests that financial well-being varied meaningfully among respondents based on their accommodation ownership status during the COVID-19 pandemic and the Movement Control Order (MCO) in Malaysia. It also indicates that the type of accommodation ownership explained financial well-being of respondents during the crises by 3%. This means that, while not the sole determinant, accommodation ownership type had a noticeable impact on financial resilience during the crisis. In practical terms, the 3% variance explained by accommodation ownership suggests that respondents who owned their homes may have experienced different financial pressures than those renting or living in other forms of housing. For example, homeowners might have felt more secure if they owned their property outright, while those with mortgages or rent payments might have experienced heightened financial stress due to monthly housing payments. Renters, in particular, may have faced more immediate financial uncertainty if they lost income or experienced job instability during the pandemic. These findings suggest that housing-related financial obligations played a role in individuals' financial well-being during the pandemic. They also highlight the potential benefit of housing-related support measures, such as mortgage or rent relief, especially during economic disruptions, to help mitigate financial strain and improve resilience across different housing ownership types.

Table 6. ANOVA results for types of accommodation ownership.

		Sum of Squares	df	Mean Square	F	Sig.
Financial Well-Being	Between Groups	8.182	5	1.636	2.648	0.023
	Within Groups	253.983	411	0.618		
	Total	262.165	416			

Additionally, Table 7 shows the results of the ANOVA analysis related to the differences in the family type on the aspects of financial well-being related to dealing with the COVID-19 pandemic and the MCO. This analysis reflects that there is a significant difference from the perspective of the family type on financial well-being with $p = 0.007$. For the effect of size, the eta-squared is $\eta^2 = 0.04$ (small to medium effect). This finding suggests that the financial well-being of respondents varied significantly based on their family structure during the COVID-19 pandemic and the Movement Control Order (MCO) period in Malaysia. It also indicates that the type of family explained the financial well-being of respondents during the crises by 4%. While not a large effect, this finding suggests that family structure played a meaningful role in shaping financial stability and resilience during the crisis. In practical terms, the 4% variance explained by family type implies that respondents from different family structures—such as single-parent households, nuclear families, or extended families—may have faced unique financial challenges during the pandemic. For example, single-parent families might have encountered more financial strain due to a single income source, while extended families may have had additional dependents, increasing financial pressure. Conversely, nuclear families with dual incomes could have potentially experienced more financial stability, depending on job security. These findings highlight family type as an influential factor in financial well-being during crisis periods. They suggest that family-oriented financial support, such as targeted assistance for single-parent households or larger families, could be beneficial in bolstering financial resilience and reducing stress for family structures more susceptible to economic hardship during periods of crisis.

Table 7. ANOVA results for types of families.

		Sum of Squares	df	Mean Square	F	Sig.
Financial Well-Being	Between Groups	9.998	5	2.000	3.259	0.007
	Within Groups	252.166	411	0.614		
	Total	262.165	416			

Then, Table 8 shows the results of the ANOVA analysis relating the highest level of education to the aspects of financial well-being related to dealing with the COVID-19 pandemic and the MCO. The analysis reflects that there is a significant difference from the perspective of the highest level of education on financial well-being with $p = 0.029$. For the effect of size, the eta squared is $\eta^2 = 0.05$ (small to medium effect). This result suggests that the respondents' financial well-being during the COVID-19 pandemic and the Movement Control Order (MCO) in Malaysia differed based on their education level. It also indicates that the highest education qualification explained financial well-being of respondents during the crisis by 5%. This suggests that education played a modest yet meaningful role in shaping individuals' financial resilience and stability during the crisis. In practical terms, the 5% variance explained by education level implies that respondents with higher education qualifications might have had different financial outcomes compared to those with lower educational attainment. Higher education levels are often associated with access to higher-paying and more stable employment, which could contribute to greater financial security. Conversely, those with lower education levels might have been more vulnerable to job losses or income reduction, especially in sectors hit hardest by the pandemic. These findings underscore the role of educational attainment as a factor influencing financial well-being in times of economic disruption. They suggest that individuals with lower educational qualifications may benefit from targeted financial support and employment opportunities, especially during crises, to help enhance financial resilience and mitigate vulnerability associated with lower education levels.

Table 8. ANOVA results for highest education qualification.

		Sum of Squares	df	Mean Square	F	Sig.
Financial Well-Being	Between Groups	12.473	10	1.247	2.028	0.029
	Within Groups	249.691	406	0.615		
	Total	262.165	416			

4. Discussion

The results show that monthly household income, types and sectors of employment, types of families, types of accommodation ownership, and education qualification have significantly different impacts toward financial well-being. The findings are consistent with AKPK (2018), where 53% of Malaysian working adults earning less than RM 2000 a month cannot afford the RM 1000 emergency expenses and are financially challenged when it comes to savings. Additionally, those who are self employed have the lowest propensity to save. Additionally, the self-employed group was most affected by the income reduction due to the crisis compared to the other groups of employment sectors and types. The findings also corroborate the previous results of Mahdzan et al. (2020) as there were significant differences in financial well-being by education level and employment sectors. In addition, earlier, Abdul Rahim et al. (2021) showed that single mothers earning a monthly income of less than RM 1000 and renting a house experienced more suffering in terms of finances due to the pandemic and the MCO. Additionally, Abdul Hamid et al. (2019) and Chong and Khong (2018) agreed that different levels of income influence the level of financial well-being. Moreover, like Megat Muzafar and Kunasekaran (2020) and Lim (2020), types and sectors of employment associated with being low skilled and having low academic qualifications experienced more unfavorable financial well-being. The lower-income household groups are more financially vulnerable to crisis compared to higher-income groups (Benyamin et al. 2022; Wei et al. 2022; Abdullah et al. 2022).

In addition, this analysis exhibits that the types and sectors of employment, as well as education qualifications, have significantly different impacts toward government assistance. Respondents with a higher education or higher academic qualifications tend to be more informative, have a higher level of awareness, and are in a better position to respond swiftly toward announced government assistance schemes during the crisis, or are in a better state of financial literacy (Magli et al. 2021; Lee et al. 2021; Sabri et al. 2021). A similar application also applies to those working in the public sector or private sector than respondents who are not working and are self-employed.

5. Conclusions

Achievement of research objectives

Objective 1: To examine the impact of the COVID-19 pandemic and the MCO on the financial well-being of low-income urban families.

This analysis finds that the impact of the COVID-19 pandemic and the MCO on the financial well-being of urban B40 families is worrying because the mean score for the financial well-being domain is only 2.312. In general, the respondents express a lack of agreement toward the indicators of financial well-being in the survey form.

Objective 2: To assess the impact of the COVID-19 pandemic and the MCO on financial well-being across selected sociodemographic attributes of low-income urban families.

The ANOVA analysis shows significant differences between respondents on financial well-being based on monthly household income, types and sectors of employment, types of accommodation ownership, highest education qualification, and types of families. Hence, it concludes that demographic characteristics have a significantly different effect on financial well-being among low-income urban families.

The practical implications of the findings

From the findings, this study proposes recommendations to improve policies and practices. These recommendations are as follows:

1. The rebranding of government financial aid schemes starts with data transparency.

Efforts to ensure financial well-being and financial resilience of low-income urban families through the rebranding of government assistance schemes should begin with data transparency. Currently, there is no single comprehensive database related to low-income urban families. Moreover, such data or information are managed by various agencies and government bodies such as Pusat Pungutan Zakat (PPZ), Islamic Religious Council of Federal Territory of Kuala Lumpur, Kuala Lumpur City Hall, National Housing Department, District Education Office, State Education Department, Ministry of Education, the Employees' Provident Fund, the Social Security Organization, Welfare Department, Economic Planning Unit, Prime Minister's Department, Inland Revenue Board, and the Ministry of Finance. This situation leads to a redundancy of data, inefficient distribution of financial aids, and subsequently a waste of resources. Therefore, the authorities must speed up the process of cleaning and empowering related data to enable government aid schemes to be carried out in a targeted, focused, and systematic manner. The transparent and comprehensive data shall help the authorities, regulators, and the relevant agencies to provide targeted financial assistance to low-income urban families by considering not only the monthly household income, in fact, also weighing other crucial demographic information like types and sectors of employment, types of accommodation ownership, highest education qualification, and types of families. Low-income urban families with the head of the family possessing lower educational qualification, being self-employed, living with extended families, and renting accommodation shall be assisted with a higher amount of financial quantum. Furthermore, at this moment, the existing financial assistance from the government such as Sumbangan Tunai Rahmah (STR) only considers the amount of household income and the size of the family or the number of dependents. The same consideration is applied by the Welfare Department through its monthly financial assistance scheme. However, the aspect of the types of accommodation ownership is not considered, even though low-income urban families allocate a substantial amount from their monthly income to pay rent. Additionally, based on the findings, the government shall consider introducing a universal payment scheme, particularly to low-income urban families whose head of the family retires from non-public sector, for instance, those who are self-employed, running their own small businesses, informal workers, and private sector workers, since they do not have fixed pension payment like their public service retiree counterparts. The appropriate amount of universal payment could be adjusted more effectively and efficiently when the data from all relevant ministries, departments, and agencies are comprehensively gathered and analyzed. This shall ensure the right amount of financial assistance is distributed to the appropriate target groups; thus, enhancing the financial well-being of low-income urban families.

2. Reform of social protection and security net programs

Next, to build resilience and ensure the financial well-being of low-income urban families to deal with future challenges, efforts to reform social security and protection programs should be strengthened. Based on the findings, types and sectors of employment significantly contributed to the financial well-being of low-income urban families. However, the majority of the groups work independently such as running their own small businesses and taking up informal jobs including gig work and being self employed. These sectors are highly exposed to a lack of social security protection, as they are not compelled to make compulsory contributions for retirement funds, or mandated contributions to employment insurance schemes. Therefore, introducing a form of law enforcement or persuasion to obligate EPF contributions and employment protections or employment insurance under SOCSO, covering workers in the informal sector, hawkers and small traders, freelancers, and workers in the gig economy sector (p-hailing and e-hailing), which are synonymous with the low-income urban family is essential. The reform of social protection and security net programs better protects the low-income urban families for the post-retirement period, and such programs prepare them to better confront future economic and health crises similar to the COVID-19 pandemic, where movement restriction negatively impacted the household's income. Moreover, better social protection and security net programs enables the low-income urban families to tap into the mandated contribution fund or employment insurance scheme for financing self-enhancement initiatives such as upskilling, reskilling, and cross skilling particularly relating to technical and vocational-based training, which upon completion permit them to enjoy better and higher levels of income, given low-income urban families generally possess lower educational qualification.

Limitations

There are several limitations inherit in this study. First, the study used cross-sectional design. Thus, the feedback received from the respondents is influenced by the situation or condition when the data collection process ends. Moreover, it prevents understanding low-income urban families' financial well-being changes over the time. It is possible that some responses were formed by the perception of major events that happened at the national level at a single point in time. As a consequence, the mitigation plan or assistance programs based on the findings of cross-sectional design may not be able to be replicated for medium-term approaches and long-term strategies. Additionally, the respondents involved families are living in the PPR area in the Federal Territory of Kuala Lumpur. There is another public housing area called Perumahan Awam (PA) which was not involved in this survey. Additionally, this study excluded other B40 vulnerable groups such as people with different abilities, traditional village residents, homeless groups, hawkers, and small traders. Despite the inherited limitation of the cross-sectional design, the outcomes of the study offer insights to policy makers and relevant agencies on the expected challenges and impacts experienced by low-income urban families in urban area based on selected demographic information. Therefore, a more targeted approach can be carried out to assist these vulnerable groups if similar economic and health crises re-emerge in the future. Furthermore, more specific or customized upskilling and reskilling programs could be crafted for low-income urban families to prepare them better for future calamities.

Suggestions for future studies

Since the current study employs the cross-sectional design, it limits an assessment of longitudinal changes and the enduring effects of the COVID-19 pandemic and the MCO on low-income urban families' financial well-being. Hence, implementing a longitudinal approach in the future could offer more comprehensive insights into these impacts on low-income urban families, as well as the mitigation that needs to be conducted to deal with these impacts. Additionally, future comparative studies may involve other vulnerable groups in urban areas like gig workers, informal sector employees, and women and youth microentrepreneurs, or low-income urban families in other states.

Summary

This study informs that the COVID-19 pandemic and the MCO affect the urban B40 family in terms of financial well-being. Although there is government assistance to reduce the negative impact, the crisis highlights the challenges related to preparedness for future shock. Looking from a more positive point of view, borrowing from the statement of the Chief of Staff of the White House during the Obama presidency who later became the Mayor of Chicago, Rahm Emanuel, "Never let a serious crisis go to waste". This became a guideline and encouragement to various agencies, authorities, stakeholders, and all citizens to redraw a social protection system that includes aspects of better financial well-being, which is more inclusive, which is more equitable, and which is more sustainable.

Author Contributions: Conceptualization, A.S.A.S. and N.M.Y.; methodology, A.M.A.S.; validation, A.S.A.S., N.M.Y. and A.M.A.S.; formal analysis, A.S.A.S. and A.M.A.S.; resources, A.S.A.S., N.M.Y. and A.M.A.S.; writing—original draft preparation, A.S.A.S.; writing—review and editing, N.M.Y.; supervision, A.S.A.S.; project administration, N.M.Y.; funding acquisition, N.M.Y. All authors have read and agreed to the published version of the manuscript.

Funding: This research was funded by the National Population and Family Development Board Malaysia (N.P.F.D.B.), research grant GPLPPKN0294, and the Multimedia University Internal Research Fund 2022, M.M.U.I./220005. Multimedia University, Malaysia, funded the A.P.C.

Informed Consent Statement: Not applicable.

Data Availability Statement: Data are not publicly available due to copyright.

Acknowledgments: The team acknowledges and expresses gratitude for the research funding from the Malaysian National Population dan Family Development Board (NPFDB)/GPLPPKN02694, Universiti Tunku Abdul Rahman, and Multimedia University toward the completion of the research.

Conflicts of Interest: The authors declare no conflicts of interest.

References

Abdul Hamid, Hawati, and Jarud Romadan Khalidi. 2020. *COVID-19 and Unequal Learning*. Kuala Lumpur: KRI.

Abdul Hamid, Hawati, Gregory Ho Wai Son, and Suraya Ismail. 2019. *Demarcating Households: An Integrated Income and Consumption Analysis*. Kuala Lumpur: KRI.

Abdul Rahim, Husniyah, Norlela Zainal, and Mohamad Fazli Sabri. 2021. Identifying the financial status risk factors for single mothers during the COVID-19 pandemic. *International Journal of Economics and Management* 15: 423–36.

Abdul Wahab, M Hafizan, Nur Areisman Salleh, Muhammad Afif Husman, Hassriq Hafize Abdul Halim Hafiz, Farah Izmyra Muzafar Shah, Iffah Khairul Anuar, Noorhafizah Ismail, and Umar Hakim M Tajuddin. 2021. Memperkasa peranan NGO dalam bentuk sistem sokongan kepada kesejahteraan golongan rentan dalam mendepani cabaran semasa dan pasca COVID-19: Satu kajian lapangan di PPR sekitar Kuala Lumpur. Prosiding. Paper presented at the Persidangan Kependudukan Kebangsaan 2021, Kuala Lumpur, Malaysia, November 16–17.

Abdullah, Azwan, Muhammad Zulfaris Mohd Salleh, Mohd Zulkifli Muhammad, and Adibah Alawiah Osman. 2022. Financial planning as catalyst for poverty eradication among B40 in Malaysia. *Journal of Wealth Management and Financial Planning* 9: 57–66.

Abdullah, Nuraini, Mohamad Fazli Sabri, and Afida Mastura Muhammad Arif. 2019. The relationship between attitude towards money, financial literacy and debt management with young worker's financial well-being. *Pertanika Journal Social Sciences and Humanities* 27: 361–78.

Agensi Kaunseling dan Pengurusan Kredit (AKPK). 2018. *Financial Behavior and State of Financial Well-Being of Malaysian Working Adults*; Research Report. Kuala Lumpur: AKPK.

Apostolopoulos, Nikolaos, Panagiotis Liargovas, Nikolaos Rodousakis, and George Soklis. 2022. COVID-19 in US Economy: Structural Analysis and Policy Proposals. *Sustainability* 14: 7925. [CrossRef]

Armstrong, Mary I., Shelly Birnie-Lefcovitch, and Michael T. Ungar. 2005. Pathways between social support, family well-being, quality of parenting, and child resilience: What we know. *Journal of Child and Family Studies* 14: 269–81. [CrossRef]

Awang Besar, Junaidi. 2018. Analisis perkembangan pembangunan perumahan awam di Selangor. *Malaysian Journal of Society and Space* 14: 40–54. [CrossRef]

Awang Besar, Junaidi, Mazlan Ali, Vivien Yew W. C., Novel Lyndon, and Mohd Nor Shahizan Ali. 2018. The socio-economic and political impact of peoples' housing programme in Lembah Subang, Selangor. *Akademika* 88: 181–91.

Barrafrem, Kinga, Daniel Västfjäll, and Gustav Tinghög. 2020. Financial well-being, COVID-19, and the financial better-than-average-effect. *Journal of Behavioral and Experimental Finance* 28: 1–5. [CrossRef]

Benyamin, Aiza Yasmin, Chin Xiao Wei, Daniel Nee, Kelvin Hii, Logenthiran Kanisan, and Yu Yen Hong. 2022. Observations from the COVID-19 Pandemic. *Journal of Wealth Management and Financial Planning* 9: 67–80.

Chan, Michelle, and Wei Ying Chong. 2022. A literature review of the relationship between social support from spouses, marital quality, and women's financial planning for retirement. *Journal of Wealth Management and Financial Planning* 9: 21–33.

Chong, Eilyn, and Farina Adam Khong. 2018. *The Living Wage: Beyond Making Ends Meet*; Kuala Lumpur: Bank Negara Malaysia.

Eadie, Pauline, and Chester Yacub. 2024. COVID-19 and aid distribution in the Philippines: A patron-clientelist explanation. *Third World Quarterly* 45: 229–46. [CrossRef]

Frey, Karin S., Mark T. Greenberg, and R. R. Fewell. 1989. Stress and coping among parents of exceptional children: A multidimensional approach. *American Journal on Mental Retardation* 94: 240–49. [PubMed]

Gogineni, Avinash, and Martin. 2022. An Analysis of COVID-19 Fiscal Policies in the US and Japan. *Journal of Student Research* 11: 1–6. [CrossRef]

Gong, Rachel. 2020. *Coping with COVID-19: Distance Learning and Digital Divide*. Kuala Lumpur: KRI.

Jabatan Perumahan Negara (JPN). 2017. *Kajian Kesejahteraan Komuniti Program Perumahan Rakyat (PPR)*; Laporan Kajian. Putrajaya: Kementerian Perumahan dan Kerajaan Tempatan.

Joo, So-Hyun, Dorothy Bahwell Durband, and John Grable. 2008. The academic impact of financial stress on college students. *Journal of College Student Retention: Research, Theory and Practice* 10: 287–305. [CrossRef]

Jusoh, Nordianah Hussain, Khairunnisa Abd Samad, Nik Rozila Nik Mohd Masdek, Nurhayati Abdul Rahman, Wan Musyirah Wan Ismail, and Bushra Mohd Zakif. 2020. Does income shock during COVID-19 make any difference on consumption among Malaysian household. *International Journal of Academic Research in Economics and Management Sciences* 9: 21–30.

Kamaruzuki, Muhammad Nazhan. 2020. *Mutu Jalur Lebar Dalam Menghadapi Kejutan COVID-19*. Kuala Lumpur: KRI.

Khazanah Research Institute (KRI). 2018. *The State of Households 2018: Different Realities*. Kuala Lumpur: KRI.

Krejcie, Robert V., and Daryle W. Morgan. 1970. Determining sample size for research activities. *Educational and Psychological Measurement* 30: 607–710. [CrossRef]

Lee, May Poh, Mohamad Fazli Sabri, Husniyah Abd Rahim, and Rusitha Wijekoon. 2021. Determinants of financial vulnerability among civil servants in Peninsular Malaysia. *Malaysian Journal of Consumer and Family Economics* 27: 113–43.

Lim, Lin Lean. 2020. *The Socioeconomic Impacts of COVID-19 in Malaysia: Policy Review and Guidance for Protecting the Most Vulnerable and Supporting Enterprises*. Kuala Lumpur: International Labour Organisation (ILO).

Magli, Amirah Shazana, Mohamad Fazli Sabri, Husniyah Abdul Rahim, Muhammad Amim Othman, Nurul Shahnaz Mahzan, Nurulhuda Mohd Satar, Roza Hazli Zakaria, and Hawati Janor. 2021. Mediation effect of financial behaviour on financial vulnerability among B40 households. *Malaysian Journal of Consumer and Family Economics* 27: 191–217.

Mahdzan, Nurul Shahnaz, Rozaimah Zainudin, Mohd Edil Abd Sukor, Fauzi Zainir, and Wan Marhaini Wan Ahmad. 2020. An exploratory study of financial well-being among Malaysian households. *Journal of Asian Business and Economic Studies* 27: 285–302. [CrossRef]

Marome, Wijitbusaba, and Rajib Shaw. 2021. COVID-19 Response in Thailand and Its Implications on Future Preparedness. *International Journal of Environmental Research and Public Health* 18: 1089. [CrossRef]

Masruki, Rosnia, and Mustafa Mohd Hanefah. 2021. Kajian Rintis Penggunaan Maklumat Perakaunan Akruan dan Impak terhadap Matlamat Pembangunan Lestari (Sustainable Development Goals, "SDG") berdasarkan Maqasid Syariah. *IPN Journal of Research and Practice in Public Sector Accounting and Management* 11: 81–102. [CrossRef]

McKeown, Kieran, Jonathan Pratschke, and Trutz Haase. 2003. *Family Well-Being: What Makes a Difference?* Kuala Lumpur: Department of Social and Family Affairs, Family Support Centre and Ceifin Centre.

Megat Muzafar, Puteri Marjan, and Theebalakshmi Kunasekaran. 2020. *The Impact of COVID-19 on the Urban Poor: Three Major Threats–Money, Food and Living Conditions*. Kuala Lumpur: KRI.

Mohamed, Shafizan, Saodah Wok, Wan Norshira Wan Ghazali, and Shakira Nasir. 2021. *Investigating the Level of Digital Literacy Among Children of B40 Income Earners: Focusing on Children Living in the Pusat Perumahan Rakyat (PPR)*; Research Report. Cyberjaya: Suruhanjaya Komunikasi dan Multimedia Malaysia (SKMM).

National Population and Family Development Board Malaysia (NPFDB). 2015. *Family Well-Being Index Report Malaysia 2011*. Research Report. Kuala Lumpur: NPFDB.

National Population and Family Development Board Malaysia (NPFDB). 2017. *Report on Malaysian Family Well-Being Index 2016*. Research Report. Kuala Lumpur: NPFDB.

National Population and Family Development Board Malaysia (NPFDB). 2020a. *The Impact of COVID-19 on Behavioural and Lifestyle Changes, Work from Home and Family Planning*. Kuala Lumpur: NPFDB.

National Population and Family Development Board Malaysia (NPFDB). 2020b. *Report on Malaysian Family Well-Being Index 2019*. Research Report. Kuala Lumpur: NPFDB.

Neuman, William Lawrence. 2007. *Basics of Social Research: Qualitative and Quantitative Approaches*. Boston: Pearson Allyn and Bacon.

Newland, Lisa A. 2015. Family well-being, parenting, and child well-being: Pathways to healthy adjustment. *Clinical Psychologist* 19: 3–14. [CrossRef]

Nunally, Jum C., and Bernstein. 1994. *Psychometric Theory*. New York: McGraw Hill.

Pallant, Julie. 2005. *SPSS Survival Manual*. Philadelphia: Open University Press.

Roziqin, Ali, Syasya Y. F. Mas'udi, and Iradhad T. Sihidi. 2021. An analysis of Indonesian government policies against COVID-19. *Public Administration and Policy: An Asia-Pacific Journal* 24: 92–107. [CrossRef]
Sabri, Mohamad Fazli, and Leila Falahati. 2012. Estimating a model of subjective financial well-being among college students. *International Journal of Humanities and Social Science* 2: 191–99.
Sabri, Mohamad Fazli, Eugene Cheng-Xi Aw, Husniyah Abd Rahim, Nik Ahmad Sufian Burhan, Mohd Amim Othman, and Megawati Simanjuntak. 2021. Financial literacy, behavior and vulnerability among Malaysian households: Does gender matter? *International Journal of Economics & Management* 15: 241–56.
Sazali, Nur Thuraya, and Tan Zhai Gen. 2019. *The Demise of Formal Employment?—A Literature Update on Informality*. Kuala Lumpur: Khazanah Research Institute.
Sekaran, Umar. 2000. *Research Methods for Business: A Skill-Building Approach*. New York: John Wiley & Sons.
United Nations Childrens' Fund, Malaysia (UNICEF), and the United Nations Population Fund (UNFPA). 2020. *Families on the Edge*. Kuala Lumpur: UNICEF and UNFPA.
Wei, Ying Chong, Grace Swee Hoon Ling, Hartini Mohammad, and Zakia Ahmed Mohamed Meshal. 2022. Savings for retirement: The COVID-19 Conundrum. *Journal of Wealth Management and Financial Planning* 9: 81–83.
Zainol, Siti Subaryani, Suhaili Mohd Hussin, Maisarah Syazwani Othman, and Nur Hazrini Mohd Zahari. 2021. Challenges of online learning faced by the B40 income parents in Malaysia. *International Journal of Education and Pedagogy* 3: 45–52.

Journal of
Risk and Financial Management

MDPI

Article

Environmental, Social and Governance Awareness and Organisational Risk Perception Amongst Accountants

Hok-Ko Pong [1,*] and Chun-Cheong Fong [2]

1 Faculty of Management and Hospitality, Technology and Higher Education Institute of Hong Kong, Hong Kong, China
2 Faculty of Business, Macao Polytechnic University, Macau, China
* Correspondence: hkpong@thei.edu.hk

Abstract: The relationships between accountants' environmental, social and governance (ESG) awareness and their perceptions of organisational risk are examined in this study. The emphasis is on the operational, strategic, financial and compliance risks of business organisations. A total of 462 accountants in Hong Kong were included via stratified random sampling and snowball sampling to ensure population diversity. A stratified random approach was used to include factors such as age, gender, income and experience, and snowball sampling amongst professional networks was used to ensure representativeness. A significant positive relationship exists between ESG awareness and risk perception, with environmental and governance factors emerging as the strongest predictors. Accountants with deep ESG awareness, especially in the aforementioned areas, can successfully identify and manage nontraditional risks such as regulatory changes and environmental threats. The findings highlight the need for institutionalising ESG-focused education in accounting and corporate governance to improve risk management capabilities. Increased ESG awareness can ensure responsible and sustainable business behaviour. Future research can expand the sample of accountants to executives and use longitudinal designs to capture the dynamic nature of ESG awareness and risk perception.

Keywords: environmental, social and governance (ESG); ESG awareness; accountants; organisational risk perception

1. Introduction

An increasing number of publicly listed business organisations have been sharing nonfinancial data about environmental, social and governance (ESG) issues. Some of them have voluntarily disclosed this information, whereas others proceed with their ESG reporting as required by law (Jackson et al. 2020). For example, organisations listed on stock markets in the United Kingdom must report risks related to climate change (Alsaifi et al. 2020). In the United States, the Securities and Exchange Commission has proposed rules to assist business organisations in disclosing climate-related risks, although such disclosure is not yet mandatory (Carattini et al. 2022; South et al. 2021). In Asia, businesses listed on the Singapore Exchange must submit sustainability reports (Nilipour et al. 2020). The Hong Kong Stock Exchange also requires business organisations to share ESG information (Leung and Xiang 2022). Interestingly, report submissions have shifted from solely declaring financial performance to measuring ESG indicators (Eccles et al. 2014). This transformation may be explained by the shift to comprehensively supporting long-term business sustainability.

Accountants are expected to include ESG principles in their work and contribute considerably to improving corporate governance and financial oversight. ESG practices contribute to long-term financial stability and improved organisational performance. Integrating sustainable development goals (e.g., ESG indicators) into accounting practices also improves transparency (Yu et al. 2018) and reduces information gaps, which are valuable for the effective management of risks (Tsang et al. 2023).

Hence, accountants need to expand their technical expertise beyond merely applying their financial–technical duties. Accountants need to understand how ESG factors affect the risks faced by business organisations. This improved level of understanding can help accountants manage risks and support their organisation's long-term success.

The literature has provided examples from around the world depicting faulty decision-making processes by large organisations due to the lack of consideration of ESG factors at different levels, which eventually led to their collapse. Failure to consider ESG factors in risk management has severe consequences, including environmental catastrophes, such as dam collapse under the supervision of BHP–Vale Samarco or oil spills caused by BP Deepwater Horizon, which have led to tremendous financial problems and irreparable harm to the environment and the business reputation of organisations (The Guardian 2010, 2018). Businesses should have strong environmental management systems so that they can recognise risks early enough to prevent them from happening via mitigation measures (Kazancoglu et al. 2021).

The labour practice scandal of the Boohoo Group illustrates the consequences of failing to take social responsibility seriously in the 'social' terms of ESG reporting; it has damaged both the reputation and financial leverage of the organisation (The Guardian 2021a). Hence, for present-day accountants, these dimensions need to be integrated into their risk evaluation, especially given the increasing correlation between social performance, particularly labour practices, and financial results (Lisi 2018).

Wirecard fraud is undeniably one of many types of governance failure, which emphasises the immediate need to enhance the consciousness of accountants about good governance (BBC News 2022). Accountants who have extensive knowledge of governance principles might be able to successfully avoid similar fraud, thus protecting their organisations from governance-related risks (Sadaf et al. 2018).

The role of accountants is central to recognising and managing risks in various sectors. The relationship between ESG awareness and organisational risk perception is truly relevant for them, given that lapses in governance and strategic risk management have catastrophic results, as seen in the cases of the Boeing 737 Max and the Facebook–Cambridge Analytica data privacy problem (The New York Times 2019; The Guardian 2019). Furthermore, the lapses highlight the need for comprehensive financial and compliance risk management, as evidenced by events such as Greensill Capital's failure or Wells Fargo's fake accounts scandal (The Guardian 2021b; BBC News 2017). These examples imply that high levels of ESG awareness enable accountants to detect and reduce risks at opportune times, further suggesting enhanced capabilities in averting potential crises.

2. Significance of the Study

This research, which is the first to investigate the relationship between the ESG awareness of accountants and their risk perceptions, intends to contribute substantially to the extant literature. Although prior studies have discussed improved risk management outcomes with increased ESG awareness, empirical evidence explicitly citing the role of accountants is lacking. Practitioners, business leaders and policymakers can gather invaluable information from such research explorations, thereby providing evidence that increased ESG awareness can help accountants manage risks effectively and efficiently. How to increase ESG awareness, which might lead to improved risk management amongst accounting professionals, is another focus of this study.

3. Problem Statement

Despite the growing recognition of ESG reporting, the understanding of how the ESG awareness of accountants affects their perceptions of organisational risk still remains limited. Accountants contribute considerably to assessing financial stability and risk, but their ability to connect these risks to ESG factors has not yet been fully established. This gap in the literature is addressed in this research by investigating the relationship between the ESG awareness of accountants and their perceptions of organisational risk.

4. Research Gaps

Although sustainability and responsibility towards the Earth are receiving widespread attention, little is known about how these factors impact individual views, such as how they relate to risk management. Most studies, including those of Chen et al. (2023) and El Khoury et al. (2023), have focused primarily on financial performance at the organisational level, often ignoring how individual accountants perceive and deal with ESG-related risks, including the impact on nonfinancial performance. Pong and Fong (2024) recently underscored the importance of the subjective experiences of accountants in terms of handling ESG responsibilities, but this topic remains largely unexplored; the correlations of these variables are vital determinants of effective risk management. Similarly, recent studies by Karwowski and Raulinajtys-Grzybek (2021) and Sulkowski and Jebe (2022) have shown that despite the increasing corporate integration of ESG factors into business strategies, the role of individual accountants in dealing with such risks is still open to research. In the present study, these research gaps are addressed by investigating the effect of ESG awareness on organisational risk perception amongst accountants, thereby deepening the insights into the role of accountants as risk managers.

5. Research Objectives and Questions

The goal of this research is to explore the correlation between accountants' understanding of ESG and their perception of organisational risk. In particular, the study aims to accomplish the following:

1. Measure the correlation between ESG awareness and the perception of operational risk amongst accountants;
2. Evaluate the impact of ESG awareness on the perception of strategic risk;
3. Determine the extent to which ESG awareness influences financial risk perception;
4. Enhance the empirical understanding of ESG consciousness and its influence on compliance risk perceptions.

Research Questions

1. What are the relationships between the ESG awareness of accountants and their perceptions of certain organisational risks?
2. How does the ESG awareness of accountants predict their perceptions of specific risks within an organisation?

6. Theoretical Framework

The research framework developed for this study is shown in Figure 1. The relationships between the ESG awareness of accountants and their perception of organisational risk are integrated into this theoretical framework. The basis of this framework comprises stakeholder theory, risk management theory, ethical decision-making theory, institutional theory and agency theory. Collectively, these theories can elucidate how accountants might perceive risks in organisations with respect to ESG parameters.

Both stakeholder theory (Freeman 2010; Freeman et al. 2018) and agency theory (Jensen and Meckling 1976) emphasise the importance of reducing agency conflicts by aligning the decisions made by accountants with the expectations of their stakeholders. Increasingly, researchers and practitioners argue that ESG awareness allows accountants to better perceive operational and financial risks because their decisions would mirror the interests of a wider range of stakeholders (Hoang 2018; Lee and Isa 2020). This phenomenon aligns closely with the central premise of stakeholder theory, which advocates for multiple stakeholder interests. Lee and Isa (2020) established that ESG performance is positively related to performance in terms of the overall profitability of an organisation in different dimensions. However, the link between ESG performance and agency problems still lacks scholarly evidence.

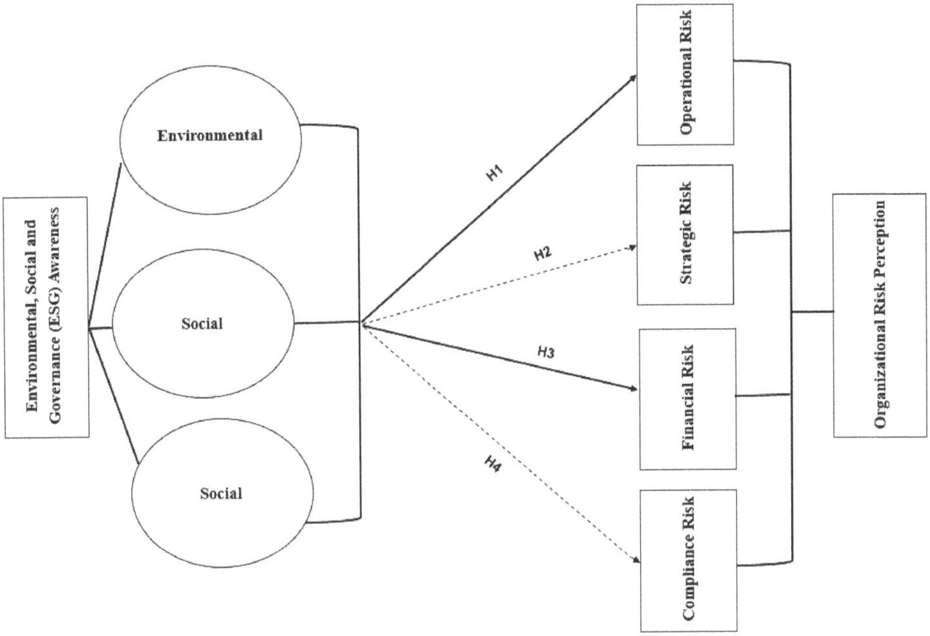

Figure 1. Research model.

Risk management theory offers a framework for incorporating ESG aspects into the identification and mitigation of various hazards or risks (Kaplan and Mikes 2012). By doing so, agents become better at identifying certain kinds of risks that traditional financial analysis would not have recognised, thereby enhancing overall risk management practices (Sassen et al. 2016).

Both ethical decision-making theory (Jones 1991) and institutional theory (DiMaggio and Powell 1983) provide a sound conceptual framework for explaining how the ESG awareness of accountants can influence their perception of risk. As accountants attempt to adapt to changing sustainability challenges, their ethical considerations also guide them in making decisions that are strategically sound and intricately linked with social responsibility. The awareness of accountants concerning compliance risks is typically fostered by social norms (Jejeniwa et al. 2024; Schwartz 2016).

The integrated framework proposed in this study not only can deepen the theoretical understanding of the relationship between ESG awareness and risk perception but also provide practical insights into ESG policies in the accounting field.

7. Literature Review

As ESG prioritisation continues to expand, business owners and managers have also begun revisiting their sustainability strategies. Such transformations can affect the decision-making and risk management processes of managers. On this basis, accountants whose role is mainly providing profitability control and governance advice should seriously consider ESG-related implications. This literature review aims to establish whether the ESG awareness of accountants affects their perceptions of operational, strategic, financial and compliance risks. Research gaps that require further investigation are also identified in this study.

7.1. ESG Awareness and Organisational Risk Perception

Stakeholders at various levels are likely involved in ESG reporting, and this situation has likely become one of the major concerns of business organisations in recent decades. Accountants in particular are expected to contribute beyond accounting matters (Pong and Fong 2023). Currently, accountants are also expected to integrate ESG aspects that could affect their respective organisations' operations (Sulkowski and Jebe 2022).

7.2. Definition and Importance of ESG Awareness

Nugroho et al. (2024) describe ESG awareness as the comprehension of ESG issues related to organisational operations and their implementation in everyday actions. Accountants in contemporary society should therefore expand their perspective of ESG rather than merely focusing on financial risk. ESG awareness is currently indispensable in risk management. According to Dechow (2023), accountants who are knowledgeable about ESG reporting are more likely to anticipate and address sustainability challenges effectively than accountants who are unaware of ESG. ESG-related capabilities enhance risk assessment and ethical decision-making processes and fortify resilience and overall corporate character (Liang and Li 2023). Recently, Armstrong (2020) and Asante-Appiah and Lambert (2023) reached similar conclusions—the mindfulness of accountants of ESG matters not only is 'more honest' but also improves their identification, management and mitigation of risks, especially in sectors requiring regulation and control, such as healthcare and financial services.

7.3. Impact of ESG Awareness on Risk Perception

The appraisal and ranking of different types of risk by accountants improve considerably as their level of ESG consciousness increases. Moffitt et al. (2024) recently showed that accountants who are deeply acquainted with ESG parameters are more aware of environmental compliance, social responsibility and governance-related risks. More importantly, such accountants can integrate other pertinent factors into risk assessments, identifying new types of risk that are otherwise disregarded by traditional models. These actions enable accountants to handle complexities in the modern business context (Atan et al. 2016). Shakil (2021) and Atif and Ali (2021) also confirm this view, stating that ESG-aware accountants are more likely to rapidly identify regulatory changes or stakeholder concerns than their ESG-unaware peers are, which further allows them to successfully recognise strategic and compliance risks.

7.4. Challenges in Integrating ESG into Risk Perception

Integrating ESG principles into risk assessments is challenging despite the widespread notion of the importance of ESG principles in the daily operations of organisations. A common challenge is the lack of a clear standard framework, leading to many inconsistencies (Singhania and Saini 2023). Moreover, contradictions arise between short-term financial objectives and long-term sustainability objectives (Caiazza et al. 2021; Zumente and Bistrova 2021). Faccia et al. (2021) suggested that a comprehensive standardised framework must be established to assist accountants in reconciling ESG parameters and economic outcomes.

8. Domains of Organisational Risk Perception

8.1. Operational Risk Perception

Inadequate processes, systems or external events often lead to operational risks that incur a variety of losses (Hubbard 2020). ESG-aware accountants can anticipate operational hazards associated with environmental regulation compliance and employee security. Saari et al. (2021) reported that organisations that are aware of risks early enough can move quickly to protect their operations, hence lessening disruptions. According to the recent studies conducted by Chen et al. (2022) and Yu et al. (2023), firms with accountants who understand ESG do not experience as many operational disruptions as compared to other companies. Overall performance is therefore improved mostly in high-risk sectors like manufacturing and energy. The present study employs multivariate regression analysis controlled for experience, industry and ESG awareness. The approach enables the examination of the relations between ESG awareness and operational risk perception in detail. ESG awareness further predicts operational risk perception, with environmentally conscious professionals recognising compliance and sustainability risks.

8.2. Strategic Risk Perception

Strategic risk is derived from long-term threats, such as unfavourable decisions, market fluctuations or shifts in corporate strategies (Kim et al. 2021). Accountants who are familiar with ESG factors might be able to identify strategic risks acutely, such as changes in stakeholder preferences, legal liability and loss of reputation. Awareness helps businesses to develop sustainable and adaptable strategies that enable organisations to remain ahead of an increasingly ESG-focused market (Bhandari et al. 2022; Liang et al. 2022). Ziolo et al. (2023) and Ishak and Asmawi (2022) have shown that integrating ESG into strategic planning allows organisations to adjust rapidly to changes in the marketplace or legislation field, thereby avoiding strategic misalignment. The current study used regression analysis to explore the direct impact of ESG awareness on strategic risk perception. Although indirect effects are testable by advanced models, such as structural equation modelling (SEM), the regression results sufficiently identify a clear positive relationship between them. This suggests that ESG-aware accountants are more proactive in identifying long-term strategic risks.

8.3. Financial Risk Perception

Monetary risk encompasses the possibility of losing finances due to market disruptions, credit difficulties or liquidity problems (Liu et al. 2023). ESG-aware accountants might be able to easily detect the financial risks associated with environmental violations or the mishandling of finances when engaging in corporate social responsibility (CSR), such as socially responsible investing (Pong and Fong 2024). Financial decisions need to consider ESG criteria to ensure that the financing strategies of organisations are in consonance with their sustainability targets (Ziolo et al. 2019; Landi et al. 2022). Apergis et al. (2022) recently established that businesses with notably high ESG scores have low capital costs and face less stringent requirements for financing. This situation illustrates how advantageous it is financially to seek ESG options. While propensity score matching (PSM) could offer additional control for selection bias, the current study used traditional covariate adjustments (e.g., experience, education levels, firm size) to mitigate this issue, ensuring that the results remain robust.

8.4. Compliance Risk Perception

Compliance risk refers to problems associated with legal fines, losing money or even ruining organisational reputation because of violations of laws and regulations (Ramos et al. 2024). ESG reporting-compliant accountants tend to actively seek governance and ethical issues (Jejeniwa et al. 2024) to assess the risks that business organisations must avoid to prevent legal perils whilst retaining a good reputation. These capabilities help promote a long business lifecycle, especially when changes vary considerably in terms of regulations (Solaimani 2024). Zhao (2022) recently reported that ESG performance has become an important consideration over the years with respect to managing compliance risk. This scenario is evident within the context of regulated industries, such as finance or pharmaceuticals, where regulators continuously observe businesses more intently than before (Lee et al. 2024). The current study utilised logistic regression to analyse the binary outcome of compliance risk perception (compliant vs. non-compliant), showing that accountants with higher ESG awareness are more likely to recognise compliance risks. While further robustness checks (e.g., bootstrapping) could enhance confidence in these results, the current model offers a solid basis for understanding ESG awareness's role in compliance risk perception.

9. Theoretical Frameworks for ESG Awareness and Risk Perception

Several theories can help explain the correlation between the ESG awareness of accountants and how they view risks. These frameworks also help researchers identify the correlations amongst various related factors.

9.1. *Stakeholder Theory and Agency Theory*

According to stakeholder theory (Freeman 2010; Freeman et al. 2018), businesses should consider all stakeholders' interests. In the context of increased ESG awareness, accountants can make decisions that are aligned with stakeholder interests, thereby mitigating agency conflicts (Jensen and Meckling 1976). This alignment facilitates accountants in understanding the perception of operational and financial risks more broadly since accountants consider the factors that are not strictly limited to finances (Chen et al. 2023). MacNeil and Esser (2022) further state that ESG-aligned decisions reduce conflicts. This focus on stakeholder interests promotes sustainability and good governance. In light of the above considerations, the current study undertakes the incorporation of multivariate regression analysis with interaction terms to study stakeholder engagement empirically in testing the hypotheses. While models like SEM could further delineate indirect effects, the regression analysis provides a clear and sufficient evaluation of the direct relationships between ESG awareness and risk perception across multiple domains.

9.2. *Risk Management Theory*

According to the risk management theory (Kaplan and Mikes 2012), ESG factors serve as significant indicators for the identification and mitigation of various risks. Accountants who incorporate ESG into their accounting practices would have their horizons expanded beyond traditional financial risks (MacNeil and Esser 2022). This also aids accountants in identifying potential hazards stemming from reputational, operational and compliance risks, which they might have overlooked otherwise. Furthermore, this improves agency conflicts and long-term stakeholder value by aligning ESG principles with risk management (MacNeil and Esser 2022).

9.3. *Ethical Decision-Making Theory and Institutional Theory*

ESG awareness has implications for accountants' perceptions of strategic and compliance risks, as evidenced by ethical decision-making theory and institutional theory. Accountants guided by ethics are in an excellent position to make decisions that resonate with both societal and organisational expectations (Lennard and Roberts 2023). Raghavan (2022) established that ESG-based training can aid accountants in dealing with complex risks, particularly in the financial and energy sectors. For example, HSBC has utilised ethical frameworks to improve their transparency mechanisms and enhance their compliance risk assessments in domains such as money laundering prevention and environmental practice (Bearpark 2022).

9.4. *Variability in the Impact of ESG Awareness on Risk Perception*

The evidence suggests correlations between ESG awareness and increased risk perception (Oh et al. 2024). The relationship, however, varies across risk categories. Several scholars have suggested that the compliance and reputational risk of accountants might be strongly influenced by strong ESG consciousness (Asante-Appiah and Lambert 2023; Tsang et al. 2023). However, such effects are less certain with respect to operational and financial risks (Park and Jang 2021). Hassanein et al. (2024) attributed this variation to organisational culture or departmental characteristics, further indicating the necessity of utilising sector-based ESG frameworks.

This literature review has examined the complex relationship between ESG awareness and risk perception by accountants of business organisations. Although ESGs have been increasingly integrated into risk management, challenges still exist. These concepts consist of ensuring standard uniformity and striking a balance between short-term profit-making and long-term sustainability. Theoretical frameworks such as stakeholder theory, risk management theory or ethical decision-making theory provide invaluable insights into these topics. However, further research should be conducted because risks are affected differently by ESG performance. With this research approach, scholars can enhance understanding at the academic level and equip practitioners with the necessary skills on how business entities can integrate ESG concepts into their organisational processes and mechanisms and their risk management systems.

10. Hypotheses

The following hypotheses are proposed on the basis of the literature review and the constructed theoretical framework:

H1: *The ESG awareness of accountants positively affects their perceptions of operational risk (Galletta et al. 2023).*

H2: *The ESG awareness of accountants improves their perceptions of strategic risk (Eccles et al. 2014).*

H3: *The ESG awareness of accountants positively affects their perceptions of financial risk (Chairani and Siregar 2021).*

H4: *The ESG awareness of accountants improves their perceptions of compliance risks (Ni 2024).*

11. Methodology

11.1. Research Design

A cross-sectional design study was used to describe how accountants perceive risks in their organisations on the basis of their awareness, including knowledge, attitudes and behaviours regarding ESG. The purpose of this design was to collect data at a specific time point, allowing the relationship between ESG awareness (independent variable) and risk perception (dependent variable) to be captured in a particular context. This approach is suitable for identifying trends and relationships between the aforementioned two variables.

A cross-sectional design was appropriate for this exploratory study, which aims to identify correlations instead of causation. Furthermore, this design provides an overall understanding of the existing level of ESG awareness performance and its effects on various risk areas.

Although PSM is often recommended in order to address selection bias, the current study employed traditional regression-based controls that included age, experience, firm size and education as important covariates which explain variations in the levels of ESG awareness amongst accountants. This approach was chosen because the current model yields robust and interpretable results, accurately depicting the ESG–risk perception relationship without the need for additional matching techniques. However, future studies could further refine these relationships by incorporating PSM.

11.2. Instruments

For the purpose of assessing accountants' comprehension of the elements pertaining to ESG, three primary instruments were utilised. The use of these instruments, as described in the literature (Gericke et al. 2019; Galletta et al. 2023; Kaplan and Mikes 2012; Turker 2009; Zaporowska and Szczepański 2024), can ensure that they possess both validity and reliability.

14. Data Collection

Data were collected between September 2023 and February 2024. For the data quality and relevance to be ensured, the survey period coincided with key financial reporting periods when accountants are most engaged with ESG-related issues.

Ethical considerations: All participants were fully informed about the purpose of the study, and their consent was obtained before participation. Data were anonymised to protect identities. The study adhered strictly to institutional review board guidelines.

15. Data Analysis

The data were analysed via SPSS version 26.0. Descriptive statistics were used to summarise the ESG awareness ratings and demographic data. Regression and correlation analyses were used to investigate the link between ESG awareness and risk perception to comprehensively investigate how risk perception might be influenced by governance and other ESG indicators within Hong Kong's accounting community.

Advanced analytical techniques: As this research is an exploratory study, structural equation modelling (SEM) was not utilised but rather regarded as an advanced analytical technique. Further studies can apply SEM to analyse possible mediating and moderating effects comprehensively.

Bias management: Instrument validation was performed carefully to eliminate any possible biases, whilst stratified sampling and questionnaire design were performed meticulously to ensure the absence of biases.

16. Results

16.1. Factor Analysis

Confirmatory factor analysis (CFA) was performed to confirm the validity of the measurement instruments. This CFA was used to assess the structure of the SCQ, which included the CSR–governance scale and the ORPS. The fit indices used in these models are shown in Table 1.

Table 1. CFA results.

Scale	Factors	CFI	TLI	SRMR	RMSEA
SCQ with CSR	Environmental, Social, Economic, Governance	0.96	0.95	0.04	0.06
ORPS	Operational, Strategic, Financial, Compliance	0.93	0.92	0.06	0.07

The instruments all indicated a good model fit, confirming their appropriateness for the further investigation of ESG awareness and risk perception. The ORPS model scored 'moderately good', within acceptable ranges.

16.1.1. SCQ with CSR–Governance Scale

The SCQ, which incorporated the three dimensions of ESG (i.e., environmental, social and economic) with governance awareness, demonstrated excellent fit indices (CFI = 0.96, TLI = 0.95, SRMR = 0.04 and RMSEA = 0.06). Thus, the SCQ with the CSR–governance scale could successfully capture the multidimensionality of the sustainability consciousness and governance awareness of accountants. Future researchers can benefit from considering the SCQ as a reliable measurement tool because of its strong modelling features.

16.1.2. ORPS

The ORPS, which comprises the operational, strategic, financial and compliance risk domains, also obtained a good model fit (CFI = 0.93, TLI = 0.92, SRMR = 0.06 and RMSEA = 0.07). The fit indices were generally within the acceptable range; however, the RMSEA indicated the need to slightly revise the model to increase the accuracy of its predictions. Nevertheless, the ORPS has been validated as a reliable instrument for measuring various dimensions of risk perception, suggesting its importance as a tool for evaluating how risk assessments of accountants are affected by ESG-related knowledge.

16.2. Internal Consistency

The internal reliability of the scales was assessed using Cronbach's α—a metric widely accepted for reliability. Although McDonald's ω represents a more detailed measure for multidimensional constructs, this analysis showed Cronbach's α to be sufficiently high (>0.70), hence indicating reliable internal consistency. Future studies can, of course, extend the current analysis by using such alternative measures as McDonald's ω, but the approach taken herein is consistent with common practices.

Cronbach's α was calculated to determine the internal consistency of the scales. All values exceeded the minimum threshold of 0.70 (Table 2), confirming the reliability of the model.

Table 2. Internal consistency (Cronbach's α).

Scale	Subscale/Dimension	Cronbach's α
SCQ	Environmental (9 items)	0.73
SCQ	Social (9 items)	0.73
SCQ	Economic (9 items)	0.74
SCQ	Overall (27 items)	0.83
CSR	Governance (4 items)	0.93
ORPS	Operational	0.82
ORPS	Strategic	0.82
ORPS	Financial	0.83
ORPS	Compliance	0.95
ORPS	Overall	0.91

The high internal consistency across the scales underscores the robustness of the constructs measured. The Cronbach's α values for the CSR–governance and ORPS compliance subscales (α = 0.93 and α = 0.95, respectively) are extremely high; therefore, whilst these scales are reliable, the potential for item redundancy should be considered in future research.

16.3. Descriptive Results

The study analysed data from 462 accountants in Hong Kong and explored their ESG awareness and organisational risk perceptions. The descriptive analysis provided insights into the demographic composition of the samples and highlighted dominant trends in ESG awareness and risk perceptions.

16.3.1. Participant Demographics

The demographics of the participants (Tables 3 and 4) help in comprehending differences in ESG consciousness and risk comprehension across the respondents. The sample was equally split between genders (51.7% female and 48.3% male participants), with most respondents aged between 26 and 36 years. In terms of educational level, approximately 38.5% had bachelor's degrees, whereas another 34% were holders of master's or postgraduate degrees. Almost all of the participants had fewer than 10 years of working experience, and only a few had worked for more than 25 years. The monthly salaries of the respondents ranged between HK$60,000 and HK$79,999, representing average remuneration levels for the financial industry in Hong Kong.

Table 3. Demographic attributes and the sustainability consciousness questionnaire (SCQ).

	N (%)	Environmental	Social	Economics	CSR Awareness in Governance
		Mean (S.D.)	Mean (S.D.)	Mean (S.D.)	Mean (S.D.)
All	462 (100%)	3.04 (0.45)	3.08 (0.39)	2.65 (0.44)	4.58 (0.54)
Gender					
(1) Male	223 (48.3%)	3.07 (0.47)	3.11 (0.41)	2.65 (0.47)	4.61 (0.55)
(2) Female	239 (51.7%)	3.01 (0.44) $t = 1.43$	3.05 (0.38) $t = 1.72$	2.64 (0.42) $t = 0.01$	4.55 (0.53) $t = 1.10$
Age					
(1) Under 26 Years Old	98 (21.2%)	2.81 (0.37)	2.99 (0.36)	2.59 (0.41)	4.23 (0.51)
(2) 26–30	118 (25.5%)	2.95 (0.40)	3.02 (0.36)	2.58 (0.40)	4.43 (0.57)
(3) 31–36	129 (27.9%)	3.16 (0.45)	3.11 (0.42)	2.68 (0.46)	4.78 (0.44)
(4) 37–43	75 (16.2%)	3.15 (0.45)	3.15 (0.40)	2.67 (0.42)	4.75 (0.48)
(5) 44 or Above	42 (9.1%)	3.30 (0.47) F = 15.99 ** (3), (4) and (5) > (1) and (2)	3.21 (0.41) F = 3.72 * (5) > (1)	2.83 (0.56) F = 3.20 * (5) > (1) and (2)	4.93 (0.22) F = 28.36 ** (3), (4) and (5) > (1) and (2); (2) > (1)
Work Experience					
(1) Less Than 4 Years	98 (21.2%)	2.81 (0.37)	2.99 (0.36)	2.59 (0.41)	4.23 (0.51)
(2) 4–9 Years	160 (34.6%)	3.02 (0.43)	3.05 (0.37)	2.61 (0.43)	4.52 (0.55)
(3) 10–16 Years	122 (26.4%)	3.11 (0.46)	3.07 (0.43)	2.63 (0.46)	4.70 (0.52)
(4) 17–24 Years	64 (13.9%)	3.29 (0.44)	3.25 (0.38)	2.81 (0.46)	4.95 (0.19)
(5) 25 Years or Above	18 (3.9%)	3.17 (0.43) F = 14.04 ** (5) > (1); (4) > (1) and (2); (3) > (1) (2) > (1)	3.15 (0.49) F = 4.73 * (4) > (1), (2) and (3)	2.76 (0.51) F = 3.13 * (4) > (1) and (2)	4.92 (0.21) F = 26.43 ** (5) > (1) and (2); (4) > (1), (2) and (3); (3) > (1) and (2) (2) > (1)
Education Level					
(1) Diploma/Associate	122 (26.4%)	2.85 (0.37)	2.98 (0.35)	2.53 (0.40)	4.31 (0.60)
(2) Bachelor	178 (38.5%)	3.11 (0.46)	3.12 (0.40)	2.66 (0.46)	4.62 (0.54)
(3) Master/Postgraduate	157 (34%)	3.11 (0.46)	3.10 (0.41)	2.72 (0.43)	4.74 (0.41)
(4) Doctoral	5 (1.1%)	3.24 (0.72) F = 11.17 ** (3) > (1); (2) > (1)	3.22 (0.48) F = 3.31 * (1) > (2)	2.93 (0.50) F = 4.92 * (3) > (1)	5.0 (0.01) F = 17.11 ** (4) > (1); (3) > (1); (2) > (1)
Religious Beliefs					
(1) No	287 (62.1%)	2.98 (0.43)	3.04 (0.39)	2.59 (0.40)	4.51 (0.57)
(2) Yes	175 (37.9%)	3.15 (0.46) $t = -4.11$ ** (1) < (2)	3.14 (0.38) $t = -2.84$ * (1) < (2)	2.74 (0.49) $t = -3.56$ ** (1) < (2)	4.70 (0.46) $t = -3.88$ ** (1) < (2)

Table 3. *Cont.*

	N (%)	Environmental	Social	Economics	CSR Awareness in Governance
Monthly Salaries					
(1) Below HK$20,000	37 (8%)	2.79 (0.43)	2.95 (0.40)	2.63 (0.37)	4.14 (0.61)
(2) HK$20,000–HK$39,999	72 (15.6%)	2.80 (0.34)	3.02 (0.33)	2.56 (0.43)	4.19 (0.55)
(3) HK$40,000–HK$59,999	104 (22.5%)	2.97 (0.40)	3.01 (0.37)	2.58 (0.39)	4.48 (0.54)
(4) HK$60,000–HK$79,999	159 (34.4%)	3.19 (0.45)	3.13 (0.41)	2.67 (0.46)	4.82 (0.35)
(5) HK$80,000–HK$99,999	69 (14.9%)	3.18 (0.45)	3.17 (0.43)	2.77 (0.48)	4.74 (0.51)
(6) HK$100,000 and Above	21 (4.5%)	3.19 (0.44) F = 13.79 ** (6) > (1) and (2); (5) > (1), (2) and (3); (4) > (1), (2) and (3)	3.11 (0.34) F = 3.02	2.75 (0.52) F = 2.47	4.92 (0.21) F = 28.88 ** (6) > (1), (2) and (3); (5) > (1), (2) and (3); (4) > (1), (2) and (3); (3) > (1) and (2)
Industries					
(1) Financial Services	117 (25.3%)	3.05 (0.46)	3.04 (0.40)	2.66 (0.43)	4.58 (0.52)
(2) Accounting and Auditing Firms	100 (21.6%)	3.18 (0.49)	3.12 (0.42)	2.72 (0.44)	4.71 (0.49)
(3) Real Estate and Construction	58 (12.6%)	2.86 (0.33)	3.08 (0.36)	2.56 (0.47)	4.47 (0.61)
(4) Manufacturing and Industrial	52 (11.3%)	3.03 (0.45)	3.11 (0.37)	2.66 (0.46)	4.57 (0.57)
(5) Retail and Consumer Goods	70 (15.2%)	2.86 (0.31)	2.97 (0.41)	2.60 (0.45)	4.36 (0.55)
(6) Government and Public Sector	40 (8.7%)	3.38 (0.41)	3.22 (0.36)	2.74 (0.46)	4.96 (0.13)
(7) Others	25 (5.4%)	2.88 (0.43) F = 10.30 ** (7) < (6) and (2); (6) > (1), (3), (4), (5) and (7); (5) < (2); (3) < (2)	3.09 (0.38) F = 2.09	2.52 (0.35) F = 1.60	4.35 (0.57) F = 7.94 ** (7) < (2) and (6); (6) > (1), (3), (4), (5); (5) < (2)
Positions					
(1) Junior Accountant/Entry-Level Accountant	49 (10.6%)	2.79 (0.40)	2.93 (0.39)	2.59 (0.40)	4.14 (0.61)
(2) Senior Accountant	56 (12.1%)	2.78 (0.33)	3.05 (0.31)	2.58 (0.43)	4.17 (0.52)
(3) Accounting Manager/Finance Manager	117 (25.3%)	2.96 (0.43)	3.00 (0.39)	2.53 (0.40)	4.45 (0.5)
(4) Internal Auditor/Compliance Officer	86 (18.6%)	3.25 (0.37)	3.19 (0.38)	2.79 (0.48)	4.92 (0.25)
(5) Controller/Financial Controller	75 (16.2%)	2.97 (0.33)	3.07 (0.38)	2.68 (0.47)	4.65 (0.55)
(6) Chief Financial Officer (CFO)/Partner	68 (14.7%)	3.36 (0.51)	3.22 (0.44)	2.77 (0.42)	4.91 (0.27)

Table 3. *Cont.*

	N (%)	Environmental	Social	Economics	CSR Awareness in Governance
(7) Others	11 (2.4%)	3.44 (0.38) F = 21.25 ** (7) > (1), (2), (3) and (5); (6) > (1), (2), (3) and (5); (4) > (1), (2), (3), (5)	3.01 (0.40) F = 4.73 ** (6) > (1) and (3); (4) > (1) and (3)	2.40 (0.25) F = 4.96 ** (6) > (3); (4) > (3)	4.91 (0.3) F = 31.59 ** (7) > (1), (2) and (3); (6) > (1), (2), (3) and (5); (5) > (1), (2) and (3); (4)> (1), (2), (3), (5) and (6); (3) > (1) and (2)

Note: **: The correlations are significant at the 0.01 level (two-tailed); *: Correlations are significant at the 0.05 level (two-tailed); Note: HK$7.8 = US$1; Bonferroni post-hoc test following a one-way ANOVA.

Table 4. Demographic attributes and the organisational risk perception scale (ORPS).

	N (%)	ORPS Operational Risk	ORPS Strategic Risk	ORPS Financial Risk	ORPS Compliance Risk
		Mean (S.D.)	Mean (S.D.)	Mean (S.D.)	Mean (S.D.)
All	462 (100%)	4.15 (0.54)	4.04 (0.59)	3.56 (0.69)	3.11 (1.07)
Gender					
(1) Male	223 (48.3%)	4.19 (0.56)	4.06 (0.62)	3.61 (0.69)	3.12 (1.10)
(2) Female	239 (51.7%)	4.11 (0.52)	4.01 (0.56)	3.51 (0.68)	3.09 (1.04)
		$t = 1.56$	$t = 0.80$	$t = 1.61$	$t = 0.29$
Age					
(1) Under 26 Years Old	98 (21.2%)	3.87 (0.56)	3.75 (0.61)	3.30 (0.60)	3.00 (0.93)
(2) 26–30	118 (25.5%)	4.01 (0.52)	3.91 (0.53)	3.43 (0.66)	2.95 (1.12)
(3) 31–36	129 (27.9%)	4.27 (0.47)	4.18 (0.52)	3.68 (0.70)	3.17 (1.14)
(4) 37–43	75 (16.2%)	4.28 (0.48)	4.15 (0.59)	3.69 (0.65)	3.26 (1.01)
(5) 44 or Above	42 (9.1%)	4.53 (0.47)	4.42 (0.48)	3.91 (0.70)	3.36 (1.09)
		F = 18.87 ** (5) > (1), (2) and (3); (4) > (1) and (2); (3) > (1) and (2)	F = 16.10 ** (5) > (1) and (2); (4) > (1) and (2); (3) > (1) and (2)	F = 9.91 ** (5) > (1) and (2); (4) > (1); (3) > (1) and (2)	F = 2.03
Work Experience					
(1) Less Than 4 Years	98 (21.2%)	3.87 (0.56)	3.75 (0.61)	3.30 (0.60)	3.00 (0.93)
(2) 4–9 Years	160 (34.6%)	4.11 (0.53)	4.01 (0.56)	3.53 (0.68)	3.11 (1.13)
(3) 10–16 Years	122 (26.4%)	4.17 (0.47)	4.05 (0.56)	3.57 (0.67)	3.02 (1.10)
(4) 17–24 Years	64 (13.9%)	4.53 (0.42)	4.42 (0.49)	3.90 (0.73)	3.38 (1.06)
(5) 25 Years or Above	18 (3.9%)	4.43 (0.42)	4.37 (0.38)	3.92 (0.50)	3.31 (1.06)
		F = 18.13 ** (5) > (1); (4) > (1), (2), (3); (3) > (1); (2) > (1)	F = 15.80 ** (5) > (1); (4) > (1), (2), (3); (3) > (1); (2) > (1)	F = 9.61 ** (5) > (1); (4) > (1), (2), (3); (3) > (1)	F = 1.62

Table 4. *Cont.*

	N (%)	ORPS Operational Risk	ORPS Strategic Risk	ORPS Financial Risk	ORPS Compliance Risk
Education Level					
(1) Diploma/Associate	122 (26.4%)	3.91 (0.49)	3.79 (0.58)	3.41 (0.58)	2.79 (0.98)
(2) Bachelor	178 (38.5%)	4.23 (0.55)	4.09 (0.61)	3.60 (0.73)	3.16 (1.09)
(3) Master/Postgraduate	157 (34%)	4.22 (0.51)	4.15 (0.51)	3.61 (0.70)	3.27 (1.06)
(4) Doctoral	5 (1.1%)	4.52 (0.54)	4.72 (0.41)	4.00 (0.68)	4.04 (1.17)
		F = 12.06 ** (3) > (1); (2) > (1)	F = 12.92 ** (4) > (1); (3) > (1); (2) > (1)	F = 3.17 * (1) < (2) and (3)	F = 6.36 ** (3) > (1); (2) > (1)
Religious Beliefs					
(1) No	287 (62.1%)	4.06 (0.52)	3.95 (0.56)	3.51 (0.62)	3.03 (1.04)
(2) Yes	175 (37.9%)	4.28 (0.55)	4.17 (0.61)	3.63 (0.78)	3.23 (1.10)
		$t = -4.38$ ** (2) > (1)	$t = -3.90$ ** (2) > (1)	$t = -1.76$	$t = -1.98$ * (2) > (1)
Monthly Salaries					
(1) Below HK$20,000	37 (8%)	3.83 (0.66)	3.68 (0.72)	3.34 (0.58)	3.03 (0.91)
(2) HK$20,000-HK$39,999	72 (15.6%)	3.86 (0.50)	3.76 (0.52)	3.19 (0.63)	2.85 (1.00)
(3) HK$40,000-HK$59,999	104 (22.5%)	4.06 (0.49)	3.94 (0.54)	3.48 (0.65)	2.96 (1.12)
(4) HK$60,000-HK$79,999	159 (34.4%)	4.28 (0.48)	4.20 (0.52)	3.72 (0.68)	3.25 (1.06)
(5) HK$80,000-HK$99,999	69 (14.9%)	4.38 (0.50)	4.21 (0.61)	3.74 (0.71)	3.27 (1.13)
(6) HK$100,000 and Above	21 (4.5%)	4.33 (0.50) F = 13.71 ** (6) > (1) and (2); (5) > (1), (2), (3); (4) > (1), (2), (3)	4.25 (0.53) F = 12.02 ** (6) > (1) and (2); (5) > (1), (2) and (3); (4) > (1), (2), (3)	3.77 (0.59) F = 8.78 ** (6) > (2); (5) > (2); (4) > (1) and (2)	3.28 (1.01) F = 2.270 * (5) > (2); (4) > (2) and (3)
Industries					
(1) Financial Services	117 (25.3%)	4.16 (0.53)	4.05 (0.62)	3.58 (0.69)	3.00 (1.09)
(2) Accounting and Auditing Firms	100 (21.6%)	4.26 (0.54)	4.13 (0.58)	3.61 (0.69)	3.14 (1.15)
(3) Real Estate and Construction	58 (12.6%)	4.05 (0.48)	4.00 (0.53)	3.48 (0.66)	3.23 (1.01)
(4) Manufacturing and Industrial	52 (11.3%)	4.18 (0.54)	4.08 (0.60)	3.52 (0.67)	3.18 (1.11)
(5) Retail and Consumer Goods	70 (15.2%)	3.97 (0.52)	3.81 (0.59)	3.43 (0.66)	3.13 (0.97)
(6) Government and Public Sector	40 (8.7%)	4.44 (0.41)	4.30 (0.46)	3.95 (0.70)	3.18 (1.08)
(7) Others	25 (5.4%)	3.77 (0.58)	3.78 (0.52)	3.23 (0.54)	2.88 (0.99)
		F = 6.77 ** (7) < (1), (2), (4) and (6); (6) > (3) and (5); (5) < (2)	F = 4.40 ** (7) < (6); (6) > (5); (5) < (2)	F = 3.82 * (6) > (3), (5) and (7)	F = 0.62

Table 4. *Cont.*

	N (%)	ORPS Operational Risk	ORPS Strategic Risk	ORPS Financial Risk	ORPS Compliance Risk
Positions					
(1) Junior Accountant/Entry-Level Accountant	49 (10.6%)	3.82 (0.61)	3.67 (0.67)	3.34 (0.56)	3.04 (0.91)
(2) Senior Accountant	56 (12.1%)	3.85 (0.51)	3.76 (0.52)	3.13 (0.62)	2.77 (1.02)
(3) Accounting Manager/Finance Manager	117 (25.3%)	4.05 (0.49)	3.90 (0.51)	3.48 (0.66)	2.98 (1.08)
(4) Internal Auditor/Compliance Officer	86 (18.6%)	4.49 (0.43)	4.38 (0.46)	3.75 (0.74)	3.40 (1.06)
(5) Controller/Financial Controller	75 (16.2%)	4.09 (0.46)	4.01 (0.56)	3.58 (0.62)	3.05 (1.07)
(6) Chief Financial Officer (CFO)/Partner	68 (14.7%)	4.44 (0.45)	4.37 (0.54)	3.90 (0.63)	3.35 (1.12)
(7) Others	11 (2.4%)	3.98 (0.43) F = 19.49 ** (6) > (1), (2), (3) and (5); (4) > (1), (2), (3), (5) and (7)	3.95 (0.42) F = 17.91 ** (6) > (1), (2), (3) and (5); (5) > (1); (4) > (1), (2), (3) and (5)	3.67 (0.65) F = 9.77 ** (6) > (1), (2) and (3); (5) > (2); (4) > (1) and (2); (3) > (2)	3.16 (1.03) F = 3.01 * (4) > (2)

Note: **: The correlations are significant at the 0.01 level (two-tailed); *: Correlations are significant at the 0.05 level (two-tailed); Note: HK$7.8 = US$1; Bonferroni post-hoc test following a one-way ANOVA.

16.3.2. Statistical Analysis of Demographic Influences

The influence of demographic factors on ESG awareness and risk perception was analysed. The key findings included the following:

- Gender: No significant differences were found in the risk perceptions or sustainability consciousness of male and female respondents. Gender does not have a significant influence on sustainability consciousness or risk perception.
- Age: Older people are more responsible, more aware of the environment and more concerned about operational risk than other respondents are. Older participants (44 years and older) demonstrated higher levels of environmental consciousness and operational risk perception, mainly because of their greater experience with and exposure to ESG issues, than did the participants in other age groups.
- Education: Higher-level education likely increases risk perception and ESG awareness. High educational attainment, particularly at the doctoral level, is associated with increased ESG awareness and risk perception. Enhanced knowledge of ESG-related issues is facilitated by high education levels.
- Work experience and salary: A positive correlation was found between work experience and ESG awareness and risk perception and between salary level and ESG awareness and risk perception. Professional experience and high income levels contribute to improved ESG awareness and ESG-related risk perception.
- Religious belief, industry and position: High levels of sustainability consciousness and risk perception were manifested by respondents who identified themselves as being religiously affiliated, those employed in the public sector or government positions and those who held senior job titles (e.g., chief finance officers and internal auditors). Thus, people's personal values, industry setting and job roles contribute to their ESG awareness and the associated risks.

16.4. Correlation Analysis

Pearson correlation analysis was used to assess the relationship between ESG awareness and organisational risk perception. Significant positive correlations were observed across all the domains (Table 5). The samples used in the correlation and regression analyses were assumed to be independent and identically distributed (iid), as the data were collected from a random sample of individuals, without significant grouping or time dependencies. The independence of the observations was also supported with diagnostic checks that included the Durbin–Watson test (statistic = 2.12). Additional tests for heteroscedasticity (White's test) and normality (Shapiro–Wilk test) further validated the assumptions of the regression model. The test results confirmed that the residuals followed a normal distribution and that there was no evidence of volatility clustering.

Table 5. Correlations between sustainability consciousness measured by the SCQ and organisational risk perception measured by the ORPS.

Correlations					
		ORPS Operational Risk	ORPS Strategic Risk	ORPS Financial Risk	ORPS Compliance Risk
SCQ Environmental	Pearson Correlation	0.58 **	0.49 **	0.36 **	0.23 **
	Sig. (2-tailed)	0.00	0.00	0.00	0.00
	Sum of Squares and Cross-Products	64.76	60.37	50.83	51.78
	Covariance	0.14	0.13	0.11	0.11
	N	462	462	462	462
SCQ Social	Pearson Correlation	0.29 **	0.29 **	0.26 **	0.17 **
	Sig. (2-tailed)	0.00	0.00	0.00	0.00
	Sum of Squares and Cross-Products	28.16	31.48	32.25	32.40
	Covariance	0.06	0.07	0.07	0.07
	N	462	462	462	462
SCQ Economic	Pearson Correlation	0.30 **	0.25 **	0.13 **	0.17 **
	Sig. (2-tailed)	0.00	0.00	0.00	0.00
	Sum of Squares and Cross-Products	33.06	29.48	18.69	37.83
	Covariance	0.07	0.06	0.04	0.08
	N	462	462	462	462
CSR Governance	Pearson Correlation	0.64 **	0.62 **	0.40 **	0.24 **
	Sig. (2-tailed)	0.00	0.00	0.00	0.00
	Sum of Squares and Cross-Products	86.46	90.57	68.57	64.33
	Covariance	0.19	0.20	0.15	0.14
	N	462	462	462	462

**: Correlation is significant at the 0.01 level (2-tailed).

16.4.1. Correlations Between ESG Awareness and Operational Risk Perception

Environmental awareness exhibited the strongest correlation with operational risk perception (r = 0.58, $p < 0.01$). Environmental consciousness is strongly linked with the recognition of operational risk. CSR–governance awareness also showed a robust correlation (r = 0.64, $p < 0.01$), suggesting the critical role of governance in managing operational risk. Although the social (r = 0.29) and economic (r = 0.30) dimensions were positively correlated, their impact was less significant. The findings confirm the need for a holistic ESG approach for understanding operational vulnerabilities.

16.4.2. Correlations Between ESG Awareness and Strategic Risk Perception

The relationship between strategic risk perception and environmental awareness was significant (r = 0.49, $p < 0.01$), thereby emphasising the importance of strategic risk management via environmentally sustainable approaches. Furthermore, CSR–governance awareness had a very strong association (r = 0.62, $p < 0.01$), drawing attention to how important governance is in assessing strategic risk. The social (r = 0.29) and economic (r = 0.25) dimensions showed moderate correlations, indicating the broad implications of ESG parameters for perceiving strategic risk.

16.4.3. Correlations Between ESG Awareness and Financial Risk Perception

All the ESG parameters are positively correlated with financial risk perception. The link between CSR–governance awareness (r = 0.40, $p < 0.01$) and environmental awareness (r = 0.36, $p < 0.01$) was the most prominent. Thus, financial risk is directly associated with governance practices and environmental components. The social (r = 0.26) and economic (r = 0.13) facets of ESG also contribute to financial risk perception, but their correlation is relatively low; these factors might be interrelated in terms of organisational financial stability.

16.4.4. Correlations Between ESG Awareness and Compliance Risk Perception

All of the ESG parameters were positively correlated with compliance risk perception; however, the associations were generally lower than those of other risk domains. The highest correlation (r = 0.24, $p < 0.01$) was found for CSR–governance awareness, underscoring the importance of governance in guaranteeing regulatory compliance. Environmental awareness was significantly correlated with compliance (r = 0.23, $p < 0.01$), suggesting that environmental elements are becoming increasingly important in ESG compliance scenarios. The social (r = 0.17) and economic (r = 0.17) components demonstrated lower correlations than the environmental conceptions did, indicating a more incidental function for these factors in the assessment of compliance risk.

16.5. Hierarchical Regression Analysis

Hierarchical regression analyses were conducted to determine how the contributing elements of demographics and ESG awareness might affect risk perception across the four aforementioned categories. These analyses emphasised the need to explore variances that could be explained by the ESG dimensions after taking into account the demographic variables.

16.5.1. Operational Risk Domain

Demographics accounted for 19% of the variance in operational risk perception, with educational level and religion being significant predictors (Table 6). This improved the model's explanatory power after the ESG dimensions were included. Environmental awareness and CSR–governance awareness explained 20% ($\Delta R^2 = 0.20$) and 9% ($\Delta R^2 = 0.09$), respectively, of the variance. Overall, the final model explained 48% of the variance, further confirming that environmental and governance factors play critical roles in operational risk perception.

Table 6. Hierarchical regression analysis result with demographics and environmental, social and governance (ESG) awareness as predictors of accountants' organisational risk perception in the operational risk domain.

Variable		β	t	F	**R**	**R^2**	**ΔR^2**	**Adjusted R^2**
Organisational Risk Perception (Operational Risk)								
Step 1				15.32 **	0.44	0.19	0.19	0.180
	Demographics							
	Age	0.25	1.59					
	Work Experience	0.05	0.47					
	Educational Level	0.16	3.68 **					
	Religion	0.15	3.61 **					
	Monthly Salaries	−0.02	−0.16					
	Industries	−0.08	−1.80					
	Positions	0.06	0.77					

Table 6. *Cont.*

Variable		*β*	*t*	*F*	R	R^2	ΔR^2	Adjusted R^2
Step 2				35.70 **	0.62	0.39	0.20	0.38
	Demographics							
	Age	0.14	1.06					
	Work Experience	0.07	0.71					
	Educational Level	0.09	2.23 *					
	Religion	0.08	2.25 *					
	Monthly Salaries	0.04	0.35					
	Industries	−0.06	−1.73					
	Positions	−0.10	−1.56					
	SCQ Environmental	0.49	12.02 **					
Step 3				32.28 **	0.63	0.39	0.01	0.38
	Demographics							
	Age	0.14	1.04					
	Work Experience	0.06	0.65					
	Educational Level	0.08	2.19 *					
	Religion	0.08	2.12 *					
	Monthly Salaries	0.05	0.41					
	Industries	−0.07	−1.82					
	Positions	−0.10	−1.58					
	SCQ Environmental	0.47	10.94 **					
	SCQ Social	0.07	1.85					
Step 4				29.83 **	0.63	0.40	0.01	0.39
	Demographics							
	Age	0.14	1.01					
	Work Experience	0.06	0.66					
	Educational Level	0.07	1.94					
	Religion	0.07	1.91					
	Monthly Salaries	0.05	0.39					
	Industries	−0.06	−1.70					
	Positions	−0.09	−1.48					
	SCQ Environmental	0.46	10.53 **					
	SCQ Social	0.04	1.05					
	SCQ Economic	0.09	2.27 *					
Step 5				38.44 **	0.70	0.48	0.09	0.47
	Demographics							
	Age	0.28	2.19 *					
	Work Experience	−0.02	−0.26					
	Educational Level	0.02	0.50					
	Religion	0.05	1.53					
	Monthly Salaries	−0.08	−0.72					
	Industries	−0.06	−1.82					
	Positions	−0.14	−2.37 *					
	SCQ Environmental	0.23	4.76 **					
	SCQ Social	0.03	0.82					
	SCQ Economic	0.07	1.84					
	CSR Governance	0.44	8.68 **					

Note: ** $p < 0.01$; * $p < 0.05$.

16.5.2. Strategic Risk Domain

Demographics accounted for 18% of the variance in strategic risk perception, with educational level being the significant predictor (Table 7). In terms of the integration of ESG dimensions to improve the model, environmental awareness accounted for an additional 12% ($\Delta R^2 = 0.12$), and CSR–governance awareness contributed 10% ($\Delta R^2 = 0.10$). The total variance of the final model was 42%. This finding further proves that environmental sustainability and governance play key roles in strategic risk management.

Table 7. Hierarchical regression analysis results with demographics and environmental, social and governance (ESG) awareness as predictors of accountants' organisational risk perception in the strategic risk domain.

Variable		β	t	F	R	R^2	ΔR^2	Adjusted R^2
Organisational Risk Perception (Strategic Risk)								
Step 1				14.47 **	0.43	0.18	0.18	0.17
	Demographics							
	Age	0.18	1.16					
	Work Experience	0.08	0.693					
	Educational Level	0.19	4.35 **					
	Religion	0.13	3.12 *					
	Monthly Salaries	−0.09	−0.65					
	Industries	−0.05	−1.26					
	Positions	0.15	2.13 *					
Step 2				24.50 **	0.55	0.30	0.12	0.29
	Demographics							
	Age	0.10	0.70					
	Work Experience	0.09	0.87					
	Educational Level	0.13	3.22 *					
	Religion	0.08	1.98 *					
	Monthly Salaries	−0.04	−0.32					
	Industries	−0.04	−1.12					
	Positions	0.03	0.47					
	SCQ Environmental	0.39	8.81 **					
Step 3				22.89 **	0.56	0.31	0.01	0.30
	Demographics							
	Age	0.10	0.66					
	Work Experience	0.08	0.78					
	Educational Level	0.13	3.17 *					
	Religion	0.07	1.81					
	Monthly Salaries	−0.03	−0.23					
	Industries	−0.05	−1.26					
	Positions	0.03	0.44					
	SCQ Environmental	0.35	7.65 **					
	SCQ Social	0.11	2.70 *					
Step 4				20.69 **	0.56	0.31	0.00	0.30
	Demographics							
	Age	0.09	0.65					
	Work Experience	0.08	0.79					
	Educational Level	0.12	3.06 *					
	Religion	0.07	1.71					
	Monthly Salaries	−0.03	−0.24					
	Industries	−0.05	−1.20					
	Positions	0.03	0.49					
	SCQ Environmental	0.34	7.42 **					
	SCQ Social	0.10	2.27 *					
	SCQ Economic	0.04	0.95					

Table 7. *Cont.*

Variable		β	t	F	R	R^2	ΔR^2	Adjusted R^2
Step 5				29.39 **	0.65	0.42	0.10	0.40
	Demographics							
	Age	0.25	1.84					
	Work Experience	−0.01	−0.15					
	Educational Level	0.06	1.64					
	Religion	0.05	1.30					
	Monthly Salaries	−0.16	−1.43					
	Industries	−0.05	−1.29					
	Positions	−0.02	−0.27					
	SCQ Environmental	0.09	1.83					
	SCQ Social	0.09	2.13 *					
	SCQ Economic	0.02	0.40					
	CSR Governance	0.48	8.95 **					

Note: ** $p < 0.01$; * $p < 0.05$.

16.5.3. Financial Risk Domain

Demographics explained 9% of the variance in financial risk perception, with professional position identified as a significant predictor (Table 8). With respect to the ESG dimensions, environmental awareness ($\Delta R^2 = 0.07$) and CSR–governance awareness ($\Delta R^2 = 0.03$) contributed to the model's explanatory power by 20%. Although the increase is less pronounced than it is in other domains, these findings still emphasise the relevance of ESG factors in financial risk assessment.

Table 8. Hierarchical regression analysis results with demographics and environmental, social and governance (ESG) awareness as predictors of accountants' organisational risk perception in the financial risk domain.

Variable		β	t	F	R	R^2	ΔR^2	Adjusted R^2
Organisational Risk Perception (Financial Risk)								
Step 1				7.79 **	0.31	0.09	0.09	0.08
	Demographics							
	Age	0.16	0.95					
	Work Experience	0.06	0.49					
	Educational Level	0.07	1.44					
	Monthly Salaries	−0.09	−0.66					
	Industries	−0.01	−0.25					
	Positions	0.19	2.47 *					
Step 2				12.15 **	0.40	0.16	0.07	0.15
	Demographics							
	Age	0.09	0.54					
	Work Experience	0.07	0.64					
	Educational Level	0.02	0.51					
	Monthly Salaries	−0.05	−0.39					
	Industries	−0.00	−0.07					
	Positions	0.10	1.30					
	SCQ Environmental	0.28	5.90 **					

Table 8. *Cont.*

Variable		β	t	F	R	R^2	ΔR^2	Adjusted R^2
Step 3				11.94	0.42	0.17	0.02	0.16
	Demographics							
	Age	0.08	0.48					
	Work Experience	0.06	0.55					
	Educational Level	0.02	0.43 *					
	Monthly Salaries	−0.04	−0.29 *					
	Industries	−0.01	−0.21					
	Positions	0.09	1.28					
	SCQ Environmental	0.23	4.72 **					
	SCQ Social	0.14	2.99 *					
Step 4				10.63 **	0.42	0.18	0.00	0.16
	Demographics							
	Age	0.08	0.49					
	Work Experience	0.06	0.55					
	Educational Level	0.02	0.49					
	Monthly Salaries	−0.04	−0.28					
	Industries	−0.01	−0.24					
	Positions	0.09	1.25					
	SCQ Environmental	0.24	4.75 **					
	SCQ Social	0.15	3.02 *					
	SCQ Economic	−0.03	−0.57					
Step 5				11.46 **	0.45	0.20	0.03	0.19
	Demographics							
	Age	0.15	0.99					
	Work Experience	0.01	0.12					
	Educational Level	−0.01	−0.23					
	Monthly Salaries	−0.11	−0.80					
	Industries	−0.01	−0.23					
	Positions	0.07	0.91					
	SCQ Environmental	0.11	1.82 *					
	SCQ Social	0.14	2.91 *					
	SCQ Economic	−0.04	−0.88					
	CSR Governance	0.25	3.97 **					

Note: ** $p < 0.01$; * $p < 0.05$.

16.5.4. Compliance Risk Domain

Demographics explained 5% of the variation in compliance risk perception, with education level identified as a key predictor (Table 9). Environmental awareness improved the model's explanatory power by only 3% ($\Delta R^2 = 0.03$), with the total variance reaching 9%. Despite the relevance of CSR–governance awareness, its effect was not statistically significant; other factors, such as regulatory frameworks, might influence compliance risk perception to a greater extent than CSR.

Table 9. Hierarchical regression analysis results with demographics and environmental, social and governance (ESG) awareness as predictors of accountants' organisational risk perception in the compliance risk domain.

Variable		β	t	F	**R**	$\mathbf{R^2}$	$\mathbf{\Delta R^2}$	**Adjusted** $\mathbf{R^2}$
Organisational Risk Perception (Compliance Risk)								
Step 1				5.97 **	0.22	0.05	0.05	0.04
	Demographics							
	Educational Level	0.17	3.58 **					
	Religion	0.07	1.61					
	Monthly Salaries	0.08	0.99					
	Positions	0.02	0.26					
Step 2				7.66 **	0.28	0.08	0.03	0.07
	Demographics							
	Educational Level	0.14	2.98 *					
	Religion	0.05	1.03					
	Monthly Salaries	0.07	0.90					
	Positions	−0.04	−0.49					
	SCQ Environmental	0.19	3.71 **					
Step 3				6.93	0.29	0.08	0.01	0.07
	Demographics							
	Educational Level	0.14	2.99 *					
	Religion	0.04	0.91					
	Monthly Salaries	0.07	0.87					
	Positions	−0.04	−0.50					
	SCQ Environmental	0.16	3.02 *					
	SCQ Social	0.09	1.76					
Step 4				6.25 **	0.30	0.09	0.00	0.07
	Demographics							
	Educational Level	0.13	2.76 *					
	Religion	0.04	0.77					
	Monthly Salaries	0.06	0.81					
	Positions	−0.03	−0.44					
	SCQ Environmental	0.15	2.77 *					
	SCQ Social	0.06	1.22					
	SCQ Economic	0.07	1.44					
Step 5				5.78 **	0.30	0.09	0.01	0.08
	Demographics							
	Educational Level	0.12	2.43 *					
	Religion	0.03	0.69					
	Monthly Salaries	0.05	−0.61					
	Positions	−0.05	−0.59					
	SCQ Environmental	0.09	1.50					
	SCQ Social	0.06	1.17					
	SCQ Economic	0.07	1.33					
	CSR Governance	0.10	1.53					

Note: ** $p < 0.01$; * $p < 0.05$.

17. Discussion

The perceptions of risks, such as operational, strategic, financial and compliance risks, of accountants employed by business entities are correlated with their ESG awareness, including their knowledge, attitudes and behaviours. The perceptions of the organisational risk of these accountants can be predicted by ESG awareness. These findings have helped solve current research gaps, further offering insights into the hypotheses developed using the theoretical framework.

17.1. ESG Awareness and Operational Risk Perception

The ESG awareness of accountants is significantly and positively correlated with their perceptions of operational risk. The environmental and governance variables of ESG are the most prominent predictors. This finding is consistent with cognitive theory (Bandura and Cervone 1986), which suggests that increased awareness can help individuals process overly complex information and anticipate possible threats.

Accountants with a deep understanding of environmental and governance issues might be able to successfully identify operational climate-related risks, such as regulatory changes, resource scarcity, ecological responsibility and extreme weather phenomena. **Risk management theory** (Kaplan and Mikes 2012) corroborates this assertion by emphasising that awareness (e.g., ESG consciousness) enables the public to detect nontraditional risks, which otherwise might not be easily captured by conventions and agreements (e.g., traditional methods of financial analyses). This conception is further supported by **stakeholder theory** (Freeman 2010; Freeman et al. 2018), especially since accountants are beginning to pay attention to the needs of different stakeholders, subsequently considering the operational impacts of environmental and governance issues.

The current study aligns with the findings of Kandpal et al. (2024) and Khan (2024), who identified governance and environmental awareness as key drivers for mitigating operational hazards. For example, taking into account cases of pollution and poor waste management as risk factors, businesses can adopt green practices and follow policy regulations simply to prevent penalties and avoid reputational harm in general (He et al. 2023). Compared with environmental awareness, other ESG factors have more indirect effects on operations (Alkaraan et al. 2022). Moreover, agency theory (Jensen and Meckling 1976) posits that ESG awareness can help reduce agency conflicts, resulting in decision-making processes that are in consonance with stakeholder expectations, particularly in relation to operational risk management.

17.2. ESG Awareness and Strategic Risk Perception

The perceptions of the strategic risk of accountants are significantly and positively correlated with their ESG awareness, with the environmental and governance variables identified as the most important. This finding supports the stakeholder theory of Freeman (2010) and Freeman et al. (2018), who emphasised the need to intricately associate corporate strategies with stakeholder interests. Previous studies (Friede et al. 2015; Eccles et al. 2014) have also revealed that ESG-aware accountants are adept at predicting risks associated with laws and regulations, market shifts, natural hazards and environmental challenges.

In behavioural decision-making theory (Trevino and Youngblood 1990), increased ESG awareness leads to enhanced ethical judgement, which can empower accountants to analyse the long-lasting results of their decisions effectively. Individuals who intensely commit to the principles of good governance and environmentalism are likely to consider risks of different forms—ethical, reputational and ecological—to ensure the application of sustainability in business decisions (Karwowski and Raulinajtys-Grzybek 2021).

Although governance and environmental awareness are the primary drivers of strategic risk perception, ethical decision-making theory (Jones 1991) supports the idea that social awareness also fosters ethical decision-making processes; however, its influence on strategic risk is indirect and might manifest only in the long term (Zumente and Bistrova 2021). Conversely, governance and environmental factors are strongly associated with immediate operational and regulatory challenges, indicating their direct effects on strategic risk perception (Scherer and Voegtlin 2020; David et al. 2024).

Although ethical decision-making concepts (Jones 1991) suggest that social consciousness is one of the triggers of ethical decision making, this is often indirect and long-term in relation to strategic risk management (Zumente and Bistrova 2021). Conversely, governance and environmental factors are likely to focus on immediate operations and regulatory challenges. These factors might have wide implications in terms of strategic risk perception (Scherer and Voegtlin 2020; David et al. 2024).

17.3. ESG Awareness and Financial Risk Perception

ESG awareness is positively correlated with the perceptions of financial risk of accountants, whereas environmental and governance factors are the most influential predictors. This trend aligns with the arguments of Friede et al. (2015), who proposed that environmental consciousness and good governance are the building blocks of financial stability and risk management. Accountants with deep governance knowledge, especially those dealing with financial reporting, regulatory compliance and ethical practices, are likely vigilant in forecasting financial risk (Pong and Fong 2023).

Risk management theory by Kaplan and Mikes (2012) suggests that accountants with enhanced ESG awareness, especially in the areas of governance and environmental concerns, are especially fully equipped to assess financial decisions with regard to their long-term viability. This level of consciousness allows accountants to detect threats, such as environmental obligations from polluting control breakdowns and civil disturbances, that otherwise might be overlooked by traditional frameworks (Comoli et al. 2023; Mooneeapen et al. 2022).

The agency theory of Jensen and Meckling (1976) also supports the aforementioned view. In particular, ESG awareness reduces institutional conflict because the decisions of accountants could be justified by the interests of many stakeholders. Although the environmental aspect of ESG is the dominant aspect of financial risk perception, the social and governance aspects also have crucial yet secondary significance in the mitigation of financial risk. Institutional theory (DiMaggio and Powell 1983) claims that social norms and institutional pressures affect accountants' perceptions of financial risk, particularly those associated with ESG issues.

17.4. ESG Awareness and Compliance Risk Perception

ESG awareness is positively correlated with the perceptions of accountants of compliance risk, and environmental awareness is the best predictor of this risk. This result confirms the findings of Hoang (2018), who identified ESG awareness as a domain for accountants to identify compliance risks, especially those related to environmental legislation and regulations. Ding et al. (2022) presented evidence that business entities with high levels of environmental awareness tend to avoid regulatory fines.

Although ESG awareness is generally positively correlated with compliance risk perception, in this study, only environmental awareness was identified as an independent predictor of compliance risk. This finding may explain why, amongst all the factors, environmental awareness is prioritised during global regulatory shifts and public scrutiny, which is consistent with the findings of Redondo Redondo Alamillos and De Mariz (2022).

Although behaviour-based decision theory by Treviño et al. (2006) suggests that governance awareness can sharpen the ethical consideration of accountants with respect to compliance, institutional theory postulates that environmental awareness is more influential because of the pressing number of regulations, including the current pressure exerted on businesses by society to underscore environmental compliance over other ESG dimensions, such as governance or social concerns. According to Gupta and Gupta (2021), increasing institutional pressures regarding sustainability have led to the popularisation of environmental legislation, thereby shifting the focal point to environmental compliance.

Accountants who have a good understanding of environment-related issues might be able to successfully identify risks related to environmental laws and standards. Jejeniwa et al. (2024) recently established that accountants who have extensive knowledge in ecology are efficient in executing compliance strategies, allowing regulatory breaches to be prevented.

17.5. Theoretical Implications

The current study has theoretical implications, even though the findings align with several theories. According to cognitive theory (Bandura and Cervone 1986), increased awareness enables accountants to detect risks, especially those that are related to the environment and governance. According to behavioural decision-making theory (Treviño et al. 2006), ESG awareness improves ethical judgement, further enabling accountants to recognise different types of risk. Stakeholder theory (Freeman 2010; Freeman et al. 2018) and agency theory (Jensen and Meckling 1976) underscore the importance for accountants of making decisions (e.g., operational and financial risk management) that are aligned with various stakeholders' expectations. Thus, ESG awareness (Kaplan and Mikes 2012) generally helps accountants exercise extra care against risks that are usually overlooked and therefore improves risk management theory. Overall, aspects of ESG awareness shape the nature of accountants' risk perceptions and decision-making processes in many ways.

17.6. Practical Implications

The results have a meaningful impact on accountants, business leaders and policymakers. The findings also underscore the importance of ESG training in educational curricula to help accountants understand how to identify and manage ESG risk. Increased ESG awareness performance leads to improved risk management and sustainable business performance. The inclusion of ESG in corporate governance frameworks underlines the basis for good ethical behaviour in risk reduction. Policymakers should consider the influence of ESG awareness on legislation and perhaps even require ESG reporting and ESG-related risk assessments to create awareness. This scheme can be achieved by enhancing good corporate behaviour, thereby contributing to the conservation of the environment. According to Friede et al. (2015), this approach can promote common and comprehensive regulations that address ESG challenges.

17.7. Conclusions

ESG awareness is crucial in influencing the risk perceptions of accountants. This study is strongly supported by cognitive theory and behavioural decision-making theory. The findings demonstrate how ESG awareness can improve risk perception in ESG metrics, leading to enhanced risk management skills. Important theoretical and practical implications can also be drawn from this research. For example, ESG promotion must be deeply emphasised in accountancy education, corporate governance and policy-making networks. A known approach for business entities is to navigate the current global market by cultivating an understanding of ESG issues amongst accountants, thereby contributing to sustainable and responsible business practices.

17.8. Limitations and Future Research

Although this study has established that ESG awareness affects risk consciousness, further research is still needed. Firstly, the survey is limited to accountants only; therefore, the applicability of the model to other practitioners of risk management is generally low. Future studies must look into major figures such as chief executive officers, board members and investors to determine how these prominent individuals might perceive risks related to their ESG awareness.

Secondly, another factor that could influence self-reported data on ESG awareness and risk perception is social desirability bias. In future research, for the findings to be confirmed and for bias to be minimised, cognitive tests and behavioural observations may be employed to objectively measure ESG awareness.

Finally, this cross-sectional study captured only a single moment—causation is difficult to ascertain. Future research may adopt longitudinal designs to assess conditions and determine how they change over time in real ESG realms. How ESG consciousness shapes risk perception is another path for research. Experimental or quasiexperimental designs may clarify the cause–effect relationship.

Author Contributions: H.-K.P. led the data collection and analysis efforts and the writing of the original draft. C.-C.F. led the funding acquisition and the writing of the original draft and its review and editing. All authors have read and agreed to the published version of the manuscript.

Funding: This research is supported by the research project funding of Corporate Social Responsibility: Perceptions and Activities (RP/FCG-01/2022) from Macao Polytechnic University.

Data Availability Statement: All the data used in this evaluation are available and can be requested from the authors. Please contact Hok-Ko Pong (author, hkpong@thei.edu.hk) for data requests.

Conflicts of Interest: The authors declare no conflicts of interest.

References

Alkaraan, Fadi, Khaldoon Albitar, Khaled Hussainey, and V. G. Venkatesh. 2022. Corporate transformation toward Industry 4.0 and financial performance: The influence of environmental, social, and governance (ESG). *Technological Forecasting & Social Change* 175: 121423. [CrossRef]

Alsaifi, Khaled, Marwa Elnahass, and Aly Salama. 2020. Market responses to firms' voluntary carbon disclosure: Empirical evidence from the United Kingdom. *Journal of Cleaner Production* 262: 121377. [CrossRef]

Apergis, Nicholas, Thomas Poufinas, and Alexandros Antonopoulos. 2022. ESG scores and cost of debt. *Energy Economics* 112: 106186. [CrossRef]

Armstrong, Anona. 2020. Ethics and ESG. *Australasian Accounting, Business and Finance Journal* 14: 6–17. [CrossRef]

Asante-Appiah, Bright, and Tamara A. Lambert. 2023. The role of the external auditor in managing environmental, social, and governance (ESG) reputation risk. *Review of Accounting Studies* 28: 2589–641. [CrossRef]

Atan, Ruhaya, Fatin Adilah Razali, Jamaliah Said, and Saunah Zainun. 2016. Environmental, social and governance (ESG) disclosure and its effect on firm's performance: A comparative study. *International Journal of Economics and Management* 10: 355–75.

Atif, Muhammad, and Searat Ali. 2021. Environmental, social and governance disclosure and default risk. *Business Strategy and the Environment* 30: 3937–59. [CrossRef]

Bacci, Silvia, Bruno Bertaccini, Ester Macrì, and Anna Pettini. 2024. Measuring sustainability consciousness in Italy. *Quality & Quantity* 58: 4751–78. [CrossRef]

Bandura, Albert, and Daniel Cervone. 1986. Differential engagement of self-reactive influences in cognitive motivation. *Organizational Behavior and Human Decision Processes* 38: 92–113. [CrossRef]

BBC News. 2017. Wells Fargo Reveals More Fake Accounts. *BBC News*, August 31. Available online: https://www.bbc.com/news/business-41113665 (accessed on 8 July 2024).

BBC News. 2022. Wirecard Trial of Executives Opens in German Fraud Scandal. *BBC News*, December 8. Available online: https://www.bbc.com/news/world-europe-63893933 (accessed on 8 July 2024).

Bearpark, Noémi També. 2022. *Deconstructing Money Laundering Risk: De-Risking, the Risk-Based Approach and Risk Communication*, 1st ed. Cham: Springer International Publishing AG. [CrossRef]

Berglund, Teresa, Niklas Gericke, Jelle Boeve-de Pauw, Daniel Olsson, and Tzu-Chau Chang. 2020. A cross-cultural comparative study of sustainability consciousness between students in Taiwan and Sweden. *Environment, Development and Sustainability* 22: 6287–313. [CrossRef]

Bhandari, Krishna Raj, Mikko Ranta, and Jari Salo. 2022. The resource-based view, stakeholder capitalism, ESG, and sustainable competitive advantage: The firm's embeddedness into ecology, society, and governance. *Business Strategy and the Environment* 31: 1525–37. [CrossRef]

Caiazza, Stefano, Giuseppe Galloppo, and Viktoriia Paimanova. 2021. The role of sustainability performance after merger and acquisition deals in short and long-term. *Journal of Cleaner Production* 314: 127982. [CrossRef]

Carattini, Stefano, Edgar Hertwich, Givi Melkadze, and Jeffrey G. Shrader. 2022. Mandatory disclosure is key to address climate risks. *Science* 378: 352–54. [CrossRef]

Chairani, Chairani, and Sylvia Veronica Siregar. 2021. The effect of enterprise risk management on financial performance and firm value: The role of environmental, social and governance performance. *Meditari Accountancy Research* 29: 647–70. [CrossRef]

Chen, Hsiao-Min, Tsai-Chi Kuo, and Ju-Long Chen. 2022. Impacts on the ESG and financial performances of companies in the manufacturing industry based on the climate change related risks. *Journal of Cleaner Production* 380: 134951. [CrossRef]

Chen, Simin, Yu Song, and Peng Gao. 2023. Environmental, social, and governance (ESG) performance and financial outcomes: Analyzing the impact of ESG on financial performance. *Journal of Environmental Management* 345: 118829. [CrossRef]
Comoli, Maurizio, Patrizia Tettamanzi, and Michael Murgolo. 2023. Accounting for 'ESG'under disruptions: A systematic literature network analysis. *Sustainability* 15: 6633. [CrossRef]
Damodaran, Aswath. 2007. *Strategic Risk Taking: A Framework for Risk Management*. Philadelphia: Wharton School Publishing.
David, Lemuel Kenneth, Jianling Wang, Vanessa Angel, and Meiling Luo. 2024. Environmental commitments and Innovation in China's corporate landscape: An analysis of ESG governance strategies. *Journal of Environmental Management* 349: 119529. [CrossRef]
Dechow, Patricia M. 2023. Understanding the sustainability reporting landscape and research opportunities in accounting. *The Accounting Review* 98: 481–93. [CrossRef]
DiMaggio, Paul J., and Walter W. Powell. 1983. The iron cage revisited: Institutional isomorphism and collective rationality in organizational fields. *American Sociological Review* 48: 147–60. [CrossRef]
Ding, Xiangan, Andrea Appolloni, and Mohsin Shahzad. 2022. Environmental administrative penalty, corporate environmental disclosures and the cost of debt. *Journal of Cleaner Production* 332: 129919. [CrossRef]
Eccles, Robert G., Ioannis Ioannou, and George Serafeim. 2014. The impact of corporate sustainability on organizational processes and performance. *Management Science* 60: 2835–57. [CrossRef]
El Khoury, Rim, Nohade Nasrallah, and Bahaaeddin Alareeni. 2023. ESG and financial performance of banks in the MENAT region: Concavity–convexity patterns. *Journal of Sustainable Finance & Investment* 13: 406–30.
Faccia, Alessio, Francesco Manni, and Fabian Capitanio. 2021. Mandatory ESG reporting and XBRL taxonomies combination: ESG ratings and income statement, a sustainable value-added disclosure. *Sustainability* 13: 8876. [CrossRef]
Freeman, R. Edward. 2010. *Strategic Management: A Stakeholder Approach*. Cambridge: Cambridge University Press.
Freeman, R. Edward, Jeffrey S. Harrison, and Stelios Zyglidopoulos. 2018. *Stakeholder Theory: Concepts and Strategies*. Cambridge: Cambridge University Press.
Friede, Gunnar, Timo Busch, and Alexander Bassen. 2015. ESG and financial performance: Aggregated evidence from more than 2000 empirical studies. *Journal of Sustainable Finance & Investment* 5: 210–33.
Galletta, Simona, John W. Goodell, Sebastiano Mazzù, and Andrea Paltrinieri. 2023. Bank reputation and operational risk: The impact of ESG. *Finance Research Letters* 51: 103494. [CrossRef]
Gericke, Niklas, Jelle Boeve-de Pauw, Teresa Berglund, and Daniel Olsson. 2019. The Sustainability Consciousness Questionnaire: The theoretical development and empirical validation of an evaluation instrument for stakeholders working with sustainable development. *Sustainable Development* 27: 35–49. [CrossRef]
Gupta, Amit Kumar, and Narain Gupta. 2021. Environment practices mediating the environmental compliance and firm performance: An institutional theory perspective from emerging economies. *Global Journal of Flexible Systems Management* 22: 157–78. [CrossRef]
Hassanein, Ahmed, Ahmed Bani-Mustafa, and Khalil Nimer. 2024. A country's culture and reporting of sustainability practices in energy industries: Does a corporate sustainability committee matter? *Humanities and Social Sciences Communications* 11: 1140. [CrossRef]
He, Xu, Qinlei Jing, and Hao Chen. 2023. The impact of environmental tax laws on heavy-polluting enterprise ESG performance: A stakeholder behavior perspective. *Journal of Environmental Management* 344: 118578. [CrossRef]
Hoang, Thinh. 2018. The Role of the Integrated Reporting in Raising Awareness of Environmental, Social and Corporate Governance (ESG) Performance. In *Stakeholders, Governance and Responsibility*. Bingley: Emerald Publishing Limited, vol. 14, pp. 47–69. [CrossRef]
Hubbard, Douglas W. 2020. *The Failure of Risk Management: Why It's Broken and How to Fix It*, 2nd ed. Hoboken: Wiley. [CrossRef]
Ishak, Nurul Diana Intan Zafirah, and Arnifa Asmawi. 2022. Integrating ESG Framework in Corporate Strategic Planning: A Proposed Case Study of a Technology Hub Developer. *Journal of Logistics, Informatics and Service Science* 9: 53–63.
Jackson, Gregory, Julia Bartosch, Emma Avetisyan, Daniel Kinderman, and Jette Steen Knudsen. 2020. Mandatory Non-financial Disclosure and Its Influence on CSR: An International Comparison. *Journal of Business Ethics* 162: 323–42. [CrossRef]
Jejeniwa, Temitayo Oluwaseun, Noluthando Zamanjomane Mhlongo, and Titilola Olaide Jejeniwa. 2024. The role of ethical practices in accounting: A review of corporate governance and compliance trends. *Finance & Accounting Research Journal* 6: 707–20.
Jensen, Michael C., and William H. Meckling. 1976. Theory of the firm: Managerial behavior, agency costs and ownership structure. *Journal of Financial Economics* 3: 305–60. [CrossRef]
Jones, Thomas M. 1991. Ethical decision making by individuals in organizations: An issue-contingent model. *Academy of Management Review* 16: 366–95. [CrossRef]
Kandpal, Vinay, Anshuman Jaswal, Ernesto DR Santibanez Gonzalez, and Naveen Agarwal. 2024. *Sustainable Energy Transition: Circular Economy and Sustainable Financing for Environmental, Social and Governance (ESG) Practices*. Cham: Springer Nature. [CrossRef]
Kaplan, Robert S., and Anette Mikes. 2012. Managing risks: A new framework. *Harvard Business Review* 90: 48–60.
Karwowski, Mariusz, and Monika Raulinajtys-Grzybek. 2021. The application of corporate social responsibility (CSR) actions for mitigation of environmental, social, corporate governance (ESG) and reputational risk in integrated reports. *Corporate Social Responsibility and Environmental Management* 28: 1270–84. [CrossRef]
Kazancoglu, Ipek, Muhittin Sagnak, Sachin Kumar Mangla, and Yigit Kazancoglu. 2021. Circular economy and the policy: A framework for improving the corporate environmental management in supply chains. *Business Strategy and the Environment* 30: 590–608. [CrossRef]

Khan, Tariqullah. 2024. Circular-ESG Model for Regenerative Transition. *Sustainability* 16: 7549. [CrossRef]

Kim, Sol, Geul Lee, and Hyoung-Goo Kang. 2021. Risk management and corporate social responsibility. *Strategic Management Journal* 42: 202–30. [CrossRef]

Landi, Giovanni Catello, Francesca Iandolo, Antonio Renzi, and Andrea Rey. 2022. Embedding sustainability in risk management: The impact of environmental, social, and governance ratings on corporate financial risk. *Corporate Social Responsibility and Environmental Management* 29: 1096–107. [CrossRef]

Lee, Jooh, Kyungyeon Koh, and Eunsup Daniel Shim. 2024. Managerial incentives for ESG in the financial services industry: Direct and indirect association between ESG and executive compensation. *Managerial Finance* 50: 10–27. [CrossRef]

Lee, Lee Siew, and Mansor Isa. 2020. Environmental, Social and Governance (ESG) Practices and Performance in Shariah Firms: Agency or Stakeholder Theory? *Asian Academy of Management Journal of Accounting and Finance* 16: 1–34. [CrossRef]

Lennard, Jacob B., and Robin W. Roberts. 2023. The accounting profession, corporate social responsibility, and ethics. In *Research Handbook on Accounting and Ethics*. Cheltenham: Edward Elgar Publishing, pp. 35–49.

Leung, Tiffany Cheng-Han, and You Shi Xiang. 2022. The general overview of environmental, social, and governance (ESG) guidelines in Hong Kong: Past, present, and future. In *Comparative CSR and Sustainability*. London: Routledge, pp. 345–63.

Liang, Lin, and Yan Li. 2023. The double-edged sword effect of organizational resilience on ESG performance. *Corporate Social Responsibility and Environmental Management* 30: 2852–72. [CrossRef]

Liang, Yi, Min Jae Lee, and Jin Sup Jung. 2022. Dynamic capabilities and an ESG strategy for sustainable management performance. *Frontiers in Psychology* 13: 887776. [CrossRef]

Lisi, Irene Eleonora. 2018. Determinants and performance effects of social performance measurement systems. *Journal of Business Ethics* 152: 225–51. [CrossRef]

Liu, Min, Tongji Guo, Weiying Ping, and Liangqing Luo. 2023. Sustainability and stability: Will ESG investment reduce the return and volatility spillover effects across the Chinese financial market? *Energy Economics* 121: 106674. [CrossRef]

MacNeil, Iain, and Irene-Marié Esser. 2022. From a financial to an entity model of ESG. *European Business Organization Law Review* 23: 9–45. [CrossRef]

Moffitt, Jacquelyn Sue, Jeanne-Claire Alyse Patin, and Luke Watson. 2024. Corporate environmental, social, and governance (ESG) performance and the internal control environment. *Accounting Horizons* 38: 103–24. [CrossRef]

Mooneeapen, Oren, Subhash Abhayawansa, and Naushad Mamode Khan. 2022. The influence of the country governance environment on corporate environmental, social and governance (ESG) performance. *Sustainability Accounting, Management and Policy Journal* 13: 953–85. [CrossRef]

Ni, Jiahao. 2024. Research On Compliance Risk Identification and Prevention Mechanism of Enterprises in The ESG Field. *Highlights in Science, Engineering and Technology* 85: 1294–99. [CrossRef]

Nilipour, Tabatabaei A., Tracy-Anne De Silva, and Xuedong Li. 2020. The Readability of Sustainability Reporting in New Zealand over time. *Australasian Accounting, Business & Finance Journal* 14: 86–107. [CrossRef]

Nocco, Brian W., and René M. Stulz. 2006. Enterprise risk management: Theory and practice. *Journal of Applied Corporate Finance* 18: 8–20. [CrossRef]

Nugroho, Deinera P. D., Yi Hsu, Christian Hartauer, and Andreas Hartauer. 2024. Investigating the Interconnection between Environmental, Social, and Governance (ESG), and Corporate Social Responsibility (CSR) Strategies: An Examination of the Influence on Consumer Behavior. *Sustainability* 16: 614. [CrossRef]

Oh, Hyun Jung, Byoungkwan Lee, Hye Hyun Ma, Dayeoun Jang, and Sejin Park. 2024. A preliminary study for developing perceived ESG scale to measure public perception toward organizations' ESG performance. *Public Relations Review* 50: 102398. [CrossRef]

Park, So Ra, and Jae Young Jang. 2021. The impact of ESG management on investment decision: Institutional investors' perceptions of country-specific ESG criteria. *International Journal of Financial Studies* 9: 48. [CrossRef]

Pollman, Elizabeth. 2019. *Corporate Social Responsibility, ESG, and Compliance. Forthcoming, Cambridge Handbook of Compliance*. Edited by D. Daniel Sokol and Benjamin van Rooij. Loyola Law School, Los Angeles Legal Studies Research Paper, (2019-35). Cambridge: Cambridge University Press.

Pong, Hok-Ko, and Chun-Cheong Fong. 2023. The Associations of Spirituality, Adversity Quotient and Ethical Decision Making of Accounting Managers in the Contexts of Financial Management and Corporate Social Responsibility. *Sustainability* 15: 14287. [CrossRef]

Pong, Hok-Ko, and Chun-Cheong Fong. 2024. The Impact of Personal Satisfaction on the Environmental, Social, and Governance Practices of Chinese Accounting Managers. *Sustainability* 16: 5839. [CrossRef]

Raghavan, Kamala. 2022. ESG reporting impact on accounting, finance. *Journal of Global Awareness* 3: 9. [CrossRef]

Ramos, Jessica, Ella Adler, and Erietta Exarchopoulou. 2024. How to maintain a strong compliance function in a remote/hybrid working environment, using ESG as both the objective and the driver. *Journal of Financial Compliance* 8: 43–53.

Redondo Alamillos, Rocío, and Frédéric De Mariz. 2022. How can European regulation on ESG impact business globally? *Journal of Risk and Financial Management* 15: 291. [CrossRef]

Saari, Ulla A., Svenja Damberg, Lena Frömbling, and Christian M. Ringle. 2021. Sustainable consumption behavior of Europeans: The influence of environmental knowledge and risk perception on environmental concern and behavioral intention. *Ecological Economics* 189: 107155. [CrossRef]

Sadaf, Rabeea, Judit Oláh, József Popp, and Domicián Máté. 2018. An investigation of the influence of the worldwide governance and competitiveness on accounting fraud cases: A cross-country perspective. *Sustainability* 10: 588. [CrossRef]
Sassen, Remmer, Anne-Kathrin Hinze, and Inga Hardeck. 2016. Impact of ESG factors on firm risk in Europe. *Journal of Business Economics* 86: 867–904. [CrossRef]
Scherer, Andreas Georg, and Christian Voegtlin. 2020. Corporate governance for responsible innovation: Approaches to corporate governance and their implications for sustainable development. *Academy of Management Perspectives* 34: 182–208. [CrossRef]
Schwartz, Mark S. 2016. Ethical Decision-Making Theory: An Integrated Approach. *Journal of Business Ethics* 139: 755–76. [CrossRef]
Shakil, Mohammad Hassan. 2021. Environmental, social and governance performance and financial risk: Moderating role of ESG controversies and board gender diversity. *Resources Policy* 72: 102144. [CrossRef]
Sheedy, Elizabeth, Le Zhang, and Kenny Chi Ho Tam. 2019. Incentives and culture in risk compliance. *Journal of Banking & Finance* 107: 105611.
Singhania, Monica, and Neha Saini. 2023. Institutional framework of ESG disclosures: Comparative analysis of developed and developing countries. *Journal of Sustainable Finance & Investment* 13: 516–59.
Solaimani, Sam. 2024. From Compliance to Capability: On the Role of Data and Technology in Environment, Social, and Governance. *Sustainability* 16: 6061. [CrossRef]
South, David, Kaitlyn Zolton, and Andy Trump. 2021. Expanded climate risk disclosure requirements by the security and exchange commission. *Climate and Energy* 38: 1–12. [CrossRef]
Sulkowski, Adam, and Ruth Jebe. 2022. Evolving ESG reporting governance, regime theory, and proactive law: Predictions and strategies. *American Business Law Journal* 59: 449–503. [CrossRef]
The Guardian. 2010. BP Oil Spill: Timeline of Events. *The Guardian*, April 20. Available online: https://www.theguardian.com/environment/2010/jun/29/bp-oil-spill-timeline-deepwater-horizon (accessed on 8 July 2024).
The Guardian. 2018. Brazil Dam Disaster: Firm Knew of Potential Impact Months in Advance. *The Guardian*, March 1. Available online: https://www.theguardian.com/world/2018/feb/28/brazil-dam-collapse-samarco-fundao-mining (accessed on 8 July 2024).
The Guardian. 2019. Facebook to Pay $5bn Fine as Regulator Settles Cambridge Analytica Complaint. *The Guardian*, July 24. Available online: https://www.theguardian.com/technology/2019/jul/24/facebook-to-pay-5bn-fine-as-regulator-files-cambridge-analytica-complaint (accessed on 8 July 2024).
The Guardian. 2021a. Boohoo Accused of Failing to Improve Working Conditions in Its Supply Chain. *The Guardian*, June 18. Available online: https://www.theguardian.com/business/2021/jun/18/boohoo-accused-of-failing-to-improve-working-conditions-in-its-supply-chain (accessed on 8 July 2024).
The Guardian. 2021b. What Did Greensill Capital Actually Do? *The Guardian*, April 15. Available online: https://www.theguardian.com/commentisfree/2021/apr/15/what-did-greensill-capital-actually-do (accessed on 8 July 2024).
The New York Times. 2019. Boeing 737 Max: What's Happened After the 2 Deadly Crashes. *The New York Times*, October 28. Available online: https://www.nytimes.com/interactive/2019/business/boeing-737-crashes.html (accessed on 8 July 2024).
Trevino, Linda K., and Stuart A. Youngblood. 1990. Bad Apples in Bad Barrels: A Causal Analysis of Ethical Decision-Making Behavior. *Journal of Applied Psychology* 75: 378–85. [CrossRef]
Treviño, Linda K., Gary R. Weaver, and Scott J. Reynolds. 2006. Behavioral ethics in organizations: A review. *Journal of Management* 32: 951–90. [CrossRef]
Tsang, Albert, Tracie Frost, and Huijuan Cao. 2023. Environmental, Social, and Governance (ESG) disclosure: A literature review. *The British Accounting Review* 55: 101149. [CrossRef]
Turker, Duygu. 2009. Measuring Corporate Social Responsibility: A Scale Development Study. *Journal of Business Ethics* 85: 411–27. [CrossRef]
Yu, Ellen Pei-Yi, Christine Qian Guo, and Bac Van Luu. 2018. Environmental, social and governance transparency and firm value. *Business Strategy and the Environment* 27: 987–1004. [CrossRef]
Yu, Wenjun, Yu Gu, and Jun Dai. 2023. Industry 4.0-enabled environment, social, and governance reporting: A case from a Chinese energy company. *Journal of Emerging Technologies in Accounting* 20: 245–58. [CrossRef]
Zaporowska, Zuzanna, and Marek Szczepański. 2024. The Application of Environmental, Social and Governance Standards in Operational Risk Management in SSC in Poland. *Sustainability* 16: 2413. [CrossRef]
Zhao, Donghui. 2022. ESG risk management and compliance practices in China. *Law and Economy* 1: 27–32. [CrossRef]
Ziolo, Magdalena, Beata Zofia Filipiak, Iwona Bąk, and Katarzyna Cheba. 2019. How to design more sustainable financial systems: The roles of environmental, social, and governance factors in the decision-making process. *Sustainability* 11: 5604. [CrossRef]
Ziolo, Magdalena, Iwona Bąk, and Anna Spoz. 2023. Incorporating ESG risk in companies' business models: State of research and energy sector case studies. *Energies* 16: 1809. [CrossRef]
Zumente, Ilze, and Jūlija Bistrova. 2021. ESG importance for long-term shareholder value creation: Literature vs. practice. *Journal of Open Innovation* 7: 127. [CrossRef]

Journal of
Risk and Financial Management

MDPI

Article

Bayesian Lower and Upper Estimates for Ether Option Prices with Conditional Heteroscedasticity and Model Uncertainty

Tak Kuen Siu

Department of Actuarial Studies and Business Analytics, Macquarie Business School, Macquarie University, Sydney, NSW 2109, Australia; ken.siu@mq.edu.au or ktksiu2005@gmail.com; Tel.: +61-2-9850-8589

Abstract: This paper aims to leverage Bayesian nonlinear expectations to construct Bayesian lower and upper estimates for prices of Ether options, that is, options written on Ethereum, with conditional heteroscedasticity and model uncertainty. Specifically, a discrete-time generalized conditional autoregressive heteroscedastic (GARCH) model is used to incorporate conditional heteroscedasticity in the logarithmic returns of Ethereum, and Bayesian nonlinear expectations are adopted to introduce model uncertainty, or ambiguity, about the conditional mean and volatility of the logarithmic returns of Ethereum. Extended Girsanov's principle is employed to change probability measures for introducing a family of alternative GARCH models and their risk-neutral counterparts. The Bayesian credible intervals for "uncertain" drift and volatility parameters obtained from conjugate priors and residuals obtained from the estimated GARCH model are used to construct Bayesian superlinear and sublinear expectations giving the Bayesian lower and upper estimates for the price of an Ether option, respectively. Empirical and simulation studies are provided using real data on Ethereum in AUD. Comparisons with a model incorporating conditional heteroscedasticity only and a model capturing ambiguity only are presented.

Keywords: ether options; Bayesian nonlinear expectations; Bayesian lower and upper estimates; conditional heteroscedasticity; model uncertainty

1. Introduction

Cryptocurrency options are important instruments for managing risks of trading cryptocurrencies, speculating and leveraging future performances of cryptocurrencies. Bitcoin options, whose underlying assets could be Bitcoin or Bitcoin futures, appear to be the most popular among different cryptocurrency options. Indeed, Bitcoin options are less than ten years old. The first Bitcoin options were launched by Deribit (crypto options and futures exchange for Bitcoin and Ethereum) in 2016, while the first regulated Bitcoin option exchange is LedgerX, which started offering products in 2017. In the aftermath of the enlightening year of 2019 for the cryptocurrency derivatives market, other players started to roll out Bitcoin options. Some of them include Bakkt, CME, Bit.com, OKEx, Binance and Huobi futures. See Yang (2021) for related discussions and more detail about the history of the cryptocurrency derivatives market.

The highly volatile cryptocurrency market poses significant challenges to the valuation of cryptocurrency options. Some researchers have taken up the challenges and proposed quantitative models for pricing cryptocurrency options. Specifically, the uses of stochastic volatility and GARCH type models for pricing Bitcoin options have received considerable attention in the literature (see, for example, (Chen and Yang 2024; Hou et al. 2020; Jalan et al. 2021; Siu and Elliott 2021; Venter and Maré 2021)). Jump-diffusion models for pricing Bitcoin options have also been considered (see, for example, (Cao and Celik 2021; Hilliard and Ngo 2022)). The uses of machine learning techniques and neural networks for pricing Bitcoin options or cryptocurrency options were considered in (Alexander et al. 2023; Li et al. 2019; Pagnottoni 2019). Alexander et al. (2023) considered the valuation of crypto quanto and inverse options. Lucic (2024) discussed the pricing and hedging of cryptocurrency inverse options. Siu (2024) considered an application of finite-mixture models to pricing Bitcoin options.

While Bitcoin is the largest cryptocurrency in terms of market capitalization, Ethereum (ETH) is the second largest cryptocurrency. The history of the blockchain technology backing Ethereum can be traced back to its creation by Vitalik Buterin in 2013, which was then launched in 2015 (see Copeland (2023)). Ether options, which are also called ETH options, are option contracts written on Ethereum. OKEx and CME launched Ether options in 2020 and 2022, respectively (see Godbole (2020) and Chan (2022)). CME also offered options written on Ether futures. According to McGleenon (2024), the trading volume of Ether options has surged to around USD 20 billion in January 2024. However, there is a relatively small amount of studies on the pricing of Ether options compared with those on the valuation of Bitcoin options. Some works on the pricing of Ether options include, for example, Shegokar (2022) for jump-diffusion stochastic volatility models and Brini and Lenz (2024) for a machine learning regression approach.

Modelling the return dynamics of cryptocurrencies is a challenging task. This is particularly the case in light of the impact of the pandemic. It is imperative to take into account model uncertainty, or ambiguity, about the return dynamics of cryptocurrencies (see, for example, Siu (2023a)). Early works on option pricing with model uncertainty focus on incorporating volatility uncertainty. Specifically, Boyle and Ananthanarayanan (1977) introduced a Bayesian approach to incorporate volatility uncertainty into option pricing. Avellaneda et al. (1995) and Lyons (1995) introduced volatility uncertainty for pricing and hedging options through "uncertain" volatility, where volatility is assumed to take on values in a bounded interval. These works seem to have provided a practical ground for the developments of nonlinear G-expectations, including the work by Peng (1997), which gives a mathematically sound approach to describe volatility uncertainty. Some other works on option pricing with model uncertainty, or volatility uncertainty in particular, include, for example, (Agarwal et al. 2021; Beissner and Riedel 2019; Boyle et al. 2008; Buraschi and Jiltsov 2006; Chau et al. 2022; Cohen and Tegnér 2019; Cont 2006; Elliott et al. 2022; Fouque and Ren 2014; Jaroszkowski and Jensen 2022; Siu 2023a; Wilmott and Oztukel 1998). It does not seem that the impacts of model uncertainty on pricing cryptocurrency options have been well explored or well understood up to now.

This paper aims to leverage Bayesian nonlinear expectations introduced in the work of Siu (2023a) to construct Bayesian lower and upper estimates for the price of an Ether option, that is, an option on Ethereum, in the presence of conditional heteroscedasticity and model uncertainty. Specifically, a discrete-time generalized conditional autoregressive heteroscedastic (GARCH) model introduced by Bollerslev (1986) and Taylor (1986) is adopted to describe conditional heteroscedasticity in the logarithmic returns of Ethereum. To incorporate model uncertainty or ambiguity about the conditional mean and volatility of the logarithmic returns, a pair of Bayesian nonlinear expectations, that is, a Bayesian superlinear expectation and a Bayesian sublinear expectation, are used to construct the Bayesian lower and upper estimates for the price of the Ether option. Firstly, using an extended Girsanov's principle in discrete time, which is also called a discrete-time Girsanov's transform (see (Elliott and Madan 1998; Elliott and Siu 2017; Elliott et al. 1995; Siu 2023a)), a family of alternative models capturing model uncertainty about the conditional mean and volatility is introduced via perturbing the conditional mean and volatility of the GARCH model. Then, applying a "risk-neutral" extended Girsanov's principle to the family of alternative models results in a family of "risk-neutralized" alternative GARCH models. Lastly, using Bayesian credible intervals obtained from conjugate priors and residuals obtained from the estimated GARCH model, Bayesian conditional superlinear and sublinear expectations are constructed, which give the Bayesian lower and upper estimates for the price of the Ether option, respectively. Empirical and simulation studies are provided using real data on Ethereum in AUD (ETH-AUD). The impacts of model uncertainty, conditional heteroscedasticity and their interactions on the Ether option prices are explored by comparing different models.

Boyle and Ananthanarayanan (1977) seem to have been among the first to propose a Bayesian approach to incorporate model uncertainty, particularly volatility uncertainty, into option valuation. Other papers on the use of Bayesian statistics in option pricing include, for example, (Bauwens and Lubrano 2002; Darsinos and Satchell 2007; Foster and Whiteman 1999; Gzyl et al. 2022; Ho et al. 2011; Jang and Lee 2019; Karolyi 1993; Martin et al. 2005; Mozumder et al. 2021; Qin and Almeida 2020; Romboutsa and Stentoft 2014; Wang et al. 2016). Bayesian option pricing under GARCH-type models or stochastic volatility models were considered in (Bauwens and Lubrano 2002; Martin et al. 2005; Mozumder et al. 2021; Romboutsa and Stentoft 2014; Wang et al. 2016). However, it seems that those papers did not use Bayesian nonlinear expectations to describe the impacts of model uncertainty, or ambiguity, about the conditional mean and volatility on estimates for option prices. Furthermore, those papers did not consider the pricing of options on cryptocurrencies such as Ethereum. Siu (2001) considered the use of Bayesian statistics to construct Bayesian credible intervals for coherent risk measures of derivative securities under discrete-time binomial tree models. (Siu et al. 2001, 2004b) proposed the use of Bayesian statistics to construct Bayesian coherent risk measures and Bayesian Value at Risk, respectively, for derivative securities. However, these papers considered risk measures for derivative securities instead of option pricing. They did not consider cryptocurrencies.

The current paper may be thought of as a companion paper of the work of Siu (2023a). In Siu (2023a), the Bayesian nonlinear expectations were applied to provide lower and upper forecasts for Bitcoin returns and to construct lower and upper estimates for tail-based risk metrics, namely Value at Risk and Expected Shortfall, for a Bitcoin position. However, Siu (2023a) did not discuss the use of Bayesian nonlinear expectations for option valuation in general, or pricing Ether options in particular. Now, in the current paper, I endeavour to use the Bayesian nonlinear expectations for constructing Bayesian lower and upper estimates for the price of an Ether option. The current paper also aims to provide novel insights into advancing the understanding for the impacts of model uncertainty, conditional heteroscedasticity and their interactions on Ether option prices through the lens of the Bayesian nonlinear expectations. To this end, the Bayesian lower and upper estimates are interpreted as the "confidence" limits of Bayesian interval estimates for the price of an Ether option along the line of Boyle and Ananthanarayanan (1977). From the perspective of two-price conic finance (Cherny and Madan 2009; Elliott et al. 2022; Madan 2015, 2016; Madan and Cherny 2010), one may explore the possibility of studying a Bayesian version of lower and upper prices of an Ether option using the Bayesian lower and upper estimates. One may also explore the possibility of developing a Bayesian version of nonlinear valuation operators, for example, (Coque et al. 2002; Peng 2004a 2004b, 2004c, 2005). These will be briefly discussed as potential topics for further research in Section 8.

The rest of the paper is organized in the following manner. Section 2 presents a GARCH model without incorporating model uncertainty, namely a reference model, for the dynamics of the logarithmic returns from Ethereum. Then, the pricing of an Ether option under the GARCH model is discussed by reviewing some existing results on GARCH option pricing using an extended Girsanov's principle. In Section 3, the family of alternative GARCH models and its risk-neutralization were introduced using the extended Girsanov's principle, and lower and upper estimates for the price of the Ether option are constructed using nonlinear expectations. In Section 4, the Bayesian lower and upper estimates for the price of the Ether option are constructed using the Bayesian conditional superlinear and sublinear expectations, respectively. The numerical and simulation procedures are presented in Section 5. The empirical and simulation results are discussed in Section 6. Model comparisons are also presented in Section 6. The chaotic and random aspects of price fluctuations are briefly commented in Section 7. Concluding remarks are provided, and some limitations of the proposed approach are discussed in Section 8. Some potential topics for further research are briefly discussed in Section 8.

2. The GARCH Model without Model Uncertainty

A simple discrete-time market consisting of two underlying securities, namely a risk-free (zero-coupon) bond and a risky asset, that is, Ethereum, is considered. The logarithmic return process of Ethereum is modelled by a discrete-time GARCH model. Specifically, we start with a reference model under a real-world reference probability measure for the logarithmic return process of Ethereum in AUD (ETH-AUD). To simplify the discussion and notation, a GARCH(1,1) model for the logarithmic return process is considered. This simple set up can be generalized to a higher-order GARCH model. A discrete-time Girsanov's transform in, for example, Elliott et al. (1995) and Elliott and Madan (1998), is used to specify a risk-neutral probability measure for valuing an Ether option under the reference GARCH(1,1) model. A discrete-time Girsanov's transform was employed to specify an equivalent martingale measure for option pricing under discrete-time GARCH-type models (see, for example, Badescu et al. (2008) and Badescu et al. (2011)). Here, we state some relevant results and include the proofs for some of them using the results found in the work of Elliott et al. (1995). This section may serve as a recap on some existing results on GARCH option pricing in the literature. They are included here for the sake of completeness.

Let $\mathbb{T}$ denote the (finite) time parameter set $\{1, 2, \cdots, T\}$ of our discrete-time model, where $T < \infty$. A complete probability space $(\Omega, \mathcal{F}, \mathbb{P})$ is considered on which random processes are defined, where $\mathbb{P}$ is a reference (real-world) probability measure on the measurable space $(\Omega, \mathcal{F})$. $\mathbb{P}$ is interpreted as the real-world probability measure underlying the reference model, which is also called an approximating model. A sequence of independent and identically distributed (i.i.d.) standard normal random variables under $\mathbb{P}$, namely $\{\epsilon_t\}_{t\in\mathbb{T}}$, is considered. In general, one may consider a sequence of i.i.d. non-normal random variables. However, for illustration, a sequence of i.i.d. normal random variables is considered here. Write $\{Y_t\}_{t\in\mathbb{T}}$ for a time series process on $(\Omega, \mathcal{F}, \mathbb{P})$, which represents the logarithmic return process of Ethereum in AUD. That is, for each $t \in \mathbb{T}$, Y_t denotes the logarithmic return of Ethereum in AUD over the tth period. Assume that the reference model for the logarithmic return process $\{Y_t\}_{t\in\mathbb{T}}$ under $\mathbb{P}$ is governed by the GARCH(1,1) model:

$$\begin{aligned} Y_t &= \mu_Y + \sqrt{h_t}\epsilon_t, \\ h_t &= \omega + \alpha h_{t-1}\epsilon_{t-1}^2 + \beta h_{t-1}. \end{aligned} \tag{1}$$

Here, μ_Y is the mean return; h_t is the conditional variance when given the price information up to and including time t; ω, α and β are the parameters in the conditional variance process; and h_0 is a given constant.

In the sequel, a risk-neutral probability measure is specified using a discrete-time Girsanov's transform. Let $\phi_{\mu,\sigma^2}(\cdot)$ denote the probability density function (pdf) of a normal distribution with mean μ and variance σ^2. Write $\phi(\cdot)$ for $\phi_{0,1}(\cdot)$. That is, $\phi(\cdot)$ is the pdf of a standard normal distribution with zero mean and unit variance (i.e., $N(0,1)$). Let $\mathbb{F}$ denote the $\mathbb{P}$-augmentation of the natural filtration $\{\mathcal{F}_t\}_{t\in\mathbb{T}}$ generated by the logarithmic return process $\{Y_t\}_{t\in\mathbb{T}}$. That is, for each $t \in \mathbb{T}$, the σ-field $\mathcal{F}_t$ represents the information set generated by the observations $\{Y_1, Y_2, \ldots, Y_t\}$ about the logarithmic return process up to and including time t.

For each $t \in \mathbb{T}$, define the notation $\mu_Y^{\dagger}(t)$ by

$$\mu_Y^{\dagger}(t) := r - \frac{1}{2}h_t. \tag{2}$$

Then, an $\mathbb{F}$-adapted process, denoted by $\{\lambda_t^\dagger\}_{t\in\mathbb{T}}$, is defined by putting

$$\lambda_t^\dagger := \frac{\phi_{\mu_Y^\dagger(t),h_t}(Y_t)}{\phi_{\mu_Y,h_t}(Y_t)} = \frac{\phi(\frac{Y_t-\mu_Y^\dagger(t)}{\sqrt{h_t}})}{\phi(\frac{Y_t-\mu_Y}{\sqrt{h_t}})}. \tag{3}$$

Furthermore, another $\mathbb{F}$-adapted process, $\{\Lambda_t^\dagger\}_{t\in\mathbb{T}}$, is defined as follows:

$$\Lambda_t^\dagger := \prod_{k=1}^{t} \lambda_k^\dagger. \tag{4}$$

By definition, $\{\Lambda_t^\dagger\}_{t\in\mathbb{T}}$ is a positive-valued process. It is also an $(\mathbb{F},\mathbb{P})$-martingale. Consequently, a probability measure $\mathbb{P}^\dagger$, which is equivalent to $\mathbb{P}$ on $\mathcal{F}_T$, is defined by setting

$$\left.\frac{d\mathbb{P}^\dagger}{d\mathbb{P}}\right|_{\mathcal{F}_T} := \Lambda_T^\dagger. \tag{5}$$

Then, the following lemma provides the conditional distribution of Y_{t+1} when given $\mathcal{F}_t$ under the probability measure $\mathbb{P}^\dagger$.

Lemma 1. *Under the probability measure $\mathbb{P}^\dagger$, the conditional distribution of Y_{t+1}, given that $\mathcal{F}_t$ is a normal distribution with mean $r-\frac{1}{2}h_{t+1}$ and variance h_{t+1}. That is, $Y_{t+1}|\mathcal{F}_t \sim N(r-\frac{1}{2}h_{t+1}, h_{t+1})$.*

Proof. The proof follows some results or arguments in the work of Elliott et al. (1995) (Chapter 3 therein). Using a version of the Bayes' rule, the martingale property of $\{\Lambda_t^\dagger\}_{t\in\mathbb{T}}$, Equation (4), the law of iterated expectations, and the fact that $\Lambda_t^\dagger$ is $\mathcal{F}_t$-measurable,

$$\begin{aligned}
\mathbb{P}^\dagger(Y_{t+1}\le y|\mathcal{F}_t) &= \mathrm{E}^\dagger[I_{\{Y_{t+1}\le y\}}|\mathcal{F}_t] = \frac{\mathrm{E}[\Lambda_T^\dagger I_{\{Y_{t+1}\le y\}}|\mathcal{F}_t]}{\mathrm{E}[\Lambda_T^\dagger|\mathcal{F}_t]} \\
&= \frac{\mathrm{E}[\Lambda_T^\dagger I_{\{Y_{t+1}\le y\}}|\mathcal{F}_t]}{\Lambda_t^\dagger} = \frac{\mathrm{E}\{\mathrm{E}[\Lambda_T^\dagger I_{\{Y_{t+1}\le y\}}|\mathcal{F}_{t+1}]|\mathcal{F}_t\}}{\Lambda_t^\dagger} \\
&= \frac{\mathrm{E}\{I_{\{Y_{t+1}\le y\}}\mathrm{E}[\Lambda_T^\dagger|\mathcal{F}_{t+1}]|\mathcal{F}_t\}}{\Lambda_t^\dagger} \\
&= \mathrm{E}[(\Lambda_t^\dagger)^{-1}\Lambda_{t+1}^\dagger I_{\{Y_{t+1}\le y\}}|\mathcal{F}_t] \\
&= \mathrm{E}[\lambda_{t+1}^\dagger I_{\{Y_{t+1}\le y\}}|\mathcal{F}_t].
\end{aligned} \tag{6}$$

Here, $\mathbb{E}[\cdot|\mathcal{F}_t]$ is the conditional expectation given $\mathcal{F}_t$ under $\mathbb{P}$; $\mathrm{E}^\dagger[\cdot|\mathcal{F}_t]$ is the conditional expectation given $\mathcal{F}_t$ under $\mathbb{P}^\dagger$. Recall that $\{\epsilon_t\}_{t\in\mathbb{T}} \overset{i.i.d.}{\sim} N(0,1)$ under the real-world reference probability measure $\mathbb{P}$. This, together with Equation (1), imply that $Y_{t+1}|\mathcal{F}_t \sim N(\mu_Y, h_{t+1})$. Then, by Equations (3) and (6),

$$\begin{aligned}
\mathbb{P}^\dagger(Y_{t+1}\le y|\mathcal{F}_t) &= \mathrm{E}[\lambda_{t+1}^\dagger I_{\{Y_{t+1}\le y\}}|\mathcal{F}_t] \\
&= \int_{-\infty}^{y} \frac{\phi_{\mu_Y^\dagger(t+1),h_{t+1}}(z)}{\phi_{\mu_Y,h_{t+1}}(z)}\phi_{\mu_Y,h_{t+1}}(z)dz \\
&= \int_{-\infty}^{y} \phi_{\mu_Y^\dagger(t+1),h_{t+1}}(z)dz.
\end{aligned} \tag{7}$$

Recall that $\phi_{\mu_Y^\dagger(t+1),h_{t+1}}(\cdot)$ is the pdf of a normal distribution with mean $\mu_Y^\dagger(t+1)$ and variance h_{t+1}. Consequently, by Equation (7), $Y_{t+1}|\mathcal{F}_t \sim N(\mu_Y^\dagger(t+1), h_{t+1})$. Note from Equation (2) that $\mu_Y^\dagger(t+1) = r-\frac{1}{2}h_{t+1}$. Hence, the result follows. □

By the fundamental theorem of asset pricing, the absence of arbitrage opportunities in a financial market is "essentially" equivalent to the existence of an equivalent martingale measure under which the discounted price process of an asset relative to a numeraire asset is a martingale (see, for example, Delbaen and Schachermayer (1994); Hansen and Richard (1987); Harrison and Kreps (1979); Harrison and Pliska (1981, 1983)). Let $\{B_t\}_{t\in\mathbb{T}}$ denote the price process of a risk-free (zero-coupon) bond with the constant continuously compounded interest rate $r > 0$. Then, for each $t \in \mathbb{T}$,

$$B_t = e^{rt}. \tag{8}$$

The bond is the numeraire asset used for discounting.

Let $\{S_t\}_{t\in\mathbb{T}}$ denote the price process of Ethereum in AUD, where S_t is the adjusted close price of Ethereum in AUD in the tth period (i.e., the tth trading day). Let S_0 denote the initial price at the beginning of the first period. Then, $S_t = S_{t-1}\exp(Y_t)$, for each $t \in \mathbb{T}$. The following theorem shows that the discounted price process $\{B_t^{-1}S_t\}_{t\in\mathbb{T}}$ of Ethereum in AUD by the bond is an $(\mathbb{F}, \mathbb{P}^\dagger)$-martingale.

Theorem 1. *$\{B_t^{-1}S_t\}_{t\in\mathbb{T}}$ is an $(\mathbb{F}, \mathbb{P}^\dagger)$-martingale.*

Proof. It suffices to prove that

$$\mathrm{E}^\dagger[B_{t+1}^{-1}S_{t+1}|\mathcal{F}_t] = B_t^{-1}S_t. \tag{9}$$

The result is then followed by induction.
From Lemma 1, the moment-generating function of Y_{t+1} given $\mathcal{F}_t$ under $\mathbb{P}^\dagger$ evaluated at u is

$$\mathrm{E}^\dagger[e^{uY_{t+1}}|\mathcal{F}_t] = \exp\left[\left(r - \frac{1}{2}h_{t+1}\right)u + \frac{1}{2}u^2 h_{t+1}\right]. \tag{10}$$

Setting $u = 1$ in Equation (10) gives

$$\mathrm{E}^\dagger[e^{Y_{t+1}}|\mathcal{F}_t] = e^r. \tag{11}$$

From Equations (8), (9) and (11),

$$\begin{aligned} \mathrm{E}^\dagger[B_{t+1}^{-1}S_{t+1}|\mathcal{F}_t] &= \mathrm{E}^\dagger[e^{-r(t+1)}S_t e^{Y_{t+1}}|\mathcal{F}_t] = e^{-r(t+1)}S_t\mathrm{E}^\dagger[e^{Y_{t+1}}|\mathcal{F}_t] \\ &= e^{-rt}S_t = B_t^{-1}S_t. \end{aligned} \tag{12}$$

This completes the proof. □

From Theorem 1, $\mathbb{P}^\dagger$ is an equivalent martingale measure, which is a risk-neutral probability measure selected by the discrete-time Giransov's transform.

Let $\{\epsilon_t^\dagger\}_{t\in\mathbb{T}}$ denote a sequence of i.i.d. standard normal random variables under the probability measure $\mathbb{P}^\dagger$. Then, from Lemma 1, under $\mathbb{P}^\dagger$,

$$Y_{t+1} = r - \frac{1}{2}h_{t+1} + \sqrt{h_{t+1}}\epsilon_{t+1}^\dagger. \tag{13}$$

Write, for each $t \in \mathbb{T}$,

$$\eta_t := r - \mu_Y - \frac{1}{2}h_t. \tag{14}$$

Then, by comparing the real-world and risk-neutral dynamics for $\{Y_t\}_{t\in\mathbb{T}}$ in Equation (1) and Equation (13), respectively,

$$\epsilon_t = \frac{\eta_t}{\sqrt{h_t}} + \epsilon_t^{\dagger}. \tag{15}$$

Using Equation (15) and the conditional variance process in Equation (1),

$$h_t = \omega + \alpha h_{t-1}\left(\frac{\eta_{t-1}}{\sqrt{h_{t-1}}} + \epsilon_{t-1}^{\dagger}\right)^2 + \beta h_{t-1}. \tag{16}$$

Putting together Equations (13) and (16), under the risk-neutral probability measure $\mathbb{P}^{\dagger}$, the logarithmic return process $\{Y_t\}_{t\in\mathbb{T}}$ has the following GARCH dynamics:

$$\begin{aligned} Y_t &= r - \frac{1}{2}h_t + \sqrt{h_t}\epsilon_t^{\dagger}, \\ h_t &= \omega + \alpha h_{t-1}\left(\frac{\eta_{t-1}}{\sqrt{h_{t-1}}} + \epsilon_{t-1}^{\dagger}\right)^2 + \beta h_{t-1}. \end{aligned} \tag{17}$$

Note that the market described by the discrete-time GARCH model is incomplete. Consequently, there are many equivalent martingale measures under the discrete-time GARCH model. The risk-neutral probability measure $\mathbb{P}^{\dagger}$ selected by the discrete-time Girsanov's transform is one of them.

There are other approaches to specify an equivalent martingale measure under a discrete-time GARCH model and their variants. Duan (1995) introduced the locally risk-neutral valuation relationship for option pricing under a discrete-time GARCH model. Siu et al. (2004a) adopted the conditional Esscher transform to select an equivalent martingale measure under discrete-time GARCH models. Elliott et al. (2006) and Siu et al. (2006) discussed the use of the conditional Esscher transform or its variants for pricing European-style options under a discrete-time Markov-switching GARCH model and a discrete-time SETAR-ARCH model, respectively. The self-exciting threshold autoregressive (SETAR) model pioneered by (Tong 1977, 1983, 1990) is one of the major classes of parametric nonlinear time series models. Siu and Elliott (2021) studied the valuation of Bitcoin options under a discrete-time SETAR-GARCH model using the conditional Esscher transform and the variance-dependent pricing kernel.

3. Model Uncertainty via Nonlinear Expectations

In this section, model uncertainty about the conditional mean and volatility of the logarithmic returns of Ethereum is introduced using an extended Girsanov's principle under the GARCH model in Section 2. Nonlinear expectations are then used to construct lower and upper estimates for the price of an Ether option in light of the model uncertainty. To this end, the following three steps are considered:

(I) Using an extended Girsanov's principle, as in (Elliott 2017; Elliott and Siu 2017; Siu 2023a), a family of alternative GARCH models is introduced by perturbing the conditional mean and volatility of the reference GARCH model in Equation (1).

(II) As in Section 2, a "risk-neutral" extended Girsanov's principle is adopted to transform the family of alternative GARCH models into a family of "risk-neutralized" alternative GARCH models.

(III) A pair of conditional nonlinear expectations, namely a conditional superlinear expectation and a conditional sublinear expectation, is constructed based on the family of "risk-neutralized" GARCH alternative models. The conditional superlinear and sublinear expectations then give the lower and upper estimates for the price of an Ether option, respectively.

3.1. A Family of Alternative Models

Step (I) is now considered. Cryptocurrency markets are highly volatile and uncertain. Modelling price fluctuations of cryptocurrencies could be a formidable task. Consequently, model uncertainty is an important and relevant issue as far as the modelling of price fluctuations of cryptocurrencies is concerned. In practice, the mean (or drift) and the volatility of the logarithmic returns are two quantities which interest market practitioners. In the context of a discrete-time GARCH model, the two quantities of interest are the conditional mean and volatility. Accurate modelling or estimation of the conditional mean and volatility of the logarithmic returns of cryptocurrencies could be difficult in practice. Consequently, from a practical perspective, a relevant issue could be how might the model uncertainty, or ambiguity, of the conditional mean and volatility be incorporated.

When faced with model uncertainty, or ambiguity, about the conditional mean and volatility, market practitioners may form interval estimates for misspecifications in the conditional mean and volatility. These interval estimates give the ranges of the "uncertain" parameters, describing the misspecifications in the conditional mean and volatility. Specifically, as in Siu (2023a), a two-dimensional vector of "uncertain" parameters, denoted by $\boldsymbol{\theta}$, describing the misspecifications in the conditional mean and volatility under the GARCH model in Equation (1), is defined as follows:

$$\boldsymbol{\theta} := (\mu, \sigma)^\top \in \Re \times \Re_+. \tag{18}$$

Indeed, μ and σ describe perturbations in the conditional mean and volatility of the logarithmic return process $\{Y_t\}_{t \in \mathbb{T}}$ under the reference GARCH model in Equation (1). μ is the "uncertain" parameter describing the misspecification in the conditional mean (or drift), and σ is the "uncertain" parameter describing the misspecification in the conditional volatility. Specifically, if $\mu = 0$ and $\sigma = 1$, there will be no perturbations/misspecification in the conditional mean and volatility of the logarithmic return process $\{Y_t\}_{t \in \mathbb{T}}$. $\mathbf{y}^\top$ denotes the transpose of a vector, or a matrix, $\mathbf{y}$.

For practical purposes, the interval estimates for misspecifications in the conditional mean and volatility should be finite intervals. Consequently, it may not be unreasonable to assume that the perturbations in the conditional mean and volatility do not take infinite values. This assumption may also be in line with the specifications of the g-expectation for the drift uncertainty in Peng (1997) and the G-expectation for the volatility uncertainty in Peng (2006, 2019). Specifically, the vector of the "uncertain" parameters $\boldsymbol{\theta}$ in Equation (18) takes on values in the following rectangular region $\boldsymbol{\Theta}$ in $\Re \times \Re_+$:

$$\boldsymbol{\Theta} := [\mu^L, \mu^U] \times [\sigma^L, \sigma^U], \tag{19}$$

for $\mu^L, \mu^U \in \Re$ and $\sigma^L, \sigma^U \in \Re_+$ such that $\mu^L < \mu^U$ and $\sigma^L < \sigma^U$. Specifically, μ^L and μ^U are, respectively, the lower and upper limits of the interval estimate for the "uncertain" parameter μ, while σ^L and σ^U are, respectively, the lower and upper limits of the interval estimate for the "uncertain" parameter σ.

To capture volatility uncertainty in continuous time, Avellaneda et al. (1995) and Lyons (1995) introduced an "uncertain" volatility parameter and supposed that the "uncertain" volatility parameter lies in an interval whose lower and upper limits could be specified based on the extreme values of the implied volatilities of liquid securities or the high–low peaks of historical volatilities. To incorporate both drift and volatility uncertainties in continuous time, Wilmott and Oztukel (1998) and Wilmott (2007) introduced both the "uncertain" drift and volatility parameters and supposed that they lie in the respective intervals whose lower and upper limits are pre-specified. They called the intervals for the "uncertain" parameters "certainty bands". Agarwal et al. (2021) incorporated the model uncertainty about the market price of risk in a continuous-time model with multiple risk factors and adopted an ellipsoid-shaped set instead of a rectangular set to specify a statistical confidence region for the "uncertain" market price of risk. The ambiguity specified by an ellipsoid-shaped set is called an elliptical ambiguity, while the ambiguity specified by a rectangular set is called a rectangular ambiguity. The elliptical ambiguity was also considered in Cohen and Tegnér (2019). Siu (2023b) applied some asymptotic results of the maximum likelihood estimates for transition probabilities for the Markov chain to specify the lower and upper limits for the perturbations/misspecifications in the transition rates of the chain.

The aforementioned works considered the incorporation of model uncertainty in continuous time, whereas the incorporation of model uncertainty in discrete time is considered here. Indeed, as noted in Elliott and Siu (2017) and Siu (2023a), besides some advantages from an econometric perspective, in a discrete-time modelling framework, volatility uncertainty can be incorporated via the use of an extended Girsanov's principle for changing probability measures. Unlike the continuous-time situation where singular probability measures are involved (e.g., Peng (1997) and Fouque and Ren (2014)), the use of an extended Girsanov's principle involves absolutely continuous changes in probability measures, and it provides a streamlined approach to incorporate volatility uncertainty. Furthermore, in (Agarwal et al. 2021; Avellaneda et al. 1995; Lyons 1995; Wilmott 2007; Wilmott and Oztukel 1998), "uncertain" parameters were introduced to directly describe the ambiguity of the model parameters, such as the drift, volatility, and market price of risk, whereas, as in Siu (2023a), the "uncertain" parameters are introduced here to describe the perturbations/misspecifications in the conditional mean and volatility. Lastly, in some of the existing literature, confidence limits are specified by market information, such as the extreme values of implied volatilities, pre-specified or specified by classical statistical approaches. However, the confidence limits are to be specified here using Bayesian credible intervals along the lines of Boyle and Ananthanarayanan (1977) and Siu (2023a). This will be discussed in more detail in Section 4.

For each $\boldsymbol{\theta} \in \boldsymbol{\Theta}$, let $\{\lambda_t(\boldsymbol{\theta})\}_{t\in\mathbb{T}}$ denote an $\mathbb{F}$-adapted process on $(\Omega, \mathcal{F}, \mathbb{P})$ defined by putting

$$\lambda_t(\boldsymbol{\theta}) := \frac{\phi_{\mu,\sigma^2}(\epsilon_t)}{\phi(\epsilon_t)} = \frac{\phi(\frac{\epsilon_t-\mu}{\sigma})}{\sigma\phi(\epsilon_t)}, \tag{20}$$

where $\{\epsilon_t\}_{t\in\mathbb{T}} \stackrel{i.i.d.}{\sim} N(0,1)$ under the reference probability measure $\mathbb{P}$ as defined in the last section (Section 2).

For each $\boldsymbol{\theta} \in \boldsymbol{\Theta}$, the $\mathbb{F}$-adapted process $\{\Lambda_t(\boldsymbol{\theta})\}_{t\in\mathbb{T}}$ is defined as follows:

$$\Lambda_t(\boldsymbol{\theta}) := \prod_{k=1}^{t} \lambda_k(\boldsymbol{\theta}). \tag{21}$$

By definition, for each $\boldsymbol{\theta} \in \boldsymbol{\Theta}$, $\{\Lambda_t(\boldsymbol{\theta})\}_{t\in\mathbb{T}}$ is a positive-valued process. It is also an $(\mathbb{F}, \mathbb{P})$-martingale. Consequently, it can be used as a density process for changing probability measures in discrete time. Then, for each $\boldsymbol{\theta} \in \boldsymbol{\Theta}$, a probability measure $\mathbb{P}^{\boldsymbol{\theta}}$ equivalent to $\mathbb{P}$ on $\mathcal{F}_T$ is defined by putting

$$\left.\frac{d\mathbb{P}^{\boldsymbol{\theta}}}{d\mathbb{P}}\right|_{\mathcal{F}_T} := \Lambda_T(\boldsymbol{\theta}). \tag{22}$$

By a discrete-time Girsanov's theorem (see, for example, Elliott et al. (1995) and Elliott and Madan (1998)), for each $\boldsymbol{\theta} \in \boldsymbol{\Theta}$, $\{\epsilon_t(\boldsymbol{\theta})\}_{t\in\mathbb{T}}$ is defined by putting:

$$\epsilon_t(\boldsymbol{\theta}) := \frac{\epsilon_t - \mu}{\sigma}, \tag{23}$$

which is a sequence of i.i.d. standard normal random variables under the newly defined probability measure $\mathbb{P}^{\boldsymbol{\theta}}$ in Equation (22).

The family $\{\epsilon(\boldsymbol{\theta})|\boldsymbol{\theta} \in \boldsymbol{\Theta}\}$ indexed by $\boldsymbol{\Theta}$, where $\epsilon(\boldsymbol{\theta}) := \{\epsilon_t(\boldsymbol{\theta})\}_{t\in\mathbb{T}}$, defines a family of sequences of Gaussian "uncertain" noises. From Equations (17) and (23), for each $\boldsymbol{\theta} \in \boldsymbol{\Theta}$, under $\mathbb{P}^{\boldsymbol{\theta}}$, the logarithmic return process $\{Y_t\}_{t\in\mathbb{T}}$ is governed by

$$\begin{aligned} Y_t &= \mu_Y + \mu\sqrt{h_t} + \sigma\sqrt{h_t}\epsilon_t(\boldsymbol{\theta}), \\ h_t &= \omega + \alpha h_{t-1}(\mu + \sigma\epsilon_{t-1}(\boldsymbol{\theta}))^2 + \beta h_{t-1}. \end{aligned} \tag{24}$$

When $\boldsymbol{\theta} := (\mu, \sigma)^\top$ varies in $\boldsymbol{\Theta}$, a family of alternative GARCH models having the form in Equation (24) is defined under a family of probability measures $\{\mathbb{P}^{\boldsymbol{\theta}}|\boldsymbol{\theta} \in \boldsymbol{\Theta}\}$. Borrowing some terminologies from relativity in physics, each of the alternative GARCH models may be considered a reference frame to describe the dynamics of the logarithmic returns. The reference GARCH model in Equation (1) may also be thought of as a reference frame as it is included in the family of alternative GARCH models. In other words, the dynamics of the logarithmic returns are described by a family of reference frames. They may be thought of as "equivalent" reference frames in the sense that they are described by a family of equivalent probability measures.

3.2. Risk-Neutralization

In this subsection, Step (II) is considered. For each $\boldsymbol{\theta} \in \boldsymbol{\Theta}$ and each $t \in \mathbb{T}$, let

$$\mu_Y^{\boldsymbol{\theta}}(t) := \mu_Y + \mu\sqrt{h_t}. \tag{25}$$

Then, an $\mathbb{F}$-adapted process $\{\lambda_t^\dagger(\boldsymbol{\theta})\}_{t\in\mathbb{T}}$ is defined by putting

$$\lambda_t^\dagger(\boldsymbol{\theta}) := \frac{\phi_{\mu_Y^\dagger(t),\sigma^2 h_t}(Y_t)}{\phi_{\mu_Y^{\boldsymbol{\theta}}(t),\sigma^2 h_t}(Y_t)} = \frac{\phi(\frac{Y_t - \mu_Y^\dagger(t)}{\sigma\sqrt{h_t}})}{\phi(\frac{Y_t - \mu_Y^{\boldsymbol{\theta}}(t)}{\sigma\sqrt{h_t}})}, \tag{26}$$

where $\mu_Y^\dagger(t)$ and $\mu_Y^{\boldsymbol{\theta}}(t)$ are given by Equations (2) and (25), respectively.

From Equation (26), for each $\boldsymbol{\theta} \in \boldsymbol{\Theta}$, an $\mathbb{F}$-adapted process $\{\Lambda_t^\dagger(\boldsymbol{\theta})\}_{t\in\mathbb{T}}$ is defined by putting

$$\Lambda_t^\dagger(\boldsymbol{\theta}) := \prod_{k=1}^{t} \lambda_k^\dagger(\boldsymbol{\theta}). \tag{27}$$

Note that for each $\boldsymbol{\theta} \in \boldsymbol{\Theta}$, $\{\Lambda_t^\dagger(\boldsymbol{\theta})\}_{t\in\mathbb{T}}$ is a positive-valued $(\mathbb{F}, \mathbb{P}^{\boldsymbol{\theta}})$-martingale. Consequently, for each $\boldsymbol{\theta} \in \boldsymbol{\Theta}$, a new probability measure $\mathbb{P}^\dagger(\boldsymbol{\theta})$, which is equivalent to $\mathbb{P}^{\boldsymbol{\theta}}$ on $\mathcal{F}_T$, is defined by setting

$$\left.\frac{d\mathbb{P}^\dagger(\boldsymbol{\theta})}{d\mathbb{P}^{\boldsymbol{\theta}}}\right|_{\mathcal{F}_T} := \Lambda_T^\dagger(\boldsymbol{\theta}). \tag{28}$$

Using arguments similar to the proof of Lemma 1, it can be shown that for each $\boldsymbol{\theta} \in \boldsymbol{\Theta}$, under the probability measure $\mathbb{P}^\dagger(\boldsymbol{\theta})$, the conditional distribution of Y_{t+1} with $\mathcal{F}_t$ given is a normal distribution with mean $\mu_Y^\dagger(t+1) := r - \frac{1}{2}h_{t+1}$ and variance $\sigma\sqrt{h_{t+1}}$. Similarly to Equation (13), for each $\boldsymbol{\theta} \in \boldsymbol{\Theta}$, under $\mathbb{P}^\dagger(\boldsymbol{\theta})$,

$$Y_{t+1} = r - \frac{1}{2}h_{t+1} + \sigma\sqrt{h_{t+1}}\epsilon_{t+1}^\dagger(\boldsymbol{\theta}), \tag{29}$$

where $\{\epsilon_t^\dagger(\boldsymbol{\theta})\}_{t\in\mathbb{T}} \overset{i.i.d.}{\sim} N(0,1)$ under $\mathbb{P}^\dagger(\boldsymbol{\theta})$.

For each $\boldsymbol{\theta} \in \boldsymbol{\Theta}$ and each $t \in \mathbb{T}$, let

$$\eta_t(\boldsymbol{\theta}) := r - \mu_Y - \frac{1}{2}h_t - \mu\sqrt{h_t}. \tag{30}$$

Comparing the dynamics for $\{Y_t\}_{t\in\mathbb{T}}$ in Equation (24) and those in Equation (29) gives

$$\epsilon_t(\boldsymbol{\theta}) = \frac{\eta_t(\boldsymbol{\theta})}{\sigma\sqrt{h_t}} + \epsilon_t^{\dagger}(\boldsymbol{\theta}). \tag{31}$$

Substituting Equation (31) into the conditional variance process in Equation (24) gives

$$h_t = \omega + \alpha h_{t-1}\left(\mu + \frac{\eta_{t-1}(\boldsymbol{\theta})}{\sqrt{h_{t-1}}} + \sigma\epsilon_{t-1}^{\dagger}(\boldsymbol{\theta})\right)^2 + \beta h_{t-1}. \tag{32}$$

Putting together Equations (29) and (32), for each $\boldsymbol{\theta} \in \boldsymbol{\Theta}$, under $\mathbb{P}^{\dagger}(\boldsymbol{\theta})$, the logarithmic return process $\{Y_t\}_{t\in\mathbb{T}}$ has the following dynamics:

$$\begin{aligned} Y_t &= r - \frac{1}{2}h_t + \sigma\sqrt{h_t}\epsilon_t^{\dagger}(\boldsymbol{\theta}), \\ h_t &= \omega + \alpha h_{t-1}\left(\mu + \frac{\eta_{t-1}(\boldsymbol{\theta})}{\sqrt{h_{t-1}}} + \sigma\epsilon_{t-1}^{\dagger}(\boldsymbol{\theta})\right)^2 + \beta h_{t-1}. \end{aligned} \tag{33}$$

Using arguments similar to the proof of Theorem 1 and Equation (33), it can be shown that for each $\boldsymbol{\theta} \in \boldsymbol{\Theta}$, the discounted price process of ETH-AUD, i.e., $\{B_t^{-1}S_t\}_{t\in\mathbb{T}}$, is an $(\mathbb{F}, \mathbb{P}^{\dagger}(\boldsymbol{\theta}))$-martingale. Consequently, for each $\boldsymbol{\theta} \in \boldsymbol{\Theta}$, $\mathbb{P}^{\dagger}(\boldsymbol{\theta})$ is a "risk-neutral" probability measure. It defines a "risk-neutralized" alternative GARCH model in Equation (33), which incorporates the impact of model uncertainty about the conditional mean and volatility via the vector of the "uncertain" parameters $\boldsymbol{\theta} := (\mu, \sigma)^{\top} \in \boldsymbol{\Theta}$. Then, the family of "risk-neutral" probability measures $\{\mathbb{P}^{\dagger}(\boldsymbol{\theta})|\boldsymbol{\theta} \in \boldsymbol{\Theta}\}$ defines a family of "risk-neutralized" alternative GARCH models, each having the form in Equation (33).

3.3. *Lower and Upper Estimates for Ether Option Prices*

Step (III) is considered in this subsection. A European-style Ether option with maturity at time T and payoff described by a random variable X on $(\Omega, \mathcal{F}, \mathbb{P})$ is considered. Assume that the random variable X is $\mathcal{F}_T^Y$-measurable and integrable under the probability measure $\mathbb{P}$. That is, $\mathrm{E}[|X|] < \infty$.

For each $\boldsymbol{\theta} \in \boldsymbol{\Theta}$, let $\mathrm{E}^{\boldsymbol{\theta},\dagger}[\cdot|\mathcal{F}_t]$ denote the conditional expectation given $\mathcal{F}_t$ under a "risk-neutral" probability measure $\mathbb{P}^{\dagger}(\boldsymbol{\theta})$. Then, an $\mathbb{F}$-adapted process $\{X_t^{\boldsymbol{\theta}}\}_{t\in\mathbb{T}}$ is defined by putting

$$\frac{X_t^{\boldsymbol{\theta}}}{B_t} := \mathrm{E}^{\boldsymbol{\theta},\dagger}\left[\frac{X}{B_T}|\mathcal{F}_t\right]. \tag{34}$$

From Equation (34), for each $\boldsymbol{\theta} \in \boldsymbol{\Theta}$, $\{\frac{X_t^{\boldsymbol{\theta}}}{B_t}\}_{t\in\mathbb{T}}$ is an $(\mathbb{F}, \mathbb{P}^{\dagger}(\boldsymbol{\theta}))$-martingale. For a given $\boldsymbol{\theta} \in \boldsymbol{\Theta}$, if $\{X_t^{\boldsymbol{\theta}}\}_{t\in\mathbb{T}}$ is taken as a price process of the Ether option, and then the discounted price process of the Ether option $\{\frac{X_t^{\boldsymbol{\theta}}}{B_t}\}_{t\in\mathbb{T}}$ is an $(\mathbb{F}, \mathbb{P}^{\dagger}(\boldsymbol{\theta}))$-martingale, where the numeraire asset for the discounting is chosen to be the bond.

The conditional superlinear and sublinear expectations for the discounted payoff of the Ether option $\frac{X}{B_T}$ with respect to the family of "risk-neutral" probability measures $\{\mathbb{P}^{\dagger}(\boldsymbol{\theta})|\boldsymbol{\theta} \in \boldsymbol{\Theta}\}$ are now defined. Specifically, for each $t \in \mathbb{T}$, given $\mathcal{F}_t$, the conditional superlinear expectation for $\frac{X}{B_T}$ with respect to $\{\mathbb{P}^{\dagger}(\boldsymbol{\theta})|\boldsymbol{\theta} \in \boldsymbol{\Theta}\}$, denoted by $\mathcal{E}_{\boldsymbol{\Theta},L}[B_T^{-1}X|\mathcal{F}_t]$, is defined as follows:

$$\mathcal{E}_{\boldsymbol{\Theta},L}[B_T^{-1}X|\mathcal{F}_t] := \mathrm{ess} - \inf_{\boldsymbol{\theta}\in\boldsymbol{\Theta}} \mathrm{E}^{\boldsymbol{\theta},\dagger}[B_T^{-1}X|\mathcal{F}_t], \tag{35}$$

where the essential infimum ess $-$ inf is taken over $\boldsymbol{\theta} \in \boldsymbol{\Theta}$.

Similarly, for each $t \in \mathbb{T}$, given $\mathcal{F}_t$, the conditional sublinear expectation for $\frac{X}{B_T}$ with respect to $\{\mathbb{P}^{\dagger}(\boldsymbol{\theta})|\boldsymbol{\theta} \in \boldsymbol{\Theta}\}$, denoted by $\mathcal{E}_{\boldsymbol{\Theta},U}[B_T^{-1}X|\mathcal{F}_t]$, is defined as follows:

$$\mathcal{E}_{\boldsymbol{\Theta},U}[B_T^{-1}X|\mathcal{F}_t] := \text{ess} - \sup_{\boldsymbol{\theta} \in \boldsymbol{\Theta}} \mathrm{E}^{\boldsymbol{\theta},\dagger}[B_T^{-1}X|\mathcal{F}_t], \tag{36}$$

where the essential supremum ess − sup is taken over $\boldsymbol{\theta} \in \boldsymbol{\Theta}$.

Note that the conditional sublinear expectation in Equation (36) satisfies the following five properties:

(i) **Measurability:** For any integrable random variable $X \in \mathcal{F}_t$ (i.e., X is an integrable, $\mathcal{F}_t$-measurable random variable),

$$\mathcal{E}_{\boldsymbol{\Theta},U}[X|\mathcal{F}_t] = X. \tag{37}$$

(ii) **Monotonicity:** For any two integrable random variables $X, Z \in \mathcal{F}_T$, satisfying $X := X(\omega) \geq Z := Z(\omega)$ for all $\omega \in \Omega$,

$$\mathcal{E}_{\boldsymbol{\Theta},U}[X|\mathcal{F}_t] \geq \mathcal{E}_{\boldsymbol{\Theta},U}[Z|\mathcal{F}_t]. \tag{38}$$

(iii) **Translation Invariance:** For any two integrable random variables $X \in \mathcal{F}_T$ and $C \in \mathcal{F}_t$,

$$\mathcal{E}_{\boldsymbol{\Theta},U}[X + C|\mathcal{F}_t] = \mathcal{E}_{\boldsymbol{\Theta},U}[X|\mathcal{F}_t] + C. \tag{39}$$

(iv) **Positive Homogeneity:** For any two integrable random variables $X \in \mathcal{F}_T$ and $\Lambda \in \mathcal{F}_t$ such that $\Lambda := \Lambda(\omega) \geq 0$, for all $\omega \in \Omega$,

$$\mathcal{E}_{\boldsymbol{\Theta},U}[\Lambda X|\mathcal{F}_t] = \Lambda \mathcal{E}_{\boldsymbol{\Theta},U}[X|\mathcal{F}_t]. \tag{40}$$

(v) **Sub-additivity:** For any two integrable random variables $X, Z \in \mathcal{F}_T$,

$$\mathcal{E}_{\boldsymbol{\Theta},U}[X + Z|\mathcal{F}_t] \leq \mathcal{E}_{\boldsymbol{\Theta},U}[X|\mathcal{F}_t] + \mathcal{E}_{\boldsymbol{\Theta},U}[Z|\mathcal{F}_t]. \tag{41}$$

The conditional superlinear expectation in Equation (35) satisfies Properties (i)–(iv) above. However, instead of satisfying the sub-additivity property in Equation (41), the conditional superlinear expectation in Equation (35) satisfies the following super-additivity property:

(v*) **Super-additivity:** For any two integrable random variables $X, Z \in \mathcal{F}_T$,

$$\mathcal{E}_{\boldsymbol{\Theta},L}[X + Z|\mathcal{F}_t] \geq \mathcal{E}_{\boldsymbol{\Theta},L}[X|\mathcal{F}_t] + \mathcal{E}_{\boldsymbol{\Theta},L}[Z|\mathcal{F}_t]. \tag{42}$$

For each $t \in \mathbb{T}$, let $L^1(\Omega, \mathcal{F}_t, \mathbb{P})$ be the space of integrable random variables defined on $(\Omega, \mathcal{F}_t, \mathbb{P})$. Since $\{\mathrm{E}^{\boldsymbol{\theta},\dagger}[B_T^{-1}X|\mathcal{F}_t]|\boldsymbol{\theta} \in \boldsymbol{\Theta}\} \subset L^1(\Omega, \mathcal{F}_t, \mathbb{P})$, and $L^1(\Omega, \mathcal{F}_t, \mathbb{P})$ is a complete lattice, both $\mathcal{E}_{\boldsymbol{\Theta},U}[B_T^{-1}X|\mathcal{F}_t]$ and $\mathcal{E}_{\boldsymbol{\Theta},L}[B_T^{-1}X|\mathcal{F}_t]$ exist, and they are $\mathcal{F}_t$-measurable random variables (see Dunford and Schwartz (1958), p. 302 therein, and Elliott (1982), p. 225 and Lemma 16.A.2 therein).

Using the conditional superlinear expectation in Equation (35), the lower estimate for the price of the Ether option at time t, denoted by $X_t^L(\boldsymbol{\Theta})$, with respect to the family of "risk-neutral" probability measures $\{\mathbb{P}^{\dagger}(\boldsymbol{\theta})|\boldsymbol{\theta} \in \boldsymbol{\Theta}\}$ is defined by

$$X_t^L(\boldsymbol{\Theta}) := B_t \mathcal{E}_{\boldsymbol{\Theta},L}\left[\frac{X}{B_T}|\mathcal{F}_t\right] = e^{-r(T-t)} \mathcal{E}_{\boldsymbol{\Theta},L}[X|\mathcal{F}_t]. \tag{43}$$

Similarly, using the conditional sublinear expectation in Equation (36), the upper estimate for the price of the Ether option at time t, denoted by $X_t^U(\mathbf{\Theta})$, with respect to the family of "risk-neutral" probability measures $\{\mathbb{P}^\dagger(\boldsymbol{\theta})|\boldsymbol{\theta} \in \mathbf{\Theta}\}$ is defined by

$$X_t^U(\mathbf{\Theta}) := B_t \mathcal{E}_{\mathbf{\Theta},U}\left[\frac{X}{B_T}|\mathcal{F}_t\right] = e^{-r(T-t)}\mathcal{E}_{\mathbf{\Theta},U}[X|\mathcal{F}_t]. \tag{44}$$

4. Bayesian Lower and Upper Estimates

In this section, the Bayesian lower and upper estimates for the price of an Ether option under the GARCH model are constructed using Bayesian nonlinear expectations in Siu (2023a). The basic idea is to adopt the "confidence" limits of Bayesian credible intervals to specify the lower and upper limits for each of the "uncertain" parameters μ and σ describing the perturbations/misspecifications in the conditional mean and volatility, respectively. Specifically, the "confidence" limits of the Bayesian credible intervals are used to specify the lower and upper limits of the rectangular region $\mathbf{\Theta}$ in Equation (19).

Bayesian statistics provides a data analytical approach, which is supplemented by expert opinion or subjective judgement, to specify the conditional nonlinear expectations in Equations (35) and (36). The two sources of information are combined "rationally" using the Bayes' theorem. Indeed, Bayesian statistics contributes to many developments of machine learning, artificial intelligence and data science. Its relevance to model uncertainty, or ambiguity, was featured in the smooth ambiguity approach to model uncertainty proposed by Klibanoff et al. (2005). Its connection with decision theory was highlighted in the classic monograph by Bernardo and Smith (2000). See also Siu (2023a) for some related discussions. Bayesian statistics and computation can also be used to handle missing data, which may be particularly relevant as far as big data are concerned. See, for example, (Kong et al. 1994; Ramoni and Sebastiani 2001; Rubin 1976; Tanner and Wong 1987). The constructions and notation below follow those in Siu (2023a), Section 4 therein, which were based on results in Bernardo and Smith (2000).

From Equation (23),

$$\epsilon_t = \mu + \sigma\epsilon_t(\boldsymbol{\theta}). \tag{45}$$

Recall that for each $\boldsymbol{\theta} \in \mathbf{\Theta}$, under $\mathbb{P}^{\boldsymbol{\theta}}$, $\epsilon_1(\boldsymbol{\theta}), \epsilon_2(\boldsymbol{\theta}), \cdots, \epsilon_T(\boldsymbol{\theta}) \stackrel{i.i.d.}{\sim} N(0,1)$. Consequently, by Equation (45), $\epsilon_1, \epsilon_2, \cdots, \epsilon_T|\boldsymbol{\theta} \stackrel{i.i.d.}{\sim} N(\mu, \sigma^2)$ under $\mathbb{P}^{\boldsymbol{\theta}}$. The above statements still hold if the two-dimensional vector of the "uncertain" parameters $\boldsymbol{\theta} := (\mu, \sigma)^\top \in (-\infty, \infty) \times (0, \infty)$. In Bayesian statistics, the vector of the "uncertain" parameters $(\mu, \sigma)^\top$ is regarded as a random vector. When evaluating the Bayesian credible intervals for the random vector $(\mu, \sigma)^\top$, it is assumed that the state space of the random vector $(\mu, \sigma)^\top$ is $(-\infty, \infty) \times (0, \infty)$. Following Bernardo and Smith (2000), Siu (2023a) and some relevant references therein, instead of considering σ, the precision λ is considered, where $\lambda := \frac{1}{\sigma^2}$. In other words, the random vector $(\mu, \lambda)^\top$, with the same state space $(-\infty, \infty) \times (0, \infty)$, is considered. Since σ is an "uncertain" parameter, λ may also be interpreted as an "uncertain" parameter.

A Normal–Gamma conjugate prior distribution is assigned for the random vector $(\mu, \lambda)^\top$. That is,

$$\mu|\lambda \sim N\left(\mu_0, \frac{1}{t_0\lambda}\right), \quad \lambda \sim Ga(\alpha_0, \beta_0), \tag{46}$$

where μ_0 and $t_0\lambda$ are the prior mean and precision of the normal prior distribution for $\mu|\lambda$, respectively. Note that $\mu_0 \in (-\infty, \infty)$ and $t_0 \in (0, \infty)$. The prior distribution of λ is a Gamma distribution with the shape parameter α_0 and the rate parameter β_0. Note also that $\alpha_0 \in (0, \infty)$ and $\beta_0 \in (0, \infty)$. In practice, those prior parameters, which are also called hyper-parameters, can be chosen based on expert opinion or subjective judgement. See Siu

(2023a), Section 4, for discussions about the intuitions behind and interpretations for those prior parameters.

Suppose that the reference model under the reference (real-world) probability measure $\mathbb{P}$ (e.g., the GARCH model in Equation (1)) is estimated, given $\mathcal{F}_n$. That is, the GARCH model is estimated using observations about the logarithmic returns $\{Y_1, Y_2, \cdots, Y_n\}$. The estimation for the GARCH model based on the conditional maximum likelihood estimation method is performed using the R package "rugarch" Galanos and Kley (2023). Let $\mathbb{I} := \{1, 2, \cdots, n\}$, which is a set of indices of the observations. Then, from Equation (1), the standardized residuals $\{e_i\}_{i \in \mathbb{I}}$ from the model fitting are computed as follows:

$$e_i = \frac{Y_i - \widehat{\mu}_Y}{\sqrt{\widehat{h}_i}}, \tag{47}$$

where $\widehat{\mu}_Y$ is the estimate for the mean parameter μ_Y, and $\widehat{h}_i$ is the estimate for the conditional variance h_i such that

$$\widehat{h}_i = \widehat{\omega} + \widehat{\alpha}\widehat{h}_{i-1}e_{i-1}^2 + \widehat{\beta}\widehat{h}_{i-1}. \tag{48}$$

Note that $\widehat{\omega}$, $\widehat{\alpha}$ and $\widehat{\beta}$ are the conditional maximum likelihood estimates for the GARCH parameters ω, α and β, respectively.

Recall that under $\mathbb{P}^{\boldsymbol{\theta}}$, $\epsilon_1, \epsilon_2, \cdots, \epsilon_n|\boldsymbol{\theta} \overset{i.i.d.}{\sim} N(\mu, \sigma^2)$. It may not be unreasonable to assume that under $\mathbb{P}^{\boldsymbol{\theta}}$, $e_1, e_2, \cdots, e_n|\boldsymbol{\theta} \overset{i.i.d.}{\sim} N(\mu, \sigma^2)$. Let $\mathbf{e}(n) := \{e_1, e_2, \cdots, e_n\}$. Write γ_1 and γ_2 for two probability levels such that $\gamma_1, \gamma_2 \in (0, 1)$. Let $t_{2\alpha_0+n}(\frac{\gamma_1}{2})$ denote the upper-tail critical value of a t-distribution with the degree of freedom $2\alpha_0 + n$ corresponding to the probability level $\frac{\gamma_1}{2}$. Then, using results in Bernardo and Smith (2000), p. 440 (see also Siu (2023a), Section 4), the $100(1 - \gamma_1)\%$ Bayesian credible interval for the "uncertain" parameter μ given $\mathbf{e}(n)$ is $(L^{\gamma_1}(\mu|\mathbf{e}(n)), U^{\gamma_1}(\mu|\mathbf{e}(n)))$ such that

$$\begin{aligned} L^{\gamma_1}(\mu|\mathbf{e}(n)) &= \mu_n - t_{2\alpha_0+n}\left(\frac{\gamma_1}{2}\right)\frac{\sigma_n}{\sqrt{n+t_0}}, \\ U^{\gamma_1}(\mu|\mathbf{e}(n)) &= \mu_n + t_{2\alpha_0+n}\left(\frac{\gamma_1}{2}\right)\frac{\sigma_n}{\sqrt{n+t_0}}, \end{aligned} \tag{49}$$

where

$$\begin{aligned} \mu_n &= \frac{t_0\mu_0 + n\bar{e}_n}{t_0 + n}, \quad \sigma_n = \sqrt{\frac{\beta_n}{\alpha_0 + \frac{n}{2}}}, \\ \beta_n &= \beta_0 + \frac{1}{2}ns_n^2 + \frac{t_0 n(\mu_0 - \bar{e}_n)^2}{2(t_0 + n)}, \\ \bar{e}_n &= \frac{1}{n}\sum_{i=1}^{n} e_i, \quad s_n^2 = \frac{1}{n}\sum_{i=1}^{n}(e_i - \bar{e}_n)^2. \end{aligned} \tag{50}$$

Using some terminologies in machine learning, the sample mean $\bar{e}_n$ may be related to the training error, while the unknown mean μ may be related to the test error that is to be learned or estimated from the training error (see, for example, Zhang (2023), page 9 therein).

Furthermore, the $100(1 - \gamma_2)\%$ Bayesian credible interval for the "uncertain" parameter λ given $\mathbf{e}(n)$ is $(L^{\gamma_2}(\lambda|\mathbf{e}(n)), U^{\gamma_2}(\lambda|\mathbf{e}(n)))$ such that

$$\begin{aligned} L^{\gamma_2}(\lambda|\mathbf{e}(n)) &= \Gamma_{\alpha_0+\frac{n}{2},\beta_n}\left(1 - \frac{\gamma_2}{2}\right), \\ U^{\gamma_2}(\lambda|\mathbf{e}(n)) &= \Gamma_{\alpha_0+\frac{n}{2},\beta_n}\left(\frac{\gamma_2}{2}\right), \end{aligned} \tag{51}$$

where $\Gamma_{\alpha_0+\frac{n}{2},\beta_n}(\gamma)$ is the upper-tail critical value of a Gamma distribution with the shape parameter $\alpha_0 + \frac{n}{2}$ and the rate parameter β_n corresponding to the probability level γ.

Take

$$L^{\gamma_2}(\sigma|\mathbf{e}(n)) := \sqrt{\frac{1}{U^{\gamma_2}(\lambda|\mathbf{e}(n))}}, \quad U^{\gamma_2}(\sigma|\mathbf{e}(n)) := \sqrt{\frac{1}{L^{\gamma_2}(\lambda|\mathbf{e}(n))}}. \tag{52}$$

Then, the following rectangular region is defined:

$$\mathbf{\Theta}_{\gamma_1,\gamma_2}(\mathbf{e}(n)) \quad := \quad [L^{\gamma_1}(\mu|\mathbf{e}(n)), U^{\gamma_1}(\mu|\mathbf{e}(n))] \times [L^{\gamma_2}(\sigma|\mathbf{e}(n)), U^{\gamma_2}(\sigma|\mathbf{e}(n))]. \tag{53}$$

Note that $\mathbf{\Theta}_{\gamma_1,\gamma_2}(\mathbf{e}(n))$ may be called a Bayesian (posterior) rectangular region. It may be thought of as a Bayesian (posterior) estimate for the rectangular region in Equation (19). To simplify the notation, we write $\mathbf{\Theta}(\mathbf{e}(n))$ for $\mathbf{\Theta}_{\gamma_1,\gamma_2}(\mathbf{e}(n))$.

Let $\mathbb{N}_T$ denote the set of non-negative integers truncated at the terminal time $T < \infty$. That is, $\mathbb{N}_T := \{0, 1, 2, \cdots, T\}$. Define the product space $\mathbf{\Theta}(\mathbf{e})$ by

$$\mathbf{\Theta}(\mathbf{e}) := \bigotimes_{n=1}^{\mathbb{N}_T} \mathbf{\Theta}(\mathbf{e}(n)). \tag{54}$$

We consider an $\{\mathcal{F}_n\}_{n\in\mathbb{N}_T}$-adapted stochastic process, denoted by $\boldsymbol{\theta}(\mathbf{e}) := \{\boldsymbol{\theta}_n(\mathbf{e})\}_{n\in\mathbb{N}_T}$, such that for each $n \in \mathbb{N}_T$ and each $\omega \in \Omega$, $\boldsymbol{\theta}_n(\mathbf{e}) := \boldsymbol{\theta}_n(\mathbf{e}, \omega) \in \mathbf{\Theta}(\mathbf{e}(n))$.

Define, for each $n \in \mathbb{N}_T$, $\boldsymbol{\theta}_n(\mathbf{e}) := (\mu_n(\mathbf{e}), \sigma_n(\mathbf{e}))^\top \in \mathbf{\Theta}(\mathbf{e}(n))$. Note that for each $n \in \mathbb{N}_T$, $\mu_n(\mathbf{e})$ is an $\mathcal{F}_n$-measurable random variable such that for each $\omega \in \Omega$, $\mu_n(\mathbf{e}) := \mu_n(\mathbf{e}, \omega) \in [L^{\gamma_1}(\mu|\mathbf{e}(n)), U^{\gamma_1}(\mu|\mathbf{e}(n))]$. Similarly, for each $n \in \mathbb{N}_T$, $\sigma_n(\mathbf{e})$ is an $\mathcal{F}_n$-measurable random variable such that for each $\omega \in \Omega$, $\sigma_n(\mathbf{e}) := \sigma_n(\mathbf{e}, \omega) \in [L^{\gamma_2}(\sigma|\mathbf{e}(n)), U^{\gamma_2}(\sigma|\mathbf{e}(n))]$.

For each process $\boldsymbol{\theta}(\mathbf{e}) := \{\boldsymbol{\theta}_n(\mathbf{e})\}_{n\in\mathbb{N}_T} \in \mathbf{\Theta}(\mathbf{e})$, each $n \in \mathbb{N}_T$ and each $k = n+1, n+2, \cdots, T$, let

$$\mu_Y(k, \boldsymbol{\theta}_n(\mathbf{e})) := \mu_Y + \mu_n(\mathbf{e})\sqrt{h_k}. \tag{55}$$

Then, for each $\boldsymbol{\theta}(\mathbf{e}) \in \mathbf{\Theta}(\mathbf{e})$, each $n \in \mathbb{N}_T$ and each $k = n+1, n+2, \cdots, T$, we define

$$\begin{aligned} \lambda_k^\dagger(\boldsymbol{\theta}_n(\mathbf{e})) \quad &:= \quad \frac{\phi_{\mu_Y^\dagger(k),(\sigma_n(\mathbf{e}))^2 h_k}(Y_k)}{\phi_{\mu_Y(k,\boldsymbol{\theta}_n(\mathbf{e})),(\sigma_n(\mathbf{e}))^2 h_k}(Y_k)} \times \frac{\phi_{\mu_n(\mathbf{e}),(\sigma_n(\mathbf{e}))^2}(\epsilon_k)}{\phi(\epsilon_k)} \\ &= \quad \frac{\phi(\frac{Y_k - \mu_Y^\dagger(k)}{\sigma_n(\mathbf{e})\sqrt{h_k}})}{\phi(\frac{Y_k - \mu_Y(k,\boldsymbol{\theta}_n(\mathbf{e}))}{\sigma_n(\mathbf{e})\sqrt{h_k}})} \times \frac{\phi(\frac{\epsilon_k - \mu_n(\mathbf{e})}{\sigma_n(\mathbf{e})})}{\sigma_n(\mathbf{e})\phi(\epsilon_k)}, \end{aligned} \tag{56}$$

where $\mu_Y^\dagger(k)$ and $\mu_Y(k, \boldsymbol{\theta}_n(\mathbf{e}))$ are given by Equation (2) and Equation (55), respectively. Furthermore, we take

$$\lambda_n^\dagger(\boldsymbol{\theta}_n(\mathbf{e})) = 1. \tag{57}$$

For each $n \in \mathbb{N}_T$, let $\mathbb{F}_n$ denote the "tail" filtration $\{\mathcal{F}_{n,k}\}_{k=n,n+1,\cdots,T}$ generated by the logarithmic returns $\{Y_n, Y_{n+1}, \cdots, Y_T\}$ such that for each $k = n, n+1, \cdots, T$,

$$\mathcal{F}_{n,k} := \sigma\{Y_m | m = n, n+1, \cdots, k\} \vee \mathcal{N}, \tag{58}$$

where $\mathcal{A}_1 \vee \mathcal{A}_2 := \sigma(\mathcal{A}_1 \cup \mathcal{A}_2)$ for any two σ-algebras $\mathcal{A}_1$ and $\mathcal{A}_2$ on Ω; $\mathcal{N}$ is a collection of $\mathbb{P}$-null subsets in the σ-field $\mathcal{F}$.

By the definitions in Equations (56)–(58), for each $n \in \mathbb{N}_T$, the "tail" process $\{\lambda_k^\dagger(\boldsymbol{\theta}_n(\mathbf{e}))\}_{k=n,n+1,\cdots,T}$ is an $\mathbb{F}_n$-adapted stochastic process.

For each $\boldsymbol{\theta}(\mathbf{e}) \in \boldsymbol{\Theta}(\mathbf{e})$ and each $n \in \mathbb{N}_T$, using Equation (56), the $\mathbb{F}_n$-adapted process $\{\Lambda_k^{\dagger}(\boldsymbol{\theta}_n(\mathbf{e}))\}_{k=n,n+1,\cdots,T}$ is defined such that for each $k = n, n+1, \cdots, T$,

$$\Lambda_k^{\dagger}(\boldsymbol{\theta}_n(\mathbf{e})) := \prod_{m=n}^{k} \lambda_m^{\dagger}(\boldsymbol{\theta}_n(\mathbf{e})). \tag{59}$$

Then, by the definitions in Equations (56), (57) and (59), for each $n \in \mathbb{N}_T$, $\{\Lambda_k^{\dagger}(\boldsymbol{\theta}_n(\mathbf{e}))\}_{k=n,n+1,\cdots,T}$ is an $(\mathbb{F}_n, \mathbb{P})$-martingale.

Consequently, for each $\boldsymbol{\theta}(\mathbf{e}) \in \boldsymbol{\Theta}(\mathbf{e})$ and each $n \in \mathbb{N}_T$, a new probability measure $\mathbb{P}^{\dagger}(\boldsymbol{\theta}_n(\mathbf{e}))$, which is equivalent to $\mathbb{P}$ on $\mathcal{F}_{n,T}$, is defined by setting

$$\left.\frac{d\mathbb{P}^{\dagger}(\boldsymbol{\theta}_n(\mathbf{e}))}{d\mathbb{P}}\right|_{\mathcal{F}_{n,T}} := \Lambda_T^{\dagger}(\boldsymbol{\theta}_n(\mathbf{e})). \tag{60}$$

For each $n \in \mathbb{N}_T$, a family of Bayesian (posterior) "risk-neutral" probability measures, given $\mathcal{F}_n$, which is indexed by the space of processes $\boldsymbol{\Theta}(\mathbf{e})$, is defined by

$$\mathcal{P}_n^{\dagger}(\boldsymbol{\Theta}(\mathbf{e})) := \{\mathbb{P}^{\dagger}(\boldsymbol{\theta}_n(\mathbf{e})) | \boldsymbol{\theta}(\mathbf{e}) \in \boldsymbol{\Theta}(\mathbf{e})\}. \tag{61}$$

The family $\mathcal{P}_n^{\dagger}(\boldsymbol{\Theta}(\mathbf{e}))$ defines a family of probability measures underlying a family of Bayesian (posterior) "risk-neutral" alternative GARCH models given $\mathcal{F}_n$. Note that for each $n \in \mathbb{N}_T$, only the nth coordinate, i.e., $\boldsymbol{\theta}_n(\mathbf{e})$, of the process $\boldsymbol{\theta}(\mathbf{e}) \in \boldsymbol{\Theta}(\mathbf{e})$ is involved in defining the probability measure $\mathbb{P}^{\dagger}(\boldsymbol{\theta}_n(\mathbf{e}))$ corresponding to $\boldsymbol{\theta}(\mathbf{e})$ within the family $\mathcal{P}_n^{\dagger}(\boldsymbol{\Theta}(\mathbf{e}))$.

For each $n \in \mathbb{N}_T$, a Bayesian (posterior) superlinear expectation for the discounted payoff of the Ether option $\frac{X}{B_T}$ given $\mathcal{F}_n$ with respect to $\mathcal{P}_n^{\dagger}(\boldsymbol{\Theta}(\mathbf{e}))$ in Equation (61), denoted by $\mathcal{E}_{\boldsymbol{\Theta}(\mathbf{e}),L}[B_T^{-1}X|\mathcal{F}_n]$, is defined as follows:

$$\mathcal{E}_{\boldsymbol{\Theta}(\mathbf{e}),L}[B_T^{-1}X|\mathcal{F}_n] := \text{ess} - \inf_{\boldsymbol{\theta}(\mathbf{e}) \in \boldsymbol{\Theta}(\mathbf{e})} \mathrm{E}^{\boldsymbol{\theta}_n(\mathbf{e}),\dagger}[B_T^{-1}X|\mathcal{F}_n], \tag{62}$$

where $\mathrm{E}^{\boldsymbol{\theta}_n(\mathbf{e}),\dagger}[\cdot|\mathcal{F}_n]$ is the conditional expectation given $\mathcal{F}_n$ under the probability measure $\mathbb{P}^{\dagger}(\boldsymbol{\theta}_n(\mathbf{e})) \in \mathcal{P}_n^{\dagger}(\boldsymbol{\Theta}(\mathbf{e}))$. The essential infimum in Equation (62) is taken over all the probability measures in the family $\mathcal{P}_n^{\dagger}(\boldsymbol{\Theta}(\mathbf{e}))$. Note that the Bayesian (posterior) superlinear expectation in Equation (62) satisfies the five properties (Properties (i)–(iv) in Equations (37)–(40) and Property (v*) in Equation (42)).

Similarly, for each $n \in \mathbb{N}_T$, a Bayesian (posterior) sublinear expectation for the discounted payoff of the Ether option $\frac{X}{B_T}$ given $\mathcal{F}_n$ with respect to $\mathcal{P}_n^{\dagger}(\boldsymbol{\Theta}(\mathbf{e}))$ in Equation (61), denoted by $\mathcal{E}_{\boldsymbol{\Theta}(\mathbf{e}),U}[B_T^{-1}X|\mathcal{F}_n]$, is defined as follows:

$$\mathcal{E}_{\boldsymbol{\Theta}(\mathbf{e}),U}[B_T^{-1}X|\mathcal{F}_n] := \text{ess} - \sup_{\boldsymbol{\theta}(\mathbf{e}) \in \boldsymbol{\Theta}(\mathbf{e})} \mathrm{E}^{\boldsymbol{\theta}_n(\mathbf{e}),\dagger}[B_T^{-1}X|\mathcal{F}_n]. \tag{63}$$

The Bayesian (posterior) sublinear expectation in Equation (63) satisfies the five properties (Properties (i)–(v) in Equations (37)–(41)).

Using the Bayesian (posterior) superlinear expectation in Equation (62), the Bayesian (posterior) lower estimate for the price of the Ether option at time n with respect to $\mathcal{P}_n^{\dagger}(\boldsymbol{\Theta}(\mathbf{e}))$, denoted by $X_n^L(\boldsymbol{\Theta}(\mathbf{e}))$, is defined by

$$X_n^L(\boldsymbol{\Theta}(\mathbf{e})) := B_n \mathcal{E}_{\boldsymbol{\Theta}(\mathbf{e}),L}\left[\frac{X}{B_T}|\mathcal{F}_n\right] = e^{-r(T-n)}\mathcal{E}_{\boldsymbol{\Theta}(\mathbf{e}),L}[X|\mathcal{F}_n]. \tag{64}$$

Similarly, using the Bayesian (posterior) sublinear expectation in Equation (63), the Bayesian (posterior) upper estimate for the price of the Ether option at time n with respect to $\mathcal{P}_n^{\dagger}(\mathbf{\Theta}(\mathbf{e}))$, denoted by $X_n^U(\mathbf{\Theta}(\mathbf{e}))$, is defined by

$$X_n^U(\mathbf{\Theta}(\mathbf{e})) := B_n \mathcal{E}_{\mathbf{\Theta}(\mathbf{e}),U}\left[\frac{X}{B_T}|\mathcal{F}_n\right] = e^{-r(T-n)}\mathcal{E}_{\mathbf{\Theta}(\mathbf{e}),U}[X|\mathcal{F}_n]. \tag{65}$$

The Bayesian (posterior) lower and upper estimates for the price of the Ether option are interpreted as the Bayesian (posterior) lower and upper confidence limits on the option price, respectively, in the line with the interpretations adopted in Boyle and Ananthanarayanan (1977).

5. Numerical/Simulation Procedure

In this section, the numerical/simulation procedure for computing the Bayesian lower and upper estimates for the price of the Ether option is described. Given $\mathbf{e}(n)$ (i.e., the standardized residuals $\{e_i\}_{i\in\mathbb{I}}$), the Bayesian (posterior) rectangular region $\mathbf{\Theta}(\mathbf{e}(n)) := \mathbf{\Theta}_{\gamma_1,\gamma_2}(\mathbf{e}(n))$ can be computed using Equations (49)–(53). Then, the Bayesian lower and upper estimates for the price of the Ether option in Equations (64) and (65) are computed using the procedures described in Section 4. However, it does not seem that closed-form expressions for the Bayesian lower and upper estimates in Equations (64) and (65) are available. Consequently, they are computed by the numerical/simulation procedures to be described in the sequel.

To compute the Bayesian lower and upper estimates, a numerical/simulation procedure based on the Monte Carlo simulation is adopted. A European call Ether option with strike price K and maturity at time T is considered. In this case, the terminal payoff of the Ether option at time T is

$$X = \max(S_T - K, 0), \tag{66}$$

where S_T is the price of Ethereum in AUD at the maturity T.

To approximate the Bayesian (posterior) superlinear expectation $\mathcal{E}_{\mathbf{\Theta}(\mathbf{e}),L}[X|\mathcal{F}_n]$, it is conjectured that the infirmum of $\mathrm{E}^{\boldsymbol{\theta},\dagger}[X|\mathcal{F}_n]$ over $\boldsymbol{\theta} \in \mathbf{\Theta}(\mathbf{e}(n))$ is attained at the extremal point $(\mu,\sigma)^\top = (L^{\gamma_1}(\mu|\mathbf{e}(n)), L^{\gamma_2}(\sigma|\mathbf{e}(n)))^\top$. Similarly, to approximate the Bayesian (posterior) sublinear expectation $\mathcal{E}_{\mathbf{\Theta}(\mathbf{e}),U}[X|\mathcal{F}_n]$, it is conjectured that the supremum of $\mathrm{E}^{\boldsymbol{\theta},\dagger}[X|\mathcal{F}_n]$ over $\boldsymbol{\theta} \in \mathbf{\Theta}(\mathbf{e}(n))$ is attained at the extremal point $(\mu,\sigma)^\top = (U^{\gamma_1}(\mu|\mathbf{e}(n)), U^{\gamma_2}(\sigma|\mathbf{e}(n)))^\top$.

It is possible that the supremum and infimum may be attained at some interior points of the rectangular region $\mathbf{\Theta}(\mathbf{e}(n))$. However, the approximations to the Bayesian (posterior) superlinear and sublinear expectations based on the extremal points look simpler than using grid search. The latter could be computationally intensive when the number of grid points is large and it is used coupled with the Monte Carlo simulation method. Furthermore, the approximation results based on extremal, or boundary, points to be presented look reasonable at an intuitive level.

To sum up, when approximating the Bayesian (posterior) superlinear expectation $\mathcal{E}_{\mathbf{\Theta}(\mathbf{e}),L}[X|\mathcal{F}_n]$, the following extremal, or boundary, point is adopted:

$$\begin{aligned}\bar{\boldsymbol{\theta}}(L) &:= (\bar{\mu}(L), \bar{\sigma}(L))^\top \\ &= (L^{\gamma_1}(\mu|\mathbf{e}(n)), L^{\gamma_2}(\sigma|\mathbf{e}(n)))^\top.\end{aligned} \tag{67}$$

Similarly, when approximating $\mathcal{E}_{\mathbf{\Theta}(\mathbf{e}),U}[X|\mathcal{F}_n]$, the following extremal, or boundary, point is used:

$$\begin{aligned}\bar{\boldsymbol{\theta}}(U) &:= (\bar{\mu}(U), \bar{\sigma}(U))^\top \\ &= (U^{\gamma_1}(\mu|\mathbf{e}(n)), U^{\gamma_2}(\sigma|\mathbf{e}(n)))^\top.\end{aligned} \tag{68}$$

Consequently, the Bayesian (posterior) superlinear and sublinear expectations may be, respectively, approximated as follows:

$$\mathcal{E}_{\mathbf{\Theta}(\mathbf{e}),L}[X|\mathcal{F}_n] \approx \mathrm{E}^{\bar{\boldsymbol{\theta}}(L),\dagger}[X|\mathcal{F}_n], \tag{69}$$

and

$$\mathcal{E}_{\mathbf{\Theta}(\mathbf{e}),U}[X|\mathcal{F}_n] \approx \mathrm{E}^{\bar{\boldsymbol{\theta}}(U),\dagger}[X|\mathcal{F}_n]. \tag{70}$$

The Monte Carlo method is used to estimate the conditional expectations $\mathrm{E}^{\bar{\boldsymbol{\theta}}(L),\dagger}[X|\mathcal{F}_n]$ and $\mathrm{E}^{\bar{\boldsymbol{\theta}}(U),\dagger}[X|\mathcal{F}_n]$ in Equations (69) and (70), respectively. The use of the Monte Carlo method for option pricing was pioneered by Boyle (1977). See also Boyle et al. (1997) for an excellent account. Here, the Monte Carlo method with control variates is used to estimate $\mathrm{E}^{\bar{\boldsymbol{\theta}}(L),\dagger}[X|\mathcal{F}_n]$ and $\mathrm{E}^{\bar{\boldsymbol{\theta}}(U),\dagger}[X|\mathcal{F}_n]$. To illustrate this, the estimation of $\mathrm{E}^{\bar{\boldsymbol{\theta}}(U),\dagger}[X|\mathcal{F}_n]$ based on the Monte Carlo method with control variates is presented here. The estimation of $\mathrm{E}^{\bar{\boldsymbol{\theta}}(L),\dagger}[X|\mathcal{F}_n]$ follows similarly. For more detail about the Monte Carlo method with control variates and other variance reduction techniques, such as antithetic variates, please refer to Boyle (1977) and Boyle et al. (1997).

Under the probability measure $\mathbb{P}^{\dagger}(\bar{\boldsymbol{\theta}}(U))$, the estimated dynamics for the "risk-neutralized" alternative GARCH in Equation (33) are given by

$$\begin{aligned} Y_t &= r - \frac{1}{2}\widehat{h}_t + \bar{\sigma}(U)\sqrt{\widehat{h}_t}\epsilon^{\dagger}_t(\bar{\boldsymbol{\theta}}(U)), \\ \widehat{h}_t &= \widehat{\omega} + \widehat{\alpha}\widehat{h}_{t-1}\left(\bar{\mu}(U) + \frac{\widehat{\eta}_{t-1}(\bar{\boldsymbol{\theta}}(U))}{\sqrt{\widehat{h}_{t-1}}} + \bar{\sigma}(U)\epsilon^{\dagger}_{t-1}(\bar{\boldsymbol{\theta}}(U))\right)^2 + \widehat{\beta}\widehat{h}_{t-1}, \end{aligned} \tag{71}$$

whereby, from Equation (30),

$$\widehat{\eta}_{t-1}(\bar{\boldsymbol{\theta}}(U)) := r - \widehat{\mu}_Y - \frac{1}{2}\widehat{h}_{t-1} - \bar{\mu}(U)\sqrt{\widehat{h}_{t-1}}. \tag{72}$$

Recall that $\widehat{\mu}_Y$, $\widehat{\omega}$, $\widehat{\alpha}$ and $\widehat{\beta}$ are the estimates for the unknown parameters in the GARCH model with drift in Equation (1) under the reference probability measure $\mathbb{P}$. Under the probability measure $\mathbb{P}^{\dagger}(\bar{\boldsymbol{\theta}}(U))$, $\{\epsilon^{\dagger}_t(\bar{\boldsymbol{\theta}}(U))\}_{t\in\mathbb{T}} \overset{i.i.d.}{\sim} N(0,1)$.

Suppose now that a set of simulated values for the terminal payoff X in Equation (66), that is, $\{X^{(m)}(\bar{\boldsymbol{\theta}}(U))\}_{m=1,2,\cdots,M}$, is generated by simulating from the estimated dynamics in Equation (71). Then, the Monte Carlo estimate for the conditional expectation $\mathrm{E}^{\bar{\boldsymbol{\theta}}(U),\dagger}[X|\mathcal{F}_n]$ is given by

$$\mathrm{E}^{\bar{\boldsymbol{\theta}}(U),\dagger}[X|\mathcal{F}_n] \approx \frac{1}{M}\sum_{m=1}^{M} X^{(m)}(\bar{\boldsymbol{\theta}}(U)). \tag{73}$$

Using Equations (65), (70) and (73), without control variates, the Monte Carlo estimate for the Bayesian (posterior) upper price is given by

$$X^U_n(\mathbf{\Theta}(\mathbf{e})) \approx e^{-r(T-n)}\frac{1}{M}\sum_{m=1}^{M} X^{(m)}(\bar{\boldsymbol{\theta}}(U)) := \widehat{V}_n(\bar{\boldsymbol{\theta}}(U)), \quad \text{say}. \tag{74}$$

Let V^G_n denote the known price of the European call Ether option at time n, which is taken as the Black–Scholes–Merton call price at time n. Write $\widehat{V}^G_n$ for the Monte Carlo estimate for the known price V^G_n. Then, with control variates, the Monte Carlo estimate, denoted by

$\widehat{V}_n^{cv}(\bar{\boldsymbol{\theta}}(U))$, for the Bayesian (posterior) upper estimate for the price of the Ether option is given by

$$\widehat{V}_n^{cv}(\bar{\boldsymbol{\theta}}(U)) = \widehat{V}_n(\bar{\boldsymbol{\theta}}(U)) + \beta(V_n^G - \widehat{V}_n^G), \tag{75}$$

where

$$\beta = \frac{\mathrm{Cov}(\widehat{V}_n(\bar{\boldsymbol{\theta}}(U)), \widehat{V}_n^G)}{\mathrm{Var}(\widehat{V}_n^G)}. \tag{76}$$

The standard error of the Monte Carlo estimate in Equation (75) is given by

$$\mathrm{SD}(\widehat{V}_n^{cv}(\bar{\boldsymbol{\theta}}(U))) = \sqrt{\mathrm{Var}(\widehat{V}_n^{cv}(\bar{\boldsymbol{\theta}}(U))) + \beta^2\mathrm{Var}(\widehat{V}_n^G) - 2\beta\mathrm{Cov}(\widehat{V}_n(\bar{\boldsymbol{\theta}}(U)), \widehat{V}_n^G)}. \tag{77}$$

In line with Boyle and Ananthanarayanan (1977), a Bayesian model for estimating the unknown volatility parameter in the Black–Scholes–Merton (BSM) model is adopted to compute Bayesian confidence limits and a Bayesian point estimate for the price of an Ether option in the current paper. For convenience, this model is called the Bayesian BSM model here. The Bayesian BSM model corresponds to a model with volatility uncertainty (but without conditional heteroscedasticity), and it is briefly discussed in the rest of this section for the sake of completeness. In Section 6, the Bayesian confidence limits obtained from the Bayesian BSM model will be compared with those obtained from the proposed model, which incorporates both model uncertainty and conditional heteroscedasticity.

In the Bayesian BSM model, the logarithmic returns of Ethereum are directly used to compute the Bayesian credible interval for the unknown volatility parameter. Let $\mathbf{Y}(n) := \{Y_1, Y_2, \cdots, Y_n\}$ (i.e., the observations about the logarithmic returns of Ethereum up to and including time n). Define

$$\bar{Y}_n := \frac{\sum_{i=1}^n Y_i}{n}, \quad s_Y^2(n) := \frac{1}{n}\sum_{i=1}^n (Y_i - \bar{Y}_n)^2. \tag{78}$$

As in Equation (50), define β_n^Y and σ_n^Y as follows:

$$\begin{aligned} \beta_n^Y &= \beta_0 + \frac{1}{2}ns_Y^2(n) + \frac{t_0 n(\mu_0 - \bar{Y}_n)^2}{2(t_0+n)}, \\ \sigma_n^Y &= \sqrt{\frac{\beta_n^Y}{\alpha_0 + \frac{n}{2}}}. \end{aligned} \tag{79}$$

Similarly to Equations (51) and (52), the $100(1-\gamma_2)\%$ Bayesian credible interval for the unknown annualized volatility of the logarithmic returns of Ethereum, i.e., σ_Y, given $\mathbf{Y}(n)$, is $(L^{\gamma_2}(\sigma_Y|\mathbf{Y}(n)), U^{\gamma_2}(\sigma_Y|\mathbf{Y}(n)))$ such that

$$\begin{aligned} L^{\gamma_2}(\sigma_Y|\mathbf{Y}(n)) &= \left(\Gamma_{\alpha_0+\frac{n}{2},\beta_n^Y}\left(\frac{\gamma_2}{2}\right)\right)^{-\frac{1}{2}} \times \sqrt{252}, \\ U^{\gamma_2}(\sigma_Y|\mathbf{Y}(n)) &= \left(\Gamma_{\alpha_0+\frac{n}{2},\beta_n^Y}\left(1-\frac{\gamma_2}{2}\right)\right)^{-\frac{1}{2}} \times \sqrt{252}, \end{aligned} \tag{80}$$

where the scaling factor $\sqrt{252}$ is applied to annualize the lower and upper limits of the Bayesian credible interval for σ_Y under the assumption that there are 252 trading days per annum.

Let r_Y denote the annualized risk-free interest rate. Then, given the volatility σ_Y, the Black–Scholes–Merton model gives the following closed-form solution to the price of the European call Ether option with strike price K and time-to-maturity τ:

$$C(s, r_Y, \sigma_Y, K, \tau) = s\Phi(d_1) - Ke^{-r_Y\tau}\Phi(d_2), \tag{81}$$

where

$$\begin{aligned} d_1 &:= \frac{\ln(\frac{s}{K}) + (r_Y + \frac{1}{2}\sigma_Y^2)\tau}{\sigma_Y\sqrt{\tau}}, \\ d_2 &:= d_1 - \sigma_Y\sqrt{\tau}. \end{aligned} \tag{82}$$

Note that s is the current price of Ethereum in AUD; τ is measured in year(s).

The Bayesian point estimate for σ_Y given $\mathbf{Y}(n)$, denoted by $M(\sigma_Y|\mathbf{Y}(n))$, is taken as follows:

$$M(\sigma_Y|\mathbf{Y}(n)) = \sigma_n^Y \times \sqrt{252}. \tag{83}$$

Then, the (closed-form) Bayesian lower and upper estimates for the price of the European call Ether option given $\mathbf{Y}(n)$ are, respectively, given by

$$C_n^L(s, r_Y, K, \tau) = C(s, r_Y, L^{\Upsilon_2}(\sigma_Y|\mathbf{Y}(n)), K, \tau), \tag{84}$$

and

$$C_n^U(s, r_Y, K, \tau) = C(s, r_Y, U^{\Upsilon_2}(\sigma_Y|\mathbf{Y}(n)), K, \tau). \tag{85}$$

Furthermore, the (closed-form) Bayesian point estimate for the price of the European call Ether option given $\mathbf{Y}(n)$ is given by

$$C_n^P(s, r_Y, K, \tau) = C(s, r_Y, M(\sigma_Y|\mathbf{Y}(n)), K, \tau). \tag{86}$$

6. Empirical and Simulation Results

Real data on the daily adjusted close prices of Ethereum in AUD (ETH-AUD) are considered. The period of the data is from 1 January 2018 to 21 May 2024 (a total of 2333 observations) covering some periods of the COVID-19 pandemic. The data were downloaded from Ethereum AUD (ETH-AUD) price history and historical data—Yahoo Finance (https://au.finance.yahoo.com/quote/ETH-AUD/, (accessed on 15 September 2024)). Data on the daily logarithmic returns from ETH-AUD (a total of 2332 observations) are used to estimate the reference model, i.e., the GARCH(1,1) model with drift, in Equation (1). The estimation of the GARCH(1,1) model was performed using the R package "rugarch" Galanos and Kley (2023). The Monte Carlo estimates and their standard errors for the Bayesian lower and upper estimates for prices of Ether options with different strike prices and maturities are computed. The strike prices are 80%, 90%, 100%, 110% and 120% of the current adjusted close price of ETH-AUD. Consequently, in-the-money (ITM), at-the-money (ATM) and out-of-the-money (OTM) Ether options are considered. The maturities are three months, six months, nine months and one year. It is supposed that there are 252 trading days per year. Besides the Bayesian lower and upper estimates, the prices of Ether options without incorporating model uncertainty, which are called the standard prices, are also considered. Specifically, Monte Carlo estimates and their standard errors for the standard prices with different strike prices and maturities are computed. The standard prices refer to the prices of the Ether options from a model incorporating conditional heteroscedasticity only, that is, the reference model in Equation (1). The Bayesian lower and upper estimates, as well as the Bayesian point estimates, for the prices of the

Ether options are computed from the model incorporating volatility uncertainty only in line with Boyle and Ananthanarayanan (1977), as described in Section 5. All the statistical analyses, simulations and computations were performed using R.

Table 1 presents some summary statistics of the daily logarithmic returns data.

Table 1. Summary statistics of daily log returns from ETH-AUD.

Min.	1st Qu.	Median	Mean
−0.5189823	−0.0185588	0.0008816	0.0007498
3rd Qu.	Max.	Skew	Kurtosis
0.0225148	0.2283313	−0.88	10.32

From Table 1, the daily logarithmic returns from ETH-AUD have a negatively skewed and heavy-tailed distribution. Furthermore, the range of the returns is large. Similar findings were discussed in Siu (2023a) for Bitcoin returns data covering some periods of the COVID-19 pandemic.

Figure 1 depicts the time series plots for the daily adjusted close prices (a) and logarithmic returns (b) from ETH-AUD.

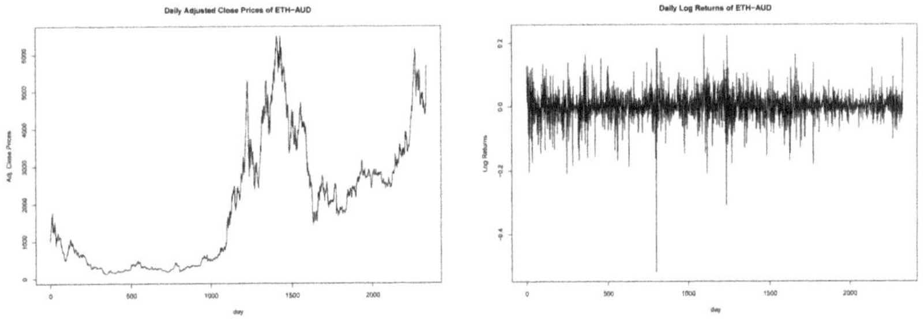

(**a**) Adjusted close prices. (**b**) Log returns.

Figure 1. Time series plots for adjusted close prices and log returns.

From Figure 1a, there was an upward trend in the adjusted close prices of ETH-AUD starting around the 1000th day and ending at around the 1500th day. This corresponds to the first half year of 2020 during which the impact of the COVID-19 pandemic started emerging. Furthermore, from Figure 1b, the daily logarithmic returns from ETH-AUD exhibit volatility clustering, that is, periods of high (low) volatility followed by periods of high (low) volatility. Similar observations were made in Siu (2023a) for Bitcoin returns data covering some periods of the COVID-19 pandemic.

Figure 2 depicts the sample ACF plot (a) and the sample PACF plot (b) for the daily logarithmic returns from ETH-AUD.

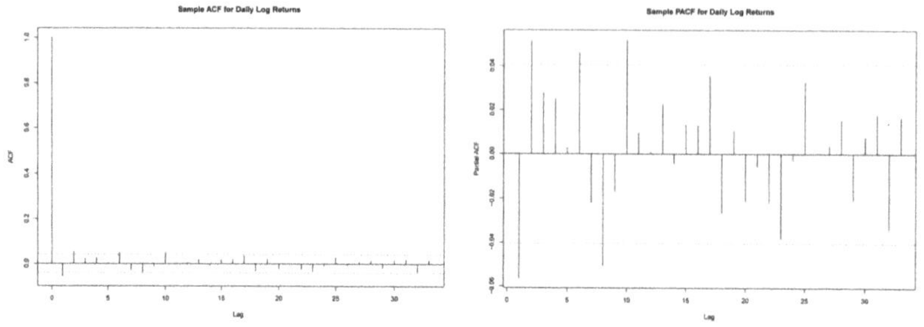

(**a**) SACF for log returns. (**b**) SPACF for log returns.

Figure 2. SACF and SPACF plots for log returns.

From Figure 2, the daily logarithmic returns from ETH-AUD appear to be stationary. To provide further evidence for the stationarity, three types of the augmented Dickey–Fuller (ADF) test were performed using the R package "aTSA" Qiu (2024). They are "Type 1: no drift no trend", "Type 2: with drift no trend", and "Type 3: with drift and trend". The alternative hypothesis of the test is "stationary". The p values of the three types of the ADF test are all less than 0.01, indicating the stationarity of the logarithmic returns data.

Table 2 provides the estimation results for the GARCH(1,1) model with drift. Note that the standard errors reported are robust standard errors.

Table 2. The estimation results of the GARCH(1,1) model with drift.

Parameter	Estimate	Std. Error	t Value	Pr(>|t|)
μ_Y	0.001097	0.000884	1.2407	0.214723
ω	0.000041	0.000035	1.1600	0.246037
α	0.071753	0.030467	2.3551	0.018517
β	0.913544	0.040071	22.7984	0.000000

From the estimation results in Table 2, the standard error of the estimate for the drift parameter μ_Y is large compared with the estimate for μ_Y. This indicates that estimating the drift parameter could be noisy, which has been documented in Merton (1980) for market returns data. Furthermore, the (G)ARCH coefficients α and β are significant at the 5% significance level. This provides evidence for the presence of conditional heteroscedasticity. To provide further evidence, a weighted Ljung–Box test on the standardized squared residuals and a weighted ARCH LM test were performed. Table 3 presents the results of the weighted Ljung–Box test on standardized squared residuals and the weighted ARCH LM test. The results of the two tests support the presence of conditional heteroscedasticity or ARCH effect in the daily logarithmic returns from ETH-AUD.

Table 3. Weighted Ljung–Box test on standardized squared residuals and ARCH LM test.

Ljung–Box			ARCH LM		
Lag	Statistic	p-Value	Lag	Statistic	p-Value
1	0.05112	0.8211	3	0.2306	0.6311
5	2.51741	0.5022	5	4.6461	0.1240
9	4.34178	0.5319	7	5.0007	0.2245

Table 4 provides the lower and upper limits of the 90% Bayesian credible intervals for the "uncertain" parameters μ and σ, which were computed using the Normal–Gamma conjugate prior and the standardized residuals from the estimated reference model. As an illustration, the assumed values for the prior parameters are $\mu_0 = 0.05$, $t_0 = 100$, $\alpha_0 = 2$

and $\beta_0 = 1$. These assumed values for the prior parameters were considered in Siu (2023a) for Bitcoin returns data.

Table 4. 90% Bayesian credible intervals for μ and σ.

Lower Limit μ	Upper Limit μ	Lower Limit σ	Upper Limit σ
−0.01795162	0.03403796	0.9814926	1.01901

From Table 4, the Bayesian credible interval for μ covers the point zero. This indicates that the Bayesian credible interval includes the situation where there are no perturbations/misspecifications in the conditional mean. Likewise, the Bayesian credible interval for σ covers the point one. This indicates that the Bayesian credible interval includes the situation where there are no perturbations/misspecifications in the conditional volatility. The Bayesian credible interval for μ appears to be relatively wide compared with that for σ. This indicates that model uncertainty about the conditional mean could be more significant than model uncertainty about the conditional volatility for the daily logarithmic returns from ETH-AUD. This appears to be in line with the finding in Merton (1980) that the drift estimate could be more noisy than the volatility estimate for market returns data. The lower and upper limits of the Bayesian credible intervals for μ and σ in Table 4 are used to compute the Monte Carlo estimates and their standard errors for the Bayesian lower and upper estimates for the prices of Ether options following the procedures described in Section 5.

Tables 5–7 give the Monte Carlo estimates for the Bayesian lower and upper estimates for the prices of the Ether options as well as their standard prices with different strike prices K and maturities T. The respective standard errors are presented in parentheses below the Monte Carlo estimates. Each Monte Carlo estimate is computed by 10,000 simulation runs. The risk-free interest rate r is taken as 5% per annum. The current adjusted close price of ETH-AUD $s_0 = 5693.319$.

Table 5. Monte Carlo estimates for lower limits.

K	T	3 Months	6 Months	9 Months	1 Year
$0.8s_0$		1614.8765	1924.207	2144.891	2291.315
		(8.543328)	(14.27263)	(20.09029)	(20.35247)
$0.9s_0$		1296.4003	1646.155	1889.479	2052.171
		(7.794544)	(13.55024)	(19.41157)	(19.73576)
s_0		1038.9999	1406.444	1669.171	1845.062
		(6.909680)	(12.77218)	(18.69219)	(19.10111)
$1.1s_0$		832.3041	1201.581	1474.649	1662.490
		(6.186688)	(12.03232)	(17.98552)	(18.49396)
$1.2s_0$		664.5770	1028.463	1305.108	1500.547
		(5.841916)	(11.40278)	(17.32325)	(17.94511)

Table 6. Monte Carlo estimates for standard prices.

K	T	3 Months	6 Months	9 Months	1 Year
$0.8s_0$		1664.5092	2018.730	2273.248	2435.673
		(9.616927)	(17.23003)	(25.58117)	(26.54255)
$0.9s_0$		1349.9941	1745.884	2024.493	2203.923
		(8.793997)	(16.40912)	(24.78752)	(25.82538)
s_0		1095.0476	1508.948	1807.992	2002.367
		(7.814137)	(15.51467)	(23.94530)	(25.08685)
$1.1s_0$		888.8722	1304.880	1615.389	1823.577
		(7.001017)	(14.64918)	(23.10734)	(24.37146)
$1.2s_0$		719.6615	1130.875	1446.286	1663.437
		(6.609144)	(13.90233)	(22.31443)	(23.71967)

Table 7. Monte Carlo estimates for upper limits.

T / K	3 Months	6 Months	9 Months	1 Year
$0.8s_0$	1734.3539 (11.278233)	2160.123 (22.56787)	2473.206 (36.63348)	2663.540 (40.43543)
$0.9s_0$	1425.0832 (10.355051)	1894.089 (21.61634)	2233.074 (35.69513)	2442.569 (39.60193)
s_0	1173.3986 (9.248022)	1661.070 (20.56020)	2022.359 (34.68488)	2249.001 (38.73560)
$1.1s_0$	968.1831 (8.306346)	1458.123 (19.51948)	1832.548 (33.65647)	2076.176 (37.88148)
$1.2s_0$	797.2568 (7.834245)	1283.132 (18.59461)	1664.871 (32.66048)	1919.336 (37.08164)

From Tables 5–7, the Bayesian lower and upper estimates as well as the standard prices increase as the maturity T increases. Furthermore, they decrease as the strike price K increases. These results are intuitively reasonable. Specifically, the results can be explained by the time value of the call option and the payoff of the call option as a decreasing function of the strike price. Furthermore, the Bayesian lower estimates are lower than the respective Bayesian upper estimates, and the standard prices lie between the respective Bayesian lower and upper estimates. This may lend support to the conjecture that the supremum and infimum of $\mathrm{E}^{\boldsymbol{\theta},+}[X|\mathcal{F}_n]$ over $\boldsymbol{\theta} \in \boldsymbol{\Theta}(\mathbf{e}(n))$ may be attained at the extremal, or boundary, points of the rectangular region $\boldsymbol{\Theta}(\mathbf{e}(n))$. The standard errors are relatively small compared with the respective Monte Carlo estimates. This indicates that the Monte Carlo estimates for the Bayesian lower and upper prices as well as the standard prices are quite precise.

Table 8 presents the differences in the Monte Carlo estimates for the Bayesian upper and lower estimates for the prices of the Ether options with different strikes K and maturities T.

Table 8. Differences in the Monte Carlo estimates for upper and lower limits.

T / K	3 Months	6 Months	9 Months	1 Year
$0.8s_0$	119.4774	235.9164	328.3146	372.2243
$0.9s_0$	128.6830	247.9340	343.5949	390.3978
s_0	134.3987	254.6257	353.1871	403.9392
$1.1s_0$	135.8790	256.5423	357.8990	413.6860
$1.2s_0$	132.6797	254.6698	359.7624	418.7889

From Table 8, for a fixed strike price K, the differences in the Monte Carlo estimates for the Bayesian upper and lower estimates for the prices of the Ether options increase as the maturity T increases. This indicates that as the maturity T of an Ether option becomes longer, the effect of model uncertainty about the conditional mean and volatility on the option prices could be more significant.

Table 9 gives the Bayesian upper, point and lower estimates for the prices of the Ether options with different strikes K and maturities T under the Bayesian BSM model. Note that the prior parameters used here are the same as those values assumed before. The 90% Bayesian credible interval for the annualized volatility parameter σ_Y is given by $(0.862603, 0.8955688)$. The Bayesian point estimate for σ_Y is given by 0.878703.

Table 9. Upper (U), point (P) and lower (L) estimates under the Bayesian BSM model.

K	T	3 Months	6 Months	9 Months	1 Year
$0.8s_0$	(U)	1619.8448	1976.500	2254.782	2487.521
	(M)	1605.4198	1955.436	2229.245	2458.637
	(L)	1591.7116	1935.352	2204.854	2431.015
$0.9s_0$	(U)	1301.2594	1703.199	2008.744	2261.713
	(M)	1284.2516	1679.555	1980.544	2230.078
	(L)	1268.0234	1656.963	1953.570	2199.788
s_0	(U)	1038.1028	1468.530	1793.441	2061.766
	(M)	1019.5382	1443.083	1763.234	2027.959
	(L)	1001.8009	1418.749	1734.321	1995.572
$1.1s_0$	(U)	824.0243	1267.552	1604.807	1884.203
	(M)	804.8823	1241.009	1573.177	1848.736
	(L)	786.6053	1215.632	1542.905	1814.758
$1.2s_0$	(U)	651.8496	1095.635	1439.256	1726.047
	(M)	632.9428	1068.601	1406.710	1689.364
	(L)	614.9288	1042.779	1375.578	1654.235

From Table 9, the Bayesian lower, point and upper estimates for the prices of the Ether options increase as the maturity T increases. They decrease as the moneyness increases. Again, these results are intuitively reasonable. The Bayesian lower, point and upper estimates for the prices of the Ether options are in correct order. That is, the Bayesian lower estimates are below the respective Bayesian upper estimates, and the Bayesian point estimates lie between the respective Bayesian lower and upper estimates. This is explained by the fact that the Black–Scholes–Merton formula for the call price is an increasing function of the annualized volatility parameter σ_Y, and the numerical results that the Bayesian point estimate for σ_Y lies within the Bayesian credible interval for σ_Y.

Table 10 presents the differences in the upper and lower estimates for the prices of the Ether options with different strikes K and maturities T under the Bayesian BSM model.

Table 10. Differences in the upper and lower estimates under the Bayesian BSM model.

K	T	3 Months	6 Months	9 Months	1 Year
$0.8s_0$		28.13318	41.14772	49.92784	56.50651
$0.9s_0$		33.23597	46.23647	55.17361	61.92441
s_0		36.30195	49.78125	59.11972	66.19463
$1.1s_0$		37.41895	51.91995	61.90179	69.44560
$1.2s_0$		36.92077	52.85592	63.67799	71.81156

From Table 10, for a fixed strike price, the differences in the upper and lower estimates for the prices of the Ether options increase as the maturity T increases. This result is consistent with that from Table 8. This reflects that as the maturity T of an Ether option becomes longer, the impact of volatility uncertainty on the option prices could be more pronounced. Comparing Tables 8 and 10, the differences in the upper and lower estimates for the prices of the Ether options under the proposed model with both model uncertainty and conditional heteroscedasticity are substantially higher than those under the Bayesian BSM model. This indicates that the combined effect of model uncertainty about the conditional mean and conditional heteroscedasticity on the option prices are more significant than the impact of volatility uncertainty.

7. Price Fluctuations: Chaotic or Random?

Are price fluctuations chaotic or random? This question has captured considerable attention from academic researchers and market practitioners. If price fluctuations are chaotic, they may be considered a deterministic (nonlinear) dynamical system. If price fluctuations are random, they are totally unpredictable and may be described by the random walk theory. The latter is related to a (weak) form of market efficiency, although rejecting random walk theory does not imply market efficiency when trading costs are taken into account (see (Taylor 1986, 2005)). Henri Poincaré realized more than a century ago that a deterministic (nonlinear) dynamical system, which is sensitive to its initial state, can generate behaviour which is reminiscent of random behaviour. In a seminal article by May (1976), a logistic map was used to illustrate chaotic dynamics in the study of animal population dynamics. Although it may not be possible to define the notion of chaos precisely, the sensitivity to the initial state is an important property of a chaotic dynamical system. See (Tong 1990, 1995, 2002) for related discussions and more detail. See also the monographs by (Gleick 1987; Palmer 2023) for an excellent account to the chaos theory and its applications to diverse fields.

Motivated by the market crash in October 1987, an early study on deterministic chaotic and nonlinear dynamical systems in financial markets was conducted in a seminal article by Hsieh (1991). Through performing a statistical test, namely the BDS test Broock et al. (1996), on weekly stock returns from the Center for Research in Securities Prices (CRSP) at the University of Chicago, the empirical results in Hsieh (1991) revealed that logarithmic stock returns are not independent and identically distributed (i.i.d.) and that conditional heteroscedasticity is the cause of the rejection of the i.i.d. logarithmic stock returns. Hsieh (1991) also pointed out that to model nonlinear behaviour in the logarithmic stock returns, instead of focusing on the conditional mean returns including chaotic dynamics, attention should be given to modelling conditional heteroscedasticity, i.e., time-varying conditional volatility. (Hsieh 1993, 1995) further explored implications of nonlinear dynamical systems for financial risk management and financial markets, respectively. Using data on four currency futures markets (the British Pound, Deutsche Mark, Japanese Yen and Swiss Franc), Hsieh (1993) found empirically that while conditional mean returns may not be predictable, the conditional variances are predictable. Using data on stock index futures prices for the S&P, Nikkei, DAX, FTSE and CAC, the empirical findings in Hsieh (1995) indicated that conditional variance models such as the ARCH-type models can account for a great deal of non-random behaviour in asset returns. For excellent accounts on chaos and nonlinear dynamical systems in financial markets and the economy, one may refer to the monographs by (Broock et al. 1991; Farmer 2024; Peters 1996). Additionally, Schefczyk (2012) may provide some discussions from a philosophical perspective.

Deterministic nonlinear dynamical systems and chaos may not provide realistic descriptions for real-world dynamics. To address some limitations of deterministic nonlinear dynamical systems and chaos, stochastic dynamical systems and noisy chaos were introduced by researchers in the 1990s. See, for example, (Bartlett 1990; Berliner 1992; Casdagli 1992; Cheng and Tong 1992, 1994; Fan et al. 1993; Tong 1990, 1992, 1995; Yao and Tong 1994a, 1994b; Chan and Tong 1994). Specifically, stochastic dynamical systems and noisy chaos are described by stochastic difference equations or nonlinear autoregressive models which generalize deterministic difference equations by introducing stochastic noise. Two important approaches have been introduced to quantify the sensitivity of stochastic dynamical systems with respect to their initial conditions. They are the conditional distribution approach and the conditional mean approach. The conditional distribution approach was considered in (Yao and Tong 1994a, 1994b). The key idea of this approach is to describe the sensitivity of the conditional distribution with respect to the initial state through the divergence of the conditional distribution relating to the Kullback–Leibler information. The conditional mean approach describes the sensitivity of the conditional mean with respect to the initial state. It aims to generalize the notion of the Lyapunov exponent in a stochastic environment. See (Chan and Tong 2001; Tong 1995, 2002; Yao and Tong 1994a) for more detailed discussions on the two approaches. Indeed, the sensitivity of stochastic dynamical systems with respect to their initial states has an important implication for nonlinear prediction. Specifically, how well you can predict depends on where you are now (Chan and Tong 2001; Fan and Yao 2003; Tong 1995; Yao and Tong 1994a). This highlights the importance of state-dependency for nonlinear prediction. Stochastic (nonlinear) dynamical systems have been explored for modelling, estimating and predicting volatility in (Elliott et al. 2012; Tong 2007). Yao and Tong (1998) introduced a bootstrap test for deterministic chaos and stochastic randomness. As a potential topic for further research, it might be interesting to explore the possibility of using this bootstrap test to examine whether price fluctuations in financial markets, or particularly in crypto markets, are chaotic or random. Indeed, Garnier and Solna (2019) and Pietrych (2021) studied the nonlinearity, chaos and multifractality in the cryptocurrency markets as well as their implications for the market efficiency of cryptocurrencies.

8. Conclusions

Using Bayesian nonlinear expectations introduced in Siu (2023a), Bayesian lower and upper estimates for the price of an Ether option are constructed with the objective of incorporating the impacts of model uncertainty and conditional heteroscedasticity. Specifically, model uncertainty about the conditional mean and volatility of the return dynamics of Ethereum modelled by a reference GARCH model is incorporated by introducing the "uncertain" parameters describing the perturbations/misspecifications in the conditional mean and volatility. Then, a family of alternative GARCH models are introduced via changing probability measures using an extended Girsanov's principle. The risk-neutralization of the family of alternative GARCH models is also performed via the extended Girsanov's principle. The Bayesian nonlinear expectations are constructed using closed-form Bayesian credible intervals with conjugate priors and the residuals from the estimated reference GARCH model. The numerical/simulation procedures for the computation of the Bayesian lower and upper estimates for the prices of Ether options are introduced based on the Monte Carlo simulation method with control variates. Empirical results from real data on the daily logarithmic returns from Ethereum in AUD are presented. Monte Carlo estimates and their standard errors for the Bayesian lower and upper estimates for the prices of the Ether options as well as their standard prices are provided. The Monte Carlo estimates are precise and consistent with intuition. It is also found that the impact of model uncertainty about the conditional mean and volatility on the Ether option prices is more significant as the maturity increases. Comparisons between the Bayesian lower and upper estimates for the prices of the Ether options under the Bayesian BSM model, which incorporates volatility uncertainty only, are provided. It is found that the combined effect of model uncertainty about the conditional mean and conditional heteroscedasticity on the option prices is more pronounced than the impact of volatility uncertainty. Some discussions about the chaotic and random aspects of price fluctuations in financial markets in general, or crypto markets in particular, are provided. The chaotic and random aspects of price fluctuations may have implications for market efficiency in cryptocurrencies (see, for example, Garnier and Solna (2019) and Pietrych (2021)). The latter is relevant to crypto option pricing as discussed in Siu and Elliott (2021). It is hoped that those discussions might provide insights and inspiration, which may be helpful for future endeavours to explore the chaotic and random aspects of price fluctuations, as well as their implications for financial markets in general, or crypto markets in particular.

Some limitations of the proposed model are briefly discussed here. Firstly, the conjugate priors for the "uncertain" parameters describing the perturbations/misspecifications in the conditional mean and volatility are adopted here. Although the conjugate priors lead to closed-form Bayesian credible intervals, it is possible that the "uncertain" parameters may be better modelled by other distributions. Indeed, one may explore the possibility of using a Bayesian nonparametric approach to construct Bayesian credible intervals for the "uncertain" parameters as noted in Siu (2023a), Online Appendix F. Secondly, to simplify the discussion, it is assumed here that the random shocks of the GARCH model are normally distributed. It is possible that the random shocks of the GARCH model follow non-normal distributions. A similar remark was made in Boyle and Ananthanarayanan (1977) for the Bayesian BSM model. Thirdly, for illustration, the GARCH model is adopted here as a reference model. It is possible that some variants of the GARCH model, such as the GJR-GARCH model and the SETAR-GARCH model, may be better candidates for a reference model. Here, it is assumed that the risk-free interest rate is a constant. However, in practice, it may be realistic to consider the situation of a stochastic interest rate. It is conjectured here that the infimum and supremum of a conditional expectation are attained at the extremal points of a rectangular region when approximating the Bayesian (posterior) superlinear and sublinear expectations. Although the numerical results presented here may lend support to this conjecture, it is possible that the the infimum and supremum may be attained at some interior points of the rectangular region. Although the chaotic and random aspects of price fluctuations are briefly touched on in Section 7, empirical studies on the chaotic and random aspects of price fluctuations in Ether and other cryptocurrencies are not provided in the current paper. The papers by Garnier and Solna (2019) and Pietrych (2021) may provide an excellent account on this topic.

As noted in Godbole (2023), bid and ask prices prevail in Bitcoin and Ether option markets. However, it seems that the literature on modelling the bid and ask prices in cryptocurrency option markets may be rather limited. In a recent paper by Madan et al. (2019), they calibrated the Bitcoin price dynamics under several Markov models using vanilla Bitcoin options and studied the implied liquidity of Bitcoin call options using conic finance theory. How might the prevalence of bid and ask prices in Bitcoin and Ether options be explained? This may be a potential topic for further research. From the perspective of a two-price economy (Cherny and Madan 2009; Madan 2015, 2016; Madan and Cherny 2010), a recent paper by Elliott et al. (2022) considered a two-price system based on a lower price process and an upper price process attributed to model uncertainty, or uncertainty in probability, for financial valuation. Suppose the Bayesian lower and upper estimates for the price of an Ether option are interpreted as a Bayesian version of the lower and upper prices of the Ether option. Then, one may consider a Bayesian two-price system for the Ether option, in which the prevalence of bid and ask prices of the Ether option is explained by the model uncertainty about the conditional mean and volatility of the logarithmic returns of Ethereum. In this case, some further questions may arise. For example, besides model uncertainty, can the prevalence of bid and ask prices of the Ether option be explained by other economic factors? If yes, what other economic factors might be included? Another potential topic for further research may be to explore the possibility of developing a Bayesian version of nonlinear valuation operators in (Coque et al. 2002; Peng 2004a, 2004b, 2004c, 2005). For example, can a Bayesian version of nonlinear valuation operators be developed in continuous time?

Funding: The author wishes to acknowledge the Discovery Grant from the Australian Research Council (ARC) (project number: DP190102674).

Data Availability Statement: The data supporting reported results can be found from Yahoo Finance (https://au.finance.yahoo.com/quote/ETH-AUD/ (accessed on 15 September 2024)).

Acknowledgments: The author sincerely thanks the three reviewers for helpful and insightful comments. The author would like to thank the comment from a referee which inspired the discussions in Section 7.

Conflicts of Interest: The author declares no conflicts of interest.

References

Agarwal, Ankush, Christian Oliver Ewald, and Yihan Zou. 2021. An RBSDE Based Monte Carlo Method for Solving Optimal Stopping Problems under Parameter Uncertainty. Available online: https://ssrn.com/abstract=3549891 (accessed on 21 June 2021).

Alexander, Carol, Ding Chen, and Arben Imeraj. 2023. Crypto quanto and inverse options. *Mathematical Finance* 33: 1005–43. [CrossRef]

Avellaneda, Marco, Arnon Levy, and Antonio Paras. 1995. Pricing and hedging derivative securities in markets with uncertain volatilities. *Applied Mathematical Finance* 2: 73–88. [CrossRef]
Badescu, Alexandru M., and Reg J. Kulperger. 2008. GARCH option pricing: A semiparametric approach. *Insurance: Mathematics and Economics* 43: 69–84. [CrossRef]
Badescu, Alexandru M., Robert J. Elliott, Reg J. Kulperger, Jarkko Miettinen, and Tak Kuen Siu. 2011. A comparison of pricing kernels for GARCH option pricing with generalized hyperbolic distributions. *International Journal of Theoretical and Applied Finance* 14: 669–708. [CrossRef]
Bartlett, Maurice S. 1990. Chance or chaos (with discussion). *Journal of Royal Statistical Society A* 153: 321–47. [CrossRef]
Bauwens, Luc, and Michel Lubrano. 2002. Bayesian option pricing using asymmetric GARCH models. *Journal of Empirical Finance* 9: 321–42. [CrossRef]
Beissner, Patrick Beissner, and Frank Riedel. 2019. Equilibria under Knightian price uncertainty. *Econometrica* 87: 37–64. [CrossRef]
Berliner, L. Mark. 1992. Statistics, probability and chaos. *Statistical Science* 7: 69–122. [CrossRef]
Bernardo, José M., and Adrian F. M. Smith. 2000. *Bayesian Theory*. New York: John Wiley & Sons, Inc.
Bollerslev, Tim. 1986. Generalized autoregressive conditional heteroskedasticity. *Journal of Econometrics* 31: 307–27. [CrossRef]
Boyle, Phelim P. 1977. Options: A Monte Carlo approach. *Journal of Financial Economics* 4: 323–38. [CrossRef]
Boyle, Phelim P., and A. L. Ananthanarayanan. 1977. The impact of variance estimation in option valuation models. *Journal of Financial Economics* 5: 375–87. [CrossRef]
Boyle, Phelim P., Mark Broadie, and Paul Glasserman. 1997. Monte Carlo methods for security pricing. *Journal of Economic Dynamics and Control* 21: 1267–321. [CrossRef]
Boyle, Phelim P., Shui Feng, Weidong Tian, and Tan Wang. 2008. Robust stochastic discount factors. *Review of Financial Studies* 21: 1077–122. [CrossRef]
Brini, Alessio, and Jimmie Lenz. 2024. Pricing cryptocurrency options with machine learning regression for handling market volatility. *Economic Modelling* 136: 106752. [CrossRef]
Broock, William A., David A. Hsieh, and Blake LeBaron. 1991. *Nonlinear Dynamics, Chaos and Instability: Statistical Theory and Economic Evidence*. Cambridge: MIT Press.
Broock, William A., José A. Scheinkman, W. Davis Dechert, and Blake Lebaron. 1996. A test for independence based on the correlation dimension. *Econometric Reviews* 15: 197–235. [CrossRef]
Buraschi, Andrea, and Alexei Jiltsov. 2006. Model uncertainty and option markets with heterogeneous beliefs. *Journal of Finance* 61: 2841–97. [CrossRef]
Cao, Melanie, and Batur Celik. 2021. Valuation of bitcoin options. *The Journal of Futures Markets* 41: 1007–26. [CrossRef]
Casdagli, Martin. 1992. Chaos and deterministic versus stochastic nonlinear modelling. *Journal of Royal Statistical Society Series B* 54: 303–28. [CrossRef]
Chan, Jeremy. 2022. CME to Launch Ether Options Contract. Financial News. Dow Jones & Company, Inc. September. Available online: https://www.fnlondon.com/articles/cme-ether-bitcoin-options-futures-crypto-merge-derivatives-contract-20220913 (accessed on 15 September 2024).
Chan, Kung-Sik, and Howell Tong. 1994. A note on noisy chaos. *Journal of Royal Statistical Society Series B* 56: 301–11. [CrossRef]
Chan, Kung-Sik, and Howell Tong. 2001. *Chaos: A Statistical Approach*. New York: Springer.
Chau, Huy N., Masaaki Fukasawa, and Miklós Rásonyi. 2022. Super-replication with transaction costs under model uncertainty for continuous processes. *Mathematical Finance* 32: 1066–85. [CrossRef]
Chen, Kuo Shing, and J. Jimmy Yang. 2024. Price dynamics and volatility jumps in bitcoin options. *Financial Innovation* 10: 132. [CrossRef]
Cheng, Bing, and Howell Tong. 1992. Consistent nonparametric order determination and chaos (with discussion). *Journal of Royal Statistical Society Series B* 54: 427–449, 451–474. [CrossRef]
Cheng, Bing, and Howell Tong. 1994. Orthogonal projection, embedding dimension and sample size in chaotic time series from a statistical perspective. *Philosophical Transactions of the Royal Society (London) A* 348: 325–41.
Cherny, Alexander, and Dilip B. Madan. 2009. New measures for performance evaluation. *The Review of Financial Studies* 22: 2571–606. [CrossRef]
Cohen, Samuel N., and Martin Tegnér. 2019. European option pricing with stochastic volatility models under parameter uncertainty. In *Frontiers in Stochastic Analysis–BSDEs, SPDEs and Their Applications*. Edited by Samuel N. Cohen, Istvan Gyongy, Goncalo dos Reis, David Siska and Lukasz Szpruch. BSDE-SPDE 2017. Springer Proceedings in Mathematics & Statistics. Cham: Springer, vol. 289. [CrossRef]
Cont, Rama. 2006. Model uncertainty and its impact on the pricing of derivative instruments. *Mathematical Finance* 16: 519–47 [CrossRef]
Copeland, Tim. 2023. A Brief History of Ethereum. The Block. September. Available online: https://www.theblock.co/learn/245716/a-brief-history-of-ethereum (accessed on 15 September 2024).
Coque, François, Ying Hu, Jean Mémin, and Shige Peng. 2002. Filtration-consistent nonlinear expectations and related *g*-expectations. *Probability Theory and Related Fields* 123: 1–27. [CrossRef]
Darsinos, Theo, and Stephen Satchell. 2007. Bayesian analysis of the Black-Scholes option price. In *Forecasting Expected Returns in the Financial Markets*. Edited by Stephen Satchell. Cambridge: Academic Press, pp. 117–50.

Delbaen, Freddy, and Walter Schachermayer. 1994. A general version of the fundamental theorem of asset pricing. *Mathematische Annalen* 300: 463–520. [CrossRef]
Duan, Jin-Chuan. 1995. The GARCH option pricing model. *Mathematical Finance* 5: 13–32. [CrossRef]
Dunford, Nelson, and Jacob T. Schwartz. 1958. *Linear Operators: Part I*. New York: Interscience.
Elliott, Robert J. 1982. *Stochastic Calculus and Applications*. Berlin/Heidelberg and New York: Springer.
Elliott, Robert J. 2017. Filtering with uncertain noise. *IEEE Transactions on Automatic Control* 62: 876–81. [CrossRef]
Elliott, Robert J., and Dilip B. Madan. 1998. A discrete time equivalent martingale measure. *Mathematical Finance* 8: 127–52. [CrossRef]
Elliott, Robert J., and Tak Kuen Siu. 2017. Stochastic volatility with regime switching and uncertain noise: Filtering with sub-linear expectations. *Discrete and Continuous Dynamical Systems Series B* 22: 59–81. [CrossRef]
Elliott, Robert J., Dilip B. Madan, and Tak Kuen Siu. 2022. Lower and upper pricing of financial assets. *Probability, Uncertainty and Quantitative Risk* 7: 45–66. [CrossRef]
Elliott, Robert J., Lakhdar Aggoun, and John B. Moore. 1995. *Hidden Markov Models: Estimation and Control*, 1st ed. New York: Springer.
Elliott, Robert J., Tak Kuen Siu, and Eric S. Fung. 2012. Filtering a nonlinear stochastic volatility model. *Nonlinear Dynamics* 67: 1295–313. [CrossRef]
Elliott, Robert J., Tak Kuen Siu, and Leunglung Chan. 2006. Option pricing for GARCH models with Markov switching. *International Journal of Theoretical and Applied Finance* 9: 825–41. [CrossRef]
Fan, Jianqing, and Qiwei Yao. 2003. *Nonlinear Time Series: Nonparametric and Parametric Methods*. New York: Springer.
Fan, Jianqing, Qiwei Yao, and Howell Tong. 1993. Estimation of conditional densities and sensitivity measures in nonlinear dynamical systems. *Biometrika* 83: 189–206. [CrossRef]
Farmer, J. Doyne. 2024. *Making Sense of Chaos: A Better Economics for a Better World*. London: Penguin.
Foster, F. Douglas, and Charles H. Whiteman. 1999. An application of Bayesian option pricing to the soybean market. *American Journal of Agricultural Economics* 81: 722–27. [CrossRef]
Fouque, Jean-Pierre, and Bin Ren. 2014. Approximation for option prices under uncertain volatility. *SIAM Journal on Financial Mathematics* 5: 360–83. [CrossRef]
Galanos, Alexios, and Tobias Kley. 2023. Univariate GARCH Models. R Package "Rugarch". Version 1.5-1. September 20. Available online: https://cran.r-project.org/web/packages/rugarch/rugarch.pdf (accessed on 15 September 2024).
Garnier, Josselin, and Knut Solna. 2019. Chaos and order in the bitcoin market. *Physica A: Statistical Mechanics and its Applications* 524: 708–21. [CrossRef]
Gleick, James. 1987. *Chaos: Making a New Science*. New York: Viking Books.
Godbole, Omkar. 2020. Crypto Derivatives Exchange OKEx Launches Options on Ether. CoinDesk. June. Available online: https://www.coindesk.com/markets/2020/06/05/crypto-derivatives-exchange-okex-launches-options-on-ether/ (accessed on 15 September 2024).
Godbole, Omkar. 2023. Bitcoin, Ether Options Order Books Signal Calm Amid Mounting Risks. CoinDesk. October. Available online: https://www.coindesk.com/markets/2023/10/10/bitcoin-ether-options-order-books-signal-calm-amid-mounting-risks/ (accessed on 15 September 2024).
Gzyl, Henryk, Enrique ter Horst, and Samuel Malone. 2022. Towards a Bayesian Framework for Option Pricing. Available online: https://arxiv.org/pdf/cs/0610053 (accessed on 15 September 2024).
Hansen, Lars Peter, and Scott F. Richard. 1987. The role of conditioning information in deducing testable restrictions implied by dynamic asset pricing models. *Econometrica* 55: 587–613. [CrossRef]
Harrison, J. Michael, and David M. Kreps. 1979. Martingales and arbitrage in multiperiod securities markets. *Journal of Economic Theory* 20: 381–408. [CrossRef]
Harrison, J. Michael, and Stanley R. Pliska. 1981. Martingales and stochastic integrals in the theory of continuous trading. *Stochastic Processes and Their Applications* 11: 215–80. [CrossRef]
Harrison, J. Michael, and Stanley R. Pliska. 1983. A stochastic calculus model of continuous trading: Complete markets. *Stochastic Processes and Their Applications* 15: 313–16. [CrossRef]
Hilliard, Jimmy E., and Julie T. D. Ngo. 2022. Bitcoin: Jumps, convenience yields, and option prices. *Quantitative Finance* 22: 2079–91. [CrossRef]
Ho, Shu Wing, Alan Lee, and Alastair Marsden. 2011. Use of Bayesian estimates to determine the volatility parameter input in the Black-Scholes and binomial option pricing models. *Journal of Risk and Financial Management* 3: 74–96. [CrossRef]
Hou, Ai Jun, Weining Wang, Cathy Y. H. Chen, and Wolfgang Karl Härdle. 2020. Pricing cryptocurrency options. *Journal of Financial Econometrics* 18: 250–79.
Hsieh, David A. 1991. Chaos and nonlinear dynamics: Application to financial markets. *Journal of Finance* 46: 1839–77. [CrossRef]
Hsieh, David A. 1993. Implications of nonlinear dynamics for financial risk management. *Journal of Financial and Quantitative Analysis* 28: 41–64. [CrossRef]
Hsieh, David A. 1995. Nonlinear dynamics in financial markets: Evidence and implication. *Financial Analyst Journal* 51: 55–62. [CrossRef]
Jalan, Akanksha, Roman Matkovskyy, and Saqib Aziz. 2021. The Bitcoin options market: A first look at pricing and risk. *Applied Economics* 53: 2026–41. [CrossRef]

Jang, Huisu, and Jaewook Lee. 2019. Generative Bayesian neural network model for risk-neutral pricing of American index options. *Quantitative Finance* 19: 587–603. [CrossRef]
Jaroszkowski, Bartosz, and Max Jensen. 2022. Valuation of European options under an uncertain market price of volatility risk. *Applied Mathematical Finance* 29: 213–26. [CrossRef]
Karolyi, G. Andrew. 1993. A Bayesian approach to modeling stock return volatility for option valuation. *Journal of Financial and Quantitative Analysis* 28: 579–94. [CrossRef]
Klibanoff, Peter, Massimo Marinacci, and Sujoy Mukerji. 2005. A smooth model of decision making under ambiguity. *Econometrica* 73: 1849–92. [CrossRef]
Kong, Augustine, Jun S. Liu, and Wing Hung Wong. 1994. Sequential imputations and Bayesian missing data problems. *Journal of the American Statistical Association* 89: 278–88. [CrossRef]
Li, Lun, Ali Arab, Jiqiang Liu, Jingxian Liu, and Zhu Han. 2019. Bitcoin options pricing using LSTM-based prediction model and blockchain statistics. Paper presented at IEEE International Conference on Blockchain (Blockchain), Atlanta, GA, USA, July 14–17; pp. 67–74.
Lucic, Vladimir, and Artur Sepp. 2024. Valuation and hedging of cryptocurrency inverse options. *Quantitative Finance* 24: 851–69. [CrossRef]
Lyons, Terry J. 1995. Uncertain volatility and the risk-free synthesis of derivatives. *Applied Mathematical Finance* 2: 117–33. [CrossRef]
Madan, Dilip B. 2015. Asset pricing theory for two price economies. *Annals of Finance* 11: 1–35. [CrossRef]
Madan, Dilip B. 2016. Benchmarking in two price financial markets. *Annals of Finance* 12: 201–19. [CrossRef]
Madan, Dilip B., and Alexander Cherny. 2010. Markets as a counterparty: An introduction to conic finance. *International Journal of Theoretical and Applied Finance* 13: 1149–77. [CrossRef]
Madan, Dilip B., Sofie Reyners, and Wim Schoutens. 2019. Advanced model calibration on bitcoin options. *Digital Finance* 1: 117–37. [CrossRef]
Martin, Gael M., Catherine S. Forbes, and Vance L. Martin. 2005. Implicit Bayesian inference using option prices. *Journal of Time Series Analysis* 26: 437–62. [CrossRef]
May, Robert M. 1976. Simple mathematical models with very complicated dynamics. *Nature* 261: 459–67. [CrossRef]
McGleenon, Brian. 2024. Ether Options Trading Volume Hits All-Time High as Price Sits around $2300. The Block. January. Available online: https://www.theblock.co/post/275300/ether-options-trading-volume-hits-all-time-high-as-price-sits-around-2300 (accessed on 15 September 2024).
Merton, Robert C. 1980. On estimating the expected return on the market: An exploratory investigation. *Journal of Financial Economics* 8: 323–61. [CrossRef]
Mozumder, Sharif, Taufiq Choudhry, and Michael Dempsey. 2021. Option pricing model biases: Bayesian and Markov Chain Monte Carlo regression analysis. *Computational Economics* 57: 1287–305. [CrossRef]
Pagnottoni, Paolo. 2019. Neural network models for Bitcoin option pricing. *Frontiers in Artificial Intelligence* 2: 5. [CrossRef]
Palmer, Tim. 2023. *The Primacy of Doubt*. Oxford: Oxford University Press.
Peng, Shige. 1997. Backward SDE and related *g*-expectation. In *Backward Stochastic Differential Equations*. Pitman Research Notes in Mathematics Series 364. London: Longman Scientific & Technical, pp. 141–59.
Peng, Shige. 2004a. Dynamical evaluations. *C. R. Acad. Sci. Paris Ser. I* 339: 585–89. [CrossRef]
Peng, Shige. 2004b. Filtration consistent nonlinear expectations and evaluations of contingent claims. *Acta Mathematicae Applicatae Sinica English Series* 20: 191–214. [CrossRef]
Peng, Shige. 2004c. Nonlinear expectations, nonlinear evaluations and risk measures. In *Stochastic Methods in Finance*. Lecture notes in mathematics 1856. New York: Springer, pp. 138–65.
Peng, Shige. 2005. Dynamically Consistent Nonlinear Evaluations and Expectations. Available online: https://arxiv.org/abs/math/0501415 (accessed on 15 September 2024).
Peng, Shige. 2006. *G*-expectation, *G*-Brownian motion and related stochastic calculus of Itô's type. In *The Abel Symposium 2005, Abel Symposia 2*. Berlin: Springer, pp. 541–67.
Peng, Shige. 2019. *Nonlinear Expectations and Stochastic Calculus under Uncertainty with Robust CLT and G-Brownian Motion*. New York: Springer.
Peters, Edgar E. 1996. *Chaos and Order in the Capital Markets: A New View of Cycles, Prices, and Market Volatility*, 2nd ed. New York: John Wiley & Sons, Inc.
Pietrych, Lukasz, Julio E. Sandubete, and Lorenzo Escot. 2021. Solving the chaos model-data paradox in the cryptocurrency market. *Communications in Nonlinear Science and Numerical Simulation* 102: 105901. [CrossRef]
Qin, Zhang, and Caio Almeida. 2020. A Bayesian nonparametric approach to option pricing. *Brazilian Review of Finance* 18: 115–37. [CrossRef]
Qiu, Debin. 2024. Alternative Time Series Analysis. R Package "aTSA". Version 3.1.2.1. February 21. Available online: https://cran.r-project.org/web/packages/aTSA/aTSA.pdf (accessed on 15 September 2024).
Ramoni, Marco, and Paola Sebastiani. 2001. Robust learning with missing data. *Machine Learning* 45: 147–70. [CrossRef]
Romboutsa, Jeroen V. K., and Lars Stentoft. 2014. Bayesian option pricing using mixed normal heteroskedasticity models. *Computational Statistics and Data Analysis* 76: 588–605. [CrossRef]
Rubin, Donald B. 1976. Inference and missing data. *Biometrika* 63: 581–92. [CrossRef]

Schefczyk, Michael. 2012. The financial crisis, the exemption view and the problem of the harmless torturer. *Philosophy of Management* 11: 25–38. [CrossRef]
Shegokar, Nikhilesh. 2022. Option Pricing on Cryptocurrency Underlying Using Diffusion and Jump-Diffusion Stochastic Volatility Models. May. Available online: https://cryptoquant.uk/assets/documentation/main.pdf (accessed on 15 September 2024).
Siu, Tak Kuen. 2001. Risk Measures in Finance and Insurance. Ph.D. thesis, The University of Hong Kong, Hong Kong SAR, China.
Siu, Tak Kuen. 2023a. Bayesian nonlinear expectation for time series modelling and its application to Bitcoin. *Empirical Economics* 64: 505–37. [CrossRef]
Siu, Tak Kuen. 2023b. European option pricing with market frictions, regime switches and model uncertainty. *Insurance: Mathematics and Economics* 113: 233–50. [CrossRef]
Siu, Tak Kuen. 2024. Finite mixture models for option pricing: An application to Bitcoin options. *Submitted.*
Siu, Tak Kuen, and Robert J. Elliott. 2021. Bitcoin option pricing with a SETAR-GARCH model. *European Journal of Finance* 27: 564–95. [CrossRef]
Siu, Tak Kuen, Howell Tong, and Hailiang Yang. 2001. Bayesian risk measures for derivatives via random Esscher transform. *North American Actuarial Journal* 5: 78–91. [CrossRef]
Siu, Tak Kuen, Howell Tong, and Hailiang Yang. 2004a. On pricing derivatives under GARCH models: A dynamic Gerber-Shiu approach. *North American Actuarial Journal* 8: 17–31. [CrossRef]
Siu, Tak Kuen, Howell Tong, and Hailiang Yang. 2004b. On Bayesian Value at Risk: From linear to non-linear portfolios. *Asia-Pacific Financial Markets* 11: 161–84. [CrossRef]
Siu, Tak Kuen, Howell Tong, and Hailiang Yang. 2006. Option pricing under threshold autoregressive models by threshold Esscher transform. *Journal of Industrial and Management Optimization* 2: 177–97.
Tanner, Martin A., and Wing Hung Wong. 1987. The calculation of posterior distributions by data augmentation. *Journal of the American Statistical Association* 82: 528–50. [CrossRef]
Taylor, Stephen J. 1986. *Modelling Financial Time Series*. Chichester: Wiley.
Taylor, Stephen J. 2005. *Asset Price Dynamics, Volatility, and Prediction*. Princeton: Princeton University Press.
Tong, Howell. 1977. Discussion of a paper by A. J. Lawrance and N. T. Kottegoda. *Journal of Royal Statistical Society: Series A* 140: 34–35.
Tong, Howell. 1983. *Threshold Models in Nonlinear Time Series Analysis*. Berlin, Heidelberg and New York: Springer Verlag.
Tong, Howell. 1990. *Non-linear Time Series: A Dynamical System Approach*. Oxford: Oxford University Press.
Tong, Howell. 1992. Some comments on a bridge between nonlinear dynamicists and statisticians. *Physica D: Nonlinear Phenomena* 58: 299–303. [CrossRef]
Tong, Howell. 1995. A personal overview of non-linear time series analysis from a chaos perspective (with discussion and rejoinder). *Scandinavian Journal of Statistics* 22: 399–445.
Tong, Howell. 2002. Nonlinear time series analysis since 1990: Some personal reflections. *Acta Mathematicae Applicatae Sinica, English Series* 18: 177–84. [CrossRef]
Tong, Howell. 2007. Exploring volatility from a dynamical system perspective. In *56th Session of the International Statistical Institute*. Lisbon: PRT.
Venter, Pierre J., and Eben Maré. 2021. Univariate and multivariate GARCH models applied to Bitcoin futures option pricing. *Journal of Risk and Financial Management* 14: 261. [CrossRef]
Wang, Ying, Sai Tsang Boris Choy, and Hoi Ying Wong. 2016. Bayesian option pricing framework with stochastic volatility for FX data. *Risks* 4: 51. [CrossRef]
Wilmott, Paul. 2007. *Paul Wilmott Introduces Quantitative Finance*, 2nd ed. Hoboken: Wiley.
Wilmott, Paul, and Asli Oztukel. 1998. Uncertain parameters, an empirical stochastic volatility model and confidence limits. *International Journal of Theoretical and Applied Finance* 1: 175–89. [CrossRef]
Yang, K. 2021. History of Crypto Derivatives. Crypto.com. February. Available online: https://crypto.com/research/history-of-crypto-derivatives (accessed on 15 September 2024).
Yao, Qiwei, and Howell Tong. 1994a. Quantifying the influence of initial values on non-linear prediction. *Journal of Royal Statistical Society Series B* 56: 701–25. [CrossRef]
Yao, Qiwei, and Howell Tong. 1994b. On prediction and chaos in stochastic systems. *Philosophical Transactions of the Royal Society (London) A* 348: 357–69.
Yao, Qiwei, and Howell Tong. 1998. A bootstrap detection for operational determinism. *Physica D: Nonlinear Phenomena* 115: 49–55. [CrossRef]
Zhang, Tong. 2023. *Mathematical Analysis of Machine Learning Algorithms*. Cambridge: Cambridge University Press.

Journal of
Risk and Financial Management

MDPI

Article

Extended Least Squares Making Evident Nonlinear Relationships between Variables: Portfolios of Financial Assets

Pierpaolo Angelini

Dipartimento di Scienze Statistiche, Università La Sapienza, 00185 Roma, Italy; pier.angelini@uniroma1.it

Abstract: This research work extends the least squares criterion. The regression models which have been treated so far in the literature do not study multilinear relationships between variables. Such relationships are of a nonlinear nature. They take place whenever two or more than two univariate variables are the components of a multiple variable of order 2 or an order greater than 2. A multiple variable of order 2 is not a bivariate variable, and a multiple variable of an order greater than 2 is not a multivariate variable. A multiple variable allows for the construction of a tensor. The α-norm of this tensor gives rise to an aggregate measure of a multilinear nature. In particular, given a multiple variable of order 2, four regression lines can be estimated in the same subset of a two-dimensional linear space over $\mathbb{R}$. How these four regression lines give rise to an aggregate measure of a multilinear nature is shown by this paper. In this research work, such a measure is an estimate concerning the expected return on a portfolio of financial assets. The metric notion of α-product is used to summarize the sampling units which are observed.

Keywords: multiple variable; tensor; correlation coefficient; CAPM; mean-variance model; expected utility model

JEL Classification: C1; C3; C5; G4

1. Introduction

Relationships between variables can be of a linear or nonlinear nature. In this paper, particular nonlinear relationships are made evident. Their intrinsic nature is multilinear. Multilinear relationships between variables take place whenever two or more than two univariate variables are the components of a multiple variable of order 2 or greater than 2. It is possible to write $X_{12} = \{_1X, _2X\}$, where $_1X$ and $_2X$ are the components of X_{12}. If one writes $X_{123} = \{_1X, _2X, _3X\}$, then $_1X$, $_2X$, and $_3X$ are the components of X_{123}. Similarly, if one writes $X_{12\ldots m} = \{_1X, _2X, _3X, \ldots, _mX\}$, then $_1X, _2X, _3X, \ldots,$ and $_mX$ are the components of $X_{12\ldots m}$. Within this context, X_{12}, X_{123}, and $X_{12\ldots m}$ are multiple variables. Their components are univariate variables which influence each other. A multiple variable of order 2 is not a bivariate variable, and a multiple variable of order greater than 2 is not a multivariate variable. This paper will clarify why multilinear indices associated with a multiple variable of order 2 are based on $2^2 = 4$ bivariate distributions of probability. Similarly, it will also be clarified why multilinear indices associated with a multiple variable of order m, where $m > 2$ is an integer, are based on m^2 bivariate distributions of probability. Each bivariate distribution of probability underlying a multilinear index is of a two-dimensional nature. Hence, it is possible to decompose it into two marginal probability distributions. This paper focuses on a multilinear approach of a Bayesian nature according to which more than two univariate variables are always studied in pairs. Since a multilinear and quadratic metric is used to study multilinear relationships between variables, various indices of a bivariate nature are firstly taken into account. This means that a disaggregation process first takes place. An aggregation process takes place second whenever a multilinear measure is shown. For these reasons, in this paper, given a multiple variable of order 2, four regression lines are estimated in the same subset of a two-dimensional linear space over $\mathbb{R}$. The multilinear regression model introduced in this research work is different from those regression models which have been treated so far in the literature (see Aneiros et al. 2022; Ewald and Schneider 2020). The multilinear regression model handled in this paper allows us to make fair estimates based on the notion of prevision (see Cassese et al. 2020). Prevision consists of considering all the observed values drawn by a given population in order to distribute among them those nonnegative and finitely additive masses such that only absolutely inadmissible evaluations have to be excluded (see Angelini 2024b). Two dynamical phases are then involved with respect to the notion of prevision. They depend on a specific state of information and knowledge associated with a given individual. This state is intrinsically variable. The first phase gives rise to a closed convex set. This is because possible opinions about the evaluations of probability are infinite in number. Strictly speaking, if the observed values are put on a straight line, then a closed line segment appears in the first phase. Every point belonging to this closed line segment is a fair estimate of the parameter under consideration. The second phase gives rise to the choice of a point belonging to the closed line segment into account. This choice avoids that an extrapolation process takes place outside the closed line segment under consideration (see Berti et al. 2001). The notion of prevision is different from the one of prediction. Within this context, to make a prediction does not mean to handle barycenters of masses in the first phase and choosing one of them in the second one. To make a prediction means to make a prophecy. Hence, one out of the possible and observed values belonging to the set of possible alternatives can arbitrarily be chosen. It is then a prophecy. For this reason, one says that a prediction transforms the uncertainty into an artificial certainty (see Angelini 2024a). The distinction between prevision and prediction is not clear-cut in a non-specific language. Nevertheless, if one wants to identify an existing dichotomy, then this distinction is appropriate and necessary. There is therefore a fundamental difference: after knowing the specific outcome, a prediction can be said to be right or wrong in an objective way; conversely, whatever happens, nothing similar in any sense can be said about a prevision. The intrinsic nature of a prevision is then subjective.

The Objectives of This Paper

Given two variables ${}_1X$ and ${}_2X$, if one writes ${}_2X = f({}_1X)$, then ${}_2X$ is the dependent or explained variable and ${}_1X$ is the independent or explanatory variable. Whenever a specific value of ${}_1X$ is predicted, the corresponding level associated with the other univariate variable ${}_2X$ can be one out of the observed values, or it can be found beyond them. If this specific value is found beyond observed values, then it can be found either to the left or right of them. The further one extrapolates beyond the observed values, the greater the risk one runs. Whenever the model under consideration is extrapolated far beyond the given sampling data, the result can become meaningless. In this paper, after studying four linear relationships between the two components, ${}_1X$ and ${}_2X$, of a multiple variable of order 2 denoted by X_{12}, one is always inclined to avoid the fact that aggregate estimates of a specific parameter take place by choosing, as their constituent elements, points outside the closed line segments belonging to the four regression lines, respectively. Such lines capture the given sampling units via the least squares criterion. For this reason, one refers oneself to the notion of prevision. Such a notion takes all given sampling units into account. It is possible to summarize them using the concept of α-product. Such a concept is of a metric nature. In Section 2, the two-variable multilinear regression model treated in this paper is conceptually and formally shown. In Section 3, a specific regression line is estimated. In Section 4, another regression line is estimated using the same observations in a different way. In Section 5, two regression lines, whose least squares residuals are intrinsically equal to zero, are handled. Section 6 shows that the notion of α-product is an essential tool of prevision. In Section 7, the bivariate correlation coefficient is obtained using an aggregate measure of a multilinear nature. This means that the bivariate correlation coefficient can intrinsically be referred to a multiple variable of order 2. Section 8 contains how the multilinear regression model treated in this paper can be used to make rational estimates related to the expected return on portfolios of financial assets. Section 9 shows that a tensor identifies a multiple variable. A fundamental difference between a multiple variable and a multivariate one is made evident. Moreover, the empirical validation of the proposed multilinear regression model is handled. Finally, Section 10 contains conclusions and some future perspectives.

2. The Two-Variable Multilinear Regression Model: Conceptual and Formal Properties

The two-variable multilinear regression model treated in this paper studies multilinear relationships between variables. X_{12} is a multiple variable of order 2. Its components are denoted by ${}_1X$ and ${}_2X$, respectively. One writes

$$X_{12} = \{{}_1X, {}_2X\}, \tag{1}$$

where ${}_1X$ and ${}_2X$ are two univariate variables. The two-variable multilinear regression model handled in this research work is composed of four regression lines. They are depicted in the same subset of a two-dimensional linear space over $\mathbb{R}$. They are studied in the same subset of the Cartesian plane. With respect to these four regression lines, two regression lines are estimated. The other two regression lines exactly coincide with the same 45-degree line. Such a model is formally given by

$$\text{two-variable multilinear regression} = \begin{cases} {}_2X = \alpha + \beta\,({}_1X), \\ {}_1X = \alpha^* + \beta^*\,({}_2X), \\ {}_2X = {}_1X, \\ {}_1X = {}_2X. \end{cases} \tag{2}$$

Since ${}_1X$ and ${}_2X$ are the two components of X_{12}, it is possible to observe that ${}_1X$ influences ${}_2X$, and ${}_2X$ influences ${}_1X$. There is no one-way causation. Hence, ${}_1X$ influences ${}_2X$. Since there is feedback in the opposite direction, ${}_2X$ influences ${}_1X$ as well. Four different pairs of marginal variables are studied. They are $({}_1X, {}_1X)$, $({}_1X, {}_2X)$, $({}_2X, {}_1X)$, and $({}_2X, {}_2X)$. For this reason, a multilinear relationship between ${}_1X$ and ${}_2X$ is dealt with.

3. An Estimated Regression Line

Let

$$({}_1X_i, {}_2X_i), \tag{3}$$

with $i = 1, \ldots, n$, be a sample of n ordered pairs of observations associated with ${}_1X$ and ${}_2X$, respectively. Given this sample, whose size is equal to n, the linear relationship between the two components of X_{12} expressed by

$${}_2X = \alpha + \beta\,({}_1X) \tag{4}$$

is first studied. It is possible to enlarge (4) by considering

$${}_2X = \alpha + \beta\,({}_1X) + u, \tag{5}$$

where u is a stochastic variable which is normally distributed. One writes

$${}_2X_i = \alpha + \beta\,({}_1X_i) + u_i, \tag{6}$$

with $i = 1, \ldots, n$, where it turns out to be

$$\begin{cases} \mathbb{E}(u_i) = 0, \quad \text{for all } i, \\ \operatorname{var}(u_i) = \mathbb{E}(u_i^2) = \sigma^2, \quad \text{for all } i, \\ \operatorname{cov}(u_i\,u_j) = \mathbb{E}(u_i\,u_j) = 0, \quad \text{for } i \neq j. \end{cases} \tag{7}$$

The disturbances denoted by u_i are independently and identically distributed, with zero mean and variance expressed by σ^2.

The scatter of n observations is conventionally studied inside the first quadrant of a two-dimensional Cartesian coordinate system. An estimation of the linear relationship coinciding with (5) is given by the straight line expressed by

$$ {}_2\hat{X} = a + b\,({}_1X), \tag{8} $$

where ${}_2\hat{X}$ indicates the height of the line at ${}_1X$. If a and b are selected to minimize the residual sum of squares given by

$$ \text{RSS} = \sum_{i=1}^{n} ({}_2e_i)^2 = \sum_{i=1}^{n} \left({}_2X_i - a - b\,({}_1X_i)\right)^2 = f(a,\, b), \tag{9} $$

then the least squares principle takes place (see Watson 1967; Bartlett and Macdonald 1968). The necessary conditions for a stationary value of RSS are such that it is possible to write

$$ a = {}_2\bar{X} - b\,({}_1\bar{X}), \tag{10} $$

and

$$ b = \frac{\sum_{i=1}^{n} {}_1x_i\, {}_2x_i}{\sum_{i=1}^{n} ({}_1x_i)^2}, \tag{11} $$

where one has

$$ {}_1x_i = {}_1X_i - {}_1\bar{X}, \tag{12} $$

with $i = 1, \ldots, n$, and

$$ {}_2x_i = {}_2X_i - {}_2\bar{X}, \tag{13} $$

with $i = 1, \ldots, n$. Once the sample means have been calculated, the data characterizing (11) are expressed using deviations from them. ${}_1\bar{X}$ and ${}_2\bar{X}$ denote the sample means of ${}_1X$ and ${}_2X$, respectively.

The least squares line passes through the mean point given by $({}_1\bar{X},\, {}_2\bar{X})$. The least squares residuals have zero correlation in the sample with the values of ${}_1X$. They have also zero correlation with the values denoted by ${}_2\hat{X}$. The decomposition of the sum of squares associated with the linear regression of ${}_2X$ on ${}_1X$ is written as

$$ \text{TSS} = \text{ESS} + \text{RSS}, \tag{14} $$

where one has

$$ \begin{cases} \text{TSS} = \text{total sum of squared deviations in the } {}_2X \text{ variable}, \\ \text{RSS} = \text{residual sum of squares from the regression of } {}_2X \text{ on } {}_1X, \\ \text{ESS} = \text{explained sum of squares from the regression of } {}_2X \text{ on } {}_1X. \end{cases} \tag{15} $$

Since it is possible to write

$$ r^2 = \frac{\text{ESS}}{\text{TSS}}, \tag{16} $$

where the coefficient of determination given by r^2 is the square of the sample correlation coefficient expressed by r, (16) is the proportion of the ${}_2X$ variation attributable to the linear regression of ${}_2X$ on ${}_1X$ (see Fisher 1922). The limits of r are ± 1. In the limiting case, the sample points all lie on a single straight line. The disturbance variance denoted by σ^2 cannot be estimated from a sample of u values denoted by u_i, $i = 1, \ldots, n$ (see Liu et al. 2020). These values are unobservable. If one knows α and β, then they can be measured. Nevertheless, α and β are unknown. It follows that the disturbance variance can be estimated from the calculated residuals. It is accordingly possible to use the following estimation expressed by

$$ {}_2s^2 = \frac{\sum_{i=1}^{n} ({}_2e_i)^2}{n-2} \tag{17} $$

to assess the disturbance variance.

Linear estimators of α and β are unbiased (see Puntanen and Styan 1989). One writes

$$ \mathbb{E}(a) = \alpha \tag{18} $$

and

$$ \mathbb{E}(b) = \beta. \tag{19} $$

Their sampling variances are the smallest that can be achieved by any linear unbiased estimator. One writes

$$ \mathrm{var}(a) = \sigma^2 \left[\frac{1}{n} + \frac{({}_1\bar{X})^2}{\sum_{i=1}^{n} ({}_1x_i)^2} \right] \tag{20} $$

and

$$ \mathrm{var}(b) = \frac{\sigma^2}{\sum_{i=1}^{n} ({}_1x_i)^2}. \tag{21} $$

The sampling distribution of the intercept term denoted by a is given by

$$ a \sim \mathrm{N}\left(\alpha, \sigma^2 \left[\frac{1}{n} + \frac{({}_1\bar{X})^2}{\sum_{i=1}^{n} ({}_1x_i)^2} \right] \right), \tag{22} $$

whereas the sampling distribution of the least squares slope denoted by b is written as

$$ b \sim \mathrm{N}\left(\beta, \frac{\sigma^2}{\sum_{i=1}^{n} ({}_1x_i)^2} \right). \tag{23} $$

Since σ^2 is unknown, it is necessary to use (17). It is an unbiased estimator because one observes

$$ \mathbb{E}\left(\frac{\sum_{i=1}^{n} ({}_2e_i)^2}{n-2} \right) = \sigma^2. \tag{24} $$

One observes

$$ \frac{\sum_{i=1}^{n} ({}_2e_i)^2}{\sigma^2} \sim \chi^2(n-2). \tag{25} $$

Also, another fundamental result associated with inference procedures is that $\sum_{i=1}^{n} ({}_2e_i)^2$ is distributed independently of $f(a, b)$. Tests on the intercept are based on the t distribution, so one writes

$$ \frac{a - \alpha}{{}_2s \sqrt{\left(\frac{1}{n} + \frac{({}_1\bar{X})^2}{\sum_{i=1}^{n} ({}_1x_i)^2} \right)}} \sim t(n-2). \tag{26} $$

Accordingly, a $100(1-\epsilon)$ percent confidence interval for α is expressed by

$$ a \pm t_{\epsilon/2}\, {}_2s \sqrt{\left(\frac{1}{n} + \frac{({}_1\bar{X})^2}{\sum_{i=1}^{n} ({}_1x_i)^2} \right)}, \tag{27} $$

whereas the null hypothesis given by $H_0\colon \alpha = \alpha_0$ is rejected at the 100ϵ percent level of significance if one observes

$$\left| \frac{a - \alpha_0}{{}_2s\sqrt{\left(\frac{1}{n} + \frac{({}_1\bar{X})^2}{\sum_{i=1}^{n}({}_1x_i)^2}\right)}} \right| > t_{\epsilon/2}. \tag{28}$$

Tests on b are based on the t distribution as well, so one writes

$$\frac{b - \beta}{\frac{{}_2s}{\sqrt{\sum_{i=1}^{n}({}_1x_i)^2}}} \sim t(n-2). \tag{29}$$

A $100(1-\epsilon)$ percent confidence interval for β is expressed by

$$b \pm t_{\epsilon/2}\frac{{}_2s}{\sqrt{\sum_{i=1}^{n}({}_1x_i)^2}}, \tag{30}$$

whereas the null hypothesis given by $H_0\colon \beta = \beta_0$ is rejected at the 100ϵ percent level of significance if one observes

$$\left| \frac{b - \beta_0}{\frac{{}_2s}{\sqrt{\sum_{i=1}^{n}({}_1x_i)^2}}} \right| > t_{\epsilon/2}. \tag{31}$$

Tests on σ^2 can be derived as well. It is possible to use a χ^2 variable to derive them.

The test for the significance of ${}_1X$ is given by $H_0\colon \beta = 0$. It is known that there are three versions connected with it. First, this test can be set out in an analysis of variance framework using the F statistic expressed by

$$F = \frac{\text{ESS}/1}{\text{RSS}/(n-2)}. \tag{32}$$

On the other hand, it is also possible to base it on the sample correlation coefficient or on the regression slope using the t distribution in both cases.

Given an estimated regression line with intercept denoted by a and slope expressed by b, it is possible to focus own attention on a specific value given by ${}_1X_0$ of the regressor variable. For example, if one is required to predict a 95 percent confidence interval for ${}_2X_0$, then one writes

$$(a + b\,({}_1X_0)) \pm t_{0.025}\,{}_2s\sqrt{\left(1 + \frac{1}{n} + \frac{({}_1X_0 - {}_1\bar{X})^2}{\sum_{i=1}^{n}({}_1x_i)^2}\right)}. \tag{33}$$

To test whether a new observation given by $({}_1X_0, {}_2X_0)$ comes from the structure generating the sample data, it is possible to compare this new observation with the confidence interval for ${}_2X_0$. If one is required to predict a 95 percent confidence interval for $\mathbb{E}({}_2X_0)$, then it is possible to write

$$(a + b\,({}_1X_0)) \pm t_{0.025}\,{}_2s\sqrt{\left(\frac{1}{n} + \frac{({}_1X_0 - {}_1\bar{X})^2}{\sum_{i=1}^{n}({}_1x_i)^2}\right)}. \tag{34}$$

In general, a sampling distribution shows the behavior of the estimators in repeated applications of the estimating formulae. A given sample provides a particular numerical estimation. Another sample from the same population will provide another numerical estimation. A sampling distribution shows the results that will be obtained for the estimators over the virtually infinite set of samples which could be drawn from the population into account. If one refers oneself to $\mathbb{E}({}_2X|{}_1X) = \alpha + \beta\,({}_1X)$ or $\mathbb{E}({}_2X|{}_1X_i) = \alpha + \beta\,({}_1X_i)$, $i = 1,\ldots,n$, then the parameters of interest are α, β, and σ^2. They are parameters of interest of a conditional distribution. In this conditional distribution, the only source of variation from one hypothetical sample to another one is a variation in the stochastic disturbance denoted by u. This stochastic disturbance, together with the given values denoted by ${}_1X_1,\ldots,{}_1X_n$, will determine the values denoted by ${}_2X_1,\ldots,{}_2X_n$. It follows that the sample values of a, b, and ${}_2s^2$ take place. Accordingly, analyzing ${}_2X$ conditional on ${}_1X$ deals with the ${}_1X_1,\ldots,{}_1X_n$ values viewed as fixed in repeated sampling. This is based on the implicit assumption that the marginal distribution for ${}_1X$ does not involve the parameters of interest. In other words, the marginal distribution for ${}_1X$ contains no information on α, β, and σ^2.

4. Another Estimated Regression Line

This paper focuses on a regression model which is not only interested in viewing ${}_1X$ as the fixed regressor. This paper focuses on a model which is also interested in viewing ${}_2X$ as the fixed regressor. Accordingly, n ordered pairs of observations of the form given by

$$({}_2X_i, {}_1X_i), \tag{35}$$

with $i = 1,\ldots,n$, are now dealt with. One takes care to interchange ${}_1X_i$ and ${}_2X_i$. One presently studies n ordered pairs of the same previous observations. Nevertheless, the first element of the previous n pairs of observations becomes the second one and vice versa. At present, one refers oneself to $\mathbb{E}({}_1X|{}_2X) = \alpha^* + \beta^*\,({}_2X)$ or $\mathbb{E}({}_1X|{}_2X_i) = \alpha^* + \beta^*\,({}_2X_i)$, $i = 1,\ldots,n$. If one refers oneself to $\mathbb{E}({}_1X|{}_2X) = \alpha^* + \beta^*\,({}_2X)$ or $\mathbb{E}({}_1X|{}_2X_i) = \alpha^* + \beta^*\,({}_2X_i)$, $i = 1,\ldots,n$, then the parameters of interest are α^*, β^*, and σ^2. They are parameters of interest of another conditional distribution (see Gilio and Sanfilippo 2014). In this conditional distribution, the only source of variation from one hypothetical sample to another one is a variation in the stochastic disturbance. It is again denoted by u. This stochastic disturbance, together with the given values denoted by ${}_2X_1,\ldots,{}_2X_n$, will determine the values denoted by ${}_1X_1,\ldots,{}_1X_n$. It follows that the sample values of a^*, b^*, and ${}_1s^2$ take place. Accordingly, analyzing ${}_1X$ conditional on ${}_2X$ deals with the ${}_2X_1,\ldots,{}_2X_n$ values viewed as fixed in repeated sampling. This is based on the implicit assumption that the marginal distribution for ${}_2X$ does not involve the parameters of interest. In other words, the marginal distribution for ${}_2X$ contains no information on α^*, β^*, and σ^2. The linear relationship between the two components of X_{12} expressed by

$${}_1X = \alpha^* + \beta^*\,({}_2X) \tag{36}$$

is studied second. It is possible to enlarge (36) by considering

$${}_1X = \alpha^* + \beta^*\,({}_2X) + u, \tag{37}$$

where u is a stochastic variable which is normally distributed. One writes

$${}_1X_i = \alpha^* + \beta^*\,({}_2X_i) + u_i, \tag{38}$$

with $i = 1,\ldots,n$, where one observes

$$\begin{cases} \mathbb{E}(u_i) = 0, & \text{for all } i, \\ \mathrm{var}(u_i) = \mathbb{E}(u_i^2) = \sigma^2, & \text{for all } i, \\ \mathrm{cov}(u_i\, u_j) = \mathbb{E}(u_i\, u_j) = 0, & \text{for } i \neq j. \end{cases}$$

The disturbances denoted by u_i are independently and identically distributed, with zero mean and variance expressed by σ^2.

An estimation of the linear relationship coinciding with (37) is given by the straight line expressed by

$$ {}_1\hat{X} = a^* + b^* \left({}_2X\right), \tag{39} $$

where ${}_1\hat{X}$ indicates the value of the straight line which is observed on the horizontal axis at ${}_2X$. If a^* and b^* are selected to minimize the residual sum of squares given by

$$ \text{RSS} = \sum_{i=1}^{n} \left({}_1e_i\right)^2 = \sum_{i=1}^{n} \left({}_1X_i - a^* - b^* \left({}_2X_i\right)\right)^2 = f(a^*, b^*), \tag{40} $$

then the least squares principle takes place. The necessary conditions for a stationary value of RSS are such that it is possible to write

$$ a^* = {}_1\bar{X} - b^* \left({}_2\bar{X}\right) \tag{41} $$

and

$$ b^* = \frac{\sum_{i=1}^{n} {}_2x_i \, {}_1x_i}{\sum_{i=1}^{n} \left({}_2x_i\right)^2}, \tag{42} $$

where one has

$$ {}_1x_i = {}_1X_i - {}_1\bar{X}, \quad i = 1, \ldots, n $$

and

$$ {}_2x_i = {}_2X_i - {}_2\bar{X}, \quad i = 1, \ldots, n. $$

Once the sample means have been calculated, the data characterizing (42) are expressed using deviations from them.

The least squares line passes through the mean point given by $\left({}_1\bar{X}, {}_2\bar{X}\right)$. The least squares residuals have zero correlation in the sample with the values of ${}_2X$. They have also zero correlation with the values denoted by ${}_1\hat{X}$. The decomposition of the sum of squares associated with the linear regression of ${}_1X$ on ${}_2X$ is written as

$$ \text{TSS} = \text{ESS} + \text{RSS}, $$

where one has

$$ \begin{cases} \text{TSS} = \text{total sum of squared deviations in the } {}_1X \text{ variable}, \\ \text{RSS} = \text{residual sum of squares from the regression of } {}_1X \text{ on } {}_2X, \\ \text{ESS} = \text{explained sum of squares from the regression of } {}_1X \text{ on } {}_2X. \end{cases} \tag{43} $$

Since it is possible to write

$$ r^2 = \frac{\text{ESS}}{\text{TSS}}, $$

r^2 is the proportion of the ${}_1X$ variation attributable to the linear regression of ${}_1X$ on ${}_2X$. The disturbance variance denoted by σ^2 cannot be estimated from a sample of u values denoted by u_i, $i = 1, \ldots, n$. These values are unobservable. If one knows α^* and β^*, then they can be measured. Unfortunately, α^* and β^* are unknown. It follows that the disturbance variance can be estimated from the calculated residuals. It is accordingly possible to use the following estimation expressed by

$$ {}_1s^2 = \frac{\sum_{i=1}^{n} \left({}_1e_i\right)^2}{n-2} \tag{44} $$

to assess the disturbance variance.

Linear estimators of α^* and β^* are unbiased. One writes

$$ \mathbb{E}(a^*) = \alpha^* \tag{45} $$

and

$$\mathbb{E}(b^*) = \beta^*. \tag{46}$$

Their sampling variances are the smallest that can be achieved by any linear unbiased estimator. One writes

$$\text{var}(a^*) = \sigma^2 \left[\frac{1}{n} + \frac{({}_2\bar{X})^2}{\sum_{i=1}^{n} ({}_2x_i)^2} \right] \tag{47}$$

and

$$\text{var}(b^*) = \frac{\sigma^2}{\sum_{i=1}^{n} ({}_2x_i)^2}. \tag{48}$$

The sampling distribution of the intercept term denoted by a^* is given by

$$a^* \sim N\left(\alpha^*, \sigma^2 \left[\frac{1}{n} + \frac{({}_2\bar{X})^2}{\sum_{i=1}^{n} ({}_2x_i)^2} \right] \right), \tag{49}$$

whereas the sampling distribution of the least squares slope denoted by b^* is written as

$$b^* \sim N\left(\beta^*, \frac{\sigma^2}{\sum_{i=1}^{n} ({}_2x_i)^2} \right). \tag{50}$$

Since σ^2 is unknown, it is necessary to use (44). It is an unbiased estimator because one observes

$$\mathbb{E}\left(\frac{\sum_{i=1}^{n} ({}_1e_i)^2}{n-2} \right) = \sigma^2. \tag{51}$$

One observes

$$\frac{\sum_{i=1}^{n} ({}_1e_i)^2}{\sigma^2} \sim \chi^2(n-2). \tag{52}$$

Also, another fundamental result associated with inference procedures is that $\sum_{i=1}^{n} ({}_1e_i)^2$ is distributed independently of $f(a^*, b^*)$. Tests on the intercept are based on the t distribution, so one writes

$$\frac{a^* - \alpha^*}{{}_1s\sqrt{\left(\frac{1}{n} + \frac{({}_2\bar{X})^2}{\sum_{i=1}^{n} ({}_2x_i)^2} \right)}} \sim t(n-2). \tag{53}$$

Accordingly, a $100(1-\epsilon)$ percent confidence interval for α^* is expressed by

$$a^* \pm t_{\epsilon/2}\, {}_1s\sqrt{\left(\frac{1}{n} + \frac{({}_2\bar{X})^2}{\sum_{i=1}^{n} ({}_2x_i)^2} \right)}, \tag{54}$$

whereas the null hypothesis given by $H_0\colon \alpha^* = \alpha_0^*$ is rejected at the 100ϵ percent level of significance if one observes

$$\left| \frac{a^* - \alpha_0^*}{{}_1s\sqrt{\left(\frac{1}{n} + \frac{({}_2\bar{X})^2}{\sum_{i=1}^{n} ({}_2x_i)^2} \right)}} \right| > t_{\epsilon/2}. \tag{55}$$

Tests on b^* are based on the t distribution as well, so one writes

$$\frac{b^* - \beta^*}{\frac{{}_1s}{\sqrt{\sum_{i=1}^{n} ({}_2x_i)^2}}} \sim t(n-2). \tag{56}$$

A $100(1-\epsilon)$ percent confidence interval for β^* is expressed by

$$b^* \pm t_{\epsilon/2} \frac{{}_1s}{\sqrt{\sum_{i=1}^{n} ({}_2x_i)^2}}, \tag{57}$$

whereas the null hypothesis given by $H_0\colon \beta^* = \beta_0^*$ is rejected at the 100ϵ percent level of significance if one observes

$$\left| \frac{b^* - \beta_0^*}{\frac{{}_1s}{\sqrt{\sum_{i=1}^{n} ({}_2x_i)^2}}} \right| > t_{\epsilon/2}. \tag{58}$$

Tests on σ^2 can be derived as well. A χ^2 variable is used to derive them.

The test for the significance of ${}_2X$ is given by $H_0\colon \beta^* = 0$. There are three versions connected with it.

Given an estimated regression line with intercept denoted by a^* and slope expressed by b^*, it is possible to focus own attention on a specific value given by ${}_2X_0$ of the regressor variable. For example, if one is required to predict a 95 percent confidence interval for ${}_1X_0$, then one writes

$$\left(a^* + b^* \left({}_2X_0\right)\right) \pm t_{0.025}\, {}_1s \sqrt{\left(1 + \frac{1}{n} + \frac{({}_2X_0 - {}_2\bar{X})^2}{\sum_{i=1}^{n} ({}_2x_i)^2}\right)}. \tag{59}$$

To test whether a new observation given by $({}_1X_0, {}_2X_0)$ comes from the structure generating the sample data, it is possible to compare this new observation with the confidence interval for ${}_1X_0$. If one is required to predict a 95 percent confidence interval for $\mathbb{E}({}_1X_0)$, then it is possible to write

$$\left(a^* + b^* \left({}_2X_0\right)\right) \pm t_{0.025}\, {}_1s \sqrt{\left(\frac{1}{n} + \frac{({}_2X_0 - {}_2\bar{X})^2}{\sum_{i=1}^{n} ({}_2x_i)^2}\right)}. \tag{60}$$

5. Two Regression Lines Whose Least Squares Residuals Are Equal to Zero

In addition to (3) and (35), this paper focuses on a regression model for which it is possible to consider n ordered pairs of observations of the form given by

$$({}_1X_i, {}_1X_i), \tag{61}$$

with $i = 1, \ldots, n$. This means that n ordered pairs of observations all lie on the 45-degree line denoted by

$${}_2X = {}_1X. \tag{62}$$

Its intercept is exactly equal to 0, whereas its slope is exactly equal to 1. The least squares residuals are intrinsically equal to 0 (see del Pino 1989). Also, in this limiting case, the least squares estimation coincides with the maximum likelihood one (see McCullagh 1983; Nelder and Pregibon 1987).

In addition to (3), (35), and (61), this paper shows a regression model for which it is also possible to study n ordered pairs of observations of the form expressed by

$$({}_2X_i, {}_2X_i), \tag{63}$$

with $i = 1, \ldots, n$. This means that n ordered pairs of observations all lie on the 45-degree line denoted by

$${}_1X = {}_2X. \tag{64}$$

Its intercept is exactly equal to 0, whereas its slope is exactly equal to 1. The least squares residuals are intrinsically equal to 0. In this limiting case, the least squares estimation coincides with the maximum likelihood one. From (62) and (64), it follows that it is true that the 45-degree line is the same graph depicted in the same subset of the Cartesian plane.

6. The Notion of α-Product as an Essential Tool of Prevision

With respect to the two estimated regression lines, one observes

$$ {}_2X = {}_2\hat{X} + {}_2e, \quad \text{with } \sum {}_2e = 0, \tag{65} $$

and

$$ {}_1X = {}_1\hat{X} + {}_1e, \quad \text{with } \sum {}_1e = 0. \tag{66} $$

This means that two n-dimensional vectors denoted by

$$ {}_2\mathbf{X} = \begin{bmatrix} {}_2X_1 \\ {}_2X_2 \\ \vdots \\ {}_2X_n \end{bmatrix} = \begin{bmatrix} {}_2X_1 \ {}_2X_2 \ \dots \ {}_2X_n \end{bmatrix} \tag{67} $$

and

$$ {}_1\mathbf{X} = \begin{bmatrix} {}_1X_1 \\ {}_1X_2 \\ \vdots \\ {}_1X_n \end{bmatrix} = \begin{bmatrix} {}_1X_1 \ {}_1X_2 \ \dots \ {}_1X_n \end{bmatrix} \tag{68} $$

are considered together with two estimated regression lines. One also writes

$$ {}_2\hat{\mathbf{X}} = \begin{bmatrix} {}_2\hat{X}_1 \\ {}_2\hat{X}_2 \\ \vdots \\ {}_2\hat{X}_n \end{bmatrix} = \begin{bmatrix} {}_2\hat{X}_1 \ {}_2\hat{X}_2 \ \dots \ {}_2\hat{X}_n \end{bmatrix} \tag{69} $$

and

$$ {}_1\hat{\mathbf{X}} = \begin{bmatrix} {}_1\hat{X}_1 \\ {}_1\hat{X}_2 \\ \vdots \\ {}_1\hat{X}_n \end{bmatrix} = \begin{bmatrix} {}_1\hat{X}_1 \ {}_1\hat{X}_2 \ \dots \ {}_1\hat{X}_n \end{bmatrix}. \tag{70} $$

These vectors belong to an n-dimensional linear space over $\mathbb{R}$ of a Euclidean nature. The last two vectors expressed by (69) and (70) are two $n \times 1$ or $1 \times n$ matrices involving regression residuals given by ${}_2e$ and ${}_1e$, respectively. In fact, one observes

$$ {}_2\hat{X} = {}_2X - {}_2e \tag{71} $$

and

$$ {}_1\hat{X} = {}_1X - {}_1e. \tag{72} $$

In general, the scalar or inner product of two n-dimensional vectors is commutative, associative, and distributive. It may also be orthogonal, so the zero-product property does not hold. Since one can always consider the transpose of an $n \times 1$ or $1 \times n$ matrix, one writes

$$ ({}_2\hat{\mathbf{X}})^T \, {}_1\mathbf{X} = \begin{bmatrix} {}_2\hat{X}_1 \ {}_2\hat{X}_2 \ \dots \ {}_2\hat{X}_n \end{bmatrix} \begin{bmatrix} {}_1X_1 \\ {}_1X_2 \\ \vdots \\ {}_1X_n \end{bmatrix}, \tag{73} $$

where $_2\hat{\mathbf{X}}$ and $_1\mathbf{X}$ are two $n \times 1$ matrices, or

$$_2\hat{\mathbf{X}}\,(_1\mathbf{X})^T = \begin{bmatrix} _2\hat{X}_1 \; _2\hat{X}_2 \; \ldots \; _2\hat{X}_n \end{bmatrix} \begin{bmatrix} _1X_1 \\ _1X_2 \\ \vdots \\ _1X_n \end{bmatrix}, \tag{74}$$

where $_2\hat{\mathbf{X}}$ and $_1\mathbf{X}$ are two $1 \times n$ matrices. Anyway, one has

$$(_2\hat{\mathbf{X}})^T \, _1\mathbf{X} = {_2\hat{\mathbf{X}}}\,(_1\mathbf{X})^T. \tag{75}$$

The two-variable multilinear regression model treated in this research work uses the metric notion of α-product (see Angelini 2023). For example, the sampling quantities of the following system

$$\begin{cases} \sum {_2X} & = na + b \sum {_1X} \\ \sum {_1X} \, {_2X} & = a \sum {_1X} + b \sum (_1X)^2 \end{cases} \tag{76}$$

are five. They are n, $\sum {_1X}$, $\sum {_2X}$, $\sum {_1X}\,{_2X}$, and $\sum(_1X)^2$. They characterize the normal equations for the linear regression of $_2X$ on $_1X$. In this paper, such quantities are α-products. For example, the following Table 1 shows that the notion of α-product of two n-dimensional vectors is used to obtain $\sum {_1X}$. The following Table 2 shows that the notion of α-product of two n-dimensional vectors is used to obtain $\sum {_1X}\,{_2X}$. Both two-way tables with n rows and n columns which have just been written use masses outside their main diagonal which are all equal to zero. In the first table, an n-dimensional vector, whose elements are all equal to 1, is used. With respect to the associative property of the notion of α-product, one can always use the constant given by $1/n$, where $1/n \in \mathbb{R}$. This constant mathematically satisfies the conditions of coherence associated with the notion of prevision of a random entity (see von Rosen 1989; Coletti et al. 2016). From Table 1, it is possible to obtain

$$\frac{\sum_{i=1}^{n} {_1X_i}}{n} = {_1\bar{X}}, \tag{77}$$

where the sum of positive and equiprobable masses associated with $_1X_1, \ldots, {_1X_n}$ is coherently equal to 1. On the other hand, if all deviations from $_1\bar{X}$ with respect to the first vector of Table 2 are considered together with all deviations from $_2\bar{X}$ with respect to the second one of the same table, then it is possible to obtain the expression given by

$$\operatorname{cov}(_1X, {_2X}) = \frac{\sum_{i=1}^{n} {_1x_i}\,{_2x_i}}{n}. \tag{78}$$

Table 1. How to obtain $\sum {_1X}$ using the notion of α-product.

Vector 1 \ Vector 2	**1**	...	**1**	**Sum**
$_1X_1$	1	...	0	1
$\vdots$	$\vdots$	$\ddots$	$\vdots$	$\vdots$
$_1X_n$	0	...	1	1
Sum	1	...	1	n

Table 2. How to obtain $\sum {}_1X\,{}_2X$ using the notion of α-product.

Vector 1 \ Vector 2	${}_2X_1$	...	${}_2X_n$	Sum
${}_1X_1$	1	...	0	1
⋮	⋮	⋱	⋮	⋮
${}_1X_n$	0	...	1	1
Sum	1	...	1	n

Let $({}_1\hat{X}, {}_1\hat{X})$, $({}_1X, {}_2\hat{X})$, $({}_2X, {}_1\hat{X})$, and $({}_2\hat{X}, {}_2\hat{X})$ be four ordered pairs of variables. They identify four two-way tables, where each of them has n rows and n columns. The n nonnegative masses appearing on the main diagonal of each two-way table are such that their sum is always equal to 1. All observed values are possible. Since there are no degrees of possibility, one can attribute to the various observed values a greater or lesser degree of a specific factor of a psychological nature expressing a more or less strong propensity to expect that a given value rather than others will turn out to be true at the right time (see Chen and Escobar-Anel 2021; Flores et al. 2021). The two-variable multilinear regression model treated in this paper can make coherent previsions. After establishing how all the n nonnegative masses appearing on the main diagonal of each two-way table are, the α-norm of a tensor of order 2 is handled (see Maturo and Angelini 2023). Such a norm coincides with the determinant of a square matrix of order 2, whose elements are all α-products. One writes

$$\begin{bmatrix} \mathbb{E}({}_1\hat{X}\,{}_1\hat{X}) & \mathbb{E}({}_1X\,{}_2\hat{X}) \\ \mathbb{E}({}_2X\,{}_1\hat{X}) & \mathbb{E}({}_2\hat{X}\,{}_2\hat{X}) \end{bmatrix}, \tag{79}$$

so it is possible to obtain

$$\mathbb{E}(\hat{X}_{12}) = \mathbf{P}(\hat{X}_{12}) = \begin{vmatrix} \mathbb{E}({}_1\hat{X}\,{}_1\hat{X}) & \mathbb{E}({}_1X\,{}_2\hat{X}) \\ \mathbb{E}({}_2X\,{}_1\hat{X}) & \mathbb{E}({}_2\hat{X}\,{}_2\hat{X}) \end{vmatrix} = \begin{vmatrix} \mathbf{P}({}_1\hat{X}\,{}_1\hat{X}) & \mathbf{P}({}_1X\,{}_2\hat{X}) \\ \mathbf{P}({}_2X\,{}_1\hat{X}) & \mathbf{P}({}_2\hat{X}\,{}_2\hat{X}) \end{vmatrix}, \tag{80}$$

where $\mathbb{E}(\hat{X}_{12}) = \mathbf{P}(\hat{X}_{12})$ is a real number. The same symbol $\mathbf{P}$ signifies the unique notion which, in general, is called prevision or mathematical expectation. In the case of single events, it is also called probability. The α-products characterizing the two elements of the main diagonal of (79) are associated with the 45-degree line, whereas the α-products characterizing the two elements of the antidiagonal of the same square matrix are connected with the two estimated regression lines. $\mathbb{E}({}_1\hat{X}\,{}_1\hat{X})$, $\mathbb{E}({}_1X\,{}_2\hat{X})$, $\mathbb{E}({}_2X\,{}_1\hat{X})$, and $\mathbb{E}({}_2\hat{X}\,{}_2\hat{X})$ are all bilinear previsions obtained by considering n nonnegative and finitely additive masses associated with n points. Each bilinear prevision is always decomposed into two linear previsions. This means that points on a specific regression line are always studied in the Cartesian plane. In the first phase, each mass of n masses can take infinite values between 0 and 1, endpoints included, into account. Hence, a closed convex set is handled with respect to each regression line. It is a closed line segment that is bounded by the two extreme points which are studied on each regression line. Given a two-way table, all the masses outside its main diagonal are always equal to zero. Straightforward cases are the following:

Example 1. *If $y = x$ is a regression line, then the following Table 3 shows how a bivariate (two-dimensional) probability distribution can be decomposed. A point belonging to $y = x$ is given by $(3.3, 3.3)$. A closed line segment appears on $y = x$ in the first phase. Its endpoints are $(0, 0)$ and $(4, 4)$. The second phase depends on the state of information and knowledge associated with a given individual. On the other hand, if $y = 2x$ is an estimated regression line, then the following Table 4 shows that a point belonging to $y = 2x$ is expressed by $(2.6, 5.2)$. A closed line segment appears on $y = 2x$ in the first phase. Its endpoints are $(0, 0)$ and $(3, 6)$. The choice of a point among infinite points on the estimated regression line depends on the state of information and knowledge associated with a given individual. This choice is absolutely rational.*

Table 3. How two marginal previsions are on $y = x$.

Vector 1 \ Vector 2	0	2	3	4	Sum
0	0	0	0	0	0
2	0	0.2	0	0	0.2
3	0	0	0.3	0	0.3
4	0	0	0	0.5	0.5
Sum	0	0.2	0.3	0.5	1

Table 4. How two marginal previsions are on $y = 2x$.

Vector 1 \ Vector 2	0	2	4	6	Sum
0	0	0	0	0	0
1	0	0.05	0	0	0.05
2	0	0	0.3	0	0.3
3	0	0	0	0.65	0.65
Sum	0	0.05	0.3	0.65	1

7. The Bivariate Correlation Coefficient Obtained Using an Aggregate Measure of a Multilinear Nature

The two-variable multilinear regression model treated in this paper focuses on a multiple variable of order 2. This section shows that the sample correlation coefficient is intrinsically associated with a multiple variable of order 2. Such a coefficient is written in the following form given by

$$r = r_{12} = \frac{\sum {}_1x\, {}_2x}{\sqrt{\sum({}_1x)^2}\,\sqrt{\sum({}_2x)^2}}, \tag{81}$$

where deviations from two mean values are considered (see Yule 1897). The population correlation coefficient is always associated with a multiple variable of order 2 in the same way as the sample correlation coefficient. If the notion of α-product of two n-dimensional vectors expressed using deviations is taken into account, then it is possible to write the sample correlation coefficient in the following form given by

$$r = r_{12} = \frac{{}_{(1)}\mathbf{d} \odot {}_{(2)}\mathbf{d}}{\|{}_{(1)}\mathbf{d}\|_\alpha \, \|{}_{(2)}\mathbf{d}\|_\alpha}, \tag{82}$$

where it turns out to be

$$\sqrt{{}_{(1)}\mathbf{d} \odot {}_{(1)}\mathbf{d}} = \sqrt{\|{}_{(1)}\mathbf{d}\|_\alpha^2} = \|{}_{(1)}\mathbf{d}\|_\alpha \tag{83}$$

and

$$\sqrt{{}_{(2)}\mathbf{d} \odot {}_{(2)}\mathbf{d}} = \sqrt{\|{}_{(2)}\mathbf{d}\|_\alpha^2} = \|{}_{(2)}\mathbf{d}\|_\alpha. \tag{84}$$

The symbol given by $\odot$ identifies the notion of α-product of two vectors. The sample correlation coefficient geometrically depends on the size of the angle between ${}_{(1)}\mathbf{d}$ and ${}_{(2)}\mathbf{d}$, where ${}_{(1)}\mathbf{d}$ and ${}_{(2)}\mathbf{d}$ are two n-dimensional vectors located at the origin of an n-dimensional linear space over $\mathbb{R}$ of a Euclidean nature. Since it is possible to write

$$-1 \le \left(1 - \frac{\|{}_{12}d\|_\alpha^2}{\|{}_{12}\hat{d}\|_\alpha^2}\right)^{1/2} \le 1, \tag{85}$$

where one has

$$\|_{12}d\|_\alpha^2 = \begin{vmatrix} \|_{(1)}\mathbf{d}\|_\alpha^2 & _{(1)}\mathbf{d} \odot _{(2)}\mathbf{d} \\ _{(2)}\mathbf{d} \odot _{(1)}\mathbf{d} & \|_{(2)}\mathbf{d}\|_\alpha^2 \end{vmatrix} \tag{86}$$

and

$$\|_{12}\hat{d}\|_\alpha^2 = \begin{vmatrix} \|_{(1)}\mathbf{d}\|_\alpha^2 & 0 \\ 0 & \|_{(2)}\mathbf{d}\|_\alpha^2 \end{vmatrix}, \tag{87}$$

the expression within the parentheses of (85) coincides with the sample correlation coefficient denoted by r_{12}. Such a coefficient is then proved to be intrinsically referred to $X_{12} = \{_1X, {}_2X\}$. The expression within the parentheses of (85) has been obtained using tensors of order 2 referred to a multiple variable of order 2. The sample correlation coefficient denoted by $r_{12} = r(_1X, {}_2X)$ is invariant with respect to rotations and translations. One writes

$$r\big(a\,(_1X) + b,\, c\,(_2X) + d\big) = r(_1X, {}_2X), \tag{88}$$

with $a,\, c \neq 0$. It is possible to verify (88) using a multilinear and quadratic metric. Moreover, one observes

$$r(_1X, {}_2X) = r(_2X, {}_1X) \tag{89}$$

and

$$r(_1X, {}_1X) = r(_2X, {}_2X) = 1. \tag{90}$$

Whenever a correlation between $_1X$ and $_2X$ is studied, it is possible to express the underlying multilinear relationship between $_1X$ and $_2X$ through the following determinant

$$\begin{vmatrix} r(_1X, {}_1X) & r(_1X, {}_2X) \\ r(_2X, {}_1X) & r(_2X, {}_2X) \end{vmatrix}. \tag{91}$$

However, in this case, it does not make sense that the calculation of (91) takes place. On the other hand, it is known that one of the most meaningful relationships constructed from a finite set of elements is a linear combination of basis vectors of a given linear space. Nevertheless, given some vectors belonging to the same linear space, an actual linear combination of them does not always make sense in practice: this observation is therefore conceptually the same as the one above related to (91).

8. The Two-Variable Multilinear Regression Model Used to Study Portfolios of Financial Assets: Fair Estimations

An n-dimensional linear space over $\mathbb{R}$ of a Euclidean nature is denoted by $\mathbb{R}^n$. $_1\mathbf{X}$ and $_2\mathbf{X}$ are elements of $\mathbb{R}^n$, where $\mathbb{R}^n$ is isomorphic to $\mathcal{R}^n$. An n-dimensional affine space is expressed by $\mathcal{R}^n$. The two elements denoted by $_1\mathbf{X}$ and $_2\mathbf{X}$ are supposed to be linearly independent. They identify a linear subspace of $\mathbb{R}^n$. Its dimension is equal to 2. One observes a reduction of dimension in this way (see Yuan et al. 2007). With respect to $_1\mathbf{X}$, all collinear vectors referred to it are considered. Their number is infinite, so a straight line of $\mathcal{R}^n$ is established. This line is a linear subspace of $\mathcal{R}^n$. Its dimension is equal to 1. It is also a linear subspace of $\mathbb{R}^n$. It is possible to prove in the form of a theorem that there is a one-to-one correspondence between the elements of a sheaf of parallel hyperplanes embedded in $\mathcal{R}^n$ and the points of intersection of them with a straight line of $\mathcal{R}^n$. This line is orthogonal to all parallel hyperplanes taken into account. The points of intersection of all these parallel hyperplanes embedded in $\mathcal{R}^n$ with a straight line of $\mathcal{R}^n$ are real numbers transferred on a one-dimensional straight line, on which an origin, a unit of length, and an orientation are established. They coincide with all the elements of $_1\mathbf{X}$. The same is true with respect to all the elements of $_2\mathbf{X}$. Two mutually orthogonal one-dimensional straight lines, on which an origin, a same unit of length, and an orientation are established, identify a two-dimensional Cartesian coordinate system. Ordered pairs of sampling units referring to two univariate variables denoted by ${}_1X$ and ${}_2X$ can be studied inside the first quadrant of a two-dimensional Cartesian coordinate system. This is because it is always possible to write

$$ {}_1X = {}_1X_1 - {}_1X_2, \tag{92} $$

with

$$ {}_1X_1 = 0 \vee {}_1X, \tag{93} $$

and

$$ {}_1X_2 = |0 \wedge {}_1X|. \tag{94} $$

Moreover, it is always possible to write

$$ {}_2X = {}_2X_1 - {}_2X_2, \tag{95} $$

with

$$ {}_2X_1 = 0 \vee {}_2X, \tag{96} $$

and

$$ {}_2X_2 = |0 \wedge {}_2X|. \tag{97} $$

In general, one has

$$ x \vee y = \max(x, y), \tag{98} $$

$$ x \wedge y = \min(x, y), \tag{99} $$

and

$$ \tilde{x} = 1 - x, \tag{100} $$

for any x and y that are real numbers.

The two-variable multilinear regression model treated in this paper shows that the real world cannot be analyzed in terms of a collection of bivariate or multivariate relationships only. The real world can also be analyzed in terms of multilinear relationships between variables (see Angelini and Maturo 2022). Surveys and technical discussions of the relationships between variables, which are studied in pairs, steadily take place. Various relationships between variables studied in pairs can be treated. Different pairs of variables are analyzed whenever a multilinear approach is used. This approach uses a multilinear and quadratic metric. For this reason, different pairs of variables have to be considered. Even though multilinear relationships between variables can be present whenever real problems are studied, one does not leave the two-dimensional diagrams behind. Bivariate relationships between variables are significant in themselves. The mathematical and statistical tools developed for them are fundamental building blocks for the analysis of multilinear situations characterizing real problems (see Bonat and Jørgensen 2016). $X_{12} = \{{}_1X, {}_2X\}$ can identify a two-financial asset portfolio. Its components can be two normally distributed variables. In other words, a bivariate normal population is considered. This means, among other things, that the ${}_1X$ values identifying observed returns on ${}_1X$ are normally distributed and so are the ${}_2X$ values identifying observed returns on ${}_2X$. A multiple variable of order 2 is associated with $\hat{X}_{12}$, where $\hat{X}_{12}$ identifies $2^2 = 4$ regression lines which are studied inside the same subset of a two-dimensional linear space over $\mathbb{R}$. In this paper, a two-financial asset portfolio is studied as a multiple random good of order 2. This matter can be extended, so

$$ X_{123} = \{{}_1X, {}_2X, {}_3X\} \tag{101} $$

can identify a three-financial asset portfolio. Its components are three normally distributed variables, so a multivariate normal population is considered. This means that the ${}_1X$ values identifying observed returns on ${}_1X$ are normally distributed. The ${}_2X$ values identifying observed returns on ${}_2X$ are normally distributed and so are the ${}_3X$ values identifying observed returns on ${}_3X$. A multiple variable of order 3 is associated with $\hat{X}_{123}$, where $\hat{X}_{123}$ identifies $3^2 = 9$ regression lines. They are studied inside the same subset of a two-dimensional linear space over $\mathbb{R}$. A quadratic metric is always used (see Markowitz 1952, 1956; Cont 2001). If $X_{12} = \{{}_1X = X, {}_2X = Y\}$ is a continuous and multiple variable of order 2, whose components are two continuous and univariate variables, then its expected return is given by the following determinant

$$\begin{vmatrix} \mathbb{E}(X^2) = \int_{-\infty}^{+\infty} x^2 f(x)\, dx & \mathbb{E}(XY) = \int_{-\infty}^{+\infty}\int_{-\infty}^{+\infty} xy\, f(x, y)\, dx\, dy \\ \mathbb{E}(YX) = \int_{-\infty}^{+\infty}\int_{-\infty}^{+\infty} yx\, f(y, x)\, dy\, dx & \mathbb{E}(Y^2) = \int_{-\infty}^{+\infty} y^2 f(y)\, dy \end{vmatrix}, \tag{102}$$

where $f(x)$ and $f(y)$ are density functions of X and Y, whereas $f(x, y)$ is a bivariate probability density function like $f(y, x)$. This determinant has the same structure as the one characterizing the α-norm of a tensor of order 2 connected with sampling quantities and their regression residuals. All elements of this determinant are integrals, so it is necessary to verify they exist. Similarly, if $X_{123} = \{{}_1X = X, {}_2X = Y, {}_3X = Z\}$ is a continuous and multiple variable of order 3, whose components are three continuous and univariate variables, then its expected return is given by the following determinant

$$\begin{vmatrix} \mathbb{E}(X^2) = \int_{-\infty}^{+\infty} x^2 f(x)\, dx & \mathbb{E}(XY) = \int_{-\infty}^{+\infty}\int_{-\infty}^{+\infty} xyf(x, y)\, dx\, dy & \mathbb{E}(XZ) = \int_{-\infty}^{+\infty}\int_{-\infty}^{+\infty} xzf(x, z)\, dx\, dz \\ \mathbb{E}(YX) = \int_{-\infty}^{+\infty}\int_{-\infty}^{+\infty} yxf(y, x)\, dy\, dx & \mathbb{E}(Y^2) = \int_{-\infty}^{+\infty} y^2 f(y)\, dy & \mathbb{E}(YZ) = \int_{-\infty}^{+\infty}\int_{-\infty}^{+\infty} yzf(y, z)\, dy\, dz \\ \mathbb{E}(ZX) = \int_{-\infty}^{+\infty}\int_{-\infty}^{+\infty} zxf(z, x)\, dz\, dx & \mathbb{E}(ZY) = \int_{-\infty}^{+\infty}\int_{-\infty}^{+\infty} zyf(z, y)\, dz\, dy & \mathbb{E}(Z^2) = \int_{-\infty}^{+\infty} z^2 f(z)\, dz \end{vmatrix}, \tag{103}$$

where $f(z)$ is a density function of Z, whereas $f(x, z)$ and $f(y, z)$ are bivariate probability density functions like $f(z, x)$ and $f(z, y)$. It is also possible to study an m-financial asset portfolio denoted by

$$X_{12\ldots m} = \{{}_1X, {}_2X, {}_3X, \ldots, {}_mX\}, \tag{104}$$

where $m > 3$ is an integer. In particular, it is possible to treat its riskiness instead of its expected return (see Cepeda and Gamerman 2000; Angelini and Maturo 2023). Conceptually, if one thinks of the case of the barycenter of a solid body, then it is possible to understand why to set up a determinant to obtain a multilinear index related to a multiple variable is meaningful. The center of mass of a distribution of mass can always be established. Conversely, it is never possible in practice to know the exact distribution of mass related to a specific solid body. Similarly, to know the exact probability distribution related to a multiple variable is of little interest in many problems, but to know its mathematical expectation is essential.

The two-variable multilinear regression model handled in this research work extends other models widely studied in the literature (see Nelder and Wedderburn 1972). It is not in conflict with them (see Yuan and Lin 2006). Since the two-variable multilinear regression model is conceptually and mathematically associated with the bivariate correlation coefficient, the null hypothesis given by

$$H_0\colon \rho = 0, \tag{105}$$

where ρ is the population correlation coefficient, is rejected if the null hypothesis given by

$$H_0\colon \beta = 0, \tag{106}$$

or

$$H_0\colon \beta^* = 0 \tag{107}$$

is rejected. To reject $\beta = 0$ or $\beta^* = 0$ implies that it is absolutely correct to reject $\rho = 0$. It follows that there is a correlation between the two components of the two-financial asset portfolio under consideration.

9. Aggregate Measures: Multiple Random Variables and Their Identification through Tensors

If one studies a multiple random variable, then one obtains an aggregate measure. This is because one has the possibility of constructing a tensor, after which one has the possibility of calculating the α-norm of this tensor by applying the techniques of multilinearity. In this way, the logical aspects of probability calculus are studied in deep. Also, they give a heuristic contribution. These aspects must be kept unconnected from the empirical ones. This approach is of a Bayesian nature. The probability distributions which are involved can first be of a nonparametric kind. In a multiple variable, the role played by the marginal variables characterized by their marginal probability distributions is essential. Within this context, the support of each marginal variable is a partition of events containing a finite number of them. An event is not a measurable set, but it is a possible alternative expressed by a real number to which a specific probability is associated. The notion of probability is not undefined, much the same as point and line are undefined in geometry. The notion of event is infinitely subdivisible. However, a subdivision stops when one studies the Cartesian product of two sets, where each set contains a finite number of possible alternatives. The Cartesian product of two sets is studied because otherwise things become unnecessarily complicated. The Cartesian product of two sets of possible alternatives identifies a bivariate variable. Nevertheless, the choice of the ordered pair of marginal variables identifying a bivariate variable is arbitrary. For this reason, it is appropriate to free oneself from the order in which the marginal variables are taken into account. Given a multiple random variable of order n containing n marginal variables written as

$$X_{12\ldots n} = \{{}_1X,\, {}_2X,\, {}_3X,\, \ldots,\, {}_nX\}, \tag{108}$$

it is possible to construct the following tensor expressed by

$$\begin{bmatrix} \mathbf{P}({}_1X\,{}_1X) & \mathbf{P}({}_1X\,{}_2X) & \ldots & \mathbf{P}({}_1X\,{}_nX) \\ \mathbf{P}({}_2X\,{}_1X) & \mathbf{P}({}_2X\,{}_2X) & \ldots & \mathbf{P}({}_2X\,{}_nX) \\ \vdots & \vdots & \ddots & \vdots \\ \mathbf{P}({}_nX\,{}_1X) & \mathbf{P}({}_nX\,{}_2X) & \ldots & \mathbf{P}({}_nX\,{}_nX) \end{bmatrix}. \tag{109}$$

Each element of the square matrix of order n given by (109) is a component of a tensor of order n. The components of this tensor are symmetric. Each element of (109) is an α-product obtained using an affine tensor of order 2. This tensor identifies the joint probabilities characterizing each bivariate probability distribution associated with a bivariate variable. Each bivariate variable is intrinsically composed of two marginal variables. The possible alternatives for each marginal variable are the components of a vector, so each bivariate probability distribution is summarized through an α-product structurally referred to the tensor product of two vectors. The tensor product of two vectors is not a scalar or inner product. The tensor product of two vectors is not commutative. Hence, n^2 ordered pairs of marginal variables are handled. The α-norm of the above-written tensor is given by

$$\mathbf{P}(X_{12\ldots n}) = \begin{vmatrix} \mathbf{P}({}_1X\,{}_1X) & \mathbf{P}({}_1X\,{}_2X) & \ldots & \mathbf{P}({}_1X\,{}_nX) \\ \mathbf{P}({}_2X\,{}_1X) & \mathbf{P}({}_2X\,{}_2X) & \ldots & \mathbf{P}({}_2X\,{}_nX) \\ \vdots & \vdots & \ddots & \vdots \\ \mathbf{P}({}_nX\,{}_1X) & \mathbf{P}({}_nX\,{}_2X) & \ldots & \mathbf{P}({}_nX\,{}_nX) \end{vmatrix}. \tag{110}$$

It is the determinant of the square matrix of order n given by (109). There is no loss of information. On the contrary, there is a gain of information. This is because an aggregate measure compatible with objects of a homogeneous nature is obtained. On the other hand, an aggregate measure expressing the riskiness of a finite set of financial assets is given by

$$\mathrm{var}(X_{12\ldots n}) = \begin{vmatrix} \frac{1}{2}\,{}^{2}\Delta^{2}({}_{1}X) & \mathrm{cov}({}_{1}X,\,{}_{2}X) & \ldots & \mathrm{cov}({}_{1}X,\,{}_{n}X) \\ \mathrm{cov}({}_{2}X,\,{}_{1}X) & \frac{1}{2}\,{}^{2}\Delta^{2}({}_{2}X) & \ldots & \mathrm{cov}({}_{2}X,\,{}_{n}X) \\ \vdots & \vdots & \ddots & \vdots \\ \mathrm{cov}({}_{n}X,\,{}_{1}X) & \mathrm{cov}({}_{n}X,\,{}_{2}X) & \ldots & \frac{1}{2}\,{}^{2}\Delta^{2}({}_{n}X) \end{vmatrix}, \tag{111}$$

where the mean quadratic difference of ${}_{i}X$ is denoted by ${}^{2}\Delta({}_{i}X), i = 1, \ldots, n$, the square of the mean quadratic difference of ${}_{i}X$ is denoted by ${}^{2}\Delta^{2}({}_{i}X), i = 1, \ldots, n$, and one writes ${}^{2}\Delta^{2}({}_{i}X) = 2\,\sigma^{2}_{{}_{i}X}, i = 1, \ldots, n$. It follows that it is possible to observe

$$\mathrm{var}(X_{12\ldots n}) = \begin{vmatrix} \mathrm{var}({}_{1}X) & \mathrm{cov}({}_{1}X,\,{}_{2}X) & \ldots & \mathrm{cov}({}_{1}X,\,{}_{n}X) \\ \mathrm{cov}({}_{2}X,\,{}_{1}X) & \mathrm{var}({}_{2}X) & \ldots & \mathrm{cov}({}_{2}X,\,{}_{n}X) \\ \vdots & \vdots & \ddots & \vdots \\ \mathrm{cov}({}_{n}X,\,{}_{1}X) & \mathrm{cov}({}_{n}X,\,{}_{2}X) & \ldots & \mathrm{var}({}_{n}X) \end{vmatrix}. \tag{112}$$

Aggregate measures are essential in many applications of an economic nature. For instance, the Sharpe ratio can be obtained using a multilinear approach. This approach gives rise to multilinear measures. If r_f is the risk-free asset paying a fixed rate of return, then the Sharpe ratio is given by

$$\mathrm{SR} = \frac{\mathbf{P}(X_{12\ldots n}) - r_f}{\sqrt{\mathrm{var}(X_{12\ldots n})}}. \tag{113}$$

The Sharpe ratio measures how risk and return can be traded off in making portfolio choices. One assumes $\mathbf{P}(X_{12\ldots n}) > r_f$. Furthermore, the beta of a given stock i is expressed by

$$\beta_i = \frac{\mathrm{cov}(r_i,\, r_m)}{\mathrm{var}(r_m)}, \tag{114}$$

so aggregate measures obtained according to a multilinear approach can operationally be associated with the capital asset pricing model (CAPM). This model has many applications in the study of financial markets. The market expected return r_m is expressed by (110). The mean-variance model based on mean return and standard deviation of return can use aggregate measures which are perfectly compatible with the satisfaction of the optimization principle by a given individual. The price of risk is then given by

$$p = \frac{r_m - r_f}{\sigma_m}, \tag{115}$$

where r_m and σ_m are always determinable within this context, and it represents the positive slope of the budget line. This is because one assumes that $r_m > r_f$. It is possible to identify a part of this budget line that is bounded by two distinct endpoints. This part is a closed line segment containing every point on the budget line that is between its endpoints. This paper focuses on a specific aspect: there are always infinitely many points for which the optimization principle can be satisfied by a given individual. They are points belonging to a closed convex set. It is known that the mean-variance model is a reasonable approximation to the expected utility model. Even the expected utility model can use aggregate measures obtained according to a multilinear approach. This means that Jensen's inequality can be extended. Studying n marginal variables, which are the components of $X_{12\ldots n}$, the certain gain, which is considered equivalent to $X_{12\ldots n}$ by a given individual who is risk neutral, is expressed by $x_{12\ldots n} = \mathbf{P}(X_{12\ldots n})$. His utility function is the 45-degree line. For a risk-loving individual, the random gain denoted by $X_{12\ldots n}$ is preferred to a certain gain denoted by $x_{12\ldots n}$, so $x_{12\ldots n}$ is greater than $\mathbf{P}(X_{12\ldots n})$ on the x-axis. His utility function is therefore convex. For a risk-averse individual, the random gain $X_{12\ldots n}$ is not preferred to a certain gain $x_{12...n}$, so $x_{12...n}$ is less than $\mathbf{P}(X_{12...n})$ on the x-axis. His utility function is then concave.

9.1. A Multiple Random Variable: Emphasis on Marginal Variables

Check the following:

Example 2. *Given $X_{123} = \{{}_1X, {}_2X, {}_3X\}$, the corresponding tensor is a square matrix of order 3. It is then possible to consider $3^2 = 9$ ordered pairs of marginal variables. Whenever $3^2 = 9$ ordered pairs of marginal variables are studied, each marginal probability distribution is summarized in such a way that one obtains a marginal measure. After summarizing, each marginal measure never changes. The joint probabilities can freely be chosen by a given individual. The only constraint for them is that the mean value associated with each marginal probability distribution does not change. The following Table 5 shows how the mean value of ${}_1X$ and ${}_2X$ can be. The following Table 6 shows how the mean value of ${}_1X$ and ${}_3X$ can be. The following Table 7 shows how the mean value of ${}_2X$ and ${}_3X$ can be. Given the mean values of ${}_1X$, ${}_2X$, and ${}_3X$, it is theoretically possible to consider all deviations from them, respectively. Thus, if the number of possible alternatives for ${}_1X$, ${}_2X$, and ${}_3X$ is not small, then the joint probabilities can be chosen in such a way that the correlation coefficient is equal to $+1$, or 0, or -1. A value of $+1$ implies that a marginal variable increases as another one increases, whereas a value of -1 implies that a marginal variable increases while another one decreases. A value of 0 implies that there is no linear dependency between the corresponding marginal variables. If a marginal variable is studied together with itself, then only the marginal probabilities of its distribution appear as joint ones. Whenever the joint probabilities are freely chosen by a given individual, they do not change. The joint probabilities can be chosen based on the state of information and knowledge associated with a given individual.*

Table 5. The mean values of ${}_1X$ and ${}_2X$ do not depend on the joint probabilities.

Vector 2 / Vector 1	0	22	41	63	Sum
0	p_{11}	p_{12}	p_{13}	p_{14}	0
10	p_{21}	p_{22}	p_{23}	p_{24}	0.2
20	p_{31}	p_{32}	p_{33}	p_{34}	0.3
30	p_{41}	p_{42}	p_{43}	p_{44}	0.5
Sum	0	0.1	0.1	0.8	1

Table 6. The mean values of ${}_1X$ and ${}_3X$ do not depend on the joint probabilities.

Vector 3 / Vector 1	0	26	45	68	Sum
0	p_{11}	p_{12}	p_{13}	p_{14}	0
10	p_{21}	p_{22}	p_{23}	p_{24}	0.2
20	p_{31}	p_{32}	p_{33}	p_{34}	0.3
30	p_{41}	p_{42}	p_{43}	p_{44}	0.5
Sum	0	0.3	0.3	0.4	1

Table 7. The mean values of ${}_2X$ and ${}_3X$ do not depend on the joint probabilities.

Vector 2 \ Vector 3	0	26	45	68	Sum
0	p_{11}	p_{12}	p_{13}	p_{14}	0
22	p_{21}	p_{22}	p_{23}	p_{24}	0.1
41	p_{31}	p_{32}	p_{33}	p_{34}	0.1
63	p_{41}	p_{42}	p_{43}	p_{44}	0.8
Sum	0	0.3	0.3	0.4	1

It is necessary to handle errors associated with the notion of prevision. Natural or intrinsic errors connected with this notion appear whenever deviations from mean values take place. These errors are not unwelcome. They identify a parametric probability distribution. They identify a normal distribution characterized by specific parameters. Conversely, logical errors appear whenever objective conditions of coherence are not satisfied. Such conditions are not satisfied when and only when one chooses a point that does not belong to the corresponding closed convex set. These errors are absolutely unwelcome. It is possible to note the following:

Remark 1. *The empirical validation of the multilinear regression model treated in this paper can easily be shown. This is because the α-norm of a tensor extends the properties of the barycenter of nonnegative and finitely additive masses. It is known that such properties are given by two distinct indices: the first index is associated with an equilibrium that is stable, the second one appears when the moment of inertia is minimum. Such properties are satisfied when and only when each component of the tensor into account is coherently expressed in a quantitative form obtained from a specific α-product. The α-norm of the tensor of order* 3 *related to Example* 2 *is given by*

$$\mathbf{P}(X_{12\ldots3}) = \begin{vmatrix} \mathbf{P}({}_1X\,{}_1X) & \mathbf{P}({}_1X\,{}_2X) & \mathbf{P}({}_1X\,{}_3X) \\ \mathbf{P}({}_2X\,{}_1X) & \mathbf{P}({}_2X\,{}_2X) & \mathbf{P}({}_2X\,{}_3X) \\ \mathbf{P}({}_3X\,{}_1X) & \mathbf{P}({}_3X\,{}_2X) & \mathbf{P}({}_3X\,{}_3X) \end{vmatrix}.$$

If each element of the following square matrix of order 3 *given by*

$$\begin{bmatrix} \mathbf{P}({}_1X\,{}_1X) & \mathbf{P}({}_1X\,{}_2X) & \mathbf{P}({}_1X\,{}_3X) \\ \mathbf{P}({}_2X\,{}_1X) & \mathbf{P}({}_2X\,{}_2X) & \mathbf{P}({}_2X\,{}_3X) \\ \mathbf{P}({}_3X\,{}_1X) & \mathbf{P}({}_3X\,{}_2X) & \mathbf{P}({}_3X\,{}_3X) \end{bmatrix}$$

is coherent, then $\mathbf{P}(X_{12\ldots3})$ *is a parameter of a coherent nature. This means that* $\mathbf{P}(X_{12\ldots3})$ *is a point belonging to the union of different closed convex sets. Each closed convex set is a part of a one-dimensional straight line that is bounded by two distinct endpoints. The product of a possible value for a marginal variable and a possible value for another one is a point of a one-dimensional straight line. This validation holds regardless of the particular masses that may be chosen by a given individual. The reader can verify this matter. As a consequence, the validation of the multilinear regression model treated in this paper is of a logical nature as well.*

Remark 2. *If the number of the possible values for two marginal variables is not the same, then this number can become the same. For instance, let*

$$\begin{bmatrix} 2 \\ 3 \\ 4 \\ 5 \end{bmatrix}, \begin{bmatrix} 0.1 \\ 0.4 \\ 0.2 \\ 0.3 \end{bmatrix}$$

and

$$\begin{bmatrix}1\\7\\8\end{bmatrix}, \begin{bmatrix}0.2\\0.6\\0.2\end{bmatrix}$$

be two ordered pairs of vectors. The second vector of each ordered pair identifies the corresponding probabilities. If one writes

$$\begin{bmatrix}2\\3\\4\\5\end{bmatrix}, \begin{bmatrix}0.1\\0.4\\0.2\\0.3\end{bmatrix}$$

and

$$\begin{bmatrix}0\\1\\7\\8\end{bmatrix}, \begin{bmatrix}0\\0.2\\0.6\\0.2\end{bmatrix},$$

then the number of the possible values for the two marginal variables under consideration becomes the same. The possible values for the two marginal variables into account identify the first vector of each ordered pair.

9.2. Difference between a Multiple Random Variable and a Multivariate One

There is a fundamental logical difference between a multiple random variable and a multivariate one. For instance, if a multivariate random variable is composed of three marginal probability distributions, then the probability distribution of this variable is of a three-dimensional nature. It is then possible to consider three axes belonging to $\mathbb{R}^3$. They are pairwise orthogonal. Each axis of them is the support of a marginal variable. Each marginal probability distribution which is summarized gives rise to a real number. Each real number associated with a marginal variable is represented on an axis belonging to $\mathbb{R}^3$. Each axis of $\mathbb{R}^3$ is a linear subspace of it. Its dimension is equal to 1. If the probability distribution of a multivariate random variable composed of three marginal probability distributions is summarized, then an ordered triplet of real numbers belonging to $\mathbb{R}^3$ has to be studied. This is because the probability distribution of a multivariate random variable composed of three marginal probability distributions is of a three-dimensional nature. Whenever the probability distribution of a multivariate random variable composed of three marginal probability distributions is summarized and a real number is handled, only empirical aspects are taken into account. Nevertheless, this paper says that it is necessary to consider logical aspects as well. For this reason, the previous real number is never an aggregate measure. A multiple random variable of order 3 logically gives rise to a tensor of order 3 which is naturally an element of a linear space over $\mathbb{R}$. Thus, $3^2 = 9$ ordered pairs of marginal variables are dealt with. Some ordered pairs out of $3^2 = 9$ give rise to a bivariate variable such that the corresponding bivariate probability distribution is summarized inside a linear subspace of $\mathbb{R}^3$ of a two-dimensional nature. This linear subspace is generated by two linear subspaces of $\mathbb{R}^3$ of a one-dimensional nature. Conversely, three ordered pairs of marginal variables out of $3^2 = 9$ give rise to a bivariate variable such that the corresponding bivariate probability distribution is summarized inside a linear subspace of $\mathbb{R}^3$ of a one-dimensional nature. It is one of the three axes of $\mathbb{R}^3$: only the squares of the possible values for each marginal variable are taken into account, so there is no loss of information. On the other hand, the same is true if a multiple random variable is of order n, where n is an integer and one has $n = 2$ or $n > 3$, and the probability distribution of a multivariate random variable is of an n-dimensional nature. Within this context, the theorem mentioned at the beginning of Section 8 does not come into play.

10. Conclusions and Some Future Perspectives

Two dynamical phases depending on the state of information and knowledge associated with a given individual always identify the notion of prevision. This notion expresses the judgment of a given individual at a given time. A given individual can criticize his previous judgment. He can therefore verify whether he forgot or underestimated or overestimated some circumstances. Such circumstances could have led him to a more accurate prevision if he had exercised better thought. Nevertheless, if his previous judgment translated into quantitative terms is an element of a closed convex set, then his past prevision is never wrong. There are only natural or intrinsic errors. New pieces of information can be used to make different previsions for more or less similar future cases. It is absolutely wrong to criticize a prevision based on a specific state of information and knowledge by referring to a different state of information and knowledge. In this paper, closed convex sets play an essential role. Closed convex sets are closed line segments. Each line segment is a part of a line regression. Fair estimations are fair previsions. They are studied inside linear spaces over $\mathbb{R}$ provided with a quadratic metric. Only their dimension can be different. Since it is possible to show that an invariant or intrinsic metric can be used, only the affine properties make sense. All indices which are obtained inside linear spaces over $\mathbb{R}$ provided with a quadratic metric do not depend on the arbitrary choice of the coordinate system. They are therefore of an intrinsic nature. This paper shows that obtaining aggregate measures is meaningful. For this reason, different applications of an economic nature are mentioned. Thus, if a given individual is indifferent to the exchange of ${}_1X$ for $\mathbf{P}({}_1X)$ and of ${}_2X$ for $\mathbf{P}({}_2X)$, then the same individual has to be indifferent to the exchange of X_{12} for $\mathbf{P}(X_{12})$, where $\mathbf{P}(X_{12})$ is an aggregate measure. $\mathbf{P}(X_{12})$ is a real number obtained from four bivariate probability distributions. They are all summarized and decomposed. In this paper, a bivariate probability distribution is of a two-dimensional nature. A bivariate probability distribution that is summarized is not properly associated with a real number. A bivariate probability distribution that is summarized is intrinsically composed of two marginal probability distributions that are summarized. A bivariate probability distribution that is summarized can then be associated with an ordered pair of real numbers. Logical aspects of probability calculus are studied in depth. Also, they give a heuristic contribution. To determine an aggregate measure is crucial in connection with the optimization of decisions of an economic nature. Such decisions usually depend on the subjective preferences associated with a given individual, who can be interested in two or more than two components of a multiple variable. These components are studied using the techniques of multilinearity. Among other things that can represent future perspectives, it is possible to prove that closed convex sets are of an essential importance in connection with stochastic models related to fair estimations. Such models are intrinsically based on a Bayesian reinterpretation of the central limit theorem. Moreover, it is possible to make evident important aspects of time series through a reinterpretation of principal component analysis based on the techniques of multilinearity.

Funding: This research received no external funding.

Institutional Review Board Statement: Not applicable.

Informed Consent Statement: Not applicable.

Data Availability Statement: The author can confirm that all relevant data are included in the article.

Conflicts of Interest: The author declares that they have no conflicts of interest.

References

Aneiros, Germán, Silvia Novo, and Philippe Vieu. 2022. Variable selection in functional regression models: A review. *Journal of Multivariate Analysis* 188: 104871. [CrossRef]

Angelini, Pierpaolo. 2023. Probability spaces identifying ordinal and cardinal utilities in problems of an economic nature: New issues and perspectives. *Mathematics* 11: 4280. [CrossRef]

Angelini, Pierpaolo. 2024a. Financial decisions based on zero-sum games: New conceptual and mathematical outcomes. *International Journal of Financial Studies* 12: 56. [CrossRef]

Angelini, Pierpaolo. 2024b. Invariance of the mathematical expectation of a random quantity and its consequences. *Risks* 12: 14. [CrossRef]

Angelini, Pierpaolo, and Fabrizio Maturo. 2022. The price of risk based on multilinear measures. *International Review of Economics and Finance* 81: 39–57. [CrossRef]

Angelini, Pierpaolo, and Fabrizio Maturo. 2023. Tensors associated with mean quadratic differences explaining the riskiness of portfolios of financial assets. *Journal of Risk and Financial Management* 16: 369. [CrossRef]

Bartlett, Maurice S., and Peter D. M. Macdonald. 1968. "Least-squares" estimation of distribution mixtures. *Nature* 217: 195–96. [CrossRef]

Berti, Patrizia, Eugenio Regazzini, and Pietro Rigo. 2001. Strong previsions of random elements. *Statistical Methods and Applications (Journal of the Italian Statistical Society)* 10: 11–28. [CrossRef]

Bonat, Wagner Hugo, and Bent Jørgensen. 2016. Multivariate covariance generalized linear models. *Journal of the Royal Statistical Society, Series C (Applied Statistics)* 65: 649–75. [CrossRef]

Cassese, Gianluca, Pietro Rigo, and Barbara Vantaggi. 2020. A special issue on the mathematics of subjective probability. *Decisions in Economics and Finance* 43: 1–2. [CrossRef]

Cepeda, Edilberto, and Dani Gamerman. 2000. Bayesian modeling of variance heterogeneity in normal regression models. *Brazilian Journal of Probability and Statistics* 14: 207–21.

Chen, Junhe, and Marcos Escobar-Anel. 2021. Model uncertainty on commodity portfolios, the role of convenience yield. *Annals of Finance* 17: 501–28. [CrossRef]

Coletti, Giulianella, Davide Petturiti, and Barbara Vantaggi. 2016. When upper conditional probabilities are conditional possibility measures. *Fuzzy Sets and Systems* 304: 45–64. [CrossRef]

Cont, Rama. 2001. Empirical properties of asset returns: Stylized facts and statistical issues. *Quantitative Finance* 1: 223–36. [CrossRef]

del Pino, Guido. 1989. The unifying role of iterative generalized least squares in statistical algorithms. *Statistical Science* 4: 394–403.

Ewald, Karl, and Ulrike Schneider. 2020. On the distribution, model selection properties and uniqueness of the Lasso estimator in low and high dimensions. *Electronic Journal of Statistics* 14: 944–69. [CrossRef]

Fisher, Ronald A. 1922. The goodness of fit of regression formulae, and the distribution of regression coefficients. *Journal of the Royal Statistical Society* 85: 597–612. [CrossRef]

Flores, Brandon, Blessing Ofori-Atta, and Andrey Sarantsev. 2021. A stock market model based on CAPM and market size. *Annals of Finance* 17: 405–24. [CrossRef]

Gilio, Angelo, and Giuseppe Sanfilippo. 2014. Conditional random quantities and compounds of conditionals. *Studia logica* 102: 709–29. [CrossRef]

Liu, Xu, Shurong Zheng, and Xingdong Feng. 2020. Estimation of error variance via ridge regression. *Biometrika* 107: 481–88. [CrossRef]

Markowitz, Harry M. 1952. The utility of wealth. *Journal of Political Economy* 60: 151–58. [CrossRef]

Markowitz, Harry M. 1956. The optimization of a quadratic function subject to linear constraints. *Naval Research Logistics Quarterly* 3: 111–33. [CrossRef]

Maturo, Fabrizio, and Pierpaolo Angelini. 2023. Aggregate bound choices about random and nonrandom goods studied via a nonlinear analysis. *Mathematics* 11: 2498. [CrossRef]

McCullagh, Peter. 1983. Quasi-likelihood functions. *The Annals of Statistics* 11: 59–67. [CrossRef]

Nelder, John A., and Daryl Pregibon. 1987. An extended quasi-likelihood function. *Biometrika* 74: 221–32. [CrossRef]

Nelder, John A., and Robert W. M. Wedderburn. 1972. Generalized linear models. *Journal of the Royal Statistical Society, Series A (General)* 135: 370–84. [CrossRef]

Puntanen, Simo, and George P. H. Styan. 1989. The equality of the ordinary least squares estimator and the best linear unbiased estimator. *The American Statistician* 43: 153–61. [CrossRef]

von Rosen, Dietrich. 1989. Maximum likelihood estimators in multivariate linear normal models. *Journal of Multivariate Analysis* 31: 187–200. [CrossRef]

Watson, Geoffrey S. 1967. Linear least squares regression. *The Annals of Mathematical Statistics* 38: 1679–99. [CrossRef]

Yuan, Ming, Ali Ekici, Zhaosong Lu, and Renato Monteiro. 2007. Dimension reduction and coefficient estimation in multivariate linear regression. *Journal of the Royal Statistical Society, Series B (Statistical Methodology)* 69: 329–46. [CrossRef]

Yuan, Ming, and Yi Lin. 2006. Model selection and estimation in regression with grouped variables. *Journal of the Royal Statistical Society, Series B (Statistical Methodology)* 68: 49–67. [CrossRef]

Yule, G. Udny. 1897. On the theory of correlation. *Journal of the Royal Statistical Society* 60: 812–54. [CrossRef]

Journal of
Risk and Financial Management

MDPI

Article

On Smoothing and Habit Formation of Variable Life Annuity Benefits

Mogens Steffensen † and Savannah Halling Vikkelsøe *,†

Department of Mathematical Sciences, University of Copenhagen, 2100 Copenhagen Ø, Denmark; mogens@math.ku.dk
* Correspondence: xgl102@alumni.ku.dk
† These authors contributed equally to this work.

Abstract: This paper studies optimal consumption and investment strategies with lifetime uncertainty to design a smooth pension product. In a simplified Black–Scholes market, we investigate three strategies for consumption and investment: the classical strategy, the habit strategy, and the hybrid strategy. Incorporating additive habit formation in preferences leads to a request for less consumption volatility. Studying the consumption dynamics, it turns out that the hybrid strategy complies with the same preferences as the habit strategy. In our design of a smooth pension product, we are highly inspired by the consumption structure under the hybrid strategy and let consumption be specified as a time-dependent weighted average of last year's consumption level and a standard market rate life annuity. We give two approaches for the investment portfolio. The numerical examples show that consumption under these approaches is less volatile than consumption under the classical strategy.

Keywords: optimal consumption and investment; consumption dynamics; smooth pension product; decumulation phase

1. Introduction

The Danish Financial Supervisory Authority frequently publishes an evaluation of the current financial risks that dominate the Danish pension and insurance market. In their latest evaluation, DFSA (2022a), the focus is on the interest rate, inflation, and the risk of recession. These factors create a volatile and insecure financial market. Thus, Danish pension companies are encouraged to revisit the pension products they offer and reassess whether these meet the investor's potential preferences for smoothing. The aim is to maintain the investor's interests and keep the investor's faith in the pension companies.

Most Danish pension companies offer market-rate pension products, where the size of the pension benefit depends on the return on investing pension savings in risky assets. Such products are comparable with variable life annuities. Thus, increased volatility and insecurity in the financial market might increase the need for the stability of pension benefits. In terms of optimal stochastic control theory with lifetime uncertainty, we think of the pension benefits as the consumption of an investor.

With stochastic optimal control theory, this paper aims to present optimal consumption and investment strategies that inspire the design of a smooth pension product. Merton (1969, 1971) formalized and solved the original problem of maximizing the total expected utility of intertemporal consumption and terminal wealth of an investor over a fixed time interval. Lifetime uncertainty was introduced to the stochastic optimal control problem by Richard (1975). The result of optimal consumption from the above literature resembles the design of a standard market rate life annuity offered by most Danish pension companies.

Introducing additive habit formation in preferences to the stochastic optimal control problem can explain the request for smooth consumption; see Bruhn and Steffensen (2013).

negative random variable τ defined on the probability space $(\Omega, \mathcal{F}, P)$. The mortality rate or the hazard function is then defined by

$$\mu_t = \lim_{z \to 0} \frac{P(t \leq \tau < t + z \mid \tau \geq t)}{z}. \tag{5}$$

As the investor has no utility from bequest, we add the income of $\mu_t^* X_t$ to the wealth dynamics (1) (see, e.g., Konicz et al. 2015). The intuition is that if there is no utility from bequest, the investor is willing to give up the wealth in case of death. For this wealth, the insurance company is willing to pay the so-called mortality credits. They work as a premium payment for reversed life insurance. It can be shown that X_t is the optimal life insurance sum (see, e.g., Richard (1975) or Kraft and Steffensen (2008)). The function μ_t^* is called the pricing intensity and is decided by the insurance company. Then, the wealth evolves by

$$\begin{aligned} dX_t &= (r + \mu_t^* + \pi_t(\lambda - r))X_t dt + \pi_t \sigma X_t dW_t - c_t dt, \\ X_0 &= x_0. \end{aligned} \tag{6}$$

Now, given the modified wealth dynamics (6), the value function is given by

$$V(t,x) = \sup_{c,\pi} E_{t,x}\left[\int_t^T e^{-\int_t^s (\rho + \mu_u) du}\left(\frac{1}{1-\gamma} c_s^{1-\gamma} ds + \frac{1}{1-\gamma} X_s^{1-\gamma} d\varepsilon_T(s)\right)\right], \tag{7}$$

where $E_{t,x}$ is the conditional expectation given that the investor is alive at time $t \in [0, T]$ and holds wealth $X_t = x$. Here, we assume that the investor retires at time 0. Thus, we focus on the decumulation phase of the investor. The utility functions are multiplied by the conditional probability that the investor survives from time t to s given that she is alive at time $t \leq s$, i.e., $\exp(-\int_t^s \mu_u du)$. Reasonably, the investor only obtains utility from consumption and terminal wealth as long as she is alive.

This paper aims to solve the utility maximization problem given by (7) under three different strategies and interpret the optimal controls as the pension benefits and the investment portfolio in the decumulation phase of the investor. We consider the classical strategy derived directly from (7) without terminal wealth in contrast to two strategies carefully chosen to achieve a smoothing effect on consumption.

3. Three Strategies for Consumption and Investment

In this section, we solve the utility maximization problem given by (7) under three different strategies. The first strategy is derived directly from the situation without terminal wealth and is considered classical. In the second strategy, we allow for additive habit formation in preferences. We will refer to this strategy as the habit strategy. Continuing to the third strategy, we examine the hybrid strategy, which is an ad hoc smoothing strategy for consumption presented by Kashif et al. (2020).

3.1. *The Classical Strategy*

Initially, we consider the classical strategy and solve the value function given by

$$V(t,x) = \sup_{c,\pi} E_{t,x}\left[\int_t^T e^{-\int_t^s (\rho + \mu_u) du} \frac{1}{1-\gamma} c_s^{1-\gamma} ds\right], \tag{8}$$

subject to the wealth dynamics (6) and the constraint $c_t \geq 0$ for all $t \geq 0$. Here, we assume that the investor has utility solely from intertemporal consumption, i.e., we omit utility from terminal wealth. Using the technique of dynamic programming, we find and solve the corresponding Hamilton–Jacobi–Bellman (HJB) equation given by

$$
\begin{aligned}
0 &= V_t - (\rho + \mu)V + \sup_{c,\pi}\left\{\frac{1}{1-\gamma}c^{1-\gamma} + ((r + \mu^* + \pi(\lambda - r))x - c)V_x \right.\\
&\quad \left. + \frac{1}{2}\pi^2\sigma^2 x^2 V_{xx}\right\}, \qquad (9)\\
V(T,x) &= 0.
\end{aligned}
$$

The dependencies have been suppressed for ease of notation, and the subscripts denote the partial derivatives. The HJB equation agrees with the one in, e.g., Merton (1969), Kashif et al. (2020) with $\mu_t = 0$ and $\mu_t^* = 0$ for all $t \geq 0$. The structure is completely maintained when we introduce lifetime uncertainty. It can also be found in Steffensen and Søe (2023) with the mortality effect present. Therefore, we neither establish a verification proof nor derive the solution to the HJB equation. We simply state its solution and the corresponding optimal controls in the following. The solution to the HJB Equation (9) is given by the following value function:

$$V(t,x) = \frac{1}{1-\gamma} a_1(t)^\gamma x^{1-\gamma}, \qquad (10)$$

where

$$a_1(t) = \int_t^T e^{-\int_t^s (\tilde{r} + \tilde{\mu}_u)du} ds, \qquad (11)$$

with

$$\tilde{r} := \frac{1}{\gamma}\rho + \left(1 - \frac{1}{\gamma}\right)\left(r + \frac{1}{2}\frac{\theta^2}{\gamma}\right), \qquad (12)$$

$$\tilde{\mu}_t := \frac{1}{\gamma}\mu_t + \left(1 - \frac{1}{\gamma}\right)\mu_t^*. \qquad (13)$$

Here, we have defined $\theta := (\lambda - r)/\sigma$, which is the market price of risk. The optimal consumption and investment portfolio, i.e., the optimal controls, under the classical strategy are given by

$$c_t^* = \frac{X_t}{a_1(t)}, \qquad (14)$$

$$\pi_t^* = \frac{\lambda - r}{\sigma^2\gamma}. \qquad (15)$$

We emphasize that the value function and the optimal controls correspond to the results in, e.g., Merton (1969) and Kashif et al. (2020) with $\mu_t = 0$ and $\mu_t^* = 0$ for all $t \geq 0$, as well as with Steffensen and Søe (2023).

Observe that optimal consumption at time t equals the wealth at time t. The proportion is determined by the function a_1, which has the interpretation of an annuity with the utility-adjusted interest rate $\tilde{r}$ as the calculation rate and the utility-adjusted mortality $\tilde{\mu}_t$ as the calculation of mortality. The utility-adjusted interest rate is a weighted average of two interest rate factors. These are the impatience factor and an interest rate obtained from investing in the financial market. The utility-adjusted mortality rate is a weighted average of the original mortality rate and the pricing intensity. The weight is determined by γ^{-1}. Optimal consumption under the classical strategy coincides with a standard market rate life annuity structure. The classical strategy considers optimal expected utility.

Moreover, the optimal proportion of wealth invested in the risky asset is constant under the classical strategy. We refer to this constant as Merton's constant. See Merton (1969, 1971).

3.2. The Habit Strategy

Now, we introduce the habit formation of the investor to the utility maximization problem. Incorporating habit formation is an additive form with respect to consumption to achieve a smoothing effect on the optimal consumption. We refer to the strategy with additive habit formation in preferences as the habit strategy. As Munk (2008), we define the habit level by

$$h_t = h_0 e^{-\beta t} + \alpha \int_0^t e^{-\beta(t-s)} c_s ds, \tag{16}$$

where h_0, α and β are assumed to be non-negative constants. Observe that the habit level at time t is the sum of the discounted, initial habit level h_0 and the discounted, weighted consumption rates from time 0 to t. The constant α is interpreted as the weight providing the relative importance to past consumption, while β is the discount rate describing the decline in the relative importance to past consumption. Hence, α and β are parameters measuring the habit preferences of the investor. The habit level follows the dynamics given by

$$\begin{aligned} dh_t &= (\alpha c_t - \beta h_t)dt, \\ h_0 &> 0. \end{aligned} \tag{17}$$

We include the habit level as an additional state variable in the utility maximization problem. Then, the value function becomes

$$V(t,x,h) = \sup_{c,\pi} E_{t,x,h}\left[\int_t^T e^{-\int_t^s (\rho+\mu_u)du} \frac{1}{1-\gamma}(c_s - h_s)^{1-\gamma} ds\right],$$

subject to the wealth dynamics (6), the habit dynamics (17) and the constraint $c_t \geq 0$ for all $t \geq 0$. Here, $E_{t,x,h}$ is the conditional expectation given that the investor is alive at time t, holds wealth $X_t = x$, and has habit level $h_t = h$. Again, exploiting the technique of dynamic programming, we find and solve the corresponding HJB equation given by

$$\begin{aligned} 0 &= V_t - (\rho+\mu)V + \sup_{c,\pi}\left\{\frac{1}{1-\gamma}(c-h)^{1-\gamma} + ((r+\mu^* + \pi(\lambda - r))x - c)V_x \right. \\ &\quad \left. + (\alpha c - \beta h)V_h + \frac{1}{2}\pi^2\sigma^2 x^2 V_{xx}\right\}, \\ V(T,x) &= 0. \end{aligned} \tag{18}$$

The HJB equation agrees with the one in, e.g., Munk (2008) and Kashif et al. (2020) with $\mu_t = 0$ and $\mu_t^* = 0$ for all $t \geq 0$. The structure is completely maintained when we introduce lifetime uncertainty. Therefore, we neither establish a verification proof nor derive the solution to the HJB equation. We simply state its solution and the corresponding optimal controls in the following. The solution to the HJB Equation (18) is given by the following value function:

$$V(t,x,h) = \frac{1}{1-\gamma} a_2(t)^\gamma (x - hb_2(t))^{1-\gamma},$$

where

$$a_2(t) = \int_t^T e^{-\int_t^s (\tilde{r}+\tilde{\mu}_u)du} (1 + \alpha b_2(s))^{1-\frac{1}{\gamma}} ds, \tag{19}$$

$$b_2(t) = \int_t^T e^{-\int_t^s (r+\mu_u^*+\beta-\alpha)du} ds, \tag{20}$$

with $\tilde{r}$ and $\tilde{\mu}$ defined as in (12) and (13), respectively. The optimal consumption and investment portfolio under the habit strategy are given by

$$c_t^* = h_t + (1 + \alpha b_2(t))^{-\frac{1}{\gamma}} \frac{X_t - h_t b_2(t)}{a_2(t)}, \tag{21}$$

$$\pi_t^* = \frac{\lambda - r}{\sigma^2 \gamma} \frac{X_t - h_t b_2(t)}{X_t}. \tag{22}$$

We emphasize that the value function as well as the optimal controls are directly comparable with the ones obtained by, e.g., Munk (2008) and Kashif et al. (2020) with $\mu_t = 0$ and $\mu_t^* = 0$ for all $t \geq 0$.

The optimal consumption at time t under the habit strategy is to consume at the current minimum level, i.e., the habit level at time t, plus a proportion of the current wealth over the price of maintaining future minimum consumption, i.e., $X_t - h_t b_2(t)$. The proportion is determined by the fraction $(1 + \alpha b_2(t))^{-1/\gamma} / a_2(t)$. We still interpret the function a_2 as an annuity with the utility-adjusted interest rate $\tilde{r}$ as the calculation rate and the utility-adjusted mortality rate $\tilde{\mu}_t$ as the calculation of mortality. Still, an extra term is added to the integral due to incorporating additive habit formation. The function b_2 is an annuity determined by the habit preferences of the investor, the interest rate, and the pricing intensity. Thus, multiplying the current habit level by b_2 is interpreted as the discounted, current habit level, i.e., the price of maintaining future minimum consumption as mentioned above. Discounting depends on the investor's habit preferences. Moreover, observe that optimal consumption under the habit strategy is affine in wealth. This implies a smoothing effect on consumption (see Bruhn and Steffensen 2013).

Unlike the classical strategy, optimal investment under the habit strategy is time-dependent. Both strategies have Merton's constant in common, but only $X_t - h_t b_2(t)$ is invested in the risky asset as the habit level is added to the strategy. Thus, habit formation reduces risk tolerance to secure consumption at the habit level as a minimum.

3.3. The Hybrid Strategy

This section presents an ad hoc smoothing strategy for consumption introduced by Kashif et al. (2020), who study different optimal consumption and investment strategies for university endowment funds. First, consider their fixed consumption–wealth ratio strategy with consumption rate specified as a proportion of the wealth, i.e.,

$$c_t = y X_t, \tag{23}$$

where y is a constant determining the consumption–wealth ratio. Then, Kashif et al. (2020) extend this strategy by a simplified version of the Yale/Stanford rule from Cejnek et al. (2014) and define the discrete-time consumption rate by

$$c_t = w c_{t-1} + (1 - w) y X_t, \tag{24}$$

where w is a weight. Thus, consumption is a weighted sum of the consumption in the previous year and a fixed proportion of the wealth in the current year. Similarly to Kashif et al. (2020), we will refer to this ad hoc strategy for consumption as the hybrid strategy, since it is a hybrid between last year's consumption rate and the fixed consumption–wealth ratio strategy.

Observe that w and y are considered to be constants. In later sections, we will allow w and y to be time-dependent such that (24) is more flexible in designing a pension product. For now, we keep w and y constants.

As consumption is already predefined by (24) before solving the utility maximization problem, we include consumption as an additional state variable, such as wealth. Thus, we assume that (24) is the optimal way to consume, and we find the corresponding optimal way to invest by maximizing the expected utility of terminal wealth with both the wealth and consumption as state variables (see Kashif et al. 2020). We must find the consumption dynamics to include consumption as a state variable. By Itô's formula, the dynamics of c are given by

$$dc_t = \frac{\partial}{\partial t}c_t dt + \frac{\partial}{\partial x}c_t dX_t + \frac{1}{2}\frac{\partial^2}{\partial x^2}c_t (dX_t)^2.$$

We can calculate the partial derivatives of c by considering (24). For the time-derivative, we consider the discrete-time version

$$c_t = (1-(1-w)\Delta)c_{t-\Delta} + (1-w)\Delta y X_t,$$

where we scale the weight on current wealth with the length of the timestep. Note that (24) is obtained as $\Delta = 1$. Now, we can calculate

$$\frac{c_t - c_{t-\Delta}}{\Delta} = (1-w)(yX_t - c_{t-\Delta}).$$

From this equation and continuity of c, we can now obtain the partial derivatives of c with respect to t by fixing $X_t = x$ and taking the limit $\Delta \to 0$. Similarly, the partial derivatives of c with respect to x are obtained directly from fixing $X_t = x$ in (24). The derivatives are given by

$$\begin{aligned} \frac{\partial}{\partial t}c_t &= (1-w)(yx - c_t), \\ \frac{\partial}{\partial x}c_t &= (1-w)y, \\ \frac{\partial^2}{\partial x^2}c_t &= 0. \end{aligned}$$

Based on the dynamics of c from Itô's formula and the derivative specified above, we obtain the continuous-time dynamics of consumption under the hybrid strategy,

$$\begin{aligned} dc_t &= (1-w)(yX_t - c_t)dt + (1-w)y dX_t \\ &= \Big(\varphi(1+r+\mu_t^* + \pi_t(\lambda - r))X_t - (1-w)(1+y)c_t\Big)dt \\ &\quad + \varphi \pi_t \sigma X_t dW_t, \\ c_0 &> 0, \end{aligned} \tag{25}$$

where we insert the wealth dynamics given by (6) and define $\varphi := (1-w)y$ in the second equality (see Kashif et al. 2020). In principle, we could consider w and y as time-dependent since we consider continuous time in (25). But we will keep w and y as constants in this section.

Observe that the consumption dynamics can be rewritten as

$$\begin{aligned} dc_t &= (1-w)(1+y)\left(\frac{y(1+r+\mu_t^* + \pi_t(\lambda - r))X_t}{1+y} - c_t\right)dt \\ &\quad + \varphi \pi_t \sigma X_t dW_t, \\ c_0 &> 0, \end{aligned} \tag{26}$$

Hence, consumption under the hybrid strategy is a mean reverting process where $(1-w)(1+y)$ is the strength of mean reversion. The process reverts toward

$$\frac{y(1+r+\mu_t^*+\pi_t(\lambda-r))X_t}{1+y}.$$

The mean reversion property results in a smoothing effect on consumption, as noticed and analyzed by Kashif et al. (2020). Hence, this is an underlying argument that the hybrid strategy is an ad hoc smoothing strategy for consumption.

Including consumption as an additional state variable, investment is the only decision variable in the utility maximization problem. We find the optimal investment portfolio by solving the value function given by

$$V(t,x,c;\pi) = \sup_{\pi} E_{t,x,c}\left[\int_t^T e^{-\int_t^s(\rho+\mu_u)du}\frac{1}{1-\gamma}X_T^{1-\gamma}\varepsilon_T(s)\right], \tag{27}$$

subject to the wealth dynamics (6) and the consumption dynamics (25). Here, $E_{t,x,c}$ is the conditional expectation given that the investor is alive at time t, holds wealth $X_t = x$, and consumes $c_t = c$. We omit the minimum subsistence level of wealth in the utility maximization problem in Kashif et al. (2020). Thus, the investor obtains utility solely from terminal wealth under the hybrid strategy. The corresponding HJB equation

$$\begin{aligned} 0 &= V_t - (\rho+\mu)V + \sup_{\pi}\Big\{\big((r+\mu^*+\pi(\lambda-r))x - c\big)V_x \\ &\quad + \big(\varphi(1+r+\mu^*+\pi(\lambda-r))x - (1-w)(1+y)c\big)V_c + \frac{1}{2}\pi^2\sigma^2x^2V_{xx} \\ &\quad + \frac{1}{2}\varphi^2\pi^2\sigma^2x^2V_{cc} + \varphi\pi^2\sigma^2x^2V_{xc}\Big\}, \\ V(T,x,c) &= \frac{1}{1-\gamma}x^{1-\gamma}. \end{aligned} \tag{28}$$

The solution to the HJB Equation (28) is given by the following value function:

$$V(t,x,c) = \frac{1}{1-\gamma}a_3(t)^{\gamma}(x-b_3(t,c))^{1-\gamma}, \tag{29}$$

where

$$\begin{aligned} a_3(t) &= e^{-\int_t^T\left(\tilde{r}+\tilde{\mu}_u-(1-\frac{1}{\gamma})(1+r+\mu_u^*)\varphi\eta(u)\right)du}, \\ b_3(t,c) &= c\eta(t). \end{aligned}$$

Here, $\eta(t)$ is the solution to the Riccati equation given by

$$\begin{aligned} \dot{\eta}(t) &= -(1+r+\mu_t^*)\varphi\eta(t)^2 + (1+r+\mu_t^*+\varphi-w)\eta(t) - 1, \\ \eta(T) &= 0, \end{aligned} \tag{30}$$

which can be rewritten as a second-order differential equation and solved numerically. The optimal investment portfolio under the hybrid strategy is given by

$$\pi_t^* = \frac{\lambda-r}{\sigma^2\gamma}\frac{X_t - c_t\eta(t)}{(1-\varphi\eta(t))X_t}. \tag{31}$$

The derivation of the results follows partially Kashif et al. (2020) with $\mu_t = 0$ and $\mu_t^* = 0$ for all $t \geq 0$. The solution of the function η differs, since we think of η as a function of time with the terminal condition $\eta(T) = 0$, whereas Kashif et al. (2020) think of η as a constant.

In line with the habit strategy, optimal investment under the hybrid strategy is time-dependent. Now, the actual investment, $\pi_t^* X_t$, is a proportion of the current wealth over a proportion of the current consumption level. The hybrid strategy reduces risk tolerance to maintain consumption at some non-guaranteed level. However, the optimal investment portfolio increases over time since the denominator of (31) decreases faster than the numerator. We found the optimal investment portfolio by maximizing the expected utility of terminal wealth. Thus, we increase the quantity invested in the risky asset to secure enough risk exposure to maximize the expected utility of terminal wealth.

It is beyond the scope of this paper to solve η as the Riccati equation given by (30). Alternatively, we present a special case where the derivation of the solution to η is more manageable, as stated in the following remark. It is attained by considering a specific construction of φ.

Remark 1. *If we consider w and y to be time-dependent and assume that*

$$\varphi(t) = (1 - w(t))y(t) = \frac{k_\eta}{\eta(t)},$$

where $0 < k_\eta < 1$ is a constant, then the Riccati equation given by (30) becomes an ODE on the form

$$\begin{aligned}\dot{\eta}(t) &= ((1 + r + \mu_t^*)(1 - k_\eta) - w(t))\eta(t) - (1 - k_\eta),\\ \eta(T) &= 0,\end{aligned}$$

which has a unique solution given by

$$\eta(t) = (1 - k_\eta) \int_t^T e^{-\int_t^s ((1+r+\mu_u^*)(1-k_\eta)-w(u))du} ds.$$

In this case, the function η is equal to a constant $(1 - k_\eta)$ multiplied by an annuity determined by $(1 + r + \mu_t^*)(1 - k_\eta) - w(t)$.

4. The Development of Consumption over Time

The dynamics of a process reveal the development of the process over time. This section aims to study the effect of optimal consumption under the three strategies. We find the optimal consumption dynamics in the classical and habit strategies by Itô's formula. In the hybrid strategy, we induce the already seen consumption dynamics by the optimal investment to find the optimal version of the dynamics.

4.1. Consumption Dynamics in the Classical Strategy

Applying Itô's formula to the optimal consumption in the classical strategy given by (14), the dynamics of optimal consumption are derived by

$$dc_t^* = \frac{\partial}{\partial t} c_t^* dt + \frac{\partial}{\partial x} c_t^* dX_t + \frac{1}{2}\frac{\partial^2}{\partial x^2} c_t^* (dX_t)^2. \tag{32}$$

Finding the derivatives of c^*, inserting these, the wealth dynamics with the optimal investment portfolio into (32) and rearranging, we can state the following result:

Theorem 1. *Consider optimal consumption in the classical strategy defined by (14). Then, the dynamics of optimal consumption are given by*

$$dc_t^* = \frac{r + \mu_t^* - \rho - \mu_t + \frac{1}{2\gamma}(1+\gamma)\theta^2}{\gamma} c_t^* dt + \frac{\theta}{\gamma} c_t^* dW_t, \tag{33}$$

$$c_0^* = \frac{x_0}{a_1(0)}, \tag{34}$$

where the deterministic function a_1 *is defined by* (11).

Proof of Theorem 1. See Appendix A.1. □

From Theorem 1, we note that optimal consumption in the classical strategy is a geometric Brownian motion. As Bruhn and Steffensen (2013), we deduce that the stock market fluctuations immediately affect the current consumption level due to the stochastic dW-term.

The dt-term reveals the expected development of consumption over time since a Brownian motion has a mean zero. Disregarding the risk aversion parameter in the denominator of the dt-term, we see that consumption increases by the interest rate, the pricing intensity, and the quantity obtained from investing in the risky asset, i.e., capital gains. Moreover, consumption decreases with the impatience factor and the mortality rate. Consequently, ignoring capital gains, an increasing or decreasing tendency in the consumption level can be explained by the relation between the interest rate and the impatience factor or the pricing intensity and the mortality rate.

Regarding the impact of the risk aversion parameter γ on the development of consumption over time, observe that the dt-term and the dW-term explode as $\gamma \to 0$. On the other hand, both terms vanish as $\gamma \to \infty$. Hence, the risk-tolerant investor experiences a highly volatile development in consumption, and the risk-averse investor prefers a less volatile or constant consumption level. Thus, the risk-averse investor is averse to variation over time.

4.2. Consumption Dynamics in the Habit Strategy

Again, by applying Itô's formula to the optimal consumption in the habit strategy given by (21), the dynamics of optimal consumption are in the following form:

$$dc_t^* = \frac{\partial}{\partial t} c_t^* dt + \frac{\partial}{\partial x} c_t^* dX_t + \frac{\partial}{\partial h} c_t^* dh_t + \frac{1}{2} \frac{\partial^2}{\partial x^2} c_t^* (dX_t)^2. \tag{35}$$

Finding the partial derivatives of c^*, inserting these, the wealth dynamics, and the habit dynamics with the optimal investment portfolio into (35) and rearranging, we obtain the following result:

Theorem 2. *Consider optimal consumption in the habit strategy defined by* (21). *Then, the dynamics of optimal consumption are given by*

$$\begin{aligned} dc_t^* = &\Bigg[\left(\frac{r + \mu_t^* - \rho - \mu_t + \frac{1}{2\gamma}(1+\gamma)\theta^2 + \kappa(t)}{\gamma} + \alpha\right) c_t^* \\ &- \left(\frac{r + \mu_t^* - \rho - \mu_t + \frac{1}{2\gamma}(1+\gamma)\theta^2 + \kappa(t)}{\gamma} + \beta\right) h_t\Bigg] dt \\ &+ \frac{\theta}{\gamma}(c_t^* - h_t) dW_t, \end{aligned} \tag{36}$$

$$c_0^* = h_0 + (1 + \alpha b_2(0))^{-\frac{1}{\gamma}} \frac{x_0 - h_0 b_2(0)}{a_2(0)},$$

where

$$\kappa(t) = \alpha\left(1 - \frac{(r+\mu_t^* + \beta)b_2(t)}{1+\alpha b_2(t)}\right). \tag{37}$$

The deterministic functions a_2 and b_2 are defined by (19) *and* (20)*, respectively.*

Proof of Theorem 2. See Appendix A.2. □

From Theorem 2, we infer that optimal consumption under the habit strategy is less volatile than optimal consumption under the classical strategy. Now, stock market fluctuations immediately affect only consumption over the current habit level. Optimal consumption over the current habit level is a geometric Brownian motion, which can be obtained by a minor rewriting of (36) (see Bruhn and Steffensen 2013). This supports the idea of using the habit strategy as a smoothing strategy for consumption.

Furthermore, the incorporation of additive habit formation impacts the expected development of consumption. Now, consumption evolves as a proportion of the current consumption level over a proportion of the existing habit level. The proportions are identical to the fraction in the dt-term of optimal consumption in the classical strategy, including a quantity, $\kappa(t)$, added to the numerator as a result of introducing habit formation. Additionally, the habit preferences are added to the fraction.

Moreover, note that for $\alpha = \beta = 0$ and $h_t = 0$ for all $t \geq 0$ in Theorem 2, we arrive at the optimal consumption dynamics from Theorem 1. Hence, the structure of the dynamics allows us to switch between the classical and the habit strategy.

For another special case, observe that for $\gamma \to \infty$, the consumption dynamics in the habit strategy are equal to the habit dynamics given by (17). Thus, the optimal consumption of a risk-averse investor with additive habit formation in the preferences evolves as the habit level.

Next, recall the expression of optimal consumption under the habit strategy given by (21). Observe that c^* is affine in h. Thus, isolating h in the expression of c^*, we obtain an expression of the habit level in terms of optimal consumption and wealth:

$$h_t = \frac{a_2(t)c_t^* - (1+\alpha b_2(t))^{-\frac{1}{\gamma}} X_t}{a_2(t) - b_2(t)(1+\alpha b_2(t))^{-\frac{1}{\gamma}}}. \tag{38}$$

Inserting (38) into the dynamics of c^* given by Theorem 2 and rearranging, we rephrase the optimal consumption dynamics as follows.

Theorem 3. *Consider the habit level given by* (38)*. Then, the dynamics of optimal consumption in the habit strategy from Theorem 2 can be rewritten as*

$$\begin{aligned} dc_t^* &= f_1(t)c_t^* dt + f_2(t)X_t dt + g_1(t)c_t^* dW_t + g_2(t)X_t dW_t, \\ c_t^* &= 0, \end{aligned} \tag{39}$$

where f_1, f_2, g_1 and g_2 are deterministic functions given by

$$f_1(t) = \frac{(\alpha-\beta)a_2(t) - \left(\frac{r+\mu_t^*-\rho-\mu+\frac{1}{2\gamma}(1+\gamma)\theta^2+\kappa(t)}{\gamma}+\alpha\right)b_2(t)(1+\alpha b_2(t))^{-\frac{1}{\gamma}}}{a_2(t)-b_2(t)(1+\alpha b_2(t))^{-\frac{1}{\gamma}}}, \tag{40}$$

$$f_2(t) = \frac{\left(\frac{r+\mu_t^*-\rho-\mu+\frac{1}{2\gamma}(1+\gamma)\theta^2+\kappa(t)}{\gamma}+\beta\right)(1+\alpha b_2(t))^{-\frac{1}{\gamma}}}{a_2(t)-b_2(t)(1+\alpha b_2(t))^{-\frac{1}{\gamma}}}, \tag{41}$$

$$g_1(t) = -\frac{\theta}{\gamma}\frac{b_2(t)(1+\alpha b_2(t))^{-\frac{1}{\gamma}}}{a_2(t)-b_2(t)(1+\alpha b_2(t))^{-\frac{1}{\gamma}}}, \tag{42}$$

$$g_2(t) = \frac{\theta}{\gamma}\frac{(1+\alpha b_2(t))^{-\frac{1}{\gamma}}}{a_2(t)-b_2(t)(1+\alpha b_2(t))^{-\frac{1}{\gamma}}}. \tag{43}$$

Proof of Theorem 3. The result of Theorem 3 follows directly from inserting the habit level given by (38) into the optimal consumption dynamics given by (36) and gathering the dt-terms and dW-terms multiplied by c^* and X, respectively. □

Hence, we have rephrased the dynamics of optimal consumption in the habit strategy without the habit level. This is reasonable when considering the design of a pension product. The visible variables in a pension product should solely be consumption and wealth, but the habit formation of the investor could reasonably drive the underlying mechanisms. But it is difficult as a pension company to form the value of the initial habit level of the investor, and now we have avoided this difficulty.

In addition, recall that the optimal investment under the habit strategy is given by

$$\pi_t^* = \frac{\lambda-r}{\sigma^2\gamma}\frac{X_t-h_tb_2(t)}{X_t}.$$

Inserting the habit level expressed by (38) into π^*, we obtain an expression of optimal investment without the habit level:

$$\pi_t^* = \frac{\lambda-r}{\sigma^2\gamma}\frac{a_2(t)(X_t-c_t^*b_2(t))}{\left(a_2(t)-b_2(t)(1+\alpha b_2(t))^{-\frac{1}{\gamma}}\right)X_t}. \tag{44}$$

Hence, the optimal investment under the habit strategy has the same structure as the optimal investment in the hybrid strategy. Now, the actual investment, $\pi_t^* X_t$, is a proportion of the current wealth over a proportion of the current consumption level.

4.3. Consumption Dynamics in the Hybrid Strategy

Recall the dynamics of consumption in the hybrid strategy:

$$\begin{aligned} dc_t &= \Big(\varphi(1+r+\mu_t^*+\pi_t(\lambda-r))X_t-(1-w)(1+y)c_t\Big)dt \\ &\quad +\varphi\pi_t\sigma X_t dW_t, \\ c_0 &> 0, \end{aligned} \tag{45}$$

with $\varphi = (1-w)y$. We found that optimal investment under the hybrid strategy is given by

$$\pi_t^* = \frac{\lambda-r}{\sigma^2\gamma}\frac{X_t-c_t\eta(t)}{(1-\varphi\eta(t))X_t}, \tag{46}$$

where η solves the Riccati equation given by (30). Inserting (46) into the dynamics of c given by (45) and doing a minor rewriting, we obtain the following result:

Theorem 4. *Consider consumption in the hybrid strategy defined by* (24) *following the dynamics given by* (45)*. With the optimal investment strategy given by* (46)*, the consumption dynamics in the hybrid strategy can be rewritten as*

$$\begin{aligned} dc_t &= \tilde{f}_1(t)c_t dt + \tilde{f}_2(t)X_t dt + \tilde{g}_1(t)c_t dW_t + \tilde{g}_2(t)X_t dW_t, \\ c_0 &> 0, \end{aligned} \tag{47}$$

where $\tilde{f}_1$, $\tilde{f}_2$, $\tilde{g}_1$ *and* $\tilde{g}_2$ *are deterministic functions given by*

$$\tilde{f}_1(t) = -\frac{\theta^2}{\gamma}\frac{\varphi\eta(t)}{1-\varphi\eta(t)} - (1-w)(1+y), \tag{48}$$

$$\tilde{f}_2(t) = \frac{\theta^2}{\gamma}\frac{\varphi}{1-\varphi\eta(t)} + \varphi(1+r+\mu_t^*), \tag{49}$$

$$\tilde{g}_1(t) = -\frac{\theta}{\gamma}\frac{\varphi\eta(t)}{1-\varphi\eta(t)}, \tag{50}$$

$$\tilde{g}_2(t) = \frac{\theta}{\gamma}\frac{\varphi}{1-\varphi\eta(t)}. \tag{51}$$

Proof of Theorem 4. The result of Theorem 4 follows directly from inserting the optimal investment strategy given by (46) into the consumption dynamics given by (45) and gathering the dt-terms and dW-terms multiplied by c and X, respectively. □

Note the astonishing similarities between the structure of the consumption dynamics from Theorems 3 and 4. We will elaborate and employ these similarities in the design of a smooth pension product in Section 5. We formalize the comparison of the two strategies in the following subsection.

4.4. Comparing Consumption Dynamics in the Habit and the Hybrid Strategy

In the preceding section, we compare the habit and hybrid strategies by comparing their consumption dynamics.

Theorem 5. *The consumption dynamics in the habit strategy given by Theorem 3 and the consumption dynamics in the hybrid strategy given by Theorem 4 coincide if*

$$f_1(t) = \tilde{f}_1(t), \tag{52}$$

$$f_2(t) = \tilde{f}_2(t), \tag{53}$$

$$g_1(t) = \tilde{g}_1(t), \tag{54}$$

$$g_2(t) = \tilde{g}_2(t). \tag{55}$$

Proof of Theorem 5. The result of Theorem 5 follows directly by comparing the consumption dynamics from Theorems 3 and 4. □

Hence, the habit strategy and the hybrid strategy for consumption are identical if Equations (52)–(55) in Theorem 5 are fulfilled. Even though the equations are not fulfilled, we still obtain that the structure of consumption and wealth is the same in the consumption dynamics under the two strategies. Thus, consumption under the two strategies evolves similarly but with (possibly) different deterministic functions. This remarkable result shows that the hybrid strategy complies with the preferences of additive habit formation. Hence, we conclude that the habit and hybrid strategies satisfy the same preferences.

5. Designing a Smooth Pension Product

This section aims to give two approaches for designing a smooth pension product, i.e., a smooth life annuity, which complies with the preferences of an investor who wants stability with respect to consumption and has no utility from their bequest. This is accomplished by inspiration of the habit and hybrid strategies and their similarities studied in Section 4. In addition, we incorporate optimal consumption under the classical strategy. We aim for a feasible, transparent, and fair design from the perspective of both the investor and the pension company. In designing a pension product, we need to specify the strategy for consumption and investment in the risky asset. With inspiration from the habit strategy and the hybrid strategy, this boils down to defining the constant and the weight in the discrete-time formulation of consumption under the hybrid strategy given by (24) and revisiting the optimal investment portfolio under the two strategies.

Consider the discrete-time formulation of consumption under the hybrid strategy given by (24), but now let w and y be time-dependent. Thus, we redefine consumption by

$$c_t = w(t)c_{t-1} + (1 - w(t))y(t)X_t. \tag{56}$$

In the design of a pension product, it is reasonable to let w and y be time-dependent. For feasibility and transparency, the liabilities of the pension company should be equal to the investor's wealth. For fairness, the investor's wealth should tend to zero as we reach termination, since we are considering a life annuity and assuming that the investor has no utility from the bequest. We can incorporate these criteria by allowing time-dependent w and y.

Let y be defined as follows

$$y(t) = \frac{1}{a_1(t)}, \tag{57}$$

where a_1 is given by (11) from the classical strategy. Recall that a_1 is interpreted as an annuity with the utility-adjusted interest rate as the calculation rate and the utility-adjusted mortality rate as the calculation of mortality. Thus, with y defined as (57), we have that $y(t)X_t$ is the optimal consumption under the classical strategy, which we interpreted as a standard market rate life annuity.

Now, let w be defined as follows

$$w(t) = \begin{cases} \frac{\alpha a_w(t)}{1+\alpha a_w(t)}, & \text{for } t \in (0, T], \\ 0, & \text{for } t = 0, \end{cases} \tag{58}$$

where α is a non-negative constant, and we define a_w as an annuity given by

$$a_w(t) = \int_t^T e^{-\int_t^s (r_w + \tilde{\mu}_u)dy} ds, \tag{59}$$

with the calculation rate given by an interest rate, r_w, and the utility-adjusted mortality rate as the calculation of mortality.

The reasoning behind the construction of w given by (58) is that the impact of last year's consumption level should depend on where the investor is in the decumulation phase. At the beginning of the decumulation phase, we want a higher weight on last year's consumption level to stabilize consumption. At the end of the decumulation phase, we want a higher weight on the future, i.e., a lower weight on past consumption, to let the standard market rate life annuity take over and the wealth go to zero. Observe that this reasoning is achieved by w defined as (58) since $\alpha a_w(t)/(1 + \alpha a_w(t)) \to 0$ for $t \to T$. We use a_w instead of a_1 since we want to change the interest rate to adjust the value of w. The higher the value of r_w, the lower the value of w. Inspired by the definition of the habit level given by (16), we weigh the annuity by α to provide relative importance to past consumption.

Requiring that $w(t) = 0$ for $t = 0$, we set the initial value of consumption equal to $x_0/a_1(0)$, where x_0 is the value of the wealth at the time of retirement. Thus, we assume that the initial consumption value in the smooth pension product is equal to that in the classical strategy. This is also reasonable when comparing the two strategies.

Summarizing the above assumptions of w and y, we rewrite consumption given by (56) as

$$\begin{aligned} c_t &= \frac{\alpha a_w(t)}{1+\alpha a_w(t)} c_{t-1} + \frac{1}{1+\alpha a_w(t)} \frac{X_t}{a_1(t)}, \\ c_0 &= \frac{x_0}{a_1(t)}. \end{aligned} \tag{60}$$

Hence, we have specified the strategy for consumption in the smooth pension product as a hybrid between a standard market rate life annuity and stability with respect to last year's consumption level.

Regarding the investment portfolio in the smooth pension product, we need to reconsider how the optimal investment portfolio in the hybrid strategy was found before using the result given by (31) from this strategy. The optimal investment portfolio was found by optimizing the expected utility of terminal wealth similar to Kashif et al. (2020). This is a somewhat artificial construction when designing a smooth pension product where we want to let the wealth go to zero as we reach termination. However, by Remark 1, we observe a simple structure of the optimal investment portfolio under the hybrid strategy. We wish to examine how this investment portfolio works with consumption specified as (60). This constitutes the first approach to a smooth pension product.

To obtain even more feasibility and transparency of the investment portfolio in the smooth pension product, we become inspired by the optimal investment portfolio under both the habit and hybrid strategies. We employ the structure of the optimal investment portfolio under the habit strategy. Instead of subtracting a proportion of the current habit level from the wealth, we subtract a proportion of the current consumption level as in the optimal investment portfolio under the hybrid strategy given by (22). Moreover, we avoid a term multiplied by the wealth in the denominator as in the optimal investment portfolio under the habit strategy. This constitutes the second approach to a smooth pension product.

Hence, we have two approaches for the investment portfolio in the smooth pension product. With y and w given by (57) and (58), respectively, such that consumption is given by (60), we formalize two approaches for the smooth pension product.

5.1. First Approach

In the first approach, we employ the simple structure obtained by Remark 1. From the remark, we have that

$$\eta(t) = \frac{k_\eta}{\varphi(t)} = \frac{k_\eta}{(1-w(t))y(t)} = \begin{cases} k_\eta a_1(t)(1+a_w(t)), & \text{for } t \in (0,T], \\ k_\eta a_1(t), & \text{for } t = 0, \end{cases} \tag{61}$$

where we insert y and w defined by (57) and (58), respectively, in the last equality. Inserting (61) into the optimal investment portfolio under the hybrid strategy given by (31), we specify the investment portfolio in the first approach for the smooth pension product by

$$\begin{aligned} \pi_t &= \frac{\lambda - r}{\sigma^2 \gamma} \frac{X_t - k_\eta a_1(t)(1+a_w(t))c_t}{(1-k_\eta)X_t}, \\ \pi_0 &= \frac{\lambda - r}{\sigma^2 \gamma} \frac{x_0 - k_\eta a_1(0) c_0}{(1-k_\eta)x_0}. \end{aligned} \tag{62}$$

Thus, the investment portfolio's denominator equals a constant multiplied by the wealth. Moreover, the proportion subtracted from the wealth is the current consumption level multiplied by a function similar to an annuity.

5.2. Second Approach

In the second approach, we set the denominator of the optimal investment portfolio under the hybrid strategy given by (31) equal to one multiplied by the wealth. Moreover, we specify the term subtracted from the wealth in the numerator by the current consumption level multiplied by an annuity. The construction is established by inspiration of the optimal investment portfolio under the habit strategy with the expression of the habit level in terms of optimal consumption and wealth inserted (see (44)). Thus, we define the investment portfolio in the second approach by

$$\pi_t = \frac{\lambda - r}{\sigma^2 \gamma} \frac{X_t - a_w(t)c_t}{X_t}, \tag{63}$$

for all $t \in [0, T]$, where the annuity a_w is given by (59). Compared to the first approach, the second approach attempts to achieve even more simplicity and transparency in the structure of the investment portfolio.

In the first and second approaches, the term multiplied by the current consumption level tends to zero as we reach termination. Furthermore, note that if we choose a high value of the interest rate, r_w, in a_w, then the term becomes small. Thus, it is interpreted as the lack of protection against a decline in the market in the attempt to achieve stability concerning consumption.

5.3. Valuation

With the structure of consumption and investment portfolio in the two approaches for a smooth pension product given above, we have that the liabilities of the pension company are precisely equal to the investor's wealth. This holds by the fact that consumption, given by (60), tends to the optimal consumption under the classical strategy such that the whole wealth is paid out when we reach termination. Thus, we omit the complexity of setting aside a buffer to achieve a smoothing effect on consumption, which is the case in the existing smooth pension product Tidspension by Bruhn and Steffensen (2013). The simplicity of the two approaches also relies on the fact that the consumption level is non-guaranteed. Instead, we aim at a less volatile development of consumption.

We have obtained two feasible, transparent, and fair designs considering everything. Compared to the existing smooth pension products, we have increased the simplicity.

6. Numerical Examples

In this section, numerical examples of consumption over time illustrate the smoothing effect on consumption under the two approaches for a smooth pension product. We compare the development of wealth, consumption, and investment portfolios under the two approaches and the classical strategy. See Munk (2008) for a numerical study of optimal consumption and investment with additive habit formation in preferences. See Kashif et al. (2020) for numerical examples of the hybrid strategy.

The first subsection below establishes the numerical setup by specifying the parameters to simulate the simplified financial market. Additionally, we decide upon a representative estimation of the mortality rate and the pricing intensity. In the second subsection, we illustrate and analyze the development of wealth, optimal consumption, and investment portfolio in the classical strategy. Continuing to the third and the fourth subsection, we give numerical examples of the two approaches for a smooth pension product from Section 5. These examples are compared with the numerical results of the classical strategy from the second subsection.

6.1. Numerical Setup

The Euler scheme is used to simulate the development of the wealth process by a time-discretized approximation with independent normal random variables representing the Brownian motion for every year in the fixed time interval $[0, T]$. The simulation is repeated $n = 100{,}000$ times under the classical strategy and the two approaches, respectively, with the chosen values of the parameters from Table 1 and a specified model for the mortality rate and the pricing intensity as described below. We let the parameter α be equal to 0.2 aligned with Munk (2008). The rest of the parameters are chosen in line with comparable life insurance literature (see, e.g., Bruhn and Steffensen (2011) or Konicz et al. (2015)). The time frame used for the simulation under the classical strategy is 3.56 s, while it is 30.08 s under the first approach, and 24.66 s under the second approach.

Table 1. Parameter values needed for simulating the simplified financial market.

Parameter	Describtion	Value
x_0	Initial wealth	100
T	Fixed time horizon	45
ρ	Impatience factor	0.04
γ	Risk aversion parameter	2
r	Drift of the risk-free asset	0.02
λ	Drift of the risky asset	0.05
σ	Volatility of the risky asset	0.2

As we only consider the decumulation phase of the investor, the fixed investment time interval $[0, T]$ represents that the investor retires at time 0 with age 65, and we assume the specified time horizon $T = 45$ at which the investor is age 110.

Regarding the lifetime uncertainty, we assume that $\mu_t = \mu_t^*$, i.e., zero market price of insurance risk, is modeled by a linear interpolation of the benchmark mortality rate for Danish women in 2021 over age 65 constituted by the Danish Financial Supervisory Authority (see DFSA 2022b). We omit to consider expected future lifetime improvements. Thus, we assume that a 65-year-old woman today in 2023 has the same mortality rate as a 65-year-old woman in 2021. Next year, when she turns 66, we think she will have the same mortality rate as a 66-year-old woman in 2021. A more realistic model for the mortality rate could have been constructed, but it is not the focus of this paper.

All numerical results are based on the assumption of no utility from bequest such that full mortality credits are assigned to the investor's wealth until death. The case of full utility from bequest, in the sense that no insurance is wanted, can, essentially, be obtained by setting $\mu_t = \mu_t^* = 0$ in all the formulas above. From a financial point of view, it corresponds to lowering the return rates r and α simultaneously by μ_t. This would lead to lower levels of consumption but along the same curvature as below. It is beyond the scope of this paper to examine in full the impact of utility from bequest, though. A different interesting case is where there is no utility from bequest but also no access to a life insurance market. The welfare loss from losing access to the insurance market is the main objective of Steffensen and Søe (2023) where there is no attention to smoothing, though.

6.2. The Classical Strategy

With the numerical setup from the preceding Section 6.1, we demonstrate the development of wealth, optimal consumption, and investment portfolio under the classical strategy. The optimal consumption and investment portfolio are given by (14) and (15), respectively. The expected development over time, accompanied by the 5% and 95% quantile, illustrates the strategy's volatility.

We leave out the graph of the optimal investment portfolio in the classical strategy as it is constant over time. With parameter values from Table 1, the optimal quantity invested in the risky asset is

$$\pi_t^* = \frac{\lambda - r}{\sigma^2 \gamma} = 0.375,$$

for all $t \in [0, T]$. Thus, about one-third of the wealth is invested in the risky asset throughout the entire decumulation phase.

Figure 1 shows that the investor is more eager to consume at the beginning of the decumulation phase than at the end, as we observe a decreasing graph of expected optimal consumption. An explanation of this development can be found by inspecting the drift term in the dynamics of optimal consumption under the classical strategy given in Theorem 1. Disregarding the return of the risky asset, the drift term contains the interest rate subtracted from the impatience factor, and as the values of these parameters are chosen such that $\rho > r$, we experience a decline in consumption over time. Hence, the investor is impatient.

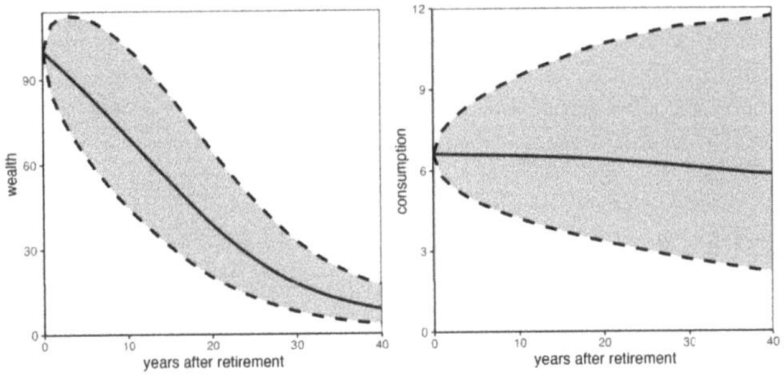

Figure 1. Wealth and consumption under the classical strategy simulated with parameter values from Table 1. The solid lines show the mean of 100,000 simulations, and the dashed lines show the 5% and 95% quantile.

Moreover, the wealth tends to zero as we reach expiry; i.e., the entire wealth is consumed since the investor has no utility from the bequest. This observation aligns with the insurance company's liabilities, which are repealed at expiry or the investor's death. Hence, the figure shows that the liabilities are equal to the wealth.

The 5% and 95% quantile emphasized by the dashed lines in Figure 1 visualize that 90% of the simulated paths of wealth and optimal consumption lie within this interval indicated by the shaded area. The path volatility expresses how the risky asset investment affects wealth development and optimal consumption over time. As observed by the dynamics of optimal consumption under the classical strategy from 1, consumption is immediately influenced by the volatility in the financial market. This uncertainty might be undesirable to an investor who favors stability in consumption over time. Hence, the optimal investment portfolio in the classical strategy is too risky to comply with the preferences of this type of investor.

6.3. The First Approach of a Smooth Pension Product

Now, we illustrate the first approach of a smooth pension product, where consumption and investment portfolio are specified as (60) and (62), respectively. The developments of wealth and consumption are shown in Figure 2. We examine the sensitivity of wealth and consumption to different values of the interest rate r_w in the annuity a_w.

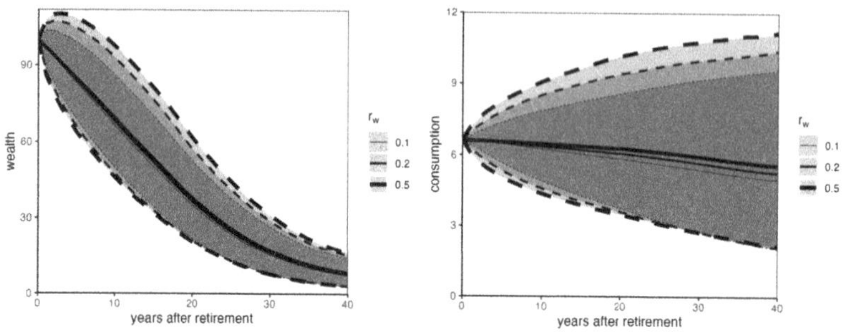

Figure 2. Wealth and consumption under the first approach of a smooth pension product simulated with different values of the interest rate r_w, $\alpha = k_\eta = 0.2$ and parameter values from Table 1. The solid lines show the mean of 100,000 simulations, and the dashed lines show the 5% and 95% quantile.

By Figure 2, we observe that the development of consumption under the first approach is less volatile than consumption under the classical strategy. The lower the value of r_w, the less volatility of consumption. This holds since the lower the value of r_w, the higher the value of w. Thus, for lower values of r_w, we maintain a higher proportion of last year's consumption level in calculating the current consumption level. At the same time, we observe that consumption under the first approach tends to consumption under the classical strategy as the value of r_w increases. This holds since the weight, w, becomes small for higher values of r_w. By constructing consumption in the smooth pension product, consumption under the classical strategy takes over. Additionally, we observe a lower expected level of consumption for lower values of r_w. It is a compensation for maintaining a higher proportion of last year's consumption level.

As we approach termination, the volatility of consumption increases. An explanation of this can be found in developing the investment portfolio under the first approach.

Unlike the classical strategy, the investment portfolio under the first approach of a smooth pension product is time-dependent. Figure 3 visualizes the impact of different values of r_w on the investment portfolio. The investment portfolio has different initial values for different values of r_w: a lower value of r_w leads to a lower initial investment portfolio value. Thus, we invest less in risky assets to maintain a higher proportion of last year's consumption.

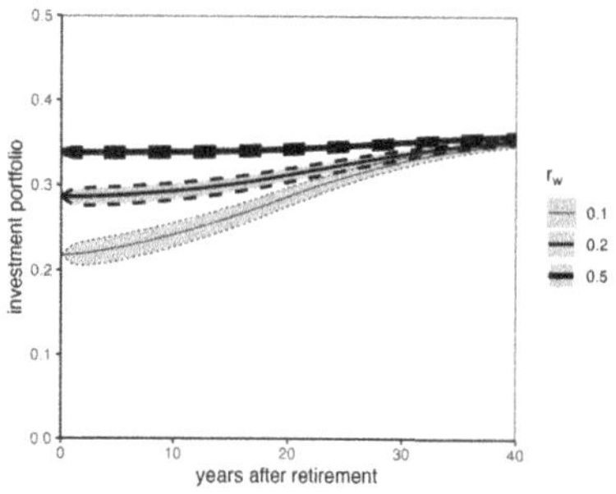

Figure 3. Investment portfolio under the first approach of a smooth pension product simulated with different values of the interest rate r_w, $\alpha = k_\eta = 0.2$ and parameter values from Table 1. The solid lines show the mean of 100,000 simulations, and the dashed lines show the 5% and 95% quantile.

Moreover, the investment portfolio is increasing and tending to the same value for the different values of r_w. The increasing development of the investment portfolio holds because the first approach is a special case of the hybrid strategy, where the optimal investment portfolio results from maximizing the expected utility of terminal wealth.

However, by constructing consumption under the smooth pension product, we let the wealth go to zero as we reach expiry, which we observe by Figure 2. The increasing investment portfolio is also why we keep increasing volatility in consumption over time.

At last, we substantiate the above analysis by illustrating the function η given by (61) and the weights, y and w, defined by (57) and (58), respectively, for different values of r_w.

By Figure 4, we only observe one graph of y, since y is independent of r_w. Thus, the graphs of y for different values of r_w are indistinguishable. Note that the graph of y is increasing over time and is rapidly closer to expiry such that the rest of the wealth is paid out by the construction of consumption under the smooth pension product.

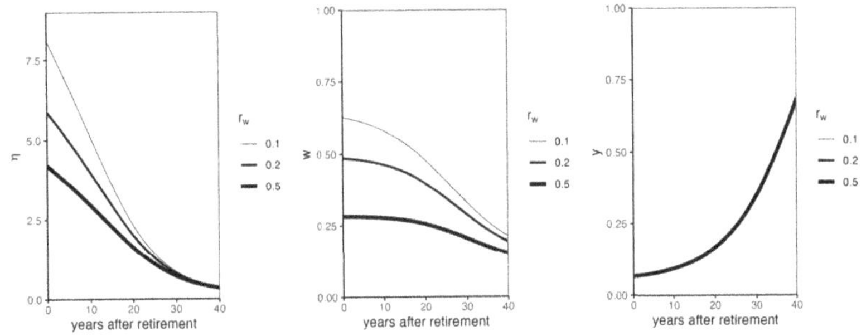

Figure 4. The function η and the weights, w and y, under the first approach of a smooth pension product with different values of the interest rate r_w, $\alpha = k_\eta = 0.2$ and parameter values from Table 1.

The graphs of w in Figure 4 show that the weight decreases over time such that the standard market rate life annuity takes over as we reach expiry. For lower values of r_w, the higher the initial value of w and vice versa. Thus, we maintain a higher proportion of last year's consumption level for lower values of r_w. Conversely, the standard market rate life annuity is more dominant for higher values of r_w.

Moreover, the function η decreases rapidly through the entire decumulation phase. This contributes to the fact that we observe an increasing investment portfolio since the numerator decreases slower than the denominator by the structure of Equation (62). Additionally, the lower the value of r_w, the higher the value of η. Thus, for higher values of r_w, we subtract a higher proportion of the current consumption level to determine the quantity invested in the risky asset. This dampens the risk taking at the beginning of the decumulation phase, as Figure 3 shows.

6.4. The Second Approach of a Smooth Pension Product

Next, we illustrate the second approach of a smooth pension product, where consumption and investment portfolio are defined by (60) and (63), respectively. The development of wealth and consumption is shown in Figure 5. Again, we study the sensitivity of wealth and consumption to different values of the interest rate r_w in the annuity a_w.

By Figure 5, we observe that the development of consumption under the second approach is less volatile than consumption under the classical strategy and consumption under the first approach. The same smoothing effect is reflected in wealth development under the second approach. Both wealth and consumption become less volatile for lower values of r_w. Note that consumption volatility increases at the beginning of the decumulation phase but stabilizes later in the decumulation phase. The stabilization of volatility happens sooner for lower values of r_w. This observation is supported by developing the investment portfolio under the second approach, as shown in Figure 6.

As in the first approach, the investment portfolio of a smooth pension product under the second approach is time-dependent. Figure 6 presents the impact of different values of r_w on the investment portfolio. Again, we observe different initial investment portfolio values for different values of r_w. In contrast to the first approach, we observe that the investment portfolio is decreasing over time, which explains the stabilization of volatility in Figure 5. As opposed to both the first approach and the classical strategy, the quantity invested in the risky asset is smaller compared to the three graphs of the expected investment portfolio with the respective corresponding value of r_w. Hence, to obtain less consumption volatility, the risk appetite is reduced.

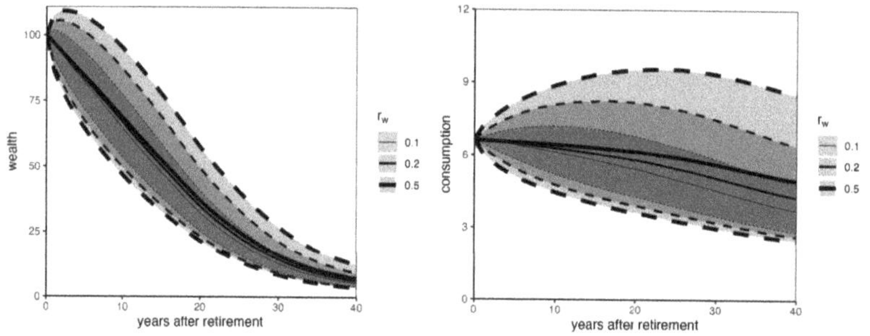

Figure 5. Wealth and consumption under the second approach of a smooth pension product simulated with different values of the interest rate r_w, $\alpha = 0.2$ and parameter values from Table 1. The solid lines show the mean of 100,000 simulations, and the dashed lines show the 5% and 95% quantile.

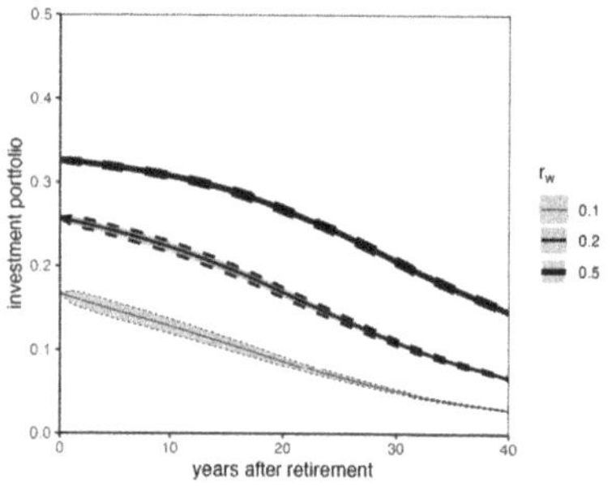

Figure 6. Investment portfolio under the second approach of a smooth pension product simulated with different values of the interest rate r_w, $\alpha = 0.2$ and parameter values from Table 1. The solid lines show the mean of 100,000 simulations, and the dashed lines show the 5% and 95% quantile.

Finally, we assist the above analysis by considering the annuity a_w given by (59), which is multiplied by the current consumption level and subtracted from the wealth in the investment portfolio under the second approach given by (63). In Figure 7, we present a_w and the weights, y and w, defined by (57) and (58), respectively, for different values of r_w.

Note that the graphs of the weights in Figure 7 are identical to those in Figure 4. This holds since the definition of consumption and the weights are similar under the two approaches. Thus, regarding the weights, the same analysis and interpretation remain as above.

Figure 7 shows that the graphs of the annuity a_w decrease over time. The higher the value of r_w, the higher the initial value of a_w. Thus, for lower values of r_w, we subtract a higher proportion, i.e., a_w, of the current consumption level directly from the actual amount invested in the risky asset by the construction of the investment portfolio in the second approach given by (63). As we subtract a proportion directly from the amount invested in the risky asset, the risk taking is dampened in the entire decumulation phase for all values of r_w as observed by Figure 6. The value of r_w dictates how much the risk taking is dampened.

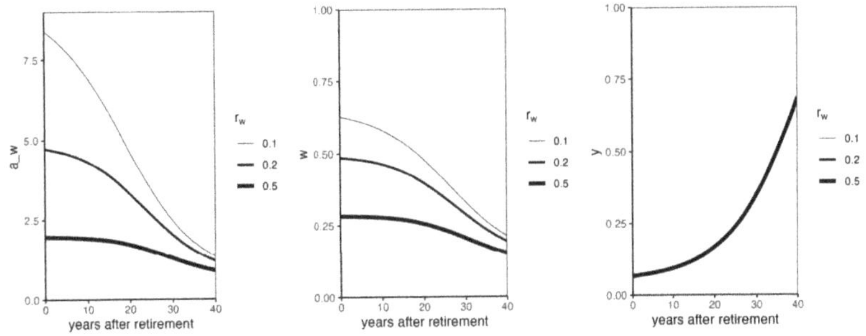

Figure 7. The annuity a_w and the weights, w and y, under the second approach of a smooth pension product with different values of the interest rate r_w, $\alpha = 0.2$ and parameter values from Table 1.

7. Conclusions

With inspiration from three strategies for consumption and investment, we have managed to design two approaches to a smooth pension product. The three strategies are the classical strategy, the habit strategy, and the hybrid strategy. Combining and modifying these strategies engenders the two approaches.

It turns out that optimal consumption under the classical strategy has the same structure as a standard market rate life annuity. Deriving the consumption dynamics under the classical and hybrid strategies, we observe that additive habit formation in preferences leads to the request for consumption stability. Comparing the consumption dynamics under the habit strategy and the hybrid strategy, we observe that the structures of the dynamics coincide. Hence, we deduce that the hybrid strategy meets the same preferences as the habit strategy. We wanted to understand these preferences to design a smooth pension product.

The objective of the smooth pension product is not to guarantee the same consumption level each year, but it is an attempt to smoothen the volatility of consumption. Moreover, we aim for a smooth pension product that is feasible, transparent, and fair from the perspective of both the investor and the pension company. Highly inspired by the consumption structure under the hybrid strategy, we let consumption be a weighted average of last year's consumption level and consumption under the classical strategy, i.e., a hybrid between stability with respect to last year's consumption level and a standard market rate life annuity. We let the weight be time-dependent such that the traditional market rate life annuity takes over as we reach termination. Hence, the pension company's liabilities equal the investor's wealth. Thus, we have obtained the smooth pension product's feasibility, transparency, and fairness. Reconsidering and inspired by both the hybrid strategy and the habit strategy, we give two approaches for the investment portfolio of the smooth pension product.

The development of the wealth process is simulated under the classical strategy and the two approaches, respectively. Each simulation is repeated $n = 100{,}000$, and the time frame under the classical strategy is 3.56 s, while it is 30.08 s under the first approach and 24.66 s under the second approach. The numerical examples show that consumption under the first and second approaches for the smooth pension product is less volatile than consumption under the classical strategy, i.e., a standard market rate life annuity. We see that consumption under the second approach is even less volatile than the first. An explanation for this result can be found in developing the investment portfolio under the respective approaches.

In the first approach, the quantity invested in the risky asset increases over time because the first approach is a special case of the hybrid strategy. The optimal investment portfolio under the hybrid strategy is found by maximizing the expected utility of terminal wealth. Thereby, we observe an increasing investment portfolio under the first approach.

The second approach is established to obtain an even simpler investment portfolio structure. It is inspired by the structure of the result obtained under the habit strategy with the expression of the habit level in terms of optimal consumption and wealth inserted.

For further research, we would study whether maximizing the expected utility of intertemporal consumption is possible given specified consumption dynamics when finding the optimal investment portfolio under the hybrid strategy. We claim that this changes the final result under the hybrid strategy.

We observed that the development of the investment portfolio impacts consumption volatility. Thus, we might have found the dynamics of the investment portfolio under the three strategies to increase the understanding of the development over time. Then, the influence of the different terms in the dynamics of the investment portfolio could be studied.

Finally, the investment portfolio under the second approach is low compared to the classical strategy. This is a result of smoothing the volatility of consumption. One might wonder whether the price of the smooth pension product is too high as the investor is dictated to take too low a risk. We need to avoid the smooth pension product becoming a guaranteed pension product. Thus, for further research, we could consider lower values of the risk aversion parameter γ such that the investment portfolio under the second approach is increased at the beginning of the decumulation phase but still decreasing over time such that the volatility of consumption is still smoothed over time. Hence, we aim to take enough risk over the entire decumulation phase.

Author Contributions: Writing—original draft preparation, S.H.V.; writing—review and editing, M.S.; Supervision, M.S. All authors have read and agreed to the published version of the manuscript.

Funding: This research received no external funding.

Institutional Review Board Statement: Not applicable.

Data Availability Statement: See DFSA (2022b).

Conflicts of Interest: The authors declare no conflicts of interest.

Appendix A. Studying Optimal Consumption

We give proof of the consumption dynamics under the classical and habit strategies in the first and the second subsections, respectively.

Appendix A.1. Proof of Theorem 1—Consumption Dynamics in the Classical Strategy

Applying Itô's formula to c^* given by (14), we find the dynamics of optimal consumption in the classical strategy by

$$dc_t^* = \frac{\partial}{\partial t}c_t^* dt + \frac{\partial}{\partial x}c_t^* dX_t + \frac{1}{2}\frac{\partial^2}{\partial x^2}c_t^*(dX_t)^2. \tag{A1}$$

By fixing $X_t = x$, the derivatives of c^* are

$$\begin{aligned}
\frac{\partial}{\partial t}c_t^* &= -\frac{x}{a_1(t)^2}\dot{a}_1(t), \\
\frac{\partial}{\partial x}c_t^* &= \frac{1}{a_1(t)}, \\
\frac{\partial^2}{\partial x^2}c_t^* &= 0.
\end{aligned}$$

Inserting the derivatives of c^* and the wealth dynamics induced by the optimal controls into (A1), we obtain that

$$dc_t^* = \left(-\frac{X_t}{a_1(t)^2}\dot{a}_1(t) + \frac{1}{a_1(t)}((r+\mu_t^* + \pi_t^*(\lambda - r))X_t - c_t^*)\right)dt + \frac{1}{a_1(t)}\pi_t^*\sigma X_t dW_t.$$

Inserting the expression of π^* given by (15), recognizing the expression of c^* and rewriting, we obtain that

$$dc_t^* = \left(-\frac{1+\dot{a}_1(t)}{a_1(t)} + r + \mu_t^* + \frac{\theta^2}{\gamma}\right)c_t^* dt + \frac{\theta}{\gamma}c_t^* dW_t. \tag{A2}$$

By Leibniz's integral rule, we have that

$$\dot{a}_1(t) = -1 + (\tilde{r} + \tilde{\mu}_t)a_1(t).$$

Thus, we see that

$$-\frac{1+\dot{a}_1(t)}{a_1(t)} = -(\tilde{r} + \tilde{\mu}_t). \tag{A3}$$

Inserting (A3) together with the expression of $\tilde{r}$ and $\tilde{\mu}$ into (A2), then by a minor rewriting, we obtain the result of Theorem 1, where the initial condition follows directly by letting $t = 0$ and $X_0 = x_0$ in (14).

Appendix A.2. Proof of Theorem 2—Consumption Dynamics in the Habit Strategy

Applying Itô's formula to c^* given by (21), we find the dynamics of optimal consumption in the habit strategy by

$$dc_t^* = \frac{\partial}{\partial t}c_t^* dt + \frac{\partial}{\partial x}c_t^* dX_t + \frac{\partial}{\partial h}c_t^* dh_t + \frac{1}{2}\frac{\partial^2}{\partial x^2}c_t^*(dX_t)^2. \tag{A4}$$

Fix $X_t = x$ and $h_t = h$. Then, by a combination of the product and the quotient rule, the derivative of c^* with respect to t is

$$\begin{aligned}\frac{\partial}{\partial t}c_t^* = &-\frac{\alpha\dot{b}_2(t)(1+\alpha b_2(t))^{-\frac{1}{\gamma}-1}}{\gamma}\frac{x - hb_2(t)}{a_2(t)} \\ &+ (1+\alpha b_2(t))^{-\frac{1}{\gamma}}\frac{-h\dot{b}_2(t)a_2(t) - (x - hb_2(t))\dot{a}_2(t)}{a_2(t)^2}.\end{aligned}$$

By Leibniz's integral rule, we have that

$$\dot{a}_2(t) = -(1+\alpha b_2(t))^{1-\frac{1}{\gamma}} + (\tilde{r} + \tilde{\mu}_t)a_2(t), \tag{A5}$$

$$\dot{b}_2(t) = -1 + (r + \mu_t^* + \beta - \alpha)b_2(t). \tag{A6}$$

Inserting the expression of $\dot{a}_2$, recognizing $c_t^* - h$ and gathering the terms multiplied by c^* and those multiplied by h, we have that

$$\begin{aligned}\frac{\partial}{\partial t}c_t^* = &\left(-\frac{\alpha\dot{b}_2(t)}{\gamma(1+\alpha b_2(t))} + \frac{(1+\alpha b_2(t))^{1-\frac{1}{\gamma}}}{a_2(t)} - \tilde{r} - \tilde{\mu}_t\right)c_t^* \\ &- \left(-\frac{\alpha\dot{b}_2(t)}{\gamma(1+\alpha b_2(t))} + \frac{\dot{b}_2(t)(1+\alpha b_2(t))^{-\frac{1}{\gamma}}}{a_2(t)} + \frac{(1+\alpha b_2(t))^{1-\frac{1}{\gamma}}}{a_2(t)} - \tilde{r} - \tilde{\mu}_t\right)h \\ =:&\ C(t) - H(t).\end{aligned}$$

The remaining necessary derivatives are

$$\frac{\partial}{\partial x}c_t^* = \frac{(1+\alpha b_2(t))^{-\frac{1}{\gamma}}}{a_2(t)},$$
$$\frac{\partial}{\partial h}c_t^* = 1 - \frac{b_2(t)(1+\alpha b_2(t))^{-\frac{1}{\gamma}}}{a_2(t)},$$
$$\frac{\partial^2}{\partial x^2}c_t^* = 0.$$

Inserting the derivatives of c^*, the wealth and the habit dynamics induced by the optimal controls into (A4), we obtain that

$$\begin{aligned}
dc_t^* = &\Bigg[C(t) - H(t) + \frac{(1+\alpha b_2(t))^{-\frac{1}{\gamma}}}{a_2(t)}((r+\mu_t^* + \pi_t^*(\lambda - r))X_t - c_t^*) \\
&+ \left(1 - \frac{b_2(t)(1+\alpha b_2(t))^{-\frac{1}{\gamma}}}{a_2(t)}\right)(\alpha c_t^* - \beta h_t)\Bigg]dt \\
&+ \frac{(1+\alpha b_2(t))^{-\frac{1}{\gamma}}}{a_2(t)}\pi_t^* \sigma X_t dW_t \\
= &\Bigg[\Bigg(-\frac{\alpha \dot{b}_2(t)}{\gamma(1+\alpha b_2(t))} + \frac{(1+\alpha b_2(t))^{1-\frac{1}{\gamma}}}{a_2(t)} - \tilde{r} - \tilde{\mu}_t \\
&+ \frac{\theta^2}{\gamma} - \frac{(1+\alpha b_2(t))^{-\frac{1}{\gamma}}}{a_2(t)} + \alpha - \frac{\alpha b_2(t)(1+\alpha b_2(t))^{-\frac{1}{\gamma}}}{a_2(t)}\Bigg)c_t^* \\
&- \Bigg(-\frac{\alpha \dot{b}_2(t)}{\gamma(1+\alpha b_2(t))} + \frac{b_2(t)(1+\alpha b_2(t))^{-\frac{1}{\gamma}}}{a_2(t)} + \frac{(1+\alpha b_2(t))^{1-\frac{1}{\gamma}}}{a_2(t)} \\
&- \tilde{r} - \tilde{\mu}_t + \frac{\theta^2}{\gamma} + \beta - \frac{\beta b_2(t)(1+\alpha b_2(t))^{-\frac{1}{\gamma}}}{a_2(t)}\Bigg)h_t\Bigg]dt \\
&+ \frac{(r+\mu_t^*)X_t(1+\alpha b_2(t))^{-\frac{1}{\gamma}}}{a_2(t)}dt + \frac{\theta}{\gamma}(c_t^* - h_t)dW_t.
\end{aligned} \tag{A7}$$

In the second equation above, we insert the expression of π^*, recognize $c_t^* - h_t$, recall the definition of $C(t)$ and $H(t)$ and gather the dt terms multiplied by c^* and those multiplied by h.

Now, observe that three of the terms multiplied by c^* vanish as

$$\frac{(1+\alpha b_2(t))^{1-\frac{1}{\gamma}}}{a_2(t)} - \frac{(1+\alpha b_2(t))^{-\frac{1}{\gamma}}}{a_2(t)} - \frac{\alpha b_2(t)(1+\alpha b_2(t))^{-\frac{1}{\gamma}}}{a_2(t)} = 0.$$

With the expression of $\dot{b}_2$ given by (A6), we see that

$$-\frac{\alpha \dot{b}_2(t)}{\gamma(1+\alpha b_2(t))} = \frac{\alpha}{\gamma}\left(1 - \frac{(r+\mu_t^* + \beta)b_2(t)}{1+\alpha b_2(t)}\right).$$

Again with the expression of $\dot{b}_2$, two of the terms multiplied by h read as

$$\frac{\dot{b}_2(t)(1+\alpha b_2(t))^{-\frac{1}{\gamma}}}{a_2(t)} - \frac{\beta b_2(t)(1+\alpha b_2(t))^{-\frac{1}{\gamma}}}{a_2(t)}$$
$$= \frac{(r+\mu_t^*)b_2(t)(1+\alpha b_2(t))^{-\frac{1}{\gamma}}}{a_2(t)} - \frac{(1+\alpha b_2(t))^{1-\frac{1}{\gamma}}}{a_2(t)}.$$

Remember that the two terms in the last equality above are multiplied by h. The last term cancels out with an identical term in the dynamics of c^*. The first term together with the dt term in line (A7) are rewritten by

$$\frac{(r+\mu_t^*)X_t(1+\alpha b_2(t))^{-\frac{1}{\gamma}}}{a_2(t)} - \frac{(r+\mu_t^*)h_t b_2(t)(1+\alpha b_2(t))^{-\frac{1}{\gamma}}}{a_2(t)} = (r+\mu_t^*)(c_t^* - h_t).$$

Combining all the observations and using the expression of $\tilde{r}$ and $\tilde{\mu}$ to undergo a final rewriting, we obtain the dynamics of c^* stated in Theorem 2. The initial condition follows directly by letting $t = 0$ and $X_0 = x_0$ in (21).

References

Bruhn, Kenneth, and Mogens Steffensen. 2011. Household consumption, investment and life insurance. *Insurance: Mathematics and Economics* 48: 315–25. [CrossRef]

Bruhn, Kenneth, and Mogens Steffensen. 2013. Optimal smooth consumption and annuity design. *Journal of Banking & Finance* 37: 2693–701.

Cejnek, Georg, Richard Franz, Otto Randle, and Neal M. Stoughton. 2014. A survey of university endowment management research. *Journal of Investment Management*, Third Quarter. [CrossRef]

DFSA. 2022a. Finanstilsynets Aktuelle Risikobillede. Available online: https://www.finanstilsynet.dk/Nyheder-og-Presse/Pressemeddelelser/2023/Risikobillede_260123 (accessed on 25 May 2023).

DFSA. 2022b. Levetidsmodel. Available online: https://www.finanstilsynet.dk/tal-og-fakta/oplysninger-for-virksomheder/oplysningstal-om-forsikring-og-pension/levetidsmodel (accessed on 15 May 2023).

Kashif, Muhammad, Francesco Menoncin, and Iqbal Owadally 2020. Optimal portfolio and spending rules for endowment funds. *Review of Quantitative Finance and Accounting* 55: 671–93. [CrossRef]

Konicz, Agnieszka Karolina, David Pisinger, Kourosh Marjani Rasmussen, and Mogens Steffensen. 2015. A combined stochastic programming and optimal control approach to personal finance and pensions. *OR Spectrum* 37: 583–616. [CrossRef]

Kraft, Holger, and Mogens Steffensen 2008. Optimal consumption and insurance: A continuous-time Markov chain approach. *ASTIN Bulletin: The Journal of the IAA* 38: 231–57.

Merton, Robert C. 1969. Lifetime portfolio selection under uncertainty: The continuous-time case. *The Review of Economics and Statistics* 51: 247–57. [CrossRef]

Merton, Robert C. 1971. Optimum consumption and portfolio rules in a continuous-time model. *Journal of Economic Theory* 3: 373–413. [CrossRef]

Munk, Claus. 2008. Portfolio and consumption choice with stochastic investment opportunities and habit formation in preferences. *Journal of Economic Dynamics and Control* 32: 3560–89. [CrossRef]

Richard, Scott F. 1975. Optimal consumption, portfolio and life insurance rules for an uncertain lived individual in a continuous time model. *Journal of Financial Economics* 2: 187–203. [CrossRef]

Steffensen, Mogens, and Julie Bjørner Søe. 2023. What is the value of the annuity market? In *Decisions in Economics and Finance*. Berlin: Springer. [CrossRef]

Journal of
Risk and Financial Management

MDPI

Article

The Duality Principle for Multidimensional Optional Semimartingales

Mahdieh Aminian Shahrokhabadi [1,*,†], Alexander Melnikov [1,†] and Andrey Pak [2,†]

[1] Mathematics and Statistical Sciences Department, Faculty of Science, University of Alberta, Central Academic Building, Edmonton, AB T6G 2G1, Canada; melnikov@ualberta.ca
[2] SS&C Technologies, Toronto, ON M5V 3K2, Canada; pak@ualberta.ca
* Correspondence: maminian@ualberta.ca
† These authors contributed equally to this work.

Abstract: In option pricing, we often deal with options whose payoffs depend on multiple factors such as foreign exchange rates, stocks, etc. Usually, this leads to a knowledge of the joint distributions and complicated integration procedures. This paper develops an alternative approach that converts the option pricing problem into a dual one and presents a solution to the problem in the optional semimartingale setting. The paper contains several examples which illustrate its results in terms of the parameters of models and options.

Keywords: optional semimartingales; derivative pricing; duality relations

1. Introduction

In this study, our objective is to build upon the exploration of the duality principle in option pricing for multidimensional optional semimartingales, as introduced in Eberlein et al. (2009). The options under consideration have payoffs dependent on various factors, such as foreign exchange rates, interest rates, and multiple stocks, including examples like swap options and quanto options.

The pricing of these complex options often necessitates a comprehensive understanding of joint probabilities and involves intricate integration procedures. A suggested alternative approach, as outlined in Eberlein et al. (2009), involves transforming the original problem into its dual option pricing problem, rather than directly solving it. The subsequent resolution of this dual problem provides valuable insights into the valuation of options characterized by intricate dependencies and multiple influencing factors.

As stated earlier, the model we employ to describe the evolution of asset price processes is in the context of multidimensional optional semimartingale models. The family of optional semimartingales constitutes a diverse class of stochastic processes that includes cadlag semimartingales as a subset. Typically, these processes lack cadlag modifications, meaning they are not inherently right-continuous with finite left-limits, particularly in unusual probability spaces. We can refer to the work by Czichowsky and Schachermayer (2016) for evidence that the theory of optional processes should be exploited more in the area of financial mathematics. In recent times, several articles have delved into the exploration of optional processes and their significance in financial and energy markets.

Applying the outcomes derived from our study, we can establish duality relationships among swap options, quanto options, and standard call and put options within the framework of optional semimartingale models. This revelation carries notable implications, primarily manifesting in a substantial reduction in the computational complexity associated with the valuation of these financial instruments.

By leveraging our findings, we unveil a practical and efficient means of interrelating swap and quanto options with their standard call and put counterparts in optional semimartingale models. This not only enhances the understanding of the intricate connections between these financial instruments but also provides a tangible advantage in terms of computational efficiency when determining their respective valuations.

Extensive literature has delved into the duality principle of option pricing for multidimensional models. Notable contributions come from studies conducted by Margrabe (1978), Geman et al. (1995), Gerber and Shiu (1996), and a lesser-known work by Fischer (1978) for the Black–Scholes model. Additionally, investigations by Eberlein and Papapantoleon (2005) focused on time-inhomogeneous Levy processes, Fajardo and Mordecki (2006) studied general Levy processes, and Schröder (2015) delved into cadlag semimartingales. In Eberlein et al. (2009), Eberlein, Papapantoleon, and Shiryaev establish a predictable characteristics triplet for one-dimensional semimartingales under the dual measure, employing the Esscher change of measure. On the contrary, limited attention has been given to optional semimartingales.

The paper is organized as follows. In Section 2, we will establish crucial definitions and notations that serve as the foundation for understanding the subsequent sections. Additionally, we will review pertinent results regarding the canonical decomposition of optional semimartingales. This includes an exploration of their quadruplet of predictable characteristics and their Laplace cumulant process. Section 3 contains details and lemmas tailored for Exponentially Optional Semimartingale models. We included the main result of this work in Section 4, where we present results concerning multidimensional optional semimartingales and the treatment of linear transformations applied to multidimensional semimartingales. In Section 5, we delve into the duality relation for optional processes, specifically examining the European, Margrabe, and quanto options. Alongside this, in Section 6, we provide explicit examples elucidating the application of the duality principles examined in the previous section.

2. Canonical Decomposition of Optional Semimartingales

Let us begin by defining key terms and notations crucial for understanding the upcoming sections. Specifically, we need to clarify the concept of an *un*usual probability space. An *un*usual probability space is $(\Omega, \mathcal{F}, \mathbf{F} = (\mathcal{F}_t)_{t\geq 0}, \mathbf{P})$, wherein the natural filtration $\mathcal{F}_t$ is characterized by the absence of both right- and left-continuity. The completeness of the space arises from the fact that $\mathcal{F}$ incorporates all its $\mathbf{P}$-null sets, and $\mathbf{P}$ serves as a completed probability measure. We define $\mathbf{F}_+ = (\mathcal{F}_{t^+})$, with $\mathcal{F}_{t^+} = \bigcap_{t\leq s} \mathcal{F}_s$. Now, considering $\mathbf{F}^* := \mathbf{F}_+^P$ as the standard filtration—both right-continuous and complete—the construction of $\mathbf{F}_+^P$ involves enriching $\mathbf{F}_+$ with $\mathbf{P}$-null sets.

Let $\mathbb{R}^d$ represent the d-dimensional Euclidean space. In this space, the scalar product between two vectors u and v, both elements of $\mathbb{R}^d$, is denoted as $\langle u, v\rangle = u'v$, where u' denotes the transpose of the vector (or matrix) u.

Moving forward, the next step involves defining optional processes, which serve as the foundational processes under consideration in this paper. All definitions in this regard are drawn from Abdelghani and Melnikov (2020). Specifically, we draw upon topics such as the definition and classifications of stopping times from Section 2, the existence and uniqueness of optional martingales from Section 5, and compensators and integration concerning optional semimartingales from Section 7, with further reference to Sections 8 and 9.

To formulate the definition of optional processes, it is essential to establish the concept of an optional σ-algebra. In this context, we designate the σ-algebra $\mathcal{O}(F)$ on the interval $[0, \infty) \times \Omega$ as optional if it is generated by all right-continuous $\mathcal{F}_t$-adapted processes with left-hand limits.

Definition 1. *A random process $X = (X_t)$, $t \in [0, \infty)$ is said to be optional if it is $\mathcal{O}(F)$-measurable. Optional processes are progressively measurable, and thus clearly measurable. In general, optional processes have right and left limits but are not necessarily continuous on the right, left, or otherwise.*

Additionally, when it comes to optional stochastic processes, we can introduce the following definitions. The left process, denoted as $X_- = (X_{t_-})_{t\geq 0}$, where $X_{0_-} = X_0$ and $X_{t_-} = \lim_{s\uparrow t} X_s$. Similarly, we have the right processes $X_+ = (X_{t_+})_{t\geq 0}$. Also, we have the regular differential process $\Delta X = (\Delta X_t)_{t\geq 0}$, where $\Delta X_t = X_t - X_{t-}$, and the forward differential process $\Delta^+ X = (\Delta^+ X_t)_{t\geq 0}$, where $\Delta^+ X_t = X_{t+} - X_t$.

It is also crucial to understand the classification of stopping times. A solid understanding of these definitions is paramount for delving into the subsequent sections. Here, we would like to briefly define stopping (or Markov) times. Then, we will restate two important categories of this random time, which is important in the rest of the paper.

Definition 2. *Let $(\mathcal{F}_t)$ be a filtration on $(\Omega, \mathcal{F}, P)$. A random variable T on Ω with values in $R_+ \cup \{+\infty\}$ is called a stopping time or optional time of the filtration $(\mathcal{F}_t)$ if, for all $t \in R_+$, the event $\{T \leq t\}$ belongs to $\mathcal{F}_t$ and belongs to the trivial filtration. The set of all stopping times is denoted by $\mathcal{T}$.*

Furthermore, stopping times are also called Markov times. Their simplest examples are $1_{T\leq t}$ and every positive constant.

Definition 3. *T is called a wide-sense stopping time if for all t,*

$$\{T < t\} \in F_t$$

Also, we can say that T as a wide-sense stopping time is optional in the wide sense if and only if it is optional to the family $\mathbf{F}_+$. Another characterization of wide-sense stopping times is, for all $t > 0$, $T \wedge t$ is F_t-measurable.

We also require another classification of these stopping times, specifically the concept of totally inaccessible stopping times, which will prove beneficial later on.

Definition 4. *$T > 0$ is totally inaccessible if, for every sequence $(T_n)_{n=1,2,\cdots}$ of stopping times that increases to T, the event $\{\lim_{n\uparrow\infty} T_n = T, T < \infty\}$ has zero probability*

Understanding the definition of a predictable process and σ-algebra is also valuable. We designate the σ-algebra $\mathcal{P}(\mathcal{F})$ on $\Omega \times [0,\infty)$ as predictable if it is generated by all left-continuous $\mathcal{F}_t$-adapted processes with right-hand limits or by sets $\{(\omega, t) : S(\omega) < t \leq T(\omega)\}$, where S, T vary across all Markov times.

Definition 5. *A random process $Y = (Y_t)$, $t \in [0,\infty)$, whose trajectories have limits from the right is said to be predictable if $P(\mathcal{F})$-measurable. Furthermore, it is termed strongly predictable if $Y_t \in P(\mathcal{F})$ and $Y_t^+ \in \mathcal{O}(\mathcal{F})$ holds for all t.*

Predictable processes are also optional, i.e., $\mathcal{P}(\mathcal{F}) \subseteq \mathcal{O}(\mathcal{F})$. Moreover, the definition of strongly predictable processes implies that for every stopping time T, the random variables $X_{T^+}1_{T<\infty}$ and $X_{T^-}1_{T<\infty}$ are $\mathcal{F}_{T^+}$-measurable and $\mathcal{F}_{T^-}$-measurable, respectively. The set of strongly predictable processes is denoted by $P_s(\mathcal{F})$ or P_s.

Let us revisit the definition of optional martingales, highlighting the difference from the definition of regular martingales on $\mathbf{F}^*$ satisfying the usual conditions. For an adapted process $X = (X_t)$ with $t \in \mathbb{R}_+$, it qualifies as a martingale (or alternatively, a supermartingale or submartingale) concerning $\mathbf{F}^*$ if, for every $t \in \mathbb{R}_+$, X_t is integrable, and the conditional expectation $X_s = \mathbb{E}[X_t|\mathbf{F}_s^*]$ (or $X_s \geq \mathbb{E}[X_t|\mathbf{F}_s^*]$, $X_s \leq \mathbb{E}[X_t|\mathbf{F}_s^*]$) holds almost surely for all $s \leq t$. Referring to the existence and uniqueness of optional martingales, we outline the definitions of optional martingales and optional local martingales here.

Definition 6. *We define $M = (M_t)_{t\in\mathbb{R}_+}$, as an optional martingale (or, alternatively, an optional supermartingale or an optional submartingale) if the following hold:*

(a) *M is an optional process (i.e., $M \in O(\mathcal{F})$);*
(b) *The random variable $M_T \cdot 1_{\{T<\infty\}}$ is integrable for any $T \in \mathcal{T}$;*
(c) *There exists an integrable random variable $\hat{M}$ such that $M_T = \mathbb{E}[\hat{M}|\mathcal{F}_T]$ (or $M_T \geq \mathbb{E}[\hat{M}|\mathcal{F}_T]$, $M_T \leq \mathbb{E}[\hat{M}|\mathcal{F}_T]$) almost surely on $\{T < \infty\}$ for any $T \in \mathcal{T}$.*

Definition 7. *A process $M = (M_t)_{t\geq 0}$ is called an optional local martingale if there exists a sequence $(R_n, M^{(n)}), n \in \mathbb{N}$, where R_n represents wide-sense stopping times, $R_n \uparrow \infty$ a.s. and $M^{(n)}$ is an optional martingale, such that $M1_{[0,R_n]} = M^{(n)}1_{[0,R_n]}$ and the random variable M_{R_n+} is integrable for any $n \in \mathbb{N}$.*

Consider $\mathcal{M}^O(P)$ ($\mathcal{M}^O_{loc}(P)$), representing the set of optional (local) martingales in relation to the probability measure P. Let $\mathcal{V}$ denote the collection of all **F**-adapted processes with a finite variation where the variation for an optional process $A = (A_t)$ is given by

$$\text{Var}(A)_t = \sum_{0\leq s\leq t} |A_{s+} - A_s| + \int_{0+}^{t} |dA^r| < \infty$$

where A^r is a right-continuous finite-variation process, and the series is absolutely convergent. This discussion lays the groundwork for the exploration of optional semimartingales and their canonical decomposition, which is the next crucial step in this study.

Definition 8. *The stochastic process X is called an optional semimartingale denoted by the set $\mathcal{S}$ if*

$$X = X_0 + M + A,$$

where $M \in \mathcal{M}^O_{loc}$, $A \in \mathcal{V}$, $A_0 = M_0 = 0$ and X_0 is an $\mathcal{F}_0$-measurable finite random variable. If this decomposition holds with a strongly predictable process A of locally integrable variation, then the optional semimartingale X attains the special designation of a special optional semimartingale, denoted by the set $\mathcal{S}_s$.

The canonical and component representation of semimartingales is also essential to our analysis of optional semimartingales. The canonical and component representation of optional semimartingales can be seen as a natural consequence of the decomposition

$$X = X_0 + X^c + X^d + X^g$$

where X^c is a continuous optional semimartingale with the decomposition $X^c = a + m$, where a is continuous and strongly predictable with locally integrable variation, and m is a continuous local martingale. The discrete optional semimartingale parts $X^d = a^d + m^d$ and $X^g = a^g + m^g$ are expressible in terms of some underlying measures of right and left jumps, respectively.

Let us proceed to define the characteristics of an optional semimartingale. Consider a d-dimensional optional semimartingale denoted as $Y = (Y_t)_{0\leq t\leq T}$, where $Y = (Y_1, \ldots, Y_d)'$ with the decomposition $Y_i = A_i + M_i$, where $M_i \in \mathcal{M}^O_{\text{loc}}$, $A_i \in \mathcal{V}$, $M_{i,0} = 0$, $i = 1, \ldots, d$. Let $(T_n)_{n\geqslant 1}$ and $(U_n)_{n\geqslant 1}$ be sequences of totally inaccessible stopping times and totally inaccessible wide-sense stopping times, respectively. For $(E, \mathcal{E})$, consider the Lusin space where $E = (\mathbb{R}^d \setminus \{0\}) \cup \{\delta^d\} \cup \{\delta^g\}$ such that δ^d and δ^g are some supplementary points or are the set of processes with finite variation on any segment $[0, t]$, **P**-a.s.; $\mathcal{E} = \mathcal{B}(E)$. On the σ-algebra $\tilde{\mathcal{E}} = \mathcal{B}(E) \times \mathcal{E}$, define integer random measures on $(\mathbb{R}_+ \times E, \tilde{\mathcal{E}})$

$$\mu^r(\Gamma) = \sum_{n\geqslant 1} \mathbf{1}_\Gamma(T_n, \beta^r_{T_n}), \qquad \mu^g(\Gamma) = \sum_{n\geqslant 1} \mathbf{1}_\Gamma(U_n, \beta^g_{U_n})$$

where $\mathbf{1}_\Gamma(\cdot)$ is an indicator function of a set $\Gamma \in \tilde{\mathcal{E}}$, $\beta^r_t = \Delta Y_t$ if $\Delta Y_t \neq 0$ and $\beta^r_t = \delta$ if $\Delta Y_t = 0$, $\beta^g_t = \Delta^+ Y_t$ if $\Delta^+ Y_t \neq 0$, $\beta^g_t = \delta$ if $\Delta^+ Y_t = 0$, $t > 0$. Under the *un*usual conditions on probability space $(\Omega, \mathcal{F}, \mathbf{F} = (\mathcal{F}_t)_{t\geq 0}, \mathbf{P})$, any optional semimartingale Y can be decomposed as follows:

$$Y_t = Y_0 + B_t + C_t + \int_{]0,t]\times E} h(x)d(\mu^r - \nu^r) + \int_{[0,t[\times E} h(x)d(\mu^g - \nu^g)$$
$$+ \int_{]0,t]\times E} (x - h(x))d\mu^r + \int_{[0,t[\times E} (x - h(x))d\mu^g$$

or in short notation

$$Y = Y_0 + B + C + \sum_{j=r,g} \Big[h(x) * (\mu^j - \nu^j) + (x - h(x)) * \mu^j\Big],$$

Y_0 is $\mathcal{F}_0$-measurable random variable, $B \in \mathcal{V}$, $B_0 = 0$, and $C \in \mathcal{M}^O_{loc}$, $C_0 = 0$, and it is continuous. ν^j represents the compensators of μ^j. The function $h(x)$ is a truncation function, meaning it is a bounded function with compact support that behaves as $h(x) = x$ around the origin. As an example, one could choose $h(x) = x1_{\{|x|\leq 1\}}$. Additionally, $W * \mu$ denotes the integral process, and $W * (\mu - \nu)$ denotes the stochastic integral with respect to the compensated random measure $(\mu - \nu)$.

The collection of the processes B, C and the measures ν^r, ν^g is called the (local) characteristics of the semimartingale Y with respect to the probability measure P. Let us call them a quadruplet and denote them by

$$Q(Y|P) = (B, C, \nu^r, \nu^g).$$

There exists an increasing predictable process A, predictable processes b and c and two transition kernels F^r and F^g from $(\Omega \times [0, T], \mathbf{P})$ into $(E, \mathcal{E})$ such that

$$B = b \cdot A, \quad B_t = \int_0^t b_s dA_s$$
$$C = c \cdot A, \quad C_t = \int_0^t b_s dA_s$$
$$\nu^j = F^j \otimes A, \quad \nu^j([0,t] \times E) = \int_0^t \int_E F^j_s(dx)dA_s,\ j = r, g$$

Optional semimartingale Y with characteristics $Q(Y|P) = (B, C, \nu^r, \nu^g)$ can be associated with an optional Laplace cumulant process defined by

$$G(u) = \langle u, B\rangle + \frac{1}{2}\langle u, Cu\rangle + (e^{\langle u,x\rangle} - 1 - \langle u, h(x)\rangle) * \nu^r + (e^{\langle u,x\rangle} - 1 - \langle u, h(x)\rangle) * \nu^g \quad (1)$$

The definition was motivated by Kallsen and Shiryaev (2002). Furthermore, expressing the optional Laplace cumulant process can be achieved using the process A, represented as $G(u) = g(u) \cdot A$ with

$$g(u) = \langle u, b\rangle + \frac{1}{2}\langle u, cu\rangle + (e^{\langle u,x\rangle} - 1 - \langle u, h(x)\rangle) * F^r + (e^{\langle u,x\rangle} - 1 - \langle u, h(x)\rangle) * F^g$$

Another significant distinction of the calculus of optional semimartingales on the *un*usual probability space, in comparison to regular semimartingales on the usual probability space, is their integration. To conclude this section and emphasize this distinction, let us briefly explore the notion of integration with respect to optional semimartingales.

The optional stochastic integral with respect to optional semimartingales X as introduced by Kühn and Stroh (2009) is defined in terms of the stochastic integrals with respect to its components A and m as

$$Y_t = \int_0^t h_s\, dX_s = h \circ X_t = \int_0^t h_s\, dA_s + \int_0^t h_s\, dm_s$$
$$= h \circ A_t + h \circ m_t = h \circ A_t^r + h \circ A_t^g + h \circ m_t^r + h \circ m_t^g,$$

where

$$h \circ A_t^r = \int_{0+}^t h_{s-} dA_s^r, \quad h \circ A_t^g = \int_0^{t-} h_s dA_{s+}^g,$$

$$h \circ m_t^r = \int_{0+}^t h_{s-} dm_s^r, \quad h \circ m_t^g = \int_0^{t-} h_s dm_{s+}^g,$$

Given that $X = X^r + X^g = X^c + X^d + X^g$, we can express the integral with respect to X as follows:

$$h \circ X = h \circ X^r + h \circ X^g = h \circ X^c + h \circ X^d + h \circ X^g,$$

where $X^r = A^r + m^r = A^c + m^c + A^d + m^d$ and $X^g = A^g + m^g$.

3. Exponentially Optional Semimartingale Models

In this section, we delve into specific details and lemmas tailored for exponentially optional semimartingale models. The forthcoming discussions will cover various results, including equivalent statements for exponentially special optional semimartingales, a martingale version of the Lévy–Khintchine formula applicable to optional semimartingales, multiplicative decomposition for optional semimartingale, and a corollary addressing the uniqueness of the exponential optional compensator.

To start this section, we present definitions for a special optional semimartingale and an exponential optional compensator. This initial step aims to show differences between the findings in this section and those in the references Jacod and Shiryaev (1987) and Eberlein et al. (2009).

Definition 9. *An optional semimartingale X is called* exponentially special optional semimartingales *if* $\exp(X - X_0)$ *is a special optional semimartingale.*

Definition 10. *Let X be an optional semimartingale. A strongly predictable process $V \in \mathcal{V}$ is called exponential optional compensator of X if* $\exp(X - X_0 - V) \in \mathcal{M}_{loc}^{O}(P)$.

In the following lemma, our objective is to reformulate the outcome presented in Corollary II.2.42 of Jacod and Shiryaev (1987) for exponentially special optional semimartingales. This restatement serves as an extension of the original result by Jacob and Shiryaev.

Lemma 1. *Suppose X is an exponentially special optional semimartingale. The following statements are equivalent:*

(a) X is an optional semimartingale, and it admits the local quadruplet of characteristics $Q(X|P) = (B, C, \nu^r, \nu^g)$.

(b) For each $z \in \mathbb{R}$, the process $e^{zX} - (e^{zX_-}) \circ G(z) \in \mathcal{M}_{loc}^{O}$.

Proof. $(a) \Rightarrow (b)$: We consider the following decomposition of X :

$$X = M + B + \sum_{s \le t} [\Delta X_s - h(\Delta X_s)] + \sum_{s<t} [\Delta^+ X_s - h(\Delta^+ X_s)]$$

Applying the change of variables formula to $f(x) = e^{zx}$ and X, we have

$$\begin{aligned} e^{zX} - e^{zX_0} =& ue^{zX_-} \circ B + ze^{zX_-} \circ M \\ & - \frac{1}{2} z^2 e^{zX_-} \cdot C \\ & + e^{zX_-} (e^{zx} - 1 - zh(x)) * \mu^r \\ & + e^{zX} (e^{zx} - 1 - zh(x)) * \mu^g. \end{aligned} \tag{2}$$

Consider the right-hand side of (2): the second term is an optional local martingale and the other terms are optional processes with a finite variation. However, since e^{zX} is a special optional semimartingale, $e^{zX_-}(e^{zx}-1-zh(x))*\mu^r + e^{zX}(e^{zx}-1-zh(x))*\mu^g$ is actually a process of locally integrable variation. Thus,

$$e^{zX_-}(e^{zx}-1-zh(x))*(\mu^r-\nu^r)+e^{zX}(e^{zx}-1-zh(x))*(\mu^g-\nu^g)\in\mathcal{M}^{O}_{loc},$$

and the result follows.

$(b)\Rightarrow(a)$: Hypothetically, e^{zX} is an optional semimartingale for each $z\in\mathbb{R}$. Then, since $\log(x)\in C^2$, X is an optional semimartingale.

Let $(B^*,C^*,\nu^{r*},\nu^{g*})$ be a good version of the characteristics of X. For each $z\in\mathbb{R}$ we associate with $(B^*,C^*,\nu^{r*},\nu^{g*})$ a process $G^*(z)$. We have proved the implication $(a)\Rightarrow(b)$, thus $e^{zX}-e^{zX}\circ G^*(z)\in\mathcal{M}^{O}_{loc}$. Then, the hypothesis and the uniqueness of the canonical decomposition of the special semimartingale e^{zX} show that $e^{zX}\circ G^*(z)=e^{zX}\circ G(z)$ up to an evanescent set. Using the orthogonality of G^r and G^g and integrating the processes e^{-zX_-} and e^{-zX}, we obtain that $G(z)$ and $G^*(z)$ are indistinguishable. Therefore, the set N of all ω for which there exists $z\in\mathbb{Q}$ and $t\in\mathbb{Q}_+$ with $G(z)_{t(\omega)}\neq G^*(z)_{t(\omega)}$ is P-null.

Now, we observe that the optional cumulant function is continuous and, as a result, completely characterized by its values on $\mathbb{Q}$. Consequently, outside of the set N, we have $B^*_t:=B^{r*}_t+B^{g*}_t$, $B_t:=B^r+B^g$, $C^*_t=C_t$ and $\nu^{j*}([0,t]\times\cdot)=\nu^j([0,t]\times\cdot), j=r,g$, for all $t\in\mathbb{Q}_+$ (see Gnedenko and Kolmogorov (1954)). This relationship also holds for all $t\in\mathbb{R}+$ due to the right-continuity of $B^{r*},B^r,C^*,C,\nu^{r*},\nu^r$, and the left-continuity of $B^{g*},B^g,\nu^{g*},\nu^g$. Therefore, (B,C,ν^r,ν^g) also serves as a version of the local characteristics of X. □

A significant finding in Jacod and Shiryaev (1987) (II.2.48 Corollary) and Eberlein et al. (2009) presents a martingale version of the Lévy–Khintchine formula specifically tailored for regular semimartingales. In this context, our goal is to broaden this result to encompass optional semimartingales.

Corollary 1. *Suppose X is an exponentially special optional semimartingale and $\mathcal{E}(G(z))\neq 0$ for all $z\in\mathbb{R}$. If for each $z\in\mathbb{R}$, $\frac{e^{zX}}{\mathcal{E}(G(z))}\in\mathcal{M}^{O}_{loc}$. Then, X is an optional semimartingale with characteristics (B,C,ν^r,ν^g).*

Proof. Denote $M(z)=\frac{e^{zX}}{\mathcal{E}(G(z))}\in\mathcal{M}^{O}_{loc}$. Then, using a similar approach as in Jacod and Shiryaev (1987) (II.2.48 Corollary) but adapted to optional semimartingales, we obtain

$$\begin{aligned}
e^{zX} =&\mathcal{E}(G(z))M(z)\\
=&e^{zX_0}+\mathcal{E}(G(z))\cdot M^r_t(z)+M_-(z)\cdot\mathcal{E}^r_t(G(z))\\
&+\mathcal{E}_+(G(z))\odot M^g_{t+}(z)+M(z)\odot\mathcal{E}^g_{t+}(G(z))\\
=&e^{zX_0}+\mathcal{E}(G(z))\cdot M^r_t(z)+M_-(z)\mathcal{E}^r_-(G(z))\cdot G^r_t(z)\\
&+\mathcal{E}_+(G(z))\odot M^g_{t+}(z)+M(z)\mathcal{E}^r(G(z))\odot G^g_{t+}(z)\\
=&e^{zX_0}+\mathcal{E}(G(z))\cdot M^r_t(z)+\mathcal{E}_+(G(z))\odot M^g_{t+}(z)\\
&+e^{zX}\circ G_t(z)
\end{aligned}$$

The definition of $\mathcal{E}(G(z))$ and the notation $\odot$ is used for the optional integral with respect to the optional martingale process. It follows from the above that $e^{zX}-e^{zX_-}\circ G(z)\in\mathcal{M}^{O}_{loc}$. The result follows from $(b)\Rightarrow(a)$ of Lemma 1. □

In addition to the canonical decomposition for an optional semimartingale, we want to establish that every optional semimartingale also allows for a multiplicative decomposition, as demonstrated in the following theorem.

Theorem 1. *Let X be an optional semimartingale with $X_0 = 1$, such that X, X_- and X_+ take their values in $(0, \infty)$. Then, X admits a multiplicative decomposition $X = LD$, where $L \in \mathcal{M}^O_{loc}$, $L > 0$ and $D \in \mathcal{V}$ is a positive strongly predictable process and $L_0 = D_0 = 1$, if and only if X is a special semimartingale.*

In this case, the multiplicative decomposition is unique (up to evanescence), and is given as follows, where $X = 1 + M + A$ is the canonical (additive) decomposition of X, and $H^r := \frac{1}{X_- + \Delta A}$ and $H^g := \frac{1}{X + \Delta^+ A}$ are necessarily locally bounded and positive:

$$L = \mathcal{E}(H \circ M), \quad D = \frac{1}{\mathcal{E}(-H \circ A)} \tag{3}$$

Proof. If a multiplicative decomposition $X = LD$ exists, we have

$$X = LD = 1 + \int_{]0,t]} D_s dL^r_s + \int_{]0,t]} L_{s-} dD^r_s + \int_{[0,t[} D_{s+} dL^g_{s+} + \int_{[0,t[} L_s dD^g_{s+}. \tag{4}$$

$\int_{]0,t]} D_s dL^r_s + \int_{[0,t[} L_s dD^g_{s+}$ is an optional local martingale and $\int_{]0,t]} L_{s-} dD^r_s + \int_{[0,t[} L_s dD^g_{s+}$ is a strongly predictable process with finite variation; thus, X is an optional special semimartingale.

Suppose that we have two multiplicative decompositions $X = LD = \hat{L}\hat{D}$, for which we can write (4). The uniqueness of the canonical decomposition yields

$$\int_{]0,t]} L_{s-} dD^r_s + \int_{[0,t[} L_s dD^g_{s+} = \int_{]0,t]} \hat{L}_{s-} d\hat{D}^r_s + \int_{[0,t[} \hat{L}_s d\hat{D}^g_{s+} \ (a.s.).$$

D^r and D^g are orthogonal, we have

$$\int_{]0,t]} L_{s-} dD^r_s = \int_{]0,t]} \hat{L}_{s-} d\hat{D}^r_s, \quad \int_{[0,t[} L_s dD^g_{s+} = \int_{[0,t[} \hat{L}_s d\hat{D}^g_{s+} \ (a.s.).$$

$L, \hat{L}, D, \hat{D}$ are positive and $L/\hat{L} = \hat{D}/D$, we deduce that

$$\int_{]0,t]} 1/D_{s-} dD^r_s = \int_{]0,t]} 1/\hat{D}_{s-} d\hat{D}^r_s$$

and

$$\int_{[0,t[} 1/D_s dD^g_{s+} = \int_{[0,t[} 1/\hat{D}_s d\hat{D}^g_{s+}$$

Then, if

$$U = \int_{]0,t]} 1/D_{s-} dD^r_s + \int_{[0,t[} 1/D_s dD^g_{s+},$$

we also have

$$\int_{]0,t]} 1/\hat{D}_{s-} d\hat{D}^r_s + \int_{[0,t[} 1/\hat{D}_s d\hat{D}^g_{s+} = U,$$

which means we have $D = \hat{D} = \mathcal{E}(U)$, and this proves the uniqueness.

Te following remains to be proven: if $X = 1 + M + A$ is the canonical decomposition of the optional special semimartingale X (with $X > 0, X_- > 0$ and $X_+ > 0$), and if $N = H \circ M$ and $B \circ A$, then the strongly predictable process H is both locally bounded and positive. Moreover, $X = LD$, where $L = \mathcal{E}(N)$ and $D = 1/\mathcal{E}(-B)$ (as defined in (3)). Note that N and L are optional local martingales, while B and D are strongly predictable with finite variation. First, we observe that

$${}^pX = {}^pA + {}^pM = A_- + \Delta A + M_- = X_- + \Delta A,$$

where the notation ^{p} denotes a predictable projection of the process. Then, for any predictable stopping time T, and since $X > 0$, we obtain $X_{T-} + \Delta A_T = \mathbf{E}(X_T | \mathcal{F}_T) > 0$

a.s. on $\{T < \infty\}$. Then, Theorem 2.4.52 in Abdelghani and Melnikov (2020) yields that $X_- + \Delta A > 0$ outside P-null set, and we deduce $0 < H^r < \infty$. Next, notice that

$$^{o}X_+ = {}^{o}A_+ + {}^{o}M_+ = A + \Delta^+ A + M = X + \Delta^+ A,$$

where ^{o} denotes an optional projection of the process. Then, for any stopping time T, and since $X > 0$, we obtain $X_T + \Delta^+ A_T = \mathbf{E}(X_{T+}|\mathcal{F}_T) > 0$ a.s. on $\{T < \infty\}$. Again, according to the aforementioned Theorem 2.4.52, we can conclude that $X + \Delta^+ A > 0$ is outside the P-null set, and we have we deduced $0 < H^g < \infty$. Furthermore, Lemma H^r and H^g are locally bounded because they both are strongly predictable. Since we know that H is locally bounded, we can define L and D as above, and it remains to prove that $X = LD = \mathcal{E}(N)/\mathcal{E}(-B)$.

Observe that $\Delta B = \frac{\Delta A}{X_- + \Delta A} < 1$ and $\Delta^+ B = \frac{\Delta^+ A}{X + \Delta^+ A} < 1$ identically; hence, $\mathcal{E}(-B) > 0$ and $\mathcal{E}(-B)_- > 0, \mathcal{E}(-B)_+ > 0$. Then, we apply the change of variables formula to the function $f(x,y) = x/y$, or rather to a C^2 function coinciding with f for y outside an arbitrary small neighborhood of 0, to obtain with $D^* = 1/D$ and $\hat{X} = LD$:

$$\begin{aligned}
\hat{X}_t =& 1 + \hat{X}_- \cdot N_t^r + \hat{X}_- \cdot B_t^r + \sum_{s \le t} \left(\frac{1 + \Delta N_s}{1 - \Delta B_s} - 1 - \Delta N_s - \Delta B_s \right) \hat{X}_{s-} \\
&+ \hat{X} \odot N^g_{t+} + \hat{X} \odot B^g_{t+} + \sum_{s<t} \left(\frac{1 + \Delta^+ N_s}{1 - \Delta^+ B_s} - 1 - \Delta^+ N_s - \Delta^+ B_s \right) \hat{X}_s \\
=& 1 + \hat{X}_- \cdot N_t^r + \hat{X}_- \cdot B_t^r + \sum_{s \le t} \hat{X}_{s-} \frac{\Delta N_s + \Delta B_s}{1 - \Delta B_s} \Delta B_s \\
&+ \hat{X} \odot N^g_{t+} + \hat{X} \odot B^g_{t+} + \sum_{s<t} \hat{X}_{s-} \frac{\Delta^+ N_s + \Delta^+ B_s}{1 - \Delta^+ B_s} \Delta^+ B_s \\
=& 1 + \hat{X}_- \left(1 + \frac{\Delta B_s}{1 - \Delta B_s} \right) \cdot N_t^r + \hat{X}_- \left(1 + \frac{\Delta B_s}{1 - \Delta B_s} \right) \cdot B_t^r \\
&+ \hat{X} \left(1 + \frac{\Delta^+ B_s}{1 - \Delta^+ B_s} \right) \odot N^g_{t+} + \hat{X} \left(1 + \frac{\Delta^+ B_s}{1 - \Delta^+ B_s} \right) \odot B^g_{t+} \\
=& 1 + \frac{\hat{X}_- H^r}{1 - \Delta B} \cdot X_t^r + \frac{\hat{X} H^g}{1 - \Delta^+ B} \odot X^g_{t+} \\
=& 1 + \frac{\hat{X}_-}{X_-} \cdot X_t^r + \frac{\hat{X}}{X} \odot X^g_{t+}.
\end{aligned}$$

$\Delta B = H^r \Delta A, \Delta^+ B = H^g \Delta^+ A$ and $1 - H^r \Delta A = H^r X_-, 1 - H^g \Delta^+ A = H^g X$; hence, $\frac{H^r}{1 - \Delta B} = \frac{1}{X_-}$ and $\frac{H^g}{1 - \Delta^+ B} = \frac{1}{X}$. Then,

$$\frac{1}{\hat{X}_-} \cdot \hat{X}^r + \frac{1}{\hat{X}} \odot \hat{X}^g = \frac{1}{X_-} \cdot X^r + \frac{1}{X} \odot X^g$$

Similarly to how we completed the proof in the beginning, we deduce that $\hat{X} = X$. □

To conclude this section, we present a corollary addressing the uniqueness of the exponential optional compensator.

Corollary 2. *A real-valued optional semimartingale X has a unique (up to indistinguishably) exponential optional compensator V if X is exponentially special optional semimartingales.*

Proof. Suppose that X is exponentially special optional semimartingales. According to Theorem 1, there exists a unique positive process $D \in \mathcal{V}$ such that $D_0 = 1$ and $L := \frac{\exp(X - X_0)}{D} \in \mathcal{M}^O_{loc}$. Since $\exp(X - X_0) > 0$ and $\frac{\exp(X_- - X_0)}{D_-} = L_- < \infty$, we have $D_- > 0$. Therefore, $V := \log(D) \in \mathcal{V}$. □

4. Multidimensional Optional Dual Measures

In this section, our objective is to extend the findings presented in Eberlein et al. (2009) to the case of optional semimartingales. Eberlein, Papapantoleon, and Shiryaev, in their study, provided a characterization for one-dimensional semimartingales. These semimartingales were defined as scalar products of the driving semimartingale and d-dimensional vectors, under a suitable equivalent probability measure. Our goal is to generalize this result for *optional* semimartingales H, emphasizing its relevance to interest rate modeling through the optional stochastic integral in the Esscher transform.

Let $L(H)$ represent the space of predictable integrable processes concerning the semimartingale H. As previously defined in Section 2, $v' \circ H$ signifies the optional stochastic integral of v' with respect to the optional semimartingale H. Additionally, $\tilde{G}(v)$ is used to denote the logarithmic transform of the cumulant process $G(v)$, expressed as $\mathcal{E}(G(v)) = \exp(\tilde{G}(v))$.

Theorem 2. *Let H be an $\mathbb{R}^d$-valued optional semimartingale with characteristics $Q(H|P) = (B, C, \nu^r, \nu^g)$. Let u be a vector in $\mathbb{R}^d$. Consider an $\mathbb{R}^d$-valued strongly predictable process v, such that $v \in L(H)$ and $v' \circ H$ is exponentially special optional semimartingale. Define the measure P_v via the Radon–Nikodym derivative*

$$\frac{dP_v}{dP} = \exp(v' \circ H_T - \tilde{G}(v)_T),$$

assuming that $e^{v' \circ H - \tilde{G}(v)} \in \mathcal{M}^O(P)$. Then, the process H^u with $H^u = \langle u, H \rangle = u'H$ is a one-dimensional optional semimartingale with characteristics $Q(H^u|P_v) = (B^u, C^u, \nu^{ur}, \nu^{ug})$ of the form

$$\begin{aligned} B^u &= u'B + u'dCv + \sum_{j=r,g} \left(h(u'x) \frac{e^{v'x}}{1 + W^j(v)} - u'h(x) \right) * \nu^j, \\ C^u &= u'Cu, \\ \nu^{ur}(\omega, t, E) &= 1_E(u'x) \frac{e^{v'x}}{1 + W^r(v)} * \nu^r, \\ \nu^{ug}(\omega, t, E) &= 1_E(u'x) \frac{e^{v'x}}{1 + W^g(v)} * \nu^g, \end{aligned} \tag{5}$$

where $E \in \mathcal{B}(\mathbb{R} \setminus \{0\})$, and $W^j(v)_t = \int (e^{v'w} - 1)\nu^j(\{t\} \times dw)$, $j = r, g$.

Proof. Using Corollary 1 in Section 3, it is sufficient to show that

$$\frac{e^{zH^u}}{\mathcal{E}(G^u(z))} \in \mathcal{M}^O_{loc}(P_v) \tag{6}$$

for all $z \in \mathcal{Z}$, where $\mathcal{Z} \subseteq \mathbb{R}$ open, such that

$$1_{\{|y|>1\}} e^{zy} * \nu^{ur} \in \mathcal{V}, \quad 1_{\{|y|>1\}} e^{zy} * \nu^{ug} \in \mathcal{V}. \tag{7}$$

G^u denotes the Laplace cumulant process associated with the characteristics

$$(B^u, C^u, \nu^{ur}, \nu^{ug})$$

Lemma 3.1 in Gasparyan (1988), (6) is equivalent to

$$Z \frac{e^{zH^u}}{\mathcal{E}(G^u(z))} = \frac{e^{v' \circ H}}{\mathcal{E}(G(v))} \frac{e^{zH^u}}{\mathcal{E}(G^u(z))} \in \mathcal{M}^O_{loc}(P) \tag{8}$$

Using (5), condition (7) transforms into

$$1_{\{|u'x|>1\}}e^{(zu+v)'x} * \nu^r \in \mathcal{V}, \quad 1_{\{|u'x|>1\}}e^{(zu+v)'x} * \nu^g \in \mathcal{V},$$

because $W^r(v)$ and $W^g(v)$ do not depend on x. Now, the exponent of the numerator in (8) is

$$v' \circ H + zH^u = v' \circ H + zu'H = (v + zu)' \circ H,$$

which has the unique exponential optional compensator presented by Corollary 2 in Section 3

$$G(v + zu)$$

under the measure P for the cumulant defined in (1); that is,

$$\frac{e^{(v+zu)'\circ H}}{\mathcal{E}(G(v + zu))} \in \mathcal{M}^O_{loc}(P).$$

To complete the proof, it suffices to show

$$\mathcal{E}(G(v))\mathcal{E}(G^u(z)) = \mathcal{E}(G(v + zu)). \tag{9}$$

Using the multiplication rule for optional stochastic exponential (see Lemma 8.1.2, Abdelghani and Melnikov (2020)) we get

$$\mathcal{E}(G(v))\mathcal{E}(G^u(z)) = \mathcal{E}(G(v) + G^u(z) + [G(v), G^u(z)]).$$

(9) reduces to showing that

$$G(v) + G^u(z) + [G(v), G^u(z)] = G(v + zu). \tag{10}$$

The right-hand side of (10), we have

$$\begin{aligned} G(v + zu) =& (v + zu)' \cdot B + \frac{1}{2}\int (v + zu)'dC(v + zu) \\ &+ \sum_{j=r,g} \left(e^{(v+zu)'x} - 1 - (v + zu)'h(x)\right) * \nu^j \end{aligned}$$

where operator $\cdot$ is the Lebesgue integral. On the left-hand side, we have similarly

$$G(v) = v' \cdot B + \frac{1}{2}\int v'dCv + \sum_{j=r,g}\left(e^{v'x} - 1 - v'h(x)\right) * \nu^j. \tag{11}$$

Second term on the left-hand side of (10), using (5), is

$$\begin{aligned} G^u(z) =& zB^u + \frac{1}{2}z^2C^u + \sum_{j=r,g}(e^{zy} - 1 - zh(y)) * \nu^{uj} \\ =& zu'B + \int zv'dCu + \sum_{j=r,g} z\left(h(u'x)\frac{e^{v'x}}{1 + W^j(v)} - u'h(x)\right) * \nu^j \\ &+ \frac{1}{2}z^2u'Cu + \sum_{j=r,g}\left(e^{zu'x} - 1 - zh(u'x)\right)\frac{e^{v'x}}{1 + W^j(v)} * \nu^j \\ =& zu'B + \int zv'dCu + \frac{1}{2}z^2u'Cu \\ &+ \sum_{j=r,g}\left(\frac{e^{(zu+v)'x} - e^{v'x}}{1 + W^j(v)} - zu'h(x)\right) * \nu^j. \end{aligned} \tag{12}$$

Last term on the left-hand side of (10) is

$$[G(v), G^u(z)] = \sum_{t\leq \cdot} \Delta G(v)_t \Delta G^u(z)_t + \sum_{t<\cdot} \Delta^+ G(v)_t \Delta^+ G^u(z)_t$$

since G, G^u are optional processes of finite variation. Now, we proceed as follows. First, we show that the drift terms on the left-hand side and right-hand side of (10) are equal. Then, we show that the diffusive terms are equal. Finally, we prove that the jump terms on the left-hand side and right-hand side are equal. The drift term and the diffusive term are rather easy to handle; indeed, from (11) and (12), we have that the drift term of the left-hand side of (10) is

$$v' \cdot B + zu'B = (v + zu'B) \cdot B$$

The diffusive term of the left-hand side of (10) is

$$\frac{1}{2}\Big(\int v'dCv + \int zv'dCu + \int zu'dCv + z^2u'Cu\Big) = \frac{1}{2}\int (v+zu)'dC(v+zu),$$

since the matrix C is symmetric. Hence, both terms agree with the right-hand side.

The jump terms are more difficult to manipulate due to the presence of the fixed times of discontinuity for the optional semimartingale H, which entails that the Laplace cumulant process is discontinuous. Regarding the fixed times of discontinuity, we have

$$\Delta G(v)_t = \int (e^{v'x} - 1)\nu^r(\{t\} \times dx) = W^r(v)_t,$$
$$\Delta^+ G(v)_t = \int (e^{v'x} - 1)\nu^g(\{t\} \times dx) = W^g(v)_t,$$

and

$$\begin{aligned}\Delta G^u(z)_t &= \int (e^{zy} - 1)\nu^{ur}(\{t\} \times dy)\\ &= \int (e^{zu'x} - 1)\frac{e^{v'x}}{1 + W^r(v)_t}\nu^r(\{t\} \times dx)\\ &= \int (e^{(v+zu)'x} - e^{v'x})\frac{1}{1 + W^r(v)_t}\nu^r(\{t\} \times dx).\end{aligned}$$

$$\Delta^+ G^u(z)_t = \int (e^{(v+zu)'x} - e^{v'x})\frac{1}{1 + W^g(v)_t}\nu^g(\{t\} \times dx).$$

$W(v)$ does not depend on the integrating variable x. Hence, we can pull it out of the integration and obtain

$$\begin{aligned}\Delta G^u(z)_t &= \tfrac{1}{1+W^r(v)_t}\int (e^{(v+zu)'x} - e^{v'x})\nu^r(\{t\} \times dx),\\ \Delta^+ G^u(z)_t &= \tfrac{1}{1+W^g(v)_t}\int (e^{(v+zu)'x} - e^{v'x})\nu^g(\{t\} \times dx).\end{aligned} \tag{13}$$

For the last term in (10), we can calculate further using (13)

$$
\begin{aligned}
[G(v), G^u(z)] &= \sum_{t\leq \cdot} \Delta G(v)_t \Delta G^u(z)_t + \sum_{t<\cdot} \Delta^+ G(v)_t \Delta^+ G^u(z)_t \\
&= \sum_{t\leq \cdot} \frac{W^r(v)_t}{1+W^r(v)_t} \int (e^{(v+zu)'x} - e^{v'x}) \nu^r(\{t\} \times dx) \\
&\quad + \sum_{t<\cdot} \frac{W^g(v)_t}{1+W^g(v)_t} \int (e^{(v+zu)'x} - e^{v'x}) \nu^g(\{t\} \times dx) \\
&= \sum_{t\leq \cdot} \frac{1+W^r(v)_t - 1}{1+W^r(v)_t} \int (e^{(v+zu)'x} - e^{v'x}) \nu^r(\{t\} \times dx)
\end{aligned}
$$

$$
\begin{aligned}
&+ \sum_{t<\cdot} \frac{1+W^g(v)_t - 1}{1+W^g(v)_t} \int (e^{(v+zu)'x} - e^{v'x}) \nu^g(\{t\} \times dx) \\
&= \sum_{t\leq \cdot} \Bigg(\int (e^{(v+zu)'x} - e^{v'x}) \nu^r(\{t\} \times dx) \\
&\quad - \frac{1}{1+W^r(v)_t} \int (e^{(v+zu)'x} - e^{v'x}) \nu^r(\{t\} \times dx) \Bigg) \\
&\quad + \sum_{t<\cdot} \Bigg(\int (e^{(v+zu)'x} - e^{v'x}) \nu^g(\{t\} \times dx) \\
&\quad - \frac{1}{1+W^g(v)_t} \int (e^{(v+zu)'x} - e^{v'x}) \nu^g(\{t\} \times dx) \Bigg).
\end{aligned}
$$

Using the above observations, we can show that the jump terms on the left-hand side and right-hand side of (10) are equal. Indeed, we can express the integrals with respect to the compensators ν^r and ν^g as sums in (11) and (12). Then, we have that the jump term on the left-hand side of (10) is

$$
\begin{aligned}
&\sum_{t\leq \cdot} \int \Bigg(e^{v'x} - 1 - v'h(x) + \frac{e^{(zu+v)'x} - e^{v'x}}{1+W^r(v)_t} \\
&- zu'h(x) + e^{(v+zu)'x} - e^{v'x} \\
&- \frac{1}{1+W^r(v)_t} \int (e^{(v+zu)'x} - e^{v'x}) \Bigg) \nu^r(\{t\} \times dx) \\
&+ \sum_{t\leq \cdot} \int \Bigg(e^{v'x} - 1 - v'h(x) + \frac{e^{(zu+v)'x} - e^{v'x}}{1+W^g(v)_t} \\
&- zu'h(x) + e^{(v+zu)'x} - e^{v'x} \\
&- \frac{1}{1+W^g(v)_t} \int (e^{(v+zu)'x} - e^{v'x}) \Bigg) \nu^g(\{t\} \times dx)
\end{aligned}
$$

$$
\begin{aligned}
&= \sum_{t\leq \cdot} \int \Big(e^{(v+zu)'x} - 1 - (v+zu)'h(x) \Big) \nu^r(\{t\} \times dx) \\
&\quad + \sum_{t<\cdot} \int \Big(e^{(v+zu)'x} - 1 - (v+zu)'h(x) \Big) \nu^g(\{t\} \times dx) \\
&= \sum_{t\leq \cdot} \Big(e^{(v+zu)'x} - 1 - (v+zu)'h(x) \Big) * \nu^r \\
&\quad + \Big(e^{(v+zu)'x} - 1 - (v+zu)'h(x) \Big) * \nu^g
\end{aligned}
$$

which equals the corresponding quantity on the right-hand side of (10). The proof is finished. □

5. Duality Relations

In this section, we establish an equivalent relation, namely the duality relation, between the prices of Margrabe options and quanto options with European call and put options in a market characterized by an unusual probability space. This analysis takes into account a portfolio composed of optional processes.

To begin, we aim to establish the duality relationship between the value of a swap option, specifically a Margrabe option or Spread option, with a payoff of $M_T = (S_T^1 - S_T^2)^+$ and the payoff of teh European call and put options It is important to note that we represent the payoff of a European call option at maturity T by $C_T = (S_T - K)^+$, where K is the strike price, and the put option is denoted by $P_T = (K - S_T)^+$.

Theorem 3. *Assume that the asset price processes S^1 and S^2 are exponential special optional semimartingales and $e^{H^i} \in \mathcal{M}^O(P)$, $i = 1,2$. Then, we can relate the value of a swap option and a European option via the following equality:*

$$M_T = P_T^v(1, S_T^u) = C_T^\theta(S_T^\zeta, 1),$$

or

$$\mathbf{E}(S_T^1 - S_T^2)^+ = \mathbf{E}_v(1 - S_T^u)^+ = \mathbf{E}_\theta(S_T^\zeta - 1)^+,$$

where the characteristics $(C^u, \nu^{ur}, \nu^{ug})$ and $(C^\zeta, \nu^{\zeta r}, \nu^{\zeta g})$ of $H^u = \log S^u$ and $H^\zeta = \log S^\zeta$, respectively, are given by Theorem 2 for $v = (1,0)'$, $u = (-1,1)'$, and $\theta = (0,1)', \zeta = (1,-1)'$.

Proof. We will use asset S^1 as the numeraire asset; if we use asset S^2 instead, then we obtain the duality relationship with a call option. The value of the swap option is

$$\begin{aligned} M_T = \mathbf{E}(S_T^1 - S_T^2)^+ =& \mathbf{E}\left[e^{H_T^1}\left(1 - \frac{S_T^2}{S_T^1}\right)^+\right] \\ =& \mathbf{E}\left[e^{v' H_T}\left(1 - \frac{S_T^2}{S_T^1}\right)^+\right] \end{aligned} \tag{14}$$

where $v = (1,0)'$. Moreover, $e^{v'H} \in \mathcal{M}^O(P)$ by assumption. We define a new measure P_v via the Radon–Nikodym derivative

$$\frac{dP_v}{dP} = e^{v' H_T},$$

Then, the pricing problem (14) becomes

$$M_T = \mathbf{E}(S_T^1 - S_T^2)^+ = \mathbf{E}_v\left[\left(1 - \frac{S_T^2}{S_T^1}\right)^+\right]$$

where we define the process $S^u = (S_t^u)_{0 \le t \le T}$ via

$$S_t^u = \frac{S_t^2}{S_t^1} = \frac{e^{H_t^2}}{e^{H_t^1}} = e^{u' H_t} = e^{H_t^u}, \quad 0 \le t \le T,$$

for $u = (-1,1)'$. The triplet of local characteristics of the semimartingale H^u is given by Theorem 2 for $v = (1,0)'$ and $u = (-1,1)'$. Now, applying Lemma 3.1 in Gasparyan (1988), we obtain that

$$e^{u'H} \in \mathcal{M}^O(P_v)$$

since

$$e^{u'H}e^{v'H} = e^{H^2} \in \mathcal{M}^O(P)$$

We conclude that

$$M_T = \mathbf{E}(S_T^1 - S_T^2)^+ = \mathbf{E}_v(1 - S_T^u)^+ = P_T^v(1, S_T^u).$$

With the same methodology, we derive the proof of equivalency for the Margrabe option and the call option as well. □

Additionally, we demonstrate another duality, this time between a quanto call option, with the payoff $Q_T^C = S_T^1(S_T^2 - K)^+$, and a European call option with payoff as defined before.

Theorem 4. *Assume that the asset price processes S^1 and S^2 are exponential special optional semimartingales and $e^{H^i} \in \mathcal{M}^O(P)$, $i = 1, 2$. Then, we can relate the value of a quanto call option and a European call option via the following duality:*

$$Q_T^C = C_T^v(S_T^u, K)$$

or

$$\mathbf{E}[S_T^1(S_T^2 - K)^+] = \mathbf{E}_v(S_T^u - K)^+,$$

where the characteristics $(C^u, \nu^{ur}, \nu^{ug})$ of $H^u = \log S^u$ are given by Theorem 2 for $v = (1,0)'$, $u = (0,1)'$. An analogous duality result relates the quanto put option and the European put option.

Proof. The value of the quanto call option is

$$\begin{aligned} Q_T^C = \mathbf{E}[S_T^1(S_T^2 - K)^+] &= \mathbf{E}[e^{H_T^1}(S_T^2 - K)^+] \\ &= \mathbf{E}[e^{v'H}(e^{H_T^2} - K)^+] \\ &= \mathbf{E}_v[(e^{H_T^u} - K)^+], \end{aligned}$$

where $\frac{dP_v}{dP} = e^{v'H_T}$ for $v = (1,0)'$ and $H^u = u'H$ for $u = (0,1)'$. Hence, the statement follows. □

Additionally, we delve into the *call-put duality* within this market, exploring two relations for these two contracts. The proof for one of them (a) requires utilizing Theorem 2 to establish this duality, while the proof for the other relation (b) involves the portfolio value and the Black–Scholes model.

Theorem 5. *Assume that the asset price process S is an exponential special optional semimartingales and $e^H \in \mathcal{M}^O(P)$. Then, we can relate the value of a European call option and a European put option via the following equivalencies:*

$$(a)\ P_T(K, S_T) = KC_T^v(S_T^u, 1/K)$$

where the characteristics $(C^u, \nu^{ur}, \nu^{ug})$ of $H^u = \log S^u$ are given by Theorem 2 for $v = 1$, $u = -1$. Furthermore, we can relate the value of a standard put option with volatility σ to a standard call option via the following equality with volatility $-\sigma$, as follows:

$$(b)\ P_T(K, S_T) = C_T(-S_T, -k),\ \text{Or}\ P_T(K, S_T, \sigma) = C_T(-S_T, -k, -\sigma)$$

Proof of Theorem 5(a). Put option value is

$$\begin{aligned} P_T(K, S_T) = \mathbf{E}[(K - S_T)^+] &= \mathbf{E}[e^{H_T}(Ke^{-H_T} - 1)^+] \\ &= K\mathbf{E}[e^{H_T}(e^{-H_T} - 1/K)^+] \\ &= K\mathbf{E}[e^{vH_T}(e^{-H_T} - 1/K)^+] \\ &= K\mathbf{E}_v[(e^{-H_T} - 1/K)^+] \end{aligned}$$

where $\frac{dp_v}{dp} = e^{vH_T}$ for $v = 1$ and $H^u = uH$ for $u = -1$. Thus, the statement (a) follows. □

Proof of Theorem 5(b). By a different approach than the previous, specifically utilizing the Black–Scholes model. In the following, we provide detailed proof of the pricing of a European call option and subsequently investigate the pricing of a European put option. We then establish the relationship between these two.

Assume that the market consists of two types of securities B and S and a portfolio $\pi = (\eta, \xi)$ which is composed of the optional processes η and $\eta.\xi$ is the volume of the reference asset B, while ξ is the volume of the security S. Suppose $B_t > 0$ and $S_t \geq 0$ for all $t \geq 0$ and write the ratio process $R_t = S_t/B_t$. Then, the discounted value of the portfolio is $Y_t = \eta_t + \xi_t R_t$ which is a real-valued optional semimartingale that had right and left limits. Furthermore, we restrict the portfolio, π, to be self-financing, that is, $dY_t = \xi dR_t$, where the interest rate is zero. Now let us consider the augmented Black–Scholes model with left and right jumps as described in Chapter 9 of Abdelghani and Melnikov (2020),

$$\begin{aligned} B_t =& B_0 + \int_{]0,t]} rB_s ds \\ S_t =& S_0 + \int_{]0,t]} S_{s-}(\mu ds + \sigma dW_s + a dL^r_s) + \int_{[0,t[} bS_s dL^g_{s+} \end{aligned}$$

where $L^r_t = L_t - \lambda t$, $L^g_t = -\bar{L}_{t-} + \gamma t$, r, μ, σ, a, and b are constants. W is a diffusion term and L and $\bar{L}$ are independent Poisson terms with constant intensity λ and γ, respectively. Let the initial wealth account for B_0 and the initial price be S_0. We can write S as $S_t = S_0\mathcal{E}(H)$, where $H_t = \mu t + \sigma W_t + a(L_t - \lambda t) + b(\gamma t - \bar{L}_{t-})$, with $H_0 = 0$, and $B_t = B_0 \exp(h_t)$, where $h_t = rt$. Furthermore, we will use the following stochastic exponential form:

$$\mathcal{E}(H)_t = \exp[H_t - \frac{1}{2}\langle H^c, H^c\rangle] \prod_{0<s\leq t} (1 + \Delta S_s)e^{-\Delta S_s} \prod_{0\leq s<t} (1 + \Delta^+ S_s)e^{-\Delta^+ S_s}$$

The ratio process is:

$$\begin{aligned} R_t = S_0 \exp\left\{\left(\mu - r - \frac{1}{2}(\sigma^2 - \lambda a^2 - \gamma b^2)\right)t + \sigma W_t\right\} \times \\ \prod_{0<s\leq t}\left[(1 + a\Delta L_t)e^{-a\Delta L_t}\right] \prod_{0\leq s<t}\left[(1 - b\Delta^+ \bar{L}_{s-})e^{-b\Delta^+ \bar{L}_{s-}}\right] \end{aligned}$$

and is not a local optional martingale. So, we need to find a suitable derivative to transfer this ratio under a martingale measure Q such that Y_t is a local optional martingale with respect to Q (see Melnikov and Shiryaev (1996) for further explanation). In the following, we repeat some of the key concepts. So, we want the derivative $Z = \mathcal{E}(N)$ for which we have to find a local martingale N such that $\Psi(h, H, N)$ is a local martingale:

$$\begin{aligned} \Psi(h, H, N) =& N_t + H_t - h_t + \langle h^c - N^c, h^c - H^c\rangle_t \\ &+ \sum_{0<s\leq t} \frac{(\Delta h_s - \Delta N_s)(\Delta h_s - \Delta H_s)}{1 + \Delta h_s} \\ &+ \sum_{0<s\leq t} \frac{(\Delta^+ h_s - \Delta^+ N_s)(\Delta^+ h_s - \Delta^+ H_s)}{1 + \Delta^+ h_s} \end{aligned}$$

Thus, for the case of European options, let us take $N_t = \varsigma W_t + c(L_t - \lambda t) + d(\gamma t - \bar{L}_{t-})$, which is an optional local martingale that will render Z as an optional scaling factor. By this choice of N, we obtain the following:

$$\begin{aligned}\Psi(h,H,N) =&(\varsigma+\sigma)W_t + (a+c+ac)(L_t - \lambda t)\\ &+(b+d-bd)(\gamma t - \bar{L}_{t-})\\ &+(\mu - r + \varsigma\sigma + 2ac\lambda + 2bd\gamma)t\end{aligned}$$

is a local martingale if

$$\mu - r + \varsigma\sigma + 2ac\lambda + 2bd\gamma = 0 \tag{15}$$

Thus, we have to find (ς, σ, d) such that (15) is satisfied. We find the martingale measure Q by solving this equation, which has infinitely many solutions that mean the market of Black–Scholes with left and right jumps is incomplete.

Now letus turn our attention to the problem at hand, pricing a European call option. As outlined in Chapter 9, Section 6 of Abdelghani and Melnikov (2020), the choice of parameters for Equation (15)

$$\left\{c = \frac{-a}{1+a}, d = \frac{-b}{1-b}, \varsigma = \frac{r - \mu + 2\lambda\frac{a^2}{1+a} + 2\gamma\frac{b^2}{1+b}}{\sigma}\right\} \tag{16}$$

leads to the normalized price of R under Q; that is,

$$\begin{aligned}R_t =&R_0\mathcal{E}(\Psi(h,H,N))\\ =&R_0\mathcal{E}((\varsigma+\sigma)W_t)\\ =&S_0\exp\{(\varsigma+\sigma)W_t - \frac{1}{2}(\varsigma+\sigma)^2 t\},\\ B_0 =&1\end{aligned}$$

is just a function of the Wiener process, and all the left jumps are absorbed. Thus, R_t is $Q-$martingale. Thus,

$$E_Q[R_T|F_t] = R_t = e^{-rt}B_t \tag{17}$$

The price of a call option at arbitrary time $0 \le t < T$ is

$$C_t = e^{rt}R_t\Phi(\tilde{K}_t + (\varsigma+\sigma)\sqrt{T-t}) + e^{-r(T-t)}K\Phi(\tilde{K}_t)$$

where

$$\tilde{K} = \frac{1}{(\varsigma+\sigma)\sqrt{T}}\left[\ln\left(\frac{S_0}{K}\right) + (r - \frac{1}{2}(\varsigma+\sigma)^2)T\right] \tag{18}$$

We proceed with the pricing of a European put option for optional processes. The payoff function of a European put option can be written as:

$$P_T = (K - S_T)^+ = (S_T - K)^+ + K - S_T$$

With the payoff of the call option, we can write:

$$\begin{aligned}P_t =&E_Q[P_T|F_t]\\ =&E_Q[(S_T - K)^+|F_t] + E_Q[k - S_T|F_t]\\ =&C_t + E_Q[k - S_T|F_t]\end{aligned}$$

where C_t is the price of the call option. Now, if we denote:

$$\tilde{P}_T = \frac{P_T}{B_T} \tag{19}$$

$$\begin{aligned} \tilde{P}_t =& E_Q[\frac{P_T}{B_T}|F_t] \\ =& E_Q[\frac{C_T}{B_T}|F_t] + E_Q[\frac{K - S_T}{B_T}|F_t] \\ =& \tilde{C}_t + Ke^{-rT} - E_Q[R_T|F_t] \end{aligned} \tag{20}$$

To compute $E_Q[R_T|F_t]$, we use the same martingale measure as it is used for pricing the European call option. Thus, using (17), we can rewrite (20) using (19) as follows:

$$\begin{aligned} \tilde{P}_t =& e^{-rt}P_t \\ =& e^{-rt}C_t + Ke^{-rT} - e^{-rt}S_t \end{aligned}$$

We obtain the following relation, which is called *call-put parity*.

$$P_t = C_t + Ke^{-r(T-t)} - S_t$$

Using this call-put parity relation, we can calculate the fair price of the put option and also establish the duality relation. Using the fact that $\Phi(-x) = 1 - \Phi(x)$, we have:

$$\begin{aligned} P_0 =& C_0 + Ke^{-rT} - S_0 \\ =& S_0\Phi(\tilde{K} + (\varsigma + \sigma)\sqrt{T}) - e^{-rT}K\Phi(\tilde{K}) + Ke^{-rT} - S_0 \\ =& S_0\Big[\Phi(\tilde{K} + (\varsigma + \sigma)\sqrt{T}) - 1\Big] - e^{-rT}(-K)(\Phi(\tilde{K}) - 1) \\ =& (-S_0)\Phi(-\tilde{K} - (\varsigma + \sigma)\sqrt{T}) - e^{-rT}(-K)\Phi(-\tilde{K}) \end{aligned}$$

Using (18)'s definition, we have:

$$-\tilde{K} = \frac{1}{-(\varsigma + \sigma)\sqrt{T}}\Big[\ln\big(\frac{-S_0}{-K}\big) + (r - \frac{1}{2}(-\varsigma - \sigma)^2)T\Big] \tag{21}$$

Given the definition of ς in (16), we can see that

$$-\varsigma = \frac{r - \mu + 2\lambda\frac{a^2}{1+a} + 2\gamma\frac{b^2}{1+b}}{-\sigma}$$

is achieved simply by using $-\sigma$. Thus, we established the following relation, which is called *call-put duality*.

$$P_0(S_0, K, \sigma) = C_0(-S_0, -K, -\sigma)$$

For arbitrary time $0 \leq t < T$, we have:

$$\begin{aligned} P_t =& C_t + Ke^{-r(T-t)} - S_t \\ =& e^{rt}R_t\Phi(\tilde{K}_t + (\varsigma + \sigma)\sqrt{T-t}) - e^{-r(T-t)}K\Phi(\tilde{K}_t) + Ke^{-r(T-t)} - S_t \\ =& (-S_t)\Phi(-\tilde{K}_t - (\varsigma + \sigma)\sqrt{T-t}) - e^{-r(T-t)}(-K)\Phi(-\tilde{K}_t) \end{aligned}$$

where

$$\tilde{K}_t = \frac{1}{(\varsigma + \sigma)\sqrt{T-t}}\Big[\ln\big(\frac{S_t}{K}\big) + (r - \frac{1}{2}(\varsigma + \sigma)^2)(T-t)\Big]$$

The *call-put duality* for arbitrary time $0 \leq t < T$ is

$$P_t(S_t, K, \sigma) = C_t(-S_t, -K, -\sigma) \tag{22}$$

Examining the duality relation in Chapter 4 of Melnikov (2011), and drawing a parallel, it becomes apparent that the (22) relation bears similarity to the duality relation involving cadlag processes. □

6. Applications and Examples

In this section, we proceed with concrete examples and explicit calculations for the previously obtained results in Section 5. The first example delves into an optional version of the well-known Merton's jump-diffusion model and calculates the price of a quanto call option.

Example 1. *Let us consider an optional version of the well-known Merton's jump-diffusion model. The two assets S^1 and S^2 are modeled as optional exponential jump-diffusion processes:*

$$S_t^i = \exp\left(b_i t + W_t^i + \sum_{k=0}^{N_t^{i,r}} U_k^i + \sum_{k=0}^{N_t^{i,g}} Z_k^i\right), \quad i = 1,2,$$

where the drift terms b^i are determined by the martingale condition. A Wiener process W_t^i has a variance $\sigma_i \geq 0$ and a correlation coefficient $-1 \leq \rho \leq 1$, i.e., $\langle W^1, W^2 \rangle = \rho$ and

$$c = \begin{pmatrix} \sigma_1^2 & \rho\sigma_1\sigma_2 \\ \rho\sigma_1\sigma_2 & \sigma_2^2 \end{pmatrix};$$

the process $N_t^{i,r}, i = 1,2$ is a right-continuous Poisson process with intensity λ_i^r, while the process $N_t^{i,r}, i = 1,2$ is a left-continuous version of a Poisson process with intensity λ_i^g, the random variables being $U_k^i \sim Normal(s_i^r, 0)$ and $Z_k^i \sim Normal(s_i^g, 0)$. The Poisson processes $N_t^{i,r}, i = 1,2$ and $N_t^{i,g}, i = 1,2$ are independent. Thus, the local characteristics of $H = (H^1, H^2)$ are

$$b = \begin{pmatrix} b_1 \\ b_2 \end{pmatrix}; \; c = \begin{pmatrix} \sigma_1^2 & \rho\sigma_1\sigma_2 \\ \rho\sigma_1\sigma_2 & \sigma_2^2 \end{pmatrix};$$

and F^r and F^g have the Lebesgue densities f^r and f^g, where

$$f^j(x_1, x_2) = \frac{1}{s_1^j s_2^j 2\pi} \exp\left(-\frac{x_1^2}{2(s_1^j)^2} - \frac{x_2^2}{2(s_2^j)^2}\right)\lambda_1^j \lambda_2^j, \quad j = r, g.$$

Now, the price of a quanto call option with strike price K, according to Theorem 4, is equal to the price of a call option with the same strike K on an asset S^u with characteristics $(B^u, C^u, \nu^{ur}, \nu^{ug})$ provided by Theorem 2 for $v = (1,0)'$ and $u = (0,1)'$. Hence, we can calculate

$$b^u = b_2 + \rho\sigma_1\sigma_2, \tag{23}$$

$$c^u = \sigma_2^2; \tag{24}$$

For the Levy measures, using the independence of the normal variables and completing the square, we have for $y \in \mathbb{R}$, $E \in \mathcal{B}(\mathbb{R} \setminus 0)$:

$$
\begin{aligned}
1_E(y) * F^{uj} =& 1_E(x_2)e^{x_1} * F \\
=& \int_{\mathbb{R}^2} 1_E(x_2)e^{x_1} \frac{1}{s_1^j s_2^j 2\pi} \exp\left(-\frac{x_1^2}{2(s_1^j)^2} - \frac{x_2^2}{2(s_2^j)^2} \right) \lambda_1^j \lambda_2^j dx_1 dx_2 \\
=& \lambda_2^j \int_E \frac{1}{s_2^j \sqrt{2\pi}} \exp\left(-\frac{x_2^2}{2(s_2^j)^2} \right) dx_2 \\
& \times \lambda_1^j e^{\left(s_1^j\right)^2/2} \int_{\mathbb{R}} \frac{1}{s_1^j \sqrt{2\pi}} \exp\left(-\frac{(x_1 - \left(s_1^j\right)^2)^2}{2(s_1^j)^2} \right) dx_1 \\
=& \lambda_2^j \lambda_1^j e^{\left(s_1^j\right)^2/2} \int_E \frac{1}{s_2^j \sqrt{2\pi}} \exp\left(-\frac{x_2^2}{2(s_2^j)^2} \right) dx_2, \quad j = r, g.
\end{aligned}
\tag{25}
$$

Pricing a quanto option in case the two assets follow the optional version of Merton's jump-diffusion model is equivalent to pricing a call option in a univariate jump-diffusion model of the same class, with parameters given by (23)–(25). In particular, left jumps occur according to a compound Poisson process with intensity $\lambda^{ur} = \lambda_2^r \lambda_1^r e^{(s_1^r)^2/2}$*, and jump heights are normally distributed with jump variance* s_2^r *and zero mean, while right jumps occur according to a left-continuous compound Poisson process with intensity* $\lambda^{ug} = \lambda_2^g \lambda_1^g e^{(s_1^g)^2/2}$*, and jump heights are normally distributed with jump variance* s_2^g *and zero mean.*

Moreover, the second example extends the previous model by incorporating exponential jumps and proceeds to calculate the price of a quanto call option.

Example 2. *Let us now consider the previous example in a case when the random variables* U_k^i *and* Z_k^i *are mutually independent and exponentially distributed with parameters* α^i *and* β^i*, respectively. Thus, the density functions* f^r *and* f^g *have the following forms:*

$$
\begin{aligned}
f^r(x_1, x_2) &= \alpha^1 \alpha^2 e^{-\alpha^1 x_1 - \alpha^2 x_2}, \\
f^g(x_1, x_2) &= \beta^1 \beta^2 e^{-\beta^1 x_1 - \beta^2 x_2}.
\end{aligned}
$$

The price of a quanto call option with strike K, according to Theorem 4, is equal to the price of a call option with the same strike K, on an asset S^u *with characteristics* $(B^u, C^u, \nu^{ur}, \nu^{ug})$ *provided by Theorem 2 for* $v = (1,0)'$ *and* $u = (0,1)'$*. Consequently, in this case* b^u *and* c^u *are the same as in Example 1, and we obtain for* $y \in \mathbb{R}$*,* $E \in \mathcal{B}(\mathbb{R} \setminus \{0\})$ *:*

$$
\begin{aligned}
1_E(y) * F^{ur} =& \lambda_1^r \lambda_2^r \int_{\mathbb{R}^2} 1_E(x_2) e^{x_1} \alpha_1 \alpha_2 e^{-\alpha_1 x_1 - \alpha_2 x_2} dx_1 dx_2 \\
=& \lambda_1^r \lambda_2^r \alpha_1 \alpha_2 \int_{\mathbb{R}} e^{x_1(1-\alpha_1)} dx_1 \int_E e^{-\alpha_2 x_2} dx_2 \\
=& \lambda_1^r \lambda_2^r \frac{\alpha_1 \alpha_2}{\alpha_1 - 1} \int_E e^{-\alpha_2 x_2} dx_2.
\end{aligned}
$$

The Levy measure for left jumps is calculated in a similar way. As a result, pricing a quanto option in case of two assets are modeled as optional jump-diffusions with exponential jumps, is equivalent to pricing a call option in a univariate optional jump-diffusion model of the same class. In particular, left jumps occur according to a compound Poisson process with intensity $\lambda^{ur} = \lambda_2^r \lambda_1^r \frac{\alpha_1}{\alpha_1 - 1}$*, and jump heights are exponentially distributed with a parameter* α_2*, while right jumps occur according to a left-continuous compound Poisson process with intensity* $\lambda^{ug} = \lambda_2^g \lambda_1^g \frac{\beta_1}{\beta_1 - 1}$*, and jump heights are exponentially distributed with a parameter* β_2*.*

7. Conclusions

In conclusion, this study has successfully addressed the challenging task of pricing intricate options, particularly within the context of multidimensional optional semimartingale models. Utilizing an innovative and alternative approach grounded in the duality principle, we extended and refined the methodology initially proposed by Eberlein et al. (2009). While their work focused on general semimartingale models, our study took a step further by extending and re-evaluating the entire framework specifically for multidimensional optional semimartingale models. The key outcome and differences that delineate this approach to optional semimartingale models can be found in Sections 3–5 with related examples in Section 6.

The established duality relationships among swap options, quanto options, and standard call and put options within the realm of optional semimartingale models are pivotal contributions of this research. The significance lies not only in the theoretical framework but also in the practical implications for financial practitioners and analysts. Our findings provide a clear and efficient means of interrelating these diverse financial instruments, thereby enhancing the understanding of their complex connections.

Furthermore, the reduction in computational complexity afforded by our approach is a noteworthy advantage. This efficiency gains prominence in the valuation process, allowing for quicker and more accurate determination of the prices of these intricate financial instruments. In essence, our study bridges the gap between theoretical advancements and practical applications, offering a valuable contribution to the field of option pricing within the context of multidimensional optional semimartingale models. For future research, exploring the application of this approach to other types of options, such as power options, could provide insights into pricing and uncover connections to various European options.

Author Contributions: Conceptualization, M.A.S., A.M. and A.P.; methodology, M.A.S., A.M. and A.P.; validation, M.A.S., A.M. and A.P.; formal analysis, M.A.S., A.M. and A.P.; investigation, M.A.S., A.M. and A.P.; resources, M.A.S., A.M. and A.P.; writing—original draft preparation, M.A.S., A.M. and A.P.; writing—review and editing, M.A.S., A.M. and A.P.; supervision, A.M.; project administration, A.M.; funding acquisition, A.M. All authors have read and agreed to the published version of the manuscript.

Funding: The research was supported by the NSERC Discovery Grant RES0043487.

Data Availability Statement: This is a theoretical work, and no specific datasets were utilized in the course of this study. In this instance, no new data were created. Furthermore, data is not available due to the nature of the study, which does not involve the analysis or generation of specific datasets.

Conflicts of Interest: Author Andrey Pak was employed by the company SS&C Technologies. Other authors declare no conflicts of interest.

References

Abdelghani, Mohamed, and Alexander Melnikov. 2020. *Optional Processes*. London : Chapman & Hall/CRC.

Czichowsky, Christoph, and Walter Schachermayer. 2016. Duality theory for portfolio optimisation under transaction costs. *The Annals of Applied Probability* 26: 1888–941. [CrossRef]

Eberlein, Ernst, and Antonis Papapantoleon. 2005. Symmetries and Pricing of Exotic Options in Lévy Models. In *Exotic Option Pricing and Advanced Lévy Models*; Hoboken and Chichester : John Wiley & Sons, Inc., pp. 99–128.

Eberlein, Ernst, Antonis Papapantoleon, and Albert N. Shiryaev. 2009. Esscher transform and the duality principle for multidimensional semimartingales. *The Annals of Applied Probability* 19: 1944–71. [CrossRef]

Fajardo, José, and Ernesto Mordecki. 2006. Pricing Derivatives on Two-Dimensional Lévy Processes. *International Journal of Theoretical and Applied Finance (IJTAF)* 9: 185–97. [CrossRef]

Fischer, Stanley. 1978. Call option pricing when the exercise price is uncertain, and the valuation of index bonds. *The Journal of Finance* 33: 169–78. [CrossRef]

Gasparyan, David. 1988. *Some Results on Optional Martingales. Girsanov Theorem. Mathematical Problems of Computer Science* 15: 199–210.

Geman, Hélyette, Nicole El Karoui, and Jean-Charles Rochet. 1995. Changes of Numéraire, Changes of Probability Measure and Option Pricing. *Journal of Applied Probability: Applied Probability Trust* 32: 443–58. [CrossRef]

Gerber, Hans U., and Elias S. W. Shiu. 1996. Martingale Approach to Pricing Perpetual American Options on Two Stocks. *Mathematical Finance* 6: 303–22. [CrossRef]

Gnedenko, Boris Vladimirovich, and Andrey Kolmogorov. 1954. *Limit Distributions for Sums of Independent*. Reading and London: Addison-Wesley Publishing Co.
Jacod, Jean, and Albert N. Shiryaev. 1987. *Limit Theorems for Stochastic Processes*. Berlin and Heidelberg: Springer. Available online: https://api.semanticscholar.org/CorpusID:122222429 (accessed on 23 December 2023).
Kallsen, Jan, and Albert N. Shiryaev. 2002. The cumulant process and Esscher's change of measure. *Finance and Stochastics* 6: 397–428. [CrossRef]
Kühn, Christoph, and Maximilian Stroh. 2009. A note on stochastic integration with respect to optional semimartingales. *Electronic Communications in Probability* 14: 192–201. [CrossRef]
Margrabe, William. 1978. The Value of an Option to Exchange One Asset for Another. *The Journal of Finance* 33: 177–86. [CrossRef]
Melnikov, Alexander. 2011. *Risk Analysis in Finance and Insurance*. Boca Raton: Chapman and Hall/CRC.
Melnikov, Alexander, and Albert Shiryaev. 1996. Criteria for the Absence of Arbitrage in the Financial Market. In *Frontiers in Pure and Applied Probability*. Moscow: TVP Science Publishers, pp. 121–34.
Schröder, Mark. 2015. Changes of Numeraire for Pricing Futures, Forwards, and Options. *The Review of Financial Studies* 12: 1143–63. [CrossRef]